Acquainted with Susanne Vosmer's previous publications, I
and willingness to 'think new thoughts' about the trade o
She brings a wealth of insights from psychology and oth

I am excited to read about her new book project and admire the ambition involved, to create a handbook of research for group analysis whilst noting that group analysis can itself constitute a useful mode of re-search. This is long overdue. Wide ranging scope it aims to cover many existing nodes of research but take it further, to integrate the contribution of non-Western, non-ethnocentric modes of knowledge. Perspectives from far Eastern philosophy and practice, and indigenous experience, for examples, are seldom included in psychotherapy literature let alone research, and are welcome (essential) guests to the table for further understanding.

I heartily recommend this book proposal and believe it will address some significant gaps in our present knowledge. I do not know of another book written in this spirit.

– **Martin Weegmann**, *Clinical Psychologist, Group Analyst and writer*

In her groundbreaking book, Susanne Vosmer initiates a truly pluralistic discussion on research in Analytic and other forms of Group Psychotherapy. She constructs an alternative yet complementary framework to evidence-based research, going beyond Eurocentric and American-centered models of knowledge and research practice. Vosmer writes about research in a "re-searching" way: open, reflective, and critically engaged.

The book not only offers a more complex and nuanced perspective on research in group psychotherapy, but also introduces a wide array of methods. Importantly, Vosmer does not privilege one methodology over another; instead, she fosters a dialogue between qualitative and quantitative approaches, promoting mutual enrichment rather than competition.

This is an essential read for both researchers and clinicians interested in the evolving landscape of group psychotherapy research.

– **Anna Zajenkowska**, *Associate Professor at Vizja University in Warsaw*

This is a timely and much needed volume that will illuminate many group-analytic research projects in different countries and cultures. Susanne Vosmer has produced a comprehensive text that goes beyond conventional Western conceptions of reality, knowledge and truth. In fact, she incorporates cross-cultural and complementary philosophical conceptions, and successfully challenges unnecessary divisions between the traditional quantitative and qualitative research paradigms. Group analysts shall value the usefulness of this book, which validates clinical effectiveness and also explores research methodology into median, large, and organisational consultancy groups. I can warmly recommend it.

– **Arturo Ezquerro**, *consultant psychiatrist, group analyst, and author of Group Analysis Throughout the Life Cycle*

As Susanne Vosmer writes in her introduction to this important book, group analytic research is a "neglected child". Her book offers cogent arguments for giving this offspring proper care and attention. Dr Vosmer has been one of the relatively few passionate advocates for research in group analysis. She has pulled her ideas together and broken new ground in writing the first book in the field of Foulkesian group analysis that is dedicated to research.

As would be expected of her, this book is meticulously researched and written in an accessible and interesting manner. It should appeal to experienced and fledgling researchers. It serves as a "how to do research" guide for those wishing to step into the field of research and to the theories and philosophies underpinning research methodologies. Dr Vosmer highlights that these are rooted in Western thinking. There is a consequential need to question this thinking to ensure that practice and research are relevant to societies that group analysis seeks to serve. Hence, the need for a pluralistic paradigm.

This groundbreaking book should find a readership amongst qualified practitioners, trainees, teachers, academics and researchers. It should find its way onto course reading lists.

– **Andy Downie**, *group analyst, supervisor and trainer*

"This book is dedicated to my children."

A NEW PLURALISTIC PARADIGM FOR RESEARCH

A New Pluralistic Paradigm for Research: Diverse Methods for Researching Analytic and Other Groups is a comprehensive resource that equips a diverse audience with essential research knowledge. Fourteen informative chapters, organized into two sections, describe a new paradigm, as well as methodologies to research group analytic psychotherapy, different types of groups, and social phenomena.

In addition to making group analytic thinking accessible and offering a practical guide, the Emerging Reality Paradigm promotes the decolonization of research practices, offering an alternative to traditional Western research paradigms. While the focus is on pluralism, readers will also gain valuable insight into both quantitative and qualitative research paradigms. Western and Indigenous thinking is bridged, illustrative examples are interwoven, and real research examples are included, enabling professionals and students to research analytic groups creatively and effectively. Engaging text boxes and figures, suggestions for further research and suggested readings foster deeper understanding.

This book is ideal for researchers, psychotherapists, students, supervisors, trainees, and seminar leaders who seek to gain or deepen their knowledge of group analytic research. It serves as an essential guide for anyone interested in (analytic) groups and the methodologies that inform them.

Dr Susanne Vosmer is a practicing group analytic psychotherapist, clinical psychologist, researcher, and research supervisor. She is a seminar leader at group analytic training organizations. She carried out several studies and has written on diverse topics. Previously, she was a clinical tutor on the Doctorate for Clinical Psychology in Hull, where she also taught psychodynamic theory. She is a member of the editorial board of the *International Journal of Psychotherapy*, edited a special Women's Issue on Love, and is involved in editorial activities for other journals. Her interests include forensic psychotherapy, psychotherapy research, love studies, politics, and literature. Also trained in EMDR, Clinical Hypnosis, and Reiki, Susanne is a research supervisor at the New School for Psychotherapy and Counselling (NSPC) in London, examiner at the NSPC and the Institute of Group Analysis in London, and responsible for the academic development of the course at Group Analysis North, United Kingdom.

A NEW PLURALISTIC PARADIGM FOR RESEARCH

Diverse Methods for Researching Analytic and Other Groups

Susanne Vosmer

Routledge
Taylor & Francis Group
LONDON AND NEW YORK

Designed cover image: Getty Images

First published 2026
by Routledge
4 Park Square, Milton Park, Abingdon, Oxon OX14 4RN

and by Routledge
605 Third Avenue, New York, NY 10158

Routledge is an imprint of the Taylor & Francis Group, an informa business

British Library Cataloguing-in-Publication Data
A catalogue record for this book is available from the British Library

ISBN: 978-1-041-00385-4 (hbk)
ISBN: 978-1-041-00383-0 (pbk)
ISBN: 978-1-003-60954-4 (ebk)

DOI: 10.4324/9781003609544

Typeset in Times New Roman
by codeMantra

CONTENTS

FIGURES

TABLE

TEXTBOXES

GENERAL INTRODUCTION

This book originates in a void. Just how significant the notion of a void is, did not occur to me at the time. Its profound significance would only dawn on me much later.

Group Analysis was an innovative approach to psychotherapy when first introduced by Siegmund Heinrich Fuchs, more commonly known as Foulkes. He established the London Institute of Group Analysis (IGA) in 1971. Since then, the IGA has trained numerous group psychotherapists and additionally established training programs worldwide.

Even though research teaching forms part of the curriculum, our profession has not espoused an English group analytic research handbook that all group analytic psychotherapists and researchers could turn to. Thus, my book was born out of a desire to address this lack.

St Pierre (2011) has pointed out that studying philosophy should precede the study of research methodology. I could not agree more. Without the knowledge of philosophy, group analytic researchers cannot understand the epistemological and ontological assumptions that structure all methodologies. Separating philosophy and research, or trying to disentangle philosophy from science, is like attempting to detach the individual from the group. It is impossible. Therefore, one focus of my book is on philosophy.

I need to declare that I have used OpenAI (2023) during the process of writing this book. However, I have primarily drawn on it to check for accuracy, locate potentially missed studies, and for verification of my calculations or claims.

When looking for suitable methodologies, I read book chapters and articles. Predominantly, but not exclusively, the chapters summarized conventional outcome studies that demonstrate the effectiveness of group analytic psychotherapies. I found descriptions of methodologies in the wider group psychotherapy research literature. Most described "traditional" research approaches.

However, the application of creative methods brings more cultural richness to the growing group analytic community (Nayak, 2023). This is another purpose of this handbook. It aims to offer a diverse perspective and to contribute to the decolonization of group analytic research.

At the time, I also noticed that group analytic research is the "neglected child" of group psychotherapy research. Perhaps this is due to the complexity of analytic groups or due to the peculiarity of Group Analysis. As a hybrid, it is situated between the clinical practice of group analytic psychotherapy and the schools of social or humanistic sciences. As Anderson (2019) highlights, Group Analysis is also a rich analytic system (Lorentzen, 2022), which provides the opportunity to radically break with current discourses due to its ability to deconstruct language and analyze texts. Anderson referred to Group Analysis as a "research method" (p. 57) and "reflexive methodology for understanding the process of knowledge production" (p. 75). Unfortunately, the wider community of researchers has ignored these aspects. Thus, my book also aims to promote Group Analysis as a research method.

Research is divided into the competing quantitative and qualitative paradigm. When paradigm proliferation arose in the 1980s, the sharp distinction between the two paradigms started to weaken (Denzin & Lincoln, 2011, p. ix). The traditions no longer seemed to be at war (Cresswell, 2003). Researchers began to view mixed methodologies as unproblematic due to beliefs in the fallibility of knowledge (Tashakkori & Teddlie, 1998). Nevertheless, positivist and idealist purists advocate either the quantitative or the qualitative approach.

Many research textbooks reflect this division. Therefore, it would have been possible to restrict the scope of my book to the neat division of quantitative and qualitative methodologies/methods. I could have included a few paragraphs on their philosophical underpinnings and describe their applications in group analytic psychotherapy research. Then I would have followed the common trend that has prevailed in Western research books.

Alternatively, I could have focused either on the quantitative or the qualitative paradigm, included a chapter on Indigenous research, and described a few suitable methodologies and techniques for researching group analytic groups. This would have been in line with the tendency to choose one's preferred approach and then write about it.

After analyzing the unconscious life of research paradigms, I started to realize that dominant doctrines masquerade as inevitable truths. Ironically, Burns (2000) argued more than two decades ago that the dichotomization of the quantitative and qualitative paradigm was misleading. However, it still exists, although Ratnesar and Mackenzie (2007) have pointed out that this divide was "no longer sustainable" (p. 13). There is no logical reason why these two paradigms must be separated. Group Analysis rejects the "either or" dichotomies as well.

Therefore, another focus of my book is on formulating a new research paradigm, which is underpinned by non-Western philosophies. Its metaphysical assumptions rest on the notion that everything arose out of a void, known as "Oriental Nothingness". Before elaborating on this in the first part of my book, I need to clarify a few things.

Firstly, I am a native German, who speaks only European languages. So, I had to rely on translations and hope that the readers will forgive me, if my interpretation of Asian or African philosophy differs from theirs.

Secondly, I use singular gender pronouns ("she", "he"), instead of sticking to the new custom in the English language that uses the plural "they" and "their" when referring to a single person. Historically, women have been excluded from science and research (Haraway, 1997). Black women and other women of color are still marginalized. By using the plural ("they", "their"), which does not distinguish between female and male, I would have rendered the female voice invisible again.

Thirdly, because research can often appear dry, I adopt a literary style at times. Occasionally, my style is a bit staccato. Variations in my style of writing are intentional.

Fourthly, although several group analytic approaches will be discussed as I proceed, I tend to lean more toward Group Analysis as practiced in Britain, because this is where I trained and reside. I will use the terms "group analytic psychotherapy" and "psychodynamic group psychotherapy" interchangeably, and capitalize Group Analysis, when referring to Foulkes' approach. By no means do I suggest that all group analytic approaches are the same.

Others may disagree with my decision. However, despite their different foci, all psychoanalytically oriented group psychotherapy models nevertheless share an overarching goal: to identify clients' unconscious conflicts and motivations, defenses, transferences, and dysfunctional patterns in their relationships or behavior (Kaklauskas & Olson, 2020, p. 13). Taking into consideration also that the modern individual group psychotherapist draws on many different theories and techniques (Dalal, 2018b), which have diluted "pure approaches", my decision seems justifiable. Ultimately, this does not matter too much, because the focus of my book is on research and not on psychotherapy.

Furthermore, my proposed research paradigm and methods are not restricted to group analytic researchers only. So that, readers from other backgrounds can understand group analytic ideas and group analytic psychotherapies, important conceptualizations are outlined in the appendices. Additional information on quantum mechanics and statistics, as well as links to resources, can also be found in the appendices.

Due to space, my selection of methods is neither complete nor are the descriptions always comprehensive. Nevertheless, this book aims to firmly position group analytic research within the wider field of Indigenous, qualitative, and quantitative research. Interestingly, Group Analysis has a lot in common with Indigenous approaches: both resist.

When selecting methods, I considered guidelines that recommend the use of quantitative methods. Despite its flaws, Positivism continues to assert its influence through these methods. Methodological Positivism reminds me of the return of the repressed (Freud, 1939). It haunts. It continually returns, or threatens to return, thereby disrupting conscious thought processes. If my group analytic reading of Positivism is correct, then it will never totally go away, because it serves a defensive function, protecting against annihilatory anxiety.

I share Freud's pessimism and believe that there will always be crises in the world. Historically, whenever annihilation anxieties were high due to wars or economic hardship, Positivism's influence increased. When Western societies flourished economically, people became disenchanted with Positivism. In the 1980s, a resurgence of Positivism occurred (Steinmetz, 2005) when the world economy was suffering (Green, 1983). Unsurprisingly, modern Positivism dominates in the form of the quantitative paradigm, because the world is plagued again by wars, climate crisis, and economic insecurities.

Our post-modern world pushes us to do everything more efficiently and faster. Technological advances encourage progression. Other ways of thinking tend to be viewed as old-fashioned. They are sidelined and are often dismissed. However, when we do not pause and engage in reflection and "diffraction", i.e., understanding a process through something else, we do not really progress.

Instead of ignoring all those wise philosophers and scholars, we could learn about research through meditation, by engaging with communities, or by putting the African Ubuntu into practice by recognizing that *I exist because We are*, or by adopting a binocular vision and Yin/Yang perspective. Hopefully, the reader will feel inspired by my discussions of philosophy, group analysis, and methodologies. More importantly, I hope that (group analytic) researchers will re-negotiate the existing status quo in the world of research. This book is an invitation to do so.

Section 1

Introduction

In Britain, clinicians are expected to know a range of methodologies and engage in research activities (Vossler & Moller, 2015). Ironically, the accrediting body for group analysts, the United Kingdom Council of Psychotherapy (UKCP), only expects adult psychotherapists to be taught *basic* research methodology/methods as part of their psychotherapy training (UKCP, 2017, p. 6). I would not consider the statistical meta-analytic method or the systematic review method as basic. The latter is a "…robust, reproducible, structured critical synthesis of existing research." (Munn et al., 2018, p. 2)

So, the UKCP conveys tacitly that group analysts do not need to know more complex methods, despite the fact that systematic reviews and meta-analyses are very important, because the National Institute for Health and Care Excellence (NICE) relies heavily on the' pyramid of evidence' (Murad et al., 2016).

The National Health Service (NHS) and private providers in Britain base the provision of therapy on recommendations by NICE, which favors meta-analyses, systematic reviews and RCTs. This is echoed in the American Psychological Association (APA) by requiring that clinicians be trained in evidence-based practice (EBP) (Blease et al., 2016). Becoming an evidence-based group clinician is, however, challenging. One should not underestimate its complexity, as Burlingame et al. (2024) note. What counts as valid evidence in psychotherapy research is still debatable (see Philips & Falkenstrőm, 2021). Thus, within the hostile environment of neoliberalism (Skaife & Martyn, 2022), group analytic psychotherapists encounter several barriers. Many clients are also terrified of group therapy (Shay, 2021), so the profession is confronted with different obstacles that must be overcome. These are also discussed by Yalom and Leszcz (2005; 2020).

Recent reviews and meta-analyses on the effectiveness of group psychotherapy (e.g. Schwartze et al. 2019; Barkowski et al. 2020; Rosendahl et al. 2021; Andrews et al. 2024; Diamond et al. 2025), and their crucial ingredients (Twomey & Dowling, 2025), have demonstrated that both f-2-f and online group psychotherapy (Andrews et al., 2024) are clinically effective and economically advantageous (Whittingham et al., 2021).

DOI: 10.4324/9781003609544-1

Comparatively few studies have been carried out in the field of group analytic psychotherapies (see Karterud, 2015; Schlapobersky, 2016; Lorentzen, 2020; Ezquerro & Cañete, 2024 for summaries or references). Alas, Blackmore et al.'s (2009; 2012) systematic review is still the only comprehensive review of the effectiveness/efficacy of Group Analysis. An updated review to ascertain, which recommendations have (not) been met, has never been conducted.

On a more positive note, since their report on the 'missing' effectiveness, more qualitative, but also quantitative research studies, have been carried out. This includes Ashton et al.'s (2025) pilot study of a patient-reported outcome measure to capture the therapeutic outcomes of group analysis; Story et al.'s (2024) study, using the CORE, which supports the effectiveness of group analytic psychotherapy; Vosmer's (2024) study on lived diversity in group analytic training; Jackson et al.'s (2024) study on group members' experience of survive & thrive; McMahon's (2023) narrative literature review on supervision; Vosmer's (2022) study examining discrimination at the IGA; Cilasun et al.'s (2021) learning evaluation of the large training group; Stocks et al.'s (2020) research to identify areas of "recovery" specific to group analytic psychotherapy to facilitate the development of a suitable patient-reported outcome measure; Anderson's (2019) deconstruction of Group Analysis; O'Beney et al.'s (2019) phenomenological study of group members' experiences; Perren et al.'s (2018) study of therapists' views of working with people with dementia; Nathan and Poulsen's (2004) qualitative study of group analytic training groups; and, of course, Lorentzen's (2020, 2022) studies and works. Lorentzen is the only group analyst, who has conducted a randomized controlled trial, together with other colleagues (e.g. Lorentzen et al., 2013; 2015a; 2015b; 2018), on the effectiveness of short-term *group analytic therapy*, adopting a manualized approach (see Lorentzen, 2014).

Other studies can also be found on the website of the European Group Analytic Training Institutions Network (EGATIN).

Thanks to psychology, psychiatry, the neurosciences, and neuropsychoanalysis, psychoanalytic conceptualizations, including the unconscious, have been supported by research evidence (e.g. Schüssler, 2002; Banaji et al., 2004; Luborsky & Barnett, 2006; Eagle, 2013).

The reputation and influence of Group Analysis varies across countries. Katerud et al. (2025) wrote that group treatment is highly regarded in Norway, but their focus is more on mentalization. This has created some tension (see Staats, 2024; Karterud et al., 2024, 2025).

By and large, group analysts have been more actively engaged in research in Scandinavia, Germany, and in the United States. Research is well established in Germany: see, for example authors, such as Catina et al., 1989; Catina & Tschuschke, 1993; König & Lindner, 1993, 1994; Tschuschke et al., 2007; 2010; Staats et al., 2014; Bernard Strauß (2022) has published numerous studies (also spelt 'Strauss'; e.g., Strauß et al., 2004; 2008).

Karterud (2025) writes that research implies a willingness to enter the world of empirical evidence for validation of truth claims and that it requires an empirical stance. It is my hope that more group analytic research will be carried out as a result of this book. Hopefully, the 'neglected child of group research' will position itself firmly in the wider field of group research, Indigenous research, qualitative research, and quantitative research.

Outline of This Book

This book is arranged in two sections. While ***Section 1 is predominantly theoretical***, the focus of ***Section 2 is on methods***. Section 1 consists of three chapters, and Section 2 comprises twelve chapters. Numerous textboxes are presented alongside so that the flow of the main narrative is not disrupted. The content is related, and textboxes comprise descriptions of theories, definitions, explanations, and so forth. Additionally, I have included several figures, because visual information is often easier to understand.

Section 2 starts with a separate introduction. In my synthesis and concluding remarks, I invite readers to carry out research, because every research project matters. To avoid duplication, this book includes one overall bibliography.

Furthermore, it has ***five appendices***, which offer information on the development of group analytic psychotherapies and a summary of where group analytic psychotherapy can be situated (Appendices 1 and 2). Readers unfamiliar with group analytic psychotherapy may find these appendices useful. For readers interested in questionnaires, tests, software, and further reading, I have included relevant material in Appendix 3. Not every researcher is interested in statistics, and I respect this. Nonetheless, the curious but inexperienced reader may like to look at Appendix 4. I have written a humorous account of a group analyst's journey to master basic statistics and included further reading. Equally, not every reader may share my enthusiasm for the quantum world. But some may like to know more. Therefore, Appendix 5 includes a supplement to Chapter 2, Part 2. An index concludes this book.

More specifically, ***Section 1*** problematizes the excluding history of philosophy and science and the dominance of Modern Positivism, and discusses the consequences for group analytic research. I suggest that alternatives are needed not only for group analytic but for all researchers. After demonstrating that a paradigm shift is needed, I introduce the Emerging Reality Paradigm (ERP) in Chapters 2, Parts 1 and 2.

Section 2 presents suitable methods for group analytic research. Drawing on the group analytic and wider group literature, I will describe a wide variety of methods for studying different types of small, median, and large groups. Philosophical foundations and methodological dis/advantages are considered throughout, and illustrative examples are interwoven. I have modified some methods and models. I also suggest the inclusion of Artificial Intelligence (AI) tools. By and large, my selection of methods is underpinned by a desire for more inclusive, diverse research. Due to space, not all approaches and methods could be described. At times, I have sacrificed breadth for depth, and vice versa. Finally, I have decided to include child and adolescent research. In contrast to psychoanalysis, or countries, such as Germany, group child and adolescent practice and research have been neglected in Britain.

More specifically, ***Chapter 1*** focuses on philosophy due to its importance for research. Essential terminology, basic group dynamics and processes, and a critical examination of philosophy are presented. This includes the African Philosophy Ubuntu, and metaphysics of the Global South and North. I describe the development of science, including the isms and schisms. Research paradigms are outlined. I question whether the decolonization of research can be achieved due to the dominance of Positivism, and the exclusion of the Global South in science and philosophy.

In ***Part 1 of Chapter 2***, I build on previous arguments, showing that research paradigms underpinned by Western philosophies are no longer fit for purpose. To counter exclusionary practices and prevailing beliefs that ontology and epistemology are distinct concerns, and to eradicate the separation between the quantitative and qualitative paradigm, a paradigm shift is advocated, and the ERP is proposed as an alternative. The ERP rests on Asian and African philosophies, group analytic and Jungian theories, and psychological conceptualizations, which are described.

Part 2 introduces quantum principles, which are an integral part of the ERP. Reality, energy, consciousness, and neuroscientific findings are presented in relation to the ERP. It will be fully formulated and its limitations will be discussed.

Section 2

In ***Chapter 3***, it is acknowledged that quantitative and qualitative methodologies do speak their own language. To make it easier to understand research, including terminology, designs, and methods, Foulkes' methodology, the Northfield Experiments, and other examples from group analysis are used to make research more understandable.

Chapter 4 discusses dis/advantages of AI and outlines how to carry out a meta-analysis, a systematic review, and randomized controlled trial. Additionally, instrumentalization and operationalization are explained. When using a diffractive methodology, epistemology is viewed differently, I will suggest.

Chapter 5 discusses the benefits and disadvantages of several methods, including the use of surveys and questionnaires, the Delphi and Focus Group Method, the Matrix Representation Grid, the Repertory Grid method, Q-Methodology, (Social) Network Analysis, and Sentiment Analysis. These methods will be described. Practical examples will be provided and the use of AI will be recommended.

In Chapter 6, I will explain the difference between concepts, models, and theory. I briefly discuss 'creative' and 'superficial' theorizing, as well as the Indigenous and other theoretical frameworks. "Living" group analytic theories is suggested to foster creative theorizing and prevent superficial theorizing. Free association, reverie, or social dreaming may also foster creativity. Versions of Grounded Theory will be described and several practical examples will be presented.

In Chapter 7, the application of Meta-Synthesis, Institutional Ethnography Autoethnography, and phenomenological approaches for group (analytic) research, will be described. One focus is Bakhtinian dialogism. Additionally, I will briefly discuss whether group (analytic) researchers can escape positivist coding when carrying out qualitative studies. This has empirical and moral implications.

In Chapter 8, many methods will be outlined to research (online) groups, individuals, unconscious group processes, and sensitive topics. Due to space, most descriptions will be brief. These include interview methods (group, oral, and biographical), the visual matrix method, and the body as research tool. Transference and transference interpretations research will be discussed in more depth due to their importance for group research. Suggestions for further research will be made. Indigenous research methods, change process research, the social dreaming method, discourse analysis, and deconstruction will also be described. The Operationalized Psychodynamic Diagnostic Procedure, Jung's Word Association Experiment/Test, and the free association narrative techniques will be outlined. I query whether researchers should 'love' their participants to obtain richer data. My discussion of research ethics suggests that revisions of codes of ethics are required.

Mixing is the focus of ***Chapter 9***. Following a brief description of the mixed methods approach and compatible philosophies (Pragmatism, Critical Realism, ERP, postcolonial Indigenous Paradigm), the privileged position of the research question is challenged. Axiological considerations should not be secondary, I will argue. The application of Critical Realism as research method will be outlined and a model to inform Evidence-based Practice/Practicebased

Evidence suggested. Action research and semiotics will be one focus. Practical examples, recommendations for research, and a detailed Peircean semiotic analysis of psychosomatic symptoms will be offered to aid understanding of theoretical concepts.

Chapter 10 focuses on secondary data and the documentary method. A variety of qualitative methods will be outlined to study therapy or supervision groups, social phenomena, documents, and monuments. In addition to offering a detailed description of the diary method and outline of the biographical narrative interview method, triangulation will be discussed. Group Analysis as tool, operationalizing, The Chronogram, Cartography, and Interpersonal Circumplex will also be outlined. Some practical examples will be provided.

Chapter 11 guides the reader through archival research. My own research on the former German Democratic Republic will be used to illustrate how documentary/bibliographical research can be done and to foster learning about archival research. For educational purposes, I show how to integrate theory, apply latent analysis techniques, and use triangulation. Additionally, I consider counter-/transference reactions and attend to the emotional impact of research on the researcher. A critical discussion of the Western academic writing style will be presented. Moreover, I explain how research is written up and draw attention to a decolonizing style.

In Chapter 12, child and adolescent research will be described. Ethics, language, a semiotic approach, and a Social Phenomenological Analysis (SPA) will be described. This method is suited for studying groups of children in educational settings. Unfortunately, child research is lacking in Group Analysis. A group analytic research framework, which entails methodologies and methods that use observations, interviews, communication, conversations, drawings, photos, texts, semiotic analysis, and dreams, could be useful.

In Chapter 13, I explain why it is important to study median and large groups. I will also describe how to research them. Following a brief outline of the features of different types of median/large groups, group analytic and conventional methodologies will be described. Many methods can be used to study large groups. These include all traditional methods (e.g., critical discourse analysis, psychometric social network analysis, mapping techniques), as well as group analytic methods. Insight into interactions, sub-groupings, the effect of the convenor, and power dynamics, can be gained by researching different types of median/large groups.

1

THE EXCLUDING HISTORIES OF PHILOSOPHY & SCIENCE AND DOMINANCE OF POSITIVISM

Is an Alternative Research Paradigm Needed?

Abstract

The main emphasis is on philosophy due to its importance for research. Essential terminology, basic group dynamics and processes, are described. My critical examination of philosophy includes the African Ubuntu and Derrida's deconstruction, as well as metaphysics of the Global South and North. Furthermore, the development of science, empiricism, patriarchalism, sexism, and racism, are discussed. The conundrum of philosophical/research paradigms is also illuminated. Positivism, Interpretivism, Social Constructivism, Social Constructionism, Phenomenology, Critical Theory, Pragmatism, Critical Realism, Postmodernism, and Poststructuralism, are outlined. I query whether we need an entirely new paradigm that is not underpinned by an oppressive epistemology and racist philosophy.

Introduction

Studying philosophy should precede the study of research methodology (St Pierre, 2011). Otherwise group analytic researchers cannot understand the epistemological and ontological assumptions that structure all methodologies.

Separating philosophy and research, or trying to disentangle philosophy and science, is like attempting to detach the individual from the group. Group researchers, who have studied groups and group analytic psychotherapy for many years (Fuhriman & Burlingame, 1994), know that this is impossible. Psychoanalytically oriented group models aim to identify clients' unconscious conflicts and motivations, defenses, transferences, and dysfunctional patterns in their relationships or behavior in groups (Kaklauskas & Olson, 2020, p. 13). Researching analytic groups is complex, and researchers often encounter constraints. To understand why, I will elucidate the histories of philosophy and science. History speaks through the language of the social unconscious, that is, aspects of the social world that people are unaware of, which include collective defenses, memories, myths, and so forth (Hopper & Weinberg, 2011). Deciphering socially unconscious processes in groups is essential but difficult. Only a holistic research perspective,

DOI: 10.4324/9781003609544-2

which extends to the social world, the environment, organizations, and to culture, can capture what happens in groups. Although it is overly simplistic, I will define 'group' as an aggregate of individuals (Calder, 2014), which exists as a separate ontological entity (Zuolo, 2014, p. 199).

Several dynamics have been identified in groups. However, Thornton (2025) notes that the term "group dynamics" has become imprecise. Hence, the concept of the "group matrix", which refers to the totality of communication and experience in a group (p. 44), seems more useful.

By linking the dynamic to the foundation matrix, the founder of Group Analysis in Britain, Foulkes, captured the idea that each matrix is connected with a historical, cultural, and social "meta-matrix" (Wilke, 2018, p. 4). Furthermore, every individual is a "nodal point" (Foulkes, 2003) in the matrices of various groups. While each person has unique experiences and own perceptions of reality, they also reflect an internalized sociocultural group dimension (Bacha, 2025).

Due to advances in neuroscience, that is, the study of the nervous system (Goswami, 2020), there is little doubt about the social and emotional nature of the brain (Damasio, 2005). Moreover, neuropsychoanalytic research, i.e. the integration of neuroscience and psychoanalysis, has enabled a better understanding of unconscious processes (see Banaji et al., 2004; Flores Mosri et al., 2022; Solms, 2018; Solms & Turnbull, 2002). What we nowadays know about individuals and groups also stems from case studies, observations, and experiments (see Barkham et al., 2021). These methods are embedded in the qualitative and quantitative research paradigms, which are underpinned by philosophy. Many definitions of philosophy exist. Therefore, another challenge that group analytic researchers have to master is acquiring sufficient knowledge of philosophy and these research paradigms, so that they can study groups methodically. Being aware of one's own underlying philosophical assumptions is also crucial, because philosophical assumptions are associated with a specific paradigm, methodologies, and methods (Kamal, 2019). So, researchers must read relevant theoretical literature about groups and philosophy. If they do not, they have little that helps them think, whilst carrying out research.

Admittedly, some texts are difficult. Noting that Aristotle is not easily understood, because of the distance that separates us from him, Lacan (1966) asserted that reading does not obligate one to understand (p. 61). Several French psychoanalysts (Lacan, Guattari) and philosophers (Foucault, Deleuze & Guattari, Derrida) are deliberately challenging. These post-modernists and post-modernists dismissed the 'ideal' that says that language should be coherent, precise, and clear. They radically separated themselves from modernist philosophical assumptions and norms of Western Enlightenment (St Pierre, 2011). I will explain this further as I proceed with this book.

Here, I will first describe group dynamics and processes. Then I will critically discuss philosophy, including the African Ubuntu and Derrida's deconstruction, as well as the metaphysics of the Global North and South, the development of science and Empiricism, patriarchalism, sexism, and racism. Furthermore, I will attend to the conundrum of paradigms and philosophical frameworks, such as Positivism, Interpretivism, Social Constructivism, Social Constructionism, Phenomenology, Critical Theory, Pragmatism, Critical Realism, Postmodernism, and Poststructuralism. Moreover, problematizing that Positivism is the benchmark of science, I will query whether decolonizing research is sufficient or whether an entirely new paradigm is needed.

Groups

Simply put, groups exist because people need each other's company. From an evolutionary perspective, prototypes of human groups were of mixed age and sex. They were characterized by

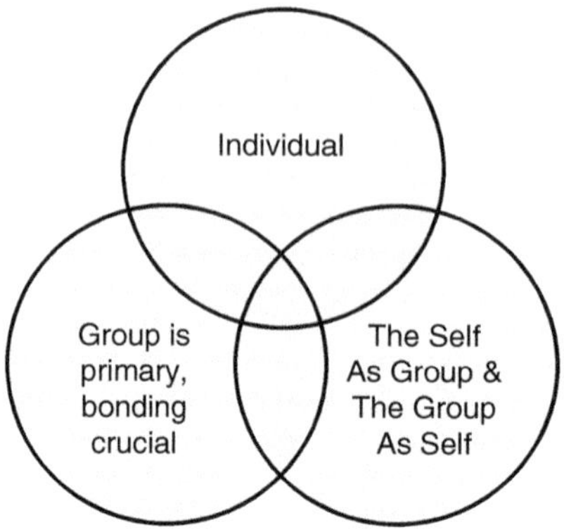

FIGURE 1.1 Relation between Individual & Group.

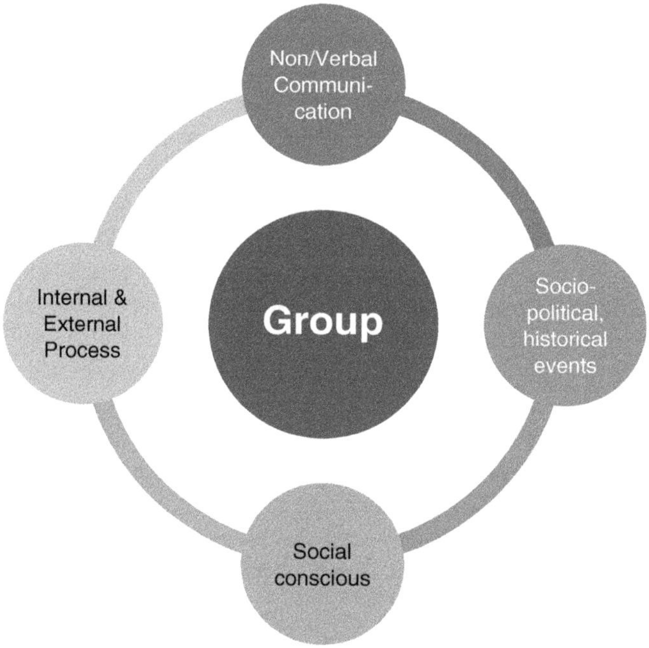

FIGURE 1.2 Influences on a Group.

intense forms of relating (Bacha, 2025). While people have a biological sociality, because bodies and social brains develop together (Schore, 2019), this development is influenced by social relationships. Our need for relating seems to be innate and is reinforced by bonding experiences in groups (Bacha, 2025). Although groups are affected by group dynamics, such as un/conscious processes, interactions, and changes, which occur in and between groups (Wilke, 2018), it is group bonding that creates and integrates the individual human being (see Figure 1.1).

Nevertheless, internalized childhood experiences of mothering, fathering, and sibling competition, or cooperation, are often neglected in the study of groups. But these group attachments form the blueprint for all other relationships (Ezquerro & Cañete, 2023, 2025). They enable the development of a coherent self, which comprises personal and group experiences, as well as un/

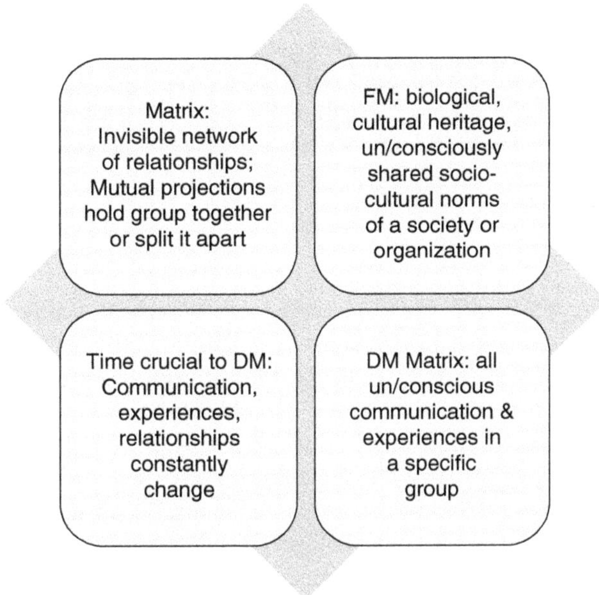

FIGURE 1.3 The Matrix, Dynamic Matrix (DM), and Foundation Matrix (FM) (see Foulkes, 1948, 2003; Thornton, 2025; Wilke, 2025).

conscious memories, and a variety of emotions. This means that people's internalized groups consist of complex dynamics, feelings, and emotional processes. If these are not well integrated, relationship difficulties and other problems arise (Bacha, 2025). However, since the underlying reasons for these problems tend to be repressed, people are unaware of them.

Furthermore, when feelings are too overwhelming, they tend to be unconsciously projected into others. A person may even become psychologically unwell (Foulkes, 1964). Foulkes (2003) emphasized the importance of language, communication, and translation, referring to the intricate process of making communication more articulate (Thornton, 2025, p. 49). Much of our communication is non-verbal, occurring at an unconscious level, and there is no barrier between an inner and outer group (Foulkes, 1973). Hence, a group is affected by several factors, see Figure 1.2.

While Foulkes (1948, 2003) explained the continually changing interdependent nature of a group by theorizing the matrix, the sociologist Elias (1978, 1987, 1994) called these "figuration", which he linked to the civilization process. Basically, both the dynamic and foundation matrices convey what happens in groups. They are characterized by specific aspects (see Figure 1.3).

Historically, the sociologist Le Bon (1896) conceptualized a dangerous crowd mentality, resulting from the unruly psychological behavior of the lower class in the French Revolution. Additionally, Freud (1913, 1921) postulated that this crowd phenomenon created something like a group mind. Collective, unconscious processes occur in groups. The individual loses the ability to think or act, independently. Wilke (2018) conceptualized the collective mind of a group and the individual mind as living networks of relationships. These relationships are formed by the dyadic and triadic alliances within these networks, and by the social matrix surrounding them, Wilke explained.

The group, group members, and the group facilitator form an interdependent Gestalt. The individual figure is brought into focus against the background of the group (Foulkes, 1975a). This means that the group has a dynamic influence on a person (Schlapobersky, 2016).

Interactions between people are always shaped by the context. To understand group processes, group analytic therapists often rely on concepts, such as mirroring, resonance, matrix, the social unconscious, and location of disturbance. They locate emotions and un/conscious processes within the invisible matrix of a group, examining dynamics on vertical and horizontal levels (Wilke, 2018). Evoked emotions are utilized. They also fulfill functions of differentiation (Elias, 1991).

What Is Philosophy?

Metaphysics, ontology, epistemology, and axiology are branches of philosophy. According to Max Horkheimer (1999), metaphysics attempts to establish a universal and fundamental structure of reality that underlies the totality of being. Metaphysics is a broader field than ontology. It tries to explain reality at the highest level of generalizability (Loux, 2006). Ontology stems from the Greek words "ontos" and "logos". Loosely translated, ontology is the study of being (Al-Amoudi & O'Mahoney, 2016). While metaphysics addresses "what is there?", seeking to explain the nature of entities ("If God exists, what is s/he like?"), epistemology (study of knowledge) tries to explain how we understand an object (meaning ascribing activity). When contemporary Western philosophers use the word "metaphysics", it tends to resemble what Aristotle spoke of, namely the "science that studies Being qua Being" (Loux, 2006, p. 11).

The branch of axiology concerns itself with questions about value and aesthetics (Honderich, 1995).

Historically, it was no earlier than 1780 that historians of philosophy began to deny that people of Africa and Asia were philosophical (Park, 2014). Distinguishing between African thought and African Philosophy, Marais (1984) was clear that it could only be a philosophy under certain conditions. If philosophy requires second-order thinking (thinking about thought), where cosmological, cosmogonical, and ontological questions are dismissed, then the rightful existence of African Philosophy may be questioned (p. 265).

Cosmological refers to the physical universe and cosmogonical ideas are astrophysical, related to the universe' origin (Shu, 2024).

When philosophizing, one distances oneself from one's world, Marais (1984) explained. For Africans, this would amount to self-annihilation as far as their view of reality is concerned. He suggested that metaphysical and existential beliefs prevented Africans from producing a philosophical system that would be considered as philosophy by Western philosophers. Hence, whether an African philosophy, a Chinese philosophy, and so forth exist, depends on which definition of philosophy one uses.

Western cultures and philosophy have been accused of oppression (Maris, 2020) and epistemological racism (Bernasconi et al., 2013). To override philosophical racism, Ramose (1999, 2002, 2003, 2015, 2016, 2017) formulated an African philosophy based on Ubuntu, the Bantu concept of humaneness (see also Ramose & Mosupyoe, 2011). Mangena (2016) clarified that the Ubuntu philosophy was united by the Bantu languages, which are spoken in Southern and Eastern Africa.

There has been some controversy about the nature of Ubuntu, which has been translated as "a person is a person, because of, or through others" (Mkhize, 2008). Nelson Mandela (2008) described Ubuntu as a philosophy that constitutes a universal truth and a way of life. It underpins a transparent society. Ubuntu emphasizes communal relationships, interconnectedness, and shared humanity. It focuses on the idea that an individual's identity and humanity are deeply rooted in their relationships with others. As articulated by Eze (1997, 2020), it emphasizes the communal essence of human existence.

Anyanwu and Ruch (1981) defined African philosophy as concerning itself with the way, in which African people make sense of their destiny, and of the world they live in. Furthermore, Imbo (1998) suggested that ethnophilosophy was an aspect of African Philosophy. Mbiti (1969) defined African philosophy as having an understanding, attitude of mind, logic, and perception to reveal what Africans think, act, or speak about in different life situations (p. 2). Bernasconi et al. (2013) argued that the critical philosophy of race was a crucial enterprise due to its critical engagement with traditional philosophical questions and answers. The view that Western philosophy played a decisive role in colonial oppression (Ramose, 1999), and that philosophical and liberal political theories are racist (Maris, 2020 citing Bracken 1978; Veraart, 2017; Mills, 1978), is shared by several philosophers (e.g. Bernasconi, 2021 Flikschuh, 2018; see also Flikschuh & Ypi, 2014; Van Norden, 2017a,b).

In a recent conversation, Mill (2021) stated that Aristotle was a pioneering racist thinker of the Western tradition. He was referring to ancient Greece, where non-Greeks (barbarians) were regarded as primitive. Aristotle had defined man as an essentially rational being. Irrational people, notably women and barbarians, were inferior human beings (Maris, 2020).

However, when women were no longer excluded from philosophy and science, some "changed the world", as Curry (2017) put it (see also Britannica, 2023; Cowen, 2024; Shearing, 2020).

Western philosophy developed in three stages in terms of metaphysics: dogmatism, skepticism, and criticism of pure reason (Park, 2014, p. 23). Philosophy, as defined by Schlegel, is knowledge of the inner human being, the cause of nature, and the relation of human beings to nature. Or, because philosophy is incomplete, as "the striving after this knowledge" (Schlegel cited in Park, 2014, p. 56).

For Kant, philosophizing was a gradual development of reason that began by concepts only. After studying Fichte's (1982) teachings on science ("Wissenschaftslehre"), the Austrian philosopher Reinhold held that "philosophy is a scientific knowledge that is independent of experience" (cited in Park, 2014, p. 97). Interestingly, for the German philosopher Ast (1807), the life of philosophy was harmonious; therefore, no philosophy should be viewed as superior or denigrated. Sadly, according to the South African philosopher Ramose (1999), Aristotle, Locke, Kant, Hume, and Hegel are among the great Western philosophers, who "... made no small contribution to the philosophical racism in the West" (p. 15).

Differentiating between philosophy, science, and the arts, the French philosopher Gilles Deleuze and the psychoanalyst Félix Guattari (1992) challenge the view that philosophy is an extension of logic. Philosophy is a disruptive act, it questions the status quo and produces concepts. Like Spinoza, both Guattari and Deleuze attend to the body and emotions. An "emotion" constitutes the psychological striation of affect (how our experiences of change are captured by subjectivity). "Affectus" refers to the materiality of change (increase/decrease occurring in relation to affecting bodies) (Hickey-Moody, 2013, pp. 80-1).

Deleuze formulated a Spinozist framework. The relationship between Spinoza's (1677/2002, 2001), and Deleuze and Guattari's (1984, 1987, 1991, 1994) philosophies is evident in conceptualizations of affects and the body. Referring to Spinoza, Hickey-Moody (2013) suggested that "affect" enabled Baruch/Benedikt Spinoza to consider the ontological constitution and power of emotions.

Dalal (2002) found that "black" is used figuratively and stands for two emotions, namely anger and sorrow (p. 154).

Ubuntu & Derrida's Deconstruction

Since the 1990s, a renewed interest in Ubuntu has been noticeable. Dladla (2017) commented that this was philosophically relevant insofar as most white South African, American, and

European scholars approach the question of Ubuntu without demonstrating that they have a working knowledge of at least one of the Bantu languages. Dladla regards this as a minimum scholarly requirement. I have no working knowledge or lived experience of "the" Ubuntu that Dladla (2017) is referring to. Like most other white Europeans, I am a stranger to it. This distance between me and Ubuntu is comparable to standing on a platform of experience, to use Ramose's (2002) analogy. This platform is an epistemological paradigm. To some extent, it determines my way of looking at and interpreting Ubuntu. However, I see it from a European perspective. Dladla (2017) seems to suggest that the scholars Praeg (2009), Cornell (Cornell & van Marle, 2005, 2015; Cornell & Muvangua, 2012), Metz (2011, 2019), and Keevy (2009) also view Ubuntu from a distance. Hence, because I am drawing on their work, I hope that the reader will forgive me, if my discussions do not reflect the "true" Ubuntu.

"Ubuntu" is a Zulu or Nguni term found among the Bantu-speaking people throughout the continent of Africa (Dladla, 2017). It has been roughly translated as "be-ing Human" or "humanness". Ramose (1999) argued that the term "ubuntu" should be hyphenated as "ubu-ntu" (prefix ubu and the stem ntu). "Ubu" evokes the notion of be-ing in general. It is an enfolded be-ing, before manifesting itself in the concrete form (or mode) of existence of any particular entity (Dladla, 2017, p. 50). However, at an ontological level, there is no strict literal separation between "ubu" and "ntu". The meaning of "Umuntu ngumuntu ngabantu" (a person is a person through other people) is inexhaustible in the English translation (Dladla, 2017).

For Ramose (1999), to be a human be-ing means to affirm one's humanity by recognizing the humanity of others, and on that basis, to establish humane relations with them (p. 37).

Dladla (2017) suggests that the core meaning of this aphorism is best expressed by Benezet Bujo, because for Black Africa, the phrase "I am related, therefore we are" (Bujo, 2001, p. 22) is decisive. Similarly, Ramose (1999) has contrasted the Cartesian "I think, therefore I am" with the African "We think". Ubuntu is central to this conceptualization. African be-ing is inseparably anchored in ubuntu, Ramose has argued, and the African tree of knowledge also originates from ubuntu. Both are connected indivisibly. This means that ubuntu is the curving connection between African ontology and epistemology (Ramose, 1999).

At an ontological level, in the African world, there is no separation between subject and object, body and mind, ratio and emotion, or thinking and acting, Ramose (2017) explains. Furthermore, the dance of be-ing is understood as an ontological and epistemological imperative. Hence, to "… dance along with be-ing means to be attuned to be-ing" (Haenen, 2017, p. 16).

For many Africans, a person is an inherently communal being. S/he is embedded in a context of social relationships and interdependence, never viewed as an isolated individual.

Gyekye (1987) has defined African communalism as a kinship-oriented social order. One is brought up with a sense of solidarity with large groups of people. During the course of this "cohabitation" (Khoza, 2005, 2006), one recognizes that one's interests are inextricably linked to the interests of the group in terms of the many crucial matters of life and well-being. According to Gyekye (1987), this sense of community is a central feature of African life. For many, this communalism defines Africanness. Ramose (2002a,b) has argued that an African community is an ongoing dynamic association of men and women, who have a special commitment to one another. They have developed a distinct sense of their communal life. "Communal" then becomes a public discursive space that people create through joint action. In this context, the history of a person's life is the story of transactions with the material and moral aspects of a community. So, it is the story of relations with specific sets of social goods (social contracts). An individual's choice of way of life is, however, constrained by the community's goals.

Discussing Ubuntu, Praeg (2009) claimed that a more radical way to conceive the construction of Africa's identity was to use the philosophy of Ubuntu as a cornerstone to challenge, subvert, and de-legitimize the hegemonic Northern epistemic power structure that determines which constructions can be ignored. Praeg regarded the traditional ways of conceptualizing the relation between epistemology and politics as inadequate. Ubuntu does not allow for such separation (p. 377). His eloquent explication of the nature of Ubuntu involves ten circumscriptions.

Praeg (2009, p. 382), referring to Hamilton and Cairns' (1961) paraphrasing of Plato's Meno (Socratic dialogue) into "Can [ubuntu] be taught?" asks Meno. Socrates replies that he certainly cannot do so for he does not know what [ubuntu] is", also draws on Socrates' geometrical hypothesis to answer what Ubuntu is. Not in the hope of arriving at demonstrative truths about ubuntu, he clarifies.

By constantly delimiting Ubuntu as a series of figures inside other figures (a fractal exploration of the infinite contained in the finite), Ubuntu is equated to an eternally receding figure, inscribed in other figures. Importantly, there is no final figure that contains all figures as one definitive answer. Even the outermost figure will, and must, be circumscribed by other figures, contexts, debates, issues, notions, and concepts, as well as by philosophies and traditions that will re-define (by circumscribing it as infinitum) the meaning and appearances of the forms inside (p. 384). Praeg (2009) expands his argument, advocating for a distinction between the work of Ubuntu and the discourse on Ubuntu. The former is irreducible to the latter.

Accepting the discursive invention of Africa, it will always remain heterogenous by others' attempts to name it. At best, the difference between the work of Ubuntu and the discourse on ubuntu can be circumscribed, he states. All past and future attempts concern themselves with reframing the debate about it. What can be "abstracted" is, at best, the pure, self-conscious logic of circumscription, where the "abstract" will only be the first frame, the epigraph inscribed at the beginning of the second frame, and so forth (p. 367).

Like the poststructuralist Derrida (see Caputo, 1996; Derrida, 1997, 1998), whose deconstruction is based on his analysis of Western philosophy, Praeg (2009) seems to deconstruct the relationship between the corpus of Ubuntu and the discourse of Ubuntu. Thus, he is turning away from Platonian ideas of true forms and essences.

Williams (2004) regarded Derrida's deconstruction as Poststructuralism, because Derrida (1998) dealt explicitly with structuralist theories of language but then transformed structuralism.

It is noteworthy that for Derrida (1990) deconstruction was neither a theory nor a philosophy. Interestingly, he wrote that it was neither a school nor method, not even a discourse or practice. Deconstruction is what happens in a so-called society, the political, historical reality, etc. (Derrida, 1990, cited in St Pierre, 2011, p. 616). Nevertheless, deconstruction is referred to as a method for interpreting texts, which shows that language is indeterminate and without limits.

Reynolds (2024) distinguishes between two types of deconstructions: literary and philosophical. While the former refers to textual interpretation, where discovery is essential to finding the hidden alternative meanings in texts, the philosophical form concerns itself mainly with deconstructing metaphysics.

Characterizing the history of Western metaphysics as logocentric, Derrida (1967a) argued that throughout history, metaphysics has presupposed that there is logos (the word). It acts as a center to all existing things.

Kakoliris (2017) explains that Derrida was influenced by Heidegger's (1962) metaphysics and his meaning of Sein (Being). It reveals itself as eidos (via presence of the thing to sight), substance (essence, existence), or temporal point (cogito, subjectivity). The search for truth ends up with finding presence, as Reynolds (2024) clarifis. Importantly, Derrida (1998) stressed intertextuality. There is nothing outside of the text. In his thinking, the outside is but another text.

Metaphysics of the Global North & South

Even though many philosophers have discussed metaphysics, scholars in the Global North have taken on a different stance than scholars in the Global South. The term "Global South" has been defined differently. However, it does not refer simply to a geographical location. As Mungwini (2024) points out, the term encapsulates that the Global South is a struggle site. Additionally, it is an analytic framework that demands equality and justice.

Descartes' metaphysical dualism suggests that humans are rational (Carreira, 2010). He has noticeably shaped Western philosophy by providing a framework in the 17th century for a specific approach to philosophy, mathematics, and science (Hatfield, 2008). The Cartesian method, expressed in his famous words "I think therefore I am" (Descartes, 1637/1998, p. 18), provided the basis for methodological skepticism. Statements about various concepts were logically/rationally appraised by Descartes (1644/2009) to show that they are true. This is known as the "Dogma of Western Philosophy", because his statements were often truisms, stating what is obviously true and nothing beyond that.

> … had I simply stopped thinking, … I would have had no reason to believe that I had existed. From this I knew that I was a substance the whole essence or nature of which is simply to think … Thus this "I" … the soul through which I am what I am, is entirely distinct from the body and is even easier to know than the body, and even if there were no body at all, it would cease to be all that it is.
>
> (Descartes, 1637/1998, pp. 18–19)

Generally cited as the most classic demonstration of private consciousness, *Discourse on Method* and *Meditations on the First Philosophy* (Descartes, 1637/1998) assumes an independent and authentic cognitive operation for all eternity. His "I" asserts itself as fully conscious, autonomous, coherent, and self-knowable, as Silverman (1983) has noted. She points out that Descartes' individual must only turn within to arrive at a direct appreciation of the truth, which exists independently of discourse (p. 128), culture, and history. The term "individual" designates a different space than the word "subject". It bears traces of Descartes' philosophy, and of other, dominant philosophies of the Renaissance (14th–17th century). Renaissance means "rebirth".

"Individual" and "man" are both stable and autonomous entities, which remain untouched by historical and cultural circumstances (p. 126). Michel Foucault (1970) would challenge this. Both the unconscious and culture could only be studied through the lens of signification.

Critiquing traditional metaphysics for its emphasis on universal categories and essences, Foucault departed as much from Descartes as the "subject" from the "I". Subjectivity marked a radical departure from the Renaissance with scholars focusing more on unconsciousness and culture than on consciousness (Silverman, 1983).

Even though the distinction between subjectivity and objectivity had been central to metaphysics, Derrida (1967a,b), in his search for the Other, formulated a new philosophy of subjectivity. In *L'écriture et la Différence,* Derrida (1967a) destabilizes oppositions, instead of reconciling them. Derrida's subject of thought, experience, and intentionality, cuts through the Hegelian dialectic of difference. There is no final unified synthesis. Instability and ongoing deferral of meaning are the essence of difference. Binaries are but limitations of Western philosophy.

Originally published in 1957, Ernst Cassirer's (2001) *Philosophy of Symbolic Forms* marks a symbolic and semiotic turn in philosophy, a shift toward understanding reality through symbols. Dieter Nitzgen (2010) wrote that the concept of the group analytic matrix owed much to Cassirer. Unfortunately, Foulkes ignored both Cassirer and Charles S Peirce (1839-1914).

What remains the most radical attack ever upon Idealism's claim that signs give expression to thought (Krois, 2004), is found in *Questions Concerning Certain Faculties Claimed for Man*, where Peirce (1868) shows that there is no intuition, but only interpretations of signs.

Known for his view on ethics, Baruch Spinoza (1632–1677) posited a single, infinite substance (God/Nature). In contrast to Descartes, Spinoza (2001) attended to the body and to emotions. Bodies are mainly made through relations with others. Like Freud, Spinoza (1677/2002) did not differentiate between human impulse and desire. The essence of man and desire is nothing but drive, and its awareness (Wróbel, 2019). This emotional congruence between Spinoza and Freud (Bernard, 1946) is not found in Group Analysis, although affective and relational dynamics bear some resemblance to Spinoza and Freud.

Whilst the German philosopher Immanuel Kant (1724–1804) referred to his philosophy as "transcendental idealism", in *Prolegomena* (Part 1 of the transcendental problem, Remark II, Carus, p. 43) (Kant, 2016), he also suggests that it be renamed to "critical realism" (Groff, 2004). He concludes in his *Critique of Pure Reason* (Kant, 1781/2003) that humans are rational and develops "Categories of the Understanding". For research purposes, one might say that "causality" constitutes a key category. Although we conceive events as having causal antecedents, we also perceive objects temporally and spatially. This makes empirical knowledge possible. The delineation of "categories" has been central to Western metaphysics since Aristotle.

Categories are the highest, or most general, types in which things are found (Cohen, 2020). Plato's metaphysics is a belief in forms that exist independently from the physical world. Platonists have used universals to explain the similarities of particulars, arguing that the former had to exist prior to the particulars that exemplify them (Loux, 2006). Thus, Platonists insist that all universals are necessary. Obviously, a form must exist; otherwise, one cannot make any statements about it, and this is necessary. Then Platonists argued that anything following from this must be true. So, they referred to pure truths and pure forms. Commonly, wisdom depends upon universals. Definitions of universals must be fixed, because a universal must be applicable to every instance, every relevant form, regardless of circumstances.

Aristotelians argued the opposite, suggesting that forms are inherent in physical objects. There are no separate domains of forms (Vezina, 2007). They advocated for a philosophy that was grounded in the observable world, emphasizing the intrinsic characteristics of individual substances. They believed that knowledge is best gained from perception and observation. A statement is true, if it corresponds to reality (Loux, 2006).

Such disagreements between idealists and Realists are found throughout history, eventually resulting in the incompatibility between qualitative and quantitative paradigms (Ladyman, 2002).

Whereas metaphysics was important to Plato and Aristotle, for the positivist Comte (1853/1988), it was just a stage between theological and positivist thinking. Hence, most Positivists have ignored metaphysics.

Metaphysics is important to many African and East Asian cultures. The metaphysical explications of Confucianism, Taoism, Buddhism, and Hinduism do not seem as sharply delineated as the expositions of Western philosophical traditions. Of course, this is simplistic. Traditions (e.g. Rationalism, Empiricism, Ubuntu, Buddhism) do have their own idiosyncratic elucidations of metaphysics. Some similarity between the philosophy and methods of the Global South and the Global North also exists.

For example, Sarkissian (2018) discussed the introspective methods (Intuitionistic School) and the investigation methods (Investigative School) of Neo-Confucianism. The Neo-Confucian philosophical tradition exemplifies the same impulse to test, question, and doubt intuition, with a drive toward investigation, as Empiricism (p. 819). There is also an overlap with Romanticism.

Romantics accept intuition as knowledge and prioritize the heart. However, they do not conceptualize the heart and mind together, as the Chinese symbol Xin (heart-mind) does.

Development of Modern Science & Consequences

Science and philosophy have been viewed as two separate disciplines, ever since Frances Bacon argued for Empiricism and rejected metaphysics (Wichert, 2023). Originally, the word "science" was derived from the Latin noun "scientia" ("knowledge) and the verb "scire", meaning "to know" (Etymonline, 2022b).

In his consolidated historical account of science, Lindberg (2010) shows that science developed over a long period of time. Research, as we know it in psychotherapy, started to develop in the European intellectual movement of the 17th and 18th centuries. However, it was not until the 19th century that modern science, and its distinguishing characteristics, began to take shape (Principe, 2011). Precision instruments emerged and Wilhelm Wundt founded the first laboratory for psychological research in 1879 (Rosa, 2023).

Disconcertingly, science is associated with colonialism (Seth, 2009). Racism and science also go together (see Mncube, 2017). Marks (2017) defined "racism" as the belief in the inequality of races, and "scientific racism" as the use of science to justify this belief (p. 126). He noted that science tolerates racism.

Furthermore, science has been patriarchal. It was Bertrand Russell (1972–1970), who pointed out, that "some men are so impressed by what science knows that they forget what it does not know" (cited in Lawson, 2020, p. 371). The sociologist Georg Simmel (1896, 1923) wrote on subordination in society Vromen, 1987), observing that we find in history the valid equation "objective equals masculine" (Keller, 1995, p. 75).

In 1956, the term "Artificial Intelligence" (AI) was coined by the mathematician McCarthy (2006), who suggested that scientists worked on natural language processing, neural networks, and machine learning. Subsequently, the symbolic approach focused on developing machines and programs that were capable of thinking, and the connectionist approach on imitating brain structures (Possati, 2021).

Partly, because technological advancements were linked to scientific research (Lem, 2014), did scholars demand that studies in the social sciences, and in psychotherapy, should also be scientific.

Evelyn Keller (1995) claimed that "... if more women were to engage in science, a different science might emerge" (p. 76). Along with Nancy Chodorow, Dorothy Dinnerstein, Jessica Benjamin, and Jane Flax, Keller argued that psychoanalytic theory was hardly exempt from the androcentric bias that permeates much of our intellectual history. Haraway (1997) highlighted that the history of science was gender in the making.

It is sobering to reflect on a history, which is permeated by sexism and the exclusion of non-White scholars. Furthermore, Keller's (1995) analysis of science found a genderization that is antithetical to Eros:

> Not only does our characterization of science thereby become colored by the biases of patriarchy and sexism, but ... what is called feminine ... becomes further devalued by its exclusion from the special social and intellectual value placed on science ...
>
> (pp. 93–94)

Although the systematization (seeking and sharing) of knowledge is important, science tends to be viewed nowadays as a socially embedded activity (Butler-Adam, 2015). Scientific objectivity stands, however, on shaky grounds (Mohamed et al., 2020) when values influence the making of "scientific" decisions in terms of the choice of research projects, recruitment of participants, and interpretation of results (Elliott & McKaughan, 2014).

Patriarchalism, Sexism & Racism: A Critical Discussion

How is it possible that Western notions of philosophy and science are still dominant? Dalal (2015) claimed that we reproduce and reinforce conventions without knowing that we are doing so. These processes are attributed to the social unconscious (Hopper, 2003a). When it was originally mentioned by Foulkes and Fromm, it overwrote notions of discourse and ideology, as used by Marx, Althusser, and Hegel (Dalal, 2015). History can be eradicated by giving concepts new names (Dalal, 2018b), and by ignoring other philosophies or knowledges altogether. This would explain why non-Western thought and research have been ignored. Furthermore, although many women have made groundbreaking contributions, very few are known (Duffy, 2016). Stokes' (2005) *Philosophy 100 Essential Thinkers* includes 98 Americo-European males, but only two female philosophers (Mary Wollstonecraft and Simone de Beauvoir). Derrida (1997) would have us search for examples of how/when it happened that these two females become recognized as philosophers, and how this disrupted prevailing patriarchal structures. From a group analytic perspective, this tendency to "forget" important figures suggests that the workings of the social unconscious enabled repression. Such "forgetting" is not limited to philosophy.

Psychotherapy has been dominated by white males since its inception. Hence, we speak of founding fathers instead of founding mothers. Pioneering female analysts, such as Deutsch, Horney, Anna Freud, and Klein, used mothering to advance Psychoanalysis from its patriarchal beginnings. Their works were regarded by many feminists and female psychotherapists as the antidote to Freud's focus on fathers, which had reinforced patriarchy and sexism in society (Sayers, 1992). Even though feminism has grappled with concepts of sexuality and desire from Mary Wollstonecraft's (1792) *A Vindication of the Rights of Women* onwards, it was only with Simone de Beauvoir's (1949) *La Deuxième Sexe* that a critical dialogue started between Psychoanalysis and Feminism. Betty Friedman's (1963) *The Feminine Mystique* also protested a psychoanalytic discourse, in which woman is defined as inferior. Woman only exists in reference to man.

Following Juliet Mitchell's (1974) critique, espoused in *Psychoanalysis and Feminism,* that men and women had internalized an oppressive ideology, alternative models of the female and of sexual identity were developed. In Group Analysis, there is no equivalent to a "feminist Psychoanalysis". This is not to say that female group analytic psychotherapists have not problematized patriarchy or group analytic practice (see, e.g., Einhorn, 2021; Rohr & Cogoy, 2024). However, there has not been a feminist group analytic movement that would be comparable to the feminist movement. Furthermore, the Oedipus Complex has not been abandoned in Group Analysis either, and non-heterosexual sexuality has not been adequately theorized (Anderson, 2019, 2022). So, Group Analysis has not rid itself from its inherent sexism and the psychoanalytic tendency to pathologize sexuality. Although it is grappling with isms, it has not yet managed to decolonize itself either (see Aiyegbusi, 2021a,b; Blackwell, 2021; Nayak, 2021), possibly because decolonization is unsettling (Tuck & Yang, 2012). This would explain why researchers have not been able to decolonize the field of group analytic research either.

Disparities continue to be found in research practices and in academia per se. For example, there is a gender bias in favor of men (Lorens et al., 2021), as well as discrimination against people of color, who encounter racist attitudes (Bhopal, 2022). Female philosophers of color might become an endangered species. Of the 11,000 members of the American Philosophical Association, only 125 were black (Gines, 2011).

Rise of Empiricism & Its Consequences

To understand why group analytic research has been sidelined, other developments are noteworthy. (Readers unfamiliar with group analytic approaches, and problems related to their statuses, can find information in Appendices 1 and 2.) Historically, Group Analysis incorporated ideas from related disciplines (e.g. social psychology, sociology) and fed on theories of psychoanalysis (Dahlin, 2003; Dalal, 1998). Loyal to Freud, Foulkes (1948) adopted his unconscious. Freud (1915b,c) had no doubt about the existence of the unconscious when postulating that the human psyche could be divided into the conscious, preconscious, and unconscious. For him, the psyche was structured in this way, and the unconscious really existed. Freud developed methods, such as free association, to reveal unconscious phenomena, which he regarded as knowledge. Equally, group analysts study socially unconscious processes through the group analytic method and accept the findings of their analyses as valid knowledge. So, it seems almost inevitable that Group Analysis' reputation was tarnished when psychoanalysis lost its credibility in Britain between the 1950s and 1960s.

From the early 1960s onwards, psychoanalysis had no place in British society, which was dominated by psychology. While psychotherapy followed a different trajectory in other countries, the influential Hans Eysenck emphasized Empiricism (Neve, 2004). Since psycho analysis, and I would add Group Analysis, did not display the right combination of statistical skill and empiricism, they became targets of disapproval (Buchanan, 2011). Karl Popper (1972) portrayed Psychoanalysis as a "pseudoscience", because it lacked the falsifiability criterion of science (Grant & Harari, 2005). Grűnbaum (1984, 1986) regarded Freud's theories as unsubstantiated, doubting their epistemic validity. With *Decline & Fall of the Freudian Empire*, Eysenck (1986/2017) contributed to the rise of Empiricism. Prior to this, the sparkling intellectual atmosphere of early 20th-century Vienna, which produced philosophers such as Popper, Wittgenstein, and Neurath, had laid the foundation for this rise (Gigerenzer, 2000).

The doctrine of the Logical Positivism/Empiricism postulated that there had to be an unambiguous relation between scientific language and sense data. Demonstrating the fallacy of the verification approach, Popper's (1983) scientific methodology and falsification theory (Popper, 1959) were highly influential among philosophers of science and practicing scientists. In his critique of Freud's Ego, Id, and Superego, Popper (1962) suggested that no stronger claim could be made for these than for Homer's collected stories involving Mount Olympus. While they contained interesting psychological suggestions, they were not testable. Equally, group analytic conceptualizations will never be as convincing as scientific explanations.

Locke's legacy was revigorated when Empiricism started to captivate psychology. With the rise of cognitive science in the 1960s and 1970s, psychology embarked on its journey to "sciencehood" (Hatfield, 2002), relying heavily on scientific experiments, observation, measurements, and statistics. These are the features of modern Positivism and scientific Empiricism, which have affected the credibility of psychoanalytically oriented psychotherapies and research practices ever since. In my opinion, it is unfortunate that Foulkes remained a Freudian, because

Group Analysis would not have escaped the prevailing criticism directed at psychoanalysis. Despite the fact that Elias and the Frankfurt School, which gave birth to Critical Theory (see TextBox 1.1), moved Group Analysis more toward sociology.

TEXTBOX 1.1 CRITICAL THEORY & POSTMODERNISM

The family of critical theory critiques normative perspectives, denoting a set of alternative paradigms to Positivism. Abend's (2008) clarified that studies by Marx, Weber, Durkheim, and Habermas are referred theories. They pose questions, provide possible answers, spell out assumptions, crucial concepts, and ideas, putting forward complex arguments to say what exactly the meaning of a topic/text is. Described as "interpretations", "analyses", or "critiques", their theories often involve meaning. Some aspects are based on phenomenology and include theoretical perspectives (e.g. feminism) that challenged Positivism (Guba & Lincoln, 1994). Critical Theory aimed at transforming society. It was developed by the Frankfurt School and social scientists, associated in/directly with it (Habermas, Horkheimer, Adorno, Elias, Fromm, Marcuse, Wertheimer) (Celikates & Flynn, 2023). While Adorno, Horkheimer, Fromm, and Marcuse belonged to the first generation, Habermas was the most distinguished theorist from the second generation of the Frankfurt School. Much of its work moved in the twilight zone between Marxism and Psychoanalysis. Emancipatory and dialectical in nature, it rejects traditional views of science and Positivism (Alvesson & Skőldberg, 2009b, p. 144).

The term "postmodernism" originated in philosophy, architecture, and literary theory in the early 20th century (Wilterdink, 2002). Modernism had reached its end and was replaced by a new epoch (Holtz, 2020). Whereas modernists regarded researchers/scientists as passive observers/analysts, postmodernists acknowledge temporal-spatial and socio-historical contexts (Alvesson, 2002). "Postmodern" and "Poststructuralism" are often used interchangeably. Postmodern discourses are all deconstructive, aiming to make us skeptical about beliefs regarding truth, knowledge, power, and the self (Flax, 1990). According to Spivak (1993), St Pierre (2011), and Jackson and Mazzei (2012), Postmodernist/Poststructuralists formulated methods, or ideas, challenged conceptualizations about language, structure, linearity, and coherence: Lacan (signifier (word), signified (idea in the mind), referent is the concrete object), Foucault (archaeology, genealogy, power/knowledge), Deleuze & Guattari (schizo-analysis, rhizo-analysis, desiring machine, deterritorialization), Derrida (deconstruction, différance, erasure), Lyotard (paralogic legitimation), Deleuze (desire, assemblage, a concept that seeks to account for multiplicity and change, or becoming; difference, immanence, intensities), Spivak (marginality), and Butler (performativity, agency, humanism).

While cognitive/behavioral psychotherapists eagerly embraced scientific concepts (Gabriel, 2023), psychoanalytic group therapists were more hesitant (Schlapobersky, 2016). Whereas psychology and cognitive behavioral therapy (CBT) use virtual reality to treat anxiety disorders (Riva & Galimberti, 2001), group analytic psychotherapists have remained conservative. With a leaning toward critical theory (TextBox 1.1), Group Analysis both positioned itself and was positioned on the outskirts of Empiricism.

I suggest that Group Analysis was sidelined, first, because it does not rely on a measurement tautology, in contrast to CBT. Postulating that specific styles of thinking result in unhelpful emotions and behavior, commonly, CBT therapists primarily focus on those thinking styles. A reduction in problematic thinking styles, and their impact on emotions and behavior, is then measured. All the things that people are not fully aware of, uncontrollable desires and unpredictable sexual eruptions, which can occur in group analytic therapy, are secondary.

Sexuality has been a taboo in British society since the Victorian era (Iqbal et al., 2009). The stirring up of desire must be restrained. So, the second reason why Group Analysis has probably never become a reputable psychotherapy like CBT is related to desire. Due to the adoption of psychoanalytic conceptualizations, Group Analysis has not defused the bomb that the compromised psychoanalysis had smuggled inside society, as Deleuze (2002) put it, forcing people to organize things differently, because psychoanalysis had uncovered their desire (Deleuze, 2002).

Postmodernists (see TextBox 1.1), such as Deleuze and Guattari (1984, 1987), talk about the machineries of desire, which churn out something to produce connections (Mazzei, 2013). Deleuze and Guattari have theorized the machine in terms of desire insofar that desire is a productive force. It forms relations between different aspects of an assemblage, Ringrose and Coleman (2013) explain, noting that their "geophilosophy" (p. 125) pays attention to the connections between various things that constitute an assemblage. Constantly seeking to produce silences, these machineries of desire have forged links. Neither rationality and intentionality, nor ontological lack, is part of Deleuzian desire (Mazzei, 2013). For Deleuze (1991), the subject of Empiricism was never given. Instead, it was made from the data and by the rules made of data. It was built on a fantasy, which goes beyond something given.

To understand the rise of Empiricism and its consequences, one being that emotions became secondary, it is useful to ask how desire works to produce a silence (Deleuze, 2002). Elucidating how the silence maintains privilege and a status quo in science and philosophy, researchers could disrupt the assemblage of power relations, and the consequences of Empiricism, thereby giving the excluded a voice.

The Conundrum of the Paradigm

What constitutes a paradigm is by no means clear. Etymologically, "paradigm" stems from the Latin "paradigma" (pattern, example). The Greek verb "paradeiknynai" means to "show side by side" (Etymonline, 2024a). The post-positivist Kuhn (1962) described it as a particular set of accepted assumptions and theories within the scientific community that explain a phenomenon. When a significant number of observational anomalies arise, and the paradigm can no longer explain the phenomenon adequately, a paradigm shift occurs.

In psychotherapy research, a paradigm is a set of interrelated ideas about the social world. It provides a conceptual framework for the organized study of the world and of people (Cottone, 2017). By subscribing to a certain paradigm, researchers are then guided by its philosophical assumptions. Traditionally, the research question determines the appropriateness of the chosen paradigm, as well as the methodology (logic of inquiry), and the methods (techniques) used to collect and analyze data (Grix, 2002).

The quantitative paradigm, the philosophy of science, and Positivism are interconnected. Positivism holds that things, people, and events in the social world are exactly as people perceive them to be. People are in contact with reality by experiencing the sensations and images of the physical world. Positivist modes of investigation can accurately trace nature itself. This ontological view reflects a "naïve" Realism (Madhill, 2008) and epistemological Objectivism.

While realists assume a reality independently of the observer (researcher), in quantum mechanics the locality of information transfer through entanglement reveals that reality is different (Barad, 2007). People"s perceptions of reality are limited and governed by probabilities. Reality is made up of mutually exclusive entities that complement each other. Quantum mechanics has discredited naïve Realism by demonstrating an inherent inseparability between the physical system being observed and the conscious mind of the observer (Barad, 2007).

The traditional scientific worldview is based on Materialism. It is opposed to Idealism, claiming that everything that exists comes from physical matter. Take, for example, the mind. While for materialists, mind and brain are the same (Pepperell, 2024), Idealists do not regard minds as products of material systems (the brain). Instead, everything is made up of ideas. The mind is a mental phenomenon, separate from the brain. Even the physical world is only a product of how people construct reality. Material objects are ideas, or impressions, generated by people's experiences (Pepperell, 2024). Hence, Idealism opposes Objectivism. It is subjectivist. Both Materialism and Idealism can be monist, that is, nature and mind are made of only *one* substance (either physical or formed by ideas). Dualism holds that nature consists of *two* essentially different kinds of things/substances, such as material or mental ideas (Pepperell, 2024).

Descartes' mind-body is a famous example of dualism. Both body and mind are separate (body is physical, the mind/soul is not physical), but they interact with each other. Broadly speaking, the traditional quantitative and qualitative research paradigms rest on a monist materialist and monist idealist worldview, respectively.

Whereas Cottone (1989) initially referred to the psycho-medical, systemic, and critical theory paradigm, more recently, Cottone (2012) has identified four psychotherapy paradigms: the Organic-Medical, Psychological, Systemic-Relational, and the Social Constructivist Paradigm (TextBox 1.2). Each of these is based on specific philosophical assumptions, although it is not entirely clear that they are proper paradigms in the Kuhnian scientific sense (Cottone, 2007).

TEXTBOX 1.2 SOCIAL CONSTRUCTIONISM & SOCIAL CONSTRUCTIVISM

Social Constructionism emerged in 1966 with *The Social Construction of Reality* (Berger & Luckmann, 1966). Unlike the historical relativists such as Feyerabend, Toulman, and Hanson (Suppe, 1977), who held that scientific knowledge is socio-historically conditioned, Social Constructionists disregard science. Social Constructionism's main tenet is that people's understanding of the world, including their own being, is a product of language. The world is constructed through language, which is influenced by the culture and time that people live in. For Kenneth Gergen science is irrelevant. Critical, emancipatory, discursive, political, and liberating research projects (Pernecky, 2016, p. 157) are more important. Constructionism differs from Constructivism, which is the philosophical explanation about the nature of learning. Jerome Bruner and Jean Piaget are chief theorists of Cognitive Constructivism. Social Constructivism is associated with the Russin psychologist Vygotsky (1978), who showed that learning occurs in sociocultural settings, mediated by language.

Developed by Ernst von Glasersfeld (1981, 1996), Radical Constructivism claims that all knowledge is constructed. It tells us nothing about the evolving reality. Knowledge is invented and can only be understood through subjective interpretation of experiences.

TEXTBOX 1.3 INTERPRETIVISM

Interpretivism consists of diverse philosophies: Constructivism, Constructionism, Hermeneutics, and Phenomenology. It has its historical roots in anthropology and rejects Positivism (Ryan, 2018). Interpretivism regards truth and knowledge as subjective, and culturally and historically situated. Therefore, researchers can never separate their own beliefs and values from the research process (collection and interpretation of data) (Ryan, 2018). Interpretivists argue that the study of human society must go beyond empirical objectives and include subjective views, opinions, emotions, and values. All those phenomena, which cannot be directly observed and require interpretation. Interpretivism is associated with action and the construction of knowledge. No uniform tradition exists. Butler (1998) identified several different variants (constructivist, conservative, critical, and deconstructionist). However, understanding subjective meaning is at the heart of Interpretivism. People, processes, and phenomena are understood through interpretation. No correct theories exist, only interesting ones (Goldkuhl, 2017).

Ponterotto (2005) identified the Positivist, Post-positivist, Interpretivist (TextBox 1.3), and the Social Constructionist research paradigms (TextBox 1.2), which have all been used in group analytic psychotherapy research.

All these paradigms are based on Western philosophical notions of reality, knowledge, consciousness, the mind, and so forth. Even though paradigms are the best organizing concepts, according to Kuhn (1962), they do not have an essence, because there is always some disagreement, or difference in emphasis among scholars, who adopt the same paradigm (Ritzer, 1981). To appreciate how influential paradigms are, let us turn to Kuhn (1962). A paradigm is a fundamental image of the subject matter within a science, he argued. It serves to define what should be studied, what questions should be asked, and what rules should be followed in interpreting the answers obtained. Furthermore, a paradigm is the broadest unit of consensus within an area of science, serving to differentiate one scientific community from another (Ritzer, 1975, p. 156). Ritzer agreed that a paradigm is important as a metasystem. A paradigm subsumes, defines, and interrelates the exemplar, theories, and methods that exist within it (Ritzer, 1975). However, Masterman (1970) identified no fewer than 21 possible meanings for paradigm. Compressing these into three categories (metaphysical, sociological, and artifact/construct paradigms), she suggested that a paradigm can function as a metaphysical worldview, a framework for research, or as a specific set of tools. She described paradigms as a way of seeing a picture that explains how the world works. So, a paradigm is a mutually supporting set of beliefs and practices. If stretched too far, it can, however, produce conceptual inconsistency, absurdity, false expectation, complexity, confusion, and disarray (p. 81). When adopted as a framework for research, Masterman's framework allows researchers to understand the underlying assumptions and practices of different scientific communities. In contrast, for Collins (1990, p. 224), a paradigm included assumptions about power, knowledge, and positionality. Paradigms were defined by Guba and Lincoln (1994) as a basic belief system, or worldview, which influence the researchers' choice of ontology, epistemology, and methodology of their research. Therefore, a paradigm is a set of philosophical beliefs, which express a worldview that defines for the beholder the nature of the world (p. 107). These are just a few definitions, and the conundrum surrounding the paradigm has not been resolved.

Philosophical Underpinnings of Common Paradigms

Positivism (TextBox 1.4) is a paradigm that relies on scientific methods and practices. In the literature, "Positivism" is often used almost as an umbrella term, comprising Logical/Modern Positivism and Empiricism. Commonly, researchers mean methodological Positivism when referring to Positivism (Riley, 2007). I will use Positivism as an umbrella term in this sense.

> **TEXTBOX 1.4 POSITIVISM**
>
> Articulated originally by Auguste Comte (1853/1988), Positivism holds that knowledge is either true by definition or derived at by logic based on sensory experience (Bourdeau, 2022). For Comte and the logical positivists, systematizing data was central (Alvesson & Skőldberg, 2009a). Positivism emerged in Austria/Germany as a philosophy of science in the form of Logical Positivism during the 1920s (Rubinstein, 2005). When the Nazis entered Vienna in early 1938, many philosophers fled to the US, where they developed Logical Empiricism (Creath, 2022). Several scholars later split, developing Post-positivism. The distinction between Logical Positivism and Logical/Scientific Empiricism is not clear cut (see Uebel & Limbeck-Lilienau, 2023).
>
> Historically, there is a strong connection between physics and philosophy (e.g. Schlick, Reichenbach). Logical positivists rejected Idealism/Rationalism, because only sense data are important. Anything else that could lead to any transcendental experiences was foregone. People relied on direct perception and were able to determine whether a particular perception (or proposition) was accurate. This thinking formed the structure of Logical Positivism.
>
> Riley (2007) clarified that *Positivism has at least three meanings. First*, Positivism is a commitment to developing sociality. Logical empiricists aimed to foster a scientific conception of the world that would create a better life (Uebel & Limbeck-Lilienau, 2023).
>
> *Second*, it refers to the articulated philosophical tradition of Logical Positivism. It aimed to formulate a scientific philosophy for understanding the relationship between science and society, combining the works of Helmholtz, Mach, Poincare, and Duhem, with the logic developed by Frege, Hilbert, and Russell. *Third*, it denotes scientific research practices (methodological Positivism).
>
> Etymologically, Positivism stems from the Latin "positum" (accusative of pono), "put, place" (Etymonline, 2023). Something (given facts, data) is put in front of the researcher, who gathers and systematize the data (Alvesson & Skőldberg, 2009a).

While Schindler (1981) surmised that group analysts had a "wide knowledge of moral philosophy" (p. 191), Jane Campbell (2006) described interrelated ideas that are inherent in clinical Group Analysis. She called these the "absurdly simple" group analytic paradigm. Its features belong to the incompatible philosophical traditions of Logical Empiricism, Rationalism (see TextBox 1.5), and Idealism. Campbell's paradigm describes the essence of Group Analysis:

> You put seven people in a circle with a conductor, who has established boundaries of time, space and confidentiality. The seven people will begin to relate to each other. While some may talk, others may be silent. They may look at each other, or not. Even if they ignore each other, they cannot help it, they will relate to each other because that is what human beings do. Then, this relating behavior is observed and reflected upon by all the members of the group,

including the conductor. This process of reflection, or thinking, involves not only the head but also the heart. And that is it.

(p. 342)

TEXTBOX 1.5 RATIONALISM VS (LOGICAL) EMPIRICISM

Philosophers, since the era of Plato (428–347 BCE), have attempted to develop an adequate theory of knowledge (epistemology). One encounters constant epistemological disputes between rationalists, e.g., René Descartes (1596–1650), and empiricists, e.g., John Locke (1632–1704). Seemingly irreconcilable disagreements persisted as to whether our human mind has a predisposition to understand, whether we have innate ideas, or whether our mind is a blank state (tabula rasa) at birth. The French Descartes and the British Locke disagreed as vehemently as their forerunners, Plato and Aristotle (384–322 BCE). Whereas Aristotele and Locke looked for answers and knowledge in the external world, Plato and Descartes sought knowledge within the internal world. Like Empiricism, Rationalism is an epistemological doctrine. It holds that the rational mind is the best way to know something. For example, when seeing a stick in the water, it might look bent but rationally we know that this is due to the water (Carreira, 2010).

Rationalists argue that people can reason. Our mind is more trustworthy than our senses. But for empiricists our senses are the ultimate source of knowledge (Allmarck & Machaczek, 2018).

In the ancient world, in religion, and in many Indigenous cultures, people believe in souls. But the soul is not physical, so how can it exist? (Al-Amoudi & O'Mahoney, 2016). Questions like this led some philosophers to become idealists. They believe that mental entities are real. Physical things exist only in the sense that we can see them. For the German Hegel (1948/2018), the ultimate structure of reality can be revealed in thought. Reality is rational in nature but unknowable in practice. Hegel's absolute Idealism differs from Berkeley's subjective Idealism and Kant's Transcendental Idealism. Simply put, Idealism asserts that reality is fundamentally formed through ideas. The physical (material) reality is secondary. Ideas are the primary source of reality (Carreira, 2010). When reality is rational, its structure can be revealed through thinking. Idealism is opposed to Realism. Idealists point out that you can think about a book. When doing so, it becomes a mental thing (concept), whose physical locality you can verify (Hegel, 1948/2018). Although Idealism is important to qualitative researchers, not everybody embraces Idealism. Its monism has become subject to criticism (Carreira, 2010). Accused of not adequately explaining an objective world by several empiricists (Locke, Hume), materialists (Hobbes, Marx), as well as realists (Russell, Moore), Idealism makes reality too dependent on ideas. When all reality is mental, how can we perceive a shared world? Idealism seems to collapse into Solipsism (only one's own mind exists) (Carreira, 2010). While idealists would study the psyche and dynamic unconscious, empiricists would not buy into the idea that a psyche existed, whose structure is partly made up of a dynamic unconscious.

Some African scholars dislike Positivism's anti-metaphysical stance. The scientific overcoming of metaphysics and eclipse of ontology under the logical positivists led to an emphasis on epistemology (Horkheimer, 2004).

Positivism is situated within epistemology, which tries to describe how knowledge is created and what counts as knowledge (Park et al., 2020). We can acquire knowledge through different sources (e.g. perception, reasoning, memory, intuition, experience, telepathy, induction, deduction). For logical/positivists/empiricists, sense data are the source and endpoint of all knowledge (Allmark & Machaczek, 2018). On epistemological grounds, they reject claims by rationalists or idealists that data derived from reasoning or introspection are knowledge sources. They would also reject experiential and intuitive knowledge, which group analysts, such as, Wilke (2018), favor. Even though positivists neglected ontology, they are realists and they believe that real entities exist. Realism is opposed to Nominalism, the belief that universals are mere names without any reality behind them, and only particulars exist (Carreira, 2010). Rationalism and Empiricism, and Idealism and Materialism, are *ontologically* opposed to each other (Carreira, 2010). This is another reason why positivists reject idealists, and why the quantitative and qualitative paradigms are incompatible.

However, Idealism and Rationalism are *epistemologically* compatible. Some monists can be idealists (everything is based on ideas, including the mind) or materialists (all ideas are ultimately products of matter) (Carreira, 2010). Idealism and Romanticism are similar (emphasize profound, often spiritual notion of reality, focus on subjective experience, hold critical stance toward Rationalism and Materialism). Notions of a higher spiritual reality that transcends the material world are also shared.

Romanticism arose as a reaction against Rationalism and the scientific approach of the Enlightenment (Boyler, 2017). It shares with psychoanalysis the focus on emotion, imagination, the sublime, and the unconscious mind (Buckley, 1997; Sigler, 2020). In the broadest sense, psychoanalysis can be defined as the domain of the unconscious (Eisold, 1995).

Romantics believed that profound truths about (subjective) experience, beauty, and the human spirit could be found in emotions, fantasies, and intuition (self and its inner life), which are sources of knowledge (Faflak, 2008). As an artistic, literary, musical, and intellectual movement, Romanticism peaked in the mid-19th century and had a lasting effect on Western culture (Ryan, 2018). It contributed to shaping modern beliefs about the value of personal expression, individualism, and expressing heart-felt emotions (Labbe & Smith, 2003).

Pragmatism (see TextBox 1.6) and Existentialism are further important traditions. For pragmatists, knowing the world is inseparable from agency within it. Pragmatism rejects unpractical ideas. It holds that propositions can be true but are unsatisfactory (McDermid, 2024). Instrumentalism is a form of Pragmatism that treats theories as instruments for prediction (Carreira, 2010).

TEXTBOX 1.6 PRAGMATISM & MIXED METHODS

Dewey (1910/1933) dismissed the Positivist notion that people are passively perceiving something. Most of our experience is learned from reflecting on experience. He rejected the "myth of the given" (Chisholm, 1964), as formulated by modern Empiricism. If we cannot take the existence of something for granted, we would have to "create meaning and knowledge ex nihilo", Garrison (2019, p. 304) argued. Dewey disputed that sensations were a separable content of consciousness. Instead, they are embedded in a larger system. Fascinated with how people think, Dewey identified several modes of thought, including belief, imagination, and stream of consciousness. However, what really captured his imagination was reflection. For Dewey (1916/1944), education was the reorganization of experience, which increases our experience. The experiential method taught us that we need to go behind the refinement of experience. An experience involves an interaction between oneself, another person, and the world. People and the environment change due to interactions. Both interaction and continuity are the elements of experience. It is not primarily cognitive (Dewey, 1916/1944). When we reflect, we create relationships and continuities. Teddlie and Tashakkori (2011) noted that Pragmatist emphasize epistemological issues. Morgan's (2007) pragmatic, reflexive research approach holds that researchers should connect methodology with epistemology and research design. Discussing paradigms as worldviews, as epistemological stances, as shared beliefs in a research field, and as model examples of research, Morgan argued that researchers should consider how their worldviews influence their research. Depending on their personal history, social background, and cultural assumptions, researchers choose what is important and appropriate to them. While abduction, intersubjectivity, and transferability are important, Morgan's approach involves oscillating between deductive and inductive reasoning, subsequently converting observations into theories and then assessing theories through action. (The traditional pragmatist approach uses theories to account for observations, which is an aspect of making inductive inferences.) Morgan (2007) attempted to demonstrate how methodology can be properly integrated in the social sciences. Uniting qualitative and quantitative approaches tallies with some group analytic researchers (e.g., Doğmuş & Canpolat, 2024; Kalleklev & Karterud, 2018; Lorentzen, 2020; McMahon, 2023; Story et al., 2024).

Existentialism concerns itself with existence. Opposed to most forms of Idealism and Scientism, it focuses on ontology. Central tenets of Existentialism are that personal freedom, individual responsibility, and deliberate choice, are essential to a person's life. Negative aspects of existence (pain, sickness, and death) are viewed as essential aspects of reality. Kierkegaard, Nietzsche, Sarte, Camus, Heidegger, and Jaspers, were prominent existential thinkers (Abbagnano, 2024).

Positivists mostly dismissed axiology, because values, ethics, and subjective experiences lie outside the domain of scientific investigation. They insisted that research was free of values, arguing that objectivity and neutrality can be achieved during the research process (Chilisa, 2020). Their rejection is related to a strict separation of metaphysics and epistemology, which occurred with the rise of Logical Positivism. Ontology was revived by Bhaskar (1998) and Heidegger. Bhaskar (1986) synthesized Realism with an epistemologically relativist view of science, viewing it as a social and historical process. In claiming that our knowledge of the

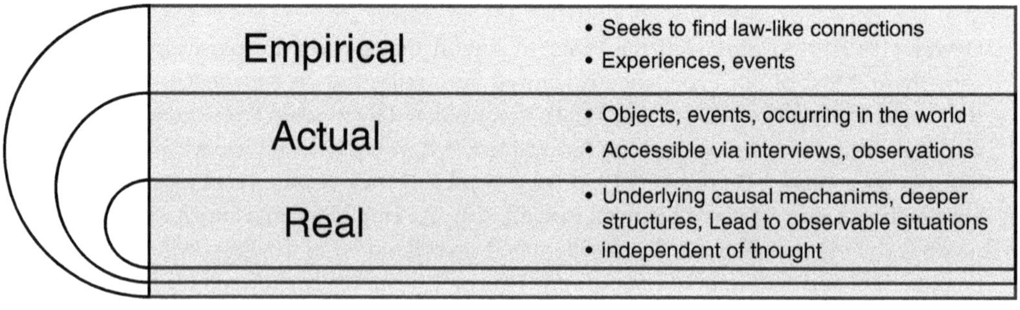

FIGURE 1.4 Critical Realism's Three Levels of Reality.

world is socially constructed, Critical Realism straddles the divide between objectivism and subjectivism, between Positivism and Interpretivism (Bhasker, 1978, 1989). However, Critical Realism (TextBox 1.7) does not agree that reality is socially constructed (Glesne & Peshkin, 1992), postulating, instead, three levels of reality, as depicted in Figure 1.4.

Critical Realism assumes that engaging in a historically situated analysis of structures is possible, due to its subjectivist epistemology, which it shares with Social Constructionism (Ellaway et al., 2020).

TEXTBOX 1.7 CRITICAL REALISM

Bhaskar (1978) viewed society as the "ever present" condition (material cause), and the continually reproduced outcome of human agency. Bhaskar acknowledged that reality is influenced by socio-historical processes (Vosmer, 2024c), but he adopts a transcendental Realism (things also exist in a non-human world). Critical Realism assumes that engaging in a historically situated analysis of structures is possible due to its subjectivist epistemology (Ellaway et al., 2020). It prioritizes reality over a system of understanding. To maintain the intelligibility and transformation of human knowledge, it holds that we must distinguish epistemology (knowledge, systems, thoughts, ideas, theories, language) from ontology (being, things, existents, reality, objects of investigation). Critical Realism makes a distinction between transitive and intransitive. While the former refers to the changing knowledge of something, the intransitive refers to the unchanging elements, which we attempt to know. From an ontological perspective, transitive refers to things that change and the intransitive refers to the unchanging dimensions of reality (e.g. aliens may inhabit a dimension in space regardless of whether humans exist).

Like pragmatists, Bhasker (1986) was committed to social justice. Bhaskar (1987) argued that there was a need for a structured and differentiated ontology. Like Heidegger (1962), he believed that it was important to say something about the things themselves. To understand the reality, the social sciences attempt to uncover, we need a differentiated account in which stratification and change feature (Bhaskar, 1978). Steinmetz (1998) clarified that a "causal" law may be defined as the characteristic pattern, or tendency, of a mechanism or activity. This all sounds very abstract. Here is an example:

An anorexic person could be defined by his/her constant tendency to avoid eating and exercise. Perhaps anorexia has psychological or biological roots. However, exercising might be influenced by health policies/guidance, which would be a causal mechanism. Differing from how positivists conceptualize causality, Bhaskar's (1989) causal mechanisms act in the domain of the "real". Critical Realism's ontology is stratified into three domains: the *real* (independent of our thoughts, our awareness and even our existence as human beings), the *actual* (observable or experienced in events), and the *empirical* (seeks to find law-like connections). Within the causal domain of the real, lower-/higher-level mechanisms exist.

If you believe that things are not exactly as you perceive them to be, that images of the physical world are deceptive and do not portray the real world exactly as it is, that not everything is directly observable, and that observations may not present the socio-political world as it actually is, then Critical Realism is a suitable paradigm.

Phenomenology rejects Positivism. Focusing on existence, Heidegger (1962) highlighted that philosophers did not question existence per se when trying to answer what exists. Metaphysical questions rest on the assumption that they already know what "to exist" meant. In contrast to his mentor Husserl, who was more concerned with epistemology, Heidegger (1962) focused on Sein (Being, Existence). He criticized Western philosophy for being reductionistic. Epistemology had reduced all "Sein" to mere presence and then forced knowledge to conform to this. Heidegger's investigation into the meaning of "Sein" focuses on the ontological *difference between Being (Sein) and Beings (entities)*. Put simply, "Being" is time. As human beings, we exist temporally. Being and time are finite, coming to an end with death. To examine this distinction, Heidegger drew on the notion of "Dasein" (Being there, Being in the world). Phenomenology was a theoretical enterprise that started from ordinary experience for him. Attentive examination of this experience can reveal the a priori transcendental conditions that structure experience.

Merleau-Ponty (1962, 1964a,b) concerned himself with the essence of perception/existence. According to Coole (2001), he believed that phenomenology consisted of so many aspects that it could *not* be described through intentionality (Husserl) or time (Heidegger). Even consciousness is perceptual, he argued. Our body is a primary site for knowing the world (Kovaly, 1977). When he died in 1961, the question about the relationship of consciousness and nature was dominated by Objectivism (naturalism in philosophy, behaviorism in psychology, mechanisms in biology) and by intellectualism (neo-Kantianism).

Moral philosophy is a branch of philosophy that is highly relevant for research. It is theoretically divided into metaethics and normative ethics. Axiology, which concerns itself with questions about value and aesthetics, is situated within normative ethics (Honderich, 1995). African (Ubuntu) and Asian philosophies, such as Confucianism, Taoism, Buddhism, and Hinduism (see Chapter 3), emphasize axiology.

Axiology is crucial to existentialists, who are deeply concerned with questions of existence, the meaning and purpose of life. Personal values/responsibility in an indifferent world, authenticity, and freedom, are crucial issues (Abbagnano, 2024). Idealists, and even more so romanticists, tend to see values as an integral part of the structure of reality. While Hegel (1948/2018) emphasized truth, morality, and beauty, which are connected to an ideal, romanticists favor aesthetics, which elevates beauty (Labbe & Smith, 2003). In contrast, rationalists prioritize reason and intellectual clarity. Rational understanding is virtuous and on a par with the "highest good", which is the ultimate end of moral action, according to Kant (1781/2003).

Knowledge, Facts & Scientific Evidence

Knowledge is always the property of the group (Dalal, 1998), and people learn or forget in groups (Elias, 1991). How knowledge, or "facts", should best be obtained has occupied many group analytic researchers. Observation is one possibility. Singular observations have led to insight into our unconscious inner world. In the natural/social sciences, observation has generated scientific statements. Inductive procedures were, therefore, regarded as producing valid knowledge. Until Popper pointed out that even if numerous observations are correct, just one differing observation will render an entire argument based on induction as false. Similarly, Foulkes (1936) held that

> [k]nowledge is never finite, it remains open to change with new experiences … a single new fact can upset all previous conceptions and require[s] a completely fresh idea that also allows a reevaluation of the old facts.
>
> (p. 52)

Popper (1959) advocated the use of deduction to produce knowledge. Deduction provides us with truths, because they are deduced from something that is based on facts. The group analyst Lorentzen (2006) suggested that facts can be integrated through observation and experimentation. In other words, researchers must use the nomothetic/quantitative paradigm. Observation, deductive logic, experimentation, and statistics, are the pillars of the quantitative paradigm. It assumes that generalizable laws exist in nature, which can be objectively discovered.

Positivism's dominance has been further strengthened by public demands for causal evidence. One consequence has been that research must produce scientific evidence for the effectiveness of their psychotherapies (Cooper, 2011). This involves designing randomized controlled trials (RCTs). Given that they are the gold standard for psychotherapy research (Park et al., 2020), Positivism dictates the norms that group analytic researchers must follow (Rutzou & Steinmetz, 2018).

When the task and the objective of research are the production of new knowledge, epistemology can resemble an intellectual battleground. Reservations toward Positivism have also been voiced within Group Analysis itself (e.g., Dalal, 2015, 2016, 2018a,b, 2023), although this critical stance is not shared by the Institute of Group Analysis (IGA) in London. Inadvertently, it endorsed the nomothetic paradigm. After the commissioning of a systematic review in the mid-2000s (Blackmore et al., 2009, 2012), it urged group analysts to carry out scientific studies, because robust evidence for Group Analysis was lacking. Once again, this resulted in debates about science and the status (see Appendix 2) of Group Analysis (Conway et al., 2003; Karterud, 2001; Knauss, 2000; Mace, 2006; Nitzgen, 2006). If it belonged to the social sciences, this would have four important consequences.

Firstly, social scientists (positivists) act as advisors to policymakers and are, therefore, agents of change.

Secondly, it would affect how group analytic psychotherapy is viewed by the public, because the term "science" enjoys unparalleled prestige in society, that is, the social organization of human life, patterns of interactions, and power relations (Erikson, 2001). Most people probably trust the word of a scientist more than that of a psychotherapist.

Thirdly, Group Analysis would potentially become a more reputable psychotherapy per se. Accepting that social scientists are widely regarded as producers of scientific evidence, researchers from other disciplines might become more interested in conducting joint studies.

Fourthly, social scientists are more likely to attract funding to carry out research.

Positivism: Benchmark of Science & Perpetrator of "Epistemicide"

When Positivism was initially celebrated in Europe for developing a scientific conception of the world, many forgot that other worldviews existed. Instead, a radical shift occurred away from superstitious beliefs (Steinmetz, 2005a). Suddenly, the philosophy of science became the conditio sine non qua. Certain philosophical postulates were regarded as an indispensable and essential ingredient of science. Positivism itself became equated with science. Once identified as the benchmark of science, its superiority was guaranteed (Steinmetz, 2005a).

That it ignored different cultural perspectives on the world (e.g., Arabian, Indian, Chinese, Persian) and equated teleological arguments (our world must have had a "designer") with being *primitive,* seemed immaterial. It was European and North American thinking that infiltrated millions of minds.

Notwithstanding that Logical/Positivism is a philosophy of science, this discipline is peculiar insofar that it seems to have justified its legitimacy through the existence of science (Benjamin, 1938).

Equally perplexing is that modern Positivism has survived (Rutzou & Steinmetz, 2018). If Positivism is an ideology, which Althusser (1969) situates in the unconscious realm, its dominance must have unconscious reasons. Steinmetz (2005b) referred to the epistemological unconscious of sociology in America, linking the dominance of Positivism to Fordism.

Be this as it may, Positivism mirrors common beliefs of a particular historical period. Hence, its texts are cultural documents that reveal how other cultures are viewed (see Erikson, 2001). Culture refers to the rich system of meanings, beliefs, practices, symbols, norms, and values, that are prevalent among people in a society (Schwartz, 2006, p. 138). It is hard to miss the air of superiority that surrounds Positivism when reading Mautner's (1997, p. 102) entry on Comte in the *Penguin Dictionary:* Comte equated primitive with theological or mysticism. His sequential three-stage theory of the historical development of peoples and the human mind divided development into the *theological stage* (primitive, characterized by superstition), the *metaphysical stage* (abstract speculation/reflection developed), and the *positive stage* (superstition and metaphysics gave way to science).

This description supports Ramose' (2001) argument that man being rational did not include the Africans. One consequence has been the erroneous belief that Africans are incapable of producing knowledge. After the "epistemicide" (Maris, 2020, p. 309; Phyak, 2021, Santos, 2014), African episteme has become an impossibility. Decolonizing black consciousness seems almost inconceivable under the reign of an oppressive Western epistemological paradigm.

Writing on philosophical racism, Maris (2020) has illuminated the British philosopher Locke from an African perspective. Locke was an empiricist, who postulated that the human mind is a blank state at birth, and that knowledge is derived from experience based on sense perception. Interestingly, because Empiricism denies the a priori existence of essences in the human mind, empiricists can compose generic concepts at will.

Examining as to whether Locke was racist, Maris (2020) drew on Farr (1986) in his conclusion:

> … whichever reading of Locke is the correct one, his silence about the Afro-American slave practices poses a great problem for understanding him as a theorist and a political actor.
>
> (p. 312)

Despite all the criticism that has been directed at Positivism, the postulate that data and facts must be observable, which links it to Empiricism, has survived the criticism of post-positivists (Harré, 1981).

Unsurprisingly, because the observable is measurable, operationalism sprung up. It is an approach within Modern Positivism or Neo-Positivism.

Neo-Positivism is regarded as a later phase of Positivism. It is committed to Empiricism, with an emphasis on statistics (Tiryakian, 1971). What distinguishes it from older forms is the method of logical analysis. Neo-Positivism was a movement in American sociology, linked to the Chicago and Columbia School (Tiryakian, 1971). It merged quantification and behaviorism in its positivist epistemology (Scott & Marshall, 2015).

Although modern positivists may collect qualitative data, they are committed to the scientific method (Open University, 2024).

Quantitative methods, such as the RCT, are still the gold standard for psychotherapy research in the Western world (Lilienfeld et al., 2018; Mohr, 2024). This guarantees Positivism's influence and dominance in research. African philosophers, such as Marais (1984), are opposed to Positivism due to its tendency to grossly oversimplify. Marais has suggested that human thought and reality are molded with the "positivist epistemological paraphernalia" (p. 264) into concepts that obscure the nature of true reality. Referring to Brokensha and Crowder (1967), Marais lamented that African thought was hardly appreciated. It may as well be nonexistent, when considered as a drearily inadequate system to approach Positivism.

Different belief systems (isms) divide. They can create schisms (break in unity). Racism is one of the most frequent contemporary isms (Kurunmäki & Marjanen, 2018).

In philosophy, racism has been acknowledged as a phenomenon with fundamental implications (Bernasconi et al., 2013). Understanding how isms affect group analytic research is necessary, because every ism creates a schism (Wahl, 2020).

Schism evokes notions of hatred. The history of schisms in psychoanalytic institutes (Wirth, 2007), among group analytic psychotherapists (see Tubert-Oklander & Hernández-Tubert, 2004), as well as the intolerance of diverse viewpoints, can be regarded as an institutional social defense that protects against uncertainty (see Pines, 1998). Equally, rigid and intolerant schismatic processes within philosophy, and the field of research, might be indicative of a social defense against cultural change.

What Can Be Done about Racism in Philosophy & Research?

Racism is hatred of one group for another, encapsulated in "racism begins where libido ends" (Dalal, 1998, p. 197). From a psychoanalytic perspective, the terms "black" and "white" belong to an empty racial category (Rustin, 1991), because "white" skin color is never literally white and brown skin has many shades (Dalal, 1999). The fact that people of color are subjected to racism, and that racism is inherent in institutions (Lazaridou & Fernando, 2022), psychotherapy (Maharaj et al., 2021), psychology (Sue et al., 2024), training programs (Wood & Patel, 2017), and in research (Bhambra, 2017; Harris, 2024; Leong et al., 2024), is a sad reality.

Although the profession is attempting to address racism (Abernathy, 2024), cultural racism can occur when researchers hold ideological beliefs in White supremacy. When researchers encounter participants from other cultures, they may be unable to relate to their participants' experiences, and pathologize communication styles or the values that people hold. They might misinterpret facial expressions, viewing passion as anger, or misinterpret difference as abnormality, and approach research through a colorblind lens. Or they may exclude certain cultural groups from research when they are lumped into the same ethnic category, for example, Asian Americans and Pacific Islanders (Yi et al., 2020).

A recent study concluded that psychological research has a racism problem, De Witte (2020) wrote. Systemic inequality exists and psychological research would benefit from diversity.

Examining more than 26,000 empirical articles published between 1974 and 2018, Roberts et al. (2020) found that psychological publications, which highlight race, are rare and remain virtually nonexistent in cognitive psychology. Most publications were edited by White editors. Many of the publications that highlight race have been written by White authors, who recruited significantly fewer participants of color.

I am not aware of a similar review in the field of group analytic therapy/research, but it would surprise me if results differed. To address the racism in research, Guo et al. (2023) have made several recommendations for antiracist research, that is, the

> … systematic theorizing, inquiry, intervention development, and program implementation that exposes, rejects, dismantles, and/or remedies racism, colonialism, antisemitism, and xenophobia with the goal of promoting social justice.
>
> (Wooten et al., 2023, p. 75)

These include using more rigorous designs to enhance internal validity and adopting advanced analytic techniques to counter selection bias. In research, bias has been defined as "the combination of various design, data, analysis, and presentation factors that tend to produce research findings when they should not be produced" (Ioannidis, 2005, cited in Leichsenring et al., 2017, p. 1000).

Psychotherapy research is full of cognitive and affective biases, because human nature confers a vulnerability to biases, blind spots, and self-enhancing illusions (MacDonald & Mellor-Clark, 2015). Biases are connected to heuristic shortcuts, that is, fast-thinking processes. Biases include publication bias (Franco et al., 2014), research bias related to replicability, or allegiance bias (Leichsenring et al., 2017). Considering that countertransference is linked to biases regarding gender, cultural ethnocentrism, religion, and social class (Yager et al., 2021), and that countertransference is used as a research tool by group analytic researchers, awareness of one's own biases is crucial when conducting research. Becoming aware of social defenses and addressing exclusion are equally important. According to Park (2014), non-European philosophies, such as East Asian and African philosophies, were excluded from influential accounts of the history of philosophy. Worse still, racism is inherent in Western philosophy, which mainly rests on the worldview of Euro-American, White males. Hence, according to Bernasconi (2021, p. 16), saying one was a Kantian is like saying

> Well, my philosophy … I'm a white guy. So, I'm going to do white guy philosophy.

Writing about the contested meaning of philosophy, Ramose (2015) demanded that the colonized people's conception of reality, knowledge, and truth should be released from slavery and the dominance from the European epistemological paradigm. Toward the last millennium, Foucault (1999) wrote that the crisis of Western thought was identical to the end of Imperialism and that the philosophy of the future had to be born outside Europe. Referring to Foucault, Chimakonam (2017) suggested that the venture of philosophy in our postcolonial age could be sought outside of the Greco-European world and might as well be in Africa.

Chapter Summary

Patriarchalism, sexism, and racism, are endemic in philosophy, science, and research. If researchers do not become aware of their own prejudices, these may be projected into an entire group of participants or one person. Furthermore, the dominance of some, and exclusions of others, has become apparent in my critical discussion of groups, paradigms, philosophy, and science.

Regarded as a family of philosophies that evaluated science very favorably, Positivism seeks to identify scientific knowledge by uncovering laws (if A occurs, B will follow). It emphasizes objectivity and relies on quantitative methods (Park et al., 2020).

Here, I have mainly focused on methodological Positivism and neglected its other sides. Logical positivists believed that scientific methods would reform philosophy and society for the better (New World Encyclopedia, 2022). So, like other philosophers and movements, the logical positivists had benevolent intentions. Sadly, Carnap (1928/1967, 1958, 1963) was mistaken in thinking that scientific methods were steps toward the emancipation of society. As evidenced by colonialism, slavery, two World Wars, and the atomic bomb, scientific methods have contributed to destruction. It is a moot point to speculate whether the world would have been a better place, if women and/or non-White scholars had played a more prominent part in Western philosophy and science. But the absence of non-Western philosophies in the history of science and research, as well as the identified sexism and racism, is likely to stir up strong negative emotions. It is equally likely that it will affect contemporary researchers and research practices. Why? Group analytic theory explains this through the concept of the social unconscious and transgenerational transmission. Unless trauma and overwhelming emotions are psychologically processed, they will be transmitted to future generations of philosophers, researchers, scholars, and so forth. Derrida's deconstruction and the analysis of the social unconscious lend themselves to explicating this. While important, analyzing and deconstructing fail to undo isms and schisms.

I have introduced the African Ubuntu philosophy and discussed what can be done about racism in philosophy and research. Within neoliberal politico-economic systems, science generates unprecedented faith in its methods. This guarantees the dominance of Positivism. Group analytic researchers are also expected to conduct quantitative studies. Some will happily do so, because quantitative methods can demonstrate the effectiveness of group analytic psychotherapies.

However, the dominance of Positivism also leads us to its perpetration of "Epistemicide" (Santos, 2014). Would it, therefore, not be time that we faced up to how Western philosophy and dominant research paradigms have failed so many researchers? Is decolonizing research truly sufficient?

Or, do we need an entirely new paradigm that reflects the possibility of becoming undone, an assemblage, a research paradigm, that is not underpinned by an oppressive epistemology and racist philosophy?

2

WHY A PARADIGM SHIFT IS NEEDED

Introducing the Emerging Reality Paradigm (ERP) Part 1

Abstract

To counter exclusionary practices, as well as philosophical beliefs that ontology and epistemology are distinct concerns, and that the quantitative and qualitative paradigm should be separate, a paradigm shift is suggested. In addition to describing the African philosophy Ubuntu, important concepts of Confucianism, Taoism, and Buddhism are outlined, which are crucial to the "Emerging Reality Paradigm" (ERP). It is proposed as an alternative research paradigm. The ERP prioritizes matter and nature. Contributing to the decolonization of research, it rests on the metaphysical assumption that everything is created from Oriental Nothingness and Qi. It emphasizes the notion of "I Am because We Are", axiology, interconnectedness, holism/unity, relationality, and complementary. Furthermore, it integrates energy psychology, group analytic and Jungian conceptualizations, which are all outlined. The ERP is fully formulated in Part 2 of Chapter 2

Introduction

One of the difficulties when writing chapters critical of Western philosophies and existing paradigms is that this might be misconstrued as me being against Western thought as such. This is not so. But I do think that paradigms should become more inclusive, which necessitates critical engagement with all their facets and underlying assumptions. And, of course, I acknowledge that it is too simplistic to speak of "Western", "Eastern", "European", "Buddhism", and so forth. Referring to "Eastern", or "Eastern philosophies", suggests that they are all the same, reflecting a blindness to difference (Dalal, 2012). Many versions of Eastern philosophies exist and within these further differentiations are found. Hence, it is deeply problematic to refer to "Western", "Southern", etc. From a psychoanalytic perspective, one could interpret this universalization as an illusion. However, writing appears unruly without the use of categories. So, the reader should bear in mind that I do not suggest that *all* African, or East Asian, philosophy is the same.

DOI:10.4324/9781003609544-3

Instead, terms (e.g. "Buddhism") should be seen as headings of a main category, which includes many subcategories, although I do not explicitly name these when referring to the key category.

Some readers may agree that research has often been portrayed as if it must rest on Western epistemologies, which are rooted in European philosophies (Bernasconi, 1997a). Critics have pointed out that we might as well say that philosophy started and ended with Plato and Aristotle (see Davis, 2022). As extreme as it may sound, when research paradigms are based on Western thought only, and researchers do not challenge this, they endorse an exclusionary philosophical research matrix. Nothing is more ignorant, as Nietzsche (1962) once pointed out, than to claim an autochthonous development for the Greeks. Although Pythagoras coined philosophy, he was influenced by Egyptian, Persian, and Indian schools of thought (Bernasconi, 1997a). So, Nietzsche's observation that the Greeks absorbed other living cultures, needs to be taken seriously particularly by group analytic researchers. Furthermore, as Bernasconi (1997a,b) noted, throughout Western philosophy we can identify exclusion. Hegel excluded Africa, China, and India. The philosophical character of the European colonization intended to establish and maintain in Africa, and in all the colonized parts of the world, the "European conception of reality, knowledge, and truth", according to Ramose (1999, p. 45). Similarly, Xiang (2023) highlights that Chinese philosophy has been "selectively amputated and ritually sacrificed as a particular that proves the universalism of Western paradigms" (p. 195).

What we call modernity has separated expert knowledge from other knowledges, such as, Indigenous knowledge. Chilisa (2020) clarified that Indigenous knowledge is specific to groups of people, regions, and locations. It can include cultures in Africa, the Māori, disabled people, the poor, women, and so forth. However, the term is commonly used to refer to cultures of the Global South.

One could say that over the past two centuries, the creation of knowledge has turned into a practice of "witnessing" (Haraway, 1997). A special community, such as scientists, witnesses each other's explications in the privacy of their laboratories and the public is excluded. Ironically, the experimental way of life was not just the production of groundbreaking scientific discoveries but also reflected "gender in the making" (Haraway, 1997). From a feminist and postcolonial perspective, the discourse of science could be construed as exclusionary, and the structure of science as misogynist and racist, reflecting "the culture of no culture", where individuals, instead of social communities, are the knowers of scientific knowledge claims (Haraway, 1997).

Except that scholars, such as Bonnie Wheeler (1992), Margo Hendricks (1994), Donna Haraway (1997), and Elizabeth Potter (1988, 2001, 2006), also point to the relationship between intersectionality and science. Gender is a relationship, as Haraway (1997) has highlighted. Thus, societal prescriptions affect men just as much as they affect women. Society, a large group, molds people according to its norms and conventions. The social unconscious is structured by power relations (Dalal, 2002), which are also influenced by capitalism (Dalal, 2012). In turn, they impact on our beliefs and behavior, but without us noticing. Researchers are not immune to the workings of the social unconscious.

A Western conception of science may have also tainted the research lens through which group analytic researchers perceive, understand, and judge, research methodologies. To be deemed robust, results must stem from methods rooted in Positivism, and by implication in a realist worldview. The widely held assumption that quantitative positivist methods must be used in (psychotherapy) research, has been problematized in Chapter 1, where Ubuntu has been contrasted with Western philosophy.

Mungwini (2022) argues that non-African researchers have to recognize that their techniques are worse than inadequate for understanding African tradition, identity, and lived experience. He regards the rejection of ethnophilosophy as a starting point for African philosophy. *Being* is an emancipatory practice, and the Philosophy of Ubuntu has positioned itself at the center of the struggle for philosophical participation (p. 165). According to Mungwini (2024), Ubuntu stands out in terms of its politico-ethical aspects.

East Asian philosophies have equally strong ethical and political dimensions. Rejecting that racism is intrinsic to human nature, Xiang (2023) states that there is a strong connection between Western metaphysics and racism. While she defines racism as a "Western phenomenon that reifies fear of difference into a systematic worldview even after this fear has outlasted its practical purpose" (p. 26), another definition simply says that "racism equals power plus prejudice" (Operario & Fiske, 1998, p. 33). Whatever definition one uses, philosophy, psychotherapy, and research, must guard against those overpowering racist structures and conceptual models, which have infiltrated contemporary thinking (see Eze, 1997). Thus, I agree that re-assessments of philosophical assumptions are needed. Research paradigms, which almost exclusively rest on Western philosophies that are plagued with the racist notion that most of the world's thought is beneath them (Xiang, 2023), are not fit for purpose. This stance is in line with group analytic authors, such as Nayak and Forrester (2024), who emphasize including marginalized voices into group analytic conceptualizations. Furthermore, the Institute of Group Analysis in London has adopted a commitment to non-discriminatory theoretical perspectives and clinical practice (see Nayak, 2023). Group analytic researchers must do the same, I contend. This involves developing a new research paradigm that re-conceptualizes philosophical assumptions.

In the social sciences, research has commonly been divided into the quantitative and qualitative paradigm. Group analytic outcome and process research seems to fit neatly into these two competing research paradigms. Such division is reflected in many research textbooks However, as Burns (2000) argued, such dichotomization is misleading. Ratnesar and Mackenzie (2007) went a step further, stating that this divide was "no longer sustainable" (p. 13).

Equally, there is good reason to question the traditional Western philosophical belief that ontology and epistemology are distinct concerns (Barad, 2007). To transcend dichotomies, it seems necessary to replace the traditional paradigms and their underlying philosophies with conceptualizations that unite rather than divide paradigms.

Concurring with Barad (2007) that epistemology, ontology, and axiology are inseparable, I will formulate an alternative transdisciplinary research paradigm. Instead of repeating tired arguments for or against the existing paradigms, I will propose an entirely new one: the Emerging Reality Paradigm (ERP). It is based on African and East/South Asian philosophies due to their foci on holism, unity, relationality, and ethical values, which is in line with group analytic thinking. Here, philosophy is viewed as an interdependent, emancipatory expression, and critique of cultural values (Mungwini, 2022).

The revival of ancient metaphysics has resulted in new conceptualizations of philosophy in Japan.

Taking a similar approach to the formulation of the ERP as the Japanese philosopher Nishida (1921/1990, 1923, 1970), I seek inspiration in East Asian metaphysics, particularly in his conceptualizations of Nothingness. Nishida (1927/1978–1979) wrote that

> … Western culture, which is persistently theoretical, the life that drives it as its foundation … We must … return to the structure … and formative function of the historical world.
>
> (Collective Works, Vol. 12, p. 288)

Furthermore, I believe that

> … we have to meet the universe halfway. Nothing will unfold for us unless we move toward what looks to us like nothing: faith is a cascade …
>
> (Alice Fulton, cited in Barad, 2007, p. 39)

Hence, the new paradigm builds on continuous, flowing movement and momentum. Energy, matter, and nature, are constituent components of this paradigm. Like Haraway (1988), I believe that it is important to understand the interplay of the natural, the material, and the cultural world.

The proposed paradigm prioritizes considerations of matter and nature. It views the body not as a mute substance, because this would deprive matter of its own historicity (Butler, 1990), but as a dynamic, relational organism. Bodies are viewed as constituted through entangled bio-energetic physical fields and processes. The psychodynamics of mind manifest in the body's energy system. Mind-body energy is linked to thought fields (Callahan, 2001). Drawing on a psychoanalytic energy approach (Mollon, 2008), which is congruent with Freud's (1905b) concept of libido, an instinctual psychic energy, a "qualitatively variable force … occurring in the field of sexual excitation" (p. 217), the Asian Qi (subtle energy), as used in Chinese Medicine, and a quantum physics energy perspective, are integrated in the ERP. It postulates that people's energy fields communicate with each other. This is conceptualized as one person "reading" the unconscious mind of another person (Freud, 1912), facilitated by the right hemisphere of the brain (Schore, 2019).

I will elaborate my ideas as I proceed. Like other societies, African and Asian cultures have strong ethical values. Ethics forms an important aspect of life. It is also crucial for research. Therefore, I will outline important ethical principles first. Then relevant ideas of the African philosophy Ubuntu, and of East/South Asian philosophies, will be discussed. In addition to explaining relevant concepts of Jungian Psychoanalysis and energy psychology, a brief comparison will be made between group analytic concepts, philosophical, Jungian, and quantum conceptualizations. Their compatibility is regarded as important, because the ERP is primarily formulated as a research paradigm for group analytic researchers. However, it is also a generic paradigm.

Ethical Considerations

"Ethics" is a broad term that covers morals and specific choices that human beings make (Varkey, 2020, p. 17). It is crucial for research. Normative ethics concerns itself with moral norms in relation to correct conduct. "Particular morality" refers to norms that bind groups together based on their culture, religion, or profession. Morality includes responsibilities and standards (p. 18). In Western cultures, the four principles of ethics (beneficence, nonmaleficence, autonomy, and justice) can be traced to Hippocrates (p. 19). Autonomy refers to research participants' rights to determine what shall be done to their bodies and to researchers respecting their participants' autonomy. It includes issues, such as informed consent, being truthful, and respecting confidentiality (p. 21).

Research Ethics Codes may vary slightly from country to country. However, European and world-wide standards have been published:

- The European Code of Conduct for Research Integrity includes the principles of reliability, honesty, respect, and accountability (ALLEA, 2023).

- The International Compilation of Human Research Standards enumerates over 1,000 laws, regulations, and guidelines that govern the protection of research participants in more than 130 countries, as well as standards from various international and regional organizations (OASH, 2024).
- The World Health Organization has issued ethical guidelines for the governance of artificial intelligence for health (WHO, 2024).
- In America, the three ethical principles of *Respect for Persons, Beneficence* (researchers act to promote the well-being of their participants, protect them from harm, discomfort, exploitation), and *Justice* (fair, equitable, appropriate treatment of participants; study should benefit them and their community) apply (Barrow et al., 2022).
- In the UK, the British Psychological Society emphasizes these principles: respect for the autonomy, privacy and dignity of individuals, groups, and communities; scientific integrity; social responsibility; and maximizing benefit and minimizing harm (BPS, 2021, p. 7).

Some Basics of Non-Western Philosophies

Over the past decades, the African philosophy Ubuntu has gained prominence. I first came across the word "ubuntu" when exploring how group analytic research could be decolonized and reading about group analytic training courses in Rwanda (see Phipps, 2023). Ubuntu was briefly discussed in Chapter 1. The word "ubuntu" is derived from a Nguni aphorism "Umuntu Ngumuntu Ngabantu" (Broodryk, 2005). This saying means that "a person is a person through other people" (Ngubane-Mokiwa, 2018, p. 460; Tuto, 2004). Ancient Nguni philosophers described the principles of Ubuntu, by which communities defined themselves, their customs, and their laws. One of Ubuntu's main characteristics is communal well-being, which is based on the belief that our humanness is dependent on relationships with others. Described also as a research paradigm, Ubuntu places much importance on ethical values (Mungwini, 2024). Hence, researchers will pay special attention to axiology.

By prioritizing relationships, groupishness, and We, the Ubuntu Philosophy has much in common with group analytic thought. So, there is a good fit between the two. Integrating Ubuntu into the Emerging Reality research Paradigm is, therefore, not only logical and an attempt to decolonize group analytic research. This integration also increases its methodological scope.

The emphasis on communality, harmony, and on "I am because we are", is found in the philosophies of many Indigenous cultures, signifying a relational ontology. While Confucianism, Taoism, and Buddhism, are the most prominent philosophies in East Asia, in South Asia, Indian philosophy comprises many other traditions. However, as Natayanan (2005) explained, Buddhism (ca. 500 BCE) originated in India. It is based on the teachings of Gautama Buddha (ca. 563–483 BCE). Significant texts of Indian philosophy are the "Vedas" (Sanskrit, meaning "Knowledge"), the "Aranyakas" (describe acquisition of knowledge and actions taken in life), and the "Upanishads" (Hindu sacred texts written ca. 600 BCE, postulating an interconnected universe with a single "supreme being", *Brahman*) (Natayanan, 2005). Most of the later literature deals with *Dharma* (truth, law). The Upanishads, the Bhagavad Gita, and the Brahma Sutra, form the nexus around the philosophical tradition of "Vedanta". For the prominent philosopher Shankara (ca. 788–820 CE), whose teaching revolved around the concept of "Advaita Vedanta", our phenomenal reality was of limited usefulness. Instead, he advocated that there was only one reality, found in the unity of the *Brahman* and *Atman* (human soul) (Natayanan, 2005).

Initially, Confucianism (ca. 1766 BCE) and Taoism (403 BCE) were the two poles of traditional Chinese culture, with Buddhism appearing much later (100–200 CE). Even though these "Three Teachings" together with the folk tradition were originally an amalgamation of Chinese religion (Oldstone-Moore, 2005a), more contemporary East Asian philosophers have not restricted their views to religion. Philosophers from the Japanese Kyoto School, for example, have also incorporated physics (Brink, 2021).

The *Analects*, a collection of sayings by Confucius (551–479 BCE) and his pupils, is the most reliable source of Confucius' teachings (Wing-Tsit, 1973). Confucius turned humanism into the driving force in Chinese philosophy. His primary concern was a good society that was based on harmonious human relations and good government. He developed the new concept of humanity (Jen), advocating the correspondence of words and actions (name and actuality). Confucius transformed Jen into a general virtue. It expressed itself in terms of conscientiousness and altruism, known as "Chung and Shu" (Wing-Tsit, 1973). The Chinese *Book of Changes* (Yijing or I-Ching, written 1000–400 BCE) is a common source for both Taoist and Confucianist philosophers. According to The Yijing, everything that exists (e.g., matter, mind, spirit) is created from the life energy, known as Qi (or Chi; Leong, 2023, p. 209). Such thinking is found in Neo-Confucian philosophy, which spread to Korea and Southeast Asia. (Neo-)Confucianist, Taoist, and Buddhist philosophical schools of thought, are prevalent in Japan (Bol, 2008).

At the heart of Taoism is the *Tao Te Ching*. It is a brief text with just over 5,000 Chinese characters, written by the Chinese philosopher Lao Tzu, approx. 600 BCE (Oldstone-Moore, 2005a). Known also as Laozi, he was the founder of Taoism. The *Tao Te Ching* has been translated as "The Classics of the Way and its Power" (p. 242) or as "The Book of the Immanence of the Way" (Mitchell, 2006, p. vii). Alongside the "Zhuangzi", it is central to religious and philosophical Taoism. Many interpretations and translations are found of Lao Tsu's book. The prominent Chinese philosopher Wang Pi (226–249 BC) offered one such interpretation. In his commentary on the Lao Tsu, Wang Pi wrote: "All being originated from non-being" (cited in Wing-Tsit, 1973, p. 321). Non-being, Nothingness, and Emptiness, are crucial conceptualizations in most South/East Asian philosophies. And so is the life energy Qi ("Prana" in Indian traditions, Shakti in Hinduism).

Adopting the Philosophy Ubuntu & Its Values in the ERP

Harmonious Communal Group Relationships

According to Metz (2019), Indigenous black Africans tend to believe that their basic aim in life should be to exhibit Ubuntu. This is achieved by prioritizing communal relationships with others rather than focusing on oneself. These principles of Ubuntu are shared by all tribes of Bantu origin (Rwelamila et al., 1999). As an ethical perspective and way of life, Ubuntu has been in existence for hundreds of years among the peoples of sub-Saharan Africa. Most written scholarship, however, has only emerged in the last 60 years or so (Praeg & Magadla, 2014). Ubuntu's focus on community and relationships, and its notion that an individual exists only within the context of groups, is also central to group analytic theories. So, it seems logical to include these ethical aspirations in the ERP. Ideals associated with Ubuntu, such as harmonious communal relationships, realizing oneself through relationships with others, and cultivating one's humanity, could be a source of inspiration for group analytic researchers as well.

Due to the dominance of Western paradigms, African philosophy and methodologies were devalued. However, a research approach informed by Ubuntu would benefit communities, which should be an aim of every research project. Historically, social communities have not been regarded as the knowers of scientific knowledge claims (Haraway, 1997). Slowly, this has started to shift. Western researchers in the field of health have started to recognize that studies should benefit the wider community from which knowledge has been taken (Banzi et al., 2011). Equally, group analytic researchers should ask themselves, when designing studies, who would benefit the most from their research projects: they, their participants, or both parties?

The history of research is contaminated with unethical experiments (see Jarrett, 2024; Sade, 2003; Weidling et al., 2016). It is marked by the exclusion of Indigenous knowledges. This includes the epistemic saliency of cultural traditions, values, belief systems, and worldviews of any Indigenous culture. As Dei (2000) explained, Indigenous knowledge is the product of the direct experience of nature and its relationship with the physical, spiritual, and social world. Castellano (2000) has distinguished between traditional, empirical, and revealed knowledge. Trends in postmodernism and postcolonial theorizing show a shift in the focus of research toward studying lived experiences (Dei, 2000). Alas, they often deny collective histories, prioritizing individual renditions (p. 116). Scholars have highlighted the disturbing tendency of postcolonial discourses to ignore the histories of the Indigenous peoples in the Global South. Initially, it was Fanon (1963), who insisted that decolonization could only be understood as a historical process. But it seems to be a very lengthy and exhausting process (Tiffin, 1995). Considering that the end goal of decolonization is to change the social order, it may be met with resistance. In academia, there is a tendency to accept the authority of Western knowledge and negate, or devalue, the knowledge of local people (Dei, 2000). Sadly, the exclusion of African philosophy, and a perception that African knowledge is inferior, is not new. It is closely linked to Colonialism and epistemological racism (Bernasconi, 1997a,b). To appreciate why the decolonization of research is so painful, but important, an understanding of the effects of Colonialism is necessary.

European's encounter with difference led to Colonialism, Xiang (2023) writes after the scramble for Africa in the 19th century, missionaries aimed to convert Indigenous people to Christianity. By 1914, Colonialism had brought 85% of the globe under European rule as colonies, protectorates, dependencies, dominions, and the Commonwealth (Mills, 1997). One could argue that religion became a means of oppression with the rise of Christian churches. The other oppressor was capitalism (see Kobe, 2021).

Decolonial discourses that focus on advancing a culture of African spirituality as part of the liberation of Black people (Vellem, 2014) have gained importance. Kobe (2021) argued that spiritual liberation is as important as liberating Africa per se. Such considerations contributed to his reconceptualizing Ubuntu outside of Christianity and Western epistemologies. According to Chigevenga (2022), the African continent is unified by the Ubuntu Philosophy. Developing this further, Ramose (1999) has suggested that a person would be instructed by Ubuntu to become a human being. Based on the belief that humanness is dependent on relationships with others, Ubuntu has been described as a worldview, a moral ethic, a research paradigm, and a framework that guides research practices. Its philosophical assumptions about social reality, ways of knowing, and ethical values can be integrated into Western research methodologies (Chigevenga, 2022). Several postulates of Ubuntu, which are important to the ERP, will be outlined below.

"I Am Because We Are"

Ubuntu can be described as the capacity of an African culture to express compassion, reciprocity, dignity, humanity, and mutuality, in the interest of forming, and maintaining, just and mutually caring communities (Khoza, 2006, p. 6; Mandela, 2008, p. xxv). Communities and communal relations are based on mutual identification with each other and on exhibiting solidarity with others (Metz, 2019). It is striking that Ubuntu's notion of "I am because we are" has been applied to every area of African life. For example, it is found in the law, in politics, and business. In philosophical terms, "umuntu" (person, human being) precedes Ubuntu ontologically and epistemologically Dladla (2017).

Highlighting that the exact meaning would be difficult to convey in English, Dladla (2017) endorsed Ramose's (2009) translation of the Nguni aphorism into "to be a human be-ing". Ramose aimed to affirm a person's humanity by recognizing the humanity of others. It is on this basis that human relationships are established.

Discussing Ubuntu as a Philosophy of Liberation, Kobe (2021) drew on Ramose (2009), who argues that "Ubu" (to become) always orients itself toward "Ntu" (person), at an ontological level. But both are two aspects of "be-ing" (p. 36). Kobe (2021) suggestes that "Ntu" could be regarded as distinctly epistemological. Both Ramose (2009) and Dladla (2017) insist that Ubuntu is always a "ness". It was never an "ism" due to the logic of "Ubu" (being). Motion is a principle of "be-ing". Since "be-ing" is understood as verbal and continual movement, translating ubuntu into "human-ism" would be wrong. It has to be "humanness", according to these two scholars.

Expanding his philosophical argument, Dladla (2017) drew on Bénézet Bujo's (1997) reasoning. Bujo (2001) stated that it was not the Cartesian "I think therefore I am" that was important to Black Africa, but rather the existential "I am related, therefore, we are" (pp. 22–23). Using this interpretation of Ubuntu, Dladla (2017) asserted that humaneness is an ethical imperative and a dictum that promotes life. He concurred with Bujo (2009) that different ethical systems with similar ideas exist. They are not always identical.

For the Bantu-speaking people, Ubuntu is the source and embodiment of ethics. However, humanness is not a given. To be born as *Homo sapiens* is a necessary, but insufficient, condition. One must become a human being in an ethical sense. Hence, Dladla (2017) argues that "be-ing" always depends on doing. It involves recognizing another person's humanity and the formation of humane relationships with her or him. From a Bantu perspective, law and politics have no meaning, if they do not include others. To prove oneself as the "embodiment of ubuntu" is important (Bujo, 2001). Determining whether one embodies ubuntu, or not, is based on the known history of a person's actions and her/his humane conduct (Dladla, 2017). This also applies to a group or groups of people (see Metz, 2019). So, Ubuntu is an ethical evaluation rather than a biological given. However, because Ubuntu is the history of the Bantu people, White people cannot embody Ubuntu due to the ethically unjustified violation of sovereign title to territory, history of political subjugation, economic exploitation, and racism. To embody Ubuntu, a White person must counter this history (Dladla, 2017).

Comparing Ubuntu with Western axiological assumptions, Metz (2019) claimes that its self-realization ethics differed from Aristotelian conceptions of the good life, which are found in contemporary Western cultures. African ethics does not have hedonic aspirations, such as individual pleasure or satisfaction. Instead, its focus is on "We" and on communal thriving.

Even though there is not one version of ubuntu that every scholar subscribes to, there are similarities between writers. According to Mokoena (2024), the holistic, ethical approach of Ubuntu includes considerations of *humanity* (our relationships as human beings, rooted in human dignity), *spirituality* (our relationship with the Supreme Being, God, the living, and our ancestors), and the *environment* (our relationship with the land, sea, sky, nature, and animals). While Mangena (2016) holds a similar view, Chiorazzi (2015) points out that African spirituality is diverse. One premise of Ubuntu entails that humans are not the center of the universe but merely a part of it. Everything must be viewed in relation to each other. In African philosophy, individual identity forms part of a larger whole (Ramose, 2015). However, this does not mean that the experience of individual reality is denied. It simply means that the community is valued more. Because it enables a person to understand her/his own identity and the environment better. Of course, Ubuntu is not static. It is a process of be-ing, signifying movement, which involves the process of becoming more humane (Ramose, 2015). Although Ubuntu could be regarded as anthropocentric, LenkaBula (2008) asserts that it transcends anthropocentricity. People form ontological, sociopolitical, economic, ecological, and religious relationships among themselves, and with their environment. This points to the inseparability of human and ecological life, demonstrating that Ubuntu is holistic. Ubuntu is expressed in art, symbolism, music, dance, proverbs, riddles, individuals' names, myths, legends, beliefs, and spiritual practices (Mbiti, 1999). Consequently, African spirituality is a lived experience (Ramose, 2005). It encompasses all facets of socio-politico-economic life, which are shaped by Ubuntu (Masango, 2006). Unfortunately, Christianization and Colonialism interfered with African spirituality (Kobe, 2021). This led to a rise in Western science and technology, altering Africans' view of themselves (Dolamo, 2013). As noted by several scholars, Ubuntu is not beyond criticism (Mbazzi, 2023). It may be experienced as an obligation or prescription that one must adhere to, Ubuntu has also been criticized for being too Indigenous, romantic, idealistic, universalistic, or even utopian and vague (see Marx, 2002; Metz, 2011; Richardson, 2008; Van Binsbergen, 2001).

Compatibility of Perspectives

Philosophy and religion were originally undifferentiated and inseparable in Hinduism, Confucianism, Taoism, and Buddhism. However, as Wing-Tsit (1973) pointed out, the interpretations of Confucian teachings have differed in the last 2,000 years. While some were more interested in historical facts, other interpretations were more subjective, interpretative, and philosophical. For example, Menicus developed his teachings from Confucius. But he was more idealistic, viewing human beings as originally good (Wing-Tsit, 1973).

Despite their differences, these philosophies rest on a relational ontology and shared ethical values. So does Ubuntu. It is compatible with East/South Asian philosophies, which also emphasize harmony, humanism, spirituality, community, and "We". There is a similarity with group analytic conceptualizations as well. Even though compatibility is not a research requirement, it aligns with the notion of harmony. Xiang (2023) defines harmony as the "creative organizing function that brings differences into complementary and productive relationship with one another" (p. 35). Admittedly, harmony is an ideal. However, "[w]hen we live in harmony with the self … we feel 'this is really me'" (Foulkes, 2003, p. 318). So, people could strive toward living in harmony with others, the environment, and themselves.

Life Energy Qi, Yin-Yang & Xi

Since the beginning of time have the teachings of Indigenous peoples emphasized the unity of body, mind, and spirit (Mark & Lyons, 2010). This means that an aspect of ourselves, which is connected to something non-material, is larger than our own existence (Ogden, 2021). In Taoism, the source of the divine is Tao (path, way). Tao begins as primordial chaos, then gives rise to Qi, then to Ying and Yang, and finally to countless forms of creation (Oldstone-Moore, 2005a). More specifically, Qi is a vital substance in its primordial state. Divided into Yin Qi (heavy, sinks down) and Yang Qi (light, ascends), the universe is created from this basic binary relationship, manifesting in a variety of groupings and divisions. According to an ancient understanding of how the cosmos functions, everything that exists (humans, deities, heaven, Earth, etc.) is made up of the life energy Qi (Ki in Japanese, Korean). Qi flows through channels and grids, giving life to all creatures (pp. 272–273). It manifests in the two forces of Yin and Yang.

The principle of Yin and Yang is a foundational concept in Taoism, Confucianism, and Buddhism. It describes seemingly opposite forces that operate in an interconnected, interdependent, and complementary manner. Inherent in Yin and Yang is transformation. Yin transforms into Yang, and vice versa (Oldstone-Moore, 2005b). All things in the universe, including people, consist of both Yin and Yang to varying proportions (Oldstone-Moore, 2005b, p. 318). While Yin is dark, feminine, passive, receptive, soft, night, cold, nurturing, rest, and introspection, Yang is bright masculine, active, assertive, hard, day, warmth, dominating, and action expressing. Yin and Yang cannot exist independently. For example, Yang's light has no meaning without Yin's darkness. Day evolves into night and activity alternates with rest. Good health depends on the balance between Yin and Yang in Chinese medicine (Hammer, 2010).

Discussing Chinese Philosophy and gender, Ann Pang-White (2018a) has noticed differences between Western and Chinese conceptualizations of gender. Masculinity and femininity are rooted in the concept of Yin-Yang, which operates with a very fluid conception. Thus, a gender discourse, as employed in Western cultures, is inadequate when applied within Chinese contexts. An "either or" thinking has dominated the patriarchal Western philosophical traditions (Pang-White, 2006). Furthermore, philosophy has not been kind to women. While Aristotle proclaimed that women are "mutilated males", for Kant women were "only beautiful" and "men sublime" (Pang-White, 2018a, p. 3). Chinese traditions also have a troubled history in dealing with gender relations. Gender remains "relatively marginalized in Chinese philosophical and in cultural discourse" (p. 1). Analyzing the view of the Neo-Confucian Zhu Xi on women, Pang-White (2018b) suggests that gender could become more interrelational and equal by modifying the metaphysics of Yin-Yang, with the different, but equal, li-qi complementarity. This could create a more "diverse and egalitarian socio-political philosophy" (p. 82). Interestingly, Sin Yee Chan's (2017) analysis of ancient Confucianism in relation to Yin-Yang has revealed that homosexuality might be acceptable. Overall, when comparing the role of women in Chinese philosophy, Buddhism's adherence to non-dualism seems to offer a philosophy beyond gender, as opposed to the engrained gender bias in most philosophical traditions (see Lu, 2018; Pang-White, 2018c; Wawrytko, 2018).

According to Shun (1997), the Chinese character "Xin" means heart. Xin has been translated as heart-mind, which preludes a distinction between thinking and feeling. In Chinese philosophy, Xin is a unified center of cognition and emotion. Romanticism also focuses on the heart and its ethos seems to be best captured in Blaise Pascal's (1958) poetic aphorism "The Heart has its reason, which Reason does not understand" (cited in *Pensées*, Section IV: Of the Means of Belief, 277, p. 99). But the Romantics turned away from the mind. They did not conceptualize the heart and mind together. So, their thinking is dissimilar from the unified notion of heart-mind (Xin).

The Book Lao Tzu

The Taoist Lao Tzu had a profound impact on Chinese civilization and philosophy (Wing-Tsit, 1973). By opposing Confucian conformity, and its emphasis on social order and an active life, Taoism cultivated a transcendental spirit, simplicity, spontaneity, tranquility, and non-action. The Lao Tzu is divided into two sections: Tao Ching and Te Ching. It means "the Classic of the Way and its Virtue". Embodying only 5,250 words, the Tao Te Ching is a metaphysical book (Wing-Tsit, 1973). One passage says that

> ... Being and non-being produce each other ... Therefore, the sage manages affairs without action (Wu-Wei). And spreads doctrines without words ...
>
> (p. 140)

Teaching without words is diametrically opposed to the Confucian ideal, where man speaks. However, it is in line with Buddhism, where silent transmission is valued. Two Taoist ideas, namely vacuity (Hsű, purity) and non-being (Wu), were subsequently elaborated by Buddhists.

Wing-Tsit (1973) commented that Chapter 21 of the Lao Tzu was of vital importance, because "The essence is very real" constituted the foundation of Chou Tuni's philosophy (1017–1073; often known as the Master of Lien-his). He developed a philosophy based on Ying and Yang. The "Explanation of the Diagram of the Great Ultimate" focuses on the reality of the "Non-Ultimate" and the essence of Yin and Yang. According to Wing-Tsit (1973), Chou's work formed the foundation of the entire metaphysics of Neo-Confucianism (p. 151), although he acknowledged that its metaphysics was more directly derived from The Yijing. However, the concepts of reality are similar in both books. Furthermore, Laozi's writing about existence and Nothingness has been interpreted as "existence and Nothingness begetting each other", meaning that Nothing is invisible. Our human senses cannot perceive, smell, hear, touch, or see "Nothing". Therefore, it is very hard to be named. That is why it is referred to as "Nothing" or "Nothingness" (Zhengkun, n.d.). One can think of it as energy fields. Even though energy exists in the universe, we do not see it. Nevertheless, energy affects us, and we would cease to exist without it.

Wu Wei: Acting without Conscious Thought

No civilization is monochrome, as Smith (1991, p. 95) put it. In China, the classical tones of Confucianism have been balanced by the spiritual shades of Buddhism, and by the romantic hues of Taoism, where De/Te is usually translated as "inherent character, inner power, or integrity" (Stefon, 2012). Being is a result of non-doing. It requires Emptiness, which is achieved through emptying one's mind of egocentric notions, desires, and one's behavior of ways of behaving that are antagonistic with nature. According to Ames (1989), "inaction" (Wu Wei) is not passive. It results from being attuned to the rhythms and harmonies of all aspects of life. It entails the awareness that each moment is the end point of all that has come before, even from the beginning of time (Ming-Dao, 1990). So, when a person is doing Wu Wei, s/he is "doing nothing" by being in harmony with nature. Like a sailor who sets the sail and rides the wind. Tao never acts yet nothing is left undone, which is the paradox of Wu Wei. Integrated with Qi, creative energies unite the doer with the deed (Ming-Dao, 1990). Truly doing Wu Wei entails living in accord with the universe. Such thinking is in stark contrast to the Western idea of doing, which often entails acting or doing something. Taoist "acting" is different. There is nothing to accomplish. In daily life, Wu Wei will only come when a person has wisdom and maturity. Then s/he responds to life spontaneously, because s/he acts with unconscious insight and without doubt, as nature itself acts (Ming-Dao, 1990).

The Yijing

Referred to as the "Book of Changes", The Yijing (or I-Ching) is 3,000 years old. Scholars have ranked it in the same league as the Christian Bible, the Jewish Talmud, the Buddhist Lotus Sutra, the Muslim's Qur'an, and the Hindu's Bhagavad Gita (Gregg, 2014). After Confucius' death (479 BCE), The Yijing formed the basis of a scholar's education in China (Shen et al., 2006). Different aspects of The Yijing have been emphasized. Zeng (2023) writes that in ancient China two Schools of Yiology (divinatory techniques and theories derived from The Yijing) dominated: the Xiang Shu (emphasizing images and numbers) and the Yi Li (focusing on implicated connotation in the philosophy of The Yijing). Karcher (1999) insisted that many translations of The Yijing are "simplistic re-hashings of older material made without recourse to the Chinese texts" (p. 303). "Yijing" literally means the Class of Yi. The sign "Yi" has two faces, regular change, such as the change of the seasons, or transformation, such as the change of water into ice (p. 292). Karcher (1999) translates this first meaning as destabilizing change, a storm threatening to devastate the fields, or when the unconscious breaks down the conscious order (p. 292). Another set of meanings tells people how to deal with difficulties through versatility, imaginative mobility, and the ability to change quickly. This quality of Yi forces people to consciously change their identity, enabling a reconnection, with the Way. It is this pattern of disruption, change, and reconnection that is central to The Yijing (p. 292).

Rinzai Zen: Ultimate Antinomy, Oriental Nothingness & Interconnectedness

Interestingly, philosophers of the Kyoto School of philosophy drew on East Asian and Western philosophy, as well as on physics (Parkes, 2008). However, the philosophy espoused by Nishida Kitarô, Tanabe Hajime, and Tosaka Jun, has challenged the Western notion of "being", which has been prevalent since Parmenides (Brink, 2021). According to the Kyoto School, absolute Nothingness underpins the Self. Instead of embracing the Western dialectics of subject and object (or Self and nature), these philosophers have focused on being and non-being. Nothing (mu), or absolute Nothingness, is the beginning of "being".

Nishida (1870–1945) is one of the greatest philosophers of modern Japan. In Brink's (2021) words, Nishida "deployed emptiness as nothingness in order to diffuse space as a site of mastery in ways that may overcome pseudo colonial relation with another" human being (p. 4). It is noteworthy that Neo-Confucianist metaphysics, which is based on the principle of Ultimate Nothingness, is identical to the Buddhist notion of Emptiness (Ozaki, 2019). Asking what ultimate reality is in *An Inquiry into the Good,* Nishida (1921/1990) wanted to formulate a different ontology and epistemology by explaining everything through pure experience. Pure experience is the sole reality. Zen provided the direction of his philosophy. Nishida was a Zen Buddhist and a philosopher, who transformed Zen into philosophy for the first time in the history of this religious tradition (Masao, 1990). Nishida looked for answers that had been dealt with before by Buddhist metaphysics. Commenting on Western culture, Nishida (1927/1978–1979) wrote that

> … there are many things to be esteemed and learnt … However, at the basis of Asian culture … lies something that can be called seeing the form of the formless and hearing the sound of the soundless. Our minds are compelled to seek this. I would like to give a philosophical foundation to this demand.
>
> (Collective Works, Vol 4, p. 6)

In Japan, the Zoto and Rinzai Zen versions of Buddhism are practiced (Barnhart, 1992). Hisamatsu Shin'ichi (1889–1980) was a Zen master in the Rinzai School. He took a slightly different angle than Zoto Zen philosophers, because Rinzai always pairs "Great Trust" with "Great Doubt". Hence, the negative must be complemented with the positive (Hisamatsu, 2002). Describing Zen as "formless" (p. 90), Hisamatsu (1971) explained that in Japanese, forms of Self are a "Self without Self" (p. 92). There are similarities but also differences between Nishida and Hiramatsu. Nishida (1993) has theorized a rigorous structure to absolute Nothingness, where we find traces of Kant, Hegel, and Bergson integrated with Zen Buddhism and Daoist ideas (see Ames & Takeuchi, 2024; Dalissier, 2007, 2009; Maraldo, 2005). Hiramatsu has developed a broader framework for Nothingness that captures East Asian perspectives (Daoism, Zen, Kyoto School, Hisamatsu 1982, 2002). However, like Nishida, Hisamatsu (1959, 2005) viewed Nothingness as the emerging foundation of reality, even though Hiramatsu seems to lean more toward traditional East Asian thought (see Masao & Ives, 1981) and has not developed a rigorous structure. Hisamatsu (2002) argued that the Self becomes inflexible, if people are clinging to the positive part of dualities (clinging to life and rejecting death). Conceptualizing "ultimate antinomy", Hisamatsu (1975) pointed out that we cannot have a life without death. To overcome this one-sided tendency, we must face the ultimate antinomy (death). Hisamatsu used the word "ultimate", which is his term for "Mu" (nothingness). It is the supreme negative principle in Rinzai Zen. Kyoto School philosophers of the Zoto tradition refer to it simply as "Nothingness" (Barnhart, 1992). Critical of Japanese Zen for its focus on awakening (Van der Braak, 2019) and for referring to "The Existence that is Nothing" (FAS, 2012, p. 42), for Hisamatsu (1959), Oriental Nothingness was the ground of everything. Oriental Nothingness encapsulates the connection between confirmation and negation, it is the voiding of voidness (Hiramatsu, 2005). What is important, however, is the relational dynamic. Anything considered in isolation and aloneness is subject to the function of complete negation in the sense that each thing is a dimensionless point of unity, relative to everything else. Absolute negation and confirmation are reversible, if exercised rigorously. Like other South/East Asian and African philosophers, Hisamatsu emphasized interconnectedness. Everything in the universe and in people's lives is interconnected. People do not exist outside the complex web of relationships and are in "inter-being" with every other thing (Hanh, 2001).

Coined by the Vietnamese Thich Nhat Hanh, "interbeing" is a philosophical concept and contemplation practice rooted in Zen Buddhism, conveying the interconnectedness of being (Hanh, 2001). The Zen Circle, which is a representation of interbeing (see also Abe, 1967; Abe, 1997; Aśvaghosha, 2003, 2008), is perhaps comparable to the circle in group analytic psychotherapies.

Interconnectedness is firmly embedded in Buddhism, Taoism, Confucianism, and in Ubuntu. "Dependent Origination" is a Buddhist notion. It emphasizes that nothing can be created on its own, all things are interdependent. Everyone and everything are emerging in parallel with everyone and everything else. Hence, the notion of an isolated, independent Self is but an illusion (Hanh, 2001). It is interconnectedness that becomes a felt and lived reality. If researchers operationalized Asian concepts, such as "Dependent Origination", they could study emerging group processes that reveal such interdependence in the group.

Ultimate Reality & Oriental Nothingness

Although ultimate reality can only be found within the Self, the Self is neither a specific thing, nor does it have a body. Knowledge of Ultimate Reality itself is an exemplification of Nothingness. What takes shape is a formless self as a "no-thing", as Barnhart (1992) put it. In genuinely knowing it, we immanently transcend ourselves and become Oriental Nothingness. This shows that "Ultimate Reality" itself is, indeed, ultimate. Hence, any notion of finiteness will be problematic. According to Hisamatsu (1959, 1971, 1975), it leads either to "Great Doubt" or to "Awakening". The barrier that needs to be crossed is the "taxonomizing mentality", because as soon as we seek a descriptive differentiation of Ultimate Reality, we encounter paradox and contradictions (Barnhart, 1992). Ultimate Reality, Oriental Nothingness, and Ultimate Antinomy, are related to Emptiness, Dependent Origination, and Non-Self, as conceptualized by Madhyamaka Buddhism, founded by Nagarjuna (see Houshmand et al., 1999). According to Capra (1991), our human mind can generate two types of knowledge, or two modes of consciousness: One is rational and associated with science. The other is intuitive and associated with religion.

Sunyata – Emptiness

In contrast to the Western notion, the "Void" has infinite potential for creation. What Buddhists call "Emptiness" (Sunyata) affirms a living Emptiness, or Void, giving birth to all forms in the phenomenal world (Capra, 1991). Hence, Sunyata also implies that all phenomena are interdependent, and an inherently independent existence is impossible. The concepts of Pratityasmutpada (Dependent Origination) and Anatta (Non-Self) assert that all phenomena arise in interdependence. So, there is no permanent, fixed Self, but only an emerging Self (Houshmand et al., 1999). (See also Abe, 1967 for awakening of faith.)

Although group analysis also rejects the notion of a static Self and of binary logic, cognitive behavioral therapy tends to view individuals as encapsulated Selves, implying that all their qualities are properties of the Self. It is a kind of thinking that follows the binary logic of opposites (individual vs group, positive vs negative, etc.). However, in East Asian philosophies, opposites are dialectically conjoined and function together. They are not viewed in the same way as opposites in Western conceptualizations (Houshmand et al., 1999). Opposites are complementary, one creating the other, because holism is very important in East Asian thought.

Buddhist Consciousness

The Treatise of the Consciousness School holds that root consciousness is the storehouse of consciousness, from which all pure and impure consciousness grows (Wing-Tsit, 1973). Cause is regarded as the rising activities of the mind, of sense organs, and spheres of objects. Consciousness manifests itself in the five sense organs. At times, consciousness manifests itself together, at other times separately, because the external causes may be combined either suddenly or gradually (Wing-Tsit, 1973, p. 385). Hence, the various forms of consciousness transform and change. Everything is only consciousness. The mistaken discrimination against the notion of "only" is recognized as a fact. Because "only" does not deny the existence of Dharmas, which are not separated from consciousness. True Emptiness is, therefore, the nature of things (p. 387).

Hence, the denial of the ego is the starting point of Buddhist philosophizing, and of the Consciousness School, in particular (Wing-Tsit, 1973).

Resting on the Metaphysical Notion of Nothingness: The ERP

Metaphysics was eradicated by Positivism (Horkheimer, 1999, 2004). In the formulation of the ERP, I am re-vitalizing ancient Eastern traditions. The ERP rests on their metaphysical notion of Nothingness. It is Nothingness that creates everything. As such, it determines how individuals exist. Brink (2021) suggested that Void (Nothingness) may be understood in the sense of non-existing singularity.

In Eastern philosophies, Ultimate Reality is regarded as the essence of the universe. It unifies everything and is beneath the multitude of things and events that we observe. Ultimate Reality is referred to as "Brahman" in Hinduism, or as the "Body of Being" (Dharmakaya) in Buddhism, or as "Tao" in Taoism (Capra, 1991). The reality underlying all phenomena is beyond all forms, defying all description and specification. Hence, it is referred to as Empty or Void, even though this Emptiness should not be understood as emptiness in a Western sense. On the contrary, as Capra (1991) explained, it is the source of all life.

Concepts from Psychoanalytic Energy Psychotherapy

The psychoanalyst Phil Mollon (2008) has integrated energy psychology into psychoanalysis, demonstrating how existing psychic conflicts and traumata are encoded within the energy system of the body. His work draws on the psychologist Callahan, who developed Thought Field Therapy, as well as on Freud's Psychoanalysis. Energy psychology itself is rooted in Applied Kinesiology (see Goodheart, 1989), which incorporated concepts from Chinese Medicine and acupuncture. Building on the psychiatrist John Diamond (1978, 1979, 1985), Roger Callahan (1985, 2001) regarded the "thought field" as an informational field that exists within the energy system of the body. Callahan suggested that the client's thoughts are expressed within the thought field of his/her body. Noticing that thought is encoded in the patterning of the energy field, expressed in the sequence of meridians that require treatment, Callahan found that this sequence was analogous to a code for a combination lock. Importantly, it was not merely a blockage in a meridian, which caused illness, but the encoded information was responsible by generating disturbance in the body (perturbation). These blockages had to be cleared away. In nature, when flows of energy are blocked, they may cause diversions or blockages. This is comparable with Freud's (1905b) concept of libido. Lying at the border between the psyche and soma, when libidinal energy is blocked, one might say that "it flows backwards" due to regression, which then causes neuroses. Interestingly, Foulkes (1948) also postulated that ill mental health was caused by a disturbance in the communicational field, which bears a striking resemblance to Callahan's descriptions. However, like most group analysts and objects relations psychoanalysts, Foulkes neglected the body. Freud (1912) suggested that the unconscious mind of one person can read that of another person. Energy fields can be conceptualized similarly. Energy information may be communicated through the therapists' capacity to sense the client's energy state, which is facilitated by the right brain hemisphere. It may be found via "muscle testing". This method enables the body to respond (Mollon, 2008, p. 23). Muscle testing was first developed by the orthopedic surgeon Lovett (Kendall et al., 1949).

Clarifying what the nature of energy was in energy psychology, Mollon (2008) wrote that energy had electrical qualities that were measurable by conventional voltmeters. Furthermore, the energy meridians of the body have similar electrical resistance, compared to other parts of the skin. He pointed out that the bioenergy and its energy fields seem to have additional qualities that are beyond those of electricity (p. 329). In its various forms, this energy (Qi and libido) is the very essence of life. Both sex and the sacred appear as different forms of the same energy that pulsates through meridians, as well as through the subtle organizing fields of mind and body. Even though this life energy is benign, reversed energy due to its links to chaos, destructiveness, and entropy, is a parasite, feeding on the healthy Qi (p. 332). Advocating for the integration of findings from energy psychology into our knowledge systems and theories, Mollon (2008) states in his conclusion that psychotherapists are "… mere technicians of the energy system. We know what to do to bring about a certain result in some, but not all, cases" (p. 473).

Jungian Conceptualizations Rooted in Eastern Philosophies

Historically, when physicists became convinced that the world could not be fully explained by Newton's laws (see Verlinde, 2011), Freud (1900) postulated that dreams were the royal road to the unconscious. While Planck and Einstein were reforming physics, Freud founded Psychoanalysis by developing a theory of dreams and of the unconscious. Initially, the Swiss psychiatrist Carl Gustav Jung was one of Freud's disciples. Freud met him in 1907 (Grunther, 2024). Jung would later disagree with Freud's conceptualizations of dreams (Jung, 1963). Overall, Jung's Psychoanalysis differs starkly. Jung (1968) developed a theory of the collective unconscious, which took a much broader view of the unconscious mind than Freud (1900, 1915c) did. In 1912, Jung published the *Psychology of the Unconscious* and developed "Analytical Psychology" (Jung, 1968a). It is a depth psychology, which integrates the influence of both personal and of collective unconscious dynamics'. Jung's conceptualization of the psyche differs from the Freudian psyche. Jung (1921/1971) defined it as "the totality of all psychic processes, conscious, as well as unconscious" (p. 463). The primary components of the psyche are the ego, the persona, and the unconscious. Jung (2011) also conceptualized the Self differently. Rather than the ego, Jung placed the Self at the center of consciousness and unconsciousness, postulating that the Self was the whole circumference that embraced un/consciousness. Jung's conceptualizations of archetypes, and of the collective unconscious, imply a quantum reality. Even though Jung was inspired by Einstein's view that one had to accept the paradox of the duality of wave and particle to understand light, the achievement of a larger cosmological vision was aided by his collaboration with the Nobel Laureate physicist Wolfgang Pauli (Moore, 2019). Synchronistic phenomena were thought to arrive from "archetypal reality". Archetypes can reveal themselves in an immediate experience or in the spoken word. They summon up a voice that is stronger than our own, and it guides us (Moore, 2019). During the 1930s, Jung spent a long time in Africa and India (Jung, 1978). His thinking became profoundly influenced by Indian philosophy, particularly, his understanding of symbolism (Jung, 1964). His interest in epistemology, alchemy, astrology, and quantum physics, is also reflected in his conceptualization of the unconscious. Jung exchanged many ideas with Pauli. Consequently, one could say that his Analytical Psychology was informed by quantum principles (see Del Medico, 2022). At the same time, Jung was intrigued by Asian philosophies. Borrowing from Taoist philosophy, Jung coined the term "Synchronicity" (meaningful coincidences) in 1929. Jung had noticed that The Yijing established a relationship with the unconscious. This was the origin of his Theory of Synchronicity, enabling Jung to additionally theorize personality (Karcher, 1999). It also reflects his quantum thinking. Synchronicity works on the assumption that events, which are separated by distance, can occur at the same time (Jung, 1960). It describes meaningful coincidences that occur with no apparent causal connection. So, it is based on an acausal connecting principle. One of Jung's (1960) most famous examples of Synchronicity involves a patient and a beetle. At the very moment when the patient was narrating a dream about a golden scarab beetle, an actual beetle turned up at the window. After catching it, Jung showed this beetle, which closely resembled the golden scarab, to his patient. It was a moment of profound psychological significance for the patient. The scarab was the link between her dream and the external world. Jung viewed the beetle as an archetypal symbol of rebirth (transformation following death), in line with ancient Egyptian mythology. Interestingly, the scarab also served as the external event that coincided with the mental events of two people (Jung and his patient). For Jung, this incident lend support to his concept of archetypes and led to the introduction of "Unus Mundus" (one world). The story itself became the prototype of Synchronicity (Breitman, 2020). For Jung, the universe was not divided. Instead, it consists of one single reality that is made up of spirit and matter (Del Medico, 2022). This is the reality that Jung and Pauli called "Unus Mundus" (p. 17). Both matter and psyche are equally important. Together they contribute to the existence of the world. Even though Jung borrowed the term "Unus Mundus" from the 16th-century alchemist Gerhard Dorn, the idea of a transcendental unity of all phenomena (e.g., cosmos, the divine, people, consciousness) is found in many Indigenous wisdom traditions (Le Mouel, 2021).

Although our internal "mental time" knows past, present, and future, in quantum physics, time is tenseless. It only equates events with "earlier than", "simultaneous with", and "later than" (Segawa, 2017). The theoretical chemist Hans Primas (2003, 2009) has postulated that the Unus Mundus is timeless. The concept of time emerged through a contextual breaking of the primordial symmetry. While the mental domain became associated with a "tenses" time, the material domain was linked to tenseless time. Primas calculated an entanglement in time, between mind and matter (Segawa, 2017). In her reflections on Unus Mundus, and the historical considerations of the spiritualization of matter, the Jungian analyst Marie Louise von Franz suggests that "being is endowed with meaning. Our basic materialistic outlook, raw like a piece of coal, is transformed into the purified gold of a worldview, where spirit and matter are no longer opposed" (Le Mouel, 2021, p. 441). One could say that Jung (1934/1969) offered us an alternative model of reality. Rather than restricting reality to either the physical or spiritual realm, Jung stated that all experiences are psychic. He held that humans exist in a psychic reality created by the physical *and* the spiritual world. Ego consciousness, Jung (1921/1971) wrote, is inherently selective. It excludes everything irrelevant that is does not need at that moment, relegating what is painful to the unconscious, until this painful material finds a way to break into conscious awareness once again. The ego interacts with the external world through the persona, which is the part of the personality that comes into existence for reasons of adaptation. Jung criticized psychology for its failure to acknowledge the psyche's grounding in the spiritual realm.

Psychotherapists acknowledge that certain events are linked through meaning rather than physical interactions. This conceptualization is also reflected in philosophical and scientific perspectives, which hold that the universe operates in a way that is not explicable by traditional views of physics and mechanics (Becker, 2019). Possibly attempting to straddle the divide between Western psychology and East Asian religion (Clarke, 1994), Jung's thinking was significantly influenced by Pauli, who was one of the architects of quantum theory, which predicts correlations that cannot be explained by classical physics (Atmanspacher & Fuchs, 2014). When wholes are decomposed into parts, and systems into subsystems, the properties of emerging parts exhibit a correlation, which is known as quantum entanglement (p. 5).

Similarity between Group Analysis, Jungian Concepts & Eastern Philosophy

When group analytic psychotherapists, who are positively inclined toward Jungian psychology, carry out research, they may readily adopt East/South Asian philosophy. Due to Freud's striving to secularize the mind, the spiritual was disavowed by him. According to Cooper (1998), Freud was transporting Enlightenment philosophy into psychoanalytic theory. Ironically, he rejected Buddhism without having knowledge of the analytic forms of Buddhist meditation (Epstein, 1998). These are fundamental to the process of transformation in Buddhism (Cooper, 1998). Despite Freud's (1927) severing of psychoanalysis from religion and spirituality, because religion was a cultural neurosis and the pursuit of spirituality indicated pathology, a few psychoanalysts embraced religion and spirituality. Jung (1938) was one of them. Moreover, Erich Fromm (1960) was more positively inclined toward Zen Buddhism and its methods (meditation). Nevertheless, throughout the history of psychoanalysis, meditation was equated with a preverbal, symbiotic union with the mother, or with a regressive oneness with her (Epstein, 1998). Whereas Jung (1938) was very interested in Indian philosophy, the available literature does not suggest that Foulkes drew on East Asian philosophy. However, his emphasis on interconnectedness bears some resemblance with Confucianism, Taoism, and Buddhism, Foulkes (1964) also conceptualized the primordial level of communication, adopting Jung's collective unconscious. It comprises cultural memories and myths, which influence every individual (Usandivaras, 1986). Zinkin (1989) asserted that even though religion had significance for Jung, and not for Foulkes, the collective unconscious could nevertheless be integrated into the levels of communication (see Figure 2.1).

Several group analysts (e.g., Lear, 1983; Usandivaras, 1993) have explicitly integrated religious or spiritual ideas into their practice. Although Bion's (1967) notion of "thoughts without a thinker" also points to a spiritual source, overall, spirituality seems to be outside the realm of group analysis. Possibly due to his loyalty to the atheist Freud, Foulkes (1948, 1964) never did adopt Jung's (1961) spiritual and East Asian thinking. Instead, Foulkes (2003) favored science. To use his words, "as scientists we have no reason to adhere to [religious] assumptions" (p. 316). This might explain why spiritually is so poorly researched in Group Analysis. However, the literature indicates some connection between Jung, Buddhism, and Group Analysis. Davidson and Thomas (2002) referred to Jung's *Introduction in the Tibetan Book on Dying*, as well as to Fromm's exposition of fundamental Buddhist ideas, to the link between the Gestalt School and Buddhism, and to the connection between Buddhism and psychotherapy organization that offer training in Buddhist-oriented psychotherapy. They suggested that Group Analysis and Buddhism shared similar ethical values. But emptying one's mind does not form part of traditional group analytic practice. Neither does meditation.

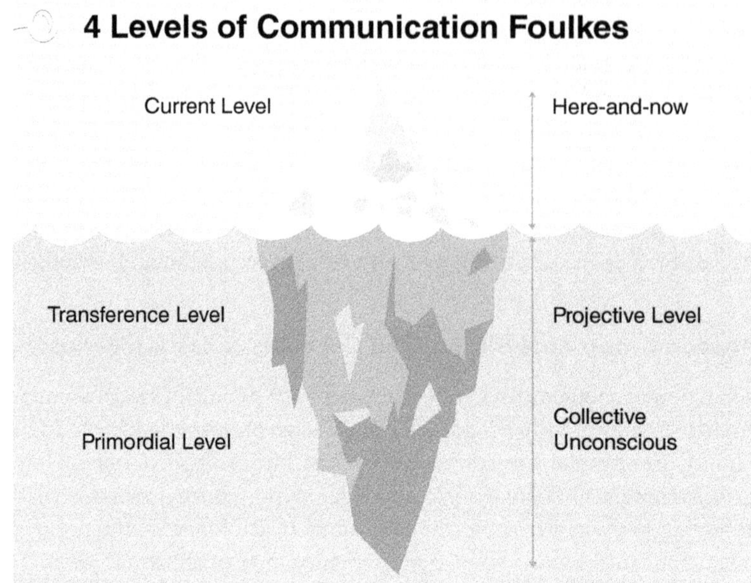

FIGURE 2.1 Foulkes' Four Levels

Kasulis (1977) suggested that Freud's Psychoanalysis and Buddhism bore some similarity, even though Buddhism focuses on consciousness, which consists of levels, and the unconscious is not normally conceptualized in Buddhism. It is nevertheless noteworthy that in a conversation between His Holiness the 14th Dalai Lama of Tibet and experts on brain science, the translator, Thubten Jinpa, asserted that there

> … is a certain misunderstanding of this "consciousness". In the Western philosophical or psychological term, consciousness is conscious, whereas, when Buddhist translators use the term, it has a wider meaning. It includes both the subconscious and unconscious levels as well.
>
> *(Houshmand, 1999, p. 107)*

If Buddhism does view the subconscious as a level of consciousness, then a link to group analysis is possible due to the conceptualization of the preconscious. In Freud's (1915b,c) model, the preconscious occupies a space between the unconscious and the conscious aspects of our psyche. As in Group Analysis, in East Asian thought, the process of becoming whole requires continuous inner work and deep engagement. Stevens (2007) described the essence of Buddhism as seeing our true nature ("kensho"). Commonly translated as Enlightenment, Kensho is sometimes equated with "prajna" (the Sanskrit meaning is best knowledge) in the Western discourse on Buddhism. Prajna entails types of wisdom. When our mind has been trained to realize a state of perfect void, there is no trace of consciousness. Even the unconscious parts have departed. Hence, the mind is left devoid of everything and "abrupt seeing" occurs, which is a special process of knowing (Zuzuki, 1949/1998). Through Dhyana (meditation), reality itself (Dharma) may be reached. Dharma is synonymous with supreme Enlightenment, it is not subject to birth, or death, and cannot be transferred from one person to another (Zuzuki, 1993). Stevens (2007) stated that becoming whole entails working with negative aspects of being (hurt, anger, etc.). For Jung (1961), this was the Shadow, the dark and unknown aspects of human consciousness. Trauma may even reside in the Shadow of the collective unconscious (Jung, 1961). Moreover, Jung drew on The Yijing for his theory of Synchronicity (Ma, 2016). However, Jung (1950) seemed more interested in images and numbers, using The Yijing as a clinical and practical framework (Zeng, 2023). His conceptualizations of the archetypes "Anima" (unconscious feminine side of a man) and "Animus" (unconscious masculine side of a woman) reflect the principle of Yin and Yang (see Jung, 1960, 1968b). What Jung referred to as projection, or transference, seems to form a vital part of the relation between the "oracle and inquirer", as conceptualized in The Yijing (Karcher, 1999). Fiumara (1989) has noticed a significant convergence between Jung's Analytical Psychology and Foulkesian Group Analysis, which is noticeable in Boyd (1989), Usandivaras (1989a), Migliorati (1989), and Zinkin (1989).

Conceptualizations of Mind

Interestingly, there seems to be a similarity between Foulkes' and Buddhists' conceptualizations of the mind. For Foulkes (2003), the mind was not confined to any one individual. Because we are born with a mother and grow up in families, we are treated as an entity by others, and we experience ourselves as separate. In our minds, this experience extends to the entire world. So, a living mind exists, which is perhaps the most undoubted of all of our experiences. According to Pines (2003), Foulkes had no doubts that the mind was identical to life and that its energies are completely dependent on the body. Acknowledging that the mind itself has a phenomenological reality, Foulkes has suggested that there is an interdependence with consciousness and unconscious mental processes, that is, the unconscious mind. To Foulkes, the individual mind is an abstraction (Pines, 2003).

Foulkes (1973) regards the group as a psychic system, in which mental processes of group members are instinctively, intuitively, and unconsciously interlocked. He has insisted that the mind is not the private possession of the individual but consists of interacting processes in the group. When two people form a relationship, they create a new phenomenon. Hence, the mind is a series of events, moving and proceeding all the time. It is through a relationship between people that the mind unfolds (Lintott, 1983). Foulkes (2003) has suggested that even though a person thinks by himself in his own mind, mind is, at the same time, a shared property of the group.

De Maré and Schőllberger (2004) have claimed that mind is the ultimate a priori. Mind is not an epiphenomenon but reflects matter. For them, the concrete presence of the brain was in sharp contradistinction to the abstract presence of the mind, which entailed the connection of one or more brains (Schőllberger, 2009). Based on the observation that every individual has his/her own body and brain, Foulkes (2003) nevertheless held that mental and bodily processes do not explain the phenomenon of mind (p. 317). Whereas mental processes depend upon the existence of a central nervous system, they are also distinct. For Freud (1940), and other group analysts who did not equate mental processes with brain functioning either, mind ends with death.

Why Should Group Analytic Researchers Bother with Quantum Theory?

Researchers should know about Quantum Theory, because Group Analysis has integrated quantum principles. Emphasizing that it belonged to Psychoanalysis (see Elizabeth Foulkes, 1990), Foulkes viewed Group Analysis as science. He integrated Freudian and Jungian conceptualizations of the unconscious into his theoretical thinking. One notices the influence of the hard sciences and of Quantum Theory in Foulkes' terminology of group analytic concepts ("basic law of group dynamics", "matrix"), and in his conceptualizations of reality (there is no difference between inner/outer reality). Additionally, Foulkes (1948) seemed to have embraced the quantum principle of randomness/uncertainty in his basic law of group dynamics, which postulates that collectively a group constitutes the very norm from which group members individually deviate. It is uncertain how an individual will randomly deviate. By implication, it seems likely that interactions in any social field are unpredictable.

Foulkes (1973) also considered the distinction of the internal psyche and the external world as "artificial". By stating "what is inside is also outside" (Foulkes, 1971, pp. 226–7), Foulkes accepted a notion of reality, where boundaries do not exist, as postulated by Quantum Theory (see Becker, 2019). There are further similarities in terms of terminology and in his conceptualizations. Whereas Foulkes (1936) was clearly influenced by neurology, viewing the group as an organism (healthy organism is a system in dynamic equilibrium that is continually adjusting and adapting to its environment), he also referred to disturbance in the network. This theorizing of the matrix is in line with quantum physics/mechanics. In my understanding, they bear a similarity to the electromagnetic field and the matrix, even though Foulkes did not use mathematical equations, as quantum scholars do (Cresser, 2011). According to Foulkes (1971), the group is a matrix of the individual's mental life. His "network of relations/relationships" (Roseneil, 2019, p. 499), is premised on the notion that people are impacted upon by social, political, personal, familial, and hereditary networks of relations. Not only does it blur the classical distinction between past and present, but it also does away with the classic separation between spaces. Hence, I would argue that the matrix rests on quantum principles. It is obvious that Foulkes (1946b/1990) adopted the terminology of physics (dynamics forces, law, matrix, abstraction, field, resonance, mirroring). Interestingly, Foulkes' idea of the observer seems akin to "Tunneling". As an integral part of the situation that is being observed, the observer introduces "dynamic forces into the field and is permeated by forces emanating from it" (pp. 129–130). Being permeated by forces assumes that these dynamic forces can travel through the skin barriers between people. This implies a quantum conceptualization. He also suggested that the observer impacted on the situation, which is the observer effect.

His theorizing does make sense. Particularly, when considering that the human body is made of atoms, such as oxygen, hydrogen, carbon, and nitrogen (Clegg, 2020), which means that Quantum Theory applies to human beings as well. And therefore, to group members in the therapy group.

Interestingly, the group analyst Stacey (2006) directly applied complexity theory to Group Analysis, offering a radically different social understanding of individuals and group processes.

The concept of complexity has its origins in quantum information science, which is an area that developed within the framework of quantum mechanics (Max Planck Institute, 2019).

Furthermore, the group analyst Barbara Dick directly linked Quantum Theory to group analytic psychotherapy. Dick (1981) outlined what her friend, a nuclear physicist, had told her about Quantum Theory. She thought that there was a connection between quantum principles and relationship dynamics in the therapy group. Referring to Einstein, Dick (1981) remarked that when he was confronted with the quantum, where almost anything can happen, he retorted that "God does not play dice" (p. 129).

The examples given show that group analysts have integrated quantum principles into theories, and at least one group analyst, has used Quantum Theory to think about group dynamics. Hence, it seems justified to incorporate this theory into the ERP to explain group processes and dynamics.

Metaphysics & Nothingness & Scientific Explanations

African and Eastern philosophers are not the only ones, who cast doubt on the Western metaphysics of individualism. Molecular biology, quantum mechanics, and neuroscience, do as well. Biochemists and molecular biologists have explained how life may have naturally evolved from inanimate beginnings through abiogenesis (Pross, 2016). Processes initiated by the evolution of a simple replicating system seem to be the building blocks of life. What makes this system special is how much it produces. This replication reaction is unique, insofar that kinetics is the dominant directive, making actions appear purposeful. Life is a network of chemical reactions (Pross, 2016). Every human individual is an ecological network rather than a single living entity. From a biological perspective, individuality does not exist. Humans are part of a biosphere, an ever-expanding living network. Interestingly, although some components of the giant replicative network appear to be individual, this is rather "illusory", because in a deeper sense "we are one" (Pross, 2016, pp. 190–191).

There is a striking similarity between the Eastern philosophical Nothingness, Non-Being, Ubuntu's "I am because We are", and scientific principles. It is a plausible possibility, as Krauss (2012) put it, that our universe emerged from nothing. Stephen Hawking (1989) has emphasized that a quantum theory of gravity allows for the creation of space itself where "none existed before" (Krauss, 2012, p. 164). As Einstein (2013) has demonstrated, energy does not merely arise from gravity. Energy and mass are equivalent, obeying the same formula. In any case, universes can, and always will, appear from nothing. Krauss (2012) made it clear that a universe emerging from nothing seemed by far the most compelling of all explanations of existence. This nothing is unstable in the world of quantum mechanics. One notices the resemblance between physical instability and Buddhist impermanence (Houshmand et al., 1999).

Chapter Summary

The African Ubuntu and Group Analysis prioritize the group over the individual. In East Asian cultures, such as China, people aspire to achieve balance and harmony, integrating knowing and doing (Si, 2017). One might argue somewhat simplistically that it is this strong desire to achieve unity that distinguishes Eastern from Western cultures. Many East/South Asian philosophies emphasize the integration of mind, spirit, and body. Their ontology and epistemology are based on a holistic conceptualization of the vitalizing field of Qi, which constitutes all natural processes. This renders discussions about psychophysical dualism moot. The relational, interconnected process of Yin and Yang is contrary to the dualistic view held by positivist purists, who divide research into subjects and objects. Often, scholars have fallen prey to binary thinking (individual vs group), where the individual is prioritized over the group. By integrating the holistic, dynamic duality of Yin and Yang, and by accepting relationality and interconnectedness, the separation between the individual and the group disappears. And so does the separation between the quantitative and qualitative research paradigms, once the paradigm is underpinned by complementary philosophical assumptions.

2

WHY A PARADIGM SHIFT IS NEEDED

Introducing the Emerging Reality Paradigm (ERP) Part 2

Abstract

Focusing on quantum mechanics/physics, the four pillars ontology, epistemology, methodology, and axiology, are described. They are viewed as inseparable in the Emerging Reality Paradigm (ERP). Research findings and theories to support the metaphysical claim that everything is created from Nothingness, are integrated. I argue that the philosophies, the ERP is based on, avoid the problem of the Western metaphysics of individualism. This is important from a group perspective. Ubuntu's "I am because we are" bypasses the Cartesian separation of body and mind, which eliminates the problem pertaining to consciousness and the mind–body. There is sufficient overlap between Eastern philosophies and quantum mechanics. By supplementing Eastern philosophy with science, a plausible, scientific explanation of Oriental Nothingness (how a universe with a positive energy in empty space could have arisen out of unstable nothingness), is possible. After fully formulating the ERP, I discuss whether it can be called "paradigm".

Introduction

Remarkably, the development of quantum physics could be viewed as the formation of a small group, which consisted of white, educated men. Not only did they share a passion for physics, but some of them were also philosophically inclined. When we consider that many philosophers are very interested in physics, then it comes as no surprise that philosophical conceptualizations verlap with quantum principles. There is a striking resemblance between Asian philosophies and quantum physics. In the Western philosophy of science, physics is viewed as an exemplar of objectivity. Herbert (1985) defined physics as the science of matter, motion, and energy. Its laws are typically expressed through mathematics.

The experimental way of life also reflected "gender in the making" (Haraway, 1997). In the history of quantum physics, women and men of color are also absent. They did not form part in the triumphant localized practices and the generation of situated knowledge. However, it would

DOI:10.4324/9781003609544-4

be impossible to understand gender in science, or in other groups, without focusing on "Dead White European Males" (p. 28).

Physicists, such as the Danish Niels Bohr (1928), the German Max Planck (1990, 1958), the Austrian Erwin Schrődinger (1926, 1944, 2020), and the German Werner Heisenberg (1927, 1945, 1949, 1956, 1960, 1971, 1977, 2014), were major contributors to the advancement of Quantum Theory. Heisenberg and Bohr created the Copenhagen School of quantum mechanics in Denmark, which was mainly active between 1925 and 1935. Key figures in this small group were Bohr, Heisenberg, the German Max Born, the Austrian Wolfgang Pauli, the German Pascual Jordan, the British Paul Dirac, and the Hungarian János von Neumann.

We encounter allegiances and frictions. The law-of-the-father (Murray, 1995) decided whose theories would be excluded or advanced. Dismissing Everett's Copenhagen Interpretation of Many Worlds (Barrett & Byrne, 2012), the influential Bohr (1928) postulated that every energy change of atomic processes results from an indivisible transition between different states, which are not continuously linked. Put differently, quantum objects behave like a wave or a particle, depending on the nature of the experiment and its setting.

Einstein (2005, 2013) severely disliked the idea of a reality, in which objects lacked definitive states, and could be in two places at the same time. For him, there was too much indeterminacy in quantum mechanics. His reservations are famously expressed in his exclamation of "God does not play dice with the Universe" (Frank, 2023). Others were less skeptical.

In his quest to unravel the mysteries of atomic structures, the theoretical physicist Max Planck introduced the concept of "discreteness in energy" (Nauenberg, 2016). What makes his constant h so crucial is its universality and constancy in time (Butto, 2021, p. 210).

While particles have a definite position and momentum in classical mechanics, in quantum mechanics this differs (Faye & Jaksland, 2011). Albert Einstein referred to it as "spooky", because it is impossible to determine both the position and speed of a particle at the same time. Captured in the famous Uncertainty Principle (Heisenberg, 1956, 1975), Schrődinger (1926) showed that a quantum particle can be described mathematically by a "wavefunction". The particle-wave duality has become an established fact of quantum mechanics. While Schrődinger devised an equation of the probability of finding a particle at a given time, Born statistically demonstrated how waves function.

Heisenberg's (1927, 1975) Uncertainty Principle still attracts researchers. That measurement (observation) can affect the system in a random fashion has been termed the "observer effect" in other disciplines, such as psychology. It has become difficult to accept a division of the world into subjects and objects, and into observer and observed.

Examining whether observation creates reality, Song (2021) took the view that mass, or energy, is transferred from the quantum vacuum filled with negative sea (representing the mind of the observer) to the observed physical world. What is seen appears to have resulted from what was unseen. Song concluds: what is being observed physically, could have already been determined. This implies that it has moved backward. Rather than moving forward as we do, Becker (2019) has remarked wryly that the atom suffers a *crisis of indecision over where to be* (p. 1). At first glance, the probabilistic nature of Quantum Theory sounds like a science fiction story. If reality can change depending on observation, can reality then be created from nothing?

This seems to be one implication. Max Born's pupil, the theoretical physicist Ernst Pascual Jordan, who contributed significantly to quantum mechanics and to Quantum Field Theory (O'Connor & Robertson, 2015), declared with emphasis that *observations not only disturb what has to be measured, they produce it!* (Jammer, 1934, cited in The Information Philosopher, 2025, chapter 1.5, para. 3).

Measurement is a fascinating aspect of the quantum world, which shows that physical systems are restrained as to how they behave. So, they have a lot in common with social systems and analytic groups. Furthermore, volatile group dynamics can abrupt rather randomly in a large group. Randomness is an intrinsic property of quantum systems. Moreover, we can neither actually see unconscious processes nor a wave accompanying its particle.

How can one determine the exact position and momentum of a particle? Only by measurement, but results will vary randomly from one measurement to the next due to uncertainty (Cresser, 2011). Einstein tried very hard to show that this could not be a complete description of reality. Surprisingly, the wavefunction does represent the full picture of the natural world (Wichert, 2023). A particle cannot have zero uncertainty in both position and momentum at the same time (Capra, 1991). And that is it.

Admittedly, not every group analytic researcher would like to explore the secrets of the atom and examine "the culture of no culture" (Haraway, 1997), where individuals, instead of social communities, are the knowers of scientific knowledge claims. From a feminist or Post-Colonial perspective, the discourse of quantum physics/mechanics is as exclusionary, as the discourse in classic physics (Greek "φύσις", Physis, natural world). Group analytic researchers might also regard Quantum Theory as irrelevant to the study of groups. However, it seems that Group Analysis has incorporated ideas from quantum mechanics/physics into its theories and group analysts, such as Dick (1981), have used quantum ideas to make sense of group processes (see Part 1). Furthermore, as Heisenberg (1949) pointed out, this theory casts doubt on a clear formulation of causality (p. 2). One consequence of discontinuous changes is that every experiment performed renders the knowledge of other experiments illusory (p. 3). This means that an objective reality has become questionable (Heisenberg, 2014). So, Quantum Theory is very relevant to ontology, to critiquing the ontological underpinnings of research paradigms. Considering that Quantum Theory is one of the most successful theories in human history that can explain *almost* everything (Becker, 2019), integrating its components into a research paradigm seems beneficial. Quantum Theory has affected assumptions about consciousness and notions of the Self (Becker, 2019). Although our lives are organized around clock time, our experiences of time and space are subjective. Immediate contact with reality is but an illusion (Metzinger, 2010), created through the temporal inwardness of the appearance of the "now" in our consciousness. Whereas time and space are commonly perceived as separate, objective, and absolute, they are not. Only spacetime exists and slicing it up is merely a useful convention (Carroll, 2022). This is relevant to group analytic researchers, because consciousness and unconsciousness belong together. Furthermore, group analytic research is about people and their interactions. This type of research is interested in emotions, experiences, relationships, unconscious motivations, and the psychological and mental health of group members. All these aspects cannot be fully researched without taking into consideration people's bodies. Emotions occur within the body. Freud (1915c) was very clear that the ego is a bodily ego.

Subatomic particles make up the appearances of people and objects. Ninety-nine percent of our bodies consist of atoms, such as hydrogen, carbon, nitrogen, and oxygen (Sundermier, 2015). Protons and neutrons form the nucleus of an atom. The protons (positively charged particles) and neutrons (particles with no charge), inside the nucleus, are made up of quarks (Cooper, 2022). Electrons, negatively charged particles, orbit the nucleus (Wood & Sherman, 2022). Scientists who concern themselves with energy believe that almost the entire mass of our body comes from the kinetic energy of quarks, and from the binding energy of gluons. Hundreds of thousands of particles (muons, neutrinos, and photons) might be passing through our bodies every second (Sundermier, 2015).

Given that people consist of atoms and are the "subject matter" of group analytic research, taking into consideration quantum principles would seem necessary. This is why I will integrate them into the Emerging Reality Paradigm (ERP). Emerging and emergence are at its heart. The ERP is supported by the four pillars of metaphysics, ontology, epistemology, and axiology. To understand the essence of quantum principles, and their link to Asian philosophies, and to Jungian and group analytic theories, I will start by outlining Quantum Theory. Fuller descriptions can be found in Appendix 3. Reality, energy, consciousness, and neuroscientific findings, will be discussed. I will formulate the ERP, discuss its limitations, and consider whether it can be called a "paradigm".

Quantum Principles Relevant to the ERP

Conceptually, Quantum Theory is *a broad framework* that describes the behavior of matter and energy at the smallest scale. So, it governs all subatomic interactions. It includes several theories and areas, for example, Quantum Field Theory, which describes fields, and not just particles, and quantum mechanics. Max Planck (1900) thought that the energy emitted from an atom could only be found in tiny discrete packs of energy (quanta). He formulated the correct curve (constant h) that connected temperature and the energy of light. This solved the conundrum of a blackbody, which was supposedly emitting infinite amounts of energy continuously (Butto, 2021, p. 213). It would lead to the development of Quantum Theory, which comprises important principles, such as Superposition, Entanglement, Sum over paths, and Tunneling (Kaku, 2024). *Superposition* means that a particle exists in multiple states simultaneously, for example, an electron can be in two places simultaneously. Superposition can only be maintained when a quantum system is unobserved. Schrődinger's famous thought experiment about a cat is an example of Superposition. He assumed that a cat would be in a sealed box (containing vial poisonous gas), which is connected to a hammer that is attached to a Geiger counter next to a quantity of uranium. If an atom of uranium decays, it would activate this counter and the hammer, thereby releasing the poison and killing the cat, as Kaku (2024) explains. The interesting question was this: "Before you open the door of the box, is the cat dead or alive?" In Newtonian law, the cat is either dead or alive. But not according to Heisenberg and Bohr, who reached a radically different point of view. Representing the cat as a sum of two waves (wave of alive and dead cat), when the box is sealed, it exists as Superposition only (or sum of two simultaneous waves). In the microworld, things exist as the sum of all possible states rather than in one definitive state. By opening the door, the wave collapses miraculously. Only this reveals whether the cat is alive or dead. Therefore, the process of measurement collapses the wave. Measurement links the microworld with the macroworld, which has profound philosophical implications with regard to Solipsism. *To be, is to be perceived*, Kaku's (2024, p. 51) writes. He referred to the finding that elements do not really exist unless someone observes them. Furthermore, when two particles are coherent and are separated, they will continue to influence each other instantly, even when divided by a huge distance. This is known as *Entanglement* (p. 81).

"Sum over paths" refers to a particle that moves between two points and sums over all possible paths that link these two points. Even though the classic, non-quantum, path is the most likely path, all other paths contribute to the final quantum path of this particle, too. So, they could affect it (p. 82).

"Tunneling" is a quantum mechanical phenomenon. It refers to penetrating a large energy barrier that is higher in energy than the particle's kinetic energy. The faster an object moves, the more kinetic energy it has. Normally, this barrier would prevent a particle from tunneling through. When a particle reaches a barrier that it cannot overcome, its wavefunction changes, thus, it can penetrate the barrier (Flowers & Theopold, 2015).

Heisenberg's *Uncertainty Principle* underpins many of the peculiarities of quantum mechanics. It offers a probabilistic description of nature. One implication is that *knowledge is probabilistic* (see Schrődinger, 1944, 2020) and imprecise. The wave-particle *duality*, where particles can exhibit both wave and particle properties, has been demonstrated by double-split experiments (see Dunning, 2023). This means that *the nature of matter depends on the experimental condition*. The Uncertainty Principle supports the assumption that matter is inherently elusive.

With the concepts of *entanglement* and *non-locality* (Bell, 1964), quantum mechanics suggests that once connected particles influence the state of the other, after their separation, regardless of the distance between them. The wavefunction, *Superposition*, and *Complementarity* (Bohr, 1928) all point to probabilities. Since the velocity, or position, of particles cannot be determined until the time of measurement, this implies that the *act of observation* itself is intrinsically linked to quantum reality. The initial Copenhagen Interpretation by Niels Bohr in the 1920s posited that only by observing the state of a quantum particle is it forced to choose a single state. That is the state we observe (Faye, 2024). However, because the particle may be forced in a different observable state each time, it behaves randomly. The particle's coherent Superposition refers to the state of existence in all possible states at once. When observing a particle, the wavefunction collapses. It has been suggested that consciousness itself is required for the collapse of the wavefunction (Faye, 2024). This is linked coherence. Quantum *decoherence* describes the process whereby a quantum system loses its coherence, during its interaction with its environment, when not perfectly isolated (Wichert, 2023). Decoherence offers a framework for the collapse of the wavefunction but does not explain the collapse itself (Wichert, 2023).

Several Interpretations have been made. An interpretation is the story told in ordinary language about mathematical equations of a theory. Everett's Interpretation, the Many Worlds Interpretation (Barrett & Byrne, 2012), postulates that there is more than one reality (Byrne, 2007). Most Copenhagen Interpretations hold that there is one reality, which could be viewed as emerging, indeterminate, and interconnected, with the observation. When a particle reaches a barrier that it cannot overcome, its wavefunction changes, so that it can *tunnel* through the barrier. Tunneling and diffraction have something in common. *Diffraction* results the Superposition, or interference, of waves. It involves the spreading out of waves, as they pass through an aperture or pass an obstruction (Barad, 2007). Both tunneling and diffraction involve the propagation of a wavefunction through a barrier.

Questioning why Bohr's Copenhagen Interpretation was relying on classic terminology, Kober (2010) suggested that the reason had to be found in the relationship between the human mind and nature. Kober theorized that space and time, in line with Kantian philosophy, are both fundamental constituents of human experience. They are the prerequisite for the mind to be in contact with the world. Therefore, they are also constitutive of experience. Space and time are the a priori of all experience (p. 77).

Even though they play a crucial role in The Yijing, space, time, and numbers, are always combined within it, demonstrating the process of cosmic change (Yang, 2022). As Yang explained, this notion of change is based on metaphors for the experience of growth. For a long time, conceptualizations of wholeness and a collective way of thinking have been dominant in China, where space has a profound connotation.

The ancient Chinese understanding of time began with the observation of spatially objective things (gestation, growth, proliferation, and wilting plants). These observations are from the compositions and elements of the hexagram in The Yijing (Yang, 2022).

The Complexity of Reality: Metaphysical & Ontological Considerations

Existence and reality are important considerations for psychotherapists and researchers. Depending on their philosophical perspectives, they will hold certain views about "Being", which they perceive to be true. Napolitani (1981) regarded the group as a mediator between individual and macrosocial reality, where need and imaginary merge. Marrone (1998) stated that the group forces individualistic-oriented psychotherapies to re-examine their ontological worldview.

Metaphysical positions between Western and Eastern traditions differ starkly. With a few exceptions, Western philosophers have ignored metaphysics. However, it is crucial to the ERP. An important metaphysical passage from the *Nature and Reality of Tao* (or the Taoist *Book of Changes*, Yijing) states that

> [i]n the beginning there was non-being. The One originates from it. It has oneness but not yet physical form. When things obtain it and come into existence, that is called virtue (which gives them their individual character). That which is formless is divided into Yin and Yang.
>
> (Wing-Tsit, 1973, p. 202)

When things are produced in accordance with the life energy, Qi, they take physical form. And when they embody and preserve the spirit, that is nature. When one is united with the universe (Ma, 2016, p. 33)

> [T]his unity is ultimate … this is complete harmony.
>
> (Wing-Tsit, 1973, p. 202)

Aristotelians did not embrace the dual ontology of Plato's forms, which exist independently of the physical world. Instead, Aristotle favored an actual reality, where forms are instantiated (Loux, 2006). In contrast, Buddhists, Confucianists, and Taoists, believe in a reality that is grounded in Emptiness, or (Oriental) Nothingness. This implies that emerging, interconnected processes are involved in the creation of such reality. It can include matter and energy. And relationality, as found in African and Indigenous cultures, the *I am related, therefore, we are,* instead of the Cartesian *I think therefore I am* (Bujo, 2001, p. 23) reality. It can also include a quantum reality, which may be generated from nothing, as implied by Jordan (Jammer, 1975). In quantum mechanics, reality is regarded as emergent (Byrne, 2007). It can also include the reality of the unconscious and virtual reality. From analytic perspectives, internal representations also comprise unconscious phantasy, and there is a fine line between different kinds of reality. Freud's (1915c) dynamic unconscious does not adhere to conscious logic. Consisting of contradictions, there are no temporal-spatial boundaries in this illogical and timeless, naturally occurring, phenomenon (Vosmer, 2021, p. 43). Unconscious reality differs from "external reality", as used in colloquial language, and from naïve Realism, which insists that there is one objective reality. Features of the unconscious overlap with virtual reality.

Etymologically, virtual stems from the Latin words "virtualis" and "virtus", meaning something in effect and not in fact (Etymonline, 2025a). Reality means "real existence" (Etymonline, 2021). Virtual environments were developed when technology became more sophisticated. Virtual Reality refers to a system that enables one, or more, users to move and react within an environment simulated by a computer (Yasar & Sheldon, 2024). This reality is as infinite as human imagination, and as vast as unconscious reality. Through philosophical reasoning, Zhai (1998) demonstrated that reality can be *created* by using Virtual Reality. The combination of digital simulation, sensory immersion, and functional teleoperation, amounts to a re-creation of the entire perceived universe, which incorporates a first-person perspective, enabling people to create their own reality. Over the past decades, the combination of Artificial Intelligence (AI), Virtual Reality, and Virtual Environments has given rise to "intelligent virtual environments" (Luck & Aylett, 2000, p. 4). The applicability of Virtual Reality ranges from gaming over to treating psychological disorders (Barnard, 2024), and to higher education, where it offers learners maximum realism and immersion that is unbounded by physical reality (Luo et al., 2019). Various types of technology allow users to sense and manipulate virtual objects to the same extent as they would do with real objects.

Being positioned inside the virtual environment enables a feeling of immersion in the simulated world, according to Barnard (2024). He explains that users are highly interactive in this world, which is created through computer programs, various software, and devices, such as headsets. In the virtual environment, the computer programmer re-creates reality (Zhai, 1998, p. 54). Agents are as constrained as people in the non-digital world. When equipped with devices that enable some control of Virtual Reality, they only *seem* to have more autonomy (Zhai, 1998). Even though the virtual environment enables a person to be what and how s/he wants to be and get rid of insecurities, once lured into the virtual world, the ego surrenders to the desire of the id, because it is lured into the imaginary realm (Vosmer, 2010). It gets even more complex in the metaverse. Originally coined by Stephenson (1992), the term "metaverse" denotes people interacting with each other as avatars in virtual environments. In 2021, the concept made it into the vernacular when Facebook changed its name to "Meta". So, it is not just Zuckerberg who is interested in the metaverse (see Thompson, 2021). Broadly speaking, the metaverse is a three-dimensional immersive version of the internet that incorporates mixed and virtual reality technologies (Turner, 2023). It is envisioned, according to Franke (2024), as some form of digital extension of the physical world. By using augmented reality technologies, the web can be experienced three dimensionally in this world of extended reality.

The "Philosophy of the Metaverse" has emerged as a growing subfield within the philosophy of technology (Chalmers, 2022; Chen, 2023; Turner, 2022). Ethical, metaphysical, and political, concerns have been raised (McStay, 2023; Turner, 2023). Arguments for, and against, the notion of "virtual fictionalism" (McDonnell & Wildman, 2019), i.e., whether experiences in virtual worlds are valuable to people, have resulted in debates about Virtual Reality and metaphysics (Ali, 2023; Chalmers, 2022; Floridi, 2011; Franke, 2024; Osler, 2022; Turner, 2023).

Modern technologies do significantly affect the construction of our Selves, identities, and belief systems (Chisnall, 2020). Notions of "digitally extended Selves" have metaphysical, ontological, relational, and epistemological, implications with regard to groups. A group consisting of digitally extended Selves, whose egos are autopoietic (self-created), is likely to inhabit a different reality than a "traditional" group, as commonly studied by group analytic researchers. With the emergence of Virtual Reality, the question as to what constitutes reality has shifted to *how* one can *create reality*, and how to *differentiate between the actual and Virtual Reality*. Due to a similarity between the dynamic unconscious, the collective unconscious, the social unconscious, and Virtual Reality, the virtual world may be particularly relevant for group analytic researchers.

Interestingly, virtual worlds must begin with information influx from "nothing", like the powering of a computer system before the virtual world is created (Zhai, 1998). This notion that everything originates from nothing is a building block of the ERP. It postulates that *reality is emerging from nothing, or Nothingness.* Stephen Hawking (1989) has emphasized that a quantum theory of gravity allows for the creation of space itself, where *none existed before*

(Krauss, 2012, p. 164). The physicist Krauss (2012) asserts that a universe emerging from nothing seems by far the most compelling of all explanations of existence. This nothing is unstable in the world of quantum mechanics. One notices the resemblance between physical instability and Buddhist impermanence. This "nothing" is similar to "Oriental Nothingness", as formulated by East Asian philosophers, such as Hisamatsu (1959, 1965, 1971, 1975, 2005).

Integrating Psychophysics into the ERP

For Newton, matter consisted of these small, solid, and indestructible objects (Capra, 1991). His equations reflect rigid determinism. Because classical physics was based on principles that were incompatible with conceptualizations of the psyche, consequently the two had to be conceptualized differently (Carminati et al., 2017). Over the past decades, several attempts have been made to describe the psyche physically, using quantum mechanics (Atmanspacher & Primas, 2009). Remarkably, Jung's (1968, 1960) collective unconscious and Synchronicity, and Pauli's Exclusion Principle (Fierz & Weisskopf, 1960), envisaged many future developments in quantum physics/mechanics and neuroscience. Their dialogue developed into working on the psychophysical conundrum. The mental and material domains were seen as complementary, emerging from a symmetry that broke away from Jung's initial conceptualization of the Unus Mundus (Segawa, 2017).

Carminati et al. (2017) developed a model of the interaction between Physis and psyche, as if time could flow in both directions. Physis and the psyche were represented through vectors that represent the quantum states of the respective qubits.

A qubit is the simplest possible quantum system. Its states are described by a two-dimensional Hilbert space and a qubit that carries a single bit of information. Qubits are the conceptual building block of quantum computing and in the physical world, they describe a 1/2 spin system. Using mathematical formulas, Carminati et al. (2017) describe a combination of two qubits, one supposed to represent Physis and the other the psyche. Their model of the interaction of Physis and psyche is a product of two Hilbert spaces, each one with a single qubit. The analysis of the Hamiltonian, governing the evolution of this system, suggests a simple description of Jung's archetypes. Eigenvalues came in opposite pairs, as if time could flow in both directions (p. 199).

The authors' perspective is novel and very interesting. Such explanations are important for the ERP and for group analytic research. A flow of time in both directions is necessary for communication to occur between the conscious and the unconscious, which is in contradistinction to the materialistic view that the mind is created by the brain. Unfortunately, these explanations are explanatory, rather than definitive, due to the speculative nature. The same applies to Pradhan's (2018) study, which has united Quantum Theory with the Special Relativity Theory to form Quantum Field Theory. This was used to provide a psychophysical explication of consciousness. By factoring in "mental/psyche" aspects alongside physical ones, these were explained. It is an innovative approach.

The above explanations are encouraging and thought-provoking. They are relevant to the ERP, because it must be able to offer some evidence for its assertion that a psychophysical mind and consciousness exist. The foundation of consciousness is conceptualized in the wavefunction, particularly, in its collapse. Recent applications of quantum mechanics to psychological concepts are equally interesting. Whether they can be used as a bridge between the mind and matter, remains to be seen.

Researching Un/Consciousness

The unconscious, in all its variations, forms the bedrock of group analytic theories, therapy, and research. Making these unconscious aspects conscious is a major task of the therapeutic work in the group. However, since unconsciousness and consciousness belong together, researchers cannot ignore consciousness.

Is the unconscious searching for a solution "computationally", or is it capable to access an eternal world of ideas (Penrose, 1989)? To answer this question, researchers have examined the implicit, unconscious realm of human experience. Intuition has been conceptualized as subjective experience. It is associated with the use of knowledge gained from implicit learning and through indirect knowing, which do not require conscious awareness, or rational processes (Schore, 2019, p. 247). Hence, sudden conscious illumination can appear after lengthy prior unconscious "work" (see Poincaré, 2015).

Neuropsychoanalysis, "the study of the interpersonal neurobiological development of the unconscious mind" (Schore, 2019, p. 246), has increased our insight into unconscious processes. In particular, the right hemisphere is crucial to the experience of emotions, allocation of attention, regulation of stress, self-awareness, relationality, and to our ability to read and respond empathically, or intuitively, to the emotional states of others.

Neuroscience has also provided us with a better understanding of intergroup relations and the underpinnings of intergroup behavior (Molenberghs, 2022). However, Wendt (2015) has noted that certain aspects of memory and consciousness are still not completely understood. In contrast, Hill (2021) has highlighted that impaired states of consciousness can offer an entry into the mystery of consciousness.

Impaired States of Consciousness

Affects have been conceptualized as indicators of bodily states, and hyperarousal results in dysregulation. Trauma is often characterized by a loss of temporality and coherence. Commonly, the subsequent experienced discontinuity of time, and impaired consciousness, are caused by dissociation (Maeres, 2012). Detachment from the environment and from others, however, affects consciousness and the person's sense of identity.

Furthermore, past traumatic events often intrude on both the present and the future. As a result, the present and future cease to exist. Consequently, time is no longer experienced as linear. From a neuroscientific perspective, the mind has been severed from the body, resulting in altered states of consciousness and different experiences of the Self (see Maeres, 2000, 2005).

Due to the integration of neurobiological theories (Schore's 2003 affect regulation theory; Porges' 2001 polyvagal theory) and research findings related to clinical practice, group analytic psychotherapists can gain a better understanding of the psychophysiology that underpins the behaviors of group members. Interestingly, Montgomery (2013) applied features of affect regulation theory to group work.

Specialized Functions

Schore (2019) explains that functional magnetic resonance imaging has resulted in better understanding of brain functioning, subcortical structures, and our central nervous system. Each brain hemisphere functions independently, so there is more than one form of consciousness. Due to the profound differences between the left and right hemisphere, it is more accurate to conceptualize the brain as a dual system (Schore, 2019). Our central nervous system consists of billions of neurons that communicate with each other, resulting in complex systems of trillions of connections between neurons. Findings from neuroscientific research have shown that neurons, and certain areas of the cerebral cortex, are specialized in their function. Higher cognitive processes (attention, perception, memory, and language) arise from neuronal rhythmic, or synchronous, activities, and the communication between them, referred to as "neural oscillations" (Singer, 2018). These oscillations can become synchronized within specific groups of neurons (local synchronization) and even physically spaced-out groups of neurons can synchronize (global synchronization) (Singer, 2018).

Neuronal activities can be observed through various methods (e.g., magnetic resonance tomography, magnetoencephalography). Singer and his colleagues demonstrated that groups of neurons, which were evenly located in separate areas of the brain, were firing at the same time, within intervals of a few milliseconds, when processing the features that belonged to the same object (Scientia, 2019).

When Does Consciousness Emerge?

His Holiness the 14th Dalai Lama (1999) explained that consciousness comprises different levels. When the body ceases to exist, there is still a subtle form of consciousness, which is independent of the body. So, there is a form of consciousness that itself does not depend on the brain. This means that it exists prior to the formation of the brain.

From a neuroscientific point of view, consciousness begins as early as in late pregnancy. An infant's brain can form conscious experiences that shape the developing Self and the baby's understanding of the environment (Bayne et al., 2023). Using the simple definition of consciousness as sensory awareness of the body, the Self, and the world, Lagercrantz and Changeux (2009, p. 255) have suggested that the fetus may be aware of the body, and it responds to external stimuli. These reactions seem to have subcortical, non-conscious origins and are probably innate. If we accept that consciousness is mainly located in the cortex, then consciousness cannot emerge before the 24th gestational week, when the thalamocortical connections from the sense organs are formed (Lagercrantz, 2014).

What Are the Neural Correlates of Consciousness?

Neuroimaging studies have shown that the dynamic flow of conscious experience results from continuous processes (see Lutz et al., 2004, 2008), whereby the brain draws on prior knowledge, and applies it to the current situation (Metzinger, 2010). The overall process of perceiving, learning, and living does create a context for itself, when we are conscious of something. This is how reality is transformed into lived reality (Metzinger, 2012). According to Baars (1988), conscious information is a type of information, which must be made available to every single one of our cognitive capacities at the same time. However, only if we do not know what will happen, do we require a conscious representation.

Metzinger (2012) pointed out that consciousness is epistemologically irreducible to first-person and third-person knowledge, but ontologically, it is constituted by one reality. His conceptualization is roughly in line with Buddhist conceptualizations.

For the past decades, neuroscientists have tried to find the neuronal correlates of human consciousness, known as the "hard problem" of consciousness research (Dennett, 2012). Neurobiology posits that all the mental phenomena we experience are the result of neuronal processes. Attempts to provide naturalistic explanations for the phenomenon of consciousness have been hindered by (1) the fact that the explanandum is ill-defined, (2) a rudimentary understanding of neuronal processes, and (3) issues surrounding the hard problem (Ibid.).

For example, even if a comprehensive account of consciousness was possible, researchers would still be unable to explain how qualia (first-person experiences arising from neuronal interactions), develop from neuronal interactions described from a third-person perspective (Singer, 2019). To overcome this conundrum, Singer (2019) has suggested a synthesis that should be realizable within a naturalistic evolutionary framework based on empirical evidence. This approach is incompatible with ontological dualism. It conceptualizes the spiritual dimension as a cognitive construct, thereby allowing sufficient space for the integration of immaterial entities that are constitutive of identity. Admitting that coming to grips with two orthogonal sources of knowledge (natural sciences and the wisdom inherent in Buddhism and other religious/cultural traditions) was challenging, Singer said that it was a challenge for neuroscience to come up with naturalistic explanations for the rise of these immaterial realities (Strűngmann, 2023).

Combining Neuroscience with Quantum Theory

Recently, neuroscience has been combined with Quantum Theory. It seems possible to measure conscious and unconscious processes, and to theorize them by using quantum principles (Carminati et al., 2017). Wendt (2015, p. 92) explained this well: the basic idea of quantum consciousness theory is that it solves (*1*) *the problems related to reality*, which are inherent in the materialistic worldview, and (*2*) *the difficulty of explaining the variety of metaphysical interpretations of quantum mechanics.* More specifically, quantum consciousness theory attempts to explicate how the brain can sustain coherent quantum states, and how consciousness inheres in the very structures of matter. Simply put, the conundrum surrounding consciousness pertains to the mind–body. If scholars were no longer sure of the Cartesian *I think therefore I am*, there would be no need to problematize the materialists' failure to explain consciousness. How can conscious experience develop from physical matter? This question, as well as others like it, has haunted materialists. Why does "being conscious" feel like anything at all? So, what is recalcitrant here is the body, a body that is conscious (Wendt, 2015, p. 92).

Over the past decades, several quantum theories of consciousness have been proposed. However, direct experimental evidence in favor of the quantum brain/mind hypothesis is still missing (De Benedittis, 2020).

Explanations of Consciousness & of the Unconscious

Wendt (2015) proposed a single underlying reality that is neither material nor mental, but one from which the distinction itself arises. Epistemologically, he has pointed out that the subjective–objective distinction is built in and could be criticized for privileging subjectivity. However, as Wendt eloquently argues, the taboo regarding subjectivity originates from an inability of the classical worldview to explain the first-person experience. Subjectivity is not a taboo for Quantum Theory, because it purports to provide this missing explanation (p. 93). Like Wendt, I attempt to provide an explanation of consciousness from within a quantum context. However, I link this to Oriental Nothingness, Qi, and other forms of energy, as explicated in psychoanalytic energy therapy (Mollon, 2008), because physics is not separated from philosophy in my conceptualizations (see Part 1).

Accepting that Buddhism, as conceptualized by the 14th Dalai Lama, regards the subconscious as a level of consciousness, then it is possible to link the Buddhist subconscious to group analysis through the concept of the preconscious (Freud's, 1915b,c). It occupies a space between the unconscious and the conscious in our psyche. However, the preconscious is still partially unconscious.

Initially, Khrennikov (2010) mathematically modeled the interaction between conscious and unconscious domains (as in Freud's 1915c model). Subsequently, Khrennikov (2023) conceptualized the unconscious as a black box, which he mathematically described by a quantum information space (unconscious state). A quantum state has been defined as "an agent's encoding of her own personal expectations for what she might experience as a consequence of her action" (Stacey, 2023, p. 1). The unconscious state probabilistically determines decision-making through interaction with consciousness. It changes in accordance with the previous unconscious state and the previously made decisions. Khrennikov (2023) suggested that Quantum Theory can be applied to measure the structures of the human mind (consciousness and the unconscious), and decision-making, through indirect observations, when conceptualized as inaccessible information systems (e.g. the unconscious). A quantum measurement refers to "an act that an agent performs on the external world" (Stacey, 2023, p. 1).

Baaquie and Martin (2005), and Eccles (1994), have suggested that consciousness could be a particular excitation of an underlying universal mental quantum field. These scholars have argued that consciousness was correlated to the neuronal structures via neural pathways in the brain, through quantum entanglement. Similarly, Khrennikov (2006, 2007, 2008) did propose that brain functioning could be modeled by using the mathematical formalism of quantum mechanics, although his model is also based on traditional neurophysiological conceptualizations of the functioning of the brain.

Detailed Description of the ERP

The transdisciplinary ERP is underpinned by several assumptions and principles:

1. Everything emerges from Oriental Nothingness and the invisible energy Qi.
2. Thus, in line with Hisamatsu (1959) and other Kyoto School philosophers, (Oriental) Nothingness is the underlying metaphysical reality that encompasses everything and determines how individuals exist (Brink, 2021).
3. Reality is created from nothing (similarly to Zhai; Jordan), in line with Hiramatsu. However, because everything is interdependent, ultimately, there is only one emerging reality. This reality may not be perceived as *one* due to the invisibility of Qi and Nothingness.
4. For some people, it may seem that multiple realities exist due to unconscious projections and splitting. This is an illusion, akin to the concept of Maya in the Advaita Vedanta (cosmic illusion that makes Brahman, the one ultimate realty, appear as a diverse world). However, the ERP favors psychoanalytic explanations of illusion.
5. Qi exists everywhere, forming nature and matter. Different forms of energy exist (kinetic energy, electrical energy, electromagnetic energy, bioelectromagnetic energy, libido, and subtle energy). Bioelectromagnetic energy and its surrounding energy fields differ from electrical energy. In Chinese medicine and acupuncture, bioelectromagnetic energy, the subtle energy of Qi, plays a crucial role in the functioning of the body and psyche (see Mollon, 2008). Kinetic energy and libido are also implicated in wellbeing.

6 Oriental Nothingness encapsulates the connection between confirmation and negation (relational dynamic).
7 Forms of consciousness, the unconscious, the mind, Nothingness, and different forms of energy are interconnected.
8 Quantum principles are crucial: Duality, Coherence and Entanglement (once coherent particles when separated influence each other), Superposition (existence in multiple states), the Superposition of states, Tunneling (penetrating through barriers), the Uncertainty Principle, and probability (see Kaku, 2024).
9 Diffraction (resulting from the Superposition or interference of waves) is marked by patterns of difference. It is also a useful methodology and tool of analysis (Barad, 2007).
10 Unconscious states are equated with quantum states (e.g. Khrennikov, 2023).
11 Temporal-spatial non-locality suggests the inseparability of time and space, an entanglement, or Superposition of mental states at different times. By incorporating non-locality in space and in time, a spatially and temporally holistic perspective arises.
12 Relational ontology in line with Ubuntu (Bujo, 2001) and East Asian philosophy (Parkes, 2018).
13 Processes of Yin and Yang, opposites that are dialectically conjoined and function together (Houshmand et al., 1999), and Wu Wei, acting in accordance with nature.
14 Impermanence (everything always changes) (Houshmand et al., 1999) and Nishida's (1921/1990) postulate that the "process of becoming whole requires ongoing meditation".
15 Ubuntu, with its emphasis of interconnectedness, "I am because we are", and the human capacity to express compassion, reciprocity, dignity, humanity, mutuality, and justice (Khoza, 2006), fits with East Asian values (harmony, balance, relationality, and equality) (Xiang, 2023).
16 Combining neuroscience with quantum principles and philosophy. Psychophysics, as envisaged by Jung and Pauli (see Del Medico, 2022).
17 Jung's (1961, 1960) collective unconscious and Synchronicity.
18 The social unconscious (Foulkes, 1964). Bion's (1967) "thoughts without a thinker" and Bion's (1961) basic assumptions; Foulkes' (1973) notion of what is inside is also outside, there is no difference between inner/outer reality, his "basic law of group dynamics", the matrix, resonance, mirroring, field (Foulkes, 1948, 1973, 2003); complexity theory (Stacey, 2006); how Dick (1981) conceptualized Quantum Theory and the group, Burrow's (1925) view of the unconscious in relation to Relativity Theory, Usandivaras' (1989b) use of meditation in groups, Lear (1983), Usandivaras (1993) integration of spiritual ideas; Fiumara's (1976, 1983, 1989) use of Jungian concepts.

It should be noted that the ERP is inspired predominantly by Wichert (2023) and Metzinger (2010). I refer interested readers to their writings, since it is impossible to offer a more detailed description here. However, there is one notable difference: the ERP rests on African and East/South Asian philosophies. Therefore, wanting to view it through the lens of Western philosophy would lead to misconstruing the ERP.

Oriental Nothing Is the Emerging Metaphysical Reality Underlying the ERP

That everything begins with "nothing", or was created from Oriental Nothingness, has been postulated by both the quantum physicist Krauss (2012) and the East Asian philosopher Hisamatsu (1959). Regarding the combination of physics with philosophy as important, the ERP rests on the same premise. Qi, translated as energy or natural force (Yang, 2022), is equated with Nothingness, which generates everything. Due to this assertion, no distinction is made between humans and non-humans. Groups with digitally extended Selves inhabit a reality that traditional research paradigms do not capture, in contrast to the ERP. Extended Selves are viewed as emergent. By "emergent" I mean that something has already become apparent, or has appeared, as a result of the emerging virtual world. Selves arise from their surroundings, according to the ERP, both digitally extended and non-digital Selves. While the former Selves are made entirely from electricity, the latter are constituted by bioelectromagnetic energy. In line with Mollon's (2008) psychoanalytic energy psychotherapy, the ERP embraces the idea that different forms of energy exist.

Reality is viewed as ***emerging***, which is in the process of coming into existence and coming to light. Being newly created, reality is in constant flux and always temporal, ephemeral (lasting for a short time). Qi, Nothingness, mind, consciousness, the unconscious, time, and space, are constitutive of experience and reality. They are regarded as emerging. Oriental Nothingness is the underlying metaphysical reality, which encompasses everything. I conceptualize it as a void that is full of the invisible life energy Qi, which connects each person with the universe and others. This explains the interconnectedness of everything, as postulated by the African philosophy Ubuntu (Ramose, 1999) and the group analytic matrix.

Whereas Qi exists everywhere, forming nature and matter, bioelectromagnetic energy and its surrounding energy fields, are important for the non-digital body and psyche. Additionally, Freud's (1905b) concept of libido, an instinctual, psychic energy, a *qualitatively variable force ... occurring in the field of sexual excitation* (p. 217), as well as kinetic and electromagnetic energy, influence humans (Figgess, 2018; Mollon, 2008). Electric energy is crucial for digital Selves. Drawing on a psychoanalytic energy approach (Mollon, 2008), which is congruent with Freud's (1905b) libido, I concur that people's energy fields communicate with each other. Chinese Medicine and acupuncture regard Qi as a subtle energy system. Subtle energy is energy activated by the mind and it can affect physical matter. It is a biofield, connected by meridians, the electrical "wiring" and network in the body, and chakras (energy centers) (Mollon, 2008). This biofield is also known as "Bioelectromagnetic Energy" (Yang, 2022). Additionally, the electromagnetic energy system within the body enables the interaction between the brain and cells of the nervous system. Each cell can be thought of as functioning like a miniature battery that produces chemical reactions and electrical currents. This creates an electromagnetic field (see Figgess, 2018). Our human body generates electricity that flows through it. Take the heart, it produces an electric current that runs through the body and to every cell, generating an electromagnetic field (McCraty, 2003). Consequently, our body is subject to the laws of electromagnetism. Most of the body's electromagnetic activity occurs in the cell membrane. Cell matter comprises charged particles. This explains why the electric and magnetic fields in our environment influence the interactions of chemicals and molecules in our body, as Valdez (2023) explains (see also National Academy of Sciences, 1993). When people's energy systems communicate with each other, one person is "reading" the unconscious mind of another person (Freud, 1912). It is a process facilitated by the right hemisphere of the brain. Neuroscientific findings lend support to this conceptualization (Schore, 2019).

The Illusion of Multiple Realities

Ultimately, there is only one reality that underpins the ERP. It resembles Jung's (1934/1969) conceptualization of one single reality, which is made up of spirit and matter, a reality that Jung and Pauli called "Unus Mundus" (Del Medico, 2022, p. 17). Hence, conceptions of multiple realities are an illusion. What do I mean by this?

Reality may not be perceived as one reality due to the invisibility of Qi and Nothingness. For some people, it may seem that multiple realities exist. However, this is an illusion, akin to the concept of "Maya" in the Advaita Vedanta Philosophy. "Maya" is the cosmic illusion that makes Brahman, the one ultimate realty, appear as a diverse world. Considering that group analysis has incorporated psychoanalytic theories and draws on the same unconscious defenses, I favor psychoanalytic explanations of illusions. Illusions can occur due to unconscious projections and splitting, for example. A perception of, or belief in, multiple realities can also be based on an unconscious need for wish fulfillment.

According to Freud (1927), an illusion differs from an error insofar that the illusion is derived predominantly from unconscious human wishes. When wish fulfillment is a prominent factor of a belief, then it is an illusion. Furthermore, an illusion differs from a delusion. The latter is in contradistinction with reality (Freud, 1927).

As Chasseguet-Smirgel and Grunberger (1986) pointed out, the unconscious aim of an illusion is the idealization of the ego, brought about by the fusion of the ego and the ego ideal. No realization can occur without projection, the unconscious defense mechanism, whereby feelings or thoughts are expelled from the Self. As a result of this process, they are located in another person or thing. Concepts, people, and other things are used as screens for such projections, because they are an obstacle to the realization of an illusion. Closely related to projection is splitting. Thus, an illusion is also bolstered by the unconscious defense mechanism of splitting. Such processes are not only confined to individuals but are group processes. The group acts out unconscious tendencies from each individual (Chasseguet-Smirgel & Grunberger, 1986). From a Freudian and group analytic perspective, one could say that conceptions of multiple realities are no more than a reflection of the dynamic conflicts between the ego, id, and the superego.

Consciousness, Unconscious Processes & Memory

The ERP is not plagued by the Cartesian "I think therefore I am", because it rests on Ubuntu, and its notion "I am because we are", and "I am related, therefore, we are" (Bujo, 2001).

Hence, it asserts that consciousness arises through energy, which flows through regions of space and time. Since I am neither a physicist nor a mathematician, I cannot offer any mathematical explanation However, Silverberg (2020) developed a theory that does seem to suggest something very similar. Conceptualizing a "fragment" of energy, rather than the particle-wave, as the fundamental building block of the universe, he offered a mathematical equation for this flow of energy.

Unconscious states are equated with quantum states, in line with Martin et al. (2009), Dravogich et al. (2009), and Orlov (1982). Regarding unconscious processes as emerging, they are emergent properties of a group-as-a-whole, and not just the sum of its individual members. I draw on theories and models by scholars, who have measured unconscious processes indirectly (see Dragovic et al., 2009). Some have linked quantum physics and neurophysiology to un/consciousness. By applying Hilbert spaces and using both p-adic and m-adic numbers, "Ultrametric Spaces" (space of the unconscious) have been produced mathematically. These are methods to research unconscious dynamics in the group. (See Appendix 5, Weisstein (n.d.) and Dolgopolov & Zubarev 2011 for explanations.)

Integrating psychoanalytic, group analytic, and quantum thinking, I view the unconscious as a non-local, entangled field of meaning. Mental states are characterized by temporal-spatial, non-locality occurring at different times (inseparability of time and space, Entanglement, or Superposition). By incorporating this non-locality, a holistic conceptualization of mental states is possible. Non-locality also extends to memory and assumptions of a "Quantum Brain Theory". While the physical basis of memories is not well understood (Wendt, 2015), we do know that memory is constituted by experiences. These seem to have the character of a wavefunction collapse taking place in the actual world, where experiences are being automatically imprinted into memory, and where neurons are spreading across the brain. To use Wendt's (2015) words,

> memory is printed to vacuum. Minimum energy states of equation fields extend over macroscopic distances in the brain. Our memories exist there in an entangled states in the superposition that is our unconscious. It is this vacuum that allows memories to surface and be recalled. (p. 200)

The Relational Nature of Difference: Diffraction

When two stones are simultaneously dropped into a calm pond, the disturbances in the water that are caused by each stone propagate outward and overlap with each other. A pattern is produced as a result of the relative difference between the overlapping wave component. The created diffraction pattern is called interference, because the waves are said to interfere with each other (Barad, 2007, p. 77). Diffraction, which is characterized by patterns of difference, is regarded as a useful metaphor for critical consciousness (Haraway, 1992), and as a methodology (Barad, 2007, 2014; Barla, 2021; Geerts & van de Tuin, 2021).

Like Haraway (1992), I regard diffraction as important, because it draws attention to the relational nature of difference. It can be used as a method (or tool of analysis) to present difference as "difference within" (p. 299).

Playing a crucial role in quantum optics, diffraction is a remarkable phenomenon that reveals the intriguing effects of the nature of light and the mysterious reality of entanglement. The famous two-split experiment used a diffraction grating with only two slits to measure the effects of difference. It showed how waves combined when they overlap, as Barad (2007) explained. So, diffraction has to do with the apparent bending and spreading of waves, occurring when waves encounter an obstruction (p. 74). Waves differ from particles. The latter are material entities. In contrast, waves are disturbances that propagate as oscillating fields like electromagnetic waves.

However, there is much more to diffraction. Imagine water waves. If the crest of a water wave overlaps with the trough of another, the disturbances partly (or in some cases completely) cancel one another out. This results in relative calm. It is known as the sum of effects. The resultant wave is a sum of the effects of each individual component wave (combination of disturbances created by each wave individually). In the language of physics, this is referred to as Superposition. It is central to understanding the nature of a wave (p. 76).

We find ubiquitous diffractive examples in nature (rainbows, ocean waves). When ocean waves pass through an opening in a barrier, it serves as a diffraction apparatus for them, diffracting the ocean waves and forming a pattern. Surfers, who catch great waves, take advantage of the diffraction patterns that are created by rocks, literally riding the diffraction pattern (p. 80).

Mind–Body

Drawing on Quantum Theory, the traditional positivist notions of linear causality, determinism, and separateness have been replaced with conceptualizations of non-linearity, a-causality, emerging, probabilistic, and interconnectedness in the ERP.

According to Quantum Theory, particles become linked in such a way that the state of one particle affects the state of another, irrespective of the distance between them. Human beings are made of particles, therefore, the assumption that quantum principles can be applied to humans follows logically.

Interestingly, the unity of body and mind seemed clear to the pioneers of both quantum mechanics and psychoanalysis, Pauli, Jung, and Freud, who did not share the ontic dualism between physis and psyche (Greek "ψυχή", soul). This division can be traced to the Greek atomists, who drew a clear line between spirit/psyche and matter (Capra, 1991).

In both quantum mechanics and group analytic theories, particles (people, group members) are not regarded as separate entities with predictable trajectories, but as interdependent and unpredictable. Quantum uncertainty characterizes the unpredictable nature of unconscious group processes, where people and processes are interdependent, influencing each other in complex ways.

Evidence for these effects has been generated by Zapirain et al. (2014), who drew on Bion's basic assumptions, and applied concepts from quantum physics to study the onset of unconscious processes in the group. Results have demonstrated that group dynamics have some effects on the individual. The initial choice of selecting images from a questionnaire seemed to have been affected by group dynamics. Thus, the ERP assumes that emotional and psychological states, as well as behaviors, are molded by unconscious group dynamics.

How Research Is Conceptualized from the Perspective of the ERP

Drawing on (Oriental) Nothingness (Nishida, 1958/1966; 1958/1973, 1993; Hisamatsu, 1959; 2005; Barnhart, 1992; FAS Society, 2012), research is regarded as Nothingness. By using the Buddhist "water and waves" metaphor (see Aśvaghosha, 2003, 2008; Hisamatsu, 2002), research paradigms are viewed like waves. Knowledge is like water.

Although each research paradigm has its own limited form and exists in relation to other research paradigms, originally, research paradigms were formless knowledge. The analogy of water and waves is used to illustrate what this means.

Water transcends the relative wave and exists absolutely. Similarly, knowledge transcends the relative nature of research paradigms, including their methodologies and methods, and exists absolutely. Research paradigms arise out of, and return to, knowledge. In this sense, while they have a relative meaning within the world, they are at the same time an absolute nothingness. These paradigms do not depart from knowledge, they disappear and return to knowledge. This allows for the creation of one pluralistic paradigm, the ERP.

From the viewpoint of knowledge, research paradigms, methodologies, and methods, are just movements of knowledge. Knowledge is non-dually one with the ERP research paradigm. And yet, the arising and perishing of research paradigms does not entail the arising and perishing, or the increasing and decreasing of knowledge. Knowledge arises and perishes as research paradigms, and yet, knowledge itself, neither arises nor perishes.

Viewed through the lens of impermanence, disagreements between positivists and critical realists, or between social constructionists and positivists, lose meaning. The question of whether there is one reality (Realism), or multiple realities (Relativism), becomes irrelevant. Hence, irreconcilable positions, such as Positivism versus Social Constructionism, are no longer irreconcilable, because the reason for their irreconcilability has ceased to exist. It allows for harmony and pluralism.

Philosophical Assumptions the ERP Rests On

Metaphysics, ontology, epistemology, and axiology are inseparable.

Metaphysical

Everything is made up of the invisible energy Qi and Oriental Nothingness, forming the underlying metaphysical reality. Nothingness is akin to Zen Buddhism' "Sunjata", Emptiness. Oriental Nothingness is not viewed as absence but potentiality for creation. Hisamatsu's (1959) and Nishida's (1927/1978–1979) emphasis on relational existence and Nothingness differs from Western metaphysics, which often avoids nothingness, or treats it as the absence of being, instead of a generative (creating) concept. Furthermore, Krauss' (2012) and Pross' (2016) explanations of how the universe and life emerged from nothing are part of the metaphysical basis of the ERP (see also Pross & Pascal, 2013).

Ontological

Reality, existence, body, being, consciousness, the unconscious, mind, and self are regarded as emerging processes, arising from Oriental Nothingness and from different types of energy, Tunneling through barriers. These phenomena are joined by a relational ontology, which arises through dynamic relationships rather than fixed substances. Hence, it is also a process ontology. Interactions between phenomena are viewed as primary. Reality is constantly in flux, shaped by emerging relational context-dependent and probabilistic processes, in line with the quantum principles of uncertainty, entanglement, and Superposition. There is no separation between the environment, nature, the universe, humans, and non-humans. Everything is interdependent. Hence, ultimately, there is only one emerging reality. If multiple realities are perceived, this is due to illusions. The relational ontology is underpinned by the African philosophy of Ubuntu, which is similar to Confucianism, Taoism, and Buddhism.

Epistemological

One implication of quantum mechanics is that knowledge is probabilistic and imprecise. So, there are limits to what we can know in terms of accuracy. Based on a relational epistemology, knowledge is viewed as emerging. It is arising and shaped by interactions. There is no delineation between knower and known, between observer and observed. Pure objectivity is viewed as an illusion. It is recognized that acts of observation may alter the observed phenomenon. Hence, there is no such thing as "the" truth, because knowledge emerges through dynamic, interconnected processes.

Axiological

The ERP emphasizes compassion, reciprocity, dignity, humanity, mutuality, justice, harmony, equality, balance, and relationality. "I am, because we are" is a main premise. Ecological balance and the collective are prioritized over the individual, in line with African and East Asian philosophies.

Methodology & Methods

Diffraction is one methodology, and the ERP enables the application of many methods. In addition to using traditional Western research methods, several Indigenous and "quantum methods" can be applied. A diffractive methodology comprises reading one approach attentively through another one to come to a more creative critique and insight (Bozalek & Murris, 2022). These will be described further in other chapters. Quantum principles and neurophysiology can be used to study consciousness and unconsciousness. For example, by producing ultrametric spaces, whereby unconscious processes can be measured indirectly (see Dragovic et al., 2009). Or, by using the method used by Zapirain et al. (2014). Other tools include the application of modern technologies and AI.

Intuitionist and introspective methods, such meditation, can also be used as a means to gather knowledge.

How the ERP Differs from Other Research Paradigms

The ERP emphasizes "emerging", which differs from being constructed (built, created) as conceptualized by many social constructionists. They argued that society and Selves are created by humans and their interactions through repeated action that becomes a habit. For them, reality is socially constructed (Berger & Luckmann, 1966). Reality may be influenced by our symbolic interactions and culturally specific knowledge. In my conceptualization, this would be emergent. More importantly, the ERP prioritizes considerations of matter and nature. Even though one reality underpins the ERP, its ontology differs from naïve Realism, which many positivists adopt. Thus, it rests on very different philosophical assumptions than the traditional quantitative and qualitative paradigms. Multiple realities are regarded as an illusion. Again, it differs from Social Constructionism, or Constructivism, which both assume that multiple realities exist. As the name ERP suggests, emerging is one of its crucial features, which differs from "emergent".

Primas (1998) argued that emergence and theory reduction are related, which are inherent in the Interpretivist (Idealist) research paradigms. Furthermore, even though the ERP has a transcendental quality, it should not be equated with mysticism. Whereas Bhasker's Critical Realism and Heidegger's Phenomenology also have a transcendental dimension, the ERP integrates conceptualizations of Oriental Nothingness and Qi. So, it is distinct from all the other research paradigms.

Is It Justified to Refer to the ERP as a Paradigm?

One requirement of a Kuhnian paradigm is scientific consensus and institutional acceptance. The ERP does not meet this requirement, so it could not be classed as a paradigm in the Kuhnian sense. However, the ERP is new. It could not have achieved acceptance. However, it is not necessary to use Kuhn's notion, but other definitions of paradigm can be used (see Masterman,

1970; Collins, 1990, p. 224; Guba and Lincoln, 1994, p. 107). The ERP is conceptually consistent, offering a metaphysical worldview, which emphasizes relationality and emergence. It incorporates marginalized epistemologies (Asian, Ubuntu) and explicitly expresses non-Western worldviews. Therefore, referring to the ERP as a paradigm seems justified.

Alternatively, it could be regarded as *one* overarching research framework, in to which other paradigms fit. Of course, the ERP has limitations. Even though an emphasis on communality, relationality, values, metaphysics, and ontology are found in many cultures, I have restricted my focus to African and East Asian cultures. This was partially done due to space. Furthermore, the quantum world was dominated by White, European males, which excluded women and males of color. By adopting these theories, the ERP could be criticized for inadvertently propagating sexism and racism. Partly, this might be compensated by the integration of Ubuntu.

Furthermore, I draw on Haraway (1997), viewing gender in the making. Gender is fluid and non-binary. Over the past decade, females have also made innovative suggestions as well. I have tried to incorporate these whenever possible. As with any new paradigm or framework, the ERP is likely to be modified, as a result of fruitful discussions with others. Native speakers may be able to expand the ERP, because they are not constrained by language, as I am. I had to rely on translations of the philosophies the ERP rests on. Furthermore, while the ERP is compatible with other paradigms and methods to a certain extent, its philosophical basis is not really suitable for randomized controlled trials. Despite these limitations, the ERP increases the methodological scope, offering researchers a choice of perspectives. It also contributes to the decolonization of research and is pluralistic.

Chapter Summary

I have outlined the building blocks of the ERP. It prioritizes matter and nature, conceptualizing people as a dynamic relational organism. Bodies are constituted through entangled psycho-energetic-physical fields and processes. The ERP assumes that the psychodynamics of the mind manifest in the body's energy system. It rests on the assumption that everything is created from Nothingness. The life energy Qi, interconnectedness, holism, relationality, the complementary duality of Yin and Yang, and the notion that everything is interconnected and dynamic are crucial to the ERP. Furthermore, it emphasizes harmonious communal relationships, humaneness, "I Am because We Are", and Wu Wei (acting in line with nature). The unity of body, mind, and spirit, are important. Of all the Western psychoanalysts, Jung (1938) is probably the one who concerned himself the most with African and Asian philosophy. This is reflected in his writing on Zen Buddhism and meditation. Jung's (1968a, 1968b) conceptualizations of the collective unconscious, archetypes, and Synchronicity, offer important insight into psychic reality. Where the Jungian unconscious and the Freudian unconscious significantly differ, is Jung's emphasis on archetypes, which he considered crucial. The collective unconscious is part of the group analytic social unconscious. They are not the same. Psychoanalytic and group analytic thinking about consciousness also differ from Buddhist conceptualizations. Finding a link between Buddhism and conceptualizations of the unconscious is difficult, but not entirely impossible. Like Group Analysis, the ERP draws on quantum mechanics, asserting that there is no difference between inner and outer reality. Foulkes (1973) accepted a reality, where boundaries did not exist, as postulated in Quantum Theory (see Becker, 2019). Foulkes acknowledged the interdependence between consciousness and the unconscious. The mind itself has a phenomenological reality (Pines, 2003). Richard Dawkins (2012) wrote that "[n]othing expands the mind like the expanding universe" (p. 187). This begs the questions: Is mind not as mysterious a phenomenon as it seems? Could mind be explained by neuroscientific studies, mathematics, and Quantum Theory?

Unfortunately, space does not allow me to provide a more comprehensive account of the ERP. Depth had to be sacrificed for the sake of brevity. This was inevitable. Thus my descriptions may seem basic, incomplete, or even simplistic. However, my selection of texts has focused on philosophical concepts that are crucial to the emergent reality paradigm. Some may criticize that the ERP rests on African and Eastern Philosophies. Others may say that I have portrayed idealist versions of Eastern/African philosophies. I acknowledge their shortcomings. However, these philosophies have several advantages. Firstly, the problem of the Western metaphysics of individualism is avoided. This is important from a group analytic perspective, which is critical of prioritizing the individual. One could even say that the notion of the individual is illusionary. Secondly, Ubuntu's "I am because we are" bypasses the Cartesian separation of body and mind. This eliminates the problem pertaining to consciousness and the mind–body. Thirdly, there is sufficient overlap between Eastern philosophies and quantum mechanics. By supplementing Eastern philosophy with science, we get a plausible, scientific explanation of Oriental Nothingness. That is, how a universe with a positive energy in empty space could have arisen out of unstable nothingness (Krauss, 2012, p. 180). One implication is that the very distinction between something and nothing disappears. This provides the ERP with a coherent foundation. Fourthly, the integration of non-Western philosophies contributes to the decolonization of research. Finally, these philosophies have much in common with group analytic theories and practices. They may even revive an interest in research spirituality. Rarely have group analytic researchers concerned themselves with spirituality, or religion. This is evident in the dearth of papers (Marmarosh, 2024), and the overall paucity of research in this area, compared to outcome and process research. These are not the only areas that could be studied, and I will make suggestions when discussing methods. Of course, these, like research as such, rest on philosophical assumptions. The ERP has been formulated as an alternative to existing paradigms, which are based on Western philosophy. I have integrated research findings and theories, which support the metaphysical claim that everything is created from Nothingness. Instead of having to rely on Positivism, Social Constructionism, Critical Realism, and so forth, researchers could draw on the ERP. Its assumptions could underpin their studies.

Group analytic research is carried out worldwide, so non-Western paradigms are needed. The ERP could also be combined with Indigenous frameworks and paradigms (see Chilisa, 2012), when researching groups in Africa. Compared to traditional paradigms, the ERP is methodologically not as limiting. A wide variety of methods can be used. So, it would be suitable for all researchers. I hope that other scholars and researchers will elaborate the ERP.

Section 2

Introduction

While Section 1 is mainly theoretical, the focus of Section 2 is on methods. Chapters 3–5 comprise quantitative designs, methodologies, and methods. In Chapter 6, the conundrum of theory and other conceptual confusion are addressed. Versions of Grounded Theory are described. Qualitative methods are also explicated in Chapters 7 and 8. Mixed methods are introduced in Chapters 9 and 10, although this separation is not always that clear cut. Chapters 11–13 have a more group analytic focus. Research with children, ethics, and large groups, are briefly described in Chapters 12 and 13, respectively.

When selecting methods, I also took into consideration the guidelines that recommend the use of quantitative methods. These are in stark contrast to post-qualitative research. Inquiry should begin with provocation, the too much, because the rest is what everybody does and knows; it is the ordinary, the repetition, St Pierre (2017, p. 608) wrote. The ERP introduces something new, where the "I" is less important than the "We". For Deleuze and Guattari (1994), the "I" is a habit. Old habits die hard. Perhaps this is why the "I" and the black hole of qualitative research, positivist coding (Lather, 1991), linger on in qualitative research. It was difficult to evade it. So, I ended up with coding techniques, or operationalizing, myself, and when looking for methods. I have included my own group analytic research (Vosmer, 2022, 2024d), which is more in line with a diffractive approach.

Overall, group analytic research (see Whitaker, 1981) still seems to lack methods that capture the uniqueness of group analysis. Questionnaires were used to study analytic groups in Greece, Germany, America, and Britain. Terlidou et al. (2004) utilized the Minnesota Multiphasic Personality Inventory, and the more psychoanalytic Rorschach projective test, to assess the decrease in symptomatology and improved adaptation. Ogrodniczuk and Piper (2003) studied the effect of the group climate. Berzon et al. (1963) researched the subjective experiences of group members. Cedeño et al.'s (2020) pilot study showed that analyzing group processes in multicultural focus groups is valuable. In addition to quantitative studies (e.g., Conway et al., 2003; Dutta & Kundu, 2021), Nathan and Poulsen's (2004) interviewed students about their experiences of analytic groups. Other studies include Hummelen et al.'s (2007) interviews of borderline clients,

DOI: 10.4324/9781003609544-5

Inderhaug's (2013) video-based case study, Vosmer's (2015) content analysis of social interaction in an ADHD group, and Inderhaug and Karterud's (2015) research on mentalization. Alas, many studies have not escaped the coding black hole, despite "quantum leaps" (Denzin & Lincoln, 2000, p. xi), and the emergence of Asian epistemologies and transformative research (Denzin & Lincoln, 2011). Furthermore, Clarke and Braun (2019b) devised a checklist to assess the quality of research. So, group analytic researchers can add checklists to their repertoire of coding and operationalization.

Although qualitative methods have become more trustworthy due to systematic procedures, have researchers been sucked deeper into the black hole rather than escaping the force field of coding? Queer research seems different. Cyber ethnographies (Ashford, 2009) explore online sexual communities. Virtual research has gained prominence. Facebook, dating, and other websites lend themselves to qualitative analyses of group behavior, expressed through texts, photos, and images. So, nowadays, group analytic researchers can use different methods, ranging from narrative approaches to political action research. Grounded Theory, Discourse Analysis, Narrative Research, Intuitive Inquiry (see Wertz et al., 2011), Autoethnography, feminist and queer methods (Ashford, 2009), the Diary Method (Filep et al., 2018), and Meta-synthesis have been elaborated. Thus, the case study is no longer the method par excellence that pays close attention to idiographic descriptions. Interpretative Phenomenological Analysis (IPA) (Smith, 1996; Smith et al., 2022) focuses on idiographic aspects, which include any specific event or situation. Like other phenomenological methods (e.g. Finlay, 2006, 2008; Giorgi, 1985, 1997, 2006, 2009, 2010; Moustakas, 1994), IPA can be used to gain an in-depth understanding of lived experience. Even though phenomenological methods emphasize consciousness, interpretative phenomenological approaches, like group analysis, focus on interpretation.

In *Group Analysis*, two IPA studies (Jackson et al., 2023; O'Beney et al., 2019) were published. Therefore, I decided to include phenomenological methods. Interestingly, through careful reading of Husserl's work Geniusas (2022, 2024) demonstrated that Husserl had a distinct approach toward the unconscious. Explicating the horizontal, time-constituting, sedimented, repressed, absorbed, dormant, and instinctual unconscious, Geniusas (2024) argues that the Freudian unconscious should be considered in phenomenology. For Husserl, consciousness had a multi-layered structure. According to Geniusas, the lowest layer is the unconscious.

Innovative research tools exist to examine dialogues and group interactions. However, we also live in the era of EBP. There is no escape from the quantifying black hole. Williams' reflections on qualitative methods seem relevant even today: "[A]gain and again … we are faced with a dilemma of either refusing to quantify … or …trying to attach some quantity … in which case they misrepresent what they are about …" (cited in Barkham & Margison, 2007, p. 462). Hence, I will briefly discuss whether it is possible to evade coding in qualitative group analytic research by using phenomenological methods as an example. Moreover, while reflection is central to qualitative research, from a post-qualitative perspective, researchers' continued reliance on reflection limits their possibilities for thinking differently (Bozalek & Zembylas, 2017). Although the ERP embraces diffraction, I am wary of imposing methods on group analytic researchers. I do not insist on a diffractive methodology but encourage careful reading of the ideas of one theorist through that of another (Bozalek & Murris, 2022; Murris & Bozalek, 2019). Personally, I feel inspired by Jackson and Mazzei's (2012) postmodern approach. However, novice researchers might like to learn orthodox qualitative methods first. Therefore, I will also attend to qualitative research. In particular, research that has been, or could be, carried out in group analysis will be described in Section 2. Participants have become an integral part of the research process (McLeod, 2023a). Perhaps Western researchers have learnt from Indigenous methodologies, eventually.

3

LEARNING TRADITIONAL RESEARCH & NOMENCLATURE THROUGH GROUP ANALYSTS

Abstract

A structured research approach is commonly recommended. It entails developing a clear research question, choosing an appropriate approach to sampling, data collection and analysis, using critical appraisal strategies and clearly reporting results. To carry out trustworthy and robust studies, researchers must have a good understanding of qualitative and quantitative research. Quantitative and qualitative methodologies do speak their own language. To make it easier to understand aspects of research, including terminology, designs, and methods, Foulkes' methodology, the Northfield Experiments, and other examples from group analysts, are used to make research more understandable.

Introduction

Without terminological clarity, effective communication about research is impossible. Using the correct words is important so that researchers can achieve a shared understanding. In his discussion of language, the philosopher Wittgenstein (1921/1961) showed that it functions like a picture and has a logical structure. Importantly, in *Philosophical Investigations* (paragraph 43), Ludwig Wittgenstein (1953) suggests that the meaning and function of words (and sentences) are dependent on shared criteria, and on their use in social practices (contexts). He referred to "language games", emphasizing that language is governed by rules.

Since the quantitative and qualitative paradigms speak their own language, group analytic researchers must learn their nomenclature. Doing so can be a laborious undertaking, especially, for novice researchers.

In my experience, many clinicians and trainees are interested in research. However, some find research nomenclature confusing. Others are unclear about the difference between a research design, which is a rigorous procedure that addresses the research question (Frankfort-Nachmias & Nachmias, 1996), and methodology (approach). While some do know the different designs, others confuse methodologies with methods (techniques). They do not know how to develop good research questions or hypotheses, which determine the study design (Barroga &

DOI:10.4324/9781003609544-6

Matanguihan, 2022). Or they are not entirely clear about the difference between quantitative and qualitative research. Put simply, quantitative research aims to measure and quantify. It emphasizes objective measurement and employs statistics to analyze data. Surveys (Jamieson et al., 2023), experiments, and randomized controlled trials (RCTs) are common quantitative methods. In contrast, qualitative research, according to Denzin and Lincoln (1994, 2005a), seeks to understand the social reality of individuals, groups, and cultures. Many different methods can be used, ranging from thematic analysis to political action research. Naturalistic (e.g. Riedl et al., 2022) and other qualitative types of studies have also been carried out to research group analytic psychotherapy (e.g. Ashton et al., 2025; Baezley, 2023; Doran, 2001; Ikkos, 2000; Jackson et al., 2023; McMahon, 2023; Schermer, 2012; Stocks et al., 2020; Story et al., 2024).

In Britain, the delivery of health care has undergone significant transformations (Gupta et al., 2025). The National Institute for Health and Care Excellence (NICE) offers guidance on what kind of psychotherapies should be provided. NICE uses the pyramid model of evidence, which prioritizes meta-analyses, systemic reviews, RTCs (Murad et al., 2016), and manualized treatments. Researchers are often expected to provide quantitative evidence for the efficacy/effectiveness of psychotherapies, because NICE favors RCTs.

Over the past few years, it has, however, acknowledged the usefulness of real-world research. Its real-world evidence framework (RWEF) was published in 2022 and was updated in 2025 (NICE, 2025a).

According to the RWEF, qualitative data may be used to understand people's experiences, beliefs, preferences, attitudes, behavior, and interactions in social contexts. But recommendations for the analysis of qualitative data predominantly focus on thematic analysis. Collecting data through interviews, focus groups, or free text response in surveys, is acceptable. The Critical Appraisal Skills Program (CASP) checklist is recommended for the assessment of previously conducted primary qualitative studies (NICE, 2025b).

Overall, recommendations by NICE support a structured research approach through development of a clear research question, choice of an appropriate approach to sampling, data collection and analysis, as well as clear reporting and robust critical appraisal strategies (Gupta et al., 2025). Therefore, researchers must have a good understanding of qualitative and quantitative research.

To make it easier to understand terminology, research concepts, and components of research, I will draw on Foulkes' methodology, the Northfield Experiments, and other group analytic examples, in my following descriptions.

Viewing Research through the Group Analytic Lens & Vice Versa

Quantitative research aims to systematize experiences, explain relationships (correlations), identify the causes that influence outcome, and formulate laws, which are viewed as the basis for prediction and generalization (Park et al., 2020). Correlations and experimentation are used to reduce interactions to constituent parts. Direct experiments and observations, empirical testing, random sampling, manipulated variables, and control groups, should produce valid knowledge. Cynics say that today's research ease originated in yesterday's belief that science is based on observation/experimentation. It comprises all there is to know about human beings. Group analyst Trigant Burrow (1913, 1926a,b, 1927, 1928a,b, 1958), who applied psychoanalysis to the group during the 1920s, embraced the quantitative paradigm. His procedures involved "… consensual observations and empirical experimentations … with various types of groups" (Pertegato & Pertegato, 2013, p. 157). After studying social reactions by analyzing the individual in groups, he formulated the "mass/social unconscious" (p. 157). The analytic group was considered by Burrow also as a means of research (Pertegato, 2014). Similarly, Foulkes (1948) thought that the group analytic method "... promise[d] to be a most valuable tool for scientific investigation and therapy alike ..." (p. 37). Not only was Foulkes (1946b, 1948) scientifically minded, but he was also a researcher himself. He used the "observational method". Being acutely aware of the unconscious, he did, however, not believe that one can be completely objective, neutral, and detached from one's group members. This claim was espoused by Freud and positivists. Even though reality can only be understood imperfectly and probabilistically (Popper, 1959, 1972), objectivity is nevertheless a regulatory ideal in quantitative research. Researchers state hypotheses, that is, make statements, which are then supported, or not, by evidence (Carpiano & Daley, 2006, p. 569). This procedure is considered objective and "empirical".

Popper (1959) did not accept that *induction* was scientific. Why? Assume that the women in a therapy group talk about emotions. Using inductive reasoning (TextBox 3.1), the therapist surmises that all females talk about emotions. However, even if only one woman would not talk about emotions, the conclusion from his observation, that all females talk about emotions, would have been wrong. For this reason, Popper argued that only deduction produces scientific knowledge. The *hypothetico-deductive model* (Hempel & Oppenheim, 1948), which explicitly equates prediction with explanation (Shmueli, 2010), is favored in quantitative research.

TEXTBOX 3.1 INDUCTION, DEDUCTION & ABDUCTION

Induction is inferential reasoning. A generalization based on individual examples is being made. In deductive reasoning, a conclusion is logically reached from its premises (Godfrey-Smith, 2003). If you read theories on emotions, which explained why women talk more frequently about emotions than men, and then concluded that men do not commonly discuss emotions in group therapy, your conclusion would be based on deduction.

Poon (2005) clarified that abduction is about finding the best explanation among several plausible, or even competing, explanations. The emphasis is on the relative importance of your data. Abduction is process driven. Abductive reasoning contains extra theoretical characteristics. It is possible to withdraw hypotheses and correct mistakes.

When Foulkes started to develop the concept of the group matrix, his thinking was influenced by Freud and Goldstein, a neurologist he worked with.

Freud's (1895) *Project for a Scientific Psychology* was grounded in the anatomy of the brain, and he conceptualized the ego as a network of cathected neurons in relation to one another (p. 325).

Similarly, Foulkes and Anthony (1957) theorized the matrix as a network in quite the same way as the brain: a network of fibers and cells, which together form a complex unit (p. 258). Advocating that having knowledge of neurology was fundamental to the task of psychotherapy (Foulkes, 1990), Goldstein's neurological theories allowed Foulkes to develop *(deduce)* the theoretical concept of the matrix,

> ... the hypothetical web of communication and relationships in a given group. It is the common shared ground, which ultimately determines the meaning and significance of all events, and upon which all communications and interpretations, verbal and non-verbal, rest.
>
> (Foulkes, 1964, p. 292)

One could say that Foulkes applied the *hypothetico-deductive method* to formulate the matrix by *deducing* it from Goldstein's theory (1925). Goldstein viewed the nervous system as a functional whole, acting as a total network. Mediated by ganglia (nerve knots), it reacted to the outside world (Stahnisch, 2024).

Additionally, Foulkes' assumption *(hypothesis)* was that the mind comprised a network of relationships. He linked it to the matrix. Furthermore, Foulkes (1990) *deduced* (TextBox 3.1) that our inner world is a microcosm of the wider world, from Goldstein's epistemological principle that nothing should be considered without reference to the total situation. Moreover, Foulkes realized that psychotherapists and group members influence each other. One could extrapolate and say that the researcher and participants affect each other, which influences the research process. So, researchers cannot completely bracket' their personal assumptions, in contrast to what the phenomenologists Husserl (1980) and Heidegger (1962) believed.

Husserl (1983) argued for phenomenological reduction, epoché, which is a means of becoming aware of conscious processes by deliberately paying attention to these. Once we become detached from pondering what something is (bracketing), we have the freedom to study how its appearance is related to what it *actually* is (Husserl, 1859–1938).

Foulkes (1946) disagreed. As a result of clinically studying (observing) his therapy groups, typically comprising eight group members and lasting for 90 minutes, he reached the conclusion that

> … we are prejudiced by introducing a preconceived theory into the observation of facts without being aware that we do so. We must be in spontaneous contact with a life situation. The observer is aware of forming an integral part of the situation. He introduces dynamic forces into the field and it is permeated by forces emanating from it …
>
> (pp. 129–130)

Observation forms part of the quantitative method, which is predicated on the Correspondence Theory of Truth and an objective reality (Mondal, 2023). C causes d, and d is consistent with reality. However, Foulkes "truth" lay between subjects and objects, between word and sentence, and between parts and the whole (Powell, 1991). He was more interested in communication, in explicating meaning through interpretation and analysis. There is an affinity with hermeneutics (see TextBox 3.2), the art of interpretation, a technique that is used in phenomenological hermeneutics (see Ricoeur, 1981).

TEXTBOX 3.2 PHENOMENOLOGICAL HERMENEUTICS & INTERPRETATION

Interpretation is more akin to Phenomenological Hermeneutics (Gadamer, 2004) than to Positivism. Gadamer's Hermeneutics addresses the fundamental problem of Phenomenology, Figal (2007, p. 95) wrote. Namely, how things reveal themselves and can be arrived at. In elaborating the ontology of language, Gadamer equated the accessibility of things and their Being (Sein). For both Heidegger and Gadamer, ontology was only possible phenomenologically (Gadamer, 1987). But Gadamer (2004) did not believe in absolute consciousness. Following Plato, he described the accessibility of things as passing off their truth and presence (Figal, 2007). Philosophical hermeneutics, philosophy as a human science, and the nature of hermeneutics, were elaborated by Gadamer (1966, 1976, 1977).

By replacing Freud's method of free association with free-floating discussion, as well as emphasizing translation over interpretation to gain access to the group members' unconscious

(Foulkes, 1964), in order to hear the symptom that mumbles, hoping to be overheard (Foulkes & Anthony, 1957), Foulkes' clinical method moves into the qualitative paradigm.

Some believe that qualitative methods are more suitable for researching analytic groups. Quantitative methods clearly have their limits, despite the technique of operationalizing, which involves defining a concept and then measuring it. Dalal (2018a) claimed in *CBT, The Cognitive Behavioral Tsunami,* that it was used due to beliefs that only the quantifiable counts as science (p. 24). It gets rid of the subjective by focusing on what is objectively measurable (Green, 2001). Hence, Dalal (2023) doubts that quantitative methods can capture the intricacies of human exchange. Qualitative methods may be better suited to research the inner life of analytic groups.

A complex social world of phenomena can be revealed through the method of interpretation. It is the setting of the analytic group, in which language, symbolism, and metaphors, play a central role. Diverse personal experiences are brought together as members meet under specific circumstances, communicate, interact, and engage, with each other at an intimate level (Powell, 1982).

The group was almost like a *laboratory* for Foulkes, enabling him to observe what was happening. Described as a social field, the group setting should not be confused with an ethnographic field. So, Foulkes was not carrying out ethnographic field studies. Undoubtedly, he was examining and describing the semantic field in detail. He gathered knowledge that enabled him to develop a group analytic method. But the psychotherapy group was not a natural setting, even though Foulkes wrote about "naturally" occurring communicational exchanges.

Downplaying his influence, Foulkes exerted control over the setting by carefully selecting members after assessment interviews. He tried to "match" patients, because he wanted to ensure that at least two people shared similar characteristics (sex, ethnicity, age, etc.), so that they would not feel isolated or be scapegoated. One could say that Foulkes controlled the practical aspects of the setting. He decided where, when, and for how long the group would meet. Therefore, his analytic groups were not a natural setting in an ethnographic sense. They resembled laboratories, in which Foulkes *observed* a naturally occurring variation in individual members. But it was not a natural experiment either, because his groups were not natural groups but assembled. At first glance, his method appears to be rooted in the quantitative paradigm. Upon further inspection, the peculiar mix of qualitative techniques, such as interpretation, and seemingly quantitative techniques (observation, matching, comparison) cannot be classed as an experiment or an experimental study (TextBox 3.3). Although Foulkes conducted several groups and compared them to the group analytic model, he did not divide groups into experimental and control groups. Therefore, his study of groups was *not experimental.* Characteristically, this method comprises a control and experimental group (Singh, 2007).

TEXTBOX 3.3 EXPERIMENTS & EXPERIMENTATION

Experimentation comprises laboratory, natural, and field experiments. At times, there is no need to create an artificial setting or to introduce an intervention. Then a natural or field experiment can be designed. Harris (1994) explained that experiments are normally carried out in laboratories. Variables are controlled to test a hypothesis (statement of what will happen). However, while the experimental method is a core feature of the scientific approach, laboratory experiments, as done in the natural sciences, are ruled out in applied social research. They only tend to be used in social psychology and for small-group research in sociology (Hammersley, 1995, p. 40).

According to Singh (2007), in experimental studies participants are randomly assigned to either an experimental or control group. These are the most important designs for establishing causality between variables, because they enable researchers to manipulate a specific variable to establish what effect this manipulation has on other variables. Designs can be longitudinal (e.g. Hohls et al. 2021) or of short duration. In a repeated-measure design, the procedure starts with a pre-test and ends with one, or several post-tests. Differences in scores between the experimental and control groups form the basis of the results (p. 67).

In terms of *research methodology*, what approach did Foulkes use? Could it be described as a naturalistic study, a case-control study, or a field experiment (TextBox 3.4)? Before answering the question, let us first consider several components of research: its *purpose, nature, aim, designs, methods, types of data,* and *analysis.*

Studies can be carried out to explore, describe, explain, or evaluate. Research can also be applied to advance knowledge without wanting to find solutions to problems in the real world. Designs depend on the research question. Typically, exploratory designs seek to gain initial insights, or an understanding, of a phenomenon. They do not have to be necessarily qualitative. Commonly, quantitative designs are used for an explanatory purpose, aiming to explain causality, X causes Y. They are often evaluative, X works better than Y. Often, RCTs are done. However, evaluative research can also be quasi-experimental, which does not involve randomly assigning participants to groups (Robinson & Seale, 2018). This is a main characteristic of RCTs. Generally speaking, quantitative research is *experimental*, trying to establish causality, or *correlational*, seeking to understand the relationship between variables.

Furthermore, even though descriptive research is commonly defined as a type of quantitative research, descriptive studies can also be qualitative.

Another important aspect of designs is temporality. Cross-sectional, time-series, cohort, and longitudinal studies are good examples of different temporalities (see TextBox 3.11).

Research data can be distinguished between *primary,* newly gathered, and *secondary* data, which involves using already existing data. Frequently, quantitative data analyses involve statistics, and qualitative analyses identify patterns, or themes.

TEXTBOX 3.4 NATURALISTIC STUDIES, FIELD EXPERIMENTS & CASE-CONTROL STUDIES

In a naturalistic study, you neither manipulate variables nor offer any interventions. Take this scenario: you want to know what effect being a clergy has on mental health. You could compare members of the clergy in country X with ordinary people in country X. However, if their selection is not random, you cannot say with certainty that being a clergy affects their mental health. Commonly known factors, such as good/poor sleep, healthy/poor diet, and drinking too much alcohol can also affect mental health.

In field experiments, researchers have evaluated the effectiveness of programs that alleviate poverty (Humphreys & Weinstein 2009): again, you compare two groups, but here you offer an intervention. Then compare the experimental and control conditions.

In case-control studies, researchers select "cases" (people who have the characteristic of interest; depressed people) and compare them (with people who are not depressed). Ideally, the case and control group are similar, except for the characteristic of interest, here depression (Robinson & Seale, 2018).

Foulkes' Use of Participant Observation

Unfortunately, in the early history of psychoanalysis, some mistook their observations for evidence of causality. Foulkes' method of choice was observation, which enabled him to hypothesize that certain dynamics occurred in small groups. Notwithstanding that his promising group analytic method has quantitative features, it does not satisfy the criteria for a quantitative design. His methodology could be described as "exploratory" research of small psychotherapy groups. It might even be called "longitudinal", because the same clients tend to be in an analytic group for more than one year. Hence, Foulkes' methodology resembles "a time series within-subject design" (TextBox 3.5). Measurements are taken from the same participants, and from all participants, at two (before and after treatment), or more, time points. However, Foulkes neither used measures, such as standardized questionnaires to measure how severely depressed a person was, nor did he carry out statistical analyses. His methodology resembles a "mixed design", which combines quantitative with qualitative techniques (Cresswell, 2003; Guba & Lincoln, 1994; Letourneau & Allen, 1999).

Foulkes (1946a) was a meticulous observer, who carefully listened, offered interventions (e.g., transference interpretations), and observed what then happened in his psychotherapy groups, which he documented. By paying attention to transference and countertransference (see TextBox 3.6), Foulkes gained insight into the psyches of group members, into group dynamics, and into himself as a group psychotherapist (Ferro & França, 2024). After the end of each session, Foulkes wrote process notes.

TEXTBOX 3.5 WITHIN & BETWEEN-SUBJECT DESIGNS

In the between-subject design, responses (measurements) are taken from participants, who have been allocated into two (or more) separate groups. So, you do not compare participants of the same group with each other, as you would do in a within-subject design.

Note that researchers should no longer refer to research participants as "subjects" in contexts other than research design, according to the British Psychological Society (BPS). Referring to a person who provides data for research as a "participant" has replaced the term "subject", because "subject" is viewed as portraying people as passive. While the extent of active "participation" in the research varies, using the term "participant" acknowledges her/his autonomy and agency, and the right to withdraw. In research, a participant's experience is a valuable additional source of information, possibly enriching the interpretation of findings (BPS, 2021, p. 5).

TEXTBOX 3.6 TRANSFERENCE & COUNTERTRANSFERENCE

In the transference, something from the client's past (emotions, relationship patterns, phantasies, and attributes arising from childhood) is unconsciously transferred to the psychoanalyst, who may then identify with these transferences. When a clinician experiences what clients feel (countertransference), s/he gains insight into their inner worlds. Another meaning of countertransference is that these feelings belong to the therapist (Schlapobersky, 2016). See also Appendix 1.

Taken together, he studied a "new culture", namely that of the small group. His method entailed traces of (ethnographic) participant observation in the widest possible sense when using the description in TextBox 3.7.

For Foulkes, the group was an organism. If we accept that the group is both a field and a living organism, and that ethnography is the systematic description of a single contemporary culture, resulting from ethnographic fieldwork (Wood, 1997, p. 157), and that listening is an important aspect of it (Forsey, 2010), and that sometimes one has to remove people from their natural surroundings in order to comprehend what is really going on behind the scenes (Trow, 1957, p. 34), and that Foulkes studied a new culture (that of a small group), then the kind of observation Foulkes engaged in, has something in common with participant observation as employed in cultural anthropology.

TEXTBOX 3.7 PARTICIPANT OBSERVATION & ETHNOGRAPHY

Participant observation is an aspect of ethnography, a research method that has a long tradition in cultural anthropology. According to Gans (1999), ethnographic observation can provide detailed and authentic information, allowing researchers to observe what people do (p. 541). Ethnography is the systematic description of a single contemporary culture, often through ethnographic fieldwork (Wood, 1997, p. 157).

The anthropologist Malinowski conducted extensive fieldwork in the Trobriand Islands. He observed Indigenous cultures by living among them and then comparing their way of life with Western cultures. Malinowski (1948) subscribed to a Positivist view of the world, which is evident in Magic, Science and Religion and Other Essays. Malinowski (1947) frequently referred to "science" in Freedom and Civilization, regarding ethnography as a scientific method. His derogatory use of language is like Comte's (see Chapter 1). Calling Indigenous people and cultures "primitive", for example, "the household is the first school where the young primitive learns his language" (p. 233), Malinowski categorized these "primitives" further into the "lowest primitive". The pygmy tribes in Africa and Indonesia, and Australian Aborigines belonged to this sub-category (pp. 277–278). One could say that he exploited "primitives", because his research was not for their benefit. He himself and Western societies profited from his writing on Indigenous peoples. Through his use of language, they became positioned as inferior when compared to "civilized" Western people.

Anthropology, Ethnography & Their Use in Group Analytic Research

Anthropology and ethnography have changed over time. At one point, the former was a comparative, nomothetic discipline in Britain (Leach, 1961), until it started to focus on producing impeccably detailed historical ethnographies of particular people (Ingold, 2008, p. 76). In the social sciences, ethnomethodology is probably the closest and most fruitful descendant of Husserl. It was developed and established by Garfinkel (1967/1984) as a field of inquiry in sociology.

Starting with Freud, Jung, and discussions between Ernest Jones and Malinowski, anthropology and psychoanalysis came together after World War II. Ethnomethodology was also used by group analytic researchers but transformed into "Ethnopsychoanalysis". It refers to the combination of ethnography and psychoanalysis as employed in group analysis. This methodology regards groups as a main phenomenon of culture (Bosse, 1993, p. 228).

Group analytic knowledge and method have been acknowledged in anthropology and vice versa. Several group analytic psychotherapists (Azu-Okeke, 1993; Bosse, 1993b; Ferrante, 1993; Pisani, 1993; Usundivaras, 1993) used anthropology and ethnography for their research.

Referring to Sigmund Freud, Bosse (1993a) suggested that anthropological knowledge, theory, and/or methods enable group analysts to unveil the inner cultural objects of a group or person. An interesting example of Ethnopsychoanalysis can be found in Rohr (1993), who researched the Churches in Ecuador. Unfortunately, she did not explain the method theoretically. Her applied method involved interpretation. She used her countertransference reactions as a basis for understanding the foreign. Her case study resembles a "detective story" (Bosse, 1993a), in which what was previously hidden is unveiled. The clinical case study (TextBox 3.8) belongs to the category of non-experimental designs. Case studies do have their place in psychotherapy research. Unfortunately, inappropriate use of statistical techniques with single cases resulted in the erroneous view that single case studies cannot be carried out in psychotherapy research, Kächele et al. (2009) pointed out. They argued that we need specimen cases in psychoanalytic research. I would apply the same argument to group analytic research, suggesting that group case studies are needed. If a database were created, where longitudinal case studies were recorded, we would gain new insight into group dynamics and processes, as they develop and influence the group and its members over time.

Freud (1900) published his first "scientific" observations and case studies over a century ago. Clinical case studies have generated a rich knowledge base for psychoanalysis and group analytic psychotherapy. It may surprise you, because people tend to hide failure due to shame, but descriptions of failed cases are quite useful (TextBox 3.9). Freud himself did not shy away from publishing unsuccessful cases and one can learn from his case study of Dora. If "unsuccessful" treatment groups, failed cases, were more frequently published, researchers could analyze these data. This may advance our knowledge and understanding of groups. After all, experimental studies do have limitations, so, other methods are additionally needed. Greene (2002) highlighted an ongoing criticism of psychotherapy outcome studies, which pertains to their limited practical utility. Comparison studies and RCTs only show that a significant change has occurred. They do not tell us anything about the "how" and "why" therapeutic change happened. Even though "mediators" have been included in the data analyses to increase understanding of how change happens, quantitative psychotherapy studies still have their limitations.

TEXTBOX 3.8 THE CASE STUDY & SINGLE CASE DESIGN

A clinical case study is based on a therapist's clinical notes that are then used to write a detailed case report. Initially, all research studies were case studies, because no other methods of inquiry were available (see Flyvbjerg, 2006 for critique). Group members must be anonymized. But if their interactions are obscured too much, the group no longer is an actual exemplar.

According to McLeod et al. (2015), from the 1920s onwards psychological tests were used. Survey questionnaires and psychological experiments did not emerge until the 1930s. Case studies gradually paved the way for increasingly sophisticated psychotherapy research to be developed and applied. Rating scales, questionnaires, projective tests (e.g. Rorschach), and audio and video recordings enabled new ways of thinking about the psychotherapy process.

From the 1960s, a single case (single subject) research design was adopted. Over the coming years, researchers carried out case studies based on multiple sources of information (session recordings, completed questionnaires by patients and therapists, follow-up interviews). This made findings more reliable and valid. In the 1990s, Dan Fishman (2013) and others advocated building up a large database of pragmatic case studies. Subsequently, psychotherapists reports became comprehensive and rigorous.

In the early 2000s, adjudicated case studies emerged. A team of researchers analyzed case material independently and compared their conclusions to arrive at an agreed interpretation of the case (quasi-judicial procedure). Case studies are guided by several aspects (paying careful attention to ethical issues, creating a rich data set based on multiple information, data offering information on the psychotherapy context, using a systematic approach and standard format for the write-up) (see Fishman et al., 2016). Single case study designs should not be confused with case studies. Properly designed, they can be used for assessing causal relationships between interventions and outcome. Internal and external validity is strong, if the study design incorporates randomization and multiple participants (Lobo et al., 2018). Single case study methodology can address outcome research and theory-building questions (how can the group process in this short-term group be used to test/refine existing theoretical models?), pragmatic questions (what techniques did the conductor use that contributed to the eventual outcome?), and narrative/experiential questions (how did the group members/conductor feel?) (McLeod et al., 2015, p. 208).

TEXTBOX 3.9 CASE STUDIES OF FAILED CASES

The therapy outcome literature has been biased, because only "successful" treatment studies were published for a long time. Goldberg's (2012) investigation of failed cases in psychoanalysis and psychotherapy is informative. Freud (1905) himself published a failed case, that of 18-year-old Dora, to demonstrate the techniques (interpretation, dream analysis) he used.

The Two Northfield Experiments That Were Not Experiments

Foulkes also studied patients in large groups as part of the "Northfield Experiments". Under the leadership of the psychoanalyst Main (1946), Northfield Hospital started the therapeutic community movement (Srinath et al., 2011). Northfield was a military hospital where practical daily needs had to be met (De Maré, 1983). Harrison (2000) noted that those psychoanalysts in the British Army, who were more socially and group-oriented, were facing practical issues which demanded psychoanalytically informed solutions. None of them was trained as a group psychotherapist. So, initially they used techniques that they were familiar with.

As part of these "Experiments", the psychiatrists Bion, John Rickman, and Foulkes (1936), were also asked to treat soldiers suffering from psychoneurosis (Harrison, 2018; Jones, 1952, 2004). The First Northfield Experiment began in 1943. Initially, soldiers from military bases in Britain were treated at Northfield. Later, soldiers from active combat duty in France and Germany, and prisoners of war, arrived. Bion (1946), together with Rickman, led the First Northfield Experiment. Soldiers were treated in groups. Their purpose was the full participation of all its members, including the doctors, and their eventual aim was the re-socialization of traumatized soldiers into society (Rapoport, 1960; Srinath, 2011). The Northfield Experiments were regarded as a landmark in the evolution of group analytic psychotherapy and the therapeutic community movement (Harrison, 2018).

Too many soldiers had been traumatized during World War II to be treated individually. Hence, the large group arose as a treatment modality for severe cases. Psychoanalysis provided the theoretical structure for treatment (Harrison & Clark, 1992), because doctors had limited understanding of trauma. Individual therapies prevailed even when social approaches were emphasized. Some techniques were unconventional (TextBox 3.10) and ethically dubious.

TEXTBOX 3.10 UNORTHODOX TECHNIQUES

The psychoanalyst Tom Main is said to have used "compulsory mourning" for traumatized tank commanders. Since they were too numbed by loss, they were confined alone in a darkened room for three days, with one hour of daylight, one hour of electric light, and a diet of bread and water. Apparently, this cruel technique enabled them to release repressed emotions, which were responsible for their neuroses (Harrison & Clark, 1992).

Researchers differentiate between outcome and process research. The distinction seems blurred at Northfield. Psychotherapy groups were formed solely out of necessity. Bion (1946, 1948a,b) used a group-as-a-whole approach, was interested in the analytic field of the group, and focused on the "here and now", in his technique (Harrison, 2018). Peer group discussions were also novel. Psychiatrists openly discussed treatment difficulties and how groups operated. Various groups were run on a weekly basis for nearly one year (Harrison, 2000).

De Maré (1985) noted that the First Experiment ended due to a cultural clash with the military authorities. Bion's controversial idea of equality was met with strong opposition by the military (Trist, 1985). Superiors felt threatened when patients challenged the existing power hierarchy of the military and of psychiatry. Liberal ideas, where everybody would be given the same rights (patients/soldiers and doctors/superiors were equals), would have resulted in the elimination of the sharp separation within the military hierarchy. Chaos in the hospital cinema hall, eventually, led to the abrupt termination of the First Northfield Experiment (Jones, 2004).

According to Harrison and Clark (1992), organizational changes were made during the Second Northfield Experiment. Moreover, young and more active patients arrived. Foulkes (1948) described the conditions in the hospital as too difficult to advance therapeutic practices. Foulkes treated one soldier with intensive individual and group therapy for six months, who benefited greatly (Harrison & Clark, 1992). Various types of groups (closed therapy groups, open meetings, psychodrama, work groups, and leisure groups) were facilitated. The success of the Second Experiment was due to more attention being paid to the wider community. Furthermore, staff were more involved, and the pace was slower (Bridger, 1990).

One could say that Northfield was a *research setting*, almost like an artificial *laboratory,* in which psychiatrists and psychoanalysts experimented with both patients and staff. Ethically dubious from a contemporary perspective, their intentions were nevertheless benevolent. Psychoanalysts wanted to cure severely ill patients. However, the label "Northfield Experiments" is misleading, because they were not typical experiments, as espoused by the nomothetic paradigm. They could not even be described as a "within-subject, non-experimental design" (TextBox 3.11).

Such a design necessitates that psychotherapists systematically gather information on the same patients in the hospital setting. It is very unlikely that this happened, considering the quick turnover of patients, the chaotic conditions, and the unpredictable circumstances at that time. Therefore, Foulkes, and other psychotherapists were *not* carrying out *experiments*, because the "Northfield Experiment" lacked the essential characteristics of an experiment. One advantage of experiments and experimental studies is that these methods enable group analytic researchers to exert a great deal of control over the "independent variable" (e.g. provision of group analytic psychotherapy). Researchers can then observe the effect that this manipulation (e.g. different types of therapy) has on the patients' war neuroses (dependent variable). However, at Northfield, psychiatrists/psychotherapists did not control variables. No comparison group was used either. Comparison groups can, for example, demonstrate that two or more variables are causally related (Frankfort-Nachmias & Nachmias, 1996). Hence, the Northfield Experiments are not experiments. Nevertheless, psychotherapists carried out research, if we use the simplest definition of research "go about searching" (Etymonline, 2022a). They were searching for clinical methods that could cure traumatized patients. So, it could be viewed as explorative research.

TEXTBOX 3.11 NON-EXPERIMENTAL, QUASI-EXPERIMENTAL & EXPERIMENTAL RESEARCH DESIGNS

Quasi-experimental designs are not as preoccupied, as experiments, with proving causality. Often, they can point to causal pathways. Evaluation research that does not use RTCs and tends to be quasi-experimental (Robinson & Seale, 2018). Quantitative researchers may use cross-sectional studies, longitudinal studies, cohort studies, case-control studies, surveys, RCTs, systematic reviews, and meta-analysis. RCTs provide much more robust evidence than non-experimental studies, such as the case study (see Chapter 4). Quantitative researchers are interested in causality. Typically, they use experimental manipulation and observe its impact on the dependent variable (e.g. well-being). They deliberately alter the levels (values) of the variable they expect to be causal, that is, the independent variable (e.g. medication abuse). This is called "manipulating the variable" in research language (Harris, 1994). It enables researchers to study the impact of medication abuse on well-being, for example. According to Robinson and Seale (2018, p. 106), cross-sectional studies take a snapshot in time, where researchers select a group of people, they are interested in, and gather data on them only at that point in time. It can be used to find out how prevalent a phenomenon is (e.g. mental health problems). However, cross-sectional studies are not good in establishing causality, because the time order of events cannot be ascertained. Longitudinal studies, such as cohort studies (Glenn, 2005), panel studies, and RCTs, take place over several weeks, months, or years. They rely on different designs, such as surveys, or the collection of observations on a sample of people, documents, or artifacts, from some people on at least two points in time (Caruana et al., 2015). Panel and cohort studies (the British Household Panel Survey) use a specific group of participants to draw inferences from (see Dudley & Stenbeck, 1988). Participants must complete them over many years. Hence, drop out is likely (see also Morgan & Lee, 2021). Longitudinal studies are often quantitative, examine change over time, and can establish a causal pathway. However, they are costly. Loss to follow-up, and people's tendency to change their behavior, may make the sample less representative (Robinson & Seale, 2018).

Research Designs, Outcome & Process Research

A main worry pertaining to research designs is how well they can answer the research question and yield accurate results. Choosing the correct research design is absolutely crucial. For example, when researchers want to establish causality (X causes Y, groups result in sad people feeling happy), they must use an experimental design, and control for the influences of interfering variables. Experimental, quasi-experimental, and non-experimental designs have been used in group analytic psychotherapy research (Karterud, 2001, 2015, 2024; Lorentzen, 2014).

Evaluation research looks at how well studies have achieved what they sat out to achieve. When a researcher tries to assess whether group analytic psychotherapy has been effective, an experimental design must always be used for this type of inquiry. It is called "outcome research". It refers to results that have been accrued from the examination of group members on any number of variables, for example, reduction in mental health symptoms (Barlow, 2014, p. 5). Typically, outcome research relies on RCTs, in which clients are randomly put into at least two different groups. For example, clients might receive either group analytic therapy, or medication, for treating their depression. Researchers control the independent treatment variables (therapy, medication), and assess their impact on depression, by using measures (e.g., Beck's depression inventory, Beck & Brown, 1996).

When carrying out an RCT to answer whether group analytic psychotherapy is clinically effective or efficacious (e.g. for treating borderline personality disorder), it is important not to confuse efficacy with clinical effectiveness (Evans et al., 1998). Normally, a research question is first tested under one condition and then tested under the other. The usual direction is from efficacy to effectiveness (Barkham & Margison, 2007). Effectiveness refers to a treatment's ability to produce clinically meaningful changes (Abernethy, 2015). When results are clinically significant, a treatment has been demonstrated to work in clinical practice.

This differs from efficacy. Group analytic psychotherapy (treatment) is efficacious, if it either outperforms an alternative treatment, a placebo (no treatment), or a control group. Or, if it is equivalent to a treatment that is already established as efficacious. Furthermore, results that support its efficacy must be obtained by two independent research labs (Abernethy, 2015).

Observational studies belong to the family of non-experimental designs. Researchers might watch naturally occurring behavior (e.g., aggression) or observe another variable of interest (e.g., scapegoating), without attempting to intervene (manipulating the variable). Through accurate observation and detailed descriptions of when, how, and why, aggression, or scapegoating, have occurred in the group, researchers gain insight into aggressive or scapegoating behavior. These data are commonly referred to as "real-world evidence", because the results reflect what normal behavior may look like. Researchers may also gain insight into everyday clinical practice when observing commonly offered treatment (Bouvier & Parcher, 2023).

Additionally, observational data could offer beneficial information with regard to treatment. For example, researchers could compare two treatments, such as the use of psychoeducation and unstructured analytic group psychotherapy. In their observations, they could pay attention to fatigue, lethargy, withdrawal, and so forth. However, when group members are not randomized and many characteristics between the members of the two treatment groups vary, researchers cannot claim that one treatment has performed better than the other.

Statistical approaches can be used to estimate treatment effects. It is crucial to predefine relevant confounders (factors that can introduce bias, such as gender, age, and ethnicity). And consider these in the data analysis (Bouvier & Parcher, 2023). Failure to adjust for the confounding variable will lead to wrong conclusions (MacKinnon, 2011). A confounder is a third variable (confounding variable). It affects the variables of interest and makes them seem related when they are not (Bhandari, 2022). But a confounding variable is not a causal sequence. It differs from a moderating variable, because the relation of X to Y may not differ across values of the confounding variable.

Group analytic process research focuses on what is happening in the group (Ballhausen-Scharf & Rudnitzki, 2000). Process research has been defined as the shared examination of members' relationships in all respects relevant to their interdependence. It often utilizes measures to capture the moment-to-moment events in the group (Barlow, 2014, p. 5).

In her discussion, Barlow (2014) has alluded to the importance of moderators and mediators. Including moderators and mediators, which allows group analytic researchers to go beyond studying a simple relationship between two variables. Moderators and mediators are third variables. Obviously, with three variables, the number of possible relations among the variables increases substantially (MacKinnon, 2011). They enable a more comprehensive understanding and should be considered when examining complex causal, and correlational, relationships. Unsurprisingly, the role of mediators and moderators has become crucial to group process and outcome research (Greene, 2012).

Bhandari (2022) referred to a mediator variable as a "go-between". This variable explains the process through which two variables are related. A moderator variable acts upon the relationship between two variables. While moderators are variables that interact with an independent variable and affect the strength and direction of a dependent variable, mediators are specific, causal agents that result in change (Barlow, 2014, p. 5).

In other words, a moderator is a quantitative, or qualitative, variable that changes the strength/direction of the relationship between the independent (predictor) and dependent variables. Age, gender, race, religion, health status, and so forth are moderators. To be classed as a moderator variable, a significant ($p > .05$) statistical interaction between the predictor and moderator variables must exist (King, 2013).

Baron and Kenny (1986) discussed group level mediator constructs (role conflict, norm, Groupthink, cohesiveness). Whereas research oriented toward mediators is more interested in the mechanisms, moderator research typically has a greater interest in predictor variables. It is important to select moderators that not only improve predictive power, but also say something about the processes underlying therapeutic technique.

Other Relevant Research Concepts

When researchers worry whether they are measuring what they intend to measure, they are concerned about the "validity" of their study. According to Timulak (2015), validity comprises internal, external, construct, and statistical conclusion, validity. Let us use the "Northfield Experiments" to tease out the different forms of validity.

Internal validity refers to how certain group analysts could have been in making causal claims about the soldiers "greatly" improving. It is related to the adequacy of the research design they relied on to prove causality. As discussed above, Foulkes, and others, did not carry out experimental studies. Therefore, they cannot state that their results were valid.

External validity involves generalization (Timulak, 2015). It refers to the extent to which researchers can generalize from their "sample" (hospitalized soldiers suffering from war neuroses) to every soldier (the entire population of soldiers).

The Northfield studies were not externally valid due to the non-experimental nature of the research. If Foulkes had wanted to experimentally research "war neuroses", the independent variable (different types of groups) should have been well delineated.

Unlike traditional quantitative research, which relies on questionnaires, Foulkes used a hypothesized construct (war neurosis) and "measured" it through observation. In questionnaire design, when items are a very good representation of the hypothesized construct (depression), the "construct validity" of the questionnaire will be high.

Statistics are a crucial part of quantitative research, but analytic training courses do not commonly teach statistics. Statistical techniques/tests enable researchers to manipulate variables and to reject, or not, the Null Hypothesis. (Statistics are discussed in Chapter 4/Appendix 4). Psychotherapists at Northfield did not use any statistical techniques. Therefore, it is unknown whether their drawn conclusions are supported by statistical calculations. Other aspects also pose a threat to the validity of results and the conclusion drawn from them. Even if experimental studies had been carried out, factors, other than group treatment, could have resulted in the soldiers' improved mental health. These "confounders" could have caused a spurious association (effect). When this happens, the results are distorted. Therefore, all possible confounders must be identified. Frankfort-Nachmias and Nachmias (1996) suggest techniques to reduce the impact of confounders: restricting the treatment group to include only participants with the same potential for confounders. For example, because sex and age are common confounders, selecting only young females might reduce spurious effects (Simkus, 2023).

Results must also be reliable. Reliability refers to consistency. Other researchers should get the same results under the same conditions when repeating a study (Dawson, 2002). Obviously, the "Northfield Experiments" could not be repeated nowadays. So, it cannot be established whether the results were reliable.

In addition to the lack of validity and reliability, the Northfield Experiments are morally and ethically questionable. Ethics, which belongs to axiology, forms a crucial aspect of any research. Axiology (from the Greek "axia", worthiness, value) is a branch of philosophy, which is concerned with theories about value (Honderich, 1995). Research ethics, "the moral principles guiding research from its inception through to completion, and publication of results" (BPS, 2021), includes respect for the autonomy, privacy, and dignity, of individuals, groups, and communities. Scientific integrity, social responsibility, maximizing benefit, and minimizing harm, are equally important (p. 5).

Studies require ethical approval nowadays and researchers must follow rigorous procedures. This includes devising a participant information sheet, which summarizes details of the study so that participants can give their informed consent to take part. Each participant must sign a consent form before participating in any study (BPS, 2021). Ethics was not an issue at Northfield hospital. Many soldiers did not even know why they were there (Harrison, 2000). However, these were exceptional circumstances. In 1945, almost 1% of all military personnel could no longer perform active duty (Mayne, 1972), because soldiers were suffering from a psychiatric disorder.

Chapter Summary

Research was important to pioneers of group analytic psychotherapy. They have used different techniques to study small and large "therapy" groups. Their methodology would neither be accepted as scientific nor as ethical nowadays. While rigorous group analytic research should inform clinical practice, research should also be relevant to group members, psychotherapists, and societies. Group analytic researchers have carried out qualitative case studies and Ethnopsychoanalysis, which are as important as quantitative methods. Creating databases and recording longitudinal group case studies would allow us to gain more insight into small groups. While studies have demonstrated that group psychotherapy is effective, fewer group analytic studies have been carried out to demonstrate that it works, how it works, and why it works. Process research has been neglected, and diverse methods are needed to study the complexity of group analytic groups.

4

DIFFRACTION & QUANTITATIVE METHODS

Combining Quantitative Methods in Group Analytic Research with AI

Abstract

How to do a meta-analysis, systematic review, and a randomized controlled trial, are described. By using a diffractive methodology, naïve Realism and positivist epistemology are viewed in a different light, I suggest. Artificial Intelligence (AI) tools are integrated into the presented methods and techniques. Benefits and disadvantages of AI are discussed. I also explain instrumentation and operationalization. Although statistics are an integral part of quantitative methods, they are not integral to group analysis. To spark interest in statistics, an account of a group analyst's engagement with statistics is appended (Appendix 4).

Introduction

"Gold standards" determine which methods researchers should use. Meta-analysis is at the top of the traditional evidence pyramid, followed by systematic reviews and randomized controlled trials (RCTs), which are the gold standard even in psychotherapy research (Philips & Falkenström, 2021). Systematic reviews and meta-analyses can provide clarity on the effectiveness of an intervention, determine whether an effect is constant across studies, and discover what future studies are required to demonstrate effects, as explained by Davis et al. (2014). They have described meta-analysis as a statistical technique, which is used to combine this information to give an overall estimate of the effect of a population (p. 1).

When evidence-based practice (EBP) became popular in the 1990s, the importance of research syntheses was acknowledged (Evans & Benefield, 2001). Simply put, a research synthesis differs from the traditional, narrative literature review by employing very rigorous techniques (Chong & Plonsky, 2024). The Cochrane and Campbell Collaboratives pioneered the methodology of the systematic review. It became one of the first explicitly recognized forms of literature review in the late 20th century (Callahan, 2014). Typically, but not always, systematic

DOI:10.4324/9781003609544-7

literature reviews are based on primary empirical studies (Whittemore & Knafl, 2005). These types of review can make substantive contributions to knowledge (Siddaway et al., 2019).

Snyder (2019, 2023) offers useful guidance on literature reviews. One purpose of modern literature reviews is to summarize the current knowledge on a topic in an objective manner, based on previously published research, as explained by Cronin et al. (2008). According to Maxwell (2006), the literature review is an essential tool "any researcher must learn to use competently" (p. 30). Historically, literature reviews were mainly narrative in nature, often written to support an author's argument (Tranfield et al., 2003), and resembled a conceptual framework (Callahan, 2010). More recently, Grant and Booth (2009) identified 14 different types, and Sutton et al.'s (2019) *Literature Review Family* includes 48 types of literature reviews. Helpfully, Byrne (2016) suggests that subtypes can be distinguished depending on the methods they employ for the literature search, appraisal, synthesis, and analysis.

Many funding decisions are based on systematic reviews (Booth et al., 2022), which have been defined by Davis et al. (2014, p. 1) as the process of systematically locating and collating all available information on an effect. Systematic reviews that assess the effectiveness of an intervention, or therapy, are by far the most common forms of reviews, as Munn et al. (2018) point out.

Blackmore et al.'s (2009, 2012) systematic review is still one of the most comprehensive reviews of the effectiveness/efficacy of Group Analysis and analytic group psychotherapy.

Systematic reviews are often based on RCTs. Like other quantitative methods, they assume a reality that is independent of the researcher and insist on establishing the truth. Results are regarded as certain. However, when adopting a diffractive methodology, and the quantitative approach is read attentively through the Artificial Intelligence (AI) approach (Bozalek & Murris, 2022), assumptions about reality, truth, and certainty are questionable.

AI has become popular in many areas. McCarthy (2006) had suggested that scientists work on natural language processing (NLP), neural networks, machine learning (ML), abstract concepts, reasoning, and creativity, to develop an AI approach. While the symbolic approach in AI focused on developing machines and programs that were capable of thinking, the connectionist approach centered on imitating brain structures (Possati, 2021). The symbolic AI paradigm was dominant until the mid-1990s. It was instrumental in developing symbolic programming languages, agents, and multi-agent systems. Subsequently, AI researchers developed methods and statistical techniques to address uncertainty. Nowadays the integration of the symbolic and connectionist approaches has been advocated (Xiong et al., 2024).

AI connectionism, also known as parallel distributed processing, refers to approaches that model mental and behavioral phenomena (Smolensky, 1987). Processes are viewed as interconnected and complex systems that can be modeled. Information is processed simultaneously in the connectionist AI paradigm, where a system learns by being exposed to data. Examples of the connectionist approach include artificial neural networks, deep learning models, and recurrent neural networks (RNNs). Combining connectionist and symbolic AI paradigms can harness the strength of both approaches (Wang, 2024). Furthermore, the combination of AI, virtual reality (VR), and virtual environments (VE) has given rise to "intelligent virtual environments" (Luck & Aylett, 2000). This has implications for reality and autonomy.

From a realist perspective, the environment is separate from the individual and functions autonomously, independently. In the VE, a person can only perceive an aspect of the environment (reality) and is autonomous only to a certain extent. It is the designer who controls the environment and the agents in it and does not distinguish between the two (Heim, 1993). People associate VR mainly with computers, and various forms of AI, because computers are the only means of creating VR. Like Pragmatism, an AI approach is interested in what works now. Both regard an approach as beneficial until a better one comes along (Blank & Barnes, 1998, p. 2).

Although the quantitative approach is favored, it is not without flaws. When using a diffractive methodology, which consists of reading the quantitative approach attentively through an AI approach (Bozalek & Murris, 2022), a virtual quantitative approach becomes a possibility. Modifications can then be made to quantitative methods by integrating AI tools to overcome some of their limitations, even though these tools are not commonly used by group analytic researchers.

In what follows, AI tools will be integrated into the methods and techniques presented. These include descriptions of how to do a meta-analysis, systematic review, and RCT. I will also explain instrumentation and operationalization. Statistics are an integral part of quantitative and AI methodologies. However, they are not taught on group analytic training programs. To spark interest, an account of a group analyst's journey to master basic statistics is appended (Appendix 4).

Artificial Intelligence Algorithms Dis/Advantages & Ethical Issues

AI refers to the development and application of computer systems, which can carry out tasks that typically require human intelligence (Goraga, 2023). Simple AI tools, such as search engines are used by Google Scholar. Google Workspace is a suite of productivity tools, including Google Docs, Sheets, Slides, etc. (Shukla, 2023).

More complex areas include NLP, a branch of AI (Goraga, 2023). Using natural language, NLP focuses on the interactions between computers and humans. In the Glossary, Shukla (2023) also explains ML, a subset of AI. It can learn from experience and improve its capability without having to be programmed explicitly to do so. Neural networks are ML algorithms, which are modeled according to the structure and functioning of the human brain. One subset of ML is deep learning, involving natural neural networks with multiple layers. These allow for more complex learning and decision-making (Shukla, 2023).

In the social sciences, AI tools have recently been applied. They can automate repetitive tasks, enabling researchers to conduct certain research aspects more efficiently in terms of time and costs (Goraga, 2023). However, AI has mainly been used in fields other than psychotherapy research. Furthermore, while many novel research directions have been explored, a unified perspective on AI's role in social science research is lacking. This must be borne in mind when considering the application of AI.

A recent review by Xu et al. (2024) notes that large language models (LLMs) (e.g. ChatGPT, Open AI, GPT-4) have demonstrated the enormous possibilities of AI. Many studies have explored the combination of traditional methods and AI (see Xu et al., 2024 for references):

Evidence indicates AI's superior performance for literature searches and review, proposing questions and hypotheses, analyzing data, and assisting with writing and survey research. Some researchers have employed LLMs for labeling, or categorizing, texts according to predefined categories. LLMs can interact directly through text inputs instead of requiring complex codes/commands. So, they are more user-friendly. While their use for hypothesis generation is promising (but has limitations), their ability to identify knowledge gaps, and to establish connections between seemingly unrelated ideas, is useful.

Goraga (2023) discusses how AI techniques can be employed in quantitative methodologies, such as meta-analyses and systematic reviews, and in experimental designs. They may improve the accuracy and efficiency of data analyses.

AI algorithms can be used to examine metadata (information about sources, such as the authors, dates of publication, and subject tags) and doing the data analysis (leveraging RNNs, clustering and association rule miming, streamlining the explorative data analysis by handling missing values, normalizing variables, identifying outliers, discovering hidden patterns and relationships) (Ibid.)

Xu et al. (2024) found that the additional use of an "AI research assistant", which is based on LLMs to automate simple, but labor intense tasks, can enhance the external validity and comparability of experimental studies. Such an assistant can find relevant papers without perfect keyword match, summarize main findings, and extract crucial information from papers.

Undeniably, AI and its emerging technology (4th Industrial Revolution, 4IR or industry 4.0) have several advantages (e.g. increased productivity, medical breakthroughs, predictive abilities to explore new developments, increased security), particularly, for the Global North (Fourie, 2020). However, there are several caveats attached. They are discussed by Xu et al. (2024), Goraga (2023), Shukla (2023), Liu (2015), and others:

Directly relying on LLMs for literature recommendations and summarization is problematic, because unreliable information may be generated. LLMs are not proficient in numerical analysis. Almost all LLMs struggle with conversational data, i.e., having difficulty understanding the subtle and non-conventional language of expert taxonomies. Therefore, they may fabricate or provide incorrect information (Choudhary, 2024). Moreover, they are highly sensitive to the instruction given by the user. Even though they can act as believable proxies of human behavior (be subjects in the experiment, because they are capable of simulating responses and behaviors resembling those of humans), their utility is still limited (Schulhoff, 2025). Complex tasks seem to exceed the scope of LLMs at present. Further drawbacks include algorithmic bias, high computational cost, and difficulties in fine-tuning for specific tasks (Xu et al., 2024). Since the reliability and authenticity of generated text must be verified, additional costs for validation must also be considered when using these models. For survey research, the above authors suggest a hybrid approach. They do not recommend that LLMs should completely replace traditional sampling methods but suggest that LLMs could potentially be used in simulating population responses to assist in survey design. It is noteworthy that LLM agents seem to be exhibiting cognitive, logical reasoning, and linguistic capabilities on par with (or even surpassing those of) humans, along with unique behavioral characteristics. Whether AI can replace humans in conducting experiments and surveys, remains unknown.

Fourie (2020) discusses ethical issues regarding equality, racism, discrimination, and if humans are attempting to play God when using supercomputers and robotics. Concerns about the (im)possibility to decolonize AI with regard to its inherent racial biases and prioritization of Western ways of knowing, and living, have been discussed by Adams (2021). For example, whether AI in Africa will continue to entrench a Western hegemony and dominance of Western epistemologies. One might agree with Benjamin (2019) and Zembylas (2023) that the implementation of AI in facial recognition and surveillance is a racializing practice.

Mokoena (2024) notes that data could be regarded as a commodity that is utilized for economic growth. Hence, terms such as "data colonialism", "data capitalism", and "algorithmic coloniality" have been used. "Algorithmic coloniality", refers to how algorithms affect resource allocation, human behavior, and systems, across societies (Mohamed et al., 2020). It manifests in making algorithmic decisions and in altering geopolitical power dynamics. Indigenous knowledge and ethical value systems may also be excluded (Brokensha et al., 2023). This could result in an "AI nationalism" (Spence, 2019), if the voices of the Global South are absent at international conferences (Hogarth, 2018; Mackereth, 2021).

From a group perspective, it is interesting is that communities constituted by AI agents exhibit nascent behaviors similar to those occurring in human societies (Park et al., 2023). This presents an opportunity to re-evaluate beliefs that human behavior possesses unique social characteristics.

Pyramid of Evidence

Meta-analysis is at the top of the traditional evidence pyramid (see Figure 4.1), followed by systematic reviews, and RCTs (see Chapter 3), which are the gold standard even in psychotherapy research (Philips & Falkenstrőm, 2021).

Several RCTs (see Burlingame & Strauss, 2021; Lorentzen, et al., 2018), meta-analyses (e.g. Barkowski et al., 2020; Burlingame et al., 2018; Alldredge et al., 2021; Schwartze et al., 2019), and systematic reviews (Andrews et al., 2024; Diamond et al., 2025; Twomey & Dowling, 2025) have been carried out in group and individual psychotherapy research. This kind of research has contributed to group psychotherapy being more widely recognized (see Whittingham et al., 2021).

According to NICE (2024b, para. 1), meta-analysis is a method that combines "results from several studies, investigating the same test, treatment, or other intervention, to estimate the overall effect of the treatment". Over the past 30 years, 11 meta-analyses have been carried out (Rosendahl et al., 2021). Meta-analytic results have demonstrated that group therapy is effective in comparison with nonactive treatment. It is equivalent in effectiveness to other active treatments for several mental disorders (see also Burlingame et al., 2016).

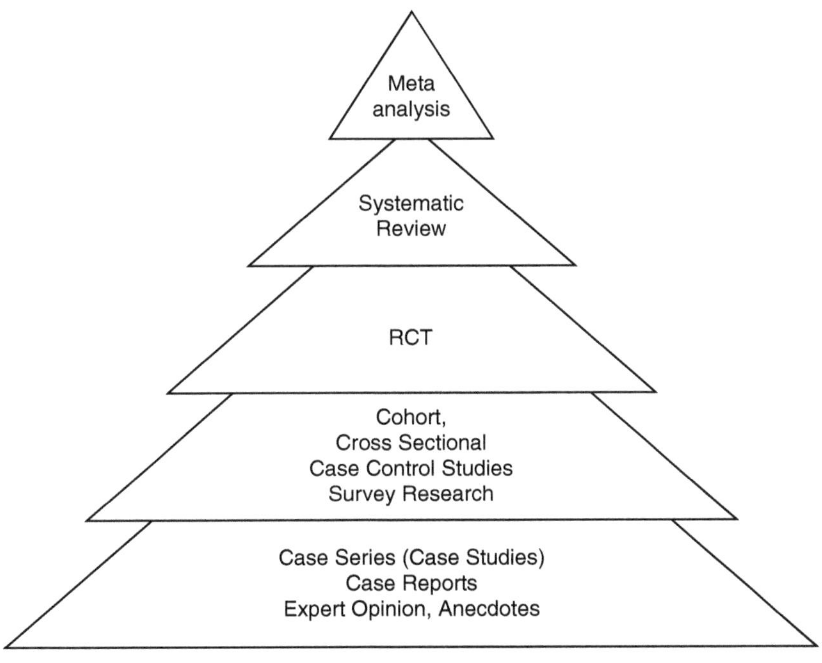

FIGURE 4.1 Evidence Pyramid, Adapted from Ingham-Broomfield (2016) and Wallace et al. (2022).

Furthermore, group therapy has been utilized for patients suffering from various medical conditions (neurological diseases, cancer, chronic pain). Rosendahl et al. (2021) emphasize the importance of conducting studies that include measures to identify, who will probably not form a therapeutic relationship with therapists, and is, therefore, unlikely to benefit from treatment.

In contrast to RCTs, which gather raw data, systematic reviews and meta-analyses use secondary (existing) data. A systematic review is a

> … review that summarizes the evidence on a clearly formulated review question according to a predefined protocol, using systematic and explicit methods to identify, select and appraise relevant studies, and to extract, analyze, collate and report their findings. It may or may not use statistical techniques.
>
> *(NICE, 2024c)*

Commonly, systematic reviews summarize different types of quantitative studies and employ a very robust approach to reviewing (Gregory & Denniss, 2018). In the field of psychotherapy, they often review the effectiveness/efficacy of psychotherapy and provide a critique of the selected literature, pointing out strengths and limitations (Fernandez, 2019).

Conducting Randomized Controlled Trials Differently

Carried out in the appropriate field, RCTs are valuable (Norcross & Wampold, 2019), because they can demonstrate the relationship between cause and effect. Inferences can be drawn that an intervention led to improvement in symptoms, and one gets an estimate of the effect (Deaton & Cartwright, 2018). Several aspects are important, such as the characteristics of the study population, the randomization method, the control, the analysis method, and all other phases/components of the trial (Saturni et al., 2014). In general, RCTs are designed to test therapeutic hypothesis under optimal conditions in the absence of confounding factors. Researchers are highly selective in choosing participants (Saturni et al., 2014).

RCTs demonstrate the "effectiveness" (Möller, 2011) and have been used in group analytic psychotherapy research (Lorentzen et al., 2013; Lorentzen, 2020). RCTs can balance unknown variables (Grossman & Mackenzie, 2005). Another advantage is that they rest on few assumptions, so they do not even require a normal distribution. The average treatment effect is commonly calculated and the mean is important (Deaton & Cartwright, 2018).

Before conducting an RCT, one of the first steps involves a statistical power calculation to establish how many participants are needed. This ensures that enough people are recruited so that statistically significant results can be detected. Researchers no longer use pen and paper, but rely on software for power calculations (see Appendix 4).

Simply put, researchers impose an intervention (group analytic psychotherapy) on some participants (experimental group), but not on others (comparison group). So, the groups differ. (Kaur and Li, 2023 also show how to design an RCT). To protect the external validity of the study so that results can be generalized to other populations and settings, researchers use "matching". It involves finding participants in the control group, who are very similar to those receiving therapy (the experimental group). To achieve this, participants with the same characteristics must be selected (e.g. severely depressed, White, single, British males, aged 40–50). They are then randomly allocated, either to the treatment, or to the control group (see

Nichol et al., 2010 for methods of randomization and pitfalls of RCTs). Several rating scales are normally administered and statistics applied to the scores. Statistics are also used for more complex issues. Thanks to advances in modern statistics, sampling theory, and experimental designs, inferences about the parameters of interest can be drawn and Bayesian statistics are also used (Msaouel et al., 2023).

Due to ethical and practical reasons, experiments are not used in group analytic psychotherapy research (de Vaus, 2008). Statistical methods (e.g. multivariate analysis) are alternatives. By statistically removing the differences between the two groups, the similarity on the specified characteristics (e.g. depressed people) is then guaranteed (p. 250). Or an intention to treat analysis is carried out when participants drop out of treatment before the end of the RCT (Grossman & Mackenzie, 2005). Finally, the results between the two groups are compared and researchers hope for statistically significant results., which show that the therapy had a positive effect. The CASP (Critical Appraisal Skills Program) and TRACT are used to assess the quality of an RCT. Moreover, Lee and Kang (2015) discuss how to evaluate RCTs.

In medicine (e.g. Mulder et al., 2018), RCTs are more straightforward than in psychotherapy research, where RCTs have resulted in debates (Wampold & Imel, 2015). Despite their benefits, RCTs have many limitations. Nonetheless, they are still the gold standard for psychotherapy research (Lilienfeld et al., 2018; Mohr, 2024). I will briefly outline their shortcomings so that the crux of the matter becomes clear with regard to Group Analysis.

RCTs create ethical challenges in terms of "un/blinding". When studying two groups, a group analytic treatment group, where additionally placebos are given to the participants (group 1), and a psychotropic drug is given to participants of the (therapy group 2, control group), participants do not know whether they have received a sugar pill (placebo), or an anti-depressant. They are "blind" to the treatment. If a participant has adverse reactions to the medication, unblinding must occur for the safety reasons. This involves telling the person, which treatment s/he has received (Bhatia et al., 2021), resulting in post-randomization bias.

More troubling is that RCTs are based on the assumption that the ingredient of the drug (treatment) is responsible for the achieved effect. Robust RCTs are based on double-blinding (neither the researcher, nor the participant, knows which treatment s/he receives).

Blinding minimizes bias, i.e., the risk that knowing which treatment one receives will influence a person (Bhatia et al., 2021). However, only single blinding is possible in group analytic psychotherapy, because the researcher knows, who receives which type of therapy, and participants often know this as well. Hence, the essential characteristic of the RCT design is violated (Tschuschke, 2016).

Moreover, RCTs are expensive, because they tend to run over many months, and it takes a long time to obtain results (Bouvier & Parcher, 2023).

Applying the Medical Model of Psychotherapy is also problematic for other reasons. Randomization of participants to intervention and control groups is neither reasonable nor possible. Firstly, even if participants have received the same diagnosis, they are not a homogenous group. Secondly, despite attempts to harmonize the Diagnostic Statistical Manual of Mental Disorders (DSM) and the International Classification of Diseases (ICD), the diagnoses from DSM-5 (APA, 2013) and ICD-11 (WHO, 2019) still differ (First et al., 2021). Thirdly, there is often an overlap in symptoms across diagnoses, so boundaries between them are fuzzy. Furthermore, diagnoses are neither valid, reliable, nor stable (Aarre, 2022). Therefore, there are no "pure" diagnostic groups of participants. Some have also pointed out that mental illness diagnoses are scientifically meaningless. Even the public does not seem to agree with all the assumptions professionals make about the diagnosis of mental disorders (Chao et al., 2022).

Fourthly, it is difficult to find participants who do not suffer from comorbidities, i.e. have multiple symptoms/diagnoses. In efficacy studies, researchers exclude such participants. That is why these trials have such low "ecological validity", i.e., they do not represent real life (Saturni et al., 2014). Research participants tend to have other difficulties in addition to mental health problems. Therefore, RCTs have insufficient "internal validity" due to the "contamination" of diagnosis with regard to homogeneity. In other words, cause and effect cannot be established.

Additionally, the control group cannot be controlled, as Tschuschke (2016) has pointed out. He has argued that a person lives 168 hours a week and attends the group analytic group (treatment) for 90 minutes. This leaves the participant uncontrolled for 166.5 hours (99%), which is another reason why internal validity is low. Furthermore, group analytic psychotherapists are not homogeneous group of people. No two psychotherapists conduct therapy in exactly the same manner, unless the treatment is manualized, e.g., Karterud's (2015) mentalization-based group analytic approach. Adherence to treatment manuals is rated and psychotherapists are not allowed to be flexible. However, unconscious motivations, desires, and nonverbal behavior cannot be manualized. Thus, the manualization of psychotherapy treatment cannot be fully achieved (Tschuschke, 2016).

Moreover, group analysts do not behave in exactly the same way with every patient. Hence, Tschuschke and Freyberger (2015) lamented the absurdity of evidence-based research in psychotherapy.

In RCTs, there are many interfering variables, which cannot be controlled for (handled by researcher). Researchers nevertheless say that the therapeutic treatment was effective for the mental disorder that was trialed. This leads to a certification of effectiveness for this treatment (Tschuschke, 2016).

Whereas RCTs offer evidence in medical research of the efficacy/effectiveness of a medical treatment, they do ***not*** in psychotherapy research due to the difficulties mentioned above.

Shifting away from the Medical Model toward a Contextual Model, where cultural and individual processes are combined, with the use of bottom-up designs (Fraser, 2020), has been suggested. Finally, considering that some psychotherapies are equally effective, but are based on different premises, this casts doubt on the validity of the basis underlying each psychotherapy. To prove that psychotherapies do not work for "unknown reasons" (Fraser, 2020), group analytic researchers would have to find the real factors of change.

I have outlined quite a few criticisms. From a diffractive perspective, criticisms result in a distancing stance toward quantitative methods. If read through AI, and researchers adopted a diffractive methodology (Bozalek & Murris, 2022), naïve Realism and positivist epistemology would appear in a different light. Probability would be more important, Realism would no longer be naïve, and modifications could be made.

In clinical settings, there is growing evidence that supports the implementation of AI-assisted tools (Lam et al., 2022). Inadequacies in methodologies and bias can interfere with the accuracy of results. Unclear reporting can also be a problem. In addition to double-blinding difficulties, other pitfalls of RCTs include poor selection of participants, inadequate randomization with residual confounders, and an insufficient sample size (Lee & Lee, 2020). To address these problems, group analytic researchers could train AI models by using available datasets. Double-blind group analytic RCTs could be carried out virtually and methodological flaws be addressed.

Researchers could use advanced statistical methods (see Lee & Lee, 2020). This could save costs and reduce ethical dilemmas. Furthermore, AI has been used for prediction (see Zhou et al., 2021). Various RCTs could be mimicked to estimate the treatment effect. Since AI could generate synthetic client data for virtual trials (Eckhardt et al., 2024), such group analytic trials could also test the effect of common factors, such as the therapeutic relationship, working alliance, positive bonds, empathy, goal consensus, collaboration, cohesion, as well as the client's readiness to change and the effect on treatment outcome. Furthermore, clients' perspectives could be incorporated into outcome research. So, researchers could conduct more process-oriented studies and consider various contexts.

By using AI, researchers they would have more time and resources to do process research with real clients. Previously, Munder et al. (2019) distinguished relative and absolute efficacy. From the perspective of the Emerging Reality Paradigm, I would suggest settling for "probable" efficacy/effectiveness (see Msaouel et al., 2023 for Bayesian statistics). When read through a group analytic lens, Positivism and quantitative methods may serve defensive functions to protect against annihilation anxiety (see introduction to Section 2). If these fears were addressed, there would be less need for certainty. Then "probable" instead of "certain" outcomes could become acceptable. Combining Indigenous and Western methods, as well as integrating communities into studies, may also become more widely accepted.

Unfortunately, for the time being, in the hierarchy of evidence (see Figure 4.1), meta-analysis provides the most robust evidence, followed by systematic reviews and RCTs (Allmark & Machaczek, 2018). Group analytic therapists and researchers could work collaboratively on achieving change to policies by explicating socially unconscious processes, in addition to conducting quantitative studies.

Carrying Out a Systematic Review

According to Branley et al. (2018), a systematic review is a specific form of reviewing the literature of interest, where the researcher formulates a clearly defined question that is researchable. Systematic reviews offer sound evidence of the effectiveness of interventions, which are used to inform clinical practice. They rely on the use of explicit methods and aim to minimize bias, and clinicians use them to draw robust conclusions about a specific treatment (Higgins et al., 2024). Munn et al. (2014) regard them as the pillar of evidence-based healthcare. While they are widely used to inform the development of clinical guidelines, when researchers want to identify knowledge gaps, the scope of a body of literature, clarify concepts, or examine already conducted research, they could also carry out a scoping review. Though useful in its own right, a scoping review (Vosmer, 2023b) can be a precursor to a systematic review (Munn et al., 2018).

Systematic reviews follow a structured process to ensure that results are valid, reliable, and meaningful. Specific components of the systematic review process include searching, screening, data extraction, and synthesis. A synthesis is performed of the included literature, which aims to provide reliable evidence by using specific procedures of selection and evaluation. It aims to distill and summarize the accumulated evidence from a wide range of sources to support clinical, or policy decisions, which render them "evidence-based". For example, Orfanos et al.'s (2020) systematic review identified a range of questionnaires that can be used by clinicians and researchers, who seek to measure either "specific therapeutic group mechanisms" or "overall group experiences" (p. 425).

Whether the synthesis procedures are quantitative or qualitative depends on the identification of eligible studies. However, these procedures must be fully described (p. 76). Normally, a qualitative synthesis is known as "meta-synthesis". For the synthesis of qualitative data, thematic analysis can be used (Mays et al., 2005). Andrews et al. (2024) draw on the six-step Reflexive Thematic Analysis process espoused by Byrne (2022).

Here is an example to give you an idea of how to conduct a systematic review: after formulating a research question (e.g. "Do transference interpretations create insight into disturbance?"), which determines the selection of the included literature in the review, you define specific inclusion and exclusion criteria. For example, including articles only published in French that report on adults. You must describe the search strategy (see Appendix 4) and inclusion/exclusion criteria regarding the literature. A crucial component of the systematic review is the literature search (information retrieval process), which informs the results. It is the underlying process that establishes which data are available for synthesis (Rethlefsen et al., 2021). Once you have identified relevant studies, the screening process begins. Titles and abstracts can be imported into "Covidence" (see Appendix 3), which is an online software used for screening, data extraction, and population of data. Covidence also removes duplicate articles. It is good practice for a second reviewer to independently screen abstracts. Having identified suitable full texts, these could be imported into Covidence and reviewed independently by another reviewer. When there is disagreement among two reviewers, this can be discussed at a consensus meeting. The quality of the structure, methodology, and the reporting of the included papers can be appraised by using specifically devised checklists (see Appendix 3). PRISMA (Page et al., 2021; Rethlefsen & Page, 2021; Rethlefsen et al., 2021; Haddaway et al., 2022) comprises an evidence-based minimum set of items for reporting systematic reviews and meta-analysis (see Appendix 3). Yazdani and Hoseini (2019) have clarified that the PRISMA flowchart enables the researcher to document the decision-making process (see Figure 4.2). It maps out the number of the identified, included/excluded records, and the reasons for their exclusion (see Rethlefsen & Page, 2021).

Systematic reviews that include RCTs will have the same limitations as discussed previously. If group analytic researchers used AI, research could be improved in several ways. The use of NLP tools allows for a quick sift through databases, including the gray literature. Hence, reviews could be more comprehensive. Such tools are also faster and probably more accurate than manual searches. ML models can be trained to recognize which study fits the inclusion criteria of a systematic review. This could reduce human error and bias. Some details of studies, such as sample size and outcomes, are extracted automatically. AI tools can also combine data from quantitative and qualitative studies. Furthermore, Sentiment or Content Analysis could be carried out to identify common themes across studies. *Rayyan* is specifically designed for systematic reviews. *Elicit* is an AI assistant that helps find relevant papers and extracts information. *RobotReviewer* is trained on the Cochrane database.

Research Suggestions for Conducting Systematic Reviews

Median and large groups have not received as much attention as therapy groups in group analytic research. However, larger groups are important and should not be neglected. Even though numbers are not the main discriminating factors between the small, median, and large group, size is nevertheless important. While group analytic psychotherapy groups do not commonly have more than eight members, psychoeducation, support, and experiential groups tend to have more participants. Some groups may comprise more than 20 members. Furthermore, the large

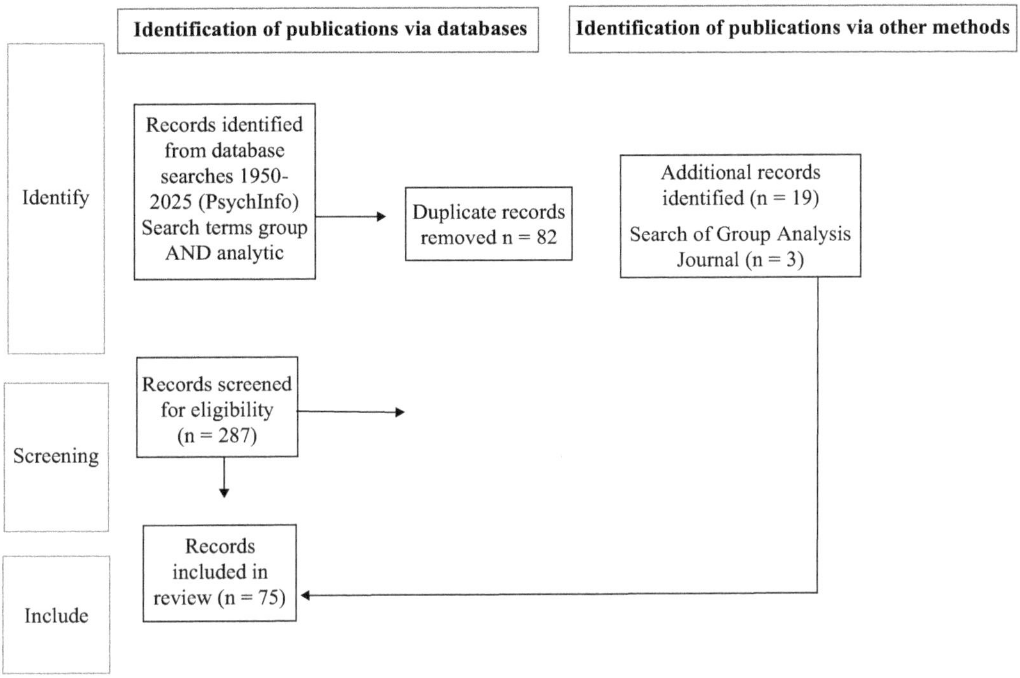

FIGURE 4.2 Fictitious Flow Diagram, Templates Available at https://www.prisma-statement.org-2020-flow-diagram.

group forms part of group analytic training. Professional development often takes place in median or large groups. At times, groups in medical, educational, and mental health settings, are also underpinned by group analytic principles.

Whether median groups dilute common factors, such as cohesion, is an interesting question that could be reviewed. Group analytic researchers could also find out whether median groups are shaped differently than small groups by culture. In large groups, fragmentation may happen. What are the factors that lead to fragmentation?

Online groups have become more popular in Group Analysis as well. Experiential, psychotherapy, and professional development groups are conducted online. Researchers could study the different types and formats (in-person small, median, large group versus online). How does the therapeutic relationship (TextBox 4.1), or working alliance, manifest in online groups? Is it affected by the online format?

In online groups, side discussions may occur. Do they interfere with the delivery of a professional development group? Online larger groups may create a different reality. Do they?

These suggestions are based on the extant group literature. Of course, researchers can think of other questions. If they cannot identify enough analytic median group studies, this would point to an overlooked area of group analytic research per se. It could generate a new impetus to carry out more studies of larger group analytic groups, or of groups based on group analytic principles. AI could be used to identify neglected areas.

TEXTBOX 4.1 THERAPEUTIC RELATIONSHIP/WORKING ALLIANCE & RUPTURE

A recent meta-analysis by Eubanks et al. (2018) illustrates the importance of monitoring the alliance and repairing ruptures, because this increases the likelihood of favorable treatment outcomes. Safran and Muran (1996) define ruptures in the therapeutic alliance as the "deteriorations in the relationship between therapist and patient" (p. 447). Having researched the alliance and ruptures extensively since the mid-1980s (e.g. Safran et al., 2002; Safran et al., 2014), Eubanks et al. (2018) presented accumulated evidence of the processes involved in ruptures and in their resolution. A rupture is a strain in the alliance that stems from difficulties with bonding, or from an inconsistency between therapists and patients with regard to the tasks/goals of therapy (Safran & Muran, 2003).

The sustained interest in the therapeutic alliance (also referred to as working alliance) has occurred due to a paradigm shift in psychotherapies that emphasizes the importance of relational factors in treatment. Safran and Muran (2006) have suggested that different methodologies would be required to research how the mutual recognition of the therapists' and patients' gender, sexual, racial, and cultural identities, relates to change.

The therapeutic relationship/alliance has also been extensively researched in group psychotherapy. Alldredge et al.'s (2021) recent meta-analysis endorses the substantial link between alliance and treatment outcome.

Meta-Analysis

Whenever possible, a review of the literature is based on meta-analysis (Egger et al., 1997). Erwin et al. (2011, p. 187) describe meta-analysis as a statistical procedure that attempts to integrate a body of quantitative research. Often, it focuses on reducing findings to a standardized metric, such as the mean effect size (see Forness, 2001). Field and Gillett (2010) have further clarified that meta-analysis is a statistical tool for estimating the "variance of underlying population effects" from a collection of empirical studies, which address the same research question (p. 665). Wampold (2001) has described how to carry out a traditional meta-analysis in psychotherapy research through an example. Andrade (2020) offers an easily understandable explanation. In group psychotherapy research, the meta-analytic method has been used widely (e.g. Burlingame et al., 2018 on the importance of group cohesion; McDermut et al. 2001 on the efficacy of group therapy for depression; McLaughlin et al., 2019 on BPD). Consequently, more is known about group processes and common factors, such as, the therapeutic relationship (TextBox 4.1), which contributes to well-functioning groups and to positive treatment outcomes.

Because research questions can be answered by conducting different types of quantitative studies (Field, 2001, 2003a), meta-analyses are useful. Sample sizes in the original studies may vary, and studies may report differing results. Doing a meta-analysis can, therefore, offer more robust results (Field, 2003b, 2005a). It enables researchers to report the variability in effects across studies, such as the influence of moderator variables (Field & Gillet, 2009). In this way, more conclusive evidence can be produced (Field, 2005b,c). Hedges and Olkin (1985) derived an estimator of the effect size that is weighted by the inverse of the variance of the individual estimates, thereby giving more weight to studies with smaller larger sample sizes. Wampold (2001) outlines three ways how to interpret an effect size: using Hedges's *g*, statistical regression, and Cohen's *d* (see Appendix 4).

Conducting a meta-analysis involves a literature search, deciding on inclusion criteria and applying these, calculating effect sizes for each included study, considering whether to do an analysis of biases, or explore moderator variables, and writing up the results (Field & Gillett, 2010). Statistical analysis can be performed using the metafor package (see Viechtbauer, 2010). Hedges *g* statistics, which expresses the difference of the means in units of the pooled standard deviation, can be used (Wampold, 2001). Higgins et al. (2003) describe how inconsistency can be measured. Higgens et al. (2009) explain how random effects can be evaluated. Missing data and bias are problematic for any quantitative study. Procedures to address these problems are described in Appendix 4.

Network meta-analysis combines data from RCTs to compare multiple interventions simultaneously, even if some treatments have never been directly compared in a trial (Verde & Ohmann, 2014). A cross-design meta-analysis is a strategy for combining evidence from different quantitative studies. It requires specific statistical methods, such as converting effect sizes to a common metric, or adjusting for different sources of bias, when RCTs and observational studies are combined (see Varadhan & Weiss, 2011). A Bayesian framework has been used to combine evidence for different study designs and biases (Droitcour et al., 2009). Since the inclusion of weaker designs, or badly conducted research, can bias the results of such meta-analysis (Droitcour et al., 2009), precise inclusion criteria must be applied, which ensures that the included studies are of similar quality. Otherwise, the overall quality of meta-analytic results will be compromised. Statistical methods must also be applied to adjust for variability. Bayesian hierarchical modeling can be used to weigh design-related heterogeneity appropriately.

Bayesian analysis is a method of statistical inference that is widely used (Lindley, 2001). It is based on Thomas Bayes (1702–1761). Bayes solved the inverse problem of how to get from sample to population. He studied the probability of hypotheses and developed a mathematical formula, the *Bayes' Theorem*. It tells researchers everything they need to know about the data in terms of probability, or likelihood. It provides a framework for working with conditional probability (Bellhouse, 2004).

Mays et al. (2005) suggested that the Bayesian approach was particularly useful when primary research data was either weak or lacking, but decisions had to be made, nonetheless. Clinical consensus statements and expert opinion (subjective judgment) could be integrated into quantitative research by combining these data with results from RCTs. When evidence is pooled together, statistical modeling can be used to provide a true overall estimate, and bias can be addressed. According to Spiegelhalter et al. (2000), the Bayesian approach involves the explicit use of external evidence regarding design, monitoring, analysis, interpretation, and the reporting of a study. The Bayesian approach is advantageous, because it can be used to draw conclusions from a range of evidence. So, a comprehensive decision analysis can be carried out.

Bayesian Decision Theory is a framework that enables researchers to make optimal decisions under uncertainty. It applies Bayesian statistical inference by incorporating Bayesian probability into the process of making decisions, as Gad (2024) explains. The decision rule predicts an outcome based on both prior and current likelihood probability. Based on previous and current observations, it is then possible to describe the most reasonable action to take. Decision Theory rests on the premise that the sum of all prior and all posterior probabilities must be 1. And that the evidence is the sum of products of the prior and likelihood probabilities of all outcomes (Gad, 2024). Although modifications of Bayesian analysis have been suggested, there is always a degree of subjectivity (choice of priors) in setting probability bounds, especially with limited data. Bayesian decision models (computational models) break down processes into interpretable and generalizable stages. Describing how these models work, Ma (2019) has clarified that they aspire to explain a decision-making process, in which variables are unknown. Decision models have been used to understand speech and inductive reasoning (Ma, 2019). Issues pertaining to feasibility are limitations of Bayesian meta-analysis (see Mays et al., 2005). So, researchers must be aware of limitations: dependence on priors, computational complexity, interpretation challenges, model specification issues, limited standardization, and software constraints, some of which can be addressed (see Gelman et al., 2013; Spiegelhalter et al., 2002).

Furthermore, researchers could utilize AI tools, such as NLP algorithms, to search databases, filter out duplicates more quickly, and identify biased studies. They could apply AI to carry out advanced statistics to provide more nuanced effect size estimates (Cui et al., 2024), giving a detailed understanding of the heterogeneity of effects, offer nuanced contextual interpretation (being more tentative), and consider the significance of results in practical terms. For example, prioritizing results with larger effect sizes and using results to guide further research. AI tools can also be used to compare multiple interventions simultaneously (see Appendix 3).

Other Quantitative Tools: Instrumentation & Operationalization

Ideally, life groups, or video-recordings of groups, offer the raw data for group research. Given how time-intense and laborious meaningful analyses are, I suggest that researchers consider using an AI assistant. Particularly, when studying analytic groups through the use of measurement instruments, or operationalization, that is, the process of providing clear measurable or observable definitions.

Instrumentation

Numerous methods have been employed to research processes and interactions in group psychotherapy. They are derivatives of Bales' (1950) Interaction Process Analysis and are listed in Fuhriman and Barlow (1994). Most of these methods focus on the content of interactions or on communication of group members. The emotional involvement and quality of the relationship among group members, and toward the therapist, are captured. Within the speech analysis tradition of empirical group therapy research, some methods focus on explicit variables, which are linked to therapeutic factors to capture dominant affects (Strauß et al., 1996). However, researchers must consider the complexity of the setting of the group, and use multiple instruments for the assessment of micro, macro, static, and dynamic influences effect size estimates (Cui et al., 2024), It is important to capture levels of interaction, nonverbal movements in the group, frequency and type of verbal statements, involvement of the facilitator, frequency of humorous, friendly, hostile remarks, types of conflict, levels of cohesiveness, satisfaction of group members with the group, bodily indicators, reduction of symptoms, and more (p. 210). Interactions and verbal behavior can be analyzed to gain insight into interpersonal and group processes. Whatever rating system researchers use, they function as coding schemes.

Provided that the selection of segments of interactions is justified, sequences have been tracked, singular, cumulative, and progressive interactions have been captured over time, and group processes are analyzed moment-by-moment, then group patterns and dynamics become visible that can reveal emotional, cognitive, and behavioral changes in interactional patterns, and in the functioning of the group-as-a-whole (Fuhriman & Barlow, 1994). Descriptions and critiques of measures are found in Fuhriman and Barlow (1994).

Specific questionnaires, Q-Sort of group factors (following Yalom), group process scales, assessment instruments, process diagnostic, the potency-valency polarity profile, the sociogram, the Hill interaction matrix, the System for Multiple Level Observation of Group (SYMLOG), the Orlik grid and other grid techniques, the Structural Analysis of Social Behavior as method of analyze group processes, the Z-HOLO, matrix representation grid, and the Gottschalk-Gleser speech content analysis, are described in Strauß et al. (1996). Appendix 3 lists additional questionnaires. Approaches to assessing group dynamics include the SYMLOG and the BECM matrix (see Bell & Morse, 2013).

Furthermore, the group emotionality rating scale (GERS) was developed by the group analyst Karterud (1989a,b, 2000b; Karterud and Foss, 1989). It aims to capture Bion's (1961) basic assumptions.

Operationalizing

Group analytic therapy loosens people's rigid personality structures, their use of primitive defenses, and their ways of relating to others. These manifest in the group (Wilke, 2018). However, conventional research instruments cannot detect and capture unconscious group dynamics and processes. Researchers could utilize the positivist technique of operationalizing, which involves defining the phenomena of interest and measuring these. Doing so necessitates a good understanding of analytic concepts, such as the unconscious, defense mechanisms, counter-/transference, and unconscious conflicts. Given the ubiquity of defenses and counter-/transference reactions, operationalizing these could be a good starting point. After having identified a working definition of these concepts, researchers then devise an operationalizing definition, or use existing ones. For example, Tschuschke et al. (2014) have operationalized several theoretical concepts in their rating manual.

When something is defensively removed from consciousness due to conflicting attitudes, this indicates that defense mechanisms have been deployed by the psyche. The psychodynamic concepts of repression, suppression, dissociation, denial, projection, projective identification, splitting, and rationalization, are examples of defense mechanisms. Suppression may be conceptualized as a "voluntary form of repression", of getting rid of unwanted thoughts, or of emotions, by consciously pushing them out of awareness (Benedittis, 2023). Suppression is more amenable to being researched than repression. Dissociation is a disruption, interruption, and/or discontinuity of the normal, subjective integration of behavior, memory, identity, consciousness, emotion, perception, body representation, and motor control (APA, 2013). Even if a person dissociates, and something is repressed or suppressed, it can still influence a person, or it may suddenly express itself through Freudian slips.

When studying defenses and resistance more generally, one working definition could be that the therapist confronts the client with matters of which the client is not aware (Tschuschke et al., 2014, p. 23). These issues are very unpleasant so that the client defends her/himself against them. On the part of the client, this entails an unconscious perceptual distortion of actual circumstances, which are ignored or suppressed. This working definition can be operationalized as follows: the therapist (1) points out the client's defense processes, (2) confronts the client with the fact that s/he is not seeing something, and (3) raises unpleasant "truths" with the client (p. 23). Practical examples would include the therapist saying: "I have the impression you would rather not look at that too closely". Or "My sense is that you, without realizing it, are putting a lot of effort into avoiding certain insights". Or "Could it be that there is something you are not seeing correctly?" (p. 23).

Stamenova (2018) operationalized psychoanalytic concepts. Furthermore, Walker (2024) discussed operationalization in psychoanalytic research. When researching or working with pre-conscious material, one possible definition is that the therapist addresses the patient's parapraxes, seemingly fleeting ideas, fantasies, and daydreams, and explores the content of reported dreams by enquiring about dreams (Tschuschke et al., 2014, p. 34). The operational definition would be that the therapist encourages working with (1) dreams, (2) daydreams, fantasies, (3) parapraxes. Practical examples include asking "How could that happen to you, do you have an opinion about it?" "Can you describe this daydream in somewhat greater detail?" "What does this element of the dream mean? Does it have any relationship to your life? What does the XYZ aspect mean for you?" (p. 34).

Additionally, some knowledge of neuroscientific findings might be useful (see Appendix 1).

Chapter Summary

Benefits and disadvantages of AI, AI algorithms, and other tools were discussed. By using a diffractive methodology, naïve Realism and positivist epistemology are viewed in a different light. Not everything can be determined with certainty. Bayesian statistics are useful to think about probabilities and calculate these. Furthermore, I described crucial aspects involved in carrying out a meta-analysis, systematic reviews, and RCTs, and explained how to instrumentalize and operationalize concepts.

AI tools have potential and might be beneficial for addressing difficulties surrounding RCTs. Systematic reviews are not commonly used in group analytic research, in comparison to the wider field of group psychotherapy, due to the lack of RCTs. Therefore, it would be more appropriate to conduct coping reviews in group analytic research. To improve the evidence for analytic psychotherapy groups, meta-analyses would be very helpful, but not enough studies exist at present. However, in group psychotherapy research, meta-analyses could be carried out. Instrumentation and operationalization are further means to study different aspects of groups. Statistics are an integral part of quantitative methodologies but are less common in Group Analysis. To spark interest in statistics, I have written a narrative of a group analyst's journey to master basic statistics, found in Appendix 4.

5

LESS FREQUENTLY USED METHODS FOR GROUP ANALYTIC RESEARCH

Abstract

Traditional and newer methods are outlined that could be used in group (analytic) research. These include the use of surveys and questionnaires, the Delphi Method, Focus Groups, the Matrix Representation Grid, the Repertory Grid Method, Q-Methodology, (Social) Network Analysis, and Sentiment Analysis. I describe these methods, provide practical examples, discuss their benefits and disadvantages, and suggest that AI may assist group analytic researchers with laborious tasks.

Introduction

Group research has significantly developed over the past 100 years (see Figure 5.1). Jacob Moreno's (1934) development of the sociogram visualization method was crucial for mapping and analyzing sets of social interactions. It provided a foundation for understanding the interconnectedness of individuals, who belong to a group.

Moreno's pioneering research laid the groundwork for the subsequent development of Social Network Analysis (SNA), which is an umbrella term for different relational statistics. It can be differentiated broadly into complete networks, ego networks, and snowball networks (Wőlfer & Hewstone, 2017). Wang et al. (2023) described SNA as a formal method to investigate relationships in groups. It involves studying the structure, or system, which are formed through individual actors (nodes) and connections (edges, ties). Hence, the basic analytic unit is the network tie that connects, different individuals, which makes this method interesting for group research. SNA considers the tie as the smallest analytic level (Wőlfer & Hewstone, 2017).

It was Lewin's (1948) field theory and his work on group dynamics that had emphasized the importance of the impact of social structures on human thought and behavior. Lewin championed a holistic approach, which recognized the reciprocal relationship between individuals and the social contexts, in which they are embedded (Forsyth, 2019). Additionally, Festinger et al.'s (1974) research on social pressures in informal groups enabled an understanding of the influence social networks have on shaping human behavior within specific contexts. All these

DOI: 10.4324/9781003609544-8

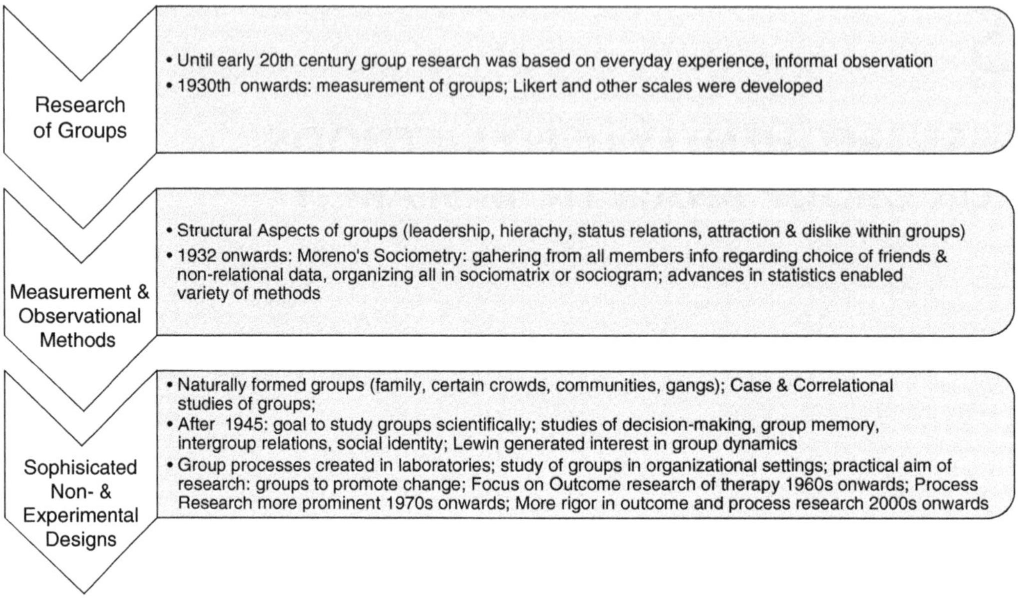

FIGURE 5.1 Development of Group Research (Extracted from Wheelan et al., 2005)

scholars laid the foundation for the subsequent advancement and application of SNA within social psychology (Mehrpour et al., 2025).

In group analytic research, SNA is underused for studying socio-psychological dimensions of intergroup contact related to prejudice, trust, threat, discrimination, or collective actions.

Possibly, because of the largely unknown advantages that SNA offers.

Numerous other methods such as surveys, questionnaires, the Delphi Method, Focus Groups, the Repertory, or the Matrix Representation Grid (MRG) methods, Q-Methodology, or Sentiment Analysis (SA), can also be used in group analytic research. Research techniques have started to increasingly rely on AI tools (see Hamed et al., 2020; Taherdoost & Madanchian, 2023; Wang et al., 2025). Traditional SA (subset of data mining) utilizes computational, natural language processing (NLP) tools (Python, NUMPY, NLTK, MATLAP), and algorithms, to identify, extract, and analyze sentiments and emotions expressed in a text, by dividing sentiments into positive, negative, and neutral categories (Sakthivel, 2021). This approach draws on Ekman's (1992) six basic emotions (happiness, sadness, surprise, disgust, fear, anger), and on Plutchik's (1991) added "trust and anticipation". In contrast, a dimensional SA enables a more nuanced expression of sentiments (see Lee et al., 2022).

In what follows, I will outline how to carry out surveys, design a questionnaire, apply the Delphi Method, conduct a Focus Group, use the Repertory Grid and MRG methods, as well as Q-Methodology, (Social) Network Analysis, and SA.

Using Survey Research in Group Analytic Research

Survey research refers to collecting "information from a sample of individuals through their responses to questions" (Ponto, 2015, p. 168). It relies on primary data, follows proven and systematic procedures to collect evidence, is replicable, and can generate both quantitative and qualitative data (Mahmutovic, 2023). Frequently, questionnaires are used. These can be mailed, emailed, or delivered online (using SurveyMonkey). Benefits of online surveys include their ability to reach a broad audience, being relatively inexpensive, and being more cost-effective than interviews (Jones et al., 2013). Unfortunately, no definitive conclusions can be drawn from surveys (Salant & Dillman, 1994). So, other methods are also needed.

Some surveys have been carried out in Group Analysis (e.g. Dutta & Kundu, 2021). Surveys can capture attitudes and opinions (Robinson & Seale, 2018). For group analytic researchers, online, mail, the Delphi method, AI (see Mahmutovic, 2023), and/or social media surveys, could be of interest, if they wanted to gather information on people's opinions (Pinsonneault & Kraemer, 1993), regarding group analytic psychotherapy. Surveys can elicit information on attitudes that cannot be obtained through observational techniques (Phillips et al., 2002).

No fixed number of participants is needed, and sample sizes vary. Large random samples increase the likelihood that the responses accurately reflect the entire population (Ponto, 2015). It is important, however, to correctly identify the population of interest, for example, relational group psychotherapists practicing in Spain versus all relational group psychotherapists worldwide. Surveys can be used to assess needs, evaluate demand, and examine impact (Salant & Dillman, 1994). For example, researchers could research if there is a need, and/or demand, for group analytic psychotherapy.

Using diverse recruitment strategies helps increase the size of the sample, for example, promoting a survey via social media or professional websites. Additionally, researchers could carry out descriptive survey research to survey group analysts' attitudes toward decolonizing Group Analysis, or any other attitudes of interest.

The structure and questions are determined beforehand in descriptive surveys. Standardized questions yield data that are statistically analyzed. Descriptive research aims to quantify and categorize the held opinions, attitudes, or beliefs of a particular population, by using existing questionnaires. Gathering demographic data, for example, participants' age, gender, ethnicity, social class, and country of residence, is also useful. Including information about the survey on the first page, and obtaining written consent, is necessary.

When developing a questionnaire yourself, it should be piloted, because an instrument must be valid and reliable to exclude measurement error (see Check & Schutt, 2012).

Frequently, a 5-point Likert-type scale (giving a score between 1 "totally unacceptable" and 5 "totally acceptable") is used to measure and compare attitudes with different "descriptors", such as a behavior. Participants are asked to rate descriptors according to perceived acceptability (Ponto, 2015). Then a descriptive analysis of the obtained data can be carried out. This involves calculating medians and interquartile ranges, which can be summarized in graphical format in box plots (Padmanathan et al., 2019; see Appendix 4). For more complicated analyses, Stata is useful, but it must be purchased. Stata is a statistical software package for data management, graphics, analysis, and automated reporting (https://www.stata.com/stata15/), and useful for comparative, cross-national surveys.

When a single method cannot sufficiently answer the research question, a mixed methods survey approach should be used (see Jones et al., 2013). For example, questionnaires can include additional open questions to better understand participants' reasons for their choices. These could be analyzed through Content Analysis. Or a telephone interview could be subsequently conducted. Researchers get a more complete picture when applying multiple methods.

In addition to studying cross-sections of psychotherapists in the same country, a comparative cross-national survey design would allow for international comparison. Psychotherapists' attitudes toward group analytic training programs could be researched. In comparative survey studies, data would be collected from individual group analytic psychotherapists, who would give their opinion regarding the training organizations. In this way, the group analytic training profile of each country would be derived from the responses of each individual group analyst, who resides in a certain country. Analysis of survey data from the cross-national survey could proceed by pooling the surveys from each country, such as attitudes of German, British, Danish, Indian, and Greek group analytic psychotherapists toward their training organizations. Then researchers would test for correlations between variables in the single dataset (de Vaus, 2008).

Assume your results show that most group analysts prefer candid communication. After the overall pattern of candid communication has been identified, you could introduce "country" as an "indicator variable" into your statistical analysis (TextBox 5.1). De Vaus (2008) explained how to do this.

He also drew attention to measurement error in comparative research. So, ensure that your results reflect "real differences".

TEXTBOX 5.1 INDICATOR/DUMMY VARIABLE

According to Garavaglia and Sharma (1998), an indicator variable (dummy) is an artificial variable that is created to represent an attribute with two or more distinct categories. The indicator variable takes on a binary value of 0 or 1, indicating the absence or presence of a specific category or characteristic. Indicator variables are used, because most statistical models require numeric inputs to function correctly. By transforming categorical into numerical data through indicator variables, you can include categorical data in statistical modeling.

If you wanted to study the relationship between candid communication and group analysts' sex, use an indicator variable to represent the candid communication of each individual female group analytic psychotherapists in your survey. It could take a value of 1, for female, and of 0 for male, or vice versa.

Hopefully, you agree that the whole is not simply the sum of its parts, which is the individualistic fallacy that cross-national comparative research is especially vulnerable to (de Vaus, 2008). And you know that culture, politico-historical contexts, and social structures affect attitudes. You should be aware that extrapolating from individual opinions to characteristics of systems is imbued with difficulties. Just because most group analytic psychotherapists prefer frank discussions and democratic participation in the large group does not mean that the training organization in that country is democratic (or the country itself).

When making sense of similarities or differences in the data, the meaning of indicators must be considered alongside their socio-cultural contexts. Take spirituality. Its expression differs across countries. In a culture where spiritual practices are commonly performed, both psychotherapists and the group analytic training program may place more emphasis on spirituality. It could mean that individuals and the organization are more likely to have the same attitude toward spirituality.

A culturally informed approach to research would take the impact of cultural norms on individual opinions into account when commenting on the differences between countries.

You may like to study attitudes toward Indigenous research or explore whether group analytic researchers have become disenchanted with the quantitative logic. Cross-national surveys could obtain information on attitudes toward research. Valbak (2022) implied that there was reticence among group analysts to adopt the nomothetic paradigm, which relies on quantitative research (Lilienfeld et al., 2013). A recent survey in Austria by Nussbaumer-Streit et al. (2022) found that psychotherapists had a negative attitude toward research per se. But their study did not include group analytic psychotherapists. However, Taubner et al. (2016) have revealed an encouraging trend. More individually trained German psychotherapists were prepared to participate in research.

Although survey research could be utilized to answer many questions, it has limitations pertaining to accuracy. Participants may not provide honest answers or not answer all questions. They may have difficulty understanding, or answering, questions. "Yes" or "No" question may be difficult for people, who want to specify their answer, i.e., "only once" (Jones et al., 2013).

Furthermore, responses may be biased and measurement errors can occur due to "wrong" responses (Mohajan, 2020). However, researchers could replicate studies to address measurement error (Fisher, 1921, 1935).

Using Questionnaires in Group Analytic Research

Aaron Beck created widely used rating scales for psychotherapy research. Questionnaires and personality inventories have also gained prominence in psychotherapy research. The same measures as used in individual psychotherapy research can also be utilized when studying groups (Conway et al., 2003; Hall and Mullee, 2000; Tschuschke and Anbeth, 2000). Due to using several measures, the benefit of group psychotherapy, including group analytic psychotherapy, has been demonstrated (e.g. Catina et al., 1989; Fuhriman & Burlingame, 1994; Heinzel et al., 1998; MacKenzie & Tschuschke, 1993; Ogrodniczuk & Piper, 2003; Staczan et al., 2015; Strauß & Burgmeier-Lohse, 1993; Strauß et al., 1993; Strauß et al., 1996; Toseland & Siporin, 1986; Tschuschke, 1993; Tschuschke, 1999, 2007; Tschuschke & Anbeh, 2000; Tschuschke & Dies, 1994; Tschuschke & Kächele, 1996; Tschuschke & MacKenzie, 1989; Tschuschke et al., 1992; Tschuschke et al., 1998; Tschuschke et al., 2007; Tschuschke et al., 2014)

However, as group analytic researchers became more focused on the effectiveness of analytic groups, specific group instruments were developed (see Appendix 3). Outcome measures are also more routinely used in clinical practice (Burlingame & Strauss, 2021). Common measures include the Group Questionnaire (GQ), the Group Readiness Questionnaire (GRQ), and the Group Climate Questionnaire (GCQ).

When considering the use of scales to assess change in psychotherapy, let us say in Spain, it is important to establish that measurements developed in the US are reliable, valid, and sensitive for Spanish clients. With regard to the questionnaire itself, item consistency, content, predictive, concurrent, and construct validity (see Appendix 4), are important. Scales must also be standardized for specific practice settings and clients, for example, depression measures developed on White males are of no use for measuring depression in ethnically diverse female groups. Furthermore, when more complex measures are used, administration and scoring accuracy/consistency are important in order to exclude errors (Creswell, 1994). More information on a measurement-based approach to group psychotherapy can be found in MacNair-Semands and Whittingham (2023).

If you would like to design your own measurement instrument, below is a summary of a simplified process (see DeVellis and Thorpe (2022), Kühne et al. (2021), Boateng et al. (2018), Graesser and Black (2019); Adams and Cox (2008); also see Appendices 3 and 4):

- a Think about what you would like to "measure" (e.g. mood).
- b Read relevant literature on mood so you know how it is conceptualized.
- c A domain, such as mood, which is developed well, provides you with a working knowledge.
- d If you want to develop a scale/questionnaire on mood, read literature on questionnaire design. Unless it is for your doctoral project, collaborate with other researchers.
- e Think about possible questions, which capture what you want to measure (aspects related to mood).

f Read about types of questions (open-ended, closed, leading, sensitive), how to group them together (logical sequence), which question to ask first and last. *Avoid* negative and ambiguous wording, sensitive questions, items that ask for more than one aspect, jargon, complicated words.

g A questionnaire must be easy to clear, brief, easy to understand and quick to complete. ("Have you felt sad yesterday?")

h Discuss questions to ensure that they are understandable.

i Use a Likert scale (Likert, 1932). Decide how many points to use (3, 5, or 7). A 5-point scale is commonly used (ranging from 0 "do not agree at all" to 5 "completely agree").

j Once you have identified all questions (let's say 20), you test their *dimensionality, validity* (discriminant, factorial, convergent, content), and *reliability* (internal consistency) by applying statistical procedures (see Appendices 3 and 4).

k Pilot your instrument on the relevant population to identify possible weaknesses and rectify these. The questionnaire must be parsimonious, so you may have to rephrase or replace questions.

l Make the physical appearance/layout attractive, user-friendly, and include brief instructions on how to complete the questionnaire.

Using the Delphi Method

Alternatives to interviewing experts are focus groups or the Delphi Method (see Jorm, 2015; Keeley et al., 2016). These two methods were originally used only quantitatively. Nowadays, researchers can employ a quantitative version, or integrate qualitative and quantitative techniques. Mixed methods make results more trustworthy. Unexploited in group analytic research, the Delphi Method (Delphi) is a user-friendly flexible method, in my experience (see Iqbal et al., 2009).

Like most people, group analytic psychotherapists and researchers disagree on numerous issues. For example, on the nature of the social unconscious, that is, the representation of social forces and power relations in the psyche (Dalal, 2001) (whether it is a separate concept, or not). What constitutes evidence and how to obtain it also remain contentious issues. To find out what views group analysts, or group analytic researchers, hold, or to establish a consensus, the "expert consensus" Delphi Method is suitable. It could also be used to guide treatment adaptation efforts (King et al., 2021), to develop new assessment questionnaires, to select the most suitable outcome measures for analytic groups and indicators of quality care, to devise policies, or to identify research priorities.

I will summarize core features of the research process. A group of participants (panelists) are specially selected for their particular expertise. Conducted over several rounds, the Delphi employs an initial "idea-generation" phase. Panelists are asked to identify salient issues, which are then used to construct the survey instrument, using a Likert scale. Open questions can also be included. This questionnaire will be distributed in Round 2. The Delphi has an evaluation phase (third or further rounds). Panelists are provided with overall responses and are asked to re-evaluate their original responses. Formation of consensus (number of panelists agreeing with each other on questionnaire items) can be achieved. Simple descriptive statistics are calculated (means, medians, modes) to reflect all views. The mean reflects the average, the median is the midpoint ordered from least to greatest, and the mode is the most frequent number in a data set.

Written answers could be analyzed by using qualitative Content Analysis (Graneheim & Lundman, 2004) or Thematic Analysis (Braun & Clarke, 2006). All results are presented to each participant (via email), who is invited to reflect on her/his responses in the light of the overall scores and themes. Changed views are analyzed again and presented to all. In this way, a consensus tends to be achieved. Final results are disseminated among participants in report format. Results can inform clinical practice or establish what further research is needed.

More information on the Delphi is found in Adler and Ziglio (1996), Sumsion (1998), Turoff (2002), Linstone and Turoff (2002), Iqbal and Pipon-Young (2009), Brady (2015), McMillan et al. (2016), and Barrett and Heale (2020).

Focus Group Method

Groups were used in the 1920s to identify survey questions, until Lazarsfeld and Merton formalized the focus group method in the 1940s. Afterwards it was predominantly used in market research. Eventually, qualitative researchers utilized focus groups in the social sciences (Morgan, 1996).

Focus groups are group interviews that rely on the interaction within the group. The group engages in a collective activity and is the focus of analysis. This format was designed to elicit participants' views, their experiences related to a topic, to understand how they interact and influence each other, and to gain an understanding of group norms and their meaning (Krueger & Casey, 2000). A group may help participants to spontaneously comment on something. Opinions tend to be voiced that may not surface in interviews (Carey, 1994).

Considering that the group process can enable people to identify and clarify their views, the focus group method seems more beneficial than individual interviews. If researchers are interested in how people have formed a "schema" of a particular topic (e.g., social justice), focus groups are a suitable method.

Through the interaction in the group difficulties, agreements, and disagreements, often come to the fore about the issues that are raised (Carey, 1994). When disagreements are resolved a consensus is built. Participants may also verbalize something that is unsaid, or express unarticulated, normative assumptions. Moreover, focus groups can facilitate public participation in the research process. They are a convenient means of providing feedback to a person with no interest in academic publications.

In focus groups, researchers speak with participants about their experiences, use this information to answer research questions, and share this information in gatherings and journals (Doria et al., 2018). Commonly, one facilitator (moderator) guides the discussion and ensures that it stays focused on the topic, because s/he wants to obtain as much information and opinions as possible. Another moderator, who takes notes, assists with equipment, sees to latecomers, and does other administrative, or analytic, tasks. Ideally, moderators are well-trained in the focus group method. It can be beneficial when they are from the population of interest themselves (Leung & Savithiri, 2009).

The optimum size of a group depends on the research topic (Bloor et al., 2001). Smaller focus groups allow for more in-depth discussions and may be more suitable for very sensitive issues. Larger groups may be dominated by vociferous participants. Recommendations about the number of participants and groups vary. As little as three participants, and two to three focus groups, have used (Guest et al., 2016). Conducting four to six groups was recommended by Krueger and Casey (2000). Four to eight groups may be sufficient, with 9–17 group interviews reaching saturation (Hennink et al., 2019). It is also a good idea to "over-recruit" due to drop out.

The researcher determines the criteria for the group composition, the type of group (heterogenous, homogenous), and how many groups/sessions to have. These decisions depend on the purpose of the study. However, participants should be reasonably diverse (age, ethnicity, gender, disability). Before carrying out a focus group, questions must be developed. These should be short, open-ended, include introductory, key, transition, and concluding questions (Leung & Savithiri, 2009).

Typically, a focus group has a duration of 60–120 minutes and consists of 6–12 participants (Onwuegbuzie et al., 2009). Focus groups can be formed by using pre-existing groups.

Alternatively, the researcher selects participants randomly or purposively. When convening a focus group, expectations should be clarified (purpose, focus, information gathered) (Leung & Savithiri, 2009).

Group analytic practitioner-researchers may appear particularly skilled in convening focus groups, because they are trained to select group members, facilitate interaction between them, identify and deal with unpredictable group dynamics, conflict, over-disclosure, and distress. However, the facilitation of a focus group is done differently, and practitioner-researchers may struggle to adopt this style.

Following a standard introduction (welcome, overview of topic, ground rules, asking general questions), the moderator may use short pauses and probes ("Could you give an example?"), according to Krueger and Casey (2008). S/he is directive and eventually brings the discussion to an appropriate end (summarizes main points; reviews if anything has been missed; thanks the participants). Other materials (articles, video/audio clips) can also be used to ask for participants' responses (Krueger & Casey, 2008).

Each focus group is the unit of analysis. Audio- or videotaping of focus group discussions, in addition to taking field notes, were recommended by Leung and Savithiri (2009). Krueger (1994) identified four possible strategies for how the data could be analyzed. These include the analysis of transcripts, analysis of tapes but not transcripts themselves, analysis of notes, and recall from memory. Analyzing focus group data may, therefore, involve multiple techniques. According to Krueger (1998), several aspects should be considered. Patterns and trends are identified of the expressed beliefs, opinions, and feelings. Doing so involves a comparison of the words that participants use, the context of the comments, identifying whether a discussion was evolving as one participant was responding to another participant, analyzing the intensity of a response and internal consistency of comments, identifying whether an individual changed her/his mind, and whether participants could provide specific examples when prompted (p. 6). Responses of individual participants can be compared when the same group meets more than once (Krueger, 1994). Whereas most focus group researchers use the group as the unit of analysis (coding data and presenting emerging themes), analyzing only the text misses all non-verbal information. Furthermore, analyzing and interpreting information about dissenters, allows determination of saturation, according to Onwuegbuzie et al. (2009). They suggested several techniques, such as Content Analysis, Keywords-in-Context (determine how words are used in relation to other words; how meaning differs), Discourse Analysis, and Constant Comparison Analysis, as used in Grounded Theory. Each focus group is analyzed at a time. Furthermore, the authors devised a simple matrix for assessing the level of consensus (recording the focus group question; each participants' verbal and non-verbal agreement, dissent, provision of significant statement, non-response).

Focus groups can also be conducted by integrating Indigenous methods, such as the talking circle. Chilisa (2020) has pointed out that it ensures that participants listen to what each person says. Talking circles symbolize equality and encourage the sharing of ideas, opinions, and beliefs. Such circles may comprise between 2 and 12 people. A complete talking circle consists of four rounds, depending on time constraints and the norms of the group (see Wilson & Wilson, 2000).

Focus groups have several advantages. Face validity is high, because the data reflect participants' comments (Nyamathi & Shuler, 1990). Researcher bias is lessened, because participants can ask questions of each other, and the group effect can be advantageous (Dawson, 2019). Focus groups can be economical, fast, and an efficient method for obtaining data from multiple participants (Krueger & Casey, 2000). They are socially oriented toward a particular environment and this sense of belonging may increase cohesiveness in the group.

However, when several focus groups and a large number of participants are used, the analyses are time-consuming. Furthermore, not everybody may contribute to the discussion in the group, and some researchers may struggle to moderate a focus group (Dawson, 2019). When researchers convene virtual focus groups, technical difficulties and connectivity problems can have a negative impact. Overall, the advantages seem to outweigh the disadvantages. And researchers could speed up data interpretation by using AI to automate transcription. NLP could identify recurrent themes and sentiments across multiple discussions. Additionally, AI could be drawn on to analyze the tone, or pitch, of voices to identify emotional undercurrents in group dynamics, or to track gestures and facial expressions to identify conflict or group cohesion.

Researchers unfamiliar with, but interested in, focus groups require some basic understanding of how to deal with silences, digressions, dominance, disruptions, and defensiveness (Dawson, 2019). Good leadership and communication skills, as well as cultural competence, are also needed. A participatory leadership skill, where the leader encourages open inquiry to yield diverse alternatives for problem solutions (Zenglo et al., 1996), makes Groupthink less likely. It refers to the tendency of groups to be in total agreement. Critical and alternative views are overridden (Janis, 1971).

Moderators should be able to identify and address Groupthink, if it occurs. Furthermore, cohesiveness enhances group effectiveness in general (Evans & Dion, 1991). Mutual trust and team orientation, or other aspects that improve group cohesion, may increase the risk of Groupthink. This could lead to making poorer decisions and to conformation bias (Kaba et al., 2016).

Attending focus groups, or watching videos of focus group discussions, would give novice researchers an idea of how such groups could be moderated. Although suitable for studying all kinds of attitudes, experiences, and opinions related to group analytic psychotherapy, training, mental health, and so forth, the focus group method has not been used that often in group analytic research. Focus groups could make a good addition to the repertoire of group analytic researchers.

The Matrix Representation Grid Method

Although psychotherapy groups are beneficial, at times, they may be damaging due to the toxicity of group dynamics and processes. Ahlin (1985, 1986, 1988) attempted to better understand therapeutic processes. Influenced by Stern's work on the interpersonal world of the infant, and by other theorists, Ahlin (1995) combined the group analytic concept of the foundation matrix (Ahlin, 1995) with different theories. Like Whitaker and Liberman (1964), and Stock and Whitaker (1982), Ahlin conceptualized the entire group when developing his group observation method.

The matrix (Foulkes, 1964; Robert, 1982) is a central concept in Group Analysis. It describes unconscious motivations and driving forces surrounding the group dynamics in an analytic psychotherapeutic group. The group-as-a whole and the matrix could be regarded as the group equivalent to the psychoanalytic conceptualizations of the individual unconscious and interpersonal unconscious dynamics (Ahlin, 2019).

Ahlin pointed out that the group has no physical body of its own. During face-to-face meetings, the group nevertheless consists of group members' bodies and minds. Resting on the premise that the group-as-a-whole differs from the sum of its component parts, something new develops, when people relate to each other as members of a group (Ahlin, 2019).

A therapy group consists of a specific matrix at a given time. Difficult to research, because the matrix has to be inferred, Ahlin (1986, 1988) developed the MRG as a research tool. This method elaborated Yalom's (1975) therapeutic factors. Additionally, Ahlin reformulated Bloch and Crouch's (1985) group specific factors as "determinants", because the group matrix determines un/conscious processes. Operationalizing eight determinants, non/-verbal communicational flow, imagery, emotional climate, self-disclosure, acceptance, relating patterns, authority patterns, and boundary character (Ahlin, 1988, pp. 216–217) into quantitative levels/scales, Ahlin (1996b) showed that they capture the communicational flow, the contents of verbal dialogues, and environmental factors (interpersonal, historical boundary of the group).

Hence, the MRG captures the entire group processes in the form of a diagram, linking it to group themes. Underlying these themes are conflicts that occur at an unconscious level in the group at that time, which the group is trying to work on (Ahlin, 1996a,b).

Group analytic theories postulate that a joint group theme develops, which is not explicitly named by group members. The group conductor, or a trained observer, is able to recognize this theme. It resembles the group focal conflict (see Stock & Whitaker, 1982; Whitaker & Liberman, 1964).

Ideally, the researcher is not the psychotherapist of the group that is being researched. Researchers must be trained in the MRG method, which takes one or more days, be familiar with transference, and have experience with group psychotherapies and interpretations (Ahlin, 1996b). Preferably, but not necessarily, the researcher (observer) is an experienced group psychotherapist. Depending on the aim of the study, more than one observer may be involved. The MRG method can be used during a group session, or afterwards, by viewing, or listening to, the recording of the session. Ahlin (1996a) recommended using video recordings, because they allow for the analysis of non-verbal communication. Ahlin et al. (1996) and Ahlin (1996a,b) clarified that the observer determines the theme the group is engaged with. In other words, the problem, or conflict, the group is grappling with. Ahlin (1996a) suggested that researchers then use eight determinants, each of which has five levels (positions). When evaluating these determinants, the observer decides which position tallies with the situation that is being assessed. Together, the five positions form the MRG diagram. It is a schema, which depicts the group climate in relation to the group theme that the group is grappling with at that time, Ahlin (1996b) explained.

Training is required to do so. Group climate refers to the manifestation of the group matrix (eight group determinants). The graphic illustration of the MRG depicts the ongoing group process and can be found in Ahlin (1988, 1996a,b).

The MRG has been validated, a computer program has been developed for the organization of observational data (Ahlin, 1996b), and it has been used in practice (see Ahlin et al., 1996). Ahlin et al. (1996) suggested that the MRG is useful for evaluating the "micro-outcomes" of group processes, because it can capture what happens in a group analytic psychotherapy session.

Repertory Grid Method

George Kelly (1955) developed personal construct theory, suggesting that people's belief systems are based on several complex bipolar personal constructs (see Fransella & Adams, 1965). They enable people to perceive similarities and differences (Bannister & Fransella, 1980, 1993). The role construct repertory grid is a research method that arose out of Kelly's theory (see e.g., Norris, 1977; Walker et al., 2013). It provides a format through which individuals can express their own views of the world. The aim of the repertory grid is to illuminate a person's, or a group's, understanding of whatever they are concerned with (Fransella & Bannister, 1977). The researcher identifies a topic that can potentially result in to new insight, but it must be relevant to the participants. Mental health legislation, politics, decolonization, and work roles, are just a few broad issues.

Label for Construct pole	Elements Role title Your mother Sandra	Elements Your Sister	Elements Your Aunt	Elements Your Cousin	Elements Your Grandpa	Label for Construct pole
Friendly	x		x	x		unfriendly
Patient	x	x	x			impatient
supportive		x	x		X	unsupportive

FIGURE 5.2 Fictitious Completed Grid

Participants choose elements, basically, anything that gives rise to construing. For Kelly, elements were roles. Nowadays, elements can be people, aspects of work, leisure activities, other group members, psychotherapists, friends, and so forth (Bannister et al., 1995). Typically, elements are people the participant knows well (Brown & Detoy, 1988). The constructs, which are bipolar dimensions defined by the participant her/himself, are the beliefs that s/he uses to organize her/his understanding of people, or of something.

The grid may be constructed by giving participants a list of role titles (e.g. mother, sister, aunt) and writing the name of specific people who fit this role (e.g. Sandra). The researcher marks three cells in each row. Participants may be asked to think about the three people (mother, aunt, cousin), say how two are alike, and how the third is different in some important way. The participant may come up with “friendly”. This label represents the first personal bipolar construct. In the same way, the procedure of “triadic elicitation of personal constructs” is done for all roles until no new constructs are generated (see Brown & Detoy, 1988). Once the grid is completed (see Figure 5.2), the researcher may carry out a Content Analysis. The content is analyzed by assigning codes (numbers or words) to specific characteristics within the text. A list of categories, a coding scheme, can be used to sort the bipolar constructs by incorporating two labels each (e.g. friendly, unfriendly) into categories.

The most important categories are identified and the construct labels assigned to them may be presented in table format.

Example of **identified categories**: social interaction, personality attributes, etc. and *construct labels* of the roles:

Social Interaction		*Personal Attributes*	
Female Relatives	*Male Relatives*	*Female Relatives*	*Male Relatives*
Good listener	unreceptive	supportive	not good with people
Verbally skilled	not tactful	patient	unfriendly

This method can also be applied to research groups (see Leach et al., 2001).

All group members are elements. Each member compares her/himself in relation to other group members along specific constructs. A grid with four group members would be constructed by giving them numbers: Ella 1, Charly 2, Leon 3, and Rosa 4. Constructs are presented in the rows of the grid and the elements in the columns. Each cell contains the corresponding rating score. Constructs for these members are, for example, smart versus dull (bipolar attributes), which the member makes to distinguish between entities of the world (different people). Elements are then rated, for example, on an ordinal scale from 1 to 6, to reflect relevance, rather than a notion of absolute quantity. Rosa rates her friend as 6, indicating that her friend is very dull.

Leach et al. (2001) described the use of the repertory grid method to study a psychotherapy group. All group members completed individual repertory grids before group therapy, after therapy, and at three- and six-month follow-ups. Using a modified grid technique, Watson (1972) measured change during psychodynamic group psychotherapy. Group processes were also studied by Watson (1970). Caplan et al. (1975), Shapiro et al. (1975), and by Fransella and Joyston-Bechal (1971). To compare specific constructs of each group member, some standardization must occur. Therefore, these researchers supplied verbal labels (adjectives, words), but not constructs, which each group member interpreted, according to her/his own constructs. Take for example the word "dislike". One member may think that others dislike him. When completing a further grid after several weeks, he may have a different perception.

Psychotherapy groups are characterized by fluctuations and change. What group members discuss (content), the group process itself, as well as emotions and perceptions, can change in analytic groups. Even though Kelly was not a group analyst, he nevertheless provided some beneficial descriptions of a psychotherapy group. Conceptualizing stages, he suggested that group members start to see the world through another person's eyes (Fransella & Bannister, 1977; Bannister & Fransella, 1993; Fransella et al., 2003). People play a role within the group and relationships are re-enactments of situations outside the group. Eventually, group members try out new roles outside the group. Bannister and Fransella (1993) suggested that the Grid technique may enable researchers to get an idea of the processes underlying group interaction, and why changes occur in the group.

Outcome was measured in diverse psychotherapy groups by Fielding (1975). Repertory Grid studies can also be done with group psychotherapists (see Morris, 1977). Hill et al. (2016) have examined clinical psychology trainees' Selves over the duration of training. Thus, group analytic trainees could be studied through grids.

Grids vary in content and form. They are designed to show the relationship between the participant's responses in mathematical terms, revealing how a person construes constructs, how they are integrated, and what implications they have (Banister et al., 1995).

Grids are a method of assessing the degree of structure and organization of construing without judgment. It is irrelevant as to whether a person's constructs are correct, or not. Instead, this technique focuses on whether a participant has a structured, coherent way of viewing the world.

The Repertory Grid method is flexible and can be adapted. Sometimes, participants prefer to use drawings to explore their construing (Banister et al., 1995). Drawings may yield more readily insight into unconscious processes than language. While it is suitable for everybody, Indigenous people, participants who are not fluent in the researcher's language, or have a learning disability, might find it easier to express themselves through creative works. Furthermore, it is not necessary to study roles. Relationships, situations, aspects of the self, and therapy sessions, are just a few foci, which show how this method has been used.

The grid data are commonly statistically analyzed. Although software packages can be used, they are not always user-friendly (Heckmann, 2024).

Winter (1992) reviewed the Grid Method with regard to its use in examining outcome, therapy process, and prediction of therapeutic change. Scapegoating, idealization of the therapist, and countertransference difficulties, have also been examined with this method. Concluding that this method could investigate the complexity of analytic groups, Winter (1992) suggested that researchers would find it a valuable tool.

Likewise, Catina and Tschuschke (1993) found it surprising that this method was not used more frequently in group analytic research, considering the impact of the group on a person's construing her/himself. They utilized it to study aspects of group members' self-image and significant others in their lives. Participants came from two psychoanalytic groups.

They assessed the correlation between the personal construing at the beginning and end of therapy, demonstrating a positive change. Furthermore, they used the grid to assess how the group was construed. Knowing how group interactions influence the individual process of construing enables therapists to intervene, the authors noted.

Leach et al. (2001) studied a group of sexual survivors. For each grid, they provided a list of elements (Child Self, Self Now, Ideal Self, Mother, Father, Abuser in Childhood, Partner, Men/Women in General). To rate the "Ideal Self", group members were asked simply to consider "myself as I would like to be". Group members can rate these nine elements on a Likert scale (7-point). Researchers and/or group members can provide constructs, and subsequently apply the standard triadic procedure developed by Bannister and Fransella (1980, 1993; Fransella et al., 2003). For some purposes, it may be helpful to select element triads systematically (Leach et al., 2001). While some comparisons may involve only family members, others may cut across different groups. In some settings, the computerized elicitation procedure based on pairs of elements (Keen & Bell, 1980), might be useful (Leach et al., 2001).

So, the Repertory Grid Method is a valuable alternative that should be utilized more often. Free-floating discussion (free association in the group), and many other aspects, could be examined in group analytic groups by using the Repertory Grid method. Furthermore, AI could be used to refine construct exploration, cluster similar constructs across participants to reveal shared or divergent views, provide visual representations of personal constructs, and perform individualized analysis.

Using Q-Methodology

Q-Methodology was initially developed by the psychologist Stephenson (1936, 1953) in the 1930s as a data collection and analytic method to empirically study human subjectivity. In mathematical terms, William Stephenson applied factor analysis to people, correlating each factor by inverting the correlation matrix, which results in Q-factors. Since then, this method has been elaborated and adapted Rost (2020) noted. The British School uses the Q-Methodology to study shared viewpoints, adopting design with multiple participants, an unusual form of qualitative analysis. In contrast, the Californian School utilizes it as a standardized observer-rated assessment tool (p. 98).

This method allows researchers to reveal the key viewpoints among a group of participants (Watts & Stenner, 2012). So, this technique is useful when trying to characterize how different people think about a particular issue, that is, group analytic psychotherapy. Or group members could be asked about their views on the "ideal" psychotherapist. Alternatively, research questions may focus on "what makes something happen", "what is it like right now", or "what should we do about it". Good Q-research questions should be simple, coherent, and tightly focused (Watts & Stenner, 2012).

The researcher's task is then to create/design a set of stimulus items (Q-set) that will enable participants to respond adequately to the research question. If a researcher asked about the main causes of why group analytic psychotherapy is not the psychotherapy of choice for commissioners, Q-set could consist of statements citing various known, or possible, causes by drawing on policies, academic articles, and so forth. Whatever sources are used, a set of opinions (statements) is developed to create the Q-set by reviewing discussions on a topic (Brown, 1986). The results are a large set of statements (concourse), which must be reduced to a manageable number constituting the Q-sample (White, 2025). Enough statements will allow sufficiently detailed responses, so, the finished Q-set may comprise between 40 and 80 items. Piloting is important to ensure that a broad coverage of the topic is achieved. Commonly, participants' effort contributes to the robustness of the results. Researchers use purposeful sampling, but recruitment also depends on the research question. Sample sizes vary, ranging from 12 to 40 participants (Webler et al., 2009). A good variety of well-formed views about the topic is needed, which allows people to describe various perspectives about an issue or research questions.

Each participant is presented with statements about the topic of interest and asked to sort these statements (can be written on cards), according to specific instructions (Q-sort). A suitable ranking system and sorting distribution are chosen. Q-sort may involve forced choice or free distribution of number of items, which are given a ranking value. Stephenson coined the term psychological significance (Burt & Stephenson, 1939). The Q-sorter is asked to give items, which have high/low psychological significance, a high/low ranking. Each item (or stimuli) is ranked relative to each other to capture their interdependence and complexity.

When used in a therapy group, Q-sort can be used to describe different and similar points of view between group members. Each Q-sort must be directly compared with each other. The final stage involves carrying out a factor analysis to identify clusters of similarly performed Q-sorts. Once these are found, it indicates a shared view among participants (or group of people). A statistical software package (see Appendix 3) can be used to determine factors, achieved through abduction.

As such, Q-factor analysis is used to derive a formulation of a theory, or hypothesis, which aims to explain why an observable phenomenon manifests in a particular way (Rost, 2020). Stephenson (1953, 1977) argued that the study of subjectivity cannot be derived through the postulation and testing of pre-formulated hypotheses. He believed that concepts do not precede operations. It is the other way around.

In Watts' (2015) study, the Q-sort has been completed using a forced choice, a quasi-normal sorting distribution, which has been designed for the use with a 48-item Q-set. This distribution and shape are considered the standard. The set contains 11 ranking values, which range from +5 to −5, indicating the number of items, which can be ranked at each value (two at +5, three at +4, and so on). Distributions, which contain 13 (+6 to −6) and 9 (+4 to −4) ranking values, are also commonly employed. The final overall pattern of items allows the researcher to capture the participants' general viewpoint. To give you an idea how a Q-sort may look like, I have created a fictious Q-sort in Figure 5.3.

The Psychotherapy Process Q-Sort (PQS) (see Ablon & Jones, 2005) is a Q-technique, which provides a set of categories across observers. They guide the observers' attention to aspects of the clinical material that would not have been noticed otherwise and can arise from the background (Jones & Windholz, 1990).

Armelius and Armelius (1992) analyzed the behavior of members in small groups. Their Q-sort was based on Bion's theoretical work. Using Bion's (1961, 1967) work group and three basic assumptions (see Appendix 1), they distinguished between manifest behavior

-5	-4	-3	-2	-1	0	+1	+2	+3	+4	+5
48	19	26	28	02	20	01	30	29	01	07
2										2
	3								3	
		4						4		
			5				5			
				6		6				
					7					

FIGURE 5.3 Fictitious Graphic Representation of a Fictitious Q-Set

and unconscious intentions/needs, creating statements and categories for the Q-sort. Relying on inferences, through the Q-sort technique, they could interpret the behavior of individuals and of the entire group (Armelius & Armelius, 1992). Group analytic researchers could do a Q-sort of Hopper's (1997) Fourth Basic Assumption to study individuals in a group and the group-as-a-whole (see Appendix 3 for further useful information on the Q-sort).

More recently, Rost (2020) concluded that the unique scientific advantages of Q-Methodology are sadly unacknowledged, and that it is underused in psychotherapy research. It could produce valuable on analytic groups. Due to modern technologies, factor analysis is no longer a barrier. AI could refine the statistical analysis, identify nuanced clusters of perspectives, and personalize the statement set. Moreover, NLP techniques could be integrated into the Q-Methodology (Wibawa & Kurniawan, 2024). Wibawa and Kurniawan discuss the complex field of text summarization in NLP, focusing on the development and importance of semantic understanding.

Social & Network Analysis Methodology

SNA is a collection of theories and methods (Freeman, 2004). Based on the assumption that individuals, groups, and organizations are influenced by their connections to othersl, and the networks they are embedded in (Fox & Everton, 2013), SNA seeks to characterize the pattern of transactions and relationships nested in the world. It wants to better understand the underlying structure of complex systems, which may be studied by using visual mapping and quantitative techniques for describing network characteristics (Rawlings et al., 2023).

Network Analysis (NA) is a broader field that can study any type of network. Network-based research questions may be answered by using statistical programming language and platforms. R is one possibility, which allows researchers to also access statistical methods other network researchers have drawn on (Rawlings et al., 2023). Software and programs make NA accessible to group analytic researchers knowledgeable of statistics and technology.

One of its beneficial aspects is that NA can reveal otherwise hidden factors that may affect clients in a therapy group, trainees or students, or members in medium and large groups. Network approaches can be applied to identify components of the system, such as actors, and the relationship among them, that is, links between nodes (Borsboom et al., 2011, 2021).

Psychological and emotional (unconscious) processes may be underpinned by specific networks, which could define the interactions among group members. Hence, NA could be used to explore the relations among them and to construct such a network.

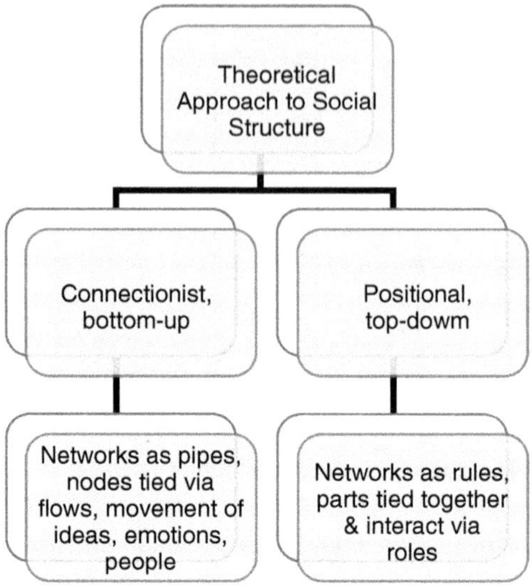

FIGURE 5.4 Main Theoretical Division between Approaches (Extracted from Rawlings et al., 2023 and Borsboom et al., 2021)

Most network modeling approaches use conditional associations to define the prevalent network structure in a set of variables (Epskamp, 2020; Robinaugh et al., 2020). Broadly defined, a structure is an arrangement of related things that form a pattern. Social structures are patterns of interactions. Whereas some structures are visible, "an invisible structure underlies society and has its influence in determining the conduct of society as a whole" (Moreno, 1933 cited in Rawlings et al., 2023, p. 2). How structure is viewed (see Figure 5.4) affects the focus of the research. The connectionist and positional approaches are commensurable, as Rawlings et al. (2023) explained, commonly working in tandem.

NA has its own distinct terminology (see Figure 5.5) to describe the connections and objects (actors) that form a network structure.

NA can examine the pattern of relationships, that is, distinguishing between simple or complex relationships. It is also suitable to establish causes. A putative cause can result in an effect (overexposure to sun causes sunburn), or several causes combined create multiple effects (overexposure to sun and environmental toxins combined with stress can cause illness). Causes may be stable or unstable (Hevey et al., 2013).

While early research applied multidimensional scaling to represent the spatial structure of causal networks (Knoke & Yang, 2008), subsequently algorithms were developed to optimally represent networks, such as qgraph (Epskamp et al., 2012). Rawlings et al. (2023) suggested that learning how to do an NA involves having theoretically guided hunches about social structures. As with other methodologies, your philosophical position and research question/aim influence which approach you use. However, you should "think structurally", Rawlings et al. (2023, p. 17) assert, offering this advice on how to carry out network research: when designing a study, you start by describing and exploring surface typologies and deeper structures. Their organizing principles can be inferred. You need to have an idea which actors and types of ties you would like to examine (p. 50). Borsboom et al. (2021), who have adopted a scientific, psychometric approach to NA, begin with the research question. Then an appropriate quantitative design is chosen for the data collection.

Network structure estimation, network description, and network stability analysis are just a few techniques that can be used (see Eskamp et al., 2018 for multivariate graphical estimation,

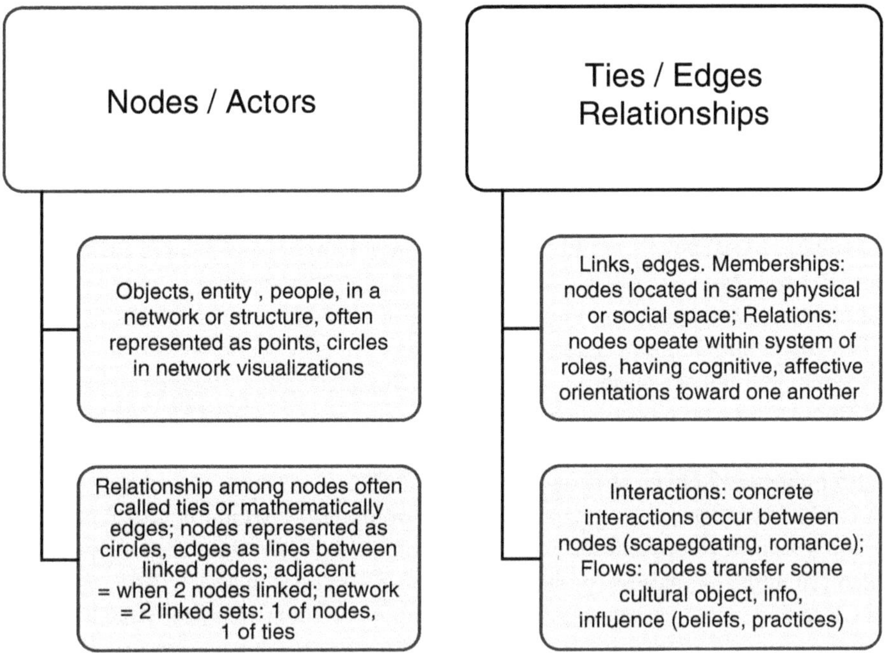

FIGURE 5.5 Conceptualization of Nodes & Social Ties (Extracted from Rawlings et al., 2023, pp. 47–49)

structural equation, and other network modeling methods). Quantitatively oriented group analytic researchers may find psychometric NA useful. However, advanced knowledge of statistics is necessary.

Network representations have a long history as research tools in statistics, where they encode important information pertaining to the joint probability distribution of a set of variables (Cox & Wermuth, 1996). Causal, structural, equation, and correlation models can be applied as part of an NA. Researchers may answer network-based research questions by using statistical programming language and platforms. R allows researchers to access statistical methods, which network researchers have used (see Rawlings et al., 2023). If you are not a technologically savvy person, you may find tutorials helpful. They also explain how to utilize software. Familiarizing yourself with the specific software will take time. Multiple measures (metrics) (Betweenness, Bridge, Centrality, Centralization, Closeness, Degree, Density, Eigenvector Centrality) are found in several software packages and platforms (Fox & Everton, 2013). I tested some for their user-friendliness and created a network graph on SocNetV, which was an interesting experience.

From an NA perspective, the network of relationships between the variables constitutes the psychological phenomenon (De Schryver et al., 2015). Hevey (2018) clarified that it is a system wherein the constituent variables mutually influence each other, and the existence of causal latent variables does not have to be hypothesized (Schmittmann et al., 2013). Network models have increasingly been applied to health psychology, personality, and research attitudes (see Hevey, 2018). I refer the interested reader to Appendix 3 for resources and literature.

While directed networks can represent causal structures (Pearl, 2000), they are based on strict assumptions. Network science has developed using graphical approaches to represent relationships between nodes. The pattern of relationships between variables and a network can be estimated using common statistical parameters that quantify relationships and be visually presented (Hevey, 2018).

Undirected network models have typically been examined by PMRF statistical models, and a time-series network of an individual may be useful for understanding the relationship between nodes (symptoms), which could inform the treatment plan (David et al., 2018). Networks can also be estimated for different groups and a direct comparison of two networks can be estimated in different subpopulations (Hevey, 2018). Alternatively, if researchers aim to examine how group members' causal beliefs are structured, and the extent to which beliefs are shared between members (Reser & Muncer, 2004), NA would be a suitable method.

What makes SNA distinct and interesting for group analytic researchers is its focus on networks, i.e., the combination of actors and ties that form a network. Actors are social entities, that is, discrete individuals, or corporate and collective social units. Relational ties are the social bonds defining a linkage between a pair of actors. The combination of actors and ties forms a network (structure), which can be studied by using visual mapping and quantitative techniques for describing network characteristics.

SNA has been used to investigate a wide range of topics, for example, the dynamics of community and group development (Monge & Contractor, 2003). While Stepanyan et al. (2014) drew attention to the availability of standardized software packages (UCINET, SIENA, ORA), which are bundled with a variety of graphical visualization tools, other software has been developed since.

Hughes et al. (2024) note the utility of network analytic approaches in mapping correlations among socio-psychological constructs of social identification and behavior in groups. A statistically informed conclusion could be drawn regarding the overall structure of identity networks.

Given the scarcity of SNA research in group analysis, exploratory methods could also be used. These include network visualization and descriptive statistics, such as the mean and standard deviations (Stepanyan et al., 2013), as well as using correlation coefficients (Bedeian, 2014) to calculate betweenness, reciprocity, and other network dynamics and effects (Stepanyan et al., 2013).

Also of interest could be an inductive NA (see Lunt, 1988, 1991; Muncer & Gillen, 1997; Muncer et al., 2001; Reser & Muncer, 2004). It can be used to understand how people make sense of events, gain insight into their beliefs or perceptions of racism, or to evaluate group analytic theories. Drawing on social identity theory, Lüders et al. (2024) suggest that network modeling can reveal and inform latent social identities, when linking intra-individual representations of group membership with attitude structures at a macro level.

If you wonder why you should use SNA to study interactive groups, Wőlfer and Hewstone (2017) give ten reasons. For group analytic research, it is relevant that SNA considers latent socio-psychological entities.

Meeussen et al. (2018) point out that Network Theory views groups as sets of individual people (nodes) in a web of interpersonal relations (ties). Hence, NA allows researchers to look at person- or team-level variables, and at dyadic relations between group members. Applying a longitudinal survey through SNA, they identified that social bonding and norming, which enable sharing of values, are main features of cohesive groups. Meeussen et al. (2018) explain that longitudinal SNA looks at social networks as they change over time. This means that group members' characteristics, such as values, and the relations between members, e.g., how much G likes O, are measured more than once. Changes in relationships and characteristics can be identified over time. Changes in people's characteristics may be predicted on the basis of social relationships, for example, does G adapt her values toward those of O, because she likes her? So, with this method researchers can trace group processes or network dynamics, while considering the interdependency of data and the network structures (Snijders, 2001).

The examples I have given demonstrate that the different approaches within the tradition of Social/Network Analysis allow for flexible and wide-ranging applications. Hence, small, medium, and large groups can be studied by applying SNA.

Assume that you would like to create a network of actors and ties (nodes and edges) about your analytic psychotherapy group. The actors/nodes are the group members. You are particularly interested in cohesion, that is, the underlying processes that create the structure you seek to measure, because cohesion is an important aspect of groups. Over time, cohesiveness tends to increase in a network, as participants start to reciprocate the ties directed at them and to connect to others.

The type of data that you will gather must tally with the aim of your research. In this case, you would like to find out how cohesive the group is. By observing members in the group, you can gather suitable data that reflect the structure of cohesion (your structure of interest).

Once you have collected the data, you prepare these by including temporal and spatial information (look at Figure 5.6). For example, when did Claude respond to Sarah, and who responded to whom. You can include representations of dyadic, triadic, or group interactions of participants. Recording these on separate Excel spreadsheets (one for nodes; another one for ties) makes it easier to extract and import them into software. Researchers have their own preferences and no "best" software package exists. Stepanyan et al. (2014) like the Pajek Arcs/Edges format (De Nooy et al., 2005).

Often, researchers depict their data in the form of a matrix:

TABLE 5.1 Fictious Correlation Matrix between Variables

Variable	*A*	*B*	*C*	*D*	*E*	*F*	*G*
B	–	7	1	5	5	–	–
C	3	2	5	4	1	3	5
D	6	1	7	1	4	2	3

The directions of the relationships represent the information flow between people (actors). If actor i replies to a message from actor j, the direction is (i → j), which can be represented in a corresponding row in the column of the matrix (Hanneman & Riddle, 2005). Depending on your data, the ties between the actors may not always be reciprocal (directed), then the matrix is asymmetric (rows and columns are not identical). Some researchers (e.g. Stepanyan et al., 2014) exclude such data from their analysis. Values appearing in the matrix are based on the number of dyadic messages exchanged between pairs of actors. Simple, descriptive network statistics can be used to calculate the density (mean, standard deviation).

A network is typically described using the language of Graph Theory, which also provides tools to measure the connectivity structure of a network, such as geodesic distance or transitivity, loosely interpreted as "the friend of my friend is my friend" (see Salter-Townshend, 2012). You might measure different network centrality parameters, such as the *degree* (i.e. number of connections) or *closeness* (i.e. distance to all network members) of a person's social contacts or connections (Wőlfer & Hewstone, 2017).

Relevant contextual network characteristics include density, network reciprocity, and centralization. While density reflects the overall connectedness within a network (total number of ties among all network members), network reciprocity specifies the total number of mutual relationships within the social network. Centralization measures the extent to which network members vary in terms of their importance, ranging from equally powered to hierarchical networks (Wőlfer & Hewstone, 2017).

While all group members in Figure 5.6 have many direct links, Claude has fewer ties. Sarah is a member with the highest degree of centrality and high betweenness, so she has a lot of influence over what does, or does not, flow through the network. Without her, the members in the periphery would be less well connected. Sarah and Li have the shortest paths compared to the other members, so they are closer to each other.

Suitable metrics to measure cohesion include density, clustering coefficient, and path length. Here, we will look at density, which tells you how connected the group members (a particular network) are. Have a look at Figure 5.6, because we will calculate the density of cohesion by using a simple formula:

> Density = Number of Actual Connections/Number of Possible Connnections*100.
> (alternatively do not multiply by the100, then 1 is the highest density).

Fictitious Network Graph of Highly Connected Therapy Group with 8 Members

Key: Nodes/circles: Members; Directed Edges/lines: Connections; Dense Structure

Networks can be directed or undirected. To determine possible connections, we need to know whether the links/edges are directed or undirected. In an *undirected* network, all relationships (ties) are mutual. The formula for possible connections is $n(n - 1)/2$ *for undirected networks* (the relationship between the two members, actors, or nodes is symmetric and mutual. So, it is the same in both directions, and if member A feels affection for B, and B for A, this is undirected). *Undirected* ties are normally represented as lines without arrows, as in Figure 5.6. In our example, the network relationships are *undirected,* resulting in this calculation: $8*(8 - 1)/2 = 28$ Actual $25/28 = 89.28$. Thus, in this group with 8 members, 25 actual connections exist out of 28 possible connections. So, the density is almost 90 (89.28), which is a high density. Derr (2024) classed everything over 50% as high density, 20–50% as moderate density, and everything under 20% as low density. When the density is higher than 70%, this may indicate that group members may feel overwhelmed by too many ties. Once the results have been interpreted, group analysts can act on them. Had the density been low, they would need to focus on building relationships in the group between those members who are in the periphery of the network. Network density is dynamic, so coherence can be monitored regularly over time to track changes and adjustments to the therapeutic techniques might be necessary.

Ties/edges are *directed* when they indicate an orientation or flow from one person to another.

The formula for number of possible connections is $n(n - 1)$ *for directed networks* (asymmetric relationship between the members, ties exhibit directionality; A feels affection for B, but B feels affection for G instead of A). Directed ties are usually represented as lines with arrows:

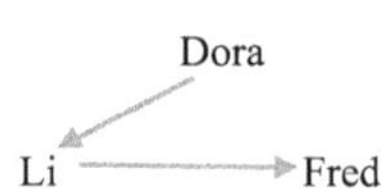

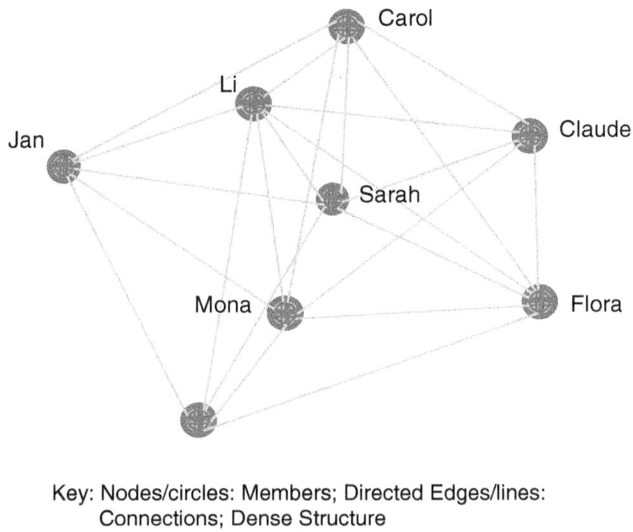

FIGURE 5.6 Fictitious Network Graph of Highly Connected Therapy Group with eight Members

Sometimes, the setting allows for either undirected or directed relations. Then it is assumed to be directed, although the extent of reciprocity depends on the empirical question (Rawlings et al., 2023).

The focus on relationships may guide group analytic researchers to find data in affiliations, connections, transactions, and comparisons across phenomena. They could identify the patterns of relations between group members (see Borsboom et al., 2021). Since group analytic researchers are often interested in relations, they could draw on Social Network Theory. Aided by a distinct set of data collection and analysis tools, it first guides the researcher to focus on specific data, representing the interrelation of objects, and later to identify the processes and patterns in these. This interrelated information allows for a holistic understanding of social structures. Generally speaking, GQs, surveys, observations, and scraping websites, or digital archives, are suitable strategies to gather data. However, when node sets are clearly delineated by time and space, they tend to be empirically valid (Rawlings et al., 2023). Crucial steps involved in doing NA research are summarized in Figure 5.7. To familiarize yourself with this method, choose the right software and tools, and practice with datasets that are publicly available.

Depending on their research focus, researchers can choose different network approaches, which have specific strengths and weaknesses. One of the difficulties with complete networks is that they are restricted to a network boundary (e.g. a medium-sized group). So, such network only captures a specific part of the population and generalization is tricky. Furthermore, SNA is particularly sensitive to missing data, because non-participating individuals may change the structure of the social network dramatically (Wőlfer & Hewstone, 2017). Thus, if researchers are interested in other contact experiences beyond a specific context, which defines the network boundary, an alternative or additional method would be snowball or ego networks (see Wőlfer & Hewstone, 2017). SNA, and NA more generally, can be time-consuming. Nevertheless, these methods have many advantages for analyzing naturally existing social structures.

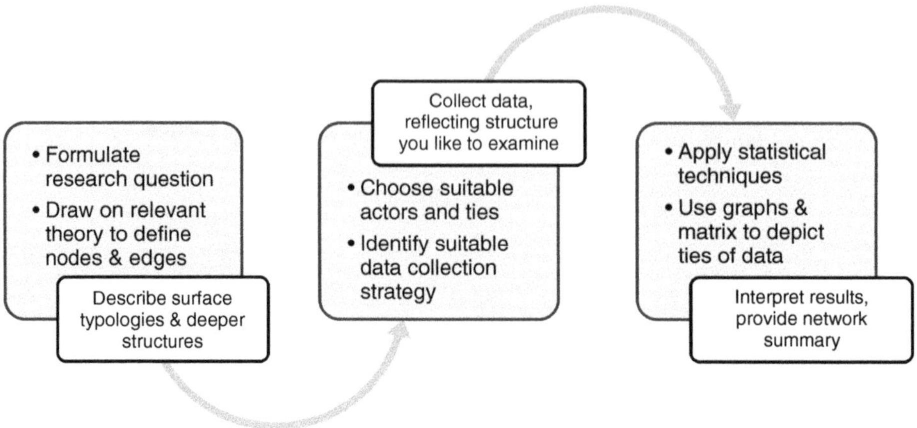

FIGURE 5.7 Procedure Involved in a (Social) Network Analysis

Benefit of AI Tools & Techniques

NLP is an area of AI that draws on linguistics, deep learning neural networks, and algorithms. Typically written in programming languages, such as Python, NLP algorithms allow computers to understand, process, and generate human languages (Gruetzemacher, 2022). Many researchers have used NLP tools and algorithms to analyze texts and speech. Such tools enable SA. It can be used for keyword extraction, text categorization, and summarization. Within the realm of NLP, SA is a crucial discipline (Wang et al., 2025). For group analytic research, its ability to analyze sentiments makes SA an attractive means to analyze the prevailing emotions within a specific group. This type of analysis aims to understand emotions within a text and has been widely used in politics, market research, and business (Khurana et al., 2023). Multilingual Sentiment Analysis (MSA) can assess the emotions and opinions in different languages (Wang et al., 2025). Considering that groups are conducted in many countries and group members speak different languages, MSA seems a useful approach to identify positive and negative emotions in a group, and/or the public sentiment toward group analytic psychotherapy. MSA, which is separated into two main techniques (see Figure 5.8), is a necessary development to shift SA away from English-speaking cultures and texts.

Pioneering approaches, such as Wang et al.'s (2025) Chinese SA, contribute to the decolonization of research per se. Dimensional SA, extending beyond the traditional binary (categorical) classification of emotions, is beneficial as well. It captures nuances, subtleties, and the intensity and specific aspects of sentiments in a text (see Lee et al., 2022; Wang et al., 2025).

Collaboration with NLP researchers seems equally useful for group analytic researchers. Language models must be trained on group analytic datasets, as well as group analytic and psychoanalytic terminology. Hence, although machine learning algorithms have significant capabilities that enable researchers to do an SA, they have limitations when applied to an MSA (see Figure 5.9).

To use AI tools, some working knowledge of language models and computational technology is required. Otherwise, researchers may neither understand limitations nor be able to deal with technical issues. Having adequate computational resources is also necessary when integrating language models into research.

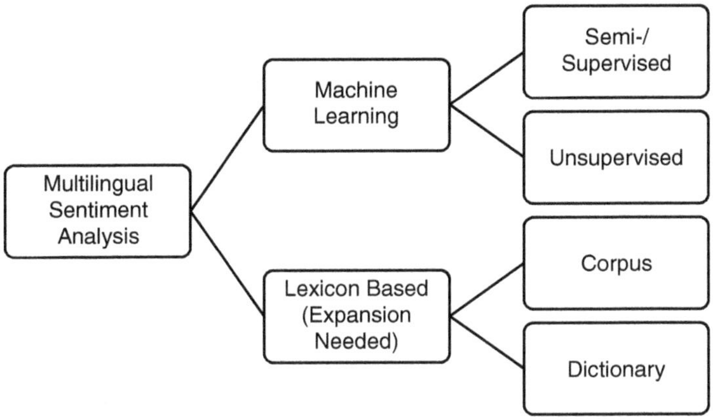

FIGURE 5.8 Multilingual Sentiment Analysis Classification (Modification of Khurana et al., 2023)

Advanced language models like ChatGPT, and other large language models, offer significant capabilities. It is a deep learning model (see Figure 5.10). Developed by OpenAI, GPT stands for "generative pre-trained transformer". A transformer is a specific type of neural network trained used to analyze the context of data input and to assign importance to each component (OpenAI, 2025). Basically, GPT is a language model used by the ChatGPT AI-bot that understands and generates coherent, human text (see also IBM, 2021).

Chatbots (computers that simulate conversations) have been used in mental health. While they may improve access to care, reduce stigma, increase engagement (D'Alfonso, 2020), they also pose ethical challenges, that is, privacy concerns, potential for harm, lack of human oversight. Overall, the pertinent literature suggests that Chatbots may potentially be an effective intervention, but more research is needed (Rad & Rad, 2023). A recent focus group study reported mixed results. Group discussions highlighted the complex psychological implications of Chatbots. The lack of empathy may limit their benefits in certain settings, although they are cost-effective. Chatbots lend themselves to being used in individual psychotherapy, but their use in analytic groups is questionable. I could not find evidence that Chatbots have been used in analytic psychotherapy groups, possibly due to the complex nature of group analytic psychotherapy. Whether they may be beneficial for assessments, such as suitability for analytic groups, would need to be researched. Furthermore, Chatbots have been used to monitor mood and reduce anxiety, for example, psychologist Alison Darcy developed Woebot, which acts as an automated therapist (Zemmelman, 2021). Evidence suggests that they are of benefit in manualized treatments (see Raile, 2024). Whether Chatbots or other apps might be of use in group analysis would need to be researched. Interestingly, ChatGPT has been used in a case study offering interpretations of dreams. Although they encouraged reflection, they lacked depth (Raile, 2024). However, ChatGPT has been used in other research with good results. One of its strengths is the ability to provide information. It can engage with a vast number of participants, ensure uniformity in interactions, and generate and organize both quantitative and qualitative data efficiently. Hence, it could assist group analytic researchers with coding, generating thematic summaries from qualitative data, identifying patterns, and extracting key findings. However, ChatGPT may misinterpret responses, it may oversimplify, overlook marginalized voices, and may not be culturally sensitive. If you do use it for your literature review or other parts of your study, reference it (see Appendix 4). As McAdoo (2024) point out, results using ChatGPT are not retrievable by other readers, unfortunately.

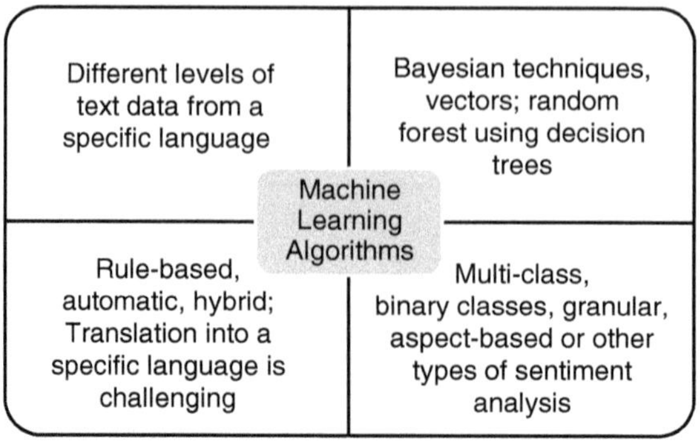

FIGURE 5.9 Capability & Limitation of Machine Learning Algorithms to Enable MSA (Extracted from Lee et al., 2022 and Wang et al., 2025)

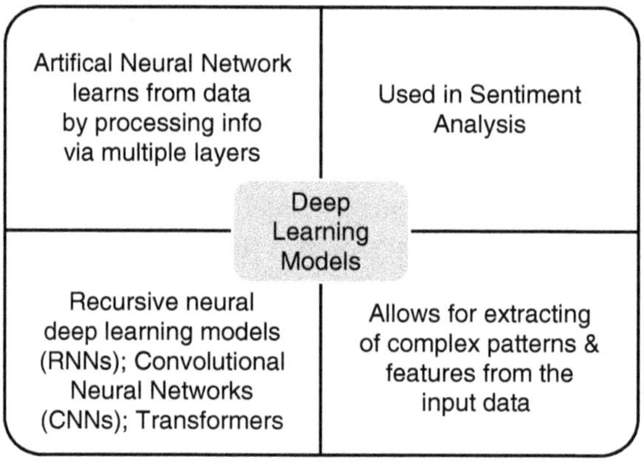

FIGURE 5.10 Deep Learning Models

Chapter Summary

Several methods were described, as well as their advantages and limitations. These included surveys and questionnaires. Although rarely used in group analytic research, the Delphi and focus group methods, the MRG, the Repertory Grid method, and Q-Methodology should not be neglected just because they seem outdated. SNA and SA could prove beneficial. AI could assist researchers in the data collection, processing, and analysis. While it cannot replace group analytic researchers, AI could assist with the laborious tasks of the research process.

6

"LIVING" GROUP ANALYTIC THEORIES TO GRASP RELATED NOTIONS, START THEORIZING & GENERATE THEORIES

Abstract

In order to provide clarity about theory and related conceptualizations, such as concepts, concept, model, theory, metatheory, and framework, their differences are discussed. Indigenous and other theoretical frameworks are described. Additionally, the related processes of modeling, conceptual analysis, and theorizing, are illuminated. I suggest that the lived experience of group analytic theories could foster imagination and understanding. This is necessary for theorizing and conceptual analyses. Furthermore, different versions of the grounded theory method are described, and practical examples are offered to aid understanding.

Introduction

Researchers should not regard theory, metatheory, concept, model, and framework as synonymous, because these have distinct characteristics (Nilson, 2015). Theoretical and terminological clarity can eliminate confusion (Nilsen & Bernhardsson, 2019). Looking at their etymological origins provides a rudimentary understanding of their differences. According to Etymonline (2024b, c, d, e, f), "theory" is derived from the Latin/Greek noun "theoria/theōria", meaning "mental scheme/contemplation". The Greek prefix "meta-" means "after". "Concept" stems from the Latin noun "conceptum". It means "draft, abstract". "Model" is derived from the Latin noun "modulus", denoting a standard. As a verb, it refers to "describing in detail". "Framework" means a "structure for enclosing or supporting". Knowing these etymological roots is useful, but insufficient. Researchers also need to know the competing definitions and not confuse them Hence, this chapter will explain these.

Furthermore, theories and theorizing have been neglected by group analytic researchers. So, I will also describe theorizing and how theories could be generated by applying the Grounded Theory method.

In what follows, I will explain concept, model, theory, metatheory, Indigenous, and other theoretical frameworks. Moreover, I will describe the related processes of modeling, conceptual analysis, and theorizing. I will suggest that the lived experience of group analytic theories could

DOI:10.4324/9781003609544-9

foster imagination and understanding, which is necessary for theorizing and conceptual analyses. Finally, the Grounded Theory method will be described. I will offer practical examples to aid understanding of the different versions of Grounded Theory.

Concepts & Conceptual Analysis

In its simplest meaning, a concept is a label that regards an abstraction, as if it had a concrete existence. Consequently, "concept" can be defined as an abstract idea that is derived from specific instances, or occurrences, of a phenomenon (Wikipedia, 2024b). Ideas and concepts are not the same. An idea is individualistic, and concepts are derived from a group of people (Trinka Blog, 2024). A concept is a mental representation of a class of things, and key concepts are particularly important in a certain context (Cambridge International Education Team, 2025). Because concepts correspond to ideas, they may be provisional rather than fixed. When concepts are viewed as comprising fundamental phenomena, or entities associated with a particular discipline, they are related to Plato's Forms or Aristotle's Universals, that is, an abstract idea or mental image (Myburgh & Tammaro, 2013, p. 133). Importantly, as Deleuze and Guattari (1994) highlighted, concepts are fabricated and created. Everyday concepts become a habit, which enable people to think or be (see Colebrook, 2002; Schulte, 2018). Concepts are crucial to the psychological processes of categorization (Margolis & Laurence, 2019) and are building blocks of theory.

Related to concepts is conceptual analysis, which concerns itself with clarifying concepts by illuminating the conditions that must be met for something to be considered a concept (Jackson, 2024). Conceptual analysis is also a philosophical method. Simply put, it centers on understanding abstract ideas. Thus, it involves the distinguishing of terms, analyzing their meanings, and representing fundamental constituent parts. Conceptual analyses have been carried out to elucidate theoretical controversies and developments (Jackson, 2024).

Kőlbel (2021) discusses the varieties of conceptual analysis and scholars have engaged in conceptual analysis in myriad ways. When used as a method, a good conceptual analysis is coherent, logically consistent, complete, pays attention to the fullest possible context, and covers as many data points as possible. It is broad and avoids unjustified extensions of concepts. It aims for precision, searches for counterexamples, looks out for semantic baggage, highlights conceptual tensions, paradoxes, and considers alternative conceptualizations (Engler & Gardiner, 2022).

Models & Modeling

According to Marrone (1984), "model" has different meanings. It is developed from research, applied in certain fields, and used by a person, group, or discipline (p. 28). Zinkin (1984) preferred the word "model" to "theory". But models are not quite the same as theories.

Descriptive models enable the visualization of a phenomenon, even though they have no substantial predictive power (Rapoport, 1972). The scope of their explanation is narrower than that of a theory. In psychoanalysis, descriptive models of the mind (id, ego, and superego) are depicted as diagrammatic representations of the components of our psyche. They consist of areas with boundaries and arrows between them to indicate the flow of energy. Such diagrams are essentially analogies or metaphors, which attempt to explain how the psyche operates.

Fried (2020) clarifies that models are instantiations of theories but are often more concrete. Models intend to explain specific processes and include a mechanism for predicting outcomes. They can be applied to a particular aspect of a given theory to provide a better understanding of it.

In group analytic research, we find the competing Medical and the Contextual Model. The five components of the Medical Model of Psychotherapy include: (1) the client disorder, problem, or complaint; (2) the psychological explanation of these; (3) the mechanism of change; (4) specific therapeutic ingredients; and (5) specificity (Wampold, 2001).

Versions of the Contextual Model emphasize a holistic common factors approach (Wampold, 2001). The components of psychotherapy include (1) client characteristics; (2) qualities of therapist; (3) treatment structures; and (4) relationship elements (Grencavage & Norcross, 1990).

When researchers compare group analytic treatment for anxiety with cognitive-behavioral treatment, they automatically compare a Contextual Model with a Medical Model, as Wampold (2001) explained. The mentalization-based and empirically-supported treatments (Karterud, 2015) are examples of manualized treatments. Manualization does not necessarily mean that a treatment has adopted the Medical Model of Psychotherapy. However, it leans toward the quantitative paradigm.

While both the Medical and Contextual Models predict that psychotherapy will be efficacious, they assume different mechanisms. Furthermore, whereas the Medical Model predicts that there will be a variation among psychotherapy treatments, the Contextual Model predicts equivalence. It means that all treatments are efficacious, known as the Dodo Bird conjecture.

These models also differ with regard to specific, general, and therapy effects, as well as allegiance and coherence (Wampold, 2001). Critics of the Medical Model of Psychotherapy advocate limited use of randomized controlled trials in therapy research.

By and large, some models are schematic representations of ideas (Rapoport, 1972). They may have only heuristic value, because they have been produced through mental shortcuts. Such models can nevertheless reveal the strength and weakness of something. Vaidyanathan (2020)

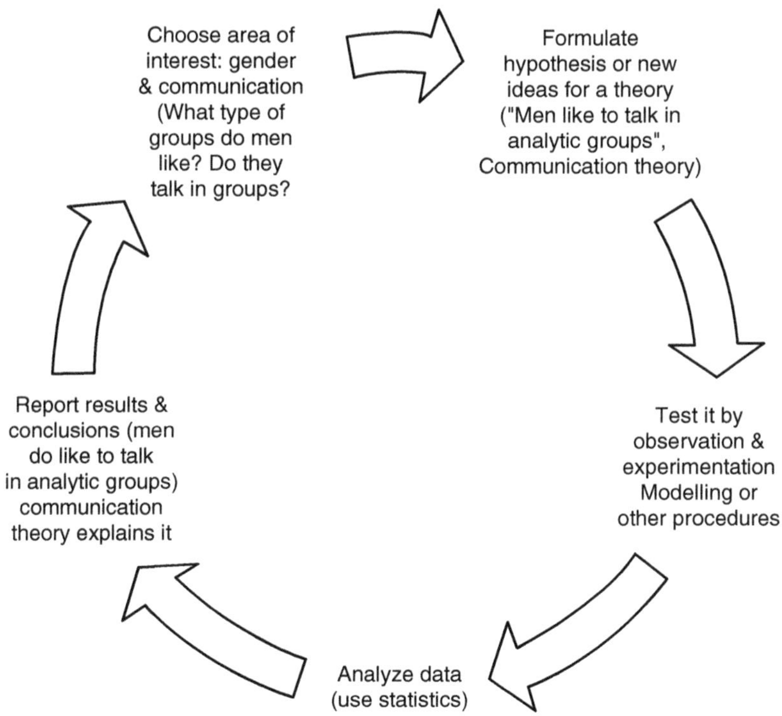

FIGURE 6.1 Scientific Cyclical Process

argue that the utility of models depends on their purpose. Fried (2020) distinguishes between theoretical and statistical models, suggesting that the broader class of models can take many forms.

According to Smaldino (2020), in order to formulate a scientific theory, it is necessary to decompose a whole phenomenon into parts, properties, and the relationship between them, and then test these through modeling. A model is a representation of these parts and relationships. It derives its power from simplicity, even revealing sometimes counterintuitive dynamics. Statistical modeling could be applied to group analytic theories to test their causal explanation, prediction, and description (see Shmueli, 2010). Page's (2018) *The model thinker. What you need to know to make data work for you*, is a useful primer for statistical modeling.

Modeling forms part of the scientific method (Figure 6.1), where researchers proceed by choosing a theory, use statistical modeling to test it, and then analyze the outcome, and refine the theory, if necessary (Shuttleworth, 2009).

The iterative cycle is also used for hypothesis testing. It was developed over centuries through philosophical and scientific contributions, drawing on the ideas of many Western male thinkers (Aristotle, Bacon, Galilei, Descartes, Newton, and Popper).

Indigenous & Other Theoretical Frameworks

Theoretical frameworks are a body of connected theories, such as Darwin's theory of natural selection, which began as one theory and has grown into a theoretical framework, in which multiple theories explain an overlapping set of phenomena (Muthukrishna & Heinrich, 2019). A framework usually denotes an overview, or system, of various descriptive categories and their relationships, used to account for a phenomenon (Nilsen, 2015). It provides a structure but does not attempt to explain the phenomena per se. Existing or developing knowledge can be integrated into frameworks. The Creative Relationship Framework is used by the Te Metahauriki Institute to research and understand the Māori culture (fundamental Māori concepts, philosophies, beliefs, values, customs, ethics, and practices), which inform the Māori law and jurisprudence (Parr, 2002).

Cribb et al. (2024) devised the Tupua te Kawa (natural law and value system) in New Zealand as a methodological framework for non-Indigenous organizations. The Kaupapa Māori literature suggests that it is a framework for doing research with, by, and for the Māori (Henry & Pene, 2001).

A framework can point to factors that have been found, or are believed to influence outcomes, such as evidence-based interventions (Damschroder, 2020). If all Western research frameworks, and Indigenous epistemology and ontology, centering on Indigenous ways of knowing, being, and doing (see Bessarab, 2015; Said, 2018), would be integrated, research could become more inclusive. In Group Analysis, intersectionality has been proposed as a framework, which provides the IGA with a structure for decolonizing Group Analysis (Nayak, 2023). Moreover, Vosmer (2023c) has introduced a rudimentary hermeneutic framework to conceptualize prejudgments and faulty/negative resonances of love in the therapy group.

Why Living Meta-/Theory Could Foster Imagination

Theories are often introduced too late, St Pierre (2017) lamented, as happens in Group Analysis. Historically, theory has been a contentious issue (Dahlin, 2003), because Foulkes was not particularly interested in theory (Brown, 2003). For Lewin (1951), there was nothing as practical as a good theory. Action researchers criticized the separation between theory and practice. Too much parsimony between the two can nevertheless be disadvantageous, particularly, when it results in neglecting other avenues of research (Yorks, 2005).

Whatever theory researchers rely on is likely to shape their study. Because theories inform intervention research, they are an integral part of the research process (see Figure 6.1). Conducting research without reference to theory could raise a few eyebrows (Greenwald, 2012). Many theories are grounded in scientific methodologies and methods (Sutton & Staw, 1995). This shows their interrelatedness.

Depending on the philosophical position a researcher adopts, s/he will rely on a specific definition of theory. Positivists demanded that every theory must be translatable into testable hypotheses. Theory is discarded, if found wanting (Rapoport, 1972). It was Popper (1959), who insisted that theory testing was deductive and that theories had to be falsifiable. Deeply influenced by Albert Einstein's insistence that if one of the predictions of his new theory unambiguously disagreed with empirical evidence the whole theory had to be given up (Krah, 2021, p. 54), Popper (1959) advocated falsification.

Hence, for Popper (1959), good scientific theories should be falsifiable, universal, testable, true, and coherent. Moreover, a good theory should make several predictions. In principle, it can be disproved or falsified by observation (Hawking, 1989, p. 11). Falsifying a theory involves demonstrating that a large part of it, if not all, is wrong insofar that it cannot fully explain the phenomena it pertains to explain. Popper posed a question that could be very useful when considering how strong a theory is. He asked: *What evidence would convince you that all of your theory is wrong?* (Dienes, 2008).

So, one could say that a theory is a self-contained system, which may prove to be true or false (Zinkin, 1984). DiMaggio (1995) suggested that all types of theories have benefits and limitations. Wong and Jeffery (2015) regarded laws and theories as distinct, even though they also overlap.

In group research, particular theories and theoretical perspectives on groups have guided how groups are conceptualized, what aspects of groups are examined, and how these aspects are studied (see Figure 6.2).

While theories can be both explanatory and descriptive (Nilsen, 2015), Van Rooij and Baggio (2020) suggest that they are primarily explanatory. Abend (2008) clarified that theories do not have to offer propositions of the world but can be a way of looking, or talking, about it. When referring to Feminist, Queer, Postcolonial Theory, and so forth, theory is often used in this

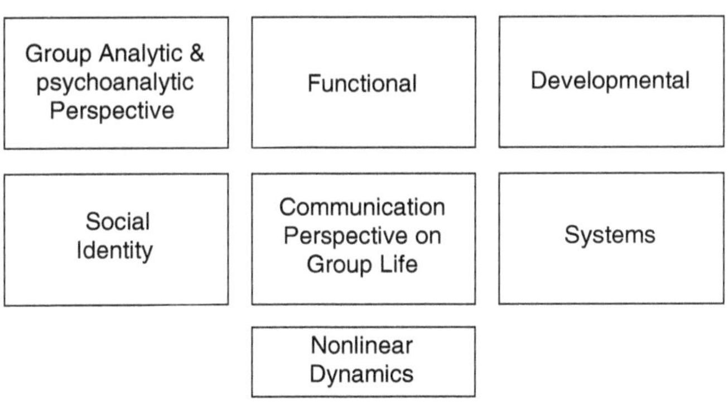

FIGURE 6.2 Theoretical Perspectives on Groups (Extracted from Barkham et al., 2021; Wheelan, 2005)

sense. The Kaupapa Māori ("general principles") is a localized critical theory (Smith, 1999). It expresses a desire to reinstate the Indigenous system mautaranga Māori, which was used before colonization. It informs methodology and has been discussed, and utilized, in several intersecting spaces to reflect the social circumstances of Māori realities. Like any other critical theory, Kaupapa Māori endeavors to seek out solutions for the benefit of the Māori. Its distinctness makes it a preferred methodology for research (Mikahere-Hall, 2017).

According to Lundberg (2004), there are two contrasting types of theories in general. While one type informs practice (Cognitive Theory), the other guides the discovery of knowledge (Relativity Theory). The Theory of Unconscious Thought (Dijksterhuis & Nordgren, 2006; Dijksterhuis et al., 2006) says that unconscious thought is relatively imprecise but can lead to better choices. Motivational processes and decision-making can take place unconsciously. Many of our motives that drive our behavior occur outside of awareness. This shows that a theory can be a creative form of scientific contribution, achieving parsimony and guiding clinical application (Greenwald, 2012). "Living" theories represent a personal and experiential process that fosters imagination and creativity (St Pierre, 2017). By and large, people like theoretical explanations, as Harvey Sacks (1995) noted. But if you do not, you will notice that there is no escape from theory.

Good theories should inform clinical practice, and theories impact each other. Take Freud's (1915b) Theory of Repression, which was integrated into group analysis. It postulates that something distressing is kept from consciousness. We deal with feelings, thoughts, and memories by "removing" these from consciousness through repression. Basically, the ego's inability to manage conflicts between the id and the superego results in anxiety. Unconscious defense mechanisms are employed to deal with this anxiety, repression being the most important of these. So, the theory of psychological defense mechanisms influences the theory of repression, and vice versa, which shows that theories impact on each other. Freud (1915b) stated that repression plays a role in distorting reality, which could result in neurosis. If repression does cause neurotic symptoms, then researchers should develop specific interventions to tackle repression. Nowadays, computer simulation models (Nguyen, 2023) often assess whether a theory is good, or not.

A good theory must be coherent and useful, according to Fried (2020), who defined theories as "bodies of knowledge that are broad in scope and aim to explain robust phenomena" (p. 336).

Theories can be conceptualized on a dimension (strong to weak). Stronger ones are clearly explicated theories that make precise, testable predictions. However, Yarkomi (2020) has highlighted that the distinction between weak and strong lies in the eye of the beholder.

Advising how a researcher can do post-qualitative inquiry, St Pierre (2017) recommends reading as many sources about specific theories as possible, until one becomes Deleuzian, Derridean, or Foucauldian. I would add becoming Foulkesian or Bionian. By "living" theories, the post-qualitative group analytic researcher will inhabit the group analytic world.

Taken together, theories have many functions (see Figure 6.3).

Half a century ago, Merton (1967) queried whether the word "theory" was becoming meaningless due to so many diverse referents. Theory' belongs to a family of words that include, guess, conjecture, and speculation (Dictionary.com, 2023). Do these many meanings obscure understanding? I agree with Levine (1979) that confusion arises when multiple, but distinct meanings are muddled. A theory can be empirical or heuristic, it can guide a hermeneutic approach or an objective scientific procedure. Thus, a positivist meaning of theory should not be confused with an interpretivist one. Being concise and consistent can eliminate misunderstanding.

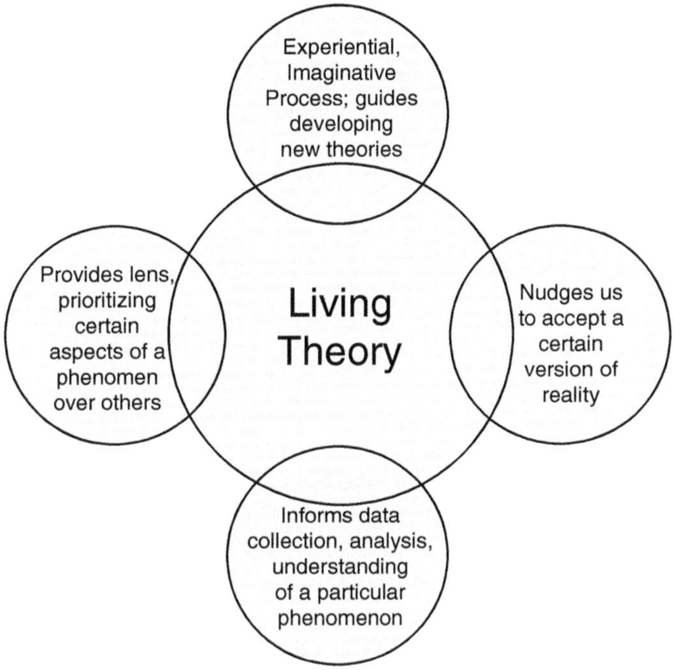

FIGURE 6.3 Distinctive Attributes & Functions of Living Theory

To achieve this, "living" theories could be a step in the right direction. It might also have a unifying effect on the many definitions of metatheory. Striving for conciseness, Wallis (2010) proposed this definition:

> Metatheory is primarily the study of theory, including the development of overarching combinations of theory, as well as the development and application of theorems for analysis that reveal underlying assumptions about theory and theorizing.
>
> (p. 78)

Creative & Superficial Theorizing

According to Weick (1995), the process of theorizing is linked to, but distinct from, theory. It consists of abstracting, generalizing, relating, selecting, explaining, synthesizing, and idealizing. Although such activities may result in hypotheses, diagrams, data, or variables, these are only *elements* of a theory. Furthermore, although testing is a means to assessing, refining, and revising theories, testing is a secondary research activity. First, theories and theorizing must be lived to foster imagination, as post-qualitative researchers have argued (e.g. St Pierre, 2011).

Engler and Gardiner (2022) caution not to reify theory when theorizing. Frequently, researchers use citations to make a copy of the theory, they like, from its original context, and then add new data to it. However, they rarely reflect upon what such superficial use of theory does to the processes of selection, reduction, translation, and appropriation (p. 117).

"Living" group analytic theories may prevent theorizing superficially (see also St Pierre, 2011, 2014). Obviously, researchers must have theoretical knowledge to theorize. Hence, before theorizing, read widely so that you are familiar with seminal and recent group analytic theories, with crucial theories about group research, and with theorizing techniques. Justify why you choose, for example, Hopper's theory of the social unconscious, and why you may like to revise it. Group analysts draw on metaphors, myths, and fairytales. So, be creative when theorizing. Engaging in free association, reverie, social dreaming, and producing mind maps, are just a few techniques that could be used.

Why Use Grounded Theory in Group Analytic Research?

Put simply, testing and developing new theories, is as important as collecting data, although some researchers focus on the latter (Simons, 2014). They choose methodological procedures over making theoretical contributions (Beller & Bender, 2017). Both are necessary. One might even argue that the methodology of Grounded Theory should be used to produce explanatory group analytic theories.

Although Grounded Theory is rooted in Positivism, Glaser and Strauss (1967) moved it away from the dominant hypothetico-deductive approach. They used induction.

Rustin (2019) has pointed that Peirce's abduction (i.e. relating observations to whatever concepts, theories, and empirical analogues are considered beneficial for their understanding) does describe Glaser and Strauss' approach better.

Be this as it may, Glaser and Strauss (1967) did emphasize the inductive generation of theory from data, which were collected through interviews and continually re-examined in the light of new information. Their production of theory involved data collection in episodes, which were punctuated by periods of data analyses (Seale, 2018b). This became the hallmark of Grounded Theory. At the time, Glaser and Strauss (1965, 1967, 1968) introduced an innovative and systematic strategy of simultaneous data collection and analysis. It differs from the typical sequential approach, where data are gathered first, and are analyzed afterwards. Unfortunately, Grounded Theory is not an easy method.

Why Does Grounded Theory Have to Be So Complicated?

Various versions of Grounded Theory have been identified (Figure 6.4), which rest on different assumptions (Figure 6.5). Chun Tie et al. (2019) have cautioned that different versions should not be used interchangeably. Methodological congruence requires that the researcher's position is congruent with her/his research question and the selected Grounded Theory approach. Hence, s/he must be aware of methodological differences in terms of how coding, analysis, theory production, and literature review are done to avoid confusion.

Morse et al. (2009) described various distinguishing features of Objectivist Grounded Theory. It assumes an independent external reality, the discovery of data, and that conceptualizations arise from the data. The neutrality, passivity, and authority of the researcher are assumed. Variables are specified, and the representations of data are regarded as unproblematic. Furthermore, it aims to achieve context-free generalizations and parsimonious conceptualizations, devoid of historical and situational contexts. It wants to create a theory that fits, works, is relevant, and is modifiable. Data analysis is viewed as objective. Categories form part of the analysis. The analytic categories are solely generated by the researcher. Reflexivity is but a data source (p. 141).

Several similarities exist between the different versions of Grounded Theory. These include the concurrent data collection/generation and doing the analyses meticulously. Analyses are

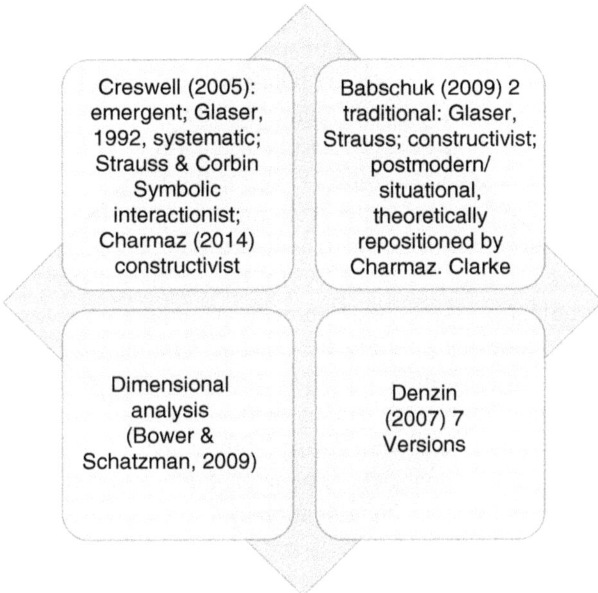

FIGURE 6.4 Different Versions of Grounded Theory (Extracted from Chun Tie et al., 2019)

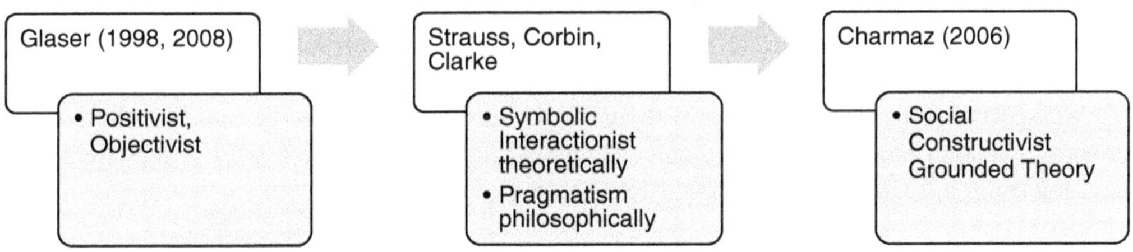

FIGURE 6.5 Philosophical Differences (Extracted from Chun Tie et al., 2019)

refined so that a comprehensive theory is produced of the studied topic or phenomenon. Scholars also agree that it is a suitable method for generating a substantive theory (Strauss & Corbin, 1998), which is grounded in rigorously collected data (see Charmaz & Thornberg, 2021). Although interviews are a common means of generating data, focus groups, questionnaires, surveys, videos, and other sources, can be used (Strauss & Corbin, 1990).

To gain a rudimentary understanding of how this could be done, I will outline the research by Johansson and Werbart (2009), who adopted the Objectivist version. They explored the negative experiences of group analytic psychotherapy. Taking into account previous research (Lilliengren & Werbart, 2005) findings, these researchers also filled a void, because others mostly focused on curative factors.

Past research (e.g. Johnson et al., 2006) indicated that conflict and avoidance contribute to negative group processes. Other group members may be experienced negatively by their mere presence (Yalom & Rand, 1966). Absences lead to the group being experienced as disjointed (Burlingame et al., 2004; Piper et al., 2002). Inconsistent membership has the same effect (Galinsky & Schopler, 1989; MacNair-Semands, 2002), affecting group cohesion (Ogrodniczuk & Piper, 2003).

Johansson and Werbart (2009) aimed to build a process model of therapeutic action, which integrates positive and negative experiences of psychotherapy, linking these to their lives outside therapy. Several aspects of their study are noteworthy. Whereas 8–20 participants are considered sufficient (Strauss & Corbin, 1998), Johansson and Werbart (2009) recruited 28 through purposive sampling. They analyzed the transcripts of the 1-h long *Private Theories Interviews* (see Appendix 3), using Strauss and Corbin's (1998) method.

In Grounded Theory, initial coding is the preliminary step in data analysis. Its purpose is to begin the process of fracturing the data, and to compare, and to seek similarities and differences in the emerging patterns (Strauss & Clarke, 1998). Researchers might find it useful to ponder over the data, for example, from which view something stems.

Inductively, as many codes as possible are created. Crucial words are labeled. Chun Tie et al. (2019) clarify that codes identify socio-psychological processes and actions. Following the initial analysis, theoretical sampling is done, which is a key aspect. It involves the process of identifying and pursuing clues that arise during analysis in a grounded theory study (Birks & Mills, 2014, p. 68). Theoretical categories are generated. Once this has been achieved, the next step involves intermediate coding, the identification of a core category, continuous and constant comparative analysis, theoretical sensitivity (what is meaningful, significant in the data), and memoing, which is an essential analytic process to ensure quality. Memos are the mortar (Stern, 2007), and the data are the building blocks, of the emerging theory (Chun Tie et al., 2019).

Furthermore, techniques of advanced coding are employed. This facilitates the integration of the final aspect of grounded theory. Storyline is one such technique (for further detail see Birks & Mills, 2014). Theoretical saturation is a core feature of Grounded Theory. It differs from the more general qualitative notion of saturation (data saturation, saturation of themes) (Yarwood-Ross & Jack, 2023). Finally, theoretical coding, which integrates and synthesizes the generated categories to produce a theory, is carried out. When two or more researchers code data, interrater agreement is calculated (TextBox 6.1).

TEXTBOX 6.1 INTERRATER AGREEMENT

To assess the reliability of codes, commonly two raters code independently. Krippendorff's alpha coefficients can be used to assess interrater agreement (Krippendorff, 2004). A coefficient of 1.0 indicates perfect reliability, above 0.64 substantial, and above 0.8 near perfect, agreement (Landis & Koch, 1977).

Conventionally, when carrying out a grounded theory study, a systematic review of the literature is done at its completion (Dey, 1999). The rationale for doing so is that researchers do not know beforehand where the data will take them. In practice, a preliminary review is often undertaken. A more robust literature review is carried out at the end of the study (Dey, 1999). Johansson and Werbart (2009) deviated from the standard Grounded Theory procedure (TextBox 6.2) by drawing on Rennie (see Rennie, 2006; Rennie et al., 1988). The phenomenologist Giorgi (2014) disagreed with Rennie's approach to combine phenomenology with Grounded Theory.

When using common software, researchers have to familiarize themselves with it. One advantage of ATLAS.ti (Muhr, 2004) is that it retains the links between meaning units, categories, and memos.

TEXTBOX 6.2 ONE POSSIBLE PROCEDURE

Johansson and Werbart (2009) used an alternative procedure (see Rennie, 2006; Rennie et al., 1988). Meaning units, expressing therapeutic action, were identified and grouped into categories. Summaries of relations between all categories were stored as memos. This enabled the movement between coding and the building of a conceptual model. They compared codes and categories, (steps 1 and 2) across all interviews, before devising the final descriptive categories for each interview. Main categories that subsumed the descriptive categories were produced through constant comparative analysis and clustering (Miles & Huberman, 1994). For the category labels, they adopted the clients' language. Each meaning unit was linked with several descriptive categories, which belong to different main categories. As an additional validity check, they followed Rennie et al. (1988) and investigated the frequencies and proportional occurrences. Then memos and graphical representations were examined so that the relations between categories could be explored. The data were analyzed by one researcher. Steps 3–5 were checked by the other researcher. To resolve disagreement, a similar method, as developed by Hill et al. (1997), was used. Finally, a theoretical model was produced, which could be regarded as exemplifying Foulkes' group matrix (Foulkes, 1964; Foulkes & Anthony, 1965), as experienced by group members.

Developing New Theories through Constructivist Grounded Theory

A substantive theory is a theoretical explanation, or interpretation, of a studied phenomenon (Bryant & Charmaz, 2007). Group Analysis is in need of substantive theories, which could be developed through the use of Grounded Theory.

Kathy Charmaz (1939–2020) was a leading scholar of Constructivist Grounded Theory. Its basic premise is that researchers develop theory from the rigorous analysis of empirical data (Charmaz, 2006). Described as a general methodology, the analytic process comprises the coding of data from interviews, the developing, checking, and integrating of theoretical categories, as well as the writing of analytic of narratives throughout the research process (Charmaz, 2014). From the start, researchers code the data, compare data and codes, and identify emerging analytic categories that will be further refined (Charmaz & Belgrave, 2015).

A grounded theory study of sexuality might begin with concrete data and end with rendering these in an explanatory theory. Group analysts could be interviewed (raw data) and transcripts (concrete data) be analyzed through the methodological grounded theory procedure.

Researchers would need to adopt a social constructivist position, which assumes multiple realties, and familiarize themselves with the method, to ensure philosophical and methodological coherence. Data are mutually constructed through interaction and the researcher constructs categories (Morse et al., 2009). The representation of data is viewed as problematic, relativistic, situational, and partial. It is assumed that the observer's values and actions affect her/his view. Constructivist Grounded Theory wants to achieve an interpretative understanding of historically situated data and to create a useful, credible, and original theory. Subjectivities are acknowledged throughout the data analysis and researchers engage in reflexivity. The co-construction of data analysis is recognized. This method seeks to re-represent the views and voices of the participants. They are integral to the analysis (Morse et al., 2009, p. 141).

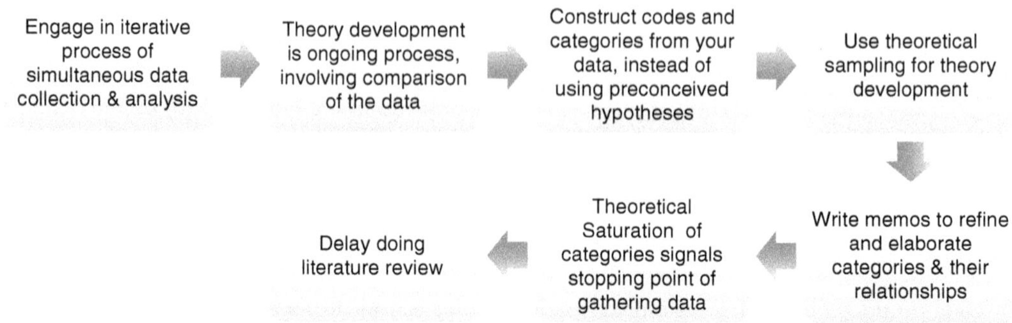

FIGURE 6.6 Basic Procedure of Constructivist Grounded Theory (Extracted from Charmaz, 2006, 2014; Charmaz & Belgrave, 2015)

Quantitative oriented group analytic researchers would need to acquire a basic understanding of qualitative research (Babchuk, 2010). Before applying Grounded Theory, it is advisable that they read key texts (e.g. Charmaz, 2006, 2008, 2014, 2017, 2020; Charmaz and Thornberg, 2021; Glasser, 2001, 2013), and familiarize themselves with the different versions. When selecting the constructivist approach, it must be applied consistently. Justifying why this version/method was chosen is also required. Viewing themselves as an active and reflexive participant of the research process is recommended (Babchuk, 2010, p. 6). Ethical considerations are important, and researchers must ensure that they adhere to ethical guidelines.

Although Grounded Theory is not that easily learnt, it can produce credible and trustworthy results, provided that the researchers' analytical conceptualizations are rigorous throughout the research process made (Chun Tie et al., 2019). When writing up a grounded theory study, researchers articulate the main components and steps, they have used. They keep an audit trail of their data collection/analysis strategies, memos, and their rationale for decisions made. Their procedure must be precise, carried out meticulously and systematically, and the iterative processes must be logical and coherent, so that the grounded theory study is done rigorously (Chun Tie et al., 2019). A basic procedure is depicted in Figure 6.6.

Ultimately, the quality of a Grounded Theory study depends on the skill, expertise, and knowledge of the researcher of the Grounded Theory procedure. It should be carried out with precision and must be philosophically and methodologically congruent with the researcher's aim of the study (Chun Tie et al., 2019). Software programs (see Appendix 3) can be useful. Further reading is suggested in Appendix 3.

Chapter Summary

My intention has been to provide some clarity about related, but often confused, terminology and conceptualizations surrounding theory. Inspired by St Pierre, I have suggested "living" group analytic theories to grasp their meaning. In this way, more creative theorizing may arise.

Furthermore, my brief discussion of Indigenous and Western theoretical frameworks has been fueled by a belief that Western and Indigenous frameworks should unite. This would be another step toward decolonizing research.

Equally important is the development of theories. Even though they have never been a priority in Group Analysis, good theories are important. They guide clinical and research practices.

Hence, Grounded Theory studies could be carried out to produce substantial group analytic theories. Our profession is fortunate, because we can build on all these great thinkers, who have produced all these wonderful techniques. We use them in clinical practice. Why not engage in free association, reverie, or social dreaming, to let your unconscious initiate the process of theorizing? Imagination precedes the more formal and cognitive aspects of theorizing. So, it is an essential aspect of refining, testing, and producing new theories. All this forms a part of "living" group analytic theory.

7

THE TROUBLE WITH QUALITATIVE METHODS

Is It Possible to Escape Positivist Coding in Group Analytic Research?

Abstract

One focus is on Bakhtin due to his emphasis on dialogue, interaction, power, polyphony, utterances, heteroglossia, and his suggestion that the Self is constituted through the Other. Meta-Synthesis, Institutional Ethnography (IE), and Autoethnography are additionally described. For studying organizational structures, work, and mental health settings, IE is relevant for group (analytic) researchers. A good Meta-synthesis is informative. Autoethnography is flexible. So, it can be combined with quantitative and qualitative methods when studying groups. Using phenomenological approaches as an example, I discuss whether group (analytic) researchers can escape positivist coding when using qualitative methods. Coding comes with baggage, namely, colonialism. Thus, relying on coding has not only empirical, but also moral, implications.

Introduction

More than three decades ago, qualitative researchers queried whether it was possible to avoid "positivist coding", or the black hole of qualitative research, as Lather (1991) called it. Despite advances in qualitative methodologies, this is still a pertinent question for qualitative group analytic researchers. Frank (2005) pointed out that qualitative researchers often adopt quantitative terminology. They refer to "raw data", which indicates that the true value of their research lies in the process of refining, finishing, and civilizing this raw material (p. 970). According to McLeod (2023a), qualitative research seeks to understand the social reality of individuals, groups, and cultures. It wants to explain how/why a certain phenomenon occurred in a particular context and what happened.

The term "qualitative research" can refer to a paradigm and philosophical perspective, or to a diverse set of methods (Devers, 1999). Qualitative research is not linear like quantitative research (Cleland, 2017). Researchers ask open-ended questions. Answers cannot be easily quantified, because qualitative research explains processes or patterns of behavior (Tenny et al., 2022).

Denzin and Lincoln (2005b) pointed out that the challenges to qualitative research are many. To fully grasp this, the political must be distinguished from the procedural role of qualitative methodology, which defines how qualitative methodology must be used to produce knowledge

DOI:10.4324/9781003609544-10

(Seale et al., 2004, p. 7). Qualitative findings are often regarded as subjective, explorative, and unscientific by policy makers. The positivist resistance toward qualitative research has maintained the distinction between hard science and soft scholarship (Denzin & Lincoln, 2005b).

Historically, qualitative researchers suffered a crisis in the 1980s when realizing that they could not directly capture the lived experience: it is created in the texts researchers write (LeGrange, 2018). In the "postmodern period" (LeGrange 2018), qualitative researchers allegedly engaged in so-called experimental ethnographic writing, and they were writing fiction not science, as positivists claimed (Denzin & Lincoln, 2005b). In the early 2000s, Elizabeth St. Pierre coined the term "post-qualitative inquiry" to describe a poststructuralist alternative to qualitative methods (St. Pierre, 2023). At that time, the social sciences were becoming increasingly positivist again. According to Giddens (1976), inquiry is based on understanding humanity through an empathetic identification with others, a grasping of their subjective experience.

Rigid ideas about what counts as valid research (St. Pierre, 2021b) also prevail in group psychotherapy research. The post-qualitative inquirer breaks with all the "conventional qualitative methods" (LeGrange, 2018). These include techniques, such as (un/ structured) interviewing of participants, observation, or focus groups (Tenny et al., 2022), and the coding of the data (St. Pierre, 2023). Qualitative research can amount to a large amount of data. The transcribed data may be coded manually or by using qualitative data analysis software.

Østern et al. (2023) explained that post-qualitative research developed due to friction with established qualitative methods that were imbued with positivist leftovers. They appear in qualitative research in the form of language, as coding, data collection, and validity. Pre-described methods were striving toward homogeneity so that qualitative research was not deemed qualitative enough (Johansson, 2016). Post-qualitative inquiry is about reading and writing in dialogue with philosophy to develop new ontologies. So, it aims to create unique ideas, something new, instead of focusing on whether findings are trustworthy or not. Of course, new does not automatically mean "better".

According to Weisser (2024), post-qualitative inquiry views identity as relational. So, it has a lot in common with group analytic thinking. For example, the notion that our identities are defined by the environment and by others around us. In post-qualitative inquiry (Flint et al., 2023), identities are fluid (see Barad, 2014) and in constant flux (see Dharani, 2025). Alas, this makes it much harder to study identities. Post-qualitative researchers may focus on how people interface with the world, for example, and at which point people become intertwined with their environment. Researchers may value a select few philosophers for elucidating being and truth (e.g. Derrida, Deleuze, Deleuze & Guattari), and are against methodological prescriptivism, i.e. the step-by-step approach. But as Weisser (2024) says, getting rid of methodology does not seem to be a good idea. Methodology is also a way to encourage greater accountability in how knowledge claims are made and constructed, so that research is more transparent and open to critique. Qualitative methodological "prescriptions" make it easier to highlight social biases in research institutions, allowing liberation-based methodologies to develop (Gerrard et al., 2017).

Qualitative research is concerned with how the social world is interpreted, understood, experienced, or constructed (Cleland, 2017). Researchers utilize qualitative approaches to understand human experience in all its complexity in natural settings. These rest on notions of reality as socially constructed. So, inquiry is unavoidably value-laden (Denzin & Lincoln, 1998). One consequence is that reality cannot be directly measured, because it only exists as perceived by people. Hence, reality is relative and multiple. It is perceived through socially constructed and subjective interpretations (Cleland, 2017).

Many qualitative methods have been developed. Data sources can be words, texts, photographs, videos, and sound recordings, which are used to understand behavior, environments, and social interactions (Denzin & Lincoln, 1994). Participants for qualitative studies can be selected based on the researcher's rationale (purposive sampling), pre-identified factors (criterion sampling), availability (convenience sampling), or based on referral from other participants (snowball sampling) (Tenny et al., 2022).

Innovative research tools exist to examine dialogues in groups. Group researchers can choose between qualitative and post-qualitative methods. Different data analysis techniques have been developed. Typically, the trustworthiness (validity) of findings is established by assessing their credibility (internal validity), dependability (reliability), transformability (external validity), and confirmability (objectivity) (see Devers, 1999 for more detail).

Popular methods include narrative research, intuitive inquiry (Wertz et al., 2011), Thematic Analysis (Braun & Clarke, 2006), Grounded Theory (Charmaz, 2014; Glaser, 2001), phenomenological approaches (e.g. Giorgi, 2009), Autoethnography (Ellis & Bochner, 2000), Institutional Ethnography (IE) (Smith, 1996), feminist, queer methods (Ashford, 2009), Meta-synthesis (Lachal et al., 2017), Interpretative Phenomenological Analysis (IPA) (Smith et al., 2022), and many more.

IPA was elaborated, and two IPA studies (Jackson et al., 2023; O'Beney et al., 2019) are also published in *Group Analysis.* So, the case study is no longer the method par excellence in psychoanalytic research that pays close attention to idiographic descriptions.

Meta-synthesis arose in the 1970s (Sandelowski & Barroso, 2007) as a procedure for synthesizing qualitative studies (Erwin et al., 2011). It is the qualitative equivalent of Meta-analysis (Noah, 2017). Thorne (2022) outlines early applications of Meta-synthesis in health. Important for systematically synthesizing primary qualitative studies to evidence the trustworthiness of qualitative research (Lachal et al., 2017; Sandelowski & Barroso, 2003, 2007; Sandelowski et al., 1998), Meta-synthesis is popular in many disciplines.

Autoethnography is a particular form of writing that seeks to unite ethnographic (looking outward) and autobiographic (gazing inward) intentions, according to Salmons (2023). The purpose of writing an autoethnographic account is to keep both the subject (knower) and the object (what is being examined) in simultaneous view (Salmons, 2023). Autoethnography builds on ethnography, but Anderson (2006) highlighted that the discourse on this genre of research referred almost exclusively to "evocative" Autoethnography, whose advocates distance themselves from realist and analytic ethnographic traditions (p. 373). More recently, Autoethnography has been used as a decolonizing tool (Nisa-Waller & Piercy, 2024). Due to its systematic engagement with culture, as a research practice, Autoethnography has a particular affinity with indigenous ways of knowing (see Nisa-Waller & Pierce, 2024; Williams, 2021; Iosefo et al., 2020; Walker, 2019; Denzin, 2018; Whitinui, 2014; Bainbridge, 2007). Defined differently by various researchers (Reed-Danahay, 1997), Autoethnography introduces a novel way of pursuing social knowledge (Ellis & Bochner, 2000). Its epistemology and ontology reflect postmodern ideas.

Postmodernism assumes that several ways of knowing and enquiring are possible. Knowledge is subjective and socially constructed. This enables researchers to question established theories, perspectives, values, and power imbalances, associated with class, gender, and ethnicity (Wall, 2006).

Autoethnographic data analysis involves shifting attention between Self and others, as well as between the personal and the social context. Vosmer (2024d) conducted an Autoethnography of the lived experience of diversity in Group Analysis. While many group analysts (in training) had recognized the need to embrace diversity (e.g. Aiyebusi, 2021b; Kent, 2021; Kinouani, 2019; Nayak, 2021), studies were lacking.

IE grew out of Dorothy Smith's (1987) feminist sociology. Smith (1996) rejected the dominance of theory and used standpoint to guide inquiry. Her standpoint as a woman is located in the historical trajectory of capitalism in Western societies (Smith, 1990, 1999). Vosmer (2022) used IE to examine whether diversity and non-discrimination of clients, students, and group analysts, is a lived actuality, because the current socio-political and economic landscape in psychotherapy demands diversity and equality.

Mikhail Bakhtin (1895–1975) is believed to have written under the names of Valentin Nikolaevich Voloshinov and Pavel Nikolaevich Medvedev (Brandist, n.d.; Morris, 1994). Bakhtin is no stranger to Group Analysis (see Pines, 2002). Bakhtin's conceptualizations have been widely applied in linguistics, cultural studies, sociology, and philosophy. They have also been used in psychology (e.g. Cresswell, 2011; Grossen & Orvig; Leiman, 2002; Richardson, 2011; Salgado & Clegg, 2011), psychotherapy research (e.g. Leiman, 2011, 2012), and group analytic research (Vosmer, 2024d). However, Bakhtin's ideas have not been taken as seriously as they should in group research.

Described as a genius by Clark and Holquist (1984), Bakhtin (1984) developed his theory of dialogism by analyzing Dostoevsky's writing. His core insight is that Dostoevsky's greatness was due to creating a new kind of literary character: a new relation of author to character (Frank, 2005). No longer determined by authorial necessity, the character appears to be free internally. However, he is formed in dialogue with other characters. The voice of any character, regardless of whether it is expressed in inner dialogue, or external talk, is never her/his own in any individualist sense, as Frank (2005) clarified. For Bakhtin, each voice is formed in a continuous process of anticipation and response to other voices. Consequently, each voice always contains the voices of others. It is the authord who hears the voices of others in a particular character. S/he leaves the character internally free to make what s/he pleases of those voices.

For Bakhtin (1984), meaning was created through a mutually constructed truth of the polyphonic voices of reader, character, and author. So, a narrative is jointly created between speakers and listeners (Frank, 2010). Moreover, Grossen and Orvig (2011) explained that heteroglossia is a broader concept than polyphony, referring to a multiplicity of languages and worldviews. Carnival is a concept, in which multiple voices, languages, and worldviews, collide due to being on an equal footing.

Viewing life as a shared interactional event (dialogical), Bakhtin has demonstrated that people participate in dialogues throughout their lives. Meaning comes about through dialogue. "Difference" is fundamental to meaning, because dissonances are the sparks that move people toward creative discourses.

Bakhtin's (1981) method can be used to analyze transcripts, documents, speeches, and interactions in groups.

One purpose of this chapter is to consider whether qualitative group analytic research can escape positivist coding. The second purpose is to outline qualitative methods that have been neglected in group (analytic) research.

First, I will describe meta-synthesis. After attending to IE and discussing Bakhtin's (1981) dialogism, I will describe Autoethnography. A discussion of phenomenological methods in relation to coding will conclude this chapter.

Meta-Synthesis

Simply put, researchers may use either an aggregative or interpretative approach when carrying out a meta-synthesis (Erwin et al., 2011). While aggregation (Hannes & Lockwood 2011) and summary (Sandelowski & Barroso, 2007) are core features of an aggregative meta-synthesis, the interpretative approach is exemplified by meta-ethnography (Noblit & Hare, 1988) and grounded theory (Kearney 1998, 2001).

According to Sim and Mengshoel (2023), aggregative meta-synthesis relies mainly on the descriptive mapping and categorization of findings. Researchers synthesize relevant primary qualitative studies by looking for patterns and commonalities, focusing more on practice-oriented issues. Interpretative meta-synthesis involves a higher level of abstraction, which relies on either a conceptual or theoretical process. It reflects Strike and Posner's (1983) view of synthesis as conceptual innovation. Researchers have used several methodologies when conducting a meta-synthesis (see Noah, 2017; Sattar et al., 2021).

The meta-synthesis process may involve extracting, separating, grouping, and abstracting text findings into numbers and statement sets. The synthesis is the final stage, which may include interpretation, conceptual models, and/or conclusions (Chrastina, 2018).

Thorne (2017) has criticized that newer forms of meta-synthesis are much more technical and theoretically superficial. Equally, Bergdahl (2019) notes that meta-aggregation falls short of being a sound method. This shows that a meta-synthesis requires expertise in qualitative methods. Combining mixed methods is a further challenge. It can be tricky to maintain the integrity of individual studies when synthesizing studies (Prasad, 2005). Determining the relationship between studies and assessing their quality can also be challenging, because qualitative research is diverse. Significant differences exist in theoretical and methodological perspectives (e.g. case studies, narrative or phenomenological approaches, Crotty, 1998). These are some challenges researchers face when trying to master the method of meta-synthesis. While their own subjectivity is important, researchers must actually make sense of the presented experiences of the participants in the primary studies. So, meta-synthesis involves third-level comprehension and interpretation (Lachal et al., 2017). This necessitates re-conceptualizing and re-interpreting existing findings to produce new knowledge. One crucial issue is how to synthesize without sacrificing the relevance, or integrity, of individual studies. Some researchers questioned whether the essence of human experiences, described in the original studies, gets lost. Is the synthesis antithetical to qualitative research by stripping away contexts? If so, then rich, thick, descriptions would be sacrificed (Erwin et al., 2011). These are all legitimate concerns.

Hence, researchers must provide a framework that includes rich contextual information about the setting and participants. Additional strategies should be used to enhance the credibility and trustworthiness of a meta-synthesis. These include triangulation, member checks, prolonged engagement, and peer debriefing (Brantlinger et al., 2005; Creswell, 2007). Limitations about subjective interpretations should be resolved through triangulation (e.g. using independent reviewers to assess and validate conclusions).

How do you conduct a meta-analysis? Erwin et al. (2011), Lachal et al. (2017), Noah (2017), Chrastina (2018), Malterud (2019), and Sattar et al. (2021) describe this. Even though these authors do not use the exact same approach, there are similarities.

First, you formulate a research question and define inclusion/exclusion criteria for your meta-synthesis. Then you conduct a comprehensive, systematic literature search to locate all relevant articles. At least two researchers scan the abstracts and articles for possible inclusion.

Select all relevant studies and document this process to ensure transparency. Extract and analyze relevant data from those studies (themes, main findings, interpretations) to answer your research question.

Be concise, clear, and coherent. To assess the quality of studies, use CASP criteria (Noyes et al., 2018; see Appendix 3), peer review, a synthesis framework and the ENTREQ, developed by Tong et al. (2012) (see Appendix 3), when integrating findings to ensure that your meta-synthesis is credible.

Do not forget to reflect on the process (Lachal et al., 2017).

Miles and Paquin (2014) concluded that there was a discrepancy between group research and group practice. They highlighted the need for collaborations between researchers and psychotherapists. Therefore, group researchers could collaborate with colleagues from other disciplines (Toye et al., 2014) and group (analytic) psychotherapists when carrying out a meta-synthesis. Having a research team tends to improve its quality (Lachal et al., 2017; Lee et al., 2014). Ideally, researchers are experts in the topic that is being synthesized and have had some training in qualitative synthesis (Atkins et al., 2008). Since there are many ways to do a qualitative synthesis, the research team will have to decide which approach to choose.

One strength of meta-synthesis is the identification of specific patterns and themes. Hence, a better understanding of the how, when, and why, of group dynamics can be achieved, although this might also increase the risk of misunderstanding (Bondas & Hall, 2007).

Turning meta-synthesis into thin descriptions is a concern (Bergdahl, 2019). Despite its benefits, the lack of clear guidance, and missing consensus on terminology and methodology (Maeda et al., 2022), are disadvantages.

Given that a meta-synthesis provides a synthesis of qualitative studies, it cannot escape the black hole of positive coding. Why? Phenomenological and narrative approaches, thematic analysis, and grounded theory are very popular methods. By synthesizing the findings from those studies, meta-synthesis automatically falls into the black hole. Furthermore, meta-synthesis has become more technical. Part of its procedure involves extraction of themes, in other words, coding.

Using Institutional Ethnography in Group Analytic Research

It was Smith (1987), who insisted that our everyday/everynight world is local and historical. She thought that we experience it directly and are connected to social relations elsewhere. Social relations are processes people enter into during our daily/nightly lives (Travers, 1996). Her idea that people are embedded in institutions and embody ruling relations, which are organized around a distinctive function such as education (Smith, 2003, 2005), has both intuitive and heuristic values.

IEs are built from the examination of work processes and study of how these are coordinated, as DeVault (2006) noted. Work activities are regarded as the basis of social life. An IE generally takes some particular experience and associated work processes as a point of entry (DeVault, 2006).

Many would agree that ruling relations coordinate and organize people's activities in, and across, local settings via the use of language (Campbell, 2001). This situation has become even more complex due to modern technologies, which transmit different forms of texts (documents, narratives, brief posts) simultaneously and instantly.

An IE analysis produces knowledge that reveals practices, which generate inequality and marginalization. So, it is a liberating method. IE starts from the standpoint of oppressed people and is accountable to them (DeVault & McCoy, 2002).

When I conducted an IE study in Britain (Vosmer, 2022), the landscape in psychotherapy was permeated by Neoliberalism. Such landscape lends itself to using IE to study psychotherapy (Kearney et al., 2019) and diversity.

IE enables an explication of how something happened (Smith, 1990, 2006). It begins with the embodied experiences of individuals. Then it systematically investigates their social and institutional determinants, before returning to individual experiences. Experiential knowing and "a problematic" (area of investigation) organize the direction of research (Smith, 2005).

Using the standpoint of marginalized people, my study (Vosmer, 2022) explored local, trans-local, and (inter)national relations, by analyzing what students at the Institute of Group Analysis (IGA), as well as group analysts' texts, said about non/discrimination, diversity, and equal opportunity. Additionally, it identified the location of authors, the purpose of texts, and how they related to each other, and to their disseminations. Mapping these connections is a vital part of IE (Campbell & Gregor, 2002).

I linked textual analyses of IGA documents to experiences. Accounts by group analysts, including mine, and by students, were additionally utilized to gain insight into discrimination. By reading across documents and relevant literature, I traced and mapped how institutional language reflected wider socioeconomic and political processes. Doing so allowed me to present a coherent description of social and ruling relations, as well as experiences of marginalization.

My study drew on Malachowski et al. (2017), who suggested that the socially coordinated character of texts is already there. In their thinking, a text is organized and waits for the reader to discover its intended meaning. Thus, to reveal the underlying meaning of documents and other texts, I mapped processes and relations, taking the standpoint of marginalized individuals.

Sadly, my analysis indicated that diversity was asserted without recognizing that this perpetuated a discriminatory, White ideological cycle. The marginalized remain outsiders due to the social relations and actions by ruling relations. Institutionalized prejudices were simply reformulated into valuing "difference".

Popular in sociology and health professions education (Kearney et al., 2019), this method has been neglected in group research. Considering that work is crucial to life, IE is useful method to study all kinds of work structures. Nguyen et al. (2023) offer guidance on IE. Due to its axiological considerations, it could be particularly valuable method for group research.

The Value of Bakhtin to Group Research

Expectations that researchers can measure (quantify) and study their participants to the last detail, and conclusions that

> *… there is nothing more to be said about you…*
>
> (Bakhtin, 1984, p. 58)

are empirically and ethically wrong, as Frank (2005) pointed out. Extending one of Bakhtin's arguments, he advocated the injunction

> *Thou shalt not Devushkinize thy research subjects.*
>
> (p. 965)

Frank (2005) refers to Bakhtin's (1984) description of Devushkin in *Problems of Dostoevsky's Poetics.* He cautions researchers in the social sciences not to make their participants feel like Devushkin did (i.e. finished off) and not to assume that they have captured "all there is" about their participants' experiences.

Frank draws our attention to finalization and monologue, two important Bakhtinian concepts which are linked to "heteroglossia". Bakhtin (1981, 1984) explained that "multiple languages" are embedded within a single national language: languages of authority, dialects, and professional jargon. They compete with each other. Language is never neutral, Bakhtin (1984) asserted, because it is born out of socio-politico and ideological contexts. Consequently, he rejected the positivist view of communication, i.e., the idea that language and texts are abstract norms that have one objective meaning.

Ostermann et al. (2023) state that Bakhtin's concepts are tools for understanding the subtleties of language and communication. One example is Bakhtin's notion of utterance, which relates to how language is used in various settings (Grossen & Orvig, 2011). Every utterance, which a speaker produces, is already pregnant with meaning. Ideological undertones are inherent in utterances (Bakhtin, 1981). An utterance (word, phrase, or sentence) is a response to previous interactions that form part of a dialogue (Bakhtin, 1986).

Bakhtin (1981) described dialogism as "… a constant interaction between meanings, all of which have the potential of conditioning others" (p. 426). Holquist (2002, p. 21) further clarified that in dialogism, all meaning is relative insofar as it comes about only as a result of the relation between two bodies, which occupy a different space at the same time (physical bodies, political bodies, bodies of ideas in general). Meaning depends on the polyphony of voices in discourses (Nikulin, 2002). For Bakhtin (1981), dialogue was an interaction that took place freely between at least two voices through the medium of language: firstly, the speaking person and secondly, the voice of the social language through which "ventriloquism" occurs (speech is influenced). Words and discourse are socially charged, dialogically engaged with past, present, and future audiences, and populated by the intentions of the individual speaker (Bakhtin, 1981, p.293).

Dialogue begins with recognizing that the other person (or text) can never be completely understood and remains "unfinalizable". Dialogism is opposed to "monologism": one authoritative voice suppresses other voices or perspectives. Bakhtin's theorizing was affected by Stalinist authoritarianism (Emerson, 1997). Unsurprisingly, he maintained that ideology can be imposed on others. As a result, a person may become finalizable (Bakhtin, 1981). By this he meant that this person has been destroyed and/or feels internally dead.

Traditionally, an author finalizes the character by having the last word about who the character is, or what s/he can become (Frank, 2005). Bakhtin's explication of Dostoevsky's author–character relationship is relevant to research practices. Comparable to Buber's (1958) "I and Thou", this distinct conceptualization is ethically important for the understanding of Self–other, clinician–patient/client, and researcher–participant relationships. The core ethical demand of this relationship is that neither party ever finalizes the other (Frank, 2005, p. 966). A (group) researcher should never finalize her/his research participants.

This is related to dialogism and "intertextuality". Meaning is shaped by other texts, conversations, and polyphony (Bakhtin, 1981). By implication, individuality is created through others, and the other is part of the Self (Bakhtin, 1990). Dialogism pays special attention to the variety of ways, in which the Self as author, incorporates the words and voices of others (Bakhtin, 1981, 1990).

Dialogism & Dialogical Narrative Analysis

Dialogism has transformed how psychologists conceive and investigate the psyche, as Salgado and Clegg (2011) explain. Conceptualizing the Self as multivoiced originates in the theoretical tradition of dialogism. The Other is part of the Self (Bakhtin, 1981, p. 354; Wertsch, 2004), and the Self relates to Others in specific ways (Marková, 2003). From a dialogical perspective, the Self thinks and speaks with the words of Others. Aveling et al. (2015) suggest that utterances often imply an Other (multivoiced nature of Self). To capture the emphasis on Self-in-relation-to-Others, they conceptualiz voices of the Self, voices of Others, and their interactions.

The dialogical narrative analysis (DNA) is associated with Arthur Frank (2010, 2012, 2013), who drew on the legacy of Bakhtin, particularly, dialogism. The dialogical approach regards people as inherently relational and views narratives (storytelling) as part of a dialogue between two, or more, voices (Frank, 2005; 2012, 2013). To practice DNA is to sustain a tension between dialogue and analysis, as Frank (2012) writes. He argues that stories play a crucial role in situating people within groups (Frank, 2006).

Strictly speaking, dialogism rejects the application of a rigid method. This would be viewed as monologizing complexity. Hence, Grossen (2010) has argued that any attempt to develop methods for the analysis of dialogue was incompatible with the assumptions of dialogism. To offer simple guidance, I will briefly summarize techniques for analysis.

Existing Research & Considerations for Group Research

Bakhtinian theory has informed many studies (e.g. Haye & Torres-Sahli, 2025), who drew on Voloshinov (1976, 1986). DNA has also been used in mental health to analyze focus groups (e.g. Buescher & McGugan, 2022). Caddick et al. (2015) used DNA in their study of veterans.

Bakhtin's (1981, 1986) language theory implies that social tensions are inevitable. Exploring social tension, Thompson et al. (2017) operationalized the stages of their theoretical interpretation (identification of ideological characteristics, conflict; examining how speakers take up ideological positions and negotiate meaning within; exploring how reality, subjectivities, affective states, cause, and effect are constructed through the argumentative texture of interactions and utterance).

Bakhtin's (1986) theory could inform group psychotherapy research on issues surrounding the dialogical Self (e.g. Grossen & Orvig, 2011). Bakhtinian theories also lend themselves to exploring tensions (e.g. Hong et al. 2016) in psychotherapy research in terms of "evidence". Or, to analyze the discourse on evidence-based practice policy in psychotherapy to elucidate whether it is an "authoritative" discourse (e.g. Wilinski, 2017; Wilinski et al., 2022), or not. Because Bakhtin (1981, p. 343) wrote that the authoritative discourse *demands our unconditional allegiance*. Alternatively, Bakhtin's notion of dialogue and dialogic interactions provides a means to study the relationship between researchers and participants (e.g. Talbot, 2015). Or, researchers could examine ideological aspects related to monological discourses on knowledge and individual therapies. Ideology resides in utterances, as Bakhtin (1986, 1990) showed, so, utterances could be used as units of analysis, but do not have to.

Bakhtin and Medvedev's (1978) conceptualizations can also be applied to faith dialogues, because all religious systems transmit and interpret holy words.

Carrying out Bakhtinian Analyses

Aveling et al. (2015) developed a method for analyzing qualitative data informed by the tradition of dialogism, but they cautioned that their method depends on significant interpretative skill and contextual knowledge. In their three-step "multivoicedness analysis", Aveling et al. (2015) distinguished between *Voices of the Self: I-Positions*, *Voices of Other: Inner-Others*, *Voices of Inner-Others*, and *The Interacting Voices* (*heterodialogue and autodialogue*). Steps 1 and 2 address the question "who is doing the talking?" by identifying, first, the multiplicity of I-positions from which Self speaks, and second, the voices of inner-Others that can be heard within the speaker's utterances. The third step then examines the nature of the autodialogue and relationships between voices within the Self. The steps can be applied to any textual data, but they used it for analyzing interview data (see Aveling et al. 2015 for further detail).

Leiman (2004, 2012) developed *dialogical sequence analysis* (DSA), a micro-analytic method that can be used to examine the dialogical organization of client and therapist utterances in the psychotherapeutic encounter. DSA originated in Bakhtin's (1984, 1986) theory of utterance. It links external actions to intra-psychic processes. At the core of his theory is the claim that every utterance expresses the speaker's position and simultaneously the referential object of speech, the addressee (Leiman, 2012, p. 133).

Every utterance has an addressee. It is the fundamental structural unit that guides researchers. In their *analysis of utterances, they start by considering To whom is the person speaking?* (Leiman, 2004, p. 3). The listener, who is present, is the only observable addressee, although her/his inner world is filled with invisible others. Their presence can be traced within the content, flow, and expressions of utterances (Leiman, 2004). Countertransference, however, is a very specific psychoanalytic form of responsive understanding (see Bakhtin, 1986).

Although considered as an adequate response to the client's projective communication, the authorship of any interpretation rests with the therapist, because the Self–other distinction no longer exists (Leiman, 2004).

By verbalizing the client's experience, the therapist uses the indirect communication to foster joint reflection. However, in therapy, the question of "Who is Speaking" is unclear for two reasons. Firstly, utterances always consist of multiple voices, because a speaker's "I" was originally formed through dis/identification with others. Secondly, initiated utterances do not reside exclusively in the client's or therapist's mind. Sometimes a client may "speak" via the therapist (countertransference). Then, the speaker of the utterance (therapist) becomes a truly dyadic subject (Leiman, 2004, p. 8).

In a psychotherapy group, this gets even more complicated due to multiple horizontal and vertical transferences. Bakhtin is relevant for psychotherapy research when client and therapist utterances are the focus (see Leiman, 2011). Then, his theory of the utterance can be used as abstraction to define the research question and purpose of research (p. 441). Leiman illustrated how utterance can be used as the unit of analysis in psychotherapy research. Leiman (2002) also drew on Bakhtinian conceptualizations of the sign and semiotics. He suggested that semiotic mediation can be used to explain utterances (Leiman 2011).

Maybin (2001) proposed that a Bakhtinian analysis primarily focuses on exploring the dialogic structure of utterances. What a person says and how s/he conveys something through intonation, body language, and gesture, are important (Hamston 2006). When performing a Bakhtinian analysis, both the verbal and extraverbal contexts, in which the utterance was produced, must be considered, according to Ostermann et al. (2023). An utterance begins when a speaker speaks, and ends when s/he finishes speaking and initiates a response. The change of speaking subjects and finalization serves to identify the *utterance*, which is the *unit of analysis*.

Ostermann et al. (2023) suggest that any analysis should be *anchored in a strong theoretical framework.* Therefore, the analysis of social tensions (or another topic) requires a theory that explains the connection of language with the social, economic, and political context.

Utterances are the basic unit of analysis. For Bakhtin (1986), an utterance was never just a reflection/expression of something given and final, but it always created something absolutely new and unrepeatable and has some relation to value (e.g. the true, good) (120).

Utterances have a basic threefold structure, according to Osterman et al. (2023). They have an author, they are addressed to somebody, and utterances are always about something. Hence, they have a referential content that is mediated by the signs that "struggle to reach at their object" in the mist of already spoken words about that object

A voice forms part of utterances. It always consists of multiple voices (Vitanova, 2013). Even though it is also unique, reflecting an aspect of one's Self (Frank, 2005), voices of others are expressed indirectly or directly, e.g., by quoting another person's words (Gillespie & Cornish, 2010). Bakhtin's (1981) notion of voice can shed new light on the group dialogue, enabling an understanding of utterances in the narrative (Frank, 2005). Within a group context, the relational Self is either reinforced or challenged through the interactions with other voices. The underlying meanings of the stories (McAdams, 1988) that people (e.g. group members) tell can be revealed (see Clandinin, 2007; Clandinin & Connelly, 2000; Polkinghorne, 1995).

Researchers should approach the analysis with an ethical attitude (Josselson, 2007) when examining how multiple voices find their expression in one single voice (narrator, speaker, author) (Frank, 2012). Bakhtinian analysis (Bakhtin, 1986) also attends to the grammatical structure of sentences (see Vosmer, 2024d).

Ostermann et al. (2023) propose a framework to inform the analysis. The steps of their framework are to (1) identify the utterance and the immediate context; (2) identify the speech genre; (3) analyze the direction and social orientation of the utterance; (4) analyze responsiveness; (5) analyze style; and (6) integrate the results into a new utterance (p. 16).

They suggest that theme, style, and the compositional structure of the utterance form the focus of the analysis. The theme is the topic that is spoken about in an utterance. The style is associated with lexical, phraseological, and syntactic choices. The compositional structure refers to the composition of the utterance (pp. 15–6).

These three characteristics are directly linked to "speech genres" (Ostermann et al., 2023), which are recognizable, relatively stable, types of utterances used in specific social situations and communication (see Bakhtin, 1986). How a certain utterance is produced depends on the context.

Furthermore, the semantic exhaustiveness of a theme is analyzed in an authors' finalization. Text and speech express the author's/speaker's intention to produce meaning. Each genre and profession have their own typical way of finishing (therapy groups, seminars).

Stefan Trausan-Matu's (2010) Polyphonic Model, which draws on Bakhtin (1981, 1984; Holquist, 1990), is interesting. Several techniques that utilize Natural Language Processing and Social Networks Analysis are combined with Bakhtinian concepts. I refer interested readers to Trausan (2010, 2013) and Trausan-Matu et al. (2014, 2021).

Developed within the field of education, these techniques seem suitable to group analytic research. The method begins with the profound dialogism of the word, as Bakhtin (1984, p. 292) put it. Traditionally, dialogue is researched as a compositional form in the structured speech, but dialogism penetrates the entire speech structure. This means that all its semantic and expressive layers cannot be ignored, as can happen in other methods.

Reading:

Whatever method is chosen, familiarity with Bakhtinian concepts is necessary. In addition to Bakhtin's (e.g. 1971, 1984, 1990) own works, Clark and Holquist (1984), Holquist (1990), Morson and Emerson (1990), Gardiner (1992), Morris (1994), Emerson (1997), Frank (2012),

Ostermann et al. (2023), Hamston (2006), Leiman (2004, 2011, 2012), and Smith (2016), are relevant.

Autoethnography

Autoethnography can be emancipatory for people, who have been silenced, because it breaks this silence. It rests on the belief that social knowledge can be acquired by using the Self and analyzing our own experiences. This may take the form of a narrative that places the Self in a social context (Reed-Danahay, 1997). For example, autoethnography can be used to tell a story that invites personal connections, or to critique the extant literature on a topic of personal significance.

Researchers vary in their emphasis on self (auto-), the cultural link (-ethno), and the application of the research process (-graphy). When the subjective Self is used as the only data source, autoethnography can be viewed as narcissistic and separated from other discourses (Wall, 2008). To avoid such separation, other sources of data collection are incorporated so that the autoethnography is done in a more scholarly way. Stories of others, documents, and reference to theory are valuable data sources. It is possible to use a mixture of analytical and evocative autoethnography in order to preserve scholarship (analytical), while also writing in an emotional, poetic manner (evocative) (Vosmer, 2024d). As an interpretivist, my study shifted the attention from the personal to the social contexts. It is comparable to the Figure-Ground. Although everything is there, not all aspects are always visible and fade into the background.

Claims of a democratic Group Analysis created unease within me so that my autoethnography arose from a reflexivity of discomfort (Pillow, 2003). Despite the uncomfortable feeling, my study aimed to create a space for silenced others and contribute to social change by explicating how marginalization occurs (Dauphinee, 2010). This is an important axiological aspect of auto-ethnographical studies.

Autoethnography can also be combined with other methods. In conjunction with a Bakhtinian analysis, it allows the use of Self to expose inequality, discrimination, and injustice, but without having to set aside one's identity. More specifically, the Theory of Dialogism (Bakhtin, 1981) can be drawn on. Dialogue, a system of languages (heteroglossia), which mutually and ideologically interanimate each other, involves polyphony (Bakhtin, 1984). This means that it places the researcher in the different social situations that are present in culture (Bakhtin, 1981). But it is the strongest voice that produces an echo of prevalent ideologies (Bakhtin, 1986). Moreover, polyphony (multiple voices) gives researchers the freedom to use many voices, but these have the overtone of other people. Texts already exist in the form of cultural dialogues (Bakhtin, 1984), long before the researcher carries out a study. So, not only the voices of ancestors are found in the language and sentence structure.

Phenomenological Methodologies

Ironically, phenomenological approaches have not escaped positivist coding upon scrutiny. Phenomenology promises to engage thoughtfully in daily situations, seeking to understand the outside world as it is interpreted by, and through, human consciousness (see Husserl, 1950–2014). It emphasizes the intentionality of human action. However, we carry out actions for specific purposes. Hofmann (2016a) reminds us that we interpret the actions of others as intentional. Consequently, our interpretation of these is also intentional, and every creation of meaning arises from such processes of understanding. Phenomenologists know this. Even though we attribute meaning to people and things in the social world, these change constantly. With every action, we influence what happens in the circular processes, as Hofmann (2016c) notes. At the very core of phenomenological inquiry lies a certain attitudinal disposition. A preparedness for relinquishing personal motivations in exchange for suffering sustained periods of unknowing (Van Manen, 2016).

Edmund Husserl (1859-1938) was critical of Objectivism. Waldenfels (1992) suggested that he developed phenomenology as a bridge between ideal laws and real experience. Husserl's (1980) epistemological system aimed to give an exact description of intentionality. It is a feature of conscious mental states, enabling us to direct consciousness toward an object and to be conscious of something (Husserl, 1983). Philosophy should concentrate on the things given directly in consciousness, according to Husserl (1950-2014). But such givenness is a theoretical construct, the German Martin Heidegger (1889-1976) objected. His philosophy centered on existence and ontology. Trying to answer what exists, philosophers do not question existence per se, Heidegger (1962) highlighted. His investigation of the meaning of "Sein" (Being) is concerned with the ontological difference between being (Sein) and beings (entities). To examine this distinction, Heidegger drew on the notion of "Dasein" (being there, being in the world). For him, phenomenology is a theoretical enterprise that starts from ordinary experience. Attentive and sensitive examination of this experience aims to reveal the a priori (transcendental conditions) that have shaped and structured experience. Therefore, the context, in which experiences and perceptions are formed, is important. Like others, Heidegger (1962) asserted that we cannot understand human existence without attending to lived experiences. Regarded as intersubjective phenomena, experience and experiencing occur in the lifeworld between people (Merleau-Ponty, 1962).

In philosophy, the term "lifeworld" refers to how we gain knowledge of the world. Lifeworld is more than just our environment and includes our experiences of the world, how we interpret it, and how it presents itself in consciousness. For Husserl (1936/2012), lifeworld was the foundation and horizon of possibilities of all experience, the source of all knowledge. While the world is perceived as given and real, presenting itself to consciousness as natural, the lifeworld is at the same time subjective and relational.

Husserl (1936/2012) held that the phenomenological analysis begins with the lifeworld, the everyday, natural, normal things in life. Thus, methods and ways of thinking had to be developed, which were derived from the lifeworld. Husserl also advocated that we look at the things themselves. They are not obvious to us, and the perception of things is not the same as these things. Waldenfels (1992) pointed out that the object is not simply one and the same, but it reveals itself as the same in the interplay of circumstances and intentions, in which it is perceived, remembered, expected, imagined, judged, treated, and thought of as real, possibly dubious, or negated (p. 15). Therefore, phenomena of the lifeworld must be differentiated from the perception that we have of them. Our only access to the world is through our own perception, so each access is also subjective. Corporeality is crucial to this, because the body is the third dimension, in addition to pure consciousness and pure nature. Paradoxically, phenomenological researchers do not use their bodies as research instrument, even though this follows logically from such thinking. Nevertheless, phenomenological methods are said to enable researchers to achieve an understanding of lived experiences. They can illuminate the specific and identify how phenomena are perceived (Moustakas, 1994). Epistemologically, phenomenological research is concerned with personal knowledge and subjectivity. While descriptive phenomenology seeks to describe, IPA also interprets.

The Husserlian method attempts to achieve phenomenological reduction by focusing on the things themselves. This involves focusing on each aspect of conscious experience, pertaining to the phenomenon of interest. The existential philosopher Emmy Van Deurzen (1998) clarified that we must step outside of our habitual way of seeing or experiencing the world. Instead, we must adopt a reflective, reflexive, and phenomenological attitude in relation to our experiences and perceptions. Doing so allows us to become more conscious of the phenomena we experience. Additionally, we may gain a deeper understanding of the meaning of people's experiences (Van Manen, 2016). Both Husserl and Heidegger argued that people are not separate from reality and a meaningful world, but part of it. Consequently, humans can only be understood by considering their involvement with the lifeworld. Distinctions between object and subject become superfluous (Hofmann, 2016c). The phenomenological method can make voices heard, and bring to the fore deeper issues, as well as the experiences and perceptions of an individual.

Conversations, interviews, and other texts can be analyzed phenomenologically. Hofmann (2015) explained that the resulting data can be aggregated and organized with mind maps. Software is available to analyze data. Alternatively, data can be entered into a database manually, organized around headings. Whatever analyses researchers choose, detailed accounts of individual experiences arise from phenomenological studies (see Crotty, 1998; Van Manen, 1990, 2014, 2017; Giorgi, 1970, 1991, 2006, 2008, 2009, 2010; Van Manen, 1990, 2014, 2017).

Interpretative Phenomenological Analysis

In clinical psychoanalytic research, IPA has been used frequently, according to Rustin (2019). He notes that it is possible to extend the IPA notion of interpretation from the sphere of conscious to that of unconscious meaning. In psychoanalysis, this is what interpretation refers to. Like psychoanalysis, group analytic theories are not exclusively concerned with the explication of meaning and people's conscious interpretations of their situation. Instead, they focus on mental structures, entities, and other unconscious aspects, which are assumed to be causal. These are distinct from people's conscious intentions. However, group analytic explanations also explain conscious, subjective states of mind, as does psychoanalysis (Rustin, 2019).

Group analysis has a broader application than IPA. Not only does it elucidate phenomenological experience, but it also attends to unconscious structures, causes, and bodily countertransference. Therefore, IPA is not the method of choice for group analytic researchers, so I will keep my descriptions brief.

Phenomenology and hermeneutics, as espoused by Husserl, Heidegger (1962), Merleau-Ponty, and Gadamer, are IPA's philosophical foundations. According to Smith et al. (2022), IPA is an idiographic methodology, paying close attention to each individual case, even during the process of comparing all cases. It aims to produce a coherent, third-person description, which captures the participant's experience. Additionally, IPA situates these descriptions in their socio-cultural and historical contexts. Although it cannot generalize, Smith et al. (2022) argue that individual experiences may nevertheless offer insight into views that are shared by others. Interpretations may be informed by theory. Furthermore, IPA focuses on how a phenomenon presents itself. However, the researcher's interpretation (double hermeneutic) should enable both its appearance and understanding (Smith et al., 2022). Few participants are needed due to the in-depth analysis. Researchers can use software, such as CAQDAS, to transcribe interviews, code data, and identify crucial themes.

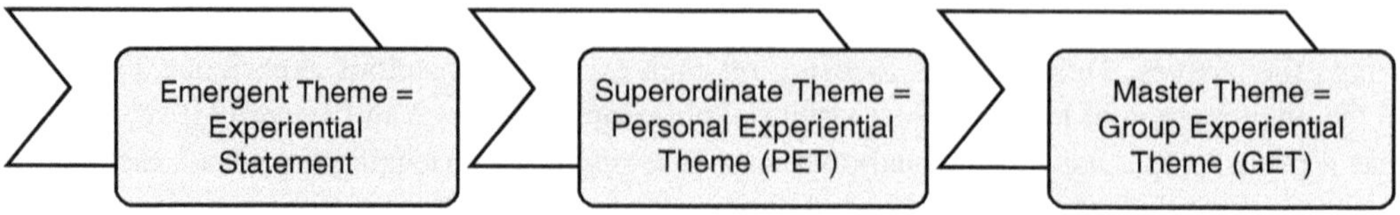

FIGURE 7.1 Old & New IPA Terminology

In *Group Analysis,* Jackson et al. (2023) described interviews of female survivors of interpersonal trauma to find out how they experienced the Survive & Thrive Course. The use of IPA (Smith, 1996) gave participants the opportunity to voice their experiences, and the meaning they assigned to these was illustrated. IPA's terminology changed in 2022 (See Figure 7.1).

Phenomenological approaches differ. Nonetheless, IPA, Van Manen's hermeneutic phenomenology (1990, 2014, 2017), and Giorgi's (1970, 2009; Giorgi et al., 2017) descriptive phenomenology have something in common: through the use of interviews, listening to these repeatedly, and reading through the transcripts several times, and the grouping of words and sentences together to identify meaning units, categories, and themes, meaning is identified. By describing everything, with or without further interpretation, researchers capture the individual lived experience, a person's meaning-making process, or the general psychological structure of an experience. In other words, the phenomenon that is being studied can be described and understood. Reflection is a crucial aspect of all phenomenological approaches. Researchers write down personal, theoretical, and other reflections. However, phenomenological methods are problematic for several reasons.

Barad (2007) and Haraway (1997) highlighted that reflection mirrors sameness. It can be regarded as a reductionist way of thinking (Bozalek & Zembylas, 2017). If one accepts this criticism, moving beyond reflection is preferable. Like Murris and Zhao (2022), group analysis would be wary of the motivations that may underpin a researcher's reflection. Furthermore, reflection seems to assume an independent individual existence, which is prior to relationality with other humans and the "more-than-human" (p. 122). Words are used to express emotions and the participant's inner thoughts. Critical of this representational ontology, Murris and Zhao (2022) focus on "be(com)ing". They prioritize the edge of awareness and affective capacities generated through remembering in-between human and more-than-human phenomena.

Commonly, researchers are advised to acquire a phenomenological attitude, which involves "bracketing" one's assumptions, also known as epoché or phenomenological reduction. Bracketing supposedly enables researchers to conduct their research and analyze the data without any, or minimal, judgment. Merleau-Ponty (1962) acknowledged that total reduction was impossible, but nonetheless believed that one can enter the lifeworld of another person via the phenomenological method. Like Derrida, St Pierre, and other scholars, I believe that language cannot transfer meaning from one person to the other (St Pierre, 2011). For me, the body is crucial and without integrating it into a method, one cannot enter the lifeworld of another person. Group analytic psychotherapists and researchers would be equally skeptical of Husserl's confidence to become conscious of a phenomenon.

Reading the transcripts several times is a must to get a good sense of the participants' experiences. Numerous textbooks say so. But why should *re-reading* enable such good understanding? I am as puzzled as St Pierre by this assumption.

Furthermore, researchers are often advised to number the lines in the transcript, mark significant statements or words related to the phenomenon of interest, and derive meaning units, themes, and so forth. Ultimately, researchers engage in coding. It is assumed that coding makes analyses rigorous, because coding is a derivative of positivist practice, where words were regarded as "brute data" (St Pierre, 2011, p. 622). Having done their final analysis, or synthesis, with/out interpretations, researchers then claim to have "revealed" the participant's lived experience, the meaning-making process, and so forth. So, phenomenological methods have not escaped the black hole of qualitative research, coding (Lather, 1991) either.

Chapter Summary

My main focus has been on Bakhtin due to his emphasis on dialogue, interaction, power, polyphony, utterances, heteroglossia, and his suggestion that the Self is constituted through the Other. While these conceptualizations are particularly important for group psychotherapy research, they are also relevant for any analysis of power hierarchies, policies, intersectionality, illness, and political events. This is not to say that meta-synthesis, IE, autoethnography, and phenomenological approaches are of no value. On the contrary, for studying organizational structures, work, and mental health settings, IE is very relevant, and a good synthesis is always informative. Autoethnography is flexible. It can be combined with quantitative and qualitative methods. Seemingly opposed to group analysis is phenomenology. It consists of diverse approaches. The problem I have with thematic analysis and phenomenology is that they are not qualitative enough.

Software makes it easier to handle vast amounts of data, and analysis techniques can be integrated into a study. I understand why this may appeal to some. I am not arguing against positivist coding procedures. The crux of the matter for me is the word "qualitative". Why not use the term "mixed method" instead? Whether one calls it identifying themes, or not, researchers still end up with codes under the label "themes", albeit more sophisticated versions than the traditional positivist content analysis.

However, coding comes with baggage, namely, colonialism. Whether group (analytic) research wants to present itself as exclusive or inclusive, and as conclusive or continuous, has empirical and ethical implications. Post-qualitative researchers criticized the black hole of qualitative research decades ago. The question as to whether qualitative group research can move beyond such coding assumes that it wants to, or should do. The entire discussion becomes redundant, if it sticks to group analytic methods, critical discourse analysis, and Bakhtinian dialogism, to name but a few. Ultimately, only group (analytic) researchers can decide in which direction research practices should develop. Whether there is a place for dialogism to make qualitative group research truly qualitative, or whether the positivist polyphony will prevail, remains to be seen.

8

APPLICATION OF DIVERSE ANALYTIC METHODS TO RESEARCH

Unconscious Group Processes, Sensitive Topics & the Hidden

Abstract

Several methods to research (online) groups, individuals, unconscious group processes, and sensitive topics are described. Due to space, methods, such as the group, oral, and biographical interview, the visual matrix method, the Operationalized Psychodynamic Diagnostic Procedure, Jung's Word Association Experiment/Test, the free association narrative techniques, and the body as research tool, are only outlined. Due to their importance, I discuss transference and transference interpretations research in more depth. Talking circles, used in Indigenous research, change process research, the social dreaming method, discourse analysis, and deconstruction, are also described. Ethical dilemmas are discussed. Whether it is necessary for researchers to "love" their participants to obtain richer data, is queried. Additionally, I make suggestions for further research and suggest that ethics codes require revisions.

Introduction

Interviews have been conducted in research for more than a century. Platt (2012) explained that the interview has changed both as a practice and as a methodological term in current use. Historically, interviewing was not a method but part of a broader methodological category (survey, case study, life story). Nora Schaeffer (1991) referred to (survey) interviews as conversations with a purpose. Similarly, group analytic researchers may regard interviews as dialogues with a purpose.

Primarily a qualitative method, the main goal of the group interview is to make the latent affective elements of participants' responses clear to the group. Aubel (1994) noted that the group interview is often known as focus groups. However, focus groups do not always attend to the hidden, in contrast to the group interview (see Small & Birnbaum, 1971). In focus groups, latent content is not usually rendered conscious through direct interpretation and involves a more subtle process.

Both the group and oral history interview methods (Sommer & Quinlan, 2024) are used when researchers want to explicate events. A community or large groups can gain insight into its past

DOI:10.4324/9781003609544-11

in this way. The group interview technique can also be combined with the visual matrix method (Froggett et al., 2019). It has been used to study non-verbal communication, and it pays attention to silence, body postures, facial expressions, body movement, personal space, variations in the quality, volume, pitch, and tone of voice (Froggett et al., 2015). Researchers try to bridge emotional distance between them and their participants.

Unconscious disturbance can become apparent when potential group members are assessed or prepared individually for joining the group. Hence, similar methods as in individual psychodynamic (therapy) research can be used for data collection and analyses. These include, for example, Rosenthal's (1998) biographical research method, the biographical and narrative interview methods (Froggett & Wengraf, 2004; Wengraf, 2001, 2011, 2018; Wengraf & Chamberlayne, 2013), and the free association narrative interview (Hollway & Jefferson, 2012). The social photo matrix (Sievers, 2008a,b, 2013) and the dream-drawing (Mersky, 2013) methods, described well by Mersky and Sievers (2018), along with psychoanalytic ethnography, developed by the French Devereux (1967) and applied by Andersen (2018), are also suitable.

Even though group analytic interviewing, observation, and interpretation of data involve considerations of embodied unconscious processes, researchers have often neglected the body. Bodies can serve as methods for experiencing and thinking about feelings, desires, actions, and corporeality (Hickey-Moody, 2013).

Group analysts work with individuals to prepare them for the group. Peter Fonagy (2004) found the German Operationalized Psychodynamic Diagnostic Procedure (OPDP) a valuable empirical tool to study individuals. Furthermore, the Word Association Experiment/Test has been used to examine the manifestation of the collective unconscious. Jung's (1968b) collective unconscious, which is characterized by archetypes, forms part of the social unconscious (Hopper, 2001). Psychoanalytic conceptualizations and techniques, such as counter-/transference and transference interpretations, have a long history in psychoanalytic research. The first experimental study of transference interpretations was carried out by Høglend et al. (2006), offering the impetus for more rigorous psychotherapy research.

The group analyst Anderson (2021) moved group analysis away from relying on psychoanalysis in terms of sexuality and gender, also discussing ethics. Anderson emphasized discourse analysis and deconstruction. Discourse analysis is a broad and diverse field, which includes a variety of approaches that study language (Wetherell et al., 2001). It examines the variability of people's accounts, rhetorical aspects, and the functions of talk (Georgaca & Avdi, 2011). Language is viewed as metaphorical rather than referential (Parker, 2005). Associated with Foucault and Derrida, discourse analysis and deconstruction have been widely used as a research method.

In this chapter, several methods to research (online) groups, individuals, unconscious group processes, and sensitive topics, will be outlined. Due to space, I will only prove a rudimentary outline of methods. After briefly outlining the group, oral, and biographical interview, I will *only* attend to the visual matrix method. Then the body as tool, the OPDP, Jung's Word Association Experiment/Test, and the free association narrative techniques will be outlined. I will *only* discuss transference and transference interpretations research in more depth due to their importance for group researchers. I will also outline methods, such as talking circles, used in Indigenous research, change process research (CPR), the social dreaming method, discourse analysis, and deconstruction. Ethical dilemmas, and whether it is necessary for researchers to "love" their participants to obtain richer data, will be briefly discussed. Additionally, I will make suggestions for further research.

Researching Unconscious Dynamics & Processes

The Group Interview, the Oral Interview & Visual Matrix Method

Small and Birnbaum (1971) clarified that the *structured* group interview procedure was originally developed in 1947 for working with large groups (25–50 persons) to bring about change in social systems, organizations, or in a community. Thompson and Demerath (1952) described their experiences with the group interview. Many people could participate in the diagnosis of, and solutions to major problems of a social system.

Also regarded as action research, a group interview with 30 participants is suitable to achieve a change process (Small & Birnbaum, 1971). Working with groups of this size has sufficient heterogeneity for the formation of sub-groups so that crucial intergroup difficulties can be explored. One main goal is on latent affective elements of participants' responses. Once these have been made visible to the group, they can be used as a source of learning, also allowing the group to be more open about feelings.

Demonstrating that latent content is not usually revealed through direct interpretation, Small and Birnbaum (1971) pointed out that interviewers cannot fake openness, but must be aware of their own feelings in the area that is being examined. When exploring sexuality this seems particularly important. Equally, when the group interview focuses on intergroup relations, researchers' unconscious communication, behavior, and verbal responses, can have a huge impact on the group process. Thus, they must have good insight into own prejudices and beliefs. Some self-disclosure may encourage open discussion and reduce projections. Additionally, researchers attend to what is missing and act as a "resource" for the group by presenting the missing perspective (Small & Birnbaum, 1971).

Through the structured group interview crucial barriers to individual and systemic change can be identified, because researchers can obtain real (genuine) information (Anme, 2004). Skill is required to prevent one person, or subgroup, from domineering, while simultaneously encouraging recalcitrant members to participate. Interviewers must be flexible, empathic, good listeners, and sensitive to the evolving patterns of group interaction (Frey & Fontana, 1991).

While unstructured interviewing tends to be dialogic, emotive, and reflexive, allowing researchers to learn from participants, post-modern interviewing is concerned with polyphonic voices, a multiplicity of perspectives, and minimal influence of the researcher (Fontana & Prokos, 2016).

Methodologically, the oral history does not differ from the unstructured interview (Fontana & Frey, 1994), but may be preferred by Indigenous or feminist researchers. In the field of oral history, the interview is viewed as joint construction, as a dynamic process of interactivity, in which the interviewer takes a crucial role in shaping the interview, Makkonen (2006) explained. The study of oral accounts is a way of seeing how narratives and oral history were shaped. Memories, interpretations, and meanings can be examined. Additionally, how narrators, groups, and societies view their own history, can be explored through oral interviews (Freund, 2009; Shopes, 2011). Makkonen (2006) taped group discussions and combined these data with one-to-one interviews, archival material, newspaper articles, letters, and photographs to "produce the past together".

Both the group and oral history interview (Portelli, 2018; Sommer & Quinlan, 2024) are useful methods when researchers want to explicate events. A community, or large groups, can gain insight into its past.

The group interview technique can also be combined with the visual matrix method (Froggett et al., 2019). It is useful to study non-verbal communication (Froggett et al., 2015).

Beneficial for researching shared experience, which is stimulated by material that is relevant to the research question, the visual matrix method may rely on sensory material, and is led by imagery, visualization, and affect in the matrix. Froggett et al. (2015) suggested that these take precedence over discourse. They enable the symbolization of creative and emotional aspects, which may not otherwise be articulated. Hence, this method allows for unthought dimensions of experience to become conscious in a group setting (p. 1).

Alas, the group format may make it more difficult to discuss sensitive topics, such as sexuality or pornography, and the group process could interfere with meaningful discussions. However, flexibility, stimulating discussions, the collection of rich data, and being relatively inexpensive, are advantages of group interviews (Fontana & Frey, 1994).

Use of the Body as Research Tool & Technique

Bodies are methods for experiencing and thinking about feelings, desires, actions, and corporeality (Hickey-Moody, 2013). The processes that make feelings are assemblages of bodies, times, places, and events (p. 83). Even though group analytic interviewing, observation, and interpretation of data involve consideration of embodied unconscious processes, researchers have neglected embodied aspects of emotions. Designs that attend to embodied responses and to the way in which different contexts (therapy, supervision, reflective, median, large groups) evoke feelings, could be informed by Deleuze and Guattari's (1994) notion of *corporeal affect*: the action by which something/someone continues to become the Other.

When emotions are viewed as the barometer of affectus, they become equated with how the body speaks (Hickey-Moody, 2013, p. 82). Affectio (affection) refers to the body and affectus (affect) to the mind (Wróbel, 2019).

The body can be used in several ways. Examining video recordings of longitudinal groups can be used to map bodily affect, and how it changes over time. This may involve paying particular attention to facial expressions. Noticing if, or when, sad expressions change into happy expressions, or when the number of angry expressions decreases, could indicate an emotional shift in the group.

Additionally, the 20-item Positive Affect and Negative Affect Schedule questionnaire (see Quiroz et al., 2018) is useful to evidence that the analytic therapy group has a transformative influence on group members' emotions.

Love is experienced within our body-mind. By applying the group analytic concept of resonance (Vosmer, 2023c), it is possible to feel the energetic vibrations of love, which merge individual group members' body-mind with the entire group. Receptively attending to changes in bodily states, sensory perceptions, and physical resonances, and using the researcher's own body as primary means, may enable an understanding of the emotions of group members, and of the dominant feeling in the entire group. Resonance is an invaluable tool to study love, unconscious affect, and affection, in the group (see Vosmer, 2023).

Emotional states may also be detected through smartwatches (Sultana et al., 2020), which have even been used as interventions in the field of health care (Triantafyllidis et al., 2024). Group members could be given smartwatches for recording and monitoring physiological responses (see Park et al., 2020; Quiroz et al., 2018). This idea is based on findings that bodily processes are indicative of emotions. Tracking *heart rates* (indicative of emotional responses), *blood pressure* (indicative of strong emotions), and *sleep*, including duration of sleep, stages and quality of sleep patterns (indicative of mental health problems), could elucidate how participants feel. Of course, any interpretation of data must take into account any existing health conditions.

Alternatively, researchers could use analytic concepts, such as projective identification, resonance, and counter/-transference, as techniques to attend to own and the emotional states in the group. Projective identification involves the transmission of psycho-somatic sensations and feelings of each individual participant, or of the entire group. By becoming the bodily and mental receiver of projective identifications, researchers reflexively pay attention to their own somatic sensations. In this way, they are in touch with an unconscious aspect of participants, which has no words (Holmes, 2019).

Everything will be documented. If a quantitative record of sensations and feelings is kept, descriptive statistics can be applied and change empirically demonstrated.

Could Researchers Obtain Richer Data If They "Loved" Their Participants?

Bion (1965) theorized about reverie, which is often regarded as a dream-like state. Discussing emotional experiences, Bion (1962b) viewed the mother-infant feeding relationship as the primary site for reverie (see Appendix 1). Love is crucial to the mother's state of reverie. Some psychoanalysts believe that love is an important aspect of the analyst–client relationship (Lev, 2023). Drawing on Bion's notion of reverie, Holmes introduced the Reverie Method (see Holmes, 2019 for further detail). Reflections form a part of this method.

Researchers are human beings, so they have feelings and emotions. Traditional research practices do not attend to researchers' feelings/emotions due to the primacy of language. Positivist neutrality, phenomenological époche, and axiology, prioritize reflection over feelings. Reflecting on feelings is not the same as feeling an emotion, because reflection is a cognitive process. Love and other strong emotions are sidelined in reflection. Furthermore, researchers are not supposed to harbor negative feelings toward their participants or love them. This could introduce bias and admitting to loving a participant would probably raise an eyebrow.

Now this creates a dilemma for the reverie technique. Citing Bion, who held that *if reverie is not associated with love, this will be communicated,* Holmes' (2019, p. 57) method seems to miss this vital ingredient of reverie: love is crucial to the mother's state of reverie. This leads us to the researcher-participant relationship. Many researchers would probably squirm when being told that love for their participants was a necessary condition for the successful completion of their studies.

Yet Ferenczi and other analysts believed that analysis cannot be successful, if they did not love their patients (Lev, 2023). By implication, how important is love for qualitative research? What effect does it have on the *richness* of the data? Would participants be able to provide fuller accounts of their experiences, if they felt loved by researchers? By love I mean non-sexual affection.

The research literature does not answer these questions. Group analytic researchers seem as hesitant as group analysts to concern themselves with love, even though love is particularly relevant to group analytic research due to the focus on emotions in group analysis.

Recently, I described techniques to assess love in the clinical interview (Vosmer, 2022). Whether researchers could use love genograms to become aware of their own love styles, and how these may influence the research relationship, and research process, would warrant further exploration in the wider research community.

Researching Individual Assessment and Preparation Sessions & Groups

The Biographical Interview/Free Association Narrative Interview,The Visual Matrix, Social Dreaming & Other Methods

Defended researchers may engage in a free associative, reflexive, process to become aware of their own defenses. Or, they could use free-floating conversations in defended groups to uncover defended content, and defensive (social) processes. Alternatively, they could use Hollway and Jefferson's (2000) free association narrative interview technique. It aims to elicit unconscious material from defended participants. Crucial to the interview techniques is that participants are given the opportunity to tell their own narratives, following an initial question by the researcher. In this way, the participants become the authors of their narratives.

Please see Chapter 10, where I describe Wengraf's bigraphical method. Here, I will only outline some crucial differences between Wengraf's and the free association narrative interview method:

Whereas Hollway and Jefferson ask "can you tell me about … can you think of something?", Tom Wengraf asks "do you remember any particular … how it all happened?" (Wengraf, 2018, p. 233). Therefore, the biographical interview technique aims to elicit a unified whole narrative over a specified life period (Wengraf, 2018). It differs from the free association technique, which does not push right from the beginning for a narrative (p. 233).

My reading of Hollway and Jefferson's (2000) method indicates that it elicits unconscious elements. Wengraf's (2001) method relies on two interviews, allowing the researcher to consider unconscious aspects that are present in the original narrative. He suggests that at least two preliminary interpretation meetings take place. A panel of four to five people, who may meet for several hours, can reveal the researcher's prejudices. Wengraf (2018) explains that puzzling aspects of the verbatim transcript are discussed and eventually everything is synthesized.

Allowing for a chronological differentiation between the told narrative and the participant's lived life, this method goes beneath rationalizations (Wengraf, 2001). Often, participants rationalize in their narratives, or they may idealize events or people.

Due to its multidimensional procedure, the biographical interview method might obtain a more "authentic" narrative, the author suggests.

Group Visual Matrix Method

Taylor (2003) proposed that cultural imaginary is an expression or representation of stories. Therefore, the visual matrix method aims to discover what the stimulus evokes in participants, and what they make of the presented imagery (Froggett et al., 2015). In line with the associative unconscious (Long & Harney, 2013), it is assumed that through associative thinking and feeling, participants provide stimuli for each other. When these become interwoven in group discussions, they are a reflection of the entire group. Even though some threads may remain uniquely personal and distinct, others merge to form patterns (see Long & Harney, 2013). This partly unconscious social process is experienced by the group.

The group visual matrix is a qualitative group-based method (Froggett, 2020), which is influenced by Deleuzian ontology and the Lorenzerian concept of scenic understanding (Manley & Roy, 2016). Researchers utilize various sensory stimuli to set thoughts and feelings in motion, using photographs, dance, drawings, and poetry. The choice of stimuli orients the group (matrix) toward a specific research problem (Froggett et al., 2015). Developed by Froggett and Trustram

(2014), the underlying premise of the visual matrix method is that it can reflect the situation of the participants and their wider social contexts. At times, words are simply not enough (Manley, 2009). Hence, this method is led by imagery and visualization. Gripsrud et al. (2018) found it beneficial for examining defended participants, who are prone to splitting and projection.

Commonly, participants (6–35; one facilitator per 10–15 participants) sit in a snowflake space for up to one hour and are presented with stimuli (Froggett et al., 2015). Following associative discussions and a short break, participants sit in a circle. They are asked to reflect on issues that have arisen (Froggett & Trustram, 2014). Clusters of imagery, thoughts, and feelings are identified (Manley & Roy, 2016). Typically, the facilitator maps these on a flipchart, and participants link the themes to the intensity of feelings. Discussions are taped for later interpretation (Manely et al., 2015).

The visual matrix method is sensitive to how particular groups produce shared experience. It offers insight into social processes that give rise to the unthought known (for more detail on this method, see Froggett & Trustram, 2014; Froggett et al., 2015; Gripsrud et al., 2018; Manley et al., 2015). This method has also been used to study death and dying (Ramvi et al., 2019), the psycho-symbolic dimensions of the breast (Gripsrud et al., 2018), recovery from substance abuse (Manley et al., 2015), and museums (Froggett et al., 2019).

Like other psychosocial methodologies, it regards the personal and social as indissolubly intertwined. Reflexivity is crucial. Researchers try to avoid reductionism to provide a useful psychosocial account of a cultural imaginary. This includes considering identifications and projections used by the group members to reproduce and relate to the world. Froggett et al. (2015) suggested that an unarticulated and partly unconscious cultural imaginary finds expression in a visual matrix. It acquires a symbolic form due to shared images and participants' figurative language.

The affect of the group can be captured, because the matrix encourages a daydreaming state of mind. One participant may say that the image reminds her/him of people protesting, which results in associations to human rights by another participant. Cultural images can have a personal referent, and the visual matrix method produces a setting for intersubjectivity (Gripsrud et al., 2018).

Sensitivity to the unarticulated tacit dimensions of experience, which also pervade the research encounter, is one feature of this method (Froggett et al., 2015). Participants have certain experiences, fantasies, anxieties, and desires, which can be expressed through shared affect, images, or ideas. They form part of the matrix, which all participants have in common, as originally suggested by Foulkes (1964).

One advantage of the visual matrix method is that hidden feelings, processes, ideas, thoughts, and sensory, emotional and intellectual experiences can be revealed. So, it captures aspects that verbal methods cannot easily discover (Froggett et al., 2015). Furthermore, this method can be applied in numerous fields (e.g., mental/health, social work, arts) and to sensitive topics.

Limitations include the complexity of the data. It may also be challenging to handle diversity and interpersonal dynamics, which may dominate the group (e.g. Froggett, 2020).

Social Dreaming Method

Social dreaming is a tool of cultural inquiry. Offered as professional development in many diverse settings (see Lawrence, 2010), this method is taught at universities in Italy (ILNodo, 2021) and has been used in the Tavistock Group Relations Conferences.

The Social Dreaming method was originally developed by Gordan Lawrence in the 1980s (Lawrence, 1998, 2005, 2012). Inspired by Charlotte Beradt (1968), this method focuses on dreaming and dreams (see Lawrence, 2007).

A social dreaming group takes place in a matrix, where people meet to explore the contents and meanings of their dreams. Lawrence (2003) chose the term "matrix", because it describes the space from which everything originates. The social dreaming matrix reflects the primordial matrix of humanity (see Manley, 2014) and is another context for dreaming (Armstrong, 1998).

It might be conceptualized as a space where the dreams are looking for a dreamer, where an individual dreams for her/himself but also for society, another group, or institution. Each dream returns to its dreamer through someone else's dream, and the metaphor of a casual tourist in the dreaming space is useful (Ofer, 2017). However, the social dreaming matrix is dissimilar to Friedman's (2008) method. It also differs from social dream drawing (Pule, 2024) and from Bernard's (2018) sociological method of interpreting dreams.

Lawrence (2005) does not view the telling of dreams as a request for containment. Counter-/transferences are not commonly a part of the social dreaming method (Ofer, 2017).

Instead, dreams are viewed as manifestations of a given social environment, which can offer insight into shared social contexts (Lawrence, 2012). Authority figures are given flesh in dreams. Aiming to transform thinking, the matrix captures the echoes of thoughts within the space of people's minds (IlNodo, 2021).

The setting has a particular configuration, which implies a change of role for the host (convenor, consultant). Seating arrangements discourage face-to-face engagement (Manley, 2014). Chairs are arranged in a beehive or snowflake format. Such spatial arrangement reflects the development of dream thinking.

Techniques to explore dreams include free association, thematic application, and systemic thinking (see Lawrence, 2007). They also aim to forge a bond, thereby identifying links, or generating new ideas. When people freely associate, they say what comes to mind, thus, bypassing their cognitive censors. Members of a social dreaming group associate freely in response to dreams, or other images, to discover the meaning of their dreams. In this way, one dream leads to another. Remembering dreams in a "social dreaming matrix group" may lead to the transformation of thinking that is embedded in dreams (see Lawrence, 2007). So, thinking can be transformed (Lawrence, 2005).

By linking dreams to one another and connecting similar dream elements, a shared theme or synthesis may develop. Through the identification of themes, the dream is situated within its original cultural context from to understand its symbolism (see IlNodo, 2021).

It is noteworthy that the term "social" was used to distinguish social dreams from individual dreams, as used in Freud's Psychoanalysis. So, this method can be used to understand the impact of "the social". It is assumed that discussions within the matrix result in working hypotheses, which are approximations of reality (Manley, 2014). They may be consistent with "factual evidence". If not, alternative hypotheses must be formulated. In practical terms, after the first dream has been shared, the host links disparate dream images in order to illuminate their arising meaning, offering working hypotheses to aid understanding.

Social dreaming groups may offer a different perspective on how to view things in organizations and society. For example, the closure of main sources of income in a community has various effects on people and communities. A social dreaming study could examine how people and communities have been affected by the closure of factories or chains of shops. Unconscious and infinite aspects of the social system can be revealed in this way.

These groups should not be confused with psychotherapy groups. Nevertheless, the social dreaming matrix can be therapeutic (Lawrence & Biran, 2002). As each person connects with the socio-cultural and natural environment while listening to the dreams of others', a different level of insight can be achieved. When regarded as a process, the matrix then becomes a network of emotions, thoughts, and connections. Although these are found in every relationships, normally they are neither recognized nor considered. Furthermore, that society is situated within the center of our psyche is often forgotten.

The social dreaming method may be attractive to group members of Indigenous cultures, who use dreams as sources of knowledge. Manley (2014) clarified that the Senoi tribe uses social dreaming (see Clare & Zarbafi, 2009). For Indigenous Australians, the dream belongs to the outside of the Self. Furthermore, Manley (2010) used social dreaming to record responses to slavery alongside an exhibition of objects and images on the abolition of the slave trade.

One strength of this method is the discovery of the interdependence of the personal, interpersonal, and transpersonal, because it postulates that thoughts arise from a shard social unconscious (Manley, 2014). Ofer (2017) provided illustrative vignettes of dreams.

Limitations include that some arising ideas, or thoughts, may not be fully understood, developed, and integrated. Due to the unpredictability of what may reveal itself in the process, group members could potentially become distressed, and the social dreaming matrix may disintegrate. To prevent this, the host must have enough skill and expertise.

This method is very suitable for practitioner-researchers, who have sufficient experience in conducting group analytic groups and are familiar with the methodology of social dreaming.

Alternatives include the social dream-drawing method (see Mersky, 2008, 2012, 2013) and the social photo matrix (see Sievers, 2007, 2008, 2013), which can be used to investigate resonances and the importance of specific photographs respectively. When social dreaming sessions are videotaped, their content can additionally be analyzed through the use of the visual matrix method.

Jung's Word Association Experiment/Test

Researchers could use Jung's Word Association Experiment/Test to examine how the collective unconscious manifests. Jung's (1968b) collective unconscious, which is characterized by archetypes, forms part of the social unconscious. Archetypes, which are beneath complexes, are universal organizing principles. They manifest as typical behavior patterns and automatic unconscious reactions (Jung, 2011). One definition of the collective unconscious says that it comprises symbols, fairytales, myths, religious stories, literature, and/or the media (Tschuschke et al., 2014, p. 114). To study complexes and the underlying archetypes of individual group members, the Word Association Test/Experiment can be used.

Assessment, preparation sessions for the group, and final sessions could be compared. However, this empirically validated test requires training and is only suitable for Jungian trained (group) researchers (see Appendix 3 for further detail).

Depending on the cultural context, researchers could also use common artifacts, other cultural objects, Indigenous stories, myths, and fairytales to research archetypes. A photo-essay interview, in which the photographs are displayed next to autobiographical text, could be used to disrupt the hegemony of Eurocentric interviews (Veeser, 2024). The transcribed data could be analyzed through content analysis (Forman & Damschroder, 2008; Hsieh & Shannon, 2005) to identify typical behavior patterns.

Operationalized Psychodynamic Diagnostic Procedure (OPDP)

Group analysts work with individuals to prepare them for the group. The German OPDP could be beneficial to identify therapeutic change in people with severe psychological difficulties, because borderline clients do not take kindly to randomization (Bateman, 2004). (For a detailed description, please see Grande et al. 2004). My outline of their *procedure* is only brief.

Basically, suitable rating scales for measuring the intensity of conflicts are chosen. Specific, identified difficulties for each participant become the focus of research. Five central problems, derived from core dysfunctional relationship patterns, are sufficient to examine the most important aspects of the participant's psychodynamics. Habitual dysfunctional patterns should be one focus. An independent observer/rater in addition to the therapist's assessment, the client's self-assessment, and data from the client's records are used, and the interviewer's countertransference is a source of information. Clients would need to be interviewed again so that results can be compared.

Tape recordings of clinical interviews are less informative than video recordings, which also enable examination of non-verbal communication, in my opinion. Due to the lengthy procedure, I also recommend AI to assist with ratings and data analysis.

The Use of Change Process Research (CPR)

Sometimes referred to a CPR (Greenberg, 1986), such research can bridge the divide between process and outcome (Elliott, 2012). CPR aims to understand how and why change occurs (Elliott, 2010). Suitable data can include therapist process notes (Todd et al., 1992). Elliott (2012) suggested that researchers ought to include "an understanding of the immediate effects (micro-outcomes) of important moments in psychotherapy" (p. 72), as well as a shift in discursive meaning. Hence, process notes are part of an array of data that may be used in descriptive studies for examining micro details of group analytic sessions (Macran & Shapiro, 1998) or for analyzing unconscious phenomena per se. Hardy and Llewelyn (2015) commented that process notes may result from interventions or interactions within sessions. Those dynamics are neither straightforward nor easily observable. Consequently, processes in group analytic psychotherapy might be missed, if process notes were excluded from research.

Anderson (2019) outlined crucial aspects of process notes research:

Process notes are written immediately after each weekly analytic group session. Then these notes are then read and reflected upon. Extracts can exemplify certain issues in relation to group analytic training, theories, group process, or group dynamics. The extract is anonymized so that aspects and material relating to individuals are not identifiable to ensure confidentiality. It is useful to consider moments of change in the group, even though an exact recollection of when discursive changes occurred is impossible.

Do reflections and recollection change the original event? This seems very likely. Furthermore, when notes are prepared for publication, the researcher may alter what happened to protect anonymity.

However, a clinical group is not a research group. Should all group members, therefore, be routinely asked to provide consent in advance, in case the group analyst or other group members would like to publish their "process notes"?

Normally, informed consent is needed. But how can someone consent to this in advance without knowing what will transpire in the group? In group analytic theory, the entire group needs to be considered alongside individual members, as well as their relationships toward each other, and toward the conductor (Foulkes, 1975). It seems reasonable that Foulkesian thinking should be applied to ethics, as Anderson (2019) suggests. Current codes do not provide sufficient guidance for group psychotherapy research and the conundrum of process notes. Whether a shift toward psychosocial ethics (Anderson, 2019) would be more appropriate for group researchers is another issue. It would require a revision of codes of ethics.

Researching Transference Interpretations

Foulkes (1984) regarded the analytic group essentially as a transference group (p. 74), suggesting that true transference neurosis could be analyzed in the group. Even though contributions of individual members also have the function of unconscious interpretations (p. 176), the conductor interprets the group's ideas and brings them to light (Foulkes, 1990b, p. 292).

While Bion's interpretations centered on the group, Foulkesians advocate that interpretations should come from the group (Halton, 1999). Foulkes (1975) held that the interpretation comes in where analysis fails (p. 117).

Transference interpretations have been studied since the 1970s, using various research designs (Banon et al., 2001; Brumberg & Gumz, 2012; Crits-Christoph & Gibbons, 2021; Gabbard & Horowitz, 2009; Giovacchini, 1979; Godwin et al., 2003; Goodman, 2011; Henriksen et al., 2021; Hobson & Kapur, 2005; Høglend, 2004, 2014; Høglend et al., 1993, 2006, 2008, 2011; Joseph, 1985; Kazdin, 2007; Levy & Scala, 2012; Ogrodniczuk et al., 1999; Piper et al., 1986, 1991; Tyndale, 1999; Ulberg et al., 2014, 2021). Numerous researchers have reported positive effects of transference interpretations on various areas of clients' functioning. Bold whole-group interpretations can, however, undermine epistemic trust (Malan et al., 1976). Mentalizing group therapists avoid interpretations, because these are not a mentalization activity (Gunnarsen, 2020). Karterud and colleagues advanced mentalization (Johnson et al., 2016; Karterud & Bateman, 2012) in group analytic psychotherapy.

Having examined transference interpretations in the analytic group, Debbane and de Carufel (1993) suggested that the complexity of the total transference situation becomes apparent. The group conductor, other members, and the group-as-a-whole become transferential objects. More primitive transference and its underlying unconscious phantasy occur in the entire group when regression prevails. Both intensity and extent of regression, and the severity of splitting, projection, and projective identification are inextricably linked. The timing and amount of the transference interpretation are important. Vertical transference interpretations without prior explanation and whole-group transference interpretations are problematic (Debbane & de Carufel, 1993). If more group sessions were videoed, the timing of transference interpretations could be studied more rigorously and in depth.

The first experimental study of transference interpretations was carried out by Høglend et al. (2006), offering the impetus for more rigorous psychotherapy research. Since then, several reviews have been published (Antichi et al., 2022; Crits-Christoph & Gibbons, 2021; Yilmaz et al., 2024; Zilcha Mano et al., 2023, 2024).

Yilmaz et al.'s (2024) systematic review found that transference interpretations in dynamic psychotherapies are often associated with significant benefits. The authors recommended that further studies ascertained whether they could sometimes be detrimental to the therapeutic process.

Unfortunately, their Anglocentric bias and focus on individual psychotherapy are common. There is a lack of reviews in group analytic psychotherapy that includes early and non-English studies.

The Norwegian group analyst Steinar Lorentzen (2006, 2012, 2014) has conducted short-/long-term groups and carried out research since the 1980s together with Per Høglend, and other colleagues. In addition to developing Focused Group Analytic Psychotherapy, he was instrumental in the development of the Short- and Long-term Group Analytic Psychotherapy Project (SALT-GAP), which intended to address several areas of concern in group psychotherapy research (Lorentzen, 2014, p. 80).

These include the scarce evidence base for their efficacy and effectiveness. Indeed, the lack of research evidence may result in group analytic therapy being perceived as less effective (Lorentzen, 2014, p. 80), because the use of experimental designs is scarce in group analytic research. Compared to the extant psychoanalytic literature, relatively few articles have been published on transference interpretations in the field of group analytic psychotherapy. The lack of research is also noticeable when comparing Group Analysis with related disciplines, such as social psychology. Notable exceptions are Lorentzen and colleagues (Høglend et al., 1993, 2006, 2008), whose research I will outline briefly.

Høglend et al.'s (2011) dismantling study, which used data from the first experimental study of transference interpretations, "FEST" (see Hersoug et al., 2006; Høglend et al., 2006; Ulberg et al., 2014), is noteworthy. In a dismantling study,

> … one component is added to, or subtracted, from an existent treatment package in order to study the causal effects of just that component.
>
> (Høglend et al., 2011, p. 420)

They used the same instruments as described by Høglend et al. (2000, 2006, 2008) and Bøgwald et al. (1999). Previously, other scales had been developed by Høglend and colleagues to measure change. Bøgwald et al. (1999) also developed the Specific Therapeutic Technique Scale to measure the use of transference interpretations. A treatment manual (Høglend, 1990) and Jacobson and Truax' (1991) statistical approach to defining meaningful change were used. Høglend et al.'s (2011) data are based on a pool of patients, who had been referred from 1993 to 2001 (total of 122). Several papers were published by studying these patients. Forty-six patients were used for the dismantling study (Høglend et al., 2011). Seven psychotherapists used a manualized treatment approach, offering weekly sessions for at least one year. Their study was specifically designed to study the long-term effects of transference interpretations in personality disordered patients.

Forty-six patients personally disordered patients, cluster C (avoidant, dependent, obsessive-compulsive), were randomly assigned to psychodynamic psychotherapy groups with and without transference interpretations. Groups lasted one year. Clients who had received interpretations improved significantly more in core psychopathology and interpersonal functioning. At three-year follow-up, 73% no longer met diagnostic criteria for any personality disorder. Høglend et al. (2011) suggested that long-term psychotherapy that includes transference interpretation is an effective treatment for cluster C and for mild cluster B personality disorders (anti-social, borderline, histrionic, narcissistic).

In contrast to the US or central Europe, group psychotherapists in South America and Portugal use a slightly different approach. South American and Portuguese group analysis is informed by Henrique Pichon-Rivière (2000, 2005), René Kaës (2011, 2017), and Eduardo Cortesão (1989). Groups have different formats. Kaës (2011) introduced the "inter-transference", which plays an important role in groups. It arises in the group situation. Pichon-Rivière (2000, 2005) developed a group model for organizations and institutions that focuses on learning. Its application has demonstrated beneficial effects for psychic health. This model is strongly influenced by social psychology and psychoanalysis (See also Pichon-Rivière et al., 1960).

Group analytic psychotherapists in South America and Portugal also engage actively in research, I noticed when reading papers in Portuguese via Google translate. Bechelli and Santos (2006) examined transference, which developed gradually in the therapeutic group. Affects and impulses, stemming from the person's early life, were transferred onto the group facilitator and other group members. Multiple transferences arose. The impact of transferences can be reduced, or even eliminated, through the use of transference interpretations and by "working through transference distortions".

Bechelli and Santos (2006) described transference and countertransference enactments, resistance, and catharsis. These are a naturally occurring phenomenon in a group.

Positive and negative transferences occurred in Bechelli and Santos' groups (see Bechelli, 1988; Bechelli & Sanots, 2002, 2004, 2005), which had also been identified by Ormont (1992). Moreover, Bechelli and Santos (2006) found that transference interpretations enabled change. A similar effect was reported by Caldeira et al. (2022). In their experiential report, which examined health aspects of employees, they drew on the theories of Freud, Pichon-Rivière, and Kaës for their data analyses. They observed employees in an operative group, which met for 12 weeks in a psychiatric institution in São Paulo. Analysis of inter-transferences allowed them to make sense of the process of group coordination.

Like other authors, Caldeira et al. (2022) recognize the importance of resistance. It requires paying attention to the space between reality and phantasy. Once anxiety is processed, one attends to other transference dynamics. Triggered inter-transferences are also affected by the group leader's countertransference. If transferences are not analyzed, the underlying motivations of behavior, feelings, and attitudes remain unconscious. Moreover, if they are repressed or denied, they will affect the relationships and pacts between group members (Ibid).

Suggestions for Research

Researching Group Processes

Here, group process is defined as everything that happens while group members interact with each other. This includes unconscious dynamics that influence the behavior, feelings, and atmosphere in the group. If group sessions are videotaped, the group analyst, an external rater, and the researcher could all independently identify important group processes and events in the groups, pinpointing when/where change occurred, so that interrater reliability is also established.

Significant events may include a shift in the atmosphere or climate in the group, in attendance rates, or when the group becomes cohesive. Group members could be interviewed and asked if, and when, they felt a sense of belonging to the group.

Belonging is a useful concept, because most people have psychological needs for belonging (Baumeister & Leary, 1995), relatedness (Deci & Ryan, 2008), and uniqueness (Synder & Fromkin, 1980) within a group. To satisfy the need to belong, people must have frequent and pleasant interactions in a temporally stable group (Baumeister & Leary, 1995). Belonging comprises group membership and group affection.

According to Jansen et al. (2014), inclusion consists of perceptions of belonging and authenticity. The group is the primary source of these perceptions. Belonging could be operationalized, and questionnaires/rating scales, such as the GCQ, GQ, and the PGIS (see Appendix 3). These could be used to measure the group's climate, change, and inclusion.

Slow open groups provide suitable clients with the opportunity to join an established group when a space becomes available (Gunnarsen, 2020). However, qualitative studies by Dyson and Brown (2016) and Lonargain et al. (2017) reported that some group members may find the uncertainty of new members joining challenging. Further research could explore whether this process is characteristic of slow open groups per se, and if, why this might be so, or if it is confined to clients with specific disturbances. A combination of the methods described in this chapter could be used.

Furthermore, group analytic psychotherapy groups are conducted worldwide. To study group processes, talking circles may be used in Canada (see Wilson & Wilson, 2000), African cultures, or within cultural contexts, where people traditionally form a circle to talk, sing, or play games (see Chilisa, 2020). In a talking circle, members of analytic therapy groups could discuss their experiences in/of their groups. In several cultures, a sacred object is passed around from speaker to speaker, which ensures that the holder of this object can speak uninterruptedly (Chilisa, 2020). Such format is beneficial, because it allows for equality and researchers are no longer the sole knowers (Quaye, 2007), as decolonial researchers have pointed out (see Daniels, 2011).

Researching Transferences & Transference Interpretations

Transference interpretations and transferences are complex. While multiple transferences are more difficult to research experimentally, they can be studied within clinical, social, political, historical contexts and in groups. Transferences manifest differently in groups, because vertical (toward therapist or leader) *and* horizontal (between members) transferences occur (see Figure 8.1).

Qualitative or mixed-method studies could be carried out in homogenous, heterogenous, short-term, and long-term *psychotherapy groups* with different client groups to gain an understanding of

1 the effects of transference
2 effects of transference interpretations
3 who makes them, clients themselves, the conductor, or both
4 how often they occur

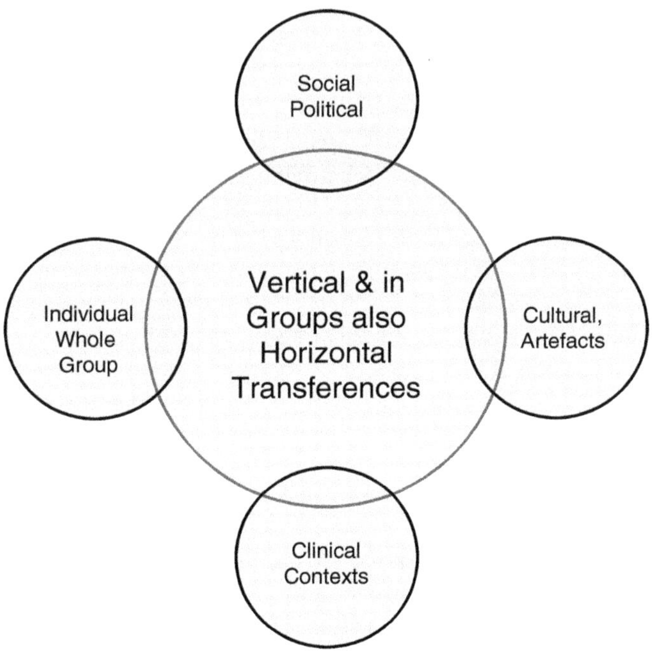

FIGURE 8.1 Manifestations of Transference

Intersectionality

Since inclusive practice is important, integration of intersectionality (Muhammad et al., 2015) in research is vital. The types of transferences that arise in culturally diverse face-to-face and online groups are another important area of research. When using a traditional mixed methods approach, standardized questionnaires and rating scales (see Appendix 3) can provide important quantitative data.

Interviewers can additionally obtain personal accounts of the experiences of receiving transference interpretations. Both psychotherapists and group members could also be interviewed to elucidate qualitative aspects of transference interpretations. Transcripts may be analyzed using thematic, content, semiotic, or other data analyses methods.

Face-to-Face & Online Psychotherapy Groups

When sessions are video-recorded, researchers can examine the nature of transferences (vertical, horizontal, whole group), the frequency of transference interpretations, and the reactions interpretations evoke. Transference interpretations can also be examined in *groups for children, adults, and older adults.*

Due to the unique technical characteristics of video-mediated group analytic psychotherapy, the onset, frequency, intensity, and forms of transference interpretations might differ from interpretations in face-to-face groups. Similar methodologies as in f-2-f groups could be used. Additionally, results from in person and online groups could be compared. Alternatively, a case study could also be used to describe transferences.

Groups delivered by videoconference can potentially improve the accessibility of group interventions for people in rural areas or with limited mobility. While teleconferencing does not seem to affect the group process negatively (Greene et al., 2010), and similar group processes as in face-to-face groups occur (Banbury et al., 2018), these findings could be replicated.

Moreover, is group cohesion *not* affected when therapy groups are conducted via video teleconferencing, as Lopez et al.'s (2020) pilot study suggested? Additionally, Pines (2002) showed that coherency differs from cohesion, denoting an organizational process. So, if and how online groups are characterized by coherence could be researched as well.

Furthermore, researchers could analyze case notes of groups, videos of experiential groups, and/or online psychotherapy groups. Agar (2020, p. 67) suggested that *idealizing, twinship, and merging transferences*, as identified by Kohut (1971, 1984), arise in online therapy. Agar (2020) found that transference occurring in video therapy is initially characterized by *projective and phantasmatic transference* and then by mutuality and intersubjectivity. These transferences undergo endless changes as the therapeutic relationship unfolds (p. 76).

It would be useful to know if other researchers reached the same conclusion as Agar. Transference could be first operationalized. Then researchers use this operational definition in multiple studies so that results can be compared.

Methods

How transferences manifest in various types of groups could be studied through postcolonial and traditional Western methods. Assessment and preparation sessions for the analytic therapy group could be researched through transference-based measures and methods. One established method is the Core Conflictual Relationship Scheme method (Luborsky et al., 1994).

Alternatives include the Consensual Response method (Horowitz & Rosenberg, 1994), Plan Formulation method (Curtis et al., 1994), and FRAMES (Dahl & Teller, 1994; Siegel et al., 2002). I refer the interested reader to Leeper and Riding (2006) for more detail.

Depending on the location and the ethnic mix of group members, Indigenous methodologies should be integrated. Researchers could follow a Postcolonial Indigenous interview process to explore transference interpretations, which could be phrased in terms of proverbs (e.g. Obiechina, 1992) that are typical for a culture or by exploring lineage and genealogy (Mishra, 2004). Postcolonial refers to an array of socio-political and aesthetic structures (Veeser, 2024).

Such interviews are guided by a relational way of knowing that recognizes participants' connections with each other (Chilisa, 2012, 2020; Roos, 2016), which lends itself to examine groups. Individual group members, participants, are viewed as knowers (see also Hlatswayo et al., 2022). Researchers listen attentively, are sensitive to cultural conventions, and enable participants to feel relaxed. They videotape the interviews but analyze them by drawing on psychoanalytic/group analytic literature from non-/Western cultures.

Group analysts also practice in Africa. Visual image methods form part of the Afrocentric methodology (Roos, 2016) and could be used to research transferences. Baart and Roos (2022) described the Mmogo (togetherness) method as a visual data collection method. Several cultural objects are selected from familiar items within a community and researchers must be familiar with these. Like Group Analysis, this method adopts an empathic stance to interpret meaning (Roos, 2016). Given that it is used to produce community-based knowledge (Roos, 2008), community leaders could assist participants in laying out cultural objects in traditional ways. Participants could be asked to talk about those items in a group. Ideally, the discussions are videotaped, the arranged cultural objects photographed (Baart & Roos, 2022), researchers take copious field notes. They may additionally ask individuals to talk about these objects in relation to their own family (for further detail, see Chilisa, 2020; Roos, 2016).

Visual objects may also be suitable for participants who find it difficult to express themselves verbally. These objects, their arrangements, individual interviews, and group discussions could be analyzed by drawing on an operationalized definition of transference. The unconscious meaning of objects could then be identified at an individual and group level. Depending on where the study is conducted, elders and leaders could assist researchers with the data analysis (see Crouch et al., 2023 for discussion). When everything has been analyzed, findings could be presented to all participants and any comments included in the final analysis.

People who suffer from neurological disorders, or who are neurodiverse, are under-researched. A single case study design could be applied to research how neurodiverse clients make sense of transference interpretations, if these are useful, or might even be harmful. This type of design uses one person (or group). The process of change can be studied by taking several measurements on the same individual (or group) over a certain period of time, so, repeatedly measuring transference interpretations. A long-term, slow open group seems ideal, because it offers the opportunity for multiple measurements over many months.

Withdrawal of treatment (transference interpretation) is the hallmark of single case designs. This involves not offering interpretations for several sessions and evaluating those sessions according to specified criteria. Afterwards, measurements taken with and without transference interpretations are compared. Unfortunately, all methods have limitations. Temporal and selective sampling are not as rigorous as purposeful case selection, which involves explicitly and thoughtfully choosing cases that are congruent with the purpose of the study (Patton, 1999).

Discourse Analysis & Group Analysis

Discourses are systems of meaning related to the interactional and wider socio-cultural context, which entail subject positions that speakers take up when using language. Wrapped up with power, discourses can marginalize certain knowledge (Keet, 2014) and practices (Georgaca & Avdi, 2011). Discourse analysis is diverse. Epistemologically and ontologically, it is social constructionist and relativist. Language is explored as a means of constructing and forming social action. Analyses of discourses have underscored the interactional nature and active role of the psychotherapist, who can promote reflexivity (Georgaca & Avdi, 2011).

In the field of psychotherapy, discourse analysis studies have examined interactional processes, dominant assumptions, and practices of psychotherapy (Avdi & Georgaca, 2007). Such studies can inform interventions.

Critical discourse analysis applies linguistically informed approaches in combination with critical theory (see Alvesson & Skőldberg, 2009c; Blommaert & Bulcaen, 2000), dealing with the relationship between discourse and power (Van Dijk, 2015). Foucauldian discourse analysis focuses on examination of power and how language shapes knowledge within the context of specific practices (Avdi & Georgaca, 2007). Foucault was influenced by Nietzsche and Wittgenstein (Powers, 2007).

Anderson (2019) suggests that Group Analysis is not governed by the domination of the subject observing the object. Instead, dialogic exchange is created through the encounter of multiple subjectivities. He refers to this as "group polyphony", because it represents the meeting of multiple speaking subjects within a contained group analytic space. Drawing on Foucault (1966, 1969, 1979, 1980) and applying Foucauldian discourse analysis (Foucault's archaeology), alongside feminist, queer, and group analytic theory, Anderson (2021) has moved Group Analysis away from relying on psychoanalysis in terms of sexuality and gender. He points out that Group Analysis has created definitions and limits, including norms that relate to knowledge of sexuality and gender. One could regard the analytic group as a "panopticon", representing the way, in which discipline and punishment work in modern society (Foucault, 1979). Power/knowledge (Foucault, 1980) is constructed through the multiple layers of surveillance of the group analyst and the group members, which become discursively instilled into each person (Anderson, 2019). An analytic group becomes the norm, even though individual members may deviate from this norm (Foulkes, 1948). While a group analytic discourse is implicated in systems of power/knowledge through its use of language, it also provides the opportunity to deconstruct language. It forces us to re-evaluate the dyadic research relationship between the observed and observer (Anderson, 2021).

Deconstruction in discourse analysis is a method where the first task is often to find and overturn oppositions inside a text (or corpus of texts). Additionally, deconstruction marks their difference (Derrida, 1997). One could regard it as an eternal interplay between opposed concepts. Derrida (1967b) suggested that metaphysics has created dualistic oppositions and installed a hierarchy within each dichotomy (presence before absence, speech before writing). The deconstructive task is to unmask these sedimented ways of thinking (Reynolds, 2024). Simply put, dichotomies are reversed, then they are corrupted (Jackson & Mazzei, 2012).

At the root of Derrida's (1998) method is the reciprocity of the sign. Where there is meaning, there are nothing but signs. Any given concept is constituted by reciprocal delimitations. Derrida (1967b) referred to a violent hierarchy when illuminating the classical philosophical opposition, where one term governs the other, where speech rules over writing (Reynolds, 2024). A deconstructive approach to data analysis is wary that something may be wrong with what researchers currently believe. Therefore, researchers seek something that is being missed, Jackson and Mazzei (2012) explained. For Derrida (1981) all knowledge (constructions) was partial.

Researchers only encounter differences, traces of traces in a text. So, they attend to these discarded traces that are available, to prevent a closure of meaning (Jackson & Mazzei, 2012). In practical terms, they re-read transcripts, data, numerous times to find inconsistency, uncertainty, what is repressed and/or concealed (for critique, see St Pierre, 2011). Preconceived notions are dismantled to expose uncertainty, the absent presence. Derrida (1998) noted that it was *not* due to the presence of the sign that language worked, but because there is difference (absence).

Do Codes of Research Ethics Require Revisions?

Good ethics and good science belong together (Welfel, 2013). Ethics requires that a detailed participant information sheet should be written so that participants can give informed consent, meaning that the person must understand the risks and benefits at stake when taking part in a study (Dooley & McCarthy, 2005). While participants must be made aware of how and by whom interviews, or any other methods, will be carried out and transcribed, whether they read and understand the information sheet is another issue (see Kim, 2024).

It is necessary to assign a pseudonym and ensure that participants are not recognizable in publications. Every attempt should be made to protect their anonymity (Welfel, 2013). Chilisa (2020) noted that codes of ethics impose constraints, such as anonymization, which some participants object to. Currently, participants cannot have their voices heard by naming them.

Researchers must adhere to data protection legislation. The wording must be appropriate for the specific country and the benefits of participation should not be overstated (Rapley, 2020). They can send the transcript to the participant to check if anything needs to be modified, deleted, or added. A debrief should happen after the interview and some researchers write "thank you" letters after the interview. It is good practice that participants receive a written report of the findings (see also Greaney et al., 2012). Being sensitive to diversity is as crucial as transparency and not harming participants. Poorly designed research on transference and transference interpretations wastes time. Welfel (2013) pointed out that it makes participants skeptical about the value of their participation and they may not take part in other studies. Rigor, good study designs, and relevance to practice are crucial ethical requirements (p. 459). Furthermore, it is important to give participants a voice.

Ethics is based on a dyadic notion, as Anderson (2021) highlights. It does not consider the social nature of the experience of group analytic psychotherapy. Hence, Group Analysis would insist that ethics must move beyond individualized conceptualizations of ethics. By being in an analytic group, consent and authorship are plural notions that can be acted upon jointly, and/or separately. One person's consent is in some sense equivalent to everyone's consent (Aderson, 2019).

This begs the questions: who "owns" experience? The ethics code? If a group member wants to publish her/his group experiences, which codes would s/he be expected to adhere to, considering that s/he is neither a therapist nor a researcher?

Further ethical dilemmas have been problematized by Jackson and Mazzei (2012). Conventional interview methods oblige researchers to center the participant. So, the interview is not a collaborative process. Participants are situated in an inferior position, even though this is not pointed out on participant information sheets.

Researchers are trained to attend to the transcripts, or their field notes, in order to sort, sift, and identify codes, categories, and themes. It is assumed that a coherent narrative emanates from participants' descriptions of a specific aspect of their experiences (Jackson & Mazzei, 2012). However, what happens during the interview or research process when the researcher projects something into the participants or the data? While group analysts learn to address projections and socially unconscious processes during their training, researchers are not required to identify their unconscious motivations. Instead, researchers are asked to "bracket" their usual ways of perceiving phenomena, so they aim to be without preconceptions. From a group analytic perspective, this seems almost impossible due to unconscious biases. So, what happens if researchers project their biases into their participants, who in projective identification, act out the researchers' prejudices? These ethical dilemmas are not addressed in guidelines.

When gathering data through in-depth semi-structured interviews, novice researchers are often advised to practice interviewing beforehand so that they know their questions. Otherwise, they may feel nervous and cannot concentrate on participants. Methodologically and ethically, it is important to make participants feel at ease to ensure a smooth research process. This is only possible when researchers themselves are calm. However, what if (novice) researchers are not? Not only will this disrupt the smooth flow of the interview, but participants themselves may become nervous, because mild anxiety (nervousness) is contagious. Participants could unknowingly be harmed. This needs to be discussed in research supervision. It should be addressed in the debrief following the interview.

In research ethics, debriefing serves the function of "dehoaxing" and desensitizing (Sommers & Miller, 2013). A debrief allows participants to reflect on their interview experience (Morley & Shashidhara, 2020). It also provides them with an opportunity to ask questions.

Taken together, an argument could be made for the revision of research ethics codes.

Chapter Summary

Despite their complexity, different types of analytic groups can and should be researched. I have described several methods to study groups, unconscious group processes, sensitive topics, and individual therapy sessions. The group interview, the oral interview, the free association narrative, the biographical interview, and the visual matrix methods can reveal tacit processes. I have also described the body as tool. The OPDP and Jung's Word Association Experiment/Test are useful for studying individual sessions. One focus has been on transference and transference interpretations due to their importance for understanding groups. Many different techniques can be applied. The Indigenous talking circle can also be used in different cultures. I have made suggestions for research and described CPR, social dreaming method, discourse analysis, and deconstruction. I have queried whether it is necessary for researchers to love their participants to obtain richer data. My discussion of research ethics indicates that ethics codes require revision.

9

ADOPTING "OTHER" PHILOSOPHIES & SHIFTING THE FOCUS TO MIXED METHODS IN GROUP (ANALYTIC) RESEARCH

Abstract

Mixing is the focus here. Following a brief description of the mixed methods approach and compatible philosophies, the privileged position of the research question is discussed. I argue that axiological considerations should be as important as the research question. Furthermore, the application of Critical Realism as research method is outlined. In addition to suggesting a model to inform evidence-based practice/practice-based evidence, action research and semiotics are described. A detailed Peircean semiotic analysis of psychosomatic symptoms is offered to aid understanding. Suggestions for research are also made throughout.

Introduction

Despite disagreements about the most suitable philosophical foundation of the mixed method approach (Biesta, 2024), Pragmatism has traditionally underpinned mixed methods research (Feilzer, 2024). Recently, the mixed methods approach has gained prominence.

Researchers can have various reasons for mixing methods, designs, or epistemologies. Being against doctrines is one reason. Howe (1988) argued against the dogma of quantitative–qualitative incompatibility, postulating a "compatibility thesis" (p. 10). The combination of qualitative and quantitative methods provides breadth, depth, and corroboration (Johnson et al., 2007). Combining methods is also in line with the group analytic "both and" approach, but not every researcher thinks like this.

While some researchers have remained philosophical purist, others focus more on methodological issues. Morgan (2007) advocated a pragmatic approach. Feminist and postcolonial (group analytic) researchers often prioritize axiological considerations and use mixed methods in the service of communities. Axiology is also of primary importance to the Emerging Realist Paradigm (ERP), which does not divide paradigms.

Searching for a philosophical foundation for mixed methods, Johnson (2017) has suggested dialectical pluralism as a meta-paradigm. Biesta (2024) thinks that Pragmatism is not the best

DOI: 10.4324/9781003609544-12

paradigm for mixed methods. Chilisa (2024) advocates the integration of Euro-Western and postcolonial Indigenous paradigms. Critical Realism and the ERP could also underpin the mixed methods approach. They place the same significance on achieving social justice as postcolonial researchers and pragmatists.

By and large, sentiments about purism have shifted more toward dialectical pluralism (Hall, 2024; Johnson, 2024). Many researchers no longer insist on one single paradigm (Hall, 2013), or on the prioritization of Pragmatism.

Originating in the United States, Pragmatism is an American philosophical school of thought. Charles Sanders Peirce (1839–1914), William James (1842–1910), John Dewey (1859–1952), and George Herbert Mead (1863–1931) are important figures of the pragmatist movement. Hookway (2008) noted that the pragmatist maxim (Peirce, James) was at the heart of classic Pragmatism. It emphasizes practical consequences, adopting a realist ontology and a distinct epistemological, anti-Cartesian, probabilistic perspective. Inquiry and the pursuit of true beliefs were important to Peirce. His method clarifies meaning and understands concepts through their practical consequences (Legg, 2024). Mead, who was close to Dewey, focused upon the relations between the Self and the community. Subsequently, Rorty, Putnam, and Brandom developed the philosophical views of the pragmatist tradition further (Hookway, 2008).

A division into three kinds of Pragmatisms (functional, referential, methodological) through the concept pair of "knowledge and action", which is at the center of Pragmatism, was described by Ågerfalk et al. (2008). They note that methodological Pragmatism (knowledge through action) has been adopted in action research (Ågerfalk et al., 2008).

For Dewey, nature was a complex field consisting of changing transactional processes that had no fixed end (Hildebrand, 2024). Dewy criticized the prevailing metaphysical and epistemological dualism. Philosophy was an instrument for living that had to go beyond traditional problems (Teddlie & Tashakkori, 2011). Viewing personal and emotional experiences as philosophically relevant, Dewey sought an account of psychological experience that respected both experimental limits and the pervasiveness of cultural influences (Hildebrand, 2024).

One notices an affinity between Pragmatism and Critical Realism (see Chapter 1 for discussion). The latter tradition, as developed by Bhasker (1978, 1986), postulates that our knowledge of the social world is inescapably socially constructed. It straddles the divide between the quantitative and qualitative paradigms (Teddlie & Tashakkori, 2010).

Pragmatic researchers often use the extant qualitative, quantitative, and mixed research literature as the foundation for their research (Onwuegbuzie & Leech, 2005), drawing on several frameworks to appraise the quality of their studies (see Leech et al., 2009; Onwuegbuzie et al., 2009a, b).

Mixing is the focus of this chapter. After challenging the privileged position of the research question, I will describe Critical Realism as a research method and make suggestions for further research. Then I will discuss action research and suggest a modified model that informs evidence-based practice/practice-based evidence (EBP/PBE). Finally, I will describe semiotics and provide several practical examples, including a detailed Peircean semiotic analysis of psychosomatic symptoms.

Challenging the Privileged Position of the Research Question

How researchers approach their projects can differ (see Vogt, 2008; Vogt et al., 2012). Grix (2002) recommended adopting a directional approach: starting with ontology, then considering epistemological assumptions, afterwards choosing a suitable methodology, selecting appropriate methods to analyze the data, and finally writing the report. I agree with Grix (2018) that an understanding of ontology and epistemology is important for students, because they need to know the logic behind research traditions. However, I would place emphasis on axiology. It is dear to many philosophers, psychotherapists, and researchers. Values and ethical commitments to social justice, and beneficence (obligation to act for the benefit of others), should guide group analytic research from the start. In my experience as research supervisor, many students do not really consider axiology. Students often start their projects by devising research questions that their studies aim to answer. It is the traditional Western way of approaching research. The fact that so-called scientific research practices reflect conventions and bear traces of Colonialism (Seth, 2009) is easily missed.

Under the "dictatorship of the research question" (Feilzer, 2024, p. 21), many researchers do not consider who benefits from their studies, or whose interests their research actually serves. Instead, they formulate research questions and choose designs. The White privilege of the research question has never been adequately addressed. White privilege hides in methodological debates. By studying socially unconscious processes surrounding the "correct" research sequence, the reasons for the neglect of axiology, and insistence on the privileged position of the research question, would become blatantly clear. Then the status quo might shift. Axiological considerations should not be secondary but the starting point of any project, together with the research question, I contend. Mixed methods group researchers could take a leading role in advocating for change to decolonize research.

Let me explain the mixed methods approach further. Referring to "dialectical pluralism", Johnson (2024) suggests that dialectical approaches and pluralism are the heart of mixed methods research. He combines ideas from different paradigms. It is not necessary to only analyze qualitative data with other qualitative methods (Biesta, 2024). Some pluralistic analytic methodologies use a mix of analyses methods (see Onwuegbuzie & Combe, 2010). Chilisa (2012, 2020, 2024) suggests a mixed methods approach that combines conventional qualitative with Indigenous methods. Instrumental in the decolonization of research, her studies focus on relationality, responsibility, reverence, reciprocity, respectful representation, reflexivity, responsivity, rights and regulations, and decolonization (Chilisa & Tsheko, 2014; Chilisa et al., 2017).

Researchers can be creative when mixing. Biesta (2010) refers to seven levels at which mixing can occur: data, methods, designs, epistemologies, ontologies, research purposes, and practical orientations. Suggestions to prioritize liberation in mixed methods research challenge conventions. Combining like with like, the sine qua none of research, has also been queried.

If (group analytic) researchers adopted the philosophical justifications, as espoused by Pragmatism, Critical Realism, the ERP, or the postcolonial Indigenous paradigms, an axiological shift toward "the other" would occur. Chilisa and colleagues have demonstrated that this is possible. Equally, for Biesta (2024), liberating (emancipating) groups and individuals from the hidden effect of social power that influences their thinking, and doing (p. 179) are a priority. Group Analysis shares this endeavor. If societal transformation, and the benefit of research to communities and participants, became the priority, then quantitative methods could form a happier relationship with qualitative methods. If Western mixed methods studies were underpinned by the ERP, or by postcolonial Indigenous paradigms, group analytic researchers would automatically expose White supremacy and prejudices about non-Western cultures. By resisting to rely on dominant knowledge systems, colonized epistemologies (Chilisa, 2024), and the dictatorship of the research question, researchers could focus on building relationships with communities.

Critical Realist As Research Method

Whereas most literature on Critical Realism concerns itself with sophisticated levels of theory and the philosophy of science, when used as a research method, it tries to explain social

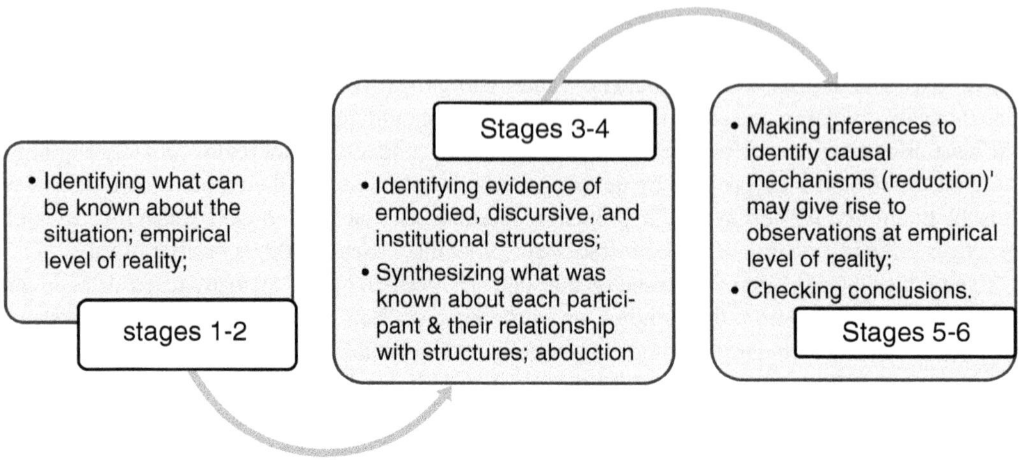

FIGURE 9.1 Stages of Data Analysis in Line with Bhaskar and Procedure Extracted from Stuchbury (2021, p. 8).

problems or inform policy. Due to these foci and its rebuttal to the positivist dogma, some view Critical Realism as liberating (Steinmetz, 1998). Not often used, the purpose of critical realist research is to determine which causal mechanisms have been triggered in a particular situation and what effect these are having. This involves understanding the relationship between structure and agency (Bhaskar, 1998), requiring the intensive study of a limited number of cases. Researchers systematically analyze the interplay between ontological layers. In this way, mechanisms, which produce the observed events, will be uncovered (see Bygstad et al., 2016). Unfortunately, even though Teddlie and Tashakkori (2010) argued that Critical Realism made it easier to design mixed method studies, few researchers have demonstrated how it has informed their data collection and analysis. Parr (2013), O'Mahoney and Vincent (2014), Bygstad et al. (2016), Fletcher (2017), and Stutchbury (2021) are notable exceptions. Furthermore, Fletcher (2017) provided a concrete example of applied qualitative research using Critical Realism as a philosophical and methodological framework. Fletcher suggested a flexible deductive process of coding and data analysis. Traditionally, Critical Realism relies on "retroduction", which involves making inferences and identifying mechanisms that could explain outcomes and testing these against the evidence. For Fletcher, this was too abstract. Therefore, her method differs from other researchers, such as Yeung (1997), Oliver (2012), and Redman-MacLaren and Mills (2015), who suggested integrating grounded theory methods into critical realist research. Simmonds and Gazley (2018) delineated the features of Critical Realism to study marketing systems. Stuchbury (2021) operationalized, drew on Constructivism, conducted interviews that were informed by theory, and presented participants with scenarios to comment on. It allowed participants to construct the "what" during the interview process. Data were analyzed through the lens of the three layers of reality which Critical Realism rests on (Bhaskar, 1989): the empirical, observable and measurable; the actual, accessible through interviews and observations; the real, underlying causal mechanisms that give rise to the observable events (Bhaskar, 1989). A modified six-stage process (Bygstad et al., 2016; Wynn & Williams, 2012) was also used by Stuchbury (2021). Analyzing data in terms of Bhaskar's three layers of reality (see Figure 9.1) is helpful when combined with the procedures Stuchbury integrated.

Recommendations for Research

Whether applied Critical Realism is suitable to study analytic groups is unknown. Nevertheless, it could be useful for researching the causal mechanisms of the therapy process. Or for the development of group analytic psychotherapies and formation of their structures, which would be viewed as a socio-historical process.

Researchers, who adopt a critical realist position, acknowledge that they are influenced by the social world they are studying (Pilgram, 2014). They start by thinking about what the world must be like for it to be knowable. So, group (analytic) researchers could conceptualize the social world in terms of societies, for example. Then they may ask *What must these societies look like so that we can know them?* Or take social class. *How does social class affect people's choice of types of psychotherapy?*

Alternatively, researchers could adopt a critical realist perspective but usc thematic analysis to analyze data, because this method allows for epistemological and theoretical flexibility (Braun & Clarke, 2006). Elaborated by Braun and Clarke (2021), reflexive thematic analysis has been applied in many fields. Thematic analysis can be used to analyze the experiences of group members in therapy groups, or in reflective practice (staff group), experiential, online, supervision, median, and large groups.

I refer the interested readers to Wilson and Ogston (2017), who analyzed patients' views on analytic groups, using thematic analysis. Both transcribed the written material from the questionnaires and coded the combined textual data by applying short descriptions to small chunks of the data. Coding aimed to extract the essence of the feedback questionnaires. Having identified the themes, these were discussed afterwards. Individually, they re-checked the analysis and calculated the inter-rater reliability.

Reflexivity is an active process, it can aid and influence interpretations, enabling researchers to gain a deeper insight into their research (Birks & Mills, 2015). It is a fundamental aspect of thematic analysis (Clarke & Braun, 2017) and of reflective practice groups.

Reflective practice groups allow multidisciplinary teams to regularly reflect on institutional dynamics (Bose, 2017), and on their clinical practice, to become more conscious of their own behavior, to develop ideas about treatment, examine psychological defenses, and become aware of ways of relating (Hartley & Kennard, 2009). Basically, practitioners and researchers critically reflect on their values and experiences. For example, how values may have shaped their theoretical perspectives and how their values impact their clinical/research practice. Researchers also write about their thoughts and feelings in a reflective journal.

Reflection and reflexivity allow for the recording of initial ideas, helping researchers to think about their own biases throughout the research process. Once coding begins, this aids the reflexive/reflective process and deepens the interpretation of the data (Braun & Clarke, 2022a,b), also connecting the stages of analysis with the write up (Tweed & Charmaz, 2012).

Forming, or attending, a peer thematic analysis group can be invaluable for several reasons. Trustworthiness and credibility can be increased by discussing one's own research and by considering the entire research process in the light of Clarke and Braun's (2019b) checklist. A peer group can also increase researchers' theoretical sensitivity by allowing them to reflect on how their own experiences may impact the meaning-making process (Charmaz, 2006).

Action Research & Its Application

The term "action research" was first coined by Kurt Lewin (1946) in *Action Research and Minority Problems.* Eric Trist and Lewin focused on multiple organizational problems, emphasizing collaboration. Through application of Field Theory and T-Groups (see Appendix 1), traditional action research was carried out to discover group dynamics (O'Brien, 2001). Over time, action research has expanded its foci. More recently, Greenwood and Levin (2007) defined it as a

> ... set of self-consciously collaborative and democratic strategies for generating knowledge and designing action in which trained experts in social and other forms of research and local stakeholders work together. The research focus is chosen collaboratively between the local stakeholders and the action researchers and the relationships among the participants are organized as joint learning processes. Action research centers on doing "with" rather than doing "for" stakeholders and credits local stakeholders with the richness of experience and reflective possibilities that long experience of living in complex situations brings with it.
>
> (Cited in Levin & Greenwood, 2011, p. 29)

Known by many different names, such as participatory research, collaborative inquiry, emancipatory research, action learning, or contextual action research, action research has often been used when the situation is too ambiguous to formulate precise research questions (O'Brien, 2001). The ideals of action research tally with Group Analysis.

Very aware of the legacy of authoritarian leaders, Foulkes (1990) believed that the group, a living organism (Foulkes, 1983), offered great scope for research. An important goal is to wean group members off their need for authoritative leadership. Group members, including the conductor, are on par, even though the conductor has knowledge of Group Analysis (Foulkes, 1984). Foulkes (1990) insisted that group analytic practices are anti-authoritarian. He advocated personal liberation from the constraints of a particular orthodoxy and dogmatism, referring to "citizenship", which is applied in the name of the community to group treatment (Cooper, 1999). Whose liberation, one may ask, the conductor's or group members'? Both, because they are the same thing (Foulkes, 1984).

Foulkes would have challenged the dominance of the research question, and does so inadvertently without ever discussing this explicitly. He captured the spirit of action research, which seeks to create participative communities of inquiry. It should be noted that citizenship and engagement with communities (Koinonia) through dialogue (De Maré et al., 1991) are important elements of Group Analysis per se.

Carrying out action research as part of group analytic research would be a logical consequence, because it is built on a commitment to democratic dialogue and social processes (Levin & Greenwood, 2011). Both group analysts and action researchers link praxis and theory, rejecting the theory/practice dichotomy (Greenwood & Levin, 1998, 2007).

As Marx (1997) highlighted, the point is not to interpret but to change the world (p. 402). Action research offers strategies to generate social change, produce empirical results, or foster methodological developments. If carried out within the different branches of group (analytic) psychotherapy, action research could potentially decolonize research practices and inform the development of new group (analytic) training practices.

For example, despite acknowledging that the group analytic curriculum must be decolonized, the teaching and assessment practices used by the Institute of Group Analysis in London are still informed by an antiquated pedagogical model. Commonly, students are given a list of papers that they are expected to read. Papers are presented and discussed in seminars. Students must write traditional essays, clinical papers, and dissertations. These academic works are marked against a set of criteria. Even though the need for reforming pedagogical systems has been recognized, changes do not seem to be informed by empirical research. Action research could be a means to achieve transformation, if carried out.

Traditionally, participants and researchers engage in cycles of action and reflection (Schön, 1983). In action phases, researchers and involved parties test practices and gather evidence. In reflection phases, they make sense of these together and plan further actions. Cycles of action and reflection integrate knowing and acting.

However, Kemmis et al. (2014) pointed out that critical participatory research does not always follow the "spiral of self-reflection". It involves cycles of planning, acting, observing, reflecting, re-planning, new action and observation, further reflection, and so on (pp. 112–3). This spiral of reflection seems useful for studying group (analytic) training practices and assessment of candidates' (students') academic work.

Researching communities would involve several stages: planning a change and then enacting this change; observing what will happen; reflecting on it to ensure that this change has been just and is inclusive; re-planning new actions, if required (p. 113).

Action research engages people who do not normally have a say in research (Park, 1993). Participation in inquiry means that participants are regarded as co-researchers, and are fully involved in the research process (Rahman, 1993). An attitude of inquiry includes developing an understanding that people are embodied human beings, who are part of a socio-ecological order, and interconnected with everybody else (Reason & Bradbury, 2008).

Words can have a slippery relationship to reality, but practices are real, Gustavsen et al. (2008) pointed out. Thus, a major advantage of action research is that it tends to create new practices. Challenges are related to the lack of freedom to participate (giving informed consent), because not everybody within a community may wish to participate, as well as to the lack of privacy, and difficulties with intervening in large scale projects. Participating communities "are made" and people can experience task exhaustion (see Bennett, 2019).

Action research is political, because people's rights to take part in the decision-making processes, which affect them, are recognized. People are viewed as capable of producing knowledge. Using their own knowledge empowers people (Freire, 1970; Reason, 2005). Within an action research project, communities of inquiry and action evolve. A project addresses questions that are significant for both participants and researchers.

From a dialogical perspective, dialogue is the key element in any emancipatory project that aims to liberate. Paulo Freire (1970, 1978) emphasized the need to "reinvent" the meaning of power by creating a different kind of power. The Indigenous Kaupapa Māori approach to research does so, because the researcher is led by members of the community. S/he does not presume to be a leader and has no power that needs to be relinquished (Denzin, 2003, p. 243). Similarly, Foulkes (1984, 1990) did not perceive the conductor to be a leader. Instead, s/he is guided by the group.

Model to Inform Evidence-Based Practice & Practice-Based Evidence

Qualitative group (analytic) researchers face the same problem as researchers in the wider field of psychotherapy research. From their perspective, it may seem reductionist to rely, for example, on an anxiety inventory, which does not capture the lived experience of anxiety. This could even be viewed as an affront to human values.

However, quantification is a crucial ingredient of EBP. Barkham and Mellor-Clark (2000, 2003) suggested that PBE was complementary to EBP.

To capture new developments and the need for decolonizing research, I have been inspired by their model, but changed it significantly. My model incorporates quantitative and qualitative methodologies, which *guide* rather than determine practices.

It prioritizes "the other" (e.g. clients, communities). Different methodologies, including group analytic, Indigenous, and AI-informed approaches/techniques, are of *equal* value and importance.

The generation of new knowledge is achieved by researching areas/topics, which have *arisen out of the research process and research evidence.* This includes essential components of group analytic psychotherapy and theory, such as therapeutic change factors (including mediators and moderators), identified by researchers, or other aspects that may have been identified as beneficial by group members, psychotherapists, or other large groups (society, communities, service user groups). Evidence generated by Indigenous and AI-informed methods is of *equal importance.*

From the perspective of the Emerging Reality Paradigm, a shift in traditional thinking would be required. It involves moving away from the traditional hierarchy of evidence to probabilistic, holistic, and integrative process-based evidence, where different forms of knowledge coalesce dynamically rather than being ranked hierarchically. This could be achieved by including relational, ecological, and qualitative data, alongside quantitative data and Bayesian statistics.

For example, group members' narratives, AI-informed sentiment analysis, and biometric measures could be integrated.

Semiotics & Semiotic Analysis

Semiotics was developed by the Swiss Ferdinand de Saussure (1959) and the American Peirce (1958).

Every sign in *langue* (whole system of language) acquires its meaning due to its difference from all the other signs in langue, according to de Saussure (1959). Any example of actual speech/writing (*parole*) uses specific elements from the entire language system (Silverman, 1983). Hence, English speakers recognize the sign "snake" by its difference from "cake" or "cat".

All languages are sign systems and non-verbal communication includes signs expressed by the body. Language enables us to communicate with linguistic signs (Bignell, 1997). It is used to examine how *langue* is structured. Researchers can examine anything where meanings are created by a system of signs. Examples of signs are images, words, objects, clothing, and anything that has a certain meaning in a particular society (Silverman, 1983). Signs are organized into groups (codes), and Bignell (1997) gives the example of dress. When wearing an evening dress or a jogging suit, their codes convey very different messages. For example, the meaning of an evening dress (formality) differs starkly from that of a jogging suit (informality).

The postulate that all signs are arbitrary leads us to the assumption that no sign has a definitive meaning. There is a paradigmatic relation between signs insofar that a sign can acquire meaning from its association with another sign (Rose, 2001). However, it can only acquire meaning from its sequential order in a sentence (syntagmatic relation), Silverman (1983) clarified. By studying the reasons for the formation of signs and the meanings behind them, semiology (or semiotics) can reveal what is hidden.

Semiotic analysis concerns itself with the relationship between the signifier and the signified, examining denoted (literal) and connoted (secondary, linked) meaning. Rose (2001) explained that, for de Saussure, there was no necessary relationship between a specific signifier and its signified. De Saussure (1959) had already demonstrated that every sign has two components: signifier and signified. The means by which the sign is expressed in the material world is the signifier. The signified is the concept that the signifier evokes. When reading the word "snake", the group of letters "s n a k e" are the signifiers. These signifiers immediately evoke the signified (Bignell, 1997), the concept of a snake in our minds. So, a sign consists of a signifier (material thing that signifies) and the signified (concept the signifier relates to).

For Peirce, Barthes, and Derrida, the signified is endlessly commutable due to the intervention of the interpretant (Peirce), due to the connotation (Barthes), or due to free play (Derrida) (Silverman, 1983, p. 38). According to Mingers and Willcocks (2017), how a semiotic analysis is carried out depends on the philosophical perspective and methodology one adopts.

Hence, a Peircean semiotic analysis differs from de Saussure's semiological analysis, from Lévi-Strauss' (1967) structural analysis, and from Roland Barthes' poststructuralist theories of discourse, who applied de Saussure's semiology to advertising. Yelle (2022) note that Silverstein's (1998, 2004; Silverstein & Urban, 1996) discourse analysis, developed in linguistic anthropology, differs from "semiotic ideologies" (Keane, 2018, p. 64), as espoused by Schieffelin et al. (1998) or Keane (2007). Poststructuralists, such as Jacques Derrida (1976), examine the denoting sign by deconstructing it into signifier(s) and signified first, before revealing its connoted symbolism through their examination of its ideology (Harvey, 2012). So, they deconstruct the denotations and connotations of signs, and their connected symbols. Whether one can separate denoted from connoted meaning is debatable, however.

Silverstein (1979) inaugurated the study of "linguistic ideology". It refers to the "politically infused ideas and rationalizations about language that explain the forms, uses, and social indexicalities of the languages their speakers use, interpret, or hear about" (Irvine, 2018, p. 25). Importantly, Janowitz (2018) observe that notions of reference and definition underpin the search for truth. She notes that "the truth", some investigators find, is limited by how they imagine language to work (p. 46).

For Peirce (1931), signification involved the interaction between the sign, the interpretant, and the object. His second triad comprises icons, indices, and symbols (sign referring to the object). He highlighted that the connections of meanings can only be made in the mind of a person. Atkin (2023) offers a detailed description of Peirce's semiotics, explaining that a sign addresses somebody, and creates in the mind of that person an equivalent sign, or even a more developed sign.

In all communication, the icon plays a crucial. Through a picture the idea of a snake can be directly communicated to people who do not speak the same language. However, to understand the word "snake", the person must know English, as Chandler (2006) noted.

Speech also tends to be accompanied by gestures and facial expressions, so-called extra linguistic indices (Chandler, 2006).

Indexical elements, which function like a pointing hand, aid the transformation of general assertions into specific statements, locating the discourse temporal-spatially (Silverman, 1983, p. 21). For instance, the name Barack Obama elicits the mental image of the former president of America. While "snake" refers to a whole class of snakes, a proper name (Obama) makes a direct and individual reference to a person.

Due to its iconicity and indexicality, Silverman preferred Peirce's semiotics. In her opinion, de Saussure's semiology does not distinguish between linguistic and photographic signifiers, but Peirce's conceptualizations enable researchers to analyze photographs and film. Indeed, Peirce does seem to make more allowance for the analysis of non-linguistic material. His semiotics could be used to analyze video-recordings of analytic therapy, or other groups, as well as for the analysis of monuments, photos and films, in archives. According to Yelle (2022), Peircean semiotic analysis commonly starts with categorizing the *iconic* (photos, images, sculptures, graphs), the *indexical* ("real thing", such as a symptom), and the *relationships* of segments in a text, ritual, or photo. Then researchers consider the temporal-spatial contexts in their final analysis.

So, an advantage of Peirce's semiotics is its suitability to analyze non-/linguistic aspects. One starts to see through communicational messages and is more aware of their implied meaning. Limitations include the complexity of the analysis, which relies heavily on the skill of the researcher (Leiss et al., 1990).

The Pragmatist Peirce & His Semiotics

According to Chandler (2006), Pierce's triadic model identifies three aspects: representamen, interpretant, and object. While the representamen is the form the sign takes, the interpretant refers to making sense of the sign. What a sign refers to is called object. For Peirce (1958), a sign was simply something that stood for something else, its object. The meaning of a sign arises in its interpretation. Silverman (1983) clarified that the "representamen" is comparable to Saussure's (1959) "signifier", but unlike the signified, the referent was an "object" for Peirce.

A sign comprises three logical relations, namely icons, indices, and symbols: *icons* (sign directly resembles what is represented; real meaning of the object), *indices* (sign is associated with what it symbolizes, smoke with fire), and *symbols* (sign is only arbitrarily linked to what it stands for, all words) (Chandler, 2006). Even though this triadic typology has been applied rigidly, Yelle (2022) suggestes that almost all signs fall into more than one of these categories.

This must be considered when doing a semiotic analysis. Litowitz (2014) also cautioned that oversimplifying the analysis could lead to errors. Each type of sign, in its triad of icon, index, and symbol, consists of a certain materiality. Furthermore, the act of interpretation transcends their individual meanings.

Understanding semiotic analysis also begins with knowing Peirce's theory of categorization. He divided experience into Firstness, Secondness, and Thirdness (Atkin, 2023), and his triadic structuralism is unlike that of Jakobson, Lévi-Strauss, and their followers. Peirce conceptualizes triads instead of duos. Put simply, while Firstness is something that exists in itself, Secondness must be related to something else. Thirdness requires a more complex relationship. Either a relationship between Firstness and Secondness, or a relation between both (Sonesson, 2013, p. 306). A more elaborate explanation views *Firstness* as the quality of a feeling, the uninterpreted qualitative experience of something. It exists in the world and can become a component of a sign. But only, if it involves an interaction or reaction, which is *Secondness*. If experience contains general principles, which transcend the individual moment, or the meaning of the sign in a cultural, or relational context, this is *Thirdness*, Litowitz (2014, p. 50) explained.

In her critical discussion of Peirce's semiotics and Freud's psychoanalysis, she concluded that semiotics could provide a better understanding of clients' symptomatic expressions. She posed a pertinent question: why do some clients predominantly communicate via their bodies?

Peircean Semiotic Analysis of Psychosomatic Symptoms

If certain clients cannot think in words, but rely on images instead, a semiotic analysis may elucidate the latent content of these images. It is important to strictly adhere to Peirce's semiotic approach when researching psychosomatic symptoms, such as chronic headaches, gastrointestinal problems, and skin eruptions. Here, I have chosen skin problems. They are the "sign" within a semiotic system. To do a Peircean analysis, you follow these procedural steps:

1 *You identify the representamen.* Ask: what is the observable form of the disturbance? Is the redness on the face, the whole body? Red skin is the sign, the thing presented to consciousness.
2 *Then you determine the object*, the sign refers to. Peirce divided it into an "immediate" and "dynamical" object. The former refers to how the object is represented within the sign. In contrast, the "dynamical object" is the real thing, the sign is trying to express. In my example, the immediate object is the redness of the skin as *experienced*, for example, through *itching*. The "dynamical object" could be a repressed emotional conflict, relational stress, or an environmental pollutant. Dynamically, the skin's redness may indicate the person's inability to express anger in a relationship.
3 *Next you analyze the interpretant*, the effect the sign produces in the person's mind (response). Peirce distinguished three types: "immediate interpretant" is the basic sense, for example, itching. The "dynamical interpretant" is the actual mental or behavioral response, e.g., scratching or using cream. The "final interpretant" represents the ultimate understanding: reddish skin is how this person expresses her unacknowledged anger.
4 You also *classify the type of sign*. The *icon* resembles its object, a drawing of the red skin. The *index* is causally, or existentially, linked. So, the skin problem could be a bodily trace of a psychological or relational reality. The *symbol* is arbitrary. Hence, the skin symptom may have symbolic overtones, an inability to psychologically digest an event. This means that a skin rash *index* could be indicative of repression. It could *symbolize* emotional stress.
5 *Apply phenomenological categories*. Firstness is the quality of the feeling, burning sensation, itching. Secondness is the reaction, the itching intrudes. Thirdness is the mediation/meaning, understanding that the rash is playing a communicative role. The skin's redness is Firstness. Its disruption of daily life is Secondness. Its meaning in a cultural or relational context is Thirdness.
6 *Construct the semiotic chain system*. Signs rarely stand alone. A psychosomatic symptom can be part of a cluster of signs, for example, skin rash, avoidance. Signs are embedded in cultural codes, how a skin rash is interpreted varies from culture to culture. Importantly, signs are reinterpreted through therapy, religion, narratives, discourse and so forth.
7 *Trace the original sign* (symptom); how it interacts with other signs to form a larger interpretative system.

How do psychosomatic skin symptoms function as *signs* within an individual?

1 *Observe shifts in the interpretant*, for example, therapeutic change. Healing or transformation involves shifts in the interpretants. From the "dynamical" to "final interpretants". From "index to symbol". For example, the skin rash no longer requires a visit to the doctor's but becomes a clue for reflection (e.g., what's happening in my life).
2 *Reflect on the semiotic habit*, Thirdness as habit. The skin rash could be the habit of signification that the body has adopted. Or it could be a patterned response to relational or affective events. The rash becomes a habitual index of relational stress. Changing the habit requires altering the triadic relation itself.
3 *Peircean analysis is pragmatic*. The meaning of a sign lies in its practical effects. Ask: what difference does this interpretation make? Can it transform the experience and guide the next

actions? If the sign now promotes awareness and better emotional regulation, it has fulfilled its semiotic function.

Alternatively, you could do a Peircean semiotic analysis of an analytic therapy group. Or you combine it with a group analytic analysis.

You use Peirce's triadic model of sign, object, and interpretant, but add an analysis of the interactions in the group. You focus on how signs circulate, are co-constructed, or resisted, in a specific group. Additionally, you examine how these signs are interpreted, reinforced, or transformed in this group.

Chapter Summary

After referring to the pragmatist, postcolonial Indigenous, and critical realist paradigms, I critically discussed the dominance of the research question, advocating that axiological considerations should be of equal importance as the research question. Additionally, the mixed methods approach, the application of Critical Realism as a research method, and a model to inform EBP/PBE, have been described. Another focus has been on action research, semiotics, and Peirce's semiotic analysis. I have made recommendations for group (analytic) research, and provided a detailed Peircean semiotic analysis of psychosomatic symptoms to aid understanding of real life research.

10

SECONDARY DATA

Analysis Methods for Documentary, Therapy & Supervision Group Research

Abstract

Secondary data are valuable and so is the diary method, which is described in-depth. In addition to providing practical examples, I show that diary studies can be combined with other methods for the study of groups. Moreover, I discuss the importance of triangulation. Researching unconscious phenomena by operationalizing concepts, and using Group Analysis as method to study unconscious aspects of groups, are suggested. I briefly outline several documentary methods, the Chronogram, Cartography, and the Interpersonal Circumplex. The methods described in this chapter are suitable for studying therapy and supervision groups, as well as documents, monuments, and other social phenomena. Whatever method researchers choose, they must first familiarize themselves with it.

Introduction

Secondary (existing) data are not commonly used in group analytic research, although secondary data analyses allow for the integration of experience, knowledge, and expertise (Hughes et al., 2022). Existing data are very valuable, particularly for lone researchers, who often do not have the opportunity to collect data themselves. Documents are secondary data. They are interesting sources, because they are produced, shared, and used, in a socially organized manner. Due to their social nature, many group (analytic) researchers may agree with Atkinson and Coffey (1997), that the documents and transcripts of certain tapes, videos, and texts, are neither transparent nor necessarily factual. Often, they reveal socially unconscious conventions. This is one reason why documentary research is important. Researchers need to consider "why" they are conducting a study, and for "whom" the study is beneficial, as they do when using primary data.

Documentary research relies on actual records produced in conditions of temporal or spatial proximity, and on data sources that have been written by people about an event from a temporal or spatial distance (Gidley, 2018). Researchers may access archives, because these are the only means to gain sufficient information on certain topics. This is why diary research is important.

DOI: 10.4324/9781003609544-13

Monuments are also secondary data. They are cultural symbols, which structure our psyche. Due to their ideological nature (Krzyzanowska, 2016), and because group analytic researchers study the human psyche, monument-research is important.

Diaries, which have existed for many centuries (The Editors, 2022), are equally important. A diary can have multiple purposes (Dincel & Savur, 2019). It can be described as a regular, personal, and contemporaneous record that is created by an individual. It consists of a narrative, which is used to track daily experiences and activities.

Throughout history, the purpose of diaries has constantly changed. Initially, diaries belonged to the collective before spreading into the private sphere. Once it was used by an individual, the diary started to form part of his/her most secretive, intimate sphere of life eventually (Alexander, 2017). In other words, intimacy only became a part of it relatively late in its history. Nowadays, forms of diaries include an interactive blog on the internet. Online, audio, verbal, photo, video, literary, and research diaries exist (Hyers, 2018).

Diary studies aim to capture events, reflections, moods, pains, or interactions, near the time these happened (Iida et al., 2012, p. 277). Diary research involves self-reports. It can have different purposes and answer various research questions. It may use time-based or event-based designs. It can be carried out electronically, or done on paper, and utilize several techniques for the analysis of the data. Diary research can also be combined with other methods, such as the biographical narrative interview (Wengraf, 2001). Additional methods can be used during, or after, the diary study has been conducted.

Whether one chooses a qualitative, quantitative, or mixed methods approach to study documents, monuments, or other texts, depends on the purpose of the study and on the research question. A combination of methods provides breadth, depth, and corroboration (Johnson et al., 2007). The logic of triangulation is based on the premise that no single method ever solves the problem of rival explanations, as Patton (2002) pointed out. That is why multiple methods of data collection, and/or analyses, increase the credibility of findings.

All methods have strengths and weaknesses. Documentary researchers (Garfinkel, Sacks, Reischl & Plotz) have developed Ethnomethodology, Conversation Analysis, and a 4-step documentary method to study documents. Discourse analysis, the group analytic method, content analysis, thematic analysis, narrative analysis, or semiotic analysis are but a few methods that could also be used.

Less commonly applied methods to study groups include the Sociogram (Moreno, 1934), Chronogram (Cox, 1989), Compendium (Okada et al., 2008; Okada, 2025), and the Interpersonal Circumplex. Used to map interactions in groups and to provide a graphic representation of interactions, these methods are useful when studying observed group phenomena from the group-as-a-whole, the individual, or an interactional perspective.

Knowledge Cartography is a specific research area, which focuses on using software tools (Okada et al., 2008). They enable mappers to think more creatively about problems through the construction of maps. The Interpersonal Circumplex is used to study interaction in groups. All these methods are suitable for researching therapy or supervision groups.

In what follows, I will further explain secondary data and the analysis of monuments. Then diary research will be described. The importance of triangulation will become clear when discussing suitable methods for researching therapy and supervision groups. Practical examples will be included. However, my intention is not to offer a full description, but instead to provide a broad overview of suitable techniques to study documents, monuments, groups, and other social phenomena.

Basics of Secondary Data & Their Use in Group Analytic Research

Collecting primary data for a study can be difficult for a lone researcher, or even impossible. Secondary data are a viable alternative (Heaton, 2011), particularly for practitioner-researchers. They offer exciting possibilities to analyze large data sets, which researchers could never gather on their own. However, the data analyses can also be complex. How would you go about using secondary data in practical terms? (see also Dale et al. 2008; Heaton, 2011; Hughes et al., 2022; see Irvine, 2024).

First of all, you locate secondary data (Vosmer, 2023b), this enables you to get a feel for what has already been researched. Unless you already have a specific research question, you need to formulate one. Often, longitudinal studies, surveys, focus groups, health records, social media, and journals are useful sources of information (see Weller, 2023). They help you to establish, which areas are under-researched. As with primary data, the research question determines whether your analysis will be quantitative (see Dale et al. 2008), qualitative, or both (mixed). Consider who would benefit from your study, what purpose it serves, and formulate an answerable research question. This ensures that your study will be valuable for clients, the community, and/or other professionals.

Let us consider this fictitious example: You heard that crime rates have increased, but so have stereotypical beliefs that black males commit them. So, it would be beneficial for the Black community, if you could show *who* actually committed these reported crimes. Additionally, you want to find out *what kind of crimes* were committed. To get an idea, you look up crime statistics and notice that hate crimes have doubled over the last year. You also find detailed demographic information. You formulate the research questions: *1) What type of hate crimes were committed by 2) which ethnic groups?* You do not have to apply for ethical approval, because you use publicly available data. Hence, the burden on participants and researchers is reduced (Irvine, 2024). You will look for quantitative data (how many crimes were committed) to answer this question. You can code ethnic categories (1 Black, 2 White, etc.). You use descriptive statistics (means, medians, modes) to analyze the data and then write a summary report.

When carrying out this study, you may communicate with other researchers. So, this type of research can also have a social dimension (see Irvine, 2024). Further advantages include not having to spend time and money gathering data (Wickham, 2019). Unnecessary duplication of research is also avoided. When the original research was sound (reliable and valid), replication (carrying out a primary study again) is not always required, although results should be replicable, as Dale et al. (2008) pointed out. By re-analyzing the data, it is possible to validate the effectiveness of an intervention. Secondary data results can also strengthen the evidence and ensure that results will not be come outdated (Dale et al., 2008).

Nevertheless, secondary data research has limitations. If you do not know exactly how the primary data were gathered, collated, and analyzed, bias can be an issue, (Irvine, 2024). While governmental data and data from reputable organizations tend to be good, you must check that the data source is dependable. Familiarizing yourself with the data, ethics, legislation, and having sufficient research knowledge, is a must (see Irvine, 2024).

Unfortunately, secondary data can restrict the choice of topic and your creativity. Unless you combine primary and secondary data, you must rely on data that were collected, possibly even for a different purpose than yours (Heaton, 2011). On the other hand, you could gain insight into what evidence is lacking. With open access and data sharing, the landscape has, however, become challenging for researchers, who are asked to make qualitative data available for re-use

(Weller, 2023). A dataset may not be available in a useful format, or it may be presented in specific categories, you are not interested in (if social class is reported instead of ethnicity). Furthermore, if you need numerical data, but only find categories, the data might be unsuitable (Dale et al., 2008). Sometimes, solutions are available.

Conceptualize datasets as a large group. When you want to explore small group dynamics, you could split the large group into several small groups first. Do the same with large datasets. Perhaps the data you are looking for are not immediately visible. They could nevertheless be hidden somewhere in the dataset.

Another problem may arise when definitions of concepts do not tally with yours. Therefore, be prepared for potential problems when utilizing secondary data (Dale et al. 2008). Furthermore, even though government sources tend to be freely available, you may have to buy secondary data sets, which could be costly. Whatever dataset you will use (see Appendix 3), bear in mind that secondary analysis is an "empirical exercise", which follows the same procedures as primary data analysis.

If you prefer qualitative studies (see Hughes & Tarrant, 2020), you could find data from interviews in so-called repositories. Think about consent when re-using those data (Irvine, 2024). You must ensure that all participants consented to their data being used by other researchers. Do not violate principles of anonymity (see Irvine, 2024; Hughes & Tarrant, 2020).

Participants should not be recognizable. Adhere to the relevant legislation when using personal data from different countries (Irwin, 2013; Hughes & Tarrant, 2020). If you would like to know more about using secondary data, Heaton's (2011) book is useful. Many videos and articles are freely available on the internet as well.

Finally, do not mistake tertiary for secondary data. Tertiary data were collected from numerous sources by third parties for various purposes rather than for a specific goal. They can be used as a quick reference or background research.

Why Use Monuments & Documents in Group Analytic Research?

When monuments are viewed in relation to collective identity, and as symbols of power, viewing them as a device for social control (Molyneux, 1995) becomes a necessity Krzyzanowska (2016) states. Many group analytic researchers probably agree.

By learning more about monuments (why, where, by whom they were erected), researchers can also gain insight into the social unconscious of nations and people. How could you analyze monuments? Contenders for analyzing artifacts are the group analytic method and semiotic analysis, which I have described in other chapters.

Associated with the structuralist Ferdinand de Saussure (1959), the pragmatist Charles Peirce (1958), and Poststructuralists, semiotics is the study of signs, symbols, and signification (Chandler, 2006). Semiology is the word that de Saussure used (Silverman, 1983). Both Roland Barthes (1973), and the philosopher/semiologist Umberto Eco (1977), are viewed as the founders of 20th century cultural semiology (Pozzo, 2006). Sociological semiology studies are important for uncovering the created meanings within society, because they reveal the ideologies underlying certain signification systems (Silverman, 1983).

The Diary Method

Diary studies can be combined with other methods, such as the biographical narrative interview (Wengraf, 2001), which can be carried out during, or after, the diary study (see section below).

The diarist writes down the date, and the words written underneath are called "entry". Without a date, the diary would be merely a notebook. This is an example of a diary entry, extracted from Läpple's (2020) documentary (translated by me):

> Even ... *border officers did not know where they [landmines] were placed. Approx. 40-50 people died, but more were injured. We could not reach them. First an officer had to come because of the mines. By that time, the injured were often dead.* X's diary serves as evidence that something dreadful happened. *"You even learn how to kill"*, he had written, *and a record was kept for every bullet that was fired.*

Commonly, a diary serves to build a memory of its authors by anchoring the past. Without such entries, we would never know what has happened. History can be erased, and atrocities are easily forgotten. When edited at a later point, the diary loses its essential characteristic, which is authenticity of the moment (Arndt & Rose, 2023). Paper frequently becomes both friend and mirror in this process. Once a person has projected herself/himself onto paper, s/he can reflect on what s/he has written. The image of the self is taking shape during this process (e.g. Fuentes & Kahlo, 1995). Written over a long period of time, a diary reveals our (un)certainties, biases, and insecurities. Such a diary may tell the story of our Selves in words.

Diaries can be solicited and unsolicited (Jones, 2000; Morrison, 2012). Many qualitative researchers keep a diary, because a reflective journal is an aspect of qualitative studies. It is solicited. The researcher may design her/his diary according to specific research aims. Hence, diaries may be a good tool for clinician-researchers who want to study analytic groups.

Keeping a diary and writing session notes have something in common (Vosmer, 2024b). The group analyst describes the activity, s/he has undertaken (led therapy group), writes about and reflects on the event (making sense of group processes/dynamics), and refers to the therapeutic and related activities that were undertaken to conduct the group (analyses, interpretations, peer discussions, supervision, reading theoretical articles about interpretation). These are all features of diary studies (see Alaszewski, 2006).

Diary research does not have to involve people. Researchers could collect data about any document they have used (NICE guidance), when it was accessed (Friday), the time it has taken to read it (ten minutes), which aspect of the guidance was helpful (recommendation for number of sessions), did they find all the information they needed. (No. Yes, on the website of the Institute of Group Analysis).

Carrying Out a Diary Study

When conducting a diary study, several research design decisions must be made (Hyers, 2018). Firstly, you must decide which format you would like to use. Do you recruit others? As a researcher, you will then be positioned outside the study (Arndt & Rose, 2023). If you yourself are the diarist, do you prefer hand-written notes or rather use an electronic version?

Secondly, will it be an unstructured diary, consisting of narratives, or will it have fixed categories? If you like structure, then you would have to devise categories.

Thirdly, how many pages should the diary have? Bear in mind that a diary should not take up too much time to write.

Fourthly, think about the timing of the entries. Ideally, they are written immediately after an event. Whatever format you choose, it should be conducive to answering your research question (Ohly et al., 2010).

Fifthly, decide whether your diary study will be exploratory or predictive. Do you want to focus on one single point in time, or capture an ongoing phenomenon? In other words, will you use a time-based or event-based design? Do time or events serve as exemplars, consisting of a repertoire of examples, images, understandings and actions (Spurling, 2015)? So, you must reflect on the temporal needs of your research, selecting the most appropriate design, format, and type of diary (Arndt & Rose, 2023).

You would need to explain to participants exactly how the diary should be kept. Events must be recorded chronologically. Hence, it is a good idea to provide written guidance, for example, what the diary study is about and what to include (Morrell-Scott, 2018). For a diary to be useful, its writer must be motivated, cooperative, and meticulous. Otherwise, your findings will be of limited value. Thus, be precise in your guidance and ensure that the participants follow it. If you ask a diarist to write about her/his feelings, and s/he records primarily activity data, you cannot answer your research question.

Narratives should also be genuine. Of course, you cannot force participants to write truthfully. Moreover, they may write what they think you would like to read. Even though diaries can generate stimulating processes, the diary method itself can also impact on the writer's reflections and experiences. Hence, you must pay the same attention to ethical aspects, as you would do, when using other methods.

Although diary studies tend to be qualitative, causality can also be inferred (Iida et al., 2012). You could carry out a quantitative (predictive), qualitative (explorative), or mixed design diary study. Assume that you are a practitioner-researcher, who wants to carry out a quantitative study (see Ciere et al., 2015).

One of your group members has consistently sworn for the past three months, always at the end of the session. Your prediction is that this person will do so in future.

In empirical terminology (see Vahle-Hinz et al., 2019), you aim to establish that the *variable X* (last ten minutes before the end of the group), which you have measured over a period of three months by keeping an accurate record of the person's behavior in the group, *predicts variable Y* (swearing). To analyze your data, you could use descriptive statistics (see Appendix 4).

Now assume that you are a researcher, who wants to research scapegoating. You recruit group analysts for your mixed design diary study. (We skip ethics here and focus on techniques.)

Devising two categories (Yes and No) of scapegoating would be an option. Alternatively, you could create a dimensional scale. Or both. With a scale, you can measure how frequent scapegoating is. From 1 to 3, where 1 means "never", 2 "sometimes", and 3 "very often". Of course, you could also use a scale with 5 or 7 points. Bear in mind that categories reduce the depth and richness, which is a valuable feature of narrative diaries.

You could give a diary pro-forma to your diarists to complete. Additionally, you could ask them to provide narratives about their experiences of scapegoating in the group. So, your diary study will have real value and produce ecologically trustworthy/valid results (Bolger et al., 2003). However, only if diarists are truthful, will your results reflect what was really happening. Commonly, a diary consists of text (narrative). However, you could also use verbal recordings, which could be transcribed by using software. Furthermore, you could supplement your study by researching the lived experience of scapegoating. (Or ask about other group dynamics and processes).

The data would be analyzed by using texts analyses techniques. Reflexive thematic analysis (Braun & Clarke, 2006) is suitable, because it does not lean toward a particular philosophical perspective (Braun & Clarke, 2006). Alternatively, narrative analysis could be used. Narrative analysis views stories as narratives. People tell stories to make sense of their experiences (see Finlay & Dela Cruz, 2025).

Various strategies can be used to analyze stories (thematic analysis focuses on stories; structural analysis, focuses on the nature of the narrative; dialogical or performative analysis, focuses on the production and content of a narrative). Narrative research tries to find out how a narrative identity has been developed, performed, or constructed. Findings are presented creatively, for example, as stories or themes.

Whatever design you choose, you must familiarize yourself first with the diary method (e.g. Bartlett & Milligan, 2015). It is often necessary to carry out a pilot study, using one diarist. You can "trial" all your categories and questions. The pilot is done prior to the actual study. However, you could include its data in your analysis, unless they are completely useless. A pilot enables you to correct design problems. You can also feel more confident that the study asks the right, correctly phrased, questions.

Descriptions of group dynamics could be analyzed qualitatively by using thematic analysis (Braun & Clarke, 2006, 2021, 2022a,b; Clarke & Braun, 2017, 2018, 2019a,b) or content analysis (Forman & Damschroder, 2008; Vaismoradi et al., 2013; Kyngäs et al., 2020).

After you have collected the data, you read the texts a few times and then start coding. This is a subjective, evolving process. For thematic analysis, Braun and Clarke (2021) recommended that the data are labeled and arranged in such a way that you can identify themes and patterns across the dataset.

Of course, you could use other qualitative methods. Diary studies have also been combined with phenomenology. Methodologically speaking, diary studies are flexible and have been employed in different fields (e.g. Bedwell et al., 2012; Dincel & Savur, 2019; Cao & Henderson, 2020).

A diary study tries to use "sampling of time" of people's lives, as can be seen in the brief extract from research my diary. Entries can be used to corroborate historical events.

> Berlin is one of those cities that excited and terrified me as a child. To get to West Berlin, we had to cross the East German border, which had been erected on 13th August 1961. It was during one of those foggy nights when the guard, for whatever reason, decided to search our car. One could tell that he was in no hurry, as he started to tear a copy of the newsmagazine *Der Spiegel* apart. Even though this happened in the 1960s, it still creates anxiety in my chest. I experienced a peculiar mixture of loss and awe. While I lacked the vocabulary to express my feelings at the time, I sensed that being separated from other human beings by borders that were surrounded by barbed wire, was a sociopolitical constraint. Perhaps this was my first encounter with the social unconscious of the former German Democratic Republic. Of course, the social unconscious is neither an object nor a person that we can see directly. It could be regarded as a psychic space where relational phenomena are located, and where sociopolitical forces and "facts" are woven into the social fabric of a society (Ettin, 2001). This psychic space may be experienced during interpersonal encounters. Without saying one single word, a shared unconscious understanding did develop amongst all of us at the time. Such understanding is possible, because we do share a common biology, and culturally embedded values as a species.

The diary method can overcome chronological inaccuracies that are associated with the use of questionnaires, interviews, and other retrospective methods of data collection. Diary studies enable researchers to follow events in a way that observation often cannot, while allowing to "observe" people in a similar way as in participant observation studies. One noteworthy benefit of a diary study is its contemporaneous nature. Events, feelings, experiences, and thoughts can be recorded in a timely manner (Iida et al., 2012).

Diary studies have other advantages. They also foster openness, because people find it easier to express intimate information in a diary than in a research interview. Diaries can be used creatively, giving an individual a voice and the space to think about what s/he would like to express. Moreover, diary studies may overcome some of the obstacles surrounding trustworthiness. When researching sensitive topics, a person might be more inclined to write how s/he genuinely feels in a diary (Day & Thatcher, 2009). Furthermore, the data are collected in a less intrusive manner than in personal interviews. Diaries are easily accessible and do not require technology. An enormous depth of information can be gathered about a topic of interest (Hyers, 2018). Diary studies can also inspire diarists to observe and reflect.

Overall, they can provide rich, meaningful data about group members, group processes/dynamics, and group conductors. They can reveal surprising content and new information. For example, certain behavior or dynamics may occur more frequently than the conductor thought. Of course, you do not have to restrict the diary studies to researching psychotherapy groups. You could research different types of groups (supervision groups, reflective practice groups, median groups etc.), asking group members to write about their reflections on a specific group in a particular diary format. Then you could analyze individual diaries and compare them.

When using group analysts as diarists, psychoanalytic and group analytic concepts (projection, projective identification, splitting, repression, regression, insecure attachment) could be used to identify defensiveness and socially unconscious constraints (see Klein, 1946; Bion, 1967, Hopper, 2003a; Ezquerro & Cañete, 2023, 2025).

Of course, diary studies have weaknesses (see Nezlek, 2012). Memory is one. The more time passes, the less accurate the content of a diary will be. Hence, writing entries immediately after an event (e.g. session, group) is advisable, because retrospective recall tends to be inaccurate. This means must be borne in mind when claiming that your results are valid or true. However, what is regarded as "truth" is an epistemological matter. You may adopt a Social Constructionist perspective when conducting a qualitative diary study. Social Constructionism views everything, including truth, as socially constructed. Therefore, objective truth is not a concern.

Keeping a diary is time-consuming. A diary must be kept for long enough to capture all events, behavior, dynamics, and feelings of interest. This may be experienced as tedious by the writer (Iida et al., 2012). Furthermore, you must know this method and any other techniques that you will apply. Learning different methods requires time and effort. However, the benefits of diary studies outweigh their drawbacks.

Use of Biographical Narrative Interviews to Supplement a Diary Study

The logic of triangulation is based on the premise that no single method ever solves the problem of rival explanations (Patton 2002). This is why multiple methods of data collection and/or analyses increase the credibility of findings. Of course, resources determine the amount of triangulation that is possible. Combinations of methods can reduce limitations, which are associated with each method, providing credibility checks across the data and analyses.

Biographical narrative interviews (Wengraf, 2001; Wengraf & Chamberlayne, 2013) could be carried out either during or after a diary study.

One aim of biographical narrative interviews is to elicit narratives of life stories. Researchers must be able to make diarists feel comfortable, and display "self-constraint" by neither probing participants, nor using directional prompts during the interview. They engage in active listening and make participants feel at ease, before asking for more stories, so that participants feel comfortable to reveal emotional aspects of their lives (Wengraf, 2001). Researchers need to respond spontaneously to unexpected stories and be able to contain distressing emotions (Wengraf & Chamberlayne, 2013). They can record the interviews, keep notes, refer to diary entries, and compare how the interview narrative may be similar, or different, from the narrative in the diary. Data can be micro-analytically analyzed, Wengraf (2001) shows. The life story is chronologically structured. Self-debriefing, or debriefing with peers, may enable researchers to dis-identify with painful aspects of stories. Readers wanting to use the biographical narrative method could start by reading Wengraf (2001, 2011, 2018).

Documents

Documentary research relies on several sources, including documents (Gidley, 2018). By examining historical events, researchers can gain insight into trends and how they have affected groups. Researchers may also access archives, because these are the only means to gain sufficient information on a topic. Documentary research is cost-effective.

Contenders for analyzing documentary data are ethnographically oriented methods, narrative methods, discourse analysis, and group analytic techniques, to name but a few. However, which method you choose, depends on your research aims.

Take for, example, discourse analysis. It attempts to understand how people's communication and descriptions of events are created, and how meaning is socially constructed (see Van Hulst et al., 2024).

Psychotherapists know that people often do not directly say what they think. Critical discourse analysis can be used to examine how socio-cultural conversation builds a concept without talking about something directly. It looks at many different kinds of texts to uncover the ideological landscape surrounding a central topic (Gournelos et al., 2019).

Michel Foucault (1969, 1970, 1977, 1978, 1983, 1994, 1998, 2019) applied it to study how language and power are used to construct the world. He also showed that madness is constructed by civilization (Foucault, 1961).

Triangulation

Documentary sources can be triangulated by using oral sources. The credibility of qualitative studies is established by several procedures, such as triangulation of data collection, and data analysis techniques (Denzin, 2012). Or, by "auditing credibility", i.e., checking that the information provided by a source is reliable. Or, through participant validation, where research participants are given the opportunity to review and validate the findings (Timulak, 2015).

Some researchers may favor content analysis. Endler et al. (2022) have used it to convey participants' perspectives. According to Lune and Berg (2017), content analysis is

> a careful, detailed, systematic examination and interpretation of a particular body of material, in an effort to identify patterns, themes, biases, and meanings.
>
> (p. 182)

Similarly, Krippendorff (2019) regarded it as a research technique for drawing valid inferences from the text to contexts (p. 24).

Quantitative content analysis can be used to determine the presence of certain words, themes, or concepts. A set of categories are established and then the number of instances, which fall into each category, are counted. Berelson (1952) asserted that categories had to be sufficiently precise. Otherwise, different coders would not arrive at the same results, when analyzing the same text. In contrast, the ethnographer Sachs (1995), who concerned himself with narratives, would listen to the same tape recording again and again. For him, this was an important research activity. When carrying out a conversational analysis, Silverman (1998) attempted to always identify the sequences of related talk, to examine how speakers took on certain identities, or roles (therapist-patient), and to look for specific outcomes in the talk such as laughter, request for clarification, and so forth. Then he would work backward to trace the trajectory by which an outcome has been produced (Silverman, 2000, p. 831).

You can be flexible and creative, as long as you are consistent, and your arguments make sense.

Specific Methods for Documentary Research

I will briefly describe several methods that can be used in documentary studies, but further reading will be required to fully understand these.

Case studies and ethnographic studies have extensively drawn on documentary sources. Many seminal studies (e.g. Erving Goffman, 1963) are based on documents. Bowen (2009) suggested that the rationale for document analysis is based on its role in methodological and data triangulation. Unless employed in ethnographic, historic, or linguistic research, it is, therefore, seldom used as the sole method (Cardno, 2018).

The context is particularly important for the analysis of documents. Establishing a conceptual or structural framework prevents confusion. While discourse and conversational analysis are useful for text analyses, a semiotic analysis is particularly suited to study monuments, the arts, non-verbal communication, and the unconscious (Silverman, 1983).

Group Analytic & Psychoanalytic Method

Group Analysis provides conceptual and methodological means to analyze dimensions of intersubjectivity. Daily conversations, written statements, films, and documents, can be used to examine intersubjectivities. Documentary, bibliographical, and narrative research may be carried out to illuminate social interactions, intersubjectivities, and so forth. These three approaches have been used to examine narratives and stories. Psychoanalysis and Foulkesian Group Analysis (or other types of group analysis) can be employed alongside documentary, bibliographical, and narrative methods. They can also be used on their own.

Like psychoanalysis, Group Analysis comprises several theoretical concepts that have been elaborated, such as counter-/transference, regression, repression, disavowal, projection, projective identification, splitting, and other defense mechanisms. However, the social context is more important for group analytic researchers. The concept of the social unconscious (Hopper & Weinberg, 2007), the matrix (Foulkes, 1973), and group analytic theories (e.g. Incohesion: Aggregation/Massification), are equally useful.

Group analysis can be used to analyze qualitative data, for example, texts and films. Its interpretative approach and conceptualizations can be incorporated into narrative, documentary, and bibliographical research. Psychoanalysis has also been used as a research method. Like Group analysis/Group, its concepts can be the basis of psychoanalytic observation.

Operationalizing concepts may enable researchers to infer and identify key characteristics of a particular unconscious process. Walker and Hinshelwood (2018) define the operationalization of terms as a process that forms a schema (set of features), which can be inferred. It involves several aspects (p. 173). So, the application of operationalization entails several steps: 1) identifying crucial features of the concept that is being used; 2) extracting its most important aspects, which are visible in observations or found in the extant literature; 3) collecting relevant data for answering the research question; 4) identifying all the necessary features in the observational data, process notes, recorded sessions etc.; 5) searching for all instances, which satisfy the necessary features (p. 173).

A common characteristic of groups and institutions involves conflict. Splitting, projection, and projective identification, are the most important defense mechanisms for understanding the dynamics of group and institutions, Skogstad (2018) states. Of further importance are transference and countertransference. Aspects from early relationships are unconsciously transferred to another person, group, or institution, who is then experienced as possessing these aspects. When a person, or groups, unconsciously experience those aspects, this is a counter-transferential reaction.

Transferences can be studied clinically, socially, politically, or historically. They can be combined with documentary research. Choose the *type of document(s)* (letter, case studies, institutional records, literary texts, media etc.), you would like to analyze, and a *framework* (group analytic, psychoanalytic, critical/cultural studies, interdisciplinary). Then you identify the transferences in the documents by using a technique that suits you, such as, textual analysis, historical conceptualizations, or comparative analysis. You could study clinical case notes from groups, historical texts related to groups, political discourse, personal stories, or narratives. You also identify your own transference reactions toward the material, such as biases, or emotional reactions.

Which concept, or defense mechanism, is considered as most important, may depend on which particular psychoanalytic, or group analytic, tradition a researcher favors.

Stamenova (2018) studied envy and frustration. A conceptual analysis can be done by *operationalizing both envy* (destructive attack, denigration of others is a defensive maneuver, envy is slit off and projected into others) *and frustration* (e.g. aggressive attacks, lack of awareness, lack of energy and stifling emotions). After having gathered data, such as observational reports, the operationalized criteria are then used to conduct a comparative data analysis (see Stamenova, 2018).

So, by operationalizing psychoanalytic and group analytic concepts, comparisons can be made between different concepts. Differentiations are also possible. The manifestations of phenomena, such as envy, can then be researched in clinical settings, in various types of groups, in daily life, in organizations, and so forth.

This procedure does not necessitate that researchers use observational data. I suggest that it can be applied to all kinds of primary and secondary data. Hence, this procedure could be incorporated into other methods. Of course, you could adopt a pragmatic stance. Instead of choosing the most popular method to answer your research question, rely on a method you know best, or consider using a method you are interested in, which tallies with your epistemological orientation. Or, think about funding and time. This may be equally useful (see Harper, 2012).

Other Documentary Methods

Documentary methods tend to be less costly than interviews. They can be used to analyze group discussions, interviews, texts, videos, and photos (Reischl & Plotz, 2020). Researchers focus on ***how*** (social reality is constructed through social practices). The following are examples, but the aim(s) of a study will determine the style of analysis.

Green and Thorogood (2005) suggested that data analysis may aim for five outcomes. Developing conceptual definitions, or typologies/classifications, exploring associations between attitudes, behaviors and experiences, developing explanations of phenomena, and generating new ideas/themes are key objectives (p. 176).

For certain research aims/questions, documents will be the only source of data.

Documentary Method of Interpretation (Garfinkel)

With its roots in the sociology of Mannheim and in Garfinkel's (1967/1984, 2002) "ethnomethodology", the documentary method was elaborated by Bohnsack. For Harold Garfinkel (1967/1984), what can be observed reflects underlying patterns of social action (Rapley, 2012). Suggesting that we constantly use ethnomethodology in daily life to understand our social world, Garfinkel (1967/1984) included reflexivity, accountability, and indexicality in ethnomethodology. Inspired by Goffman's studies of the order of interactions, Garfinkel attended to what can be observed.

Conversation Analysis (Sacks)

Developed in lectures from 1964 to 1972, Harvey Sacks elaborated his ideas in "conversation analysis". Sacks studied the sequential ordering of actions (rules, patterns, structures of interaction). How action, structures, and intersubjectivity, are achieved in talk/interaction distinguishes conversation analysis from other methods (Sacks, 1995).

Documentary Method (Reischl & Plotz)

According to Reischl and Plotz (2020), the documentary method involves four steps, namely, formulating the interpretation, reflective interpretation, case analysis, and finding the typology. Researchers read, or listen, to the material several times, select passages according to certain criteria, initially focus on the analysis of the "what", then analyze the "how", summarize the overall form of the case, and carry out a comparative analysis.

However, other researchers have omitted the case description. It is also noteworthy that the how is prioritized (Reischl & Schmőlz, 2020).

Reischl (2021) also triangulated the documentary method with depth hermeneutics by considering Goffman's conceptualizations of interaction and roles. Furthermore, Reischl and Schmőlz (2020) applied Garfinkel's documentary method to develop an ethnomethodology, which had previously been elaborated by Bohnsack (1997, 2013, 2017). Bohnsack (2014) regarded this methodology as reconstructive social research.

Reischl and Plotz' (2020) comparative analysis has a reconstructive orientation. Frames are contrasted and correlated with each other. Their process of interpretation is guided by asking *Where can this interpretation be found in the data?*. Reischl and Plotz (2020) note that depending on the research question, further forms of interpretations must be used. Reischl's depth hermeneutics and Bohnsack's conceptualizations are useful. While Reischl and Plotz' (2020) method has the same weakness as other interpretative qualitative methods, its advantage is that researchers can reveal hidden aspects of social interactions and of habitual structures.

Narrative Analysis

Narrative analysis also lends itself to analyzing documentary data. For Ricoeur (1991), the referent of narration (human action) is an action that has been (re-)symbolized over and over again (p. 469). We create and draw on narratives to give meaning to the social world. Stories and narratives are told in a certain context. By telling stories, we define ourselves. This is why narratives are crucial to understanding identity. The plot is a central structure of any story. Ricoeur regarded the process of "emplotment" (assembly of series of historical events into a narrative with a plot) as the synthesis of heterogenous elements, which is central to the formation of narratives (p. 426).

Narrative analysis focuses on the components of a narrative: plot, theme, structure, narrator, characters, time, causality, and a setting (Murray & Sargeant, 2012). Deciding which component to focus on, depends on the research question and the nature of the data. It is a good idea to base the initial analysis on themes, when most of the narrative is verbal. Examining the structure, coherence, emplotment, or positioning, also form part of narrative analysis (Murray & Sargeant, 2012).

Studying Therapy & Supervision Groups

Chronogram

Group phenomena can be observed and mapped from a group-as-a-whole, the individual, or an interactional perspective.

The sociogram (Moreno, 1934), Chronogram (Cox, 1989), Compendium (Okada et al., 2008; Okada, 2025), and the Interpersonal Circumplex, have been used to map interactions in a group, and to provide a graphic representation of these interactions.

The group analyst Murray Cox (1989) emphasized the visual and the auditory nature of the group. He devised a system using circles to represent the individuals in a group. These circles (see Figure 10.1) were divided into three, to represent the beginning, middle, and end-phases, of a group session.

In each segment, there is a space to record the contribution of the individual group member and to add other pertinent comments. Cox depicted a group session through ten of these chronograms (depending on the number group members), which he arranged in the form of a circle (see Cox, 1989, pp. 44-45). I have modified his template in Figure 10.2.

Cox used a chronogram template. Knowing exactly which of the plethora of possible observations are particularly interesting is a skill (Foulkes, 1964). In addition to recording all the information for each member, Cox (1989) used different lines to demonstrate several aspects of the interactions between members (who initiated verbal exchanges, dominated through talk or silence; main interaction patterns; jostling phenomenon) to depict these.

His group therapy interaction chronogram system is a visualization of a part of what happened in the group. Counter/transference, group processes, such as mirroring, resonance, scapegoating, location of disturbance, and so forth, can be included.

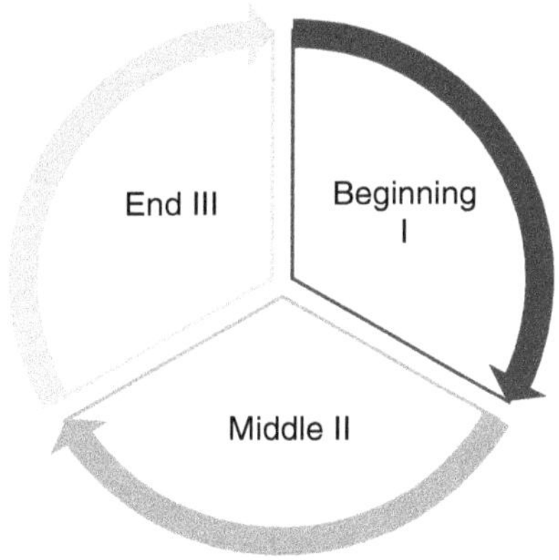

FIGURE 10.1 Chronogram Structuring a Group Session into Three Phases. Extracted from Cox (1989, p. 43)

FIGURE 10.2 Group Session: Consisting of Four Members

The chronogram is a heuristic device for the recording of sequential sessions. It does not require any technical equipment, which makes it attractive for practitioner-researchers, who are not technologically savvy. Another advantage is that the visual representation of group dynamics, and of the manifest/latent contents, is clearer than process notes.

Cartography Software & the Interpersonal Circumplex

Knowledge Cartography is a specific research area, which focuses on using software tools (Okada et al., 2008). They enable mappers to think more creatively about problems through the construction of maps. By using the software Compendium, Brown et al. (2012) tracked processes in an analytic therapy group. They mapped interactions within the group, identified significant themes and key moments, and analyzed interactional patterns among members, across the entire group, and between individuals.

Compendium allowed the group analytic researchers to incorporate the group discourse by hiding the dialogue behind individual icons (representing group members), or behind icons (representing themes between members, or the entire group). They used tags to ascribe attributes to individual members in each session.

De Haas (2025) has highlighted that participants in a group interact by evoking responses and behavior in, and between, each other. Originally developed by Leary in the 1950s, the circular model of the interpersonal domain of personality, the Interpersonal Circumplex (IPC), has been validated (e.g. Boudreaux et al., 2018), and used in research (Waldherr & Muck, 2011), since then.

It postulates that interaction involves two basic dimensional relational desires: *influence/ control*. One person wants to influence another person, so that person 2 will follow what person 1 suggests/does. And *affiliation/attachment*. A person desires contact, proximity, and wants to belong, or s/he wants to be able to be free, on her/his own, or keep a distance. These desires must be viewed on a dimension. When two people meet, they convey different desires to each other. The interactional laws of the IPC postulate that "Above" behavior evokes "Under" behavior, and vice versa. "Near" behavior evokes Near behavior. "Distant" behavior evokes Distant behavior. Taken together, each of these four quadrants is split into eight interactional variants (leading, helping, cooperative, dependent, withdrawn, rebellious, hostile, competitive). Each has its own combination of influence and affiliation behaviors. However, one of these two behavioral characteristics predominates in each case (De Haas, 2025, pp. 18-22).

Dutch researchers have confirmed the validity of the eight behavioral interaction variants. Therefore, the IPC can be regarded as a valid measure for interactional behavior, according to De Haas (2025). Traditionally, Horowitz et al.'s (1988, 2000) Inventory of Interpersonal Problems has been used to understand people's difficulties.

Both the IPC and Horowitz et al.'s inventory can be used to study interactional processes during group psychotherapy.

Additionally, the IPC model can be used to research supervision groups (see De Haas, 2025 for further information). Furthermore, chronograms with, or without, the use of software, can be utilized to map interactions, dynamics, and other unconscious phenomena in therapy, supervision, and other groups.

Chapter Summary

Secondary data are clearly valuable and so is the diary method, which I have described in-depth by providing practical examples. Any diary study can also be combined with thematic analysis, discourse narrative analysis, or other suitable methods. In addition to discussing the importance of triangulation, the biographical narrative interview method has been outlined. Group Analysis can also be used as a method. By operationalizing concepts it is possible to research unconscious phenomena. Semiology, traditional document methods, the Chronogram, Cartography, and the Interpersonal Circumplex, are all interesting tools. Due to space, I could not do justice to these methods, and I refer interested readers to the bibliography. Suffice it to say that nowadays many methods can be used to study therapy or supervision groups. Whatever method researchers choose, they must first familiarize themselves with this method, regardless of whether they study documents, monuments, social phenomena, or groups.

11

LEARNING ABOUT ARCHIVAL RESEARCH & WRITING UP OF RESEARCH THROUGH ILLUSTRATIVE EXAMPLES

Abstract

Archives offer the opportunity for conducting rich case studies and comparing past with present social patterns. My own research on the former German Democratic Republic is used to illustrate how documentary/bibliographical research can be done to foster learning about archival research. I demonstrate how to integrate theory, apply latent analysis techniques, use triangulation, consider counter-/transference reactions, reflexivity, and attend to the emotional impact of research on the researcher. In addition to critically discussing the Western academic writing style, I explain how research is written up, and draw attention to the need to decolonize research writing. Reflecting on power and privilege when drawing on colonial writers, and drafting a position statement, contributes to decolonizing research.

Introduction

Original physical and digital documents can be found in archives. The Stasi Records Archive in Berlin is one of the largest archives of its kind in the world. Comprising 111 kilometers of documents, it holds fifty kilometers of material, containing millions of magnetic tapes, disks, audio documents, and photographs (Bundesarchiv, 2025). Many different professionals have used the archives to study the former German Democratic Republic (GDR, aka East Germany). The historian Leask (2019) wrote an emotional account. For group analytic researchers, the German archives might also be interesting due to the connection between Foulkesian Group Analysis and Germany (the Federal Republic of Germany, aka FRG).

Never before has so much material been available about a State in its original form. So, the Stasi Records Archive is an excellent and unique source of information. It offers the possibility to conduct rich case studies of people, groups, organizations, structures, social practices, group dynamics, and processes within real contexts. Past and present social patterns can also be compared.

Various methods (e.g. qualitative/latent content analysis) can be used to analyze documents, recordings, and photos. Methods are more easily learnt when they are linked to real practice-based research. Hence, I will describe my own research on the GDR, including the write up of research.

DOI: 10.4324/9781003609544-14

Even though the Western style of writing has been criticized, and Harriden (2022, 2023) highlights the importance of decolonizing academic writing, and of offering a space for non-Western practices, I will adopt the Western style nevertheless, because many students and researchers are expected to write like this. Typically, the Western academic style adopts the following structure: title, abstract, key words, introduction, methodology and method(s), data analysis, results/findings, discussion, conclusion/recommendations, references, and appendices (see Rivas, 2018).

In what follows, I will briefly explain qualitative/latent content analysis. For educational purposes, I will then describe main points of my research to illustrate how data can be gathered and analyzed. This includes the use of latent techniques, triangulation, integration of theory, critical reflection, and attending to countertransference and the emotional effect of research. In addition to describing how to write up research, I will draw attention to a decolonizing style in my critical discussion of Western writing.

Qualitative Content Analysis, Latent Content, & Class Analysis

Qualitative content analysis is the systematic reduction, or condensation, of content, which is analyzed by attending to the context in which the content was created (Roller & Lavrakas, 2015). Although both qualitative and quantitative content analysis follow a methodical process, qualitative researchers emphasize the subjective interpretation of content (Hsieh & Shannon, 2005). Over time, researchers modified quantitative content analysis. They wanted to enrich an overly sterile approach that focused mainly on the surface content, largely missing the richer latent content, the underlying meaning of texts, and unconscious elements of the contents (Ho & Limpaecher, 2022). Qualitative content analysis has been used to analyze text, images, video, audio, graphics, and symbols. It is systematic, process-driven and contextual (Berg, 2001). Meaningful inferences can be drawn from the manifest and latent contents. Researchers identify patterns, categories, and themes, from the raw data to answer their research question(s), or to create new questions (Elo & Kyngäs, 2008). Zhang and Wildemuth (2009) wrote that it aims "… to understand social reality in a subjective but scientific manner" (p. 308). Rezaii et al. (2019) identified the latent content of a person's speech by comparing it to a large corpus of language.

A latent content analysis should not be confused with latent class analysis, which is a statistical procedure. A probabilistic modeling algorithm allows for clustering of data and statistical inference (Sinha et al., 2021, p. 63). Latent class analysis aims to identify qualitatively different undetected latent subgroups (classes) within a population, based on responses to categorical indicator variables. It assumes that membership in unobserved classes can cause, or explain, patterns of scores across assessment indicators, such as questionnaires, or scales (Weller et al., 2020, p. 1022).

Kleinheksel et al. (2020) explain the process of a latent content analysis by drawing on a transcribed video. After identifying in the text relevant aspects of interest, researchers then use a combination of a priori codes and codes they develop during their analysis. Basically, the authors applied a traditional content analysis (identifying of codes, categories, themes) but added other layers for the "latent projective analysis" (p. 132), which aims to identify the deeper meaning of a text, such as social rules. This is in line with Ho and Limpaecher's (2022) description.

Researchers have distinguished "latent pattern" from "latent projective" types of content (Potter & Levine-Donnerstein, 1999, p. 261). When coding the former, researchers follow the procedure of a content analysis, but also infer (identify) underlying meaning, develop themes from these, and draw conclusions, as Kleinheksel et al. (2020) explain. Understanding projective content involves the coder selecting theories and using her/his own mental schema to identify implied meaning, develop categories, identify underlying meaning, generate themes, and draw conclusions. In other words, latent content analysis requires a deeper interpretative analysis of the text than traditional versions (e.g. Graneheim & Lundman, 2004). The analysis seeks to infer the underlying meaning from words, or phrases, and focuses on the tone and implied feeling (Downe-Wamboldt, 1992). According to Potter and Levine-Donnerstein (1999, p. 261), the task for the coder of manifest content involves clerical recording. In contrast, the coder recognizes patterns, when coding latent content (theory is the basis for deductive coding scheme), or constructs interpretations (projective type of content; deductions from weak theories, inductions of results to stronger theories).

My version of latent content analysis uses this schema:

Qualitative content analysis + application of group analytic techniques (my interpretations based on concepts and clinical experience) = latent content analysis

Theoretical group analytic and psychoanalytic conceptualizations of the social unconscious, defenses, primary/secondary process, and the collective unconscious provide the framework within which latent content analysis is embedded. After carrying out a traditional qualitative analysis, I searched for meaning in written, verbal, and visual communication, which is not immediately apparent (Hsieh & Shannon, 2005). I identified the latent content through interpretations based on group analytic/psychoanalytic concepts.

Contextualizing the Research, Own Assumptions & Use of Theory

My interest in researching the former GDR arose after attending a Symposium in Berlin. Its theme was "Crossing Borders". I was reminded that Group Analysis came into existence following the emigration of Foulkes from Nazi Germany to Britain. After concerning myself with history, politics, Group Analysis, the arts, music, literature, economics, and research methods for several months, I decided to research the experiences of Germans. Influenced by my group analytic and clinical psychology training, I wanted to study unconscious psychological processes in groups, social structures, and experiences.

My conception of experience included people's encounters with others, interactions in social institutions, as well as thinking about myself and theories in certain ways. Experience is involved in our actions, through which experience becomes lived. Grosz (1995) discussed the psychic inscriptive and phenomenological side of experience, the embodiment (Joyce, 2004), and intersubjectivity of experience. It can leave lasting un/conscious memory traces by imprinting, and inscribing people's previous interactions with the world, in their own bodies and minds (Joyce, 2005). Experience grows and expands. It is the most intimate knowing of one's Self, and includes the conscious ability to say, or do, something (see Boud et al., 1994). What resides in experiences at the level of bodily inscription is often a subjective representation of the world, people, and events. Inscriptions that happen during the first years of life are *not* available to introspection, psychoanalytic theory postulates. Interpretation must occur for some aspects of this experience to become conscious. Only then can new meaning arise.

After pondering the philosophical position I favored, I thought about research designs, aims, specific research questions, methods, and my theoretical assumptions. I believe that we are all impacted by socio-economic and political structures. Matrices affect identities, subjectivities (intra-psychological relations), and intersubjectivities. Because intersubjectivity implies a permeability of the psyche, and reciprocal conscious and unconscious influences, the unconscious is also constituted intersubjectively, for example, by socialist or capitalist discourses (see Vanheule, 2016).

Rosa's (2016) theory postulates that our entire existence consists of relationships with others and the world. Without resonance in relations the consolidation of inter/subjectivity is inconceivable. Engagement in responsive interaction is necessary to develop a sense of Self, which is embedded in individual and collective identities. This is captured in Foulkes' (1990) foundation matrix. Cultural identity can be conceptualized as the internalization of norms (i.e. being part of collectives) and customs (i.e. participating in Pioneer activities) of (GDR) society.

The social contexts, in which networks of relations between people are embedded (matrix), were essential for my analysis. I was also interested in factors that shape social contexts, such as the mode of governance (democratic, authoritarian).

Institutional structures, such as educational systems, and democratic, or authoritarian, governance matter for the formation of intersubjectivity. When you directly ask people how they experience certain structures and modes of governance, you achieve a rudimentary understanding of their experiences and subjectivity. By analyzing unconscious elements, you gain a deeper understanding. Various other aspects formed part to my study, which I omit here. Suffice it to say that I have drawn on resonance theory (see also Taylor, 2018, 2023; Vendenberghe, 2023; Anderson, 2023).

Rosa (2016) defined resonance as a mode of relating to the world, in which subjects feel moved/touched or addressed by other people, objects, or places they encounter. How individuals respond depends on their previous experiences and social contexts. However, when people connect *with others* (e.g. East/West Germans being in loving relationships), or with *cultural objects* (thinking about life after watching a documentary on Berlin), Germans and their worlds are transformed, because their perceptions change. Nothing will be the same after this moment of resonance (Vorderer & Halfmann, 2019). When life stories about cultural/social life are shared, intimate and resonant relationships can develop (Mc Adams, 1988). Resonance entails openness to others and allows opposite perspectives (Susen, 2007). It is about genuine, but not necessarily harmonious, relationships. The most liberating forms of resonance may arise from profound experiences of oppression and repulsion.

Rosa (2016) conceptualized resonance as bidirectional, consisting of three axes and spheres: horizontal (social sphere: love, friendship), diagonal (material sphere: artifacts, clothes), and vertical (world sphere: existential). For my analyses of GDR structures and practices, I will identify spheres and modes of resonance, paying attention to affectivity and emotion. Affectivity refers to how we are gripped by something/someone. When reaching out, we touch/move someone, or something, which is emotion (Rosa, 2016). Resonance only occurs when these two modes, affectivity and emotion, are present at the same time. This necessitates that we must actively experience the world around us, for example, when Germans built the GDR and FRG after the war.

Rosa (2016) distinguished basic modes that can be discerned in our relationship to the world: resonance, alienation, indifference, and repulsion. Alienation is an experience of indifference *or* repulsion, involving hostile or injurious encounters. It results from damaged subjectivity and missing harmony between the subject and the world. External or internal repression can result in human alienation. Resonance is its antithesis. The dialectic relationship of resonance and alienation is at the heart of Rosa's theory (Anderson, 2023). Characterized by objectifying and cold disengagement, alienation may also be caused by disrupting or eradicating resonances. Repulsion can be an intensely embodied experience, resulting from a closing/closed off relation to the world, which happens in violent relationships. Van Egmond (2022) has highlighted that art can shock or repulse, but it nevertheless keeps us connected to it. This shows that repulsion can also be an engaged, but unpleasant, relation.

Although Rosa's (2016) theory is mainly based on capitalist world relations, and it is not without criticism (Cheng, 2023; Sigurðsson & D'Ambrosio; Rosa, 2023), he nonetheless acknowledged that fascist societies could promote relations between people of their national community (Susen, 2020). Therefore, resonance theory can be used to critique social structures and the GDR's/East German's relations with the world.

Description of Methodology

Methodologically, I combined bibliographical with documentary research.

My specific research aims were: to find out whether (a) East German subjectivities (psyches, identities, Selves) and intersubjectivities (structures and relations) were molded by socio-political, cultural, historic, and economic forces; (b) whether certain practices and power relations contributed to the formation of particular subjectivities; (c) whether the Politburo (leaders of the GDR) achieved its aim to mold a socialist personality; (d) if so, how this happened; and (e) compare East and West German arrangements, constraints, and practices to identify differences and similarities.

Intersubjectivity is an organizing principle and a complex relational field, where psychological processes unite and experiences are shaped (Weegmann, 2001).

One of my research questions was "Whether the molding of intersubjectivity/identity occurred through 'large groups'" (e.g. SED). I operationalized my question: this would be measured by identifying whether children had introjected political norms and acquired an East German identity as envisaged by the Politburo. Basically, I would compare its postulates with children's adherence to these.

Documentaries, films, texts, and songs, in which people discussed politics, or talked about their experiences and crucial events, were my data sources. I wanted to address six dimensions of experience: politics, culture, economics, religion, interpersonal, and intra-psychic (Blackwell, 2018).

I searched the Federal Archives, the Stasi Records Archive, the Federal Center for Political Education … listened to East German music, satire, and watched films and series, videos etc. My *searches* centered on finding (1) speeches by, and/or information on, leaders (Honecker, Mielke, Schalk); (2) crucial historical events, such as the formation/dissolution of the GDR, erection and demolition of borders, development of the educational system; (3) crucial organizations, the Stasi, the KoKo; and (4) descriptions of experiences from ordinary people.

After locating relevant information, I listened to these documentaries, interviews, or read about crucial events written/aired by respectable newspapers/channels (der Spiegel, ZDF) in contemporary Germany.

Saturation was used as a criterion for discontinuing data collection (Saunders et al., 2017). When informational redundancy occurred, and I found very similar comments, accounts/descriptions in terms of my research aims, the collected data were considered as sufficient (see Fofana, 2020).

During this time, I "lived" in the archives. It is a cliché that research is painless, at least not when one is German and digs in Germany's past. My engagement with German narratives, cultural objects, and events, included a very personal dimension.

While growing up in the Federal Republic of Germany, I was exposed to the sequelae of the Holocaust. As a child, I heard stories about life in Nazi Germany from my grandparents. My father had been a prisoner of war. School excursions included visiting the concentration camp in Auschwitz. Although it was meant to be more educational than experiential, walking through the triste camp troubled me deeply. The smell of horror became imprinted in my body and soul for a long time. I felt deeply ashamed and guilty. I can empathize with Foulkes' need to change his German name after having immigrated to Britain. For many years, I felt a similar need and, therefore, changed my name trying to conceal the fact that I am German. Feeling ashamed of my German nationality and cultural heritage is not unusual for my generation. Wilke (2016) found that trauma is engrained in the German social unconscious. So, I was aware that my cultural inheritance and experiences were likely to affect my research of East and West Germany. However, this experience also had an advantage. I could become an active participant and contribut to findings by including my own recollections, counter-/transference reactions, and reflections, on the "inherited" German foundation matrix and the social unconscious.

One needs to be careful not to become too enmeshed, otherwise there is a risk of confusing one's own with the experience of the other. Having resided outside Germany for many years gave me distance. I had become more aware of unconscious German assumptions and practices through my exposure of other cultures.

I adopted the philosophical perspective of critical realism (Bhaskar, 1975). It is compatible with intersubjectivity and Group Analysis. This ensured conceptual consistency and methodological coherence. I read critical realism as follows: Roy Bhasker (1978) revitalized ontology in his formulation of critical realism, postulating that our knowledge of the social world is inescapably socially constructed. For Bhaskar (1989), theories involve causal mechanisms, which act in the domain of the real. His ontology stratifies reality into three domains: the *real* (independent of our thought, awareness and even our existence as humans), the *actual* (observable or experienced in events), and the *empirical* (seeks to find lawful connections).

Like interpretivism, critical realism holds that social phenomena need interpretative understanding (Taylor, 2008). Critical realism can be used to study intersubjectivity.

Critical realism and intersubjectivity have been combined to explore the interdependence between intersubjectivity and economics (Lewis & Runde, 2001).

According to Sorrell (2018), critical realism may provide a better understanding of social structures and technical systems. A system refers to tangible and measurable elements, such as infrastructure, public opinion, artifacts, regulations, and patterns of consumption (Geels, 2002 cited in Sorrell, 2018, p. 1275). Critical realism considers the relationship between the constituent parts of structure or systems, the material/social relations, which can be interpreted causally. It prioritizes reality (the world) over practices of understanding. In order transform human knowledge, we must separate epistemology (knowledge, systems, thoughts, ideas, theories, language, etc.) from ontology. The distinction between transitive, the changing knowledge of something, and the intransitive, unchanging elements (that's how it is) that we attempt to know, is crucial to critical realism. The world as it is (intransitive) as opposed to our interpretations of it (transitive). So, our knowledge of the structured world is molded by an intransitive reality and by our own socio-cognitive processes.

Critical realism allows for the legitimate combination of methods (Zachariadis et al., 2010, 2013). I could incorporate diverse thinkers, because my epistemology was informed by interpretivism, the underlying framework of social constructivism and social constructionism. So, trustworthy knowledge could be gathered by examining communication, analyzing narrated experiences, and by interpreting symbols and texts.

Language is the medium that enables interpretation (Raphael-Leff, 2018), it plays a crucial role in the exercising of power (Foucault, 1980), and in the carrying out of research.

How would I know what happened in the GDR? Only by listening to accounts or by reading about events.

My act of interpreting can be viewed as an exposition of experiences, facilitated by language and skill (Raphael-Leff, 2018). By entering the intersubjective world in projective identification, I would gain an emotional understanding of inter/subjectivities. I aimed to illuminate the effects of political relations/relationships by analyzing leaders' use of language. Additionally, I carried out bibliographical research to support my arguments.

However, I must point out that a critical examination of Germany could fill shelves with hundreds of books due to its complexity. Therefore, I did not aspire to elucidate all possible facets of the GDR, which arose in the 40 years of its existence. Rather, I aimed to illuminate *typical practices and elements*. Due to space, my selection of, and focus on, certain topics resulted in the exclusion of other areas. I acknowledge this shortcoming of my study. To ensure that my findings were accurate (credible), that methods, data collection, and analyses were transferable (can be applied in other settings), and that my findings were dependable (consistent) and confirmable, I attempted to be as transparent as possible, and to minimize confirmation bias, *not* selecting only material in line with my beliefs (Carter, 2014).

I was methodical in my literature searches, the collection of data and their analyses. I used inclusion/exclusion criteria, when searching for material to address my research questions, and saturation, when gathering data. I checked my findings against the existing literature and other sources (triangulation), as well as for mistakes.

Shortened Description of Data Analysis

For the data analyses, I used operationalized group/psychoanalytic concepts, conceptualized society as a large group, drew on Rosa's (2016) critical theory of resonance, Foulkes' (1973) four levels of relationships and communication, applied qualitative latent content analysis and other techniques. I focused on the *latent content* in order to identify the hidden meaning of verbal, written, and visual communication. By diving under the surface of what was said (Kleinheksel et al., 2020), I revealed socially unconscious processes.

How the Stasi (secret service, see Gauck, 1994; Gieseke, 2014a,b; Bundesarchiv, 2023; Dennis & Laporte, 2003) and the Politburo (government) asserted their control was analyzed by identifying social defenses: what was defended against when people resorted to disavowals, projection, denial, repression, avoidance, etc. To elucidate further socially unconscious elements, I analyzed the *current, transference, projective, and the primordial level* of Foulkes' (1973) levels (TextBox 11.1). By analyzing assumptions, social defenses, and structural oppression, I identified how the social unconscious manifested (see Brown, 2001). Basically, I *interpreted and analyzed* narratives, stories, symbols, and descriptions, of experiences and events to make their hidden meaning conscious.

Interpretation is the *methodical activity of interpreting*, which refers to *uncovering unconscious* structural processes, conditions, motivations, behavior, and practices (Reeder, 1998). It was *operationalized* as establishing connections between problematic, or conflicting matters, of which participants (or others) are not aware of, and making unconscious connections accessible to the participants, or others (adapted from Tschuschke et al., 2014, p. 51).

Analysis is more comprehensive. *Analyzing* involves making sense of what psychotherapists discover during the interaction with group members (Foulkes, 2002). By interpreting and analyzing counter-/transference, one can gain insight into groups (see Ferro & França, 2020; Snell, 2024). Personal testimonies were analyzed by applying latent content analysis to understand the lived experience.

TEXTBOX 11.1 FOULKES' (1973) FOUR LEVELS OF RELATIONSHIPS AND COMMUNICATION

Foulkes (1964/1985) considered transference *to be operating beneath the current and above the projective level* in a psychotherapy group (pp. 114–115). Schlapobersky (2016) explained that a group's *current level is the* "reality level", the real world outside the therapy group. Underneath this level lies that of transference. Family members and significant other figures from childhood belong to it. More obscure is the projective level, dominated by part object relations (objects = people; part objects relations = splitting of people/relationships into good and bad). Fragments of past relationships are projected into others. *Projective and primordial levels work together*, generating a visible field that brings the hidden world of unconscious conflicts and anxieties to life. The primordial level belongs to the collective unconscious, characterized by archaic meanings, symbols, and metaphors (pp. 329–334).

Counter-/Transference Reactions in Research

I also examined my *transference and countertransference* reactions, a technique that has been widely used in group analytic research. As researchers, we tend to have feelings toward others, groups, and institutions, and may transfer unsolved difficulties to any, or all, aspects of the research process (Knight, 2019). Positive, or negative, transferences may also be displaced onto theories (Rangell, 2004, 2017). So researchers could have a positive, or negative, transference reaction toward certain theories. Additionally, any material may trigger countertransference reactions. Emotions arise within us due to our own personal history or due to identification with the unconscious emotions that belong to individuals, or groups, whom we encounter whilst doing research (Knight, 2019).

Countertransference can be operationalized as the researcher communicating own mental/physical experiences by voicing own emotional responses regarding another person.

In terms of the research relationship: mentioning own sensations and feelings that the researcher cannot explain. If there is a discrepancy between the feeling that the participant is expressing and the feeling the researcher has, this discrepancy must be addressed (adapted from Tschuschke et al., 2014, p. 65).

Researchers must always study countertransference together with transference, because the total situation consists of all the feelings, behavior, and attitudes that comprise both (Joseph, 1983, 1985). A good understanding of counter-/transference (see Chapter 3) is required when using them as research techniques.

Extract 1: Example of Bodily Countertransference Reaction

While listening to the speeches of former GDR leaders … I experienced strong bodily countertransference reactions. Twice, I fell asleep, even though I was not tired. Possibly, because anger and aggression may induce drowsiness.

Other Examples of Findings

Socially Unconscious Processes at Primordial Level of Communication

Throughout the separation, both Germanies fought a bitter Cold War on the running track (Balbier, 2005), a parallel process, mirroring the Russian and American conflictual relationships. … At the *primordial level of communication*, a deep archaic longing for the Great Mother (Neumann, 1972) may have occurred. The archetype, symbolically expressed in the statue/paintings of Germania. This longing had to be repressed due to the lack of protecting and comforting female leaders.

*Latent Analysis of Defense Mechanisms (see below *)*

(All translations in what follows have been done by me.)

Example of Category: Avoidance

Two ex-border guards did not want to speak in front of the camera about land mines. Exchanging knowing glances, with a wry smile on their faces, they insist that "sometimes it's wise to be a coward" (see Läpple, 2020, documentary). They referred to it as wisdom. While connecting with each other via the signifying border, they disengage by walking away.

Example of Theme: Forgetting

A former guard is asked about the bunker. Totally perplexed, he replied: "I can't remember… I'm stunned … how can something like this disappear. Without a trace, it has just disappeared" (see Läpple, 2020, documentary). A past that has disappeared, which contains the existing taboo of not talking about the 22-meter-wide Death Strip, which used to be covered with raked sand, rendering footsteps easily noticeable, providing clear fields of fire for the guards (see Lapp, 2013, 2014, 2016; Wolle, 1999, 2024, 2013).

Defenses

Codes	*Category*	*Theme*	*Conclusion*
avoiding conversations	Avoidance		Denial
distancing		Forgetting	
unease	Emotions		Repression of events, actions, emotions

Example of Socially Unconscious Processes (in Italics) from Archival Data, Verified by Bibliographical Research (Triangulation)

[triangulation, bibliographical data] According to Judt (2015), *the myth of the shady KoKo empire* (consisting of 180 companies, which traded under different names, and could not be audited by tax inspectors or banks, Judt, 2013) was disenchanted by historical research *(so it used to be denied or repressed prior to this).*

… silver lake remained a symbol of ruthless practices of the East German KoKo and Western countries (80% of waste from West Germany, 15% from the Netherlands and 5% from Austria, France, Switzerland, Italy) (Signatur: BStU, MfS, AG BKK, Nr. 55; Hauptabteilung XVIII, Information zu geleiteten Massnahmen under Vorkehrungen bezüglich der Gewährleistung der Sicherheit der Deponie Schőnberg vom 12 März 1986, 1. 124). **[archival data]**

This makes for an uncomfortable assessment of several countries, who are *repressing the consequences of actions, or denying* them, classic examples of the workings of the social unconscious (see Hopper, 2003a). **[link to theory]**

Example of Social Structure: Bibliographical Data Analyzed Using Rosa's (2016) Theory of Resonance/Alienation, Verified by Archival Research

[bibliographical data] To achieve its goals, the Politburo established the Ministry for Security (MfS or Stasi) in 1950. The MfS was one of the most intrusive secret police systems in world history (Gieseke, 2014b), extending its "octopus tentacles" into all spheres of people's lives (Dennis, 2003). So extensive was its system of surveyance that widespread paranoia and persecutory anxiety existed (see Maier, 2019) that it would listen to every conversation (Mayer, 2006a). This fear was justified, because the Stasi used informants who spied on relatives, friends, lovers, and colleagues (Mayer, 2006b).

[theory] Alienation is caused by disrupting/eradicating resonances (Rosa, 2016). Alienation among people themselves arose. Furthermore, alienation between the government and its people arose, as evidenced by the thousands of applications to leave the GDR (Gieseke, 2014a), which were mostly declined. Repulsion results from closed off relations to the world (Rosa, 2016), which made ordinary GDR citizens feel powerless.

[bibliographical] The political structure of the GDR was totalitarian (Gieseke, 2014b). Erich Honecker was instrumental in creating a totalitarian state (Poppe & Poppe, 2022). Even though the death penalty was abolished in the FRG in 1949, it took East Germany until 1987. **[archival data]** Teske was shot in his neck after his unsuccessful clemency petition, according to Stasi reports (Signatur: BStU, MfS, AU, Nr.26/90, Bd.8, BL 124–125; Signatur: BStU, MfS, AU, Nr.26/90, Bd.8, BL 166) from June 1981 (Stasi Mediathek, 2023). The full extent of this brutality only came to the fore after the German reunification. Honecker was brought to trial in 1992 but not convicted. **[bibliographical]** Judge Wassermann wrote:

> The campaign of destruction against … 'alien peoples' had its parallels in the communist struggle against the bourgeoisie as a 'class enemy.' The one group disregarded human rights from the standpoint of race … the other did … from the class standpoint. The oppression in [East Germany] was even more tangible … because communist rule had no legitimacy at all ….
>
> (Cited in McAdams, 1996, p. 5)

Example of Stasi Practice: Bibliographical Data & Rosa's (2016) Theory of Resonance

[film, biographical] The Stasi used love to obtain secret information shown in *Der gleiche Himmel* (Hirschbiegel, 2017). **[Rosa's theory]** Love is highly resonant (**Žalec**, 2021), because love relations involve *horizontal* (relationships with people), *diagonal* (use of the body as object), and *vertical* (existential elements that concern all humans) axes of resonance (Rosa, 2016). The

Stasi trained Romeo agents, who pretended to be in love and skillfully wooed their targets. *Very strong resonant relations* were formed between the female target and the Romeo agent. Secret information was revealed in bed. This explains how the Stasi acquired secret information and seemed to know everything, as the more than 100-kilometer (The Federal Archives, 2021) long shelves of files show. **[archival data]**

Examples from Reflective Journal

[theoretical]

Green and Thorogood (2005) cautioned against "routine triviality" (as a White male I'm aware of how my status had an impact on my interviews with women ...). A "confessional style of reflexivity", as Seale (2018a, p. 195) put it, that is, presenting yourself through a series of blunders or engaging in too much self-exploration, whereby you tell your story rather than that of your participants' or of the research itself, should also be avoided. Reflexivity, becoming aware of how we feel, perceive, or think about, what we are doing (see Boud et al., 1994), entails methodological and theoretical openness, awareness of the social setting of the research itself and of the wider social context (Seale, 2018a).

Journal Entry 1

While reading and listening to material in the archives, I became aware of socially unconscious dynamics that had lured me into endorsing stereotypical beliefs about the inferiority of East German culture (Sporn, 2019), although it had excelled at sports, for which it was criticized due to doping (Meier & Mutz, 2016, 2018; Meier, 2016; Meier et al., 2016; Aykroyd, 2019; Richter, 2020). Several East Germans have written about the circumstances (Budde, 1997, 2002; Geipel, 2009, 2019, 2022; Kaminsky, 2016, 2019). After listening to satire (Golm, 2022) and reading articles in a popular satire magazine, I quite liked the dry sense of humor, how commentators/writers made fun of West Germans, of our politics and capitalist way of life.

Entry 2

Bierman was one of my idols as a teenager. I knew that overt critics of the State (Biermann, 1976, Kunze, Kunert, Becker) had been stripped off their citizenship. In this way, East German intersubjectivity was pushed toward conformity (see Jarausch, 1997; Brock, 2009; Fulbrook, 2009). Critics had to be very subtle to challenge power structures. In the FRG, we had the freedom to speak one's mind, when I was growing up.

Discussion of Triangulation & Examples

Triangulation is a crucial aspect of qualitative research (Denzin, 2012). Following many recommendations by qualitative researchers, I compared documentaries with interview data, and what people said in public (in documentaries, videos, films) with what they said in private (Stasi surveillance documents). Due to the short existence of the GDR, it was possible to check for consistency of what people were saying, or not saying, over time. I was also able to compare people's perspectives from different viewpoints (patriots, dissidents, children, women, men, politicians, staff). I looked at evidence from other research (interviews) to corroborate my findings to establish whether my findings were trustworthy. So, I used data from different sources, such as the Stasi Archives, contemporary documentaries, newspaper reports, and articles in journals, and books. I checked the consistency of my findings by double checking that they yielded the same findings (Noble & Heale, 2019). I compared findings generated through latent content analysis with findings obtained by applying Rosa's (2016) theory, and with group analytic theories (social unconscious, foundation matrix). After having identified manifestations of the social unconscious and typical practices, I *identified resonant relations/relationships* and compared these to the latent analysis *(**theme**: forgetting, **conclusion** repression or denial of events, actions, emotions).*

Youth Houses Extract

Culturally unique typical institutions, Youth Houses, offer insight into the foundation matrix of the GDR. Led as if they were military institutions (Poppe & Poppe, 2021), delinquent teenagers were molded into valuable members of socialist society (Rescheleit & Krippendorf, 2002). The Politburo ***created resonant relationships with*** those who identified with its goals: thousands of volunteers. The abusive nature of practices was ***repressed, denied, disavowed***, relegated to the social unconscious. This bleak East German history, the incarceration of young people who refused to fit into the regime, remains unknown to those, who cannot read German texts (Kagel, 2020). Educational practices were based on the pedagogy of the Russian Makarenko. By adopting Russian pedagogy, resonant political relations were reinforced with the Soviet Union.

No resonant relationships between opponents and the Politburo, or minsters reporting to it, were identified. I took this as confirmation that the Politburo suppressed critical voices, and denied, or repressed, its cruel actions and showed no emotions. Newspaper reports (Paterson, 2009) and interviews with the education minister, Margot Honecker, supported this. Those East Germans, who viewed themselves as political victims, were called criminals, others who died "*... paid for their stupidity with their lives*" (Scally, 2016, p. 2), as she put it. Asked whether she experienced any guilt, Margot Honecker responded that it did not touch her at all, because she had a thick skin (Panorama, 2009). The fact that many records were destroyed (McFadden, 2016) explains why I found it difficult to locate certain information in the archives. Some files from the Education Ministry were found in 1991. They confirmed the allegations, which had never been proven, that Margot Honecker had forced alleged traitors to give up their children for adoption. The unrepentant minister (Schudel, 2016) always dismissed accusations that she had directed such program, claiming that it did not exist. Whether this is merely a sign of repression or psychopathy is beyond the scope of this chapter. That the GDR regime was totalitarian and only formed resonant relations with people, who identified with its goals, who either denied their practices or repressed what they did, is supported by bibliographical and archival evidence. Most of it only exists in German. So, my research gives people, who have been oppressed and abused, a voice outside the German speaking world.

During their book discussion, Poppe and Poppe (2022, p. 12) narrated a story from Bräunsdorf: "*When an adult* [staff member] *saw that a child was being abused, she only looked and nodded. And then she went into her* office."

(Sexual) abuse was normal. Rape or torture were also common in other Youth Houses (Sachse et al., 2017). Often rituals for newcomers did include brutal beatings. X worked in the female prison in Dessau, where similar conditions prevailed: "One girl had to stand in her nighty in the freezing cold. They had painted footsteps, and she had to stay on them. By the next day, she was gone, frozen to death", one victim mumbled. "Some tried to commit suicide. It was your only way out, it gave you hope" (Lischke, 2022, documentary). When asked whether these things had happened, X replied: "I can't confirm it, say yes or no, I've not experienced it myself." Even though the workings of the social unconscious enabled widespread repression, one officer, who had worked in Dessau, told a reporter: "Anyone who says they [youngsters] weren't beaten, is lying" (Schröter, 2004, p. 3).

Lischke (2022) highlighted how difficult it was to find any former worker, who was prepared to talk about the methods that had been used in these institutions. It indicates widespread collusion, identification with the aggressor and disavowal, but also resonant political relations between former GDR ministers and staff.

Recent German publications have drawn attention to these horrific events. What happened

> … is …hardly known to the public … left out of historical accounts … children were sedated with psychotropic drugs … education aimed at breaking the will of the child, using open or hidden … power, manipulation and blackmail to make an obedient subject … the inadequate processing of re-education practices in German history … Brandenburg … was only dissolved at the end of 2013 and proves the lack of knowledge about its consequences ….
>
> (Poppe & Poppe, 2021, p. 17)

There seem to have been little consequences for some perpetrators due to a lack of evidence or statutes of limitation. Sadly, what took place in Youth Institutions does affect inter/subjectivities.

Emotional Impact of Research on Researcher

Texts inextricably bridge the distance between readers and writers, permitting a fuller articulation of unknown facets of our Selves (Leask, 2019). Reading and listening, as part of the research, may activate several defenses to cope with traumatic and painful material. Non-clinical researchers may feel as if they have been hit by a bombshell, as Leask (2019) put it, when their studies involve traumata and violence. One never knows where the research could take one. Think very carefully about the effect that topics of research can have on you or on your participants before embarking on a project. Archival research is no different. Engaging with testimonies, recordings, texts, and other kinds of data can be an emotional experience for researchers, as the excerpt from my reflective diary shows:

Extract 1

My disbelief turned into shock when confronted with numbers and facts about capitalist exploitation and child labor: humiliation and drill were normal in Youth Houses. Teenagers had to work for 12h daily (Poppe & Poppe, 2022). *Western companies all benefitted from forced labor; children aged 14–16 worked for exports to IKEA (Fannrich-Lautenschläger, 2014). Within the matrix of secrecy, I encountered unbelievable events and experiences. Forced labor in the correctional systems* (Connolly, 2012) *contributed to the GDR economy and companies in capitalist countries benefited significantly. Not expecting to discover such ugly truths in the post-modern 'civilized' Western world, I have little sympathy for IKEA.*

IKEA Germany officially apologized on 16th November 2012 in Berlin, expressing regret, and providing financial means for research into forced labor in the GDR (Kreutzmann 2012)

In my personal and academic experience, the consequences of carrying out research on sensitive topics tend to be underestimated. Some researchers feel confused, numb, almost paralyzed, or angry, sad, anxious and overwhelmed. If the distress is too unbearable, they have to temporarily suspend their research activities. When researchers get too entangled in the traumatic stories of their participants and fall into a lasting abyss of despair, psychotherapy is a good idea. Due to the nature of group analytic research that is related to the Holocaust, to wars and international conflicts, some researchers do encounter severe suffering. Having a supportive supervisor, keeping a reflective journal, and accessing support when needed, all form part of self-care skills. Writing can also be cathartic. Joan Raphael-Leff (2018) referred to "meta-metabolizing", that is, thinking about our own feelings and behavior in terms of beliefs, purposes, reasons, and needs (p. 114). So, researchers may be able to emotionally process their painful research experiences through writing.

During his research, the historian Leask (2018) was wondering what impact the stories had on him. Almost nothing he found in the Stasi Archives was as terrible as the cases his colleagues encountered when researching the Holocaust:

> But how does the writer … cope with such horrors day after day … What does it do to me to keep discovering people's largely forgotten stories filed away in bomb-proof basements … I tell myself that these people, or their suffering relatives, have chosen to put their stories into the archives, hoping someone sometime will … be moved by them and write about them …
> (p. 89)

Decolonizing Western Academic Writing Style & Structure

I looked at numerous textbooks, articles, and blogs on the internet. Typically, authors use the same structure in academic writing. Discourse can become culturally blind if it does not acknowledge difference (Tamdgidi, 2005). The traditional Western writing style, Shajahan Naomi (2022) suggest, is focused on a singular Cartesian rational Self. Command and authority over knowledge must be demonstrated to the readers. The Subject must speak from a transparent position, and the produced research report is more read, than experienced.

For illustrative purposes, I feel obliged to explain the common Western academic structure, because this is the format that most researchers are expected to adopt. The narrative style I am supposed to use, adheres to rules of linearity, separation, and syllogism. While noticing that it makes me feel uneasy, I am nevertheless trying to be pragmatic. At the same time, I acknowledge the deficits of colonial writing and would like to draw attention to "ethical" (Harriden, 2022) writing. Being critical about privileging dominant voices and adopting a decolonial tone is one aspect of it (Harriden, 2022, 2023). Attending to the social unconscious is another. Hence, even though my research is not about Indigenous people, I can nonetheless adapt my use of language to demonstrate awareness that the Western academic context has created a specific lens. In acknowledging that I am expected to write in a particular way, and lamenting this constraint, I am starting to problematize Western academic conventions.

Several articles (e.g. Tuck, 2013; Tood, 2016; Snow et al., 2016), and books (e.g. Denzin et al., 2008), have draw attention to decolonizing research. The United Nations (2013) acknowledge the rights of Indigenous Peoples. Furthermore, Gram-Hanssen's (2021) article is said to reflect a decolonized writing style.

Perhaps it is easier to decolonize qualitative research writing. Papers are often longer than quantitative ones, because they offer rich descriptions and interpretations of data. So, it gives researchers more leverage to include position statements. The quantitative writing style tends to be more concise. Results are commonly presented in tables and figures (Rivas, 2018). There is less leeway to avert this structure. One could call it the dictatorship of the positivist writing tradition.

Commonly, researchers are also advised to think about the audience they write for and the required format of journals/universities (Reeves, 2018). There is a certain irony in suddenly privileging the Other, when the writer/researcher simultaneously adheres to the individualistic tradition, which centers on the "I", Self, Subject, or Ego.

Experience is objectified, the Subject is integrated into the big Other, the intersubjective symbolic tradition, in which the noir subject is a void (Žižek, 1993). Loewenthal (2007) recommended that researchers (students) describe main ideas related to their research in the introduction. Basically, they begin with a general description, then include theory in relation to the chosen topic, and eventually are expected to be more specific. Loewenthal's advice is sound: researchers explain how their research question tallies with the existing information, such as the theoretical literature on the topic they study. In addition to defining all terms, they may also operationalize concepts, ideas, and/or the research question. This is done in qualitative research as well. Outlining how to measure variables when doing quantitative research is important, Loewenthal (2007) reminds the researcher. All specialist terms and concepts are explained when used for the first time.

This is how I was taught in the 1980/90s as well. References must be provided in support of claims, and the cited works should be relevant to the topic.

It does not matter which book, or article, I look at, there is no escape from the Western structure and narrative style. Popular bibliographic management programs include EndNote, Bibus or RefDB, Peg Boyle Single (2009) tells her readers. These programs still are popular nowadays. Only isolated points of the system are permitted to appear, deploying in it those blank spaces, the whole without novelty except a spacing of reading, as Bass (2003) put it, in his translation of Derrida.

"… ces blancs sans lesquels aucun texte jamais ne se propose comme tel …"

(Derrida, 1967a cited in Bass, 2003, p. ix)

Blanc (blank) spaces created by the blanche (White) subject, filled with the void "noir subject" (Žižek, 1993). Within the structure of academic writing, one must adhere to a sequence. There is no blank space, because everything has been filled with the White subject.

Following on from the introduction one encounters methodology. Here, aims and research question(s) should be linked to theory and/or research. Brief literature reviews seem useful. Research findings from related studies may be included, main results of those studies are summarized, or what is unknown about the chosen topic outlined. I feel boredom creeping up from behind, as I am trying to make it sound more interesting than it is.

Having located the question/aim in the available literature, researchers also outline the theoretical orientation they draw on (group analytic, psychoanalytic, sociological). Which theory/theories will be used is clearly stated. Of course, there should be some logical progression, because the Western style of writing is logocentric.

When describing the research *approach* (methodology), researchers explain the philosophical stance they adopt, their *ontological* (how they view reality), *epistemological* (what they accept as knowledge), and *axiological* (their ethical values) *perspective*. Additionally, they describe the methods they will use to analyze the data and offer an explanation of why a specific method was (not) chosen (Rivas, 2018). Researchers provide information on search strategies, participants, and the selected material. Choosing a method is not easy. Interestingly, Patton (2002) suggested that creativity, intellectual rigor, perseverance, and insight go beyond routine application of research procedures. I was intrigued by Bridgman's (1950) view on the scientific method. He stated that there is no scientific method as such. Instead, science is what scientists do. So, there are as many scientific methods as there are individual scientists.

Paying serious attention to ethics, power, privilege, and including a position statement contributes to decolonizing research (Harriden, 2022). How much detail one can provide depends on the word count and where one would like to publish. Because researchers are viewed as an "instrument" in qualitative inquiry, it has been suggested that the report should include information about the researcher (her experience, perspective, training, personal connections to the people or the topic of research, own demographic information) (Patton, 2002).

Academic institutions and books on dissertations/theses tend to provide templates. Some researchers like templates, because it is easier to follow a structure than to create one. However, a particular colonial structure is then imposed on researchers. By sticking to traditional templates, there is little chance that academic writing will be decolonized. However, in qualitative research, conventions are slowly becoming less strict.

As the decolonization of research is gaining legitimacy, norms are changing (Harriden, 2023). The researcher as author of postmodernist inclination seems more oriented toward values (see Alveson & Skőldberg, 2009c), and adopts a respectful language (Harriden, 2023). Researchers can also be more creative in post-colonial research (see Chilisa, 2020).

Logic demands that data analysis comes after methodology. Researchers explain how they did the analysis. They describe statistical, computational, or other techniques, which they applied, before describing their results/findings.

In brief research reports, the findings and discussion are often presented together. The "findings section" is written in the past tense, because it is a description of what researchers found. At first glance, writers are given more freedom to use different styles. This is but an illusion, because the writing style reflects that of the chosen methodology.

Findings are organized around research aims/questions, report main themes, and highlight unexpected, but important aspects. Competent researchers have learnt how to separate detail from trivia Patton (1999) claimed, preventing them from feeling too overwhelmed by huge amounts of data. Knowing how to use different methods makes validating results easier, and using rigorous procedures increases the trustworthiness of the findings (Heale & Forbes, 2013). Checking with participants that the findings accurately reflect their views, before presenting these to others, is ethical (see Janesick, 2000). Select quotes that capture the essence of the findings. 'Neither overstate nor minimize what your results indicate'. This is good advice, because in the Western style of academic writing, the focus is on explaining, and accurately evaluating, what researchers have uncovered.

Researchers delve into the relevance, meaning, and importance of their findings, and relate this to the Introduction and Theory Sections (see Rivas, 2018). This also reflects a Western way of producing knowledge, where writing styles nonetheless vary between the disciplines. To make research more accessible, prose and poetry can be integrated in discussions. However, in the field of psychotherapy, students are still expected to adhere to the logocentric Western academic style, in my experience as an examiner. Group analytic researchers may be less constrained due to the variety of styles found in group analysis. Except, the marking criteria of the IGA (2024–2025) adopt the traditional marking style.

A reflexive account is commonly included, where researchers reflect on the research process, method(s) used, and their findings. Reflexivity is a conscious reflection. It is important to acknowledge that researchers are part of the process of producing the data and their meaning (Green & Thorogood, 2005). While there is some overlap between the Results and Discussion Sections, researchers should not introduce new results/findings, but only discuss the data they have already reported.

In theses and dissertations, students tend to write a summary of results/findings. Ideally, it is a descriptive, interpretative, and insightful *summary* of findings (Dawson, 2019). Visual representations, such as bubbles, circles, diagrams, and photographs, might be used. The overall conclusion arises from the (summary) findings. Dawson (2019) advised to clearly say how and why, the findings of the research are relevant. Recommendations for further research, and other recommendations (change of policies; change to clinical practice,) are also made.

Limitations of the research should be acknowledged. Do not confuse limitations of methods with flawed results. For example, qualitative studies do not aim to generalize, so this is not a limitation of your study. If your approach has been neither consistent, nor coherent, this would be a weakness of your research.

Researchers also present their main argument in the conclusion. Trying to be respectful, humble, and addressing biases, contributes to decolonizing academic writing styles (see Thambinathan & Kinsella, 2021).

Decolonial researchers concern themselves with writing ethically (Chilisa, 2012). So, researchers should review the language they have used, when writing about people, they have interviewed (Harriden, 2023). This involves thinking about what to publicly say about participants and not distorting things. In that respect, documentary research is easier, because it draws on information that is already available in the public domain. A decolonizing style may also involve drafting a positionality statement (Harriden, 2023). Self-reflection, explicating how biases and your own identity influences your approach to research, is a must.

Chapter Summary

Latent content analysis and other group analytic techniques have been illuminated. I have presented a part of my own research on the former GDR to demonstrate the value of archival/bibliographical research, and to make group analytic research more understandable. In my description of techniques I have shown how different sources of data, and theories, can be integrated in the analyses. Triangulation is important when carrying out qualitative studies. I have shown how to triangulate findings. As my examples of counter-/transference reactions, and the emotional impact of research on the researcher have shown, one encounters suffering when doing archival research. Researchers must take this into consideration before embarking on their research. Attending to self-care is necessary. This makes it less likely that they will feel emotionally overwhelmed. I have also explained the structure of Western academic writing. Reflecting on power and privilege when drawing on colonial authors, and/or drafting a positionality statement, form part of a decolonizing writing style. Using such style might move Western academics closer to researchers of the Global South.

12

CHILD AND ADOLESCENT RESEARCH & ETHICS

Abstract

Child and adolescent research, ethics, language, and Social Phenomenological Analysis (SPA), are discussed. SPA method is suited for studying groups of children in educational settings. Although group analytic child and adolescent research is lacking, it is important. Admittedly it is also challenging. Many ethical dilemmas arise, and researchers must pay attention to their use of language. Other means of communication must be considered when carrying out research with young children. Taking into consideration the extant literature, I suggest that a group analytic research framework, which entails a methodology that uses observations, interviews, communication, conversations, drawings, photos, texts, and dreams to gather data, could be beneficial.

Introduction

Writing about the foundation matrix in the context of the group, Foulkes (1971b) referred to speaking the same language. It is the common ground of communication, which is transmitted culturally (p. 213). Language is also taught at school, thus, educational systems are influential (e.g., Bernstein, 1971; Bourdieu, 1971; Hopper, 1971; Scotford Archer & Vaughan, 1971; Smith, 1971; Zeigler & Peak, 1971). While children learn language by hearing people speak, and through education, the capacity for language acquisition seems to be innate. By the age of two, both deaf and hearing children tend to acquire spoken language and grammar by moving from gesture to language, and from prelinguistic pointing to a linguistic system (see Muller, 2013). Becoming a sophisticated user of language takes time. Therefore, researchers must adjust their use of language when researching children. Also, group analytic child research is scarce. Although group analysts have worked with mothers and babies (Pedrina, 2004), children, and adolescents (Bamber, 1988; Stumptner, 2022; Woods, 1996), most group analytic research has concentrated on adults. Possibly, because children are classed as vulnerable. This means that they have limited capacity to make voluntary and informed decisions (ESOMAR, 2018, p. 8). When studying vulnerable populations, many ethical issues arise. However, in terms of young children, there

DOI: 10.4324/9781003609544-15

has been a growing recognition that they must be acknowledged as research participants. Children should have the right to influence the activities that affects them. If included in studies, their well-being should be prioritized over other research interests, and their personality and uniqueness must be respected (see Larsson et al., 2019). Hence, the perspective of the child should be reflected in the research question(s), the theoretical and methodological approach, the execution of the study, and in the reporting of findings (Larsson et al., 2019; Smith, 2007). Since Dagley et al.'s (1994) summary of group child and pre/adolescent research thirty years ago, more studies have been carried out. These are described in Ezquerro and Cañete (2023). Overall, group analytic child/adolescent therapy and research are, however, lacking, particularly, research focused on younger children. The Israeli studies on children's dreams are a notable exception (see Friedman, 2019).

My intention is primarily to draw attention to the lack of group analytic research and I will only outline some suitable methods for child and adolescent research briefly. Ethicadilemmas, In addition to discussing language and the semiotic approach, I will outline Social Phenomenological Analysis (SPA). I will suggest that a group analytic research framework, which entails methodologies and methods that use observations, interviews, communication, conversations, drawings, photos, texts, semiotic analysis, and dreams, could be beneficial.

Child & Adolescent Research

Overall, there is a paucity of services that provide child group analytic therapy (Schlapobersky, 2016). Although group analysts do work with children and adolescents (Bamber, 1988; Ezquerro & Cañete, 2023; Stumptner, 2022; Woods, 1996), group analytic child therapy has been neglected in Britain. Ezquerro and Cañete (2023) note that it does not form part of the IGA's training programs. This is in stark contrast to the London Institute of Psychoanalysis. This could partly explain the lack of group analytic research and frameworks. Compared to effectiveness research of psychodynamic therapy for children and adolescents (e.g. Abbass et al., 2013; Aitken et al., 2020; Krischer et al., 2019; Midgley et al., 2014; Midgley et al., 2021), outcome studies of group mentalization-based therapy (Bo et al., 2017), or of child and adolescent group psychotherapy research in general (Ninan et al., 2019), there is a lack of group analytic child and adolescent research.

Studies have examined children across cultural contexts (Hunleth et al., 2022) in other disciplines. Children's drawings, which are believed to reflect the child's world, are used in therapy and research. Other traditional methods include questionnaires, surveys, and experimental designs. In children aged 6–11, the most common qualitative methods used are focus groups, interviews, observational, and arts-based, methods (Hunleth et al., 2022).

Since Anna Freud started to observe children, observational infant studies have become common in psychoanalysis, but less so in Group Analysis. The Tavistock method of observation relies on induction. Researchers may take part in the family's life, or become friends with the child, to build trust (Reid, 1997). Pretorius (2024) describe the process, experience, and value, of observation of a therapeutic parent-toddler group.

Several ethical issues have, however, been raised about infant observation. For example, whether it is ethical to criticize the mother. Or, to show certain videos of infant observation and not to be aware that observation includes an attachment relationship. Or, to use infant observation for the benefit of the therapist/researcher. To determine what is an ethical response to a baby of a depressed or traumatized mother in a challenging environment (see Gillam et al., 2010; Hindle & Klauber, 2006), is equally tricky.

In the wider field, developmental theories, such as psychoanalytic, learning, or cognitive theories, inform studies (Greig & Taylor, 1999).

Many studies have demonstrated that group psychotherapy is effective. Hoag and Burlingame's (1997) meta-analysis showed that children and adolescents treated in groups improved more than waitlist or placebo controls. Comparatively little has been published on group psychotherapy for this population since. Arias-Pujol and Anguera (2017) noted that most studies report on cognitive behavioral interventions, citing only two group interventions with an analytic orientation: Shechtman (2007); Devi and Fenn (2012). Their own observational group research of six 13-15-year-old adolescents, examined group communication.

Pascual-Leone et al., 2009), and Arias-Pujol and Anguera (2017), have examined communicational change. They filmed twenty-four group sessions. Fifteen types of communication (facilitating conversation, reflective function, expressivity, defensive expressions, dislike, ordering, humor, confrontation, exclamation, degradation of vocal behavior, whispering, touching, noise, surrounding noise, silence) were captured through their observation instrument. Previously, Arias and Anguera (2004, 2005) had studied communication in a therapeutic group of adolescents. In their recent study, Arias-Pujol and Anguera (2017) have put the types of communication into categories. Turn-taking and content were analyzed. Communication changed to circular interactions, which was not facilitated by the therapist for all members equally. Arias-Pujol and Anguera (2020) have also combined qualitative with quantitative methods.

The above studies are examples of how children and adolescents could be studied in group analytic research. Additionally, children's dreams could be researched, as the Israeli studies have shown (see Friedman, 2019).

Ethical Considerations

Hill (2005) suggested that researchers should see themselves as people, who are standing alongside all individuals within society. This has several ethical implications. Although researchers must incorporate respect for human rights into their everyday research practice, ethical child research is additionally guided by specific children's rights, pertaining to protection, provision, choice, and participation (Bell, 2008, p. 19). The Declaration of Helsinki (WMA, 1964) remains an essential international ethical framework for researching humans worldwide. In October 2024, its 10th revision was issued (WMA, 2024). It states that *everybody* involved in medical research must uphold these principles (Resneck, 2024). The same holds true for psychotherapy research.

Furthermore, the United Nations (UN, 2002), children's organizations (see Bell, 2008), and professional groups have devised ethical guidelines for research with children. Informed consent must be sought from the child's legal guardian. Additionally, consent should be sought from the child. Whether children can provide informed consent, or whether they should be used in research, has been debated. However, to establish the effectiveness of child analytic groups, these groups must be examined. Adhering to ethical guidelines (e.g. ESOMAR, 2018) is paramount, when studying psychotherapy groups.

Researchers can be participant observers, only observers, or both. The different positions have their own dilemmas. For example, when filming children as part of the observation, they should have the right to withdraw. If the camera is small and not immediately visible, the researcher must use strategies to make the child aware that s/he is being filmed. Furthermore, even if legal guardians have given consent to film children, researchers should adopt an ethical position that ensures that the child does not feel distressed, or uncomfortable, when being filmed (see Larsson et al., 2019).

Recognizing uniqueness is important. Nevertheless, children have often been viewed as a homogenous group, Carter (2009) pointed out. Moreover, a tick box ethical approach automatically identifies child research as "risky" (p. 858). This might also explain why so few group analytic studies have been carried out with children, as compared to adults. However, when sensitivity to ethics silences children's voices altogether, this is not in anybody's interest (see Carter, 2009).

Several researchers have highlighted the need for reforming ethical regulations to facilitate the meaningful participation of children and adolescents (Alves, 2022). Similarly, Water (2024) notes that the United Nations Convention on the Rights of the Child (UNCRC, 1989), which underpins research, states in Article 12 that children and young people have the right to be involved in matters that concern them. Disquietudes and concerns about vulnerability should, therefore, not result in the exclusion of children's participation in research.

Group analytic researchers could employ methods that protect children, but also give them the opportunity to take part in studies. Admittedly, groups add a further layer of complexity. Knauss (2007) noted that groups are a powerful force and that youngsters are influenced by peer pressure. This has ethical implications in terms of making decisions, competence, recruitment of group members, screening and selection, informed consent, confidentiality, child abuse, and keeping records. These factors must be considered in addition to the already described aspects of ethical research. If child participants have suffered abuse, neglect, exploitation, and/or other forms of violence, ethical concerns about research are multiplied (see Roth, 2023).

Not including children in research means that their views cannot be considered in service planning, policies, and group interventions. The effectiveness of group analytic treatment cannot be evidenced, and an opportunity is missed to include children in participatory processes (see Olsen, 2025).

The Importance of Language

Exponents of the social unconscious were influenced by Mead's (1934) reasoning about the effect of language. De Zuluetta (1995) highlighted that identities are formed by language. Researchers, who engage in infant observation and child research, often notice that language is the means of orienting ourselves far beyond our personal experience (Elias, 1991). Children absorb language before they can express their thoughts. Words and their meanings are deposited in their brains below the level of consciousness, and language is the very condition that enables thinking, as Dalal (1998) noted.

At the same time, language also constrains thought, emotions, and experience itself (Elias, 1991). For Mead (1934), language involved communication through significant symbols. Our thoughts, self-concepts, and the wider community, are created through communication, symbolic interaction, and the exchange of symbols. Hence, the Self is based on our societal experience, which forms part of our personality (see Pines, 1998). So, the child incorporates the collective. Children are influenced by how others perceive them, by the looking glass (mirror). Mead (1934) regarded the "Me" as the socialized component of the individual. The "I" refers to the Self as a subject of consciousness. Both are linked to the "self-concept", which refers to how a child views, assesses, and interprets her/his own identity, and develops self-awareness (see Dalal, 1998).

Importantly, researchers must also use other means than verbal language when communicating with children. Qualitative research aims to capture how the child makes sense of research events (Greig & Taylor, 1999). Pictures, stories, photographs, physical props, or picture books, should be used when explaining both quantitative and qualitative research to young children (see Pyle & Danniels, 2016).

The Value of a Semiotic Approach

Emile Benveniste (1971) broke once and for all with the idea that language is just a system of signals. With the use of language children can say "I", or "you", constituting themselves as subjects, Benveniste argued. More specifically, subjectivity arises through intersubjectivity when the child interacts with another subject, often the mother (Silverman, 1983). Culture is transmitted via semiotic codes, which govern the mother-infant relationship, which is characterized by the rhythm of touching, gazing, and vocalizing (Muller, 2013).

Considering that language is the most well-developed sign system (de Saussure, 1959), and that almost anything that children interact with involves signs (Mingers & Willcocks, 2017), it is astonishing that semiotic analysis has been neglected. Both psychoanalysis and Group Analysis ignored Peirce (1958). He was one of the founders of semiotics. Semiotics is the study of how meaning is generated and interpreted through signs, including symbols (Mingers & Willcocks, 2017).

Litowitz (2014) drew attention to post-Freudian theories, which rely on research findings for understanding the developing brain and mind. Due to their focus on pre-verbal and psychosexual development, the significance of semiotic mediation in all mental processes from the beginning of life has been neglected.

The importance of symbol formation has been recognized in psychoanalysis (e.g. Lorenzer, 1970) and in Group Analysis (e.g. Elias, 1991). Ernest Jones (1987) believed that symbolization was crucial to healthy psychic development. Hence, semiotics is an ideal means to research symbolism and symbols. It can be applied to study all forms of communication, including drawings. Children's drawings have been used in many studies (e.g. Tűrkcan, 2013) to understand children's inner worlds, and to identify their cognitive development.

Icons, indices, and symbols, become the focus when analyzing drawings. Children are first asked to draw a specific object and then asked to talk about their drawings. Tűrkcan (2013) found the semiotic approach effective. Indeed, a semiotic approach seems valuable when researching children.

The Use of Social Phenomenological Analysis

Greig and Taylor (1999) clarified that interpretive sociology begins from the inside out. One enters the child's world to explicate her subjective experience. According to Hatch, 1995), the goal of interpretative research is to understand the meaning that children ascribe to things/people in their everyday actions.

SPA has been formulated as a sociological concept in the tradition of Schűtz. It focuses on understanding the subjective meaning of social actions (Hofmann, 2016a). Preuβ and Hofmann (2019) referred to Husserl's and Merleau-Ponty's phenomenology, and to Alfred Schűtz' life-world analysis, when discussing experience.

SPA has been used to research children in a cultural and historical setting through mutual interactions. The unit of analysis includes people and the culturally defined environment. SPA is suitable to study groups of children in kindergarten, nursery, primary school, or in group situations that involve cultural, or aesthetic, objects.

Considering the importance of sociology to Group Analysis, Hofmann's (2015) methodology is relevant. It involves reconstructing the subjective meaning that participants assign to a phenomenon to penetrate its essence. Hofmann clarified that SPA constitutes a metatheoretical position in qualitative social research. Hofmann (2016c) referred to the sociologist Hitzler, for whom the task of social phenomenology was not just reconstructing social reality (p. 6). Instead, a *preoccupation* with the experiences of others is crucial. Lived experience includes subjective reflections on observable phenomena.

SPA (Hofmann, 2015, 2016a) starts by focusing on the specific phenomenon researchers want to examine and proceeds by formulating research questions. Then researchers collect data that reveal the essence of this phenomenon. Data could be records of participatory observation, photographs, video recordings, drawings, or sculptures (Hofmann, 2015). When researching groups of children, at least two researchers gather the data. Videoing the groups is a good idea. Additionally, one researcher takes field notes to capture important aspects of the interactions. One researcher engages in participatory observation.

Hofmann (2016a, b) carried out research in museums, schools, and nurseries. He talked to a group of children in front of a piece of art. He focused on observing their interactions to reveal children's inner perspectives, as well as aspects that cannot be captured on camera. Additionally, he drew sketches of the surroundings (Hofmann, 2016c). In line with group analytic thinking, his observations focused on the individual, the whole group, and the work of art. Field notes of all observations were recorded on an observation sheet in a narrative style.

Like group analysts, who focus on the interplay between something/someone, Hofman focused his attention on the aesthetic object, the group of children, and the educator. For the analysis, interesting points from the video were jotted down after an initial scanning of the data to get a sense of the more general meaning.

Qualitative researchers do something similar with texts. A systematic analysis is carried out afterwards (see Denzin & Lincoln, 1998). In line with phenomenological research, a SPA involves two hermeneutic circles, the findings "at first sight", and the detailed analysis (Hofmann, 2016c). Even though SPA was used for art education, and interesting research can be carried out in museums (see Hofmann & Preuβ, 2017), SPA can be useful for research that involves photos, drawings, or other physical objects, and aiming to analyze children's interactions.

Depending on the setting, and how much time researchers like to spend on a SPS, this descriptive and interpretative approach does not have to be time-consuming. It is easily learnt and put into practice (Hofmann, 2015). There is no need to use special software or complicated techniques. Adopting a socio-phenomenological attitude toward research is important, Hofmann (2016c) writes.

SPA is very detailed and requires a high degree of self-reflection. Thus, researchers must be methodical, meticulous, and precise. It is noteworthy that a wide range of impressions are extracted from the video recording (actions, atmospheres, utterances, room layouts, movements), which are also analyzed (Hofmann, 2015).

Of course, this method has limitations. To present the interactions in a meaningful sentence is difficult, Hofmann (2016c) admits. It also requires skill to select the most important aspects of all the raw data for the analysis.

Researchers interested in SPA, could first read Alfred Schűtz (1972), Zahavi and Overgaard (2008), and Hofmann's work.

Chapter Summary

Both child and adolescent research is important, but challenging. Many ethical dilemmas arise, and researchers must pay attention to their use of language. Other means of communication must be considered when carrying out research with young children. A semiotic approach seems useful. I have described SPA, which is suitable for studying groups of children in educational settings. Unfortunately, most studies, which have demonstrated that groups are effective, have been carried out in the wider field of group research. Hopefully, more group analytic studies will be carried out to improve group interventions for children and adolescents. Considering the extant literature, a group analytic research framework that entails a methodology that uses observations, interviews, communication, conversations, drawings, photos, texts, and dreams, to gather data, might be beneficial.

13

RESEARCHING MEDIAN & LARGE GROUPS

Abstract

The importance of studying median and large groups is emphasized, because they do something to their members, who are exposed to regressive and progressive processes. After offering a brief description of different types of median and large groups by drawing on important authors, such as De Maré', I describe how to research such groups. Group analytic or other more traditional methods, such as critical discourse analysis, psychometric social network analysis, or mapping techniques, could be used to gain insight into interactions, subgroupings, the effect of the convenor, and power dynamics. The provocation technique is useful. Critical discourse analysis offers a detailed interpretation about the "what", "why", and "how", something happened in a specific place/space, at a particular time.

Introduction

Median and large groups are important, because they form part of everyday life. Studying them can provide useful insight into human behavior, interactions, and subgroupings. Some researchers may not know how large groups have been conceptualized group-analytically and how group analysts study them. Equally, group analytic researchers may be unaware of other methods that could be used to research these groups. Thus, this chapter offers a brief outline of conceptualizations and methods.

De Maré (1989, 1990) and colleagues (De Maré et al., 1991; De Maré & Schöllberger, 2003) described processes and dynamics of median and large groups. De Maré et al. (1991) believed that a person's sense of self arises out of the community. This is why larger groups can bring about identity change.

Median groups can be conducted for various reasons, including consultancy work or group analytic training. Despite their different purposes, median groups share certain characteristics. While they often create anxiety, they are also resourceful (Rogers, 2013). Pisani et al. (2006) summarized further aspects, processes, and dynamics. Instead of becoming an object of desire, frequently this type of group becomes an object of projections. Hence, median and large groups

DOI: 10.4324/9781003609544-16

may initially be experienced as chaotic (see De Maré et al., 1991; Island, 1995, 2003; Menoutis, 2000; Schneider, 2003; Shaked, 1995, 2003; Weinberg, 2003; Wilke, 2003). Additionally, there is a risk of persecutory attack by the group. Due to the dissolution of individual boundaries, panic may arise, which resembles psychotic anxiety (Pisani, 2013). Similar processes may happen in organizations.

Clinicians have approached large groups differently. Some convenors may interpret cultural and social dynamics, and constraints, instead of making personal, transferential interpretations, as they may do in a small group (De Maré, 1972). Transformation through dialogue is then possible.

Organizational consultants approach groups differently. Psychoanalytically oriented consultants like Obholzer and Roberts (2005), suggested that a person may perform a role on behalf of an organization, which becomes dysfunctional under the sway of unconscious processes. Group-analytically oriented consultants have successfully worked with institutions for a long time (e.g. Thornton, 2017, 2018). Von Sommaruga Howard (2024) created a series of workshops on the median group. Some have integrated De Bono's (1973) provocation technique. Overall, many different techniques have been applied, and group consultants have demonstrated that large groups are an essential tool to influence an institutional culture. So, having knowledge of large groups is useful for group researchers. Unfortunately, von Sommaruga Howard (2024) has noticed that many people in organizations have knowledge of Bion's basic assumptions. They often know Tuckman's (1965) forming, storming, norming, and performing approach. However, they have never heard of De Maré, who significantly advanced the understanding of large groups.

In what follows, I will offer a brief description of different types of median and large groups, by drawing on important authors, such as De Maré'. Then I will describe how to research median and large groups. Methods will include group analytic techniques and conventional methods.

Median & Large Groups

Several group analysts have written about the median group and explained how to "grow it" (Douglas, 2013). Situated between the small and the large group, the median group is the transitional space between the family group and society. Although median groups operate more at a projective and primordial level, similar factors as identified by Foulkes (1948) are often noticeable. A median group comprises 12–30 participants, according to Lyndon (1997), and 17 is an ideal number when used therapeutically (Schőllberger, 2013). However, there is no agreement regarding numbers. Nevertheless Schick (2013) emphasized that the size of the group is vitally important. A circular membership of 15–20 members moves from kinship, or family issues, to a sociocultural dimension. Numbers can also be impacted by the setting. The size of median groups that are conducted as part of group analytic training depends on the number of students and staff. Rogers (2013) noted that students might like to feel intimate. Due to professional rivalry, subgroupings, envy, and competition, tend to arise. As a result, intimacy is more difficult to achieve.

Median and large groups have been facilitated for decades (De Maré, 1989). Their purpose ranges from reflecting on culture, society, and institutions, to identifying the influence these have on individuals. Aims involve understanding group dynamics and processes to achieve change. As the unconscious life of groups is uncovered and dynamics are rendered conscious, they no longer make participants behave so irrationally (De Maré & Schőllberger, 2003). Group analysts, who work as consultants and coaches, have facilitated median/large groups for learning experiences. Depending on the cultural context and theoretical orientation, their techniques and styles differ.

In South America, the "Rosario Experience" was a large research-based group. It was conducted by psychoanalysts and group therapists in 1958, led by Pichon-Rivière (Pichon-Rivière et al., 1960). It was a "social laboratory", where approximately 200–300 people from various backgrounds met. A similar format, which involves a plenary meeting, introductory lecture, small groups, and a concluding meeting, has been adopted by convenors in other countries. Convenors and organizers may analyze these groups.

While there is some similarity between Lewin's social laboratories, conferences at the Tavistock Institute of Human Relations, and large groups conducted at group analytic Symposia, the latter are less structured (Tubert-Oklander & Hernández-Tubert, 2014).

Commonly, convenors of median or large groups are non-directive. Even though there is often not a specific topic or goal, convenors nevertheless endeavor to create an atmosphere, in which dialogues can occur (Tubert-Oklander & Hernández-Tubert, 2014). This is easier to achieve in groups with fewer participants.

Many Foulkesian and Kleinian thinkers are in agreement that the large group almost always regresses into a psychotic state of mind (Wilke, 2003). Hence, it is common that the large group is feared. Von Sommaruga Howard (2015) rightly queried why group analysts create too many barriers that make conversing impossible. By not carrying out the necessary dynamic administration and getting 400 people in one space, where they neither see nor hear each other, difficulties are likely to arise. She wondered whether unconsciously group analysts are too terrified of the large group due to its propensity for destruction. It frustrates the satisfaction of libidinal needs, thereby causing hate in the group-as-a-whole, and between sub-groups, and individuals (De Maré et al., 1991). Resentment builds up, finding a channel for its expression in sub-groups. These contain the hate, which needs to be turned into a desire to think and speak through dialogue.

Wilke (2003) noted that Foulkes was profoundly ambivalent about the large group methodology. Thus, conductors of large groups may un/knowingly base their interventions on Bion's (1962, 1967) concepts of basic assumptions, thinking, and linking, Wilke suggested. The second generation of group analysts holds two different views about the large group. Whereas Kreeger (1975) had an unnecessarily pessimistic view of the kind of social therapy that can be accomplished in the large group, De Maré et al. (1991) were more optimistic. Subsequently, the split between the good, benign, small group, with its tendency toward integration and relatedness, and the bad, malignant, large group, with its propensity for disintegration and fragmentation, has been partly reconciled (Wilke, 2003). Through dialogue between the sub-groups, hate is transformed into frustration (De Maré et al., 1991), a precondition for thinking and linking (Bion, 1967).

De Maré (1985) believed that a large group can weave a holding matrix between differing sub-groups. In this way, the capacity for human fellowship develops. De Maré et al. (1991) argued that this capacity makes the large group a space for processing historical traumata and intergroup conflicts. Once it has developed into a space for containment, and its capacity to tolerate frustration expands, the members' ability to think reflectively increases. As some group members start to feel heard and reconnected (De Maré, 1972), the push for thinking and linking becomes as strong as the pull toward fragmentation and disintegration within the evolving group matrix (Wilke, 2003).

Group-Analytically Oriented Consultancy Groups

Organizational consultancy, which draws on insights from psychoanalysis and group work, is important to enable organizations to perform better (Armstrong, 2005). Emotional dimensions are a crucial factor in the life of organizations. Obholzer and Roberts (2005, 2019) suggested that a person is unconsciously sucked into performing a role on behalf of others.

Rogers (2013) admitted that median/large groups can be experienced as intimidating. However, they can also be used for addressing organizational difficulties. *Larger groups are an essential tool* to influence an institutional culture.

The provocation technique (De Bono, 1973) has been used in group-analytically oriented consultancy work (Rogers, 2017). Simply put, a provocation is an idea that is too radical, unrealistic, or too stupid to "solve" a problem. By getting participants to identify what underpins the provocation, this technique tries to create a sense of security and also flexibility (De Bono, 1973). Issues are raised in median/large groups by the provocateur, who may comment on the provocation, but does not have to, as Rogers (2017) explains. As the participants listen to the provocation and form associations in their minds, they may identify with some, but question other, provocations. The underlying idea is that people move to more realistic solutions and acquire the ability for lateral (creative) thinking (De Bono, 1973). In the group, members may recognize that they do not have to respond immediately. Through scaffolding, thoughts can be elaborated and exchanged, provided that a good therapeutic alliance has been formed with the consultant, so that participants feel understood (Rogers, 2017). By raising and verbalizing issues, the consultant puts participants' concerns into words, but challenges existing negative predictions and declarative statements as well. A provocation is particularly useful, according to Rogers (2017), when an organization seems unable to respond to the stresses it encounters, or when people do not know each other, but share similar concerns.

According to group analytic theory, difficulties are always located between people (Foulkes, 1964). Consultants assume the same. Organizational problems are conceptualized interpersonally, reflecting the constraints of the institutional culture (Thornton, 2010). Hence, any provocation explicitly demonstrates a focus on the group-as-a-whole. In this way, scapegoating, and humiliation of an individual person, are minimized (Foulkes, 1964). Questions, such as "what is this culture like?", or, "why is something articulated like this?", are used to formulate a provocation (Rogers, 2017).

Groups work best when operating at an optimum level of "creative chaos" and when people utilize their feelings (Wilke, 2018). Once anxiety levels have been reduced, participants can gain new insights into the functioning of their organization. Interestingly, Wilke (2003) suggested that participants seek assurance, recognition, and social connectedness, even if they become attacking. Viewed as an act of communication and exchange, the convenor contains attacks and models a form of blind trust in the form of a free associative process, Wilke explained. This is a typical group analytic technique as espoused by De Maré et al. (1991), Thornton (2025), and others. By giving the group a feeling that it can transit from a state of disconnectedness to connectedness, an interdependent matrix develops, in which members start to feel secure and trusting (Wilke, 2003).

Many group analysts have noticed that members, who are particularly agitated, or angry, act out something unconsciously for the entire group (e.g. Wilke, 2018). The group reassures itself of its capacity for sanity, Wilke (2003) suggested. When the conductor creates a space for experiencing "mothering", this can have a civilizing effect. By tolerating and containing "chaos", destructive forms of exchange become integrated. Nitsun (2015) wrote mainly about small groups, where the good and bad relational aspects are internalized. However, the same happens in large groups.

It is noteworthy that the group analyst Wilke contributed to management research in the early 2000s, when the researchers lived alongside leaders and their organizations (Binney et al., 2012). They carried out interviews and case studies, published in *A practical guide for "ordinary heroes"*.

How to Research Median & Large Groups

Thornton (2025) observed that the group matrix, communication, translation, negative/mirroring, exchange, resonance, condenser phenomenon, and location (see Appendix 1), are features of all groups. These concepts can be operationalized to study the unconscious life of larger groups methodically to find out when and how change occurs.

Median and large group experiences in South Africa were researched by Vice in her interview study (Vice & Hildenhuys, 2016). These groups formed part of the "Working with Groups program". Although these interviews offer insight into the thoughts and emotions of participants, which they never dared to voice in the group (Rohr, 2016), the group was not researched more "neutrally". Both researchers were participants of both the small and median groups.

Filming median groups and interviewing participants offers researchers the opportunity to study them. They can validate Vice and Hildenhuys' (2016) findings by carrying out focus group research. The median group approach operates at the juncture, where personal and social aspects of identity overlap.

Vice and Hildenhuys (2016) clarified that the participants were aware of the wider scope of group analysis (see De Mendelssohn, 2000). As a participant observer in the median group, one researcher sat on the periphery of the group observing the group and taking verbatim notes. Focus groups had 12–15 participants. Provided vignettes reflect the group analytic approach. So, their study is informative for researchers unfamiliar with this approach.

Many unconscious processes operate in the median group and unprocessed traumatic experience often arise. This is also discussed by Spiro et al. (2013), Mojovic (2007), Rohr (2013), and von Sommaruga Howard (2012). Such groups can be researched by several group analytic methods (see, e.g., Chapter 8).

Provocation and creative chaos can be studied empirically. Researchers ask consultants to videotape sessions, or obtain their process notes, if they do not want to be a participant observer. Alternatively, they interview group members and consultants. Thematic analysis (Braun & Clarke, 2022), discourse analysis (e.g., Powers, 2007), or narrative analysis (e.g. Holstein & Gubrium, 2012) are just a few methods to analyze the data. Given the large volume of data that are generated, when researching median/large groups, AI tools could make data analyses easier.

It is noteworthy that large groups do something to their members due to being exposed to both regressive and progressive processes. Wilke (2003), therefore, suggested the integration of preventative and curative techniques. The conductor's view of the large group significantly shapes group members' experiences, he noted. His observations could be verified by mapping group interactions through the Interpersonal Circumplex (see De Haas, 2025). Or, a sentiment analysis could be carried out.

Given the power differential between students and staff in the median/large groups on training courses, a combination of critical discourse analysis and social network analysis (SNA) could be used. Critical discourse analysis has been used primarily to study the abuse of power, dominance, and inequality, in particular sociocultural situations. However, the discourses in larger groups on training courses could be gathered to research the training structure. Data could be interpreted reflectively by attending to power, social dynamics, and their expected effect (see Anderson, 2019, 2022).

Critical discourse analysis offers a detailed interpretation about the "what", "why", and "how", something happened in a specific place/space, at a particular time. So, researchers could carry out a trajectory analysis.

Either specific occurrences that happened in a short space of time (scapegoating), or events that occurred regularly (ignoring difficult issues) in the group, could be studied. Change is captured by attending to these occurrences/events. Of course, interpretations of qualitative data are subjective. To obtain more objective evidence of shifts in interactions, a psychometric SNA can be carried out additionally. This involves combining critical discourse analysis with network analysis at a data level (see Ryu, 2020).

When groups are videoed, and non-verbal communication is fully described/analyzed, facial expressions, gestures, pitch, emotional tones, intonations, and so forth, can be captured. This enables a better understanding of when changes have occurred in the sequences of interactions.

Ryu (2020) suggests gathering information about the setting and the participants, and to take notes during the group sessions. Historical and sociocultural information should be collected, because processes outside the group affect its inside. Establishing a good relationship with participants is equally important.

SNA (Rawlings et al., 2023) aims to evidence the findings from the critical discourse analysis. Several statistical techniques can be applied to analyze and visualize the interaction patterns in the median group, the structure of the relationships, and the positions of individual members (e.g. educational groups). Centrality measures, such as, betweenness, degree, and eigenvector, or clustering coefficients to analyze the network structure, may be used (see Borsboom et al., 2021).

Very large groups can also be studied through SNA. Groups with hundreds of participants would constitute a large network. It could be divided into a small community of closely linked nodes and ties. Both structure and related characteristics of each sub-group can be analyzed. The relationship between sub-groups, and the entire large group relationships, and interactions, can then be mapped visually.

Furthermore, large groups have convenors. Some participants tend to be more dominant in groups. Convenors can become the focus of a visualized network, and a comparison can be made between them, and domineering participants. Eigenvector measures the influence of an actor (node) within a network. It is based on "relative importance". So, it may show, whether domineering participants have more power than convenors and influence the group.

Brown et al. (2012) used cartography (Software Compendium) to map group processes and dialogue in an analytic therapy group.

Okada et al. (2008) and Okada (2025) describe cartography and mapping techniques. Visual thinking is an alternative to how Westerners traditionally conceptualize thought processes. Inspired by Paulo Freire's (1967) pioneering ideas on critical pedagogy and transformative education, Alexandra Okada promotes socio-scientific thinking through emotional, intellectual, and social engagement. Integrating AI in her research, she described many techniques and the application of knowledge mapping.

Dialogue and experiential learning can be a focus in median/large groups. Dialogic and experiential processes can be mapped in group analytic training organizations (see Okada, 2008, 2025 for me detail).

Chapter Summary

Median and large groups form a part of life. They are useful tools for studying organizations. I have described features of such groups, including group analytic and consultancy groups, and how to research them. Group analytic and other conventional methods can be used. These include operationalizing, critical discourse analysis, a combination of critical discourse analysis and psychometric SNA, and mapping techniques. Studying large groups can offer insight into interactions, subgroupings, behavior, effect of the convenor, power dynamics, and many other unconscious aspects.

CONCLUDING REMARKS: EVERY RESEARCH PROJECT MATTERS

My motivation for writing this book originated in a lack. Initially, I was motivated to fill an existing void, the absence of a group analytic research handbook. During the process of searching for material and "re-searching" research, I discovered a much deeper void: the absence of non-Western voices. While deeply immersing myself in philosophies, history, politics, physics, and research, I started to notice that research reflects a worldview, which is predominantly based on Americo-European, White males.

Many, if not most, researchers, who I had known, had also embraced Western philosophical traditions. Some might have done so inadvertently, because the traditional paradigms are underpinned by Greek philosophy. At the time, I was unaware of this.

Nowadays, I agree with Bernasconi (1997a) that one may as well say that research must rest on a Greek epistemology, because philosophy and its history started, and ended, with Plato and Aristotle. It is rather astonishing that they are still the yardstick of modern definitions of science and research. At least, this is the conclusion I have reached, after tracing the thinking of several dominant philosophers of the past centuries to its origin.

Ironically, despite claiming to have found a method of infallible abstract reasoning that would arrive at "the" truth without any bias, Plato and Aristotle themselves tried to escape the theorizing of the Skeptics, as Wilson (2016) has pointed out. Aristotle's universe assumed an assembly of things with essences inside them.

According to quantum mechanics, an electron has a different essence every time we measure it. So, it has *no* essence. This is in line with Buddhism. Furthermore, quantum physics/mechanics casts doubt on reductionist and "objective" worldviews (Barad, 2007).

Unfortunately, non-Western philosophical views have been ignored in traditional research, as I have discussed in Section 1. Possibly due to defensive maneuvers (splitting, projection, repression), known as "othering". From a group analytic perspective, one could say that exclusionary matrices of research and philosophy were formed by erasing any history that would challenge Western scholarship. As a result, non-Western knowledges were erased altogether. So, we have ended up with reductionism and racism, in my opinion.

However, the dichotomization of the quantitative and qualitative paradigms is misleading (Burns, 2000). Group (analytic) theories do not accept the prevalent individualist dichotomies, the "either or" perspective, and the prioritization of the individual. Hence, I have adopted this way of thinking and formulated one pluralistic research paradigm. It offers an alternative to the existing paradigms, which are based on Western philosophy.

As discussed in the first part of the book, the Emerging Reality Paradigm (ERP) rests on African and Eastern philosophies, thereby avoiding the problem of the Western metaphysics of individualism. This is important from a group and from a decolonizing perspective.

The ERP includes Indigenous methods. It can be combined with Indigenous frameworks and paradigms, as I have shown in Section 2. By incorporating the methodology of diffraction, a variety of methods can be used. These also include methods that draw on quantum theories. They allow us to study unconscious processes and dynamics more "scientifically".

Readers may wonder how the ERP differs from other paradigms. I have addressed this in Section 1, where I have also discussed whether it could be called a "paradigm". Suffice it here to say that, in contrast to Critical Realism, the ERP does not offer a synthesis of the quantitative and qualitative paradigms. It also departs from other Western paradigms by resting on East/South Asian and African philosophies.

I could be accused of idealizing these philosophies. Of course, they have flaws and are also plagued by isms and schisms. Furthermore, the African or Asian way of life is not as harmonious as I have made it appear. However, collectivist societies are more concerned with "We", instead of "I". And why should we not prioritize non-Western philosophies for a change?

Inevitably, my conceptualizations will involve an unlearning of Western forms of knowledge production (Mignolo & Walsh, 2017). This may be met with resistance, because old ways of thinking die hard. Nevertheless, we should at least try to be open to the decolonization of research.

The concepts used in decolonizing research methodologies are social justice, inclusion, and empowerment. However, as Barnes (2018) has highlighted, we should not ignore the causes of social injustices (capitalism, globalization, patriarchy, inequality). So, writing about decolonizing and Indigenous research is not enough.

Unfortunately, decolonizing methodologies may even reproduce unfavorable representations of groups of people, albeit inadvertently. Moreover, what constitutes "Indigenous" is not straightforward. I have tried to be mindful of these issues.

Of course, not everybody is against the decolonization of research. I have noticed a shift in thinking over the past decade. Researchers have also become more aware of the need to decolonize language.

Some have argued that the power to define what counts as "real" knowledge lies at the epistemic core of colonialism (Tuhiwai-Smith, 2021). If we accept this, European and American-centered ways of conceptualizing knowledge must be dismantled. This could be done in various ways. Hyphenating the word "re-search" can foster a decolonizing process, Ndlovu-Gatsheni (2018) suggests, because re-searching signifies that something remains unresolved: the wounds colonialism has inflicted have not yet healed. It points the finger at research by revealing that it was not innocent, thereby casting doubt on any portrayal of its benevolent nature and purpose. I have not hyphenated the word "re-search" because important researchers, such as Chilisa, have not done so. Nevertheless, I do agree with Ndlovu-Gatsheni that it can contribute to the process of decolonizing research. Undoubtedly, we must challenge how knowledge is produced to instigate change. This is not easy. However, if we want to decolonize our group (analytic) institutions, practices, discourses, and minds, we need to ask ourselves whether we allow "outsider" ideas in (Nayak, 2021). It involves questioning the dominance of Western thought in metaphysics, epistemology, ontology, and axiology (Chigevenga, 2022), which is a big undertaking.

To grasp the complexity that is hidden in research, I have argued that all researchers must first acquire a deeper understanding of the Western philosophies that underpin research methodologies. Only then will they be able to fully appreciate the need for integrating other forms of knowledge, which are located outside prevailing epistemic norms. All these ignored philosophies, methodologies, and methods that rest on notions of relationships, reciprocity, connections, and accountability. They are embedded in Indigenous understandings of knowledge and ethics, as Tuhiwai-Smith (2021) has noted.

These values are also important to Group Analysis. Some group analytic researchers and psychotherapists may, therefore, welcome my introduction of "forgotten", or "neglected", philosophies and my interweaving of these into research. But as Karl Marx (1997) has once rightly highlighted, philosophizing is not enough. We need to change the world. Hence, to instigate a change in the ways knowledge is perceived, my focus has *not only* been on challenging Western research paradigms. My intention has been to change them.

Overall, this book has achieved its objective to formulate an alternative to the dominant research paradigms and to integrate diverse methods into it. Whether this will have a positive effect on the decolonization of research, and whether it will position the methods of group analytic approaches more firmly in the world of research, remains to be seen.

I would like to extend an invitation to carry out research, because every contribution to the field of group analytic psychotherapy matters. You could (1) engage in debates about research paradigms; (2) advocate for the decolonizing of research; (3) develop group analytic theories; (4) think about how to move ethical guidelines forward; (5) study therapy, supervision, online, median, consultancy, large or experiential groups; (6) supervise students' theses; (7) carry out empirical dissertations; (8) apply methods that you favor to produce new knowledges about analytic groups; (9) advance the practice of group analytic research. Or, you could become a participant in a study and write about it.

Importantly, the pyramid of evidence is not the sine qua non. Researchers must re-negotiate existing socio-economic and political demands for the conduct of primarily quantitative studies. My book is an invitation to do so.

BIBLIOGRAPHY

Aarre TF (2022) A farewell to psychiatric diagnoses. *Tidsskriftet*. 142: 1–8. DOI: 10.4045/tidsskr.22.0386 Available at: https://tidsskrifet.no/en/2022/09/perspectives/farewell-psychiatric-diagnoses (accessed 8 July 2024).

Abbagnano N (2024) *Existentialism*. Britannica. Encyclopedia Britannica. 24 October 2024. Available at: https://www.britannica.com/topic/existentialism (accessed 10 November 2024).

Abbass AA, Rabung S, Leichsenring F, Refseth JS and Midgley N (2013) Psychodynamic psychotherapy for children and adolescents: a meta-analysis of short-term psychodynamic models. *Journal of the American Academy Child Adolescent. Psychiatry*. 52(8): 863–875. https://doi.org/10.1016/j.jaac.2013.05.014.

Abe M (1988) Nishida's philosophy of "place". *International Philosophical Quarterly*. 28(4): 355–371. https://www.pdcnet.org/ipq/content/ipq_1988_0028_0004_0355_0371

Abe M (1995) The problem of "inverse correspondence" in the philosophy of Nishida: toward a critical understanding. Trans. JL Fredericks. *International Philosophical Quarterly*. 35(4): 419–436. https://www.pdcnet.org/ipq/content/ipq_1995_0035_0004_0419_0436

Abe M (1997) *Zen and Comparative Studies: Part Two of a Two-Volume Sequel to Zen and Western Thought*. Edited by Steven Heine. Honolulu, HI: University of Hawai'i Press.

Abe M and Brűll L (1988) Kitaro Nishida bibliography. *International Philosophical Quarterly*. 28(4): 373–381. https://www.pdcnet.org/ipq/content/ipq_1988_0028_0004_0373_0381

Abe RY (1967) *The Awakening of Faith. Attributed to Açvaghosha*. Trans. YS Hakedas. New York: Dover Publications Inc. Available at: https://archive.org/details/20200427-the-awakening-of-faith

Abend G (2008) The meaning of 'theory'. *Sociological Theory*. 26(2): 173–199.

Abernathy A (Ed.) (2024) *Addressing Diversity Dynamics in Group Therapy. Clinical and Training Applications. AGPA Group Therapy Training and Practice Series*. New York: Routledge. Available at: https://www.routledge.com/AGPA-Group-Therapy-Training-and-Practice-Series/book-series/AGPA

Abernethy AD (2015) A spiritually informed approach to group psychotherapy. In Kleinberg JL (Ed.) *The Wiley Blackwell Handbook of Group Psychotherapy*. Oxford: Wiley Blackwell, pp. 681–705.

Ablon JS and Jones EE (2005) On analytic process. *Journal of the American Psychoanalytic Association*. 53(2): 541–568. https://doi.org/10.1177/00030651050530020101.

Ablon JS, Levy A and Smith-Hansen L (2011) The contributions of the psychotherapy process Q-set to psychotherapy research. *Research in Psychotherapy*. 14(1): 14–48.

Adams A and Cox AL (2008) Questionnaires, in-depth interviews and focus groups. In Cairns P and Cox AL (Eds.) *Research Methods for Human Computer Interaction*. Cambridge: Cambridge University Press, pp. 17–34.

Adams R (2021) Can artificial intelligence be decolonized? *Interdisciplinary Science Reviews*. 46(1–2): 176–197. https://doi.org/10.1080/03080188.2020.1840225.

Adelphi University (2024) *Group psychotherapy. Group Psychotherapy Training Program*. Available at: https://www.adelphi.edu/program/graduate/group-psychotherapy (accessed 18 August 2024).

Adlam J, Aiyegbusi A, Kleinot P, Motz A and Scanlon C (Eds.) (2012) *The Therapeutic Milieu under Fire: Security and Insecurity in Forensic Mental Mealth. Forensic Focus* 34. London: Jessica Kingsley.

Adler M and Ziglio E (Eds.) (1996) *The Delphi Method and Its Application to Social Policy and Public Health*. London: Jessica Kingsley Publishers.

Adler S (2019) *Sanierung von DDR Altlasten. Giftiges Erbe in Bitterfeld Wolken. [Cleaning up the old rubbish of the GDR. Toxic Inheritance in the clouds of Bitterfeld.]* Deutschlandfunk 8 April. https://www.deutschlandfunk.de/sanierung-von-ddr-altlasten-giftiges-erbe-in-bitterfeld-100.html

Adshead G (2002) Three degrees of security. Attachment and forensic institutions. *Criminal Behaviour and Mental Health*. 12(2): S31–S45. https://doi.org/10.1002/cbm.2200120605.

Adshead G (2012) Mirror mirror. Parallel processes in forensic institutions. In Adlam J, Aiyegbusi A, Kleinot P, Motz A and Scanlon C (Eds.) *The Therapeutic Milieu Under Fire. Security and Insecurity in Forensic Mental Health. Forensic Focus* 34. London: Jessica Kingsley, pp. 97–115.

Agar G (2020) The clinic offers no advantage over the screen, for relationship is everything. In Weinberg H and Rolnick A (Eds.) *Theory and Practice of Online Therapy. Internet-Delivered Interventions for Individuals, Groups, Families and Organizations*. New York: Routledge Taylor & Frances Group, pp. 66–78.

Agazarian Y (1994) The phases and development and the systems-centered group. In Pines M and Schermer V (Eds.) *Ring of Fire. Primitive Affect and Object Relations in Group Psychotherapy*. London: Routledge, pp. 36–85.

Agazarian Y (1997) *Systems-Centred Therapy for Groups*. London: Karnac.

Ågerfalk P, Aakhus M and Lind M (2008) Proceedings of the Inaugural Meeting of AIS SIGPrag. Paris, December 14, 2008. *Working Papers on Information Systems*. 8(49). http://sprouts.aisnet.org/8-49

Ahlin G (1985) On thinking about the group matrix. *Group* Analysis. 18(2): 112–124.

Ahlin G (1986) *Exploring psychotherapy group cultures. Essays on group theory and the development of Matrix Representation Grid, an observation method for studying therapeutic group processes*. Academic doctoral thesis. Sweden: Karolinska Institute and University of Stockholm.

Ahlin G (1988) Reaching for the group matrix. *Group Analysis*. 21(3): 212–226.

Ahlin G (1995) The interpersonal world of the infant and the foundation matrix of the groups and networks of the person. *Group Analysis*. 28(1): 5–20.

Ahlin G (1996a) *Exploring Psychotherapy Group Cultures*. Stockholm: Karolinska Institute, Department of Neuroscience.

Ahlin G (1996b) Der Gruppenprozeß under der Lupe: Das Matrix-Representation-Grid. In Strauß B, Eckert J and Tschuschke V (Hrsg.) *Methoden zur empirischen Forschung in der Gruppenpsychotherapie. Ein Handbuch*. [Methods on the empirical research in group psychotherapy.] Opladen: Westdeutscher Verlag, pp. 345–359.

Ahlin G (2019) The group-analytic group matrix concept. *Group-Analytic Contexts*. 84(2). Available at: https://groupanalyticsociety.co.uk/contexts/issue-84/ga-concepts-and-methods/the-group-analytic-group-matrix-concept (accessed 6 February 2025).

Ahlin G, Sandahl C, Herlitz K and Brimberg I (1996) Developing the Matrix Representation Grid (MRG): A method of observing group processes. Findings from time-limited group psychotherapy for alcohol dependent patients. *Group*. 20(2): 145–173.

Aitken M, Haltigan JD Szatmari P, Dubicka B, Fonagy P, Kelvin R, Midgley N, Reynolds S, Wilkinson PO and Goodyer IM (2020) Toward precision therapeutics: General and specific factors differentiate symptom change in depressed adolescents. *The Journal of Child Psychology & Psychiatry*. 61(9): 998–1008. https://doi.org/10.1111/jcpp.13194.

Aiyegbusi A (2021a) The white mirror: Face to face with racism in group analysis Part 1. Mainly practice. *Group Analysis*. 54(1): 421–436.

Aiyegbusi A (2021b) The white mirror: Face to face with racism in group analysis Part 2. Mainly theory. *Group Analysis*. 54(3): 402–420.

Akbarzadeh Baghban A, Younespour S, Jambarsang S, Yousefi M, Zayeri F and Azizi Jalilian F (2013a) How to test normality distribution for a variable: a real example and a simulation study. *Archives of Advances in Biosciences*. 4(1). https://doi.org/10.22037/jps.v4i1.3974.

Akbarzadeh Baghban A, Younespour S, Jambarsang S, Yousefi M, Zayeri F and Azizi Jalilian F (2013b) How to test normality distribution for a variable: a real example and a simulation study. *Journal of Paramedical Sciences*. 4(1): 73–77. https://journals.sbmu.ac.ir/index.php/aab/article/view/3974/3551

Al-Amudi I and O'Mahoney J (2016) Ontology. Philosophical discussion and implications for organization studies. In Raza M, Willmott H and Greenwood M (Eds.) *The Routledge Companion to Philosophy in Organizational Studies*. New York: Routledge & Francis Taylor, pp. 15–32.

Alaszewski A (2006) *Using Diaries for Social Research*. London: Sage.

Alexander F (2017) *The Role of the Diary Today's Diary Is Tomorrow's History*. Available at: https://lifestoriesdiary.com/about-june/the-role-of-the-diary/ (accessed 4 November 2023).

Ali R (2023) The values of the virtual world. *Journal of Applied Philosophy*. 40(2): 231–245.

Alldredge CT, Burlingame GM, Yang C and Rosendahl J (2021) Alliance in group therapy. A meta-analysis. *Group Dynamics Theory, Research, and Practice*. 25(1): 13–28. https://doi.org/10.1037/gdn0000135.

ALLEA (ALL European Academies) (2023) *The European Code of Conduct for Research Integrity*. Revised Edition. Berlin: Allea. https://allea.org/research-integrity-and-research-ethics/

Allmark P and Machaczek K (2018) Realism and pragmatism in a mixed methods study. *Journal of Advanced Nursing*. 74(6): 1301–1309.

Althusser L (1969) *For Marx*. Harmondsworth: Penguin.

Alves H, Gibbs L, Marinkovic K, Brito I and Sheikhattari P (2022) Children and adolescents' voices and the implications for ethical research. *Childhood*. 29(1): 126–143.

Alvesson M (2002) *Postmodernism and Social Research. Understanding Social Research*. Milton Keynes: Open University Press.

Alvesson M and Skőldberg K (2009a) (Post-)positivism, social constructionism, neorealism. Three reference points in the philosophy of science. In Alvesson M and Skőldberg K (Eds.) *Reflexive Methodology. New Vistas for Qualitative Research*. 2nd Edition. London: Sage Publications Ltd., pp. 15–52.

Alvesson M and Skőldberg K (2009b) Critical theory. The political and ideological dimension. In Alvesson M and Skőldberg K (Eds.) *Reflexive Methodology. New Vistas for Qualitative Research*. 2nd Edition. London: Sage Publications Ltd., pp. 144–178.

Alvesson M and Skőldberg K (2009c) *Reflexive Methodology. New Vistas for Qualitative Research*. 2nd Edition. London: Sage Publications Ltd.

Amaral MM (2024) *The Quantum Legacy of Paul Dirac: Spin, Antimatter, and the Evolution of the Scientific Method*. Available at: https://medium.com/marcelomarcielamaral/the-quantum-legacy-of-paul-dirac-spin-antimatter-and-the-evolution-of-the-scientifc-method-774c2e5f874e (accessed 7 January 2025).

American Physical Society (2025) *This Month in Physics History. January 2025: Wolfgang Pauli Announces the Exclusion Principle*. Available at: https://www.aps.org/archives/publications/apsnews/200701/history.cfm (accessed 1 February 2025).

Ames RT (1989) Putting the Te back into Taoism. In Callicott JB and Ames RT (Eds.) *Nature in Asian Thought. Essays in Environmental Philosophy*. New York: State University of New York Press, pp. 113–144.

Ames RT and Takeuchi Y (2024) *Nishida Kitaro*. Encyclopedia Britannica. 13 June. https://www.britannica.com/biography/Nishida-Kitaro

Andersen LL (2018) Psychoanalytic ethnography. In Stamenova K and Hinshelwood RD (Eds.) *Methods of Research into the Unconscious. Applying Psychoanalytic Ideas to Social Science*. London and New York: Routledge, pp. 241–255.

Anderson A (2023) The moral and political challenges of Hartmut Rosa's theory of resonance. *The Journal of Chinese Sociology*. 10: 6. https://doi.org/10.1186/s40711-023-00182-9.

Anderson D (2011) Group analysis and dementia. Reflections on conducting an Analytic Space. *Group Analysis*. 44(4): 385–394.

Anderson D (2019) Group analysis as a research method: Reflexivity, discourse, textuality and ethics. *Special Issue on Group Psychotherapy*. 64: 57–77. The British Psychological Society. Psychotherapy Section Review. https://doi.org/10.53841/bpspsr.2019.1.64.57.

Anderson D (2021) *The Body of the Group: Sexuality and Gender in Group Analysis*. London: Karnac.

Anderson L (2006) Analytic autoethnography. *Journal of Contemporary Ethnography*. 35(4): 373–395.

Andrade C (2020) Mean difference, standardized mean difference (SMD) and their use in meta-analysis: As simple as it gets. *Journal of Clinical Psychiatry*. 81(5): 20f13681. https://doi.org/10.4088/JCP.20f13681.

Andrews K, Ross D and Maroney T (2024) Online group psychotherapy. A systematic review. *Community Mental Health Journal.* 60(8): 1511–1531. Available at: https://link.springer.com/article/10.1007/s10597-024-01304-4.

Anme T (2004) *Group Interview Method: The Development of Qualitative Research Methods Based on Scientific Evidence.* Tokyo: Isiyaku Publications.

Antichi L, Giannini M and Loscalzo Y (2022) Interpretation in psychodynamic psychotherapy: A systematic review. *Psychodynamic Practice.* 28(3): 254–274.

Anyanwu KC and Ruch EA (1981) *African Philosophy: An Introduction to the main philosophical trends in Contemporary Africa.* Rome: Catholic Book Agency.

APA (2013) *Diagnostic and Statistical Manual of Mental Disorders.* Washington, DC: American Psychiatric Association.

Arato A and Gebhardt E (Eds.) *The Essential Frankfurt School Reader.* New York: Continuum.

Argelès D (2011) "Das waren wir nicht!" The Image of East Germans and the GDR as a Narrative Problem after 1989 in Klaus Schlesinger's 'Die Sachem mit Randow'. In Rechtien R and Tate D (Eds.) *Twenty Years On.* London: Boydell & Brewer, Camden House, pp. 57–68.

Arias E and Anguera MT (2004) Detección de patrones de conducta comunicativa en un grupo terapéutico de adolescents. [Detection of communicative behavior patterns in a therapeutic group of adolescents.] *Acción Psicolőgia.* 3(3): 199–206. https://revistas.uned.es/index.php/accionpsicologica/article/view/513

Arias E and Anguera MT (2005) Análisis de la comunicación en un grupo terapéutico de adolescentesestudio diacrónico. [Analysis of communication in a therapeutic group of adolescents. A diachronic study.] *Revista de Psicolőgia y Salud Mental del Nino y del Adolescente.* 1: 25–36. https://dialnet.unirioja.es/revista/5667/A/2005

Arias-Pujol E and Anguera MT (2017) Observation of interactions in adolescent group therapy. A mixed methods study. *Frontiers in Psychology.* 24(8): 1188. https://doi.org/10.3389/fpsyg.2017.01188.

Arias-Pujol E and Anguera MT (2020) A mixed methods framework for psychoanalytic group therapy. From qualitative records to a quantitative approach using T-pattern, lag sequential, and polar coordinate analysis. *Frontiers in Psychology.* 11. https://doi.org/10.3389/fpsyg.2020.01922.

Armelius BA (1982) Group personality and group behavior. An expansion of bion's model. In Pines M and Rafaelsen L (Eds.) *The Individual and the Group.* Boston, MA: Springer, pp. 353–363.

Armelius BA and Kataja P (1980) *Developing a questionnaire for measuring work-emotionality on wards.* Research report. Department of Applied Psychology. Umea: Umea University. Cited in Karterud S (1989) A study of Bion's basic assumption groups. *Human Relations.* 42(4): 315–335. https://doi.org/10.1177/001872678904200403.

Armelius K and Armelius BA (1992) Group personality, task and group culture. In Pines M (Ed.) *Bion and Group Psychotherapy.* London: Tavistock/Routledge, pp. 255–273.

Armstrong D (1998) Introduction. In Lawrence WG (Ed.) *Social Dreaming at Work.* London: Karnac, pp. xvii–xxi.

Armstrong D (2005) *Organization in the Mind: Psychoanalysis, Group Relations, and Organizational Consultancy: Occasional Papers 1989–2003.* London: Karnac.

Arnberg FK, Linton SJ, Hulterantz M, Heintz E and Jonsson U (2014) Internet-delivered psychological treatments for mood and anxiety disorders. A systematic review of their efficacy, safety, and cost-effectiveness. *PLoS One.* 9(5): e98118. https://journals.plos.org/plosone/article?id=10.1371/journal.pone.0098118

Arndt H and Rose H (2023) Capturing life as it is truly lived? Improving diary data in educational research. *International Journal of Research & Method in Education.* 46(2): 175–186.

Arndt M and Hornberger K (2014) Testing the limits of quantum mechanical superpositions. *Nature Physics.* 10(4): 271–277.

Arnheim R (1971) *Entropy and Art: An Essay on Disorder and Order.* Berkeley: University of California Press.

Arnheim R (1981) The other Gustav Theodor Fechner. In Koch S and Leary DE (Eds.) *A Century of Psychology as Science.* Washington, DC: American Psychological Association, pp. 856–865.

Ashby W (1960) *Design for a Brain.* New York: Wiley & Sons.

Ashford C (2009) Queer theory, cyber ethnographies and researching online sexual environments. *Information & Communications Technology Review.* 18(3): 297–314. https://www.tandfonline.com/doi/full/10.1080/13600830903424734

Ashton A, Chadwick H and Panteliou E (2025) Asking the right questions: Developing a patient-reported outcome measure (PROM) specific to group analytic psychotherapy. *Group Analysis*. Online. https://doi.org/10.1177/05333164251335881.

Aspect A, Dalibard J and Roger G (1982) Experimental test of bell's inequalities using time-varying analyzers. *Physical Review Letters*. 49(25): 1804–1807.

Ast F (1807) *Grundriß einer Geschichte der Philosophie.* Landshut: Joseph Thomann. https://www.digitale-sammlungen.de/de/view/bsb10045092?page=5

Aśvaghosha (2003) *The Awakening of Faith. The Classic Exposition of Mahayana Buddhism.* New York: Dover Publications Inc. (attributed to Aśvaghosha translated by Hakeda, YS in 1967). https://archive.org/details/20200427-the-awakening-of-faith

Aśvaghosha (2008) *Life of the Buddha. Translated by Patrick Olivelle.* Series Clay Sanskrit Library. New York: New York University Press. https://nyupress.org/9780814762165/life-of-the-buddha/

ATA (2020) Spectrometry and Spectroscopy: What's The Difference? 17 January. Available at: https://atascientific.com.au/spectrometry/ (accessed 8 December 2024).

Atkin A (2023) *Peirce Theory of Signs*. The Stanford Encyclopedia of Philosophy. https://plato.stanford.edu/entries/peirce-semiotics/

Atkins S, Lewin S, Smith H, Engel M, Fretheim A and Volmink J (2008) Conducting a meta-ethnography of qualitative literature: Lessons learnt. *BMC Medical Research Methodology.* 8: 21. https://doi.org/10.1186/1471-2288-8-21.

Atkinson PA and Coffrey A (1997) Analysing documentary realities. In Silverman D (Ed.) *Qualitative Research. Theory, Method and Practice.* London: Sage, pp. 45–62.

Atmanspacher H and Fuchs CA (Eds.) (2014) *The Pauli-Jung Conjecture And Its Impact Today.* Exeter: Imprint Academic Publishers.

Atmanspacher H and Primas H (Eds.) (2009) Recasting Reality, *Proceedings of the Conference on "Wolfgang Pauli's Philosophical Ideas and Contemporary Science".* May 20–25, 2007, Monte Verita, Ascona, Switzerland. Berlin: Springer Verlag.

Aubel J (1994) *Guidelines for Studies Using the Group Interview Technique*. Geneva: International Labour Office. https://digitallibrary.un.org/record/150374?ln=en

Avdi E and Georgaca E (2007) Discourse analysis and psychotherapy: A critical review. *European Journal of Psychotherapy and Counselling.* 9(2): 157–176. https://doi.org/10.1080/13642530701363445.

Aveling EL, Gillespie A and Cornish F (2015) A qualitative method for analysing multivoicedness. *Qualitative Research.* 15(6): 670–687. https://doi.org/10.1177/1468794114557991.

Ávila LA and de Macedo CRM (2012) The 'Impossible' Group. An Experience of Long-term Group Analytic Psychotherapy for Autistic People. *Group Analysis.* 45(3): 310–324.

Aykroyd L (2019) *Fall of Berlin Wall Brought Curtain Down on GDR's Doping Program.* 9 November. Global Sport Matters. Cited in Cheng OL (2025) *How the Cheating of East and West Germany Reveals a Global Trend of Doping in International Sports.* https://pdxscholar.library.pdx.edu/younghistorians/2025/papers/22/. See also: https://www.doping-archiv.de/allgemein/deutschland-doping-geschichten/doping-in-der-ddr/ddr-doping-strafrechtliche-aufarbeitung/

Azu-Okeke O (1993) Conflict in the search of an individual self as opposed to a traditional group self. A consequence of undertaking group-analytic training. *Group Analysis.* 26(3): 261–268.

Baaquie BE and Martin F (2005) Quantum psyche. Quantum field theory of the human psyche. *NeuroQuantology.* 3(1): 7–42. https://www.neuroquantology.com/open-access/Quantum+Psyche+Quantum+Field+Theory+of+the+Human+Psyche_554/

Baars BJ (1988) *A Cognitive Theory of Consciousness.* New York: Cambridge University Press.

Baart A and Roos V (2022) An analytic tool for visual data analysis. Application to the Mmogo-method R. *International Journal of Qualitative Methods.* 21. https://doi.org/10.1177/16094069221135962.

Babchuk WA (2009) Grounded theory for practice-based application "Closing the embarrassing gap between theory and empirical research. In Truty D (Ed.) *Proceedings of the 28th Annual Midwest*

Research Research-to-Practice Conference in Adult Continuing, and Community Education. Chicago: Illinois University Press, pp. 21–23. https://www.researchgate.net/publication/320353483_Grounded_theory_for_practice-based_applicationClosing_the_embarrassing_gap_between_theory_and_empirical_research

Babchuk WA (2011) Grounded theory as a "family of methods": A genealogical analysis to guide research. *US-China Education Review.* 1(3): 383–388. https://eric.ed.gov/?id=ED524803

Bacha CS (2017) Neuroscience and the social unconscious. *Group Analysis.* 50(4): 502–518.

Bacha CS (2018) Response to "everybody needs a group. A qualitative study looking at therapists' views of the role of psychotherapy groups in working with older people with dementia and complex needs". *Group Analysis.* 51(1): 102–109.

Bacha CS (2025) *The Group Dimension.* London: Karnac.

Baezley A (2023) My first experience of group analysis. *Group Analysis.* 56(4): 527–540.

Bailey AH, LaFrance M and Dovidio JF (2018) Is man the measure of all things? A social cognitive account of androcentrism. *Personality and Social Psychology Review.* 23(4): 307–331. https://doi.org/10.1177/1088868318782848 (original work published 2019).

Bainbridge R (2007) Autoethnography in Indigenous research contexts: The value of inner knowing. *Journal of Australian Indigenous Issues.* 10(2): 54–64. https://eprints.jcu.edu.au/10844/

Baker E, Burlingame GM, Cox, JC, Beecher ME and Gleave RL (2013) The group readiness questionnaire. A convergent validity analysis. *Group Dynamics. Theory, Research, and Practice.* 17(4): 299–314.

Bakhtin M (1971) *Rabelais and His World.* Trans. H Iswolsky. 2nd Edition. Cambridge, MA: MIT Press.

Bakhtin M (1981) *The Dialogic Imagination. Four Essays.* Trans. C Emerson and M Holquist. Austin: University of Texas Press.

Bakhtin M (1984) *Problems of Dostoevsky's Poetics. Theory and History of Literature. Volume 8.* Manchester: Manchester University Press.

Bakhtin M (1986) *Speech Genres and Other Late Essays.* Austin: University of Texas Press.

Bakhtin M (1990) *Art and Answerability.* Austin, TX: University of Texas Press.

Bakhtin M and Medvedev P (1978) *The Formal Method in Literary Scholarship.* Baltimore, MD: John Hopkins University Press.

Balbier U (2005) *Kalter Krieg auf der Aschenbahn. Deutsch-deutscher Sport, 1950–1972. [Cold War on the Tracks. German-German Sport, 1950–1972].* Paderborn: Schönigh. ISBN 978-3-506-75616-9.

Bales RF (1950) *Interaction Process Analysis. A Method for the Study of Small Groups.* Cambridge: Addison-Wesley.

Balint E (1979) The Balint Group approach. *Journal of the Royal Society of Medicine.* 72(6): 469–471.

Balint M (1964) *The Doctor, his Patient and the Illness.* London: Pitman Medical. https://archive.org/details/doctorhispatient0000bali_b6r0

Ballhausen-Scharf B and Rudnitzki G (2000) The group conductor and group research. ethical, conceptual and technical problems. *Group Analysis.* 33(4): 469–483.

Bamber J (1988) Grup analysis with children and adolescents. *Group Analysis.* 21(2): 99–180.

Banaji MR, Lemm KM and Carpenter SJ (2004) The social unconscious. In Brewer MB and Hewstone M (Eds.) *Social Cognition.* Oxford: Blackwell Publishing, pp. 28–53.

Banbury A, Nancarrow S, Dart J, Gray L and Parkinson L (2018) Telehealth interventions, delivering home-based support group videoconferencing. Systematic review. *Journal of Medical Internet Research.* 20(2): e25. https://doi.org/10.2196/jmir.8090.

Banerjee A, Chitnis UB, Jadhav SL, Bhawalkar JS and Chaudhury S (2009) Hypothesis testing, type I and type II errors. *Industrial Psychiatry Journal.* 18(2): 127–131. https://doi.org/10.4103/0972-6748.62274.

Banet AG and Hayden C (1977) The Tavistock primer. In Jones JE and Pfeiffer JW (Eds.) *The 1977 Annual Handbook for Group Facilitators.* San Diego, CA: University Associates, pp. 15–20.

Bannister D and Fransella F (1980) *Inquiring Man. The Psychology of Personal Constructs.* 2nd Edition. London: Penguin Books.

Bannister D and Fransella F (1993) *Inquiring Man. The Psychology of Personal Constructs.* 3rd Edition. London: Routledge.

Bannister D, Burman E, Parker I, Taylor M and Tindall C (1995) *Qualitative Methods in Psychology. A Research Guide.* Buckingham: Open University Press.

Banon E, Evan-Grenier, M and Bond M (2001) Early transference interventions with male patients in psychotherapy. *Journal of Psychotherapy Practice and Research.* 10(2): 79–92. https://pmc.ncbi.nlm.nih.gov/articles/PMC3330640/

Banzi R, Moja L, Pistotti V, Facchini A and Liberati A (2011) Conceptual frameworks and empirical approaches used to assess the impact of health research: An overview of reviews. *Health Research Policy and Systems.* 9: 26. https://doi.org/10.1186/1478-4505-9-26.

Barad K (2007) *Meeting the Universe Halfway. Quantum Physics and the Entanglement of Matter and Meaning.* London: Duke University Press.

Barad K (2014) Diffracting diffraction. Cutting-together-apart. *Parallax.* 20(3): 168–187. https://doi.org/10.1080/13534645.2014.927623.

Barkham M and Margison F (2007) Practice-based evidence as a complement to evidence-based practice: from dichotomy to chiasmus. In Freeman C and Power M (Eds.) *Handbook of Evidence-Based Psychotherapy. A Guide for Research and Practice.* Chichester: John Wiley & Sons, pp. 443–476.

Barkham M and Mellor-Clark J (2000) Rigour and relevance. The role of practice-based evidence in the psychological therapies. In Rowland N and Goss S (Eds.) *Evidence-based Counselling and Psychological Therapies. Research and Applications.* London: Routledge, pp. 127–144.

Barkham M and Mellor-Clark J (2003) Bridging evidence-based practice and practice-based evidence: Developing rigorous and relevant knowledge for psychological therapies. *Journal of Clinical Psychology and Psychotherapy.* 10(6): 319–327.

Barkham M, Evans C, Margison F, McGrath G, Mellor-Clark J, Milne D and Connell J (1998) The rationale for developing and implementing core batteries in service settings and psychotherapy outcome research. *Journal of Mental Health.* 7(1): 35–47. https://doi.org/10.1080/09638239818328.

Barkham M, Hardy GE and Startup M (1996) The IIP-32: a short version of the inventory of interpersonal problems. *British Journal of Clinical Psychology.* 35(1): 21–35. https://doi.org/10.1111/j.2044-8260.1996.tb01159.x.

Barkham M, Lutz W and Castonguay LG (2021) *Bergin and Garfield's Handbook of Psychotherapy and Behavior Change.* 7th Edition. Hoboken, NJ: John Wiley & Sons.

Barkowski S, Schwartze D, Strauss B, Burlingame GM and Rosendahl J (2020) Efficacy of group psychotherapy for anxiety disorders: A systematic review and meta-analysis. *Psychotherapy Research.* 30(8): 965–982.

Barla J (2021) Beyond reflexivity and representation: diffraction as a methodological sensitivity in science studies. *Distinktion. Journal of Social Theory.* 24(3): 444–466. https://doi.org/10.1080/1600910X.2021.1934506.

Barlow SH (2013) *Specialty Competencies in Group Psychology.* New York: Oxford University Press.

Barlow SH (2014) The history of group counselling and psychotherapy. In DeLucia-Waack, JL, Kalodner CR and Riva MT (Eds.) *Handbook of Counselling and Psychotherapy.* 2nd Edition. Thousand Oaks, CA: Sage, pp. 3–23.

Barnard A (2018) Well-being, more than a dream: women constructing metaphors of strength. *Frontiers in Psychology.* 9: 1186. https://doi.org/10.3389/fpsyg.2018.01186.

Barnard D (2024) History of VR. *Timeline of Events and Tech Development.* Virtual Speech. 17 October. Available at: https://virtualspeech.com/blog/history-of-vr (accessed 18 November 2024).

Barnes BR (2018) Decolonising research methodologies. Opportunity and caution. *South African Journal of Psychology.* 28(3): 379–387.

Barnes BR, Ernst S and Hyde K (1999) *An Introduction to Groupwork. A Group-Analytic Perspective.* Basingstoke: Palgrave MacMillan.

Barnhart MG (1992) Hisamatsu's oriental nothingness. Ultimate reality and meaning from a zen perspective. *Ultimate Reality and Meaning.* 15(1): 20–35. https://doi.org/10.3138/uram.15.1.20

Baron RM and Kenny DA (1986) The moderator-mediator variable distinction in social psychological research. Conceptual, strategic, and statistical considerations. *Journal of Personality and Social Psychology.* 51(6): 1173–1182. https://doi.org/10.1037/0022-3514.51.6.1173.

Barrett D and Heale R (2020) What are Delphi studies? *British Medical Journal.* 23(3): 68–69.

Barrett JA and Byrne P (2012) *The Everett Interpretation of Quantum Mechanics. Collected Works 1855–1980 with Commentary.* Princeton, NJ: Princeton University Press.

Barroga E and Matanguihan GJ (2022) A practical guide to writing quantitative and qualitative research questions and hypotheses in scholarly articles. *Journal of Korean Medical Science*. 37(16): e121. https://doi.org/10.3346/jkms.2022.37.e121.

Barrow JM, Brannan GD and Khandhar PB (2022) *Research Ethics*. In StatPearls [Internet]. Treasure Island, Florida: StatPearls Publishing. Available at: https://www.ncbi.nlm.nih.gov/books/NBK459281 (accessed 26 September 2024).

Barthes R (1973) *Mythologies*. Trans. A Levers. London: Granada.

Bartlett R and Milligan C (2015) *What Is Diary Method? What Is Research Methods Series*. London: Bloomsbury.

Barwick N (2018) 'I am not a philosopher?' A response to Vic Schermer's 'Four modalities of the experience of others in groups. *Group Analysis*. 51(2): 211–221.

Barwick N and Weegmann M (2018) *Group Therapy: A Group-Analytic Approach*. London: Routledge.

Bass A (2003) Translator's introduction. In Derrida J (Ed.) *Writing and Difference*. New York: Routledge, pp. ix–xxviii.

Bateman AW (2004) Psychoanalytically oriented day hospital treatment for borderline personality disorder: Theory, problems, and practice. In Richardson P, Kächele H and Renlund C (Eds.) *Research on Psychoanalytic Psychotherapy with Adults*. London: Karnac, pp. 109–132.

Baumeister RF and Leary MR (1995) The need to belong. Desire for interpersonal attachments as a fundamental human motivation. *Psychological Bulletin*. 117(3): 57–89.

Bayne T, Frohlich J, Cusack R, Moser J and Naci L (2023) Consciousness in the cradle. On the emergence of infant experience. *Trends in Cognitive Sciences*. 27(12): 1135–1149.

Bea N (n.d.) *Buddhism. The Way of Emptiness. True Emptiness, Wondrous Being*. Blog. Available at: https://buddhism-thewayofemptiness.blog.nomagic.uk/nishida-kitaro-1870-1945/ (accessed 7 April 2024).

Beaudreaux MJ, Ozer DJ, Oltmanns TF and Wright GC (2018) Development and validation of the circumplex scales of interpersonal problems. *Psychological Assessment*. 30(5): 594–609. htpps://doi.org/10.1037/pas0000505

Bechelli LPC (1988) Terapia de grupo en consultório. [Group Therapy in Group Private Practice.] Revista *Brasileiro de Psiquiatria*. 37(7): 251–255. https://pesquisa.bvsalud.org/portal/resource/pt/lil-61934

Bechelli LPC and Santos MA (2002) Psicoterapia de grupo e considerações sobre o paciente como agente da própria mudança. [Group Psychotherapy and Considerations concerning the patient as an agent for his own change.] *Revista Latino-Americana de Enfermagem*. 10(3): 383–391. https://doi.org/10.1590/S0104-11692002000300012.

Bechelli LPC and Santos MA (2004) Psicoterapia de grupo. Como surgui e evolulu. *Revista Latino-Americana de Enfermagem*. [Group Psychotherapy. How it emerged and evolved.] 12(2): 242–249. https://www.scielo.br/j/rlae/i/2004.v12n2/ https://doi.org/10.1590/S0104-11692004000200014.

Bechelli LPC and Santos MA (2005) O terapeuta na psicoterapia de grupo. *Revista Latino-Americana de Enfermagem*. 13(2): 249–254. [The therapist in Group Psychotherapy.] https://doi.org/10.1590/S0104-11692005000200018.

Bechelli LPC and Santos MA (2006) Transferência e psicoterapia de grupo. *Revista Latino-Americana de Enfermagem*. 14(1): 110–117. [Transference and Group Psychotherapy.] https://www.researchgate.net/publication/26427171_Transferencia_e_psicoterapia_de_grupo; https://doi.org/10.1590/S0104-11692006000100015.

Beck AT (1978) *Depression Inventory*. Philadelphia, PA: Center for Cognitive Therapy.

Beck AT, Epstein N, Brown G and Steer RA (1988) An inventory for measuring clinical anxiety. Psychometric properties. *Journal of Consulting and Clinical Psychology*. 56(6): 893–897. https://doi.org/10.1037//0022-006x.56.6.893.

Beck AT, Steer A and Brown GK (1996) *Manual for Beck Depression Inventory-II*. San Antonio, TX: Psychological Corporation.

Becker A (2019) *What Is Real? The Unfinished Quest For The Meaning Of Quantum Physics*. London: Clays Ltd.

Becker A (2022) What Is Spacetime Really Made Of? *Scientific American*. 1 February. Available at: https://www.scientificamerican.com/article/what-is-spacetime-really-made-of/ (accessed 8 October 2024).

Becker GK (1992) In search for the ultimate reflections on methodology in URAM research and Asian studies. *Ultimate Reality and Meaning.* 15(1): 77–88. https://doi.org/10.3138/uram.15.1.7.
Becker W (2003) *Goodbye, Lenin!* Hollywood, LA: Sony Pictures Classics.
Beckhard R (1969) *Organization Development: Strategies and Models.* Reading, MA: Addison-Wesley.
Bedeian AG (2014) "More than meets the eye": A guide to interpreting the descriptive statistics and correlation matrices reported in management research. *Academy of Management Learning & Education.* 13(1): 121–135.
Bedwell C, McGowan L and Lavender T (2012) Using diaries to explore midwives' experiences in intrapartum care: An evaluation of the method in a phenomenological study. *Midwifery.* 28(2): 150–155.
Behr H (2011) Why is the past important in group analysis? *Group Analysis.* 44(4): 454–465.
Behr H and Hearst L (2005) *Group Analytic Psychotherapy: A Meeting of Minds.* London: Whurr Publishers.
Beitmann B (2022) *Meaningful Coincidences: How and Why Synchronicity and Serendipity Happen.* Rochester, Vermont: Park Street Press.
Belinkoff J, Bross R and Stein A (1964) The effect of group psychotherapy on anaclitic transference. *International Journal of Group Psychotherapy.* 14(4): 474–481. https://doi.org/10.1080/00207284.1964.11642786.
Bell EE (2006) Infusing race into the discourse of action research. In Reason P and Bradbury H (Eds.) *Handbook of Action Research: Participative Inquiry and Practice.* Thousand Oaks, CA: Sage, pp. 48–58.
Bell JS (1964) On the Einstein Podolsky Rosen paradox. *Physics.* 1(3): 195–200. https://doi.org/10.1103/PhysicsPhysiqueFizika.1.195.
Bell JS (1989) Quantum mechanics for cosmologists. In Bell JS (Ed.) *Speakable and Unspeakable in Quantum Mechanics. Collected Papers on Quantum Philosophy*. 2nd Edition. Cambridge: Cambridge University Press, pp. 117–138.
Bell JS (2004) *Speakable and Unspeakable in Quantum Mechanics. Collected Papers on Quantum Philosophy.* 2nd Edition. Cambridge: Cambridge University Press.
Bell N (2008) Ethics in child research: Rights, reason and responsibilities. *Children's Geographies.* 6(1): 7–20. https://doi.org/10.1080/14733280701791827.
Bell S and Morse S (2013) An approach to comparing eternal and internal methods for analyzing group dynamic. *Group Dynamics, Theory Research, and Practice.* 17(4): 281–289.
Beller S and Bender A (2017) Theory, the final frontier? A corpus-based analysis of the role of theory in psychological articles. *Frontiers in Psychology.* 8: 951. https://doi.org/10.3389/fpsyg.2017.00951.
Bellhouse DR (2004) The reverend Thomas Bayes, FRS. A biography to celebrate the tercentenary of his birth. *Statistical Science.* 19(1): 3–43. https://doi.org/ 10.1214/088342304000000189 https://projecteuclid.org/journals/statistical-science/volume-19/issue-1/The-Reverend-Thomas-Bayes-FRS—A-Biography-to-Celebrate/10.1214/088342304000000189.full
Benet-Martínez V and Haritatos J (2005) Bicultural identity integration (BII): Components and psychosocial antecedents. *Journal of Personality*. 73(4): 1015–1050.
Benjamin R (2019) *Race After Technology. Abolitionist Tools for the New Jim Code.* Cambridge, MA: Polity Press.
Benkenstein H, Kirchner R and Seidler C (Hrsg.) (1995) *Die Gruppe: eine verlorene Utopie? Gruppenpsychotherapie im Ost-West-Dialog.* [The Group a lost Utopia? Group Psychotherapy in the East-West Dialogue.] Lengerich: Pabst.
Bennett M (2019) A Review of the literature on the benefits and drawbacks of participatory action research. *First Peoples Child & Family Review.* 14(1): 109–122.
Bentley SV, Greenaway KH, Haslam SA, Cruwys T, Steffens NK, Haslam C and Cull B (2020) Social identity mapping online. *Journal of Personality and Social Psychology.* 118(2): 213–241. https://doi.org/10.1037/pspa0000174.
Benveniste E (1971) *Problems in General Linguistics.* Trans. ME Meek. Coral Gables, FL: University of Miami Press.
Beradt C (1968) *The Third Reich of Dreams. Trans. A. Gottwald.* With an Essay by Bruno Bettelheim. Chicago, IL: Quadrangle Books.

Berelson B (1952) *Content Analysis in Communicative Research.* New York: Free Press.

Berendse GJ (2021) *Echoes of Surrealism. Challenging Socialist Realism in East German Literature, 1945–1990.* New York: Berghahn Books.

Berg BL (2001) *Qualitative Research Methods for the Social Sciences.* 4th Edition. Boston, MA: Allyn & Bacon.

Bergdahl E (2019) Is meta-synthesis turning rich descriptions into thin reductions? A criticism of meta-aggregation as form of qualitative synthesis. *Nursing Inquiry.* 26(1): e12273. https://doi.org/10.1111/nin.12273.

Berger PL and Luckmann T (1966) *The Social Construction of Reality. A Treatise in the Sociology of Knowledge.* New York: Anchor Books.

Berlin HA (2011) The neural basis of the dynamic unconscious. *Neuropsychoanalysis.* 13(1): 5–31. https://doi.org/10.1080/15294145.2011.10773654.

Berlin HA and Montgomery J (2017) Neural basis of intrapsychic and unconscious conflict and repetition compulsion. In Christian C, Eagle MN and Wolitzky DL (Eds.) *Psychoanalytic Perspectives on Conflict.* New York: Routledge, chapter 16, pp. 260–277.

Bernard L (2018) *L'Interprétation sociologique des rêves*, [*The sociological interpretation of dreams.*] Paris: La Découverte.

Bernard W (1946) Freud and Spinoza. *Psychiatry.* 9(2): 99–108. https://doi.org/10.1080/00332747.1946.11022590.

Bernasconi R (1997a) Philosophy's paradoxical parochialism. The reinvention of philosophy as Greek. In Ansell-Pearson, K, Parry B and Squires J (Eds.) *Cultural Readings of Imperialism: Edward Said and the Gravity of History*. London: Lawrence and Wishart, pp. 212–226.

Bernasconi R (1997b) African philosophy's challenge to continental philosophy. In Eze EC (Ed.) *Postcolonial African Philosophy: A Critical Reader.* Cambridge, MA: Blackwell Publishers, pp. 183–196.

Bernasconi R (2021) Race, Philosophy, and Political Thought. Dialogue with Owen Williams, Sharon Achinstein, Charles W Mill, Jennifer I Morgan, Robert Bernasconi. 21 June 2021. Transcript. A Folger Institute Fiftieth Anniversary Project. Supported by the Mellon Initiative in Collaborative Research. Available at: www.youtube.com (Critical Race Conversations). https://www.youtube.com/watch?v=3PkIYdkEjdY

Bernasconi R, Gines K and Taylor P (2013) Critical Philosophy of Race Journal Launched. Available at: https://www.newappsblog.com/2013/03/critical-philosophy-of-race-journal-launched-html (accessed 24 December 2024).

Bernstein B (1971) On the classification and framing of educational knowledge. In Hopper E (Ed.) *Readings in the Theory of Educational Systems*. London: Hutchinson University Library, pp. 184–209.

Berry M (2024) Paul Dirac: The purest soul in physics. *Physical World.* 1 February 1998. Available at: https://physicsworld.com/a/paul-dirac-the-purest-soul-in-physics/ (accessed 7 January 2025).

Berzon B, Pious C and Parson R (1963) The therapeutic event in group psychotherapy. A study of subjective reports by group members. *Journal of Individual Psychology*. 19(2): 204–212.

Bessarab D (2015) Editorial. Changing how and what we do: The significance of embedding aboriginal and Torres strait islander ways of knowing, being, and doing in social work education and practice. *Australian Social Work.* 68(1): 1–4. http://dx.doi.org/10.1080/0312407X.2015.973475.

Beveridge A (2023) An historical overview of psychodynamic psychotherapy. In Graham P (Series Ed.) *Cambridge Guide to Psychodynamic Psychotherapy. Cambridge Guides To The Psychological Therapies.* Cambridge: Cambridge University Press, pp. 1–17.

Bhambra GK (2017) Brexit, Trump, and 'methodological whiteness. On the misrecognition of race and class. *The British Journal of Sociology*. 68(S1): 214–234.

Bhandari P (2022) *Mediator vs Moderator Variables. Differences & Examples*. 4 May. Available at: https://www.scribbr.co.uk/research-methods/mediator-vs-moderator-variables/ (accessed 27 November 2023).

Bhaskar R (1975) *A Realist Theory of Science.* Brighton: Harvester Press.

Bhaskar R (1986) *Scientific Realism and Human Emancipation.* London: Verso.

Bhaskar R (1989) *Reclaiming Reality.* London: Verso.

Bhaskar R (1998) Facts and values: Theory and practice. In Archer M, Bhaskar R, Collier A, Lawson T and Norrie A (Eds.) *Critical Realism. Essential Readings.* Abingdon: Routledge, pp. 409–417.

Bhatia A, Appelbaum PS and Wisner KL (2021) Unblinding in randomized controlled trials. A research ethics case. *Ethics & Human Research.* 43(2): 28–34.

Bhopal K (2022) Academics of colour in elite universities in the UK and the USIhe 'unspoken system of exclusion'. *Studies in Higher Education.* 47(11): 2127–2137.

Biermann W (1976) *Und als wir ans Ufer kamen. Das Kölner Konzert.* 13 November 1976. [And when we got to the shore. The Concert in Cologne 13 November 1976.]. Available at: https://www.jpc.de/jpcng/poprock/detail/-/art/Wolf-Biermann-Das-Kőlner-Konzert-13-November-1976/hnum/1490292 (accessed 12 March 2022) https://youtu.be/GSw5H4tY29A?si=zsbVclYIPekLbhdU

Biesta G (2010) Pragmatism and the philosophical foundations of mixed methods research. In Tashakkori A and Teedlie C (Eds.) *Sage Handbook of Mixed Methods in Social & Behavioral Research.* 2nd Edition. Thousand Oaks, CA: Sage, pp. 95–117.

Biesta G (2024) Mixed methods research and deweyan pragmatism reconsidered. In Shan Y (Ed.) *Philosophical Foundations of Mixed Methods Research. Dialogues between Researchers and Philosophers.* New York: Routledge, pp. 171–193.

Bignell J 1997) *Media Semiotics. An Introduction.* Manchester: Manchester University Press.

Billow RM (2003) *Relational Group Psychotherapy. From Basic Assumptions to Passion.* London: Jessica Kingsley Publications.

Billow RM (2015) It's all about me. Introduction to relational group psychotherapy. In Kleinberg JL (Ed.) *The Wiley Blackwell Handbook of Group Psychotherapy.* Oxford: Wiley Blackwell, pp. 169–185.

Billow RM (2017a) Relational group psychotherapy. An overview. Part 1: Foundational principles and practices. *Group Analysis.* 50(1): 6–22.

Billow RM (2017b) Relational group psychotherapy. An overview. Part 2: Relational models of group process. *Group Analysis.* 50(2): 135–158.

Billow RM (2017c) Relational group psychotherapy. An overview. Part 3: Modes of therapeutic leadership *Group Analysis.* 50(3): 293–313.

Binney G, Wilke G and Williams C (2012) *Living leadership. A practical guide for ordinary heroes.* London: Pearson.

Bion WR (1946) The leaderless group project. *Bulletin of the Menninger Clinic.* 10(3): 77–81.

Bion WR (1948a) Paper on Advances in Group and Individual Therapy read at the International Congress on Mental Health 3, London 11–14 August 1948. In *Proceedings of the International Conference on Medical Psychotherapy.* New York: Columbia University Press, pp. 106–109. (Referred to by Karnac H (2008) *Bion's Legacy. Bibliography of Primary and Secondary Sources of the Life, Work and Ideas of Wilfred Rubrecht Bion.* London: Karnc; Reprinted in 2018 by Routledge).

Bion WR (1948b) Psychiatry in a time of crisis. *British Journal of Medical Psychology.* 21(2): 81–89.

Bion WR (1959/2013) Attacks on linking. *The Psychoanalytic Quarterly.* 82(2): 285–300. https://www.tandfonline.com/doi/abs/10.1002/j.2167-4086.2013.00029.x.

Bion WR (1961) *Experiences in Groups. An Other Papers.* London: Tavistock Publications Ltd. [Published in 2004 by Frances and Taylor e-book].

Bion WR (1962a) *Learning from Experience.* London: William Heinemann Medical Books Ltd.

Bion WR (1962b) The Psycho-analytic theory of thinking. *International Journal of Psychoanalysis.* 43(5): 306–310.

Bion WR (1963) *Elements of Psychoanalysis.* London: William Heinemann Medical Books Ltd. [Republished 1984 by Karnac; Reprinted in 2018 by Routledge].

Bion WR (1965) *Transformations: Change from Learning to Growth.* London: William Heinemann Medical Books Ltd. [Republished 1984 by Karnac; Republished by Routledge 2018].

Bion WR (1967) *Second Thoughts. Selected Papers on Psycho-Analysis.* London: William Heinemann Medical Books Ltd. [Published 1984 by Karnac; Reprinted 2018 by Routledge].

Bion WR (1970) *Attention and Interpretation: A scientific Approach to Insight in Psycho-Analysis and Groups. The International Behavioural and Social Sciences Library.* London: Classics from the Tavistock Press. [Reprinted 2001 by Routledge].

Bion WR (1997) *Taming Wild Thoughts.* (Foreword Parthenope Bion Talamo, Introduction Francesca Bion). London: Karnac Books. [Republished by 2018 Routledge].

Birchmore T (2015a) Group analytic concepts: Resonance. *Group Analysis*. *48*(2_suppl): 59–63. https://doi.org/10.1177/0533316415583262l.

Birchmore T (2015b) Group analytic concepts: Mirroring. *Group Analysis*. *48*(1_suppl): 57–60. https://doi.org/10.1177/0533316415569661k.

Birks M and Mills J (2015) *Grounded Theory: A Practical Guide*. London: Sage.

Black AE and Wright EL (2024) Modern psychoanalytic group therapy online: Adaptation of theory and technique. In Weinberg H, Rolnick A and Leighton A (Eds.) *The Virtual Group Therapy Circle. Advances in Online Group Theory and Practice.* New York: Routledge, pp. 89–100.

Blackmore C, Beecroft, C, Parry G, Booth A, Tantam D, Chambers E, Simpson E, Roberts E and Saxon D (2009) *A Systematic Review of the Efficacy and the Effectiveness of Group Analysis/Group Analytic Psychotherapy.* Centre for Psychological Services Research, School of Health and Related Research, University of Sheffield, UK.

Blackmore C, Tantam D, Parry G and Chambers E (2012) Report on a systematic review of the efficacy and clinical effectiveness of group analysis and analytic/dynamic group psychotherapy. *Group Analysis*. 45(1): 46–69. https://doi.org/10.1177/0533316411424356.

Blackwell D (2002) Out of their class. Class, colonisation and resistance in analytic psychotherapy and group analysis. *Group Analysis.* 35(3): 367–380.

Blackwell D (2003) Colonialism and Globalization. A group analytic perspective. *Group Analysis.* 36(4): 445–462.

Blackwell D (2015) Group analysis, racism and youth and community work training: A response to David Woodger's article. *Group Analysis.* 48(1): 90–97.

Blackwell D (2018) Cultural transition, negation and the social unconscious. *Group Analysis.* 51(3): 304–314.

Blackwell D (2020) The impenetrable wall of whiteness. A response to Guilaine Kinouani. *Group Analysis.* 53(1): 92–101.

Blackwell D (2021) A history of the struggle against racism in the social unconscious of group analysis. *Group Analysis* 54: 1–17.

Blanco Furgeri L (Ed.) (2001) *The Technique of Group Treatment. The Collected Papers of Louis R. Ormont.* Madison, CT: Psychology Press.

Bland M (2015) Estimating mean and standard deviation from the sample size, three quartiles, minimum, and maximum. *International Journal of Statistics in Medical Research.* 4(1): 57–64. https://lifescienceglobal.com/pms/index.php/ijsmr/article/view/2688/1576

Blank G and Barnes RA (1998) *The Universal Machine. A Multimedia Introduction to Computing.* New York: McGraw Hill.

Blease CR, Lilienfeld SO and Kelley JM (2016) Evidence-based practice and psychological treatments: The imperatives of informed consent. *Frontiers in Psychology*. 7: 1170. https://doi.org/10.3389/fpsyg.2016.01170.

Bloch S and Crouch E (1985) *Therapeutic Factors in Group Psychotherapy.* Oxford: Oxford University Press.

Block J (1961a) An introduction to the Q-sort method of personality description. In Block J (Ed.) *The Q-Sort Method in Personality Assessment and Psychiatric Research.* Springfield, IL: Charles C Thomas Publisher, pp. 2–26. https://doi.org/10.1037/13141-001.

Block J (1961b) *The Q-Sort Method in Personality Assessment and Psychiatric Research.* Springfield, IL: Charles C Thomas Publisher.

Block J (2008) *Q-Sort in Character Appraisal: Encoding Subjective Impressions of Persons Quantitatively*. Washington: American Psychological Association. https://doi.org/10.1037/11748-000.

Block NJ, Flanagan OJ and Gűzeldere G (Eds.) (1997) *The Nature of Consciousness. Philosophical Debates.* Cambridge: MIT Press.

Blommaert J and Bulcaen C (2000) Critical discourse analysis. *Annual Review of Anthropology.* 29: 447–466. https://www.annualreviews.org/content/journals/10.1146/annurev.anthro.29.1.447

Bloor M, Frankland J, Thomas M and Hobson K (2001) *Focus Groups in Social Research.* Thousand Oaks, CA: Sage.

Blusiewicz T (2016) The Blueprint for the East German Kommerzielle Koordinierung, or How the Stasi read Capitalism 2.0. *Cornell University*. 30 September. Available at: https://hoc.ilr.cornell.edu (accessed 4 April 2023).

Bo S, Sharp C, Beck E, Pedersen J, Gondan M and Simonsen E (2017) First empirical evaluation of outcomes for mentalization-based group therapy for adolescents with BPD. *Personality Disorders. Theory, Research, and Treatment*. 8(4): 396–401. https://doi.org/10.1037/per0000210.

Boateng GO, Neilands TB, Frongillo EA, Melgar-Quiñonez HR and Young SL (2018) Best practices for developing and validating scales for health, social, and behavioral research: a primer. *Frontiers in Public Health*. 6: 149. https://doi.org/10.3389/fpubh.2018.00149.

Bøgwald KP, Høglend P and Sørbye Ø (1999) Measurement of transference interpretations. *The Journal of Psychotherapy Practice & Research.* 8(4): 264–273.

Bohm D (1986) *Wholeness and the Implicate Order.* London: Ark.

Bohm D (1996) *On Dialogue. David Bohm.* Ed. L Nichol. New York: Routledge.

Böhme W (Hg.) (1973) *Kleines Politisches Wörterbuch.* [Short Political Dictionary]. Berlin: Dietz Verlag.

Bohnsack E (2013) Dokumentarische methode und die Logik der Praxis. [Documentary Method and the Logic of Practice]. In Lenger, A, Schneichert C and Schumacher F (Hrsg.) *Pierre Bourdieus Konzeption des Habitus. Grundlagen, Zugänge, Forschungsperspektiven. [Pierre Bourdieu's Conception of Habitus].* Wiesbaden: Springer Verlag für Sozialwissenschaften, pp. 175–200.

Bohnsack R (1997) Dokumentarische methode. [Documentary Method]. In Hitzler R and Honer A (Hrgs.) *Sozialwissenschaftliche Hermeneutik. [Social Science Hermeneutic].* Wiesbaden: Springer, Verlag für Sozialwissenschaften, pp. 191–212.

Bohnsack R (2014) *Rekonstruktive Sozialforschung. Einführung in Methodologie und Praxis Qualitativer Forschung. Neunte Auflage. [Reconstructive Social Research. Introduction to the Methodology and Practice of Qualitative Research].* 9th Edition. Opladen: Verlag Barbara Budrich.

Bohnsack R (2017) *Praxeologische Wissenssoziologie. [Praxiological Sociology of Knowledge].* Opladen: Verlag Barbara Budrich.

Bohr N (1928) The quantum postulate and the recent development of atomic theory. *Nature.* (Supplement)121: 580–590. https://doi.org/10.1038/121580a0.

Bol PK (2008) *Neo-Confucianism in History.* Cambridge, MA: Harvard University Press.

Bolger N, Davis A and Rafaeli E (2003) Diary methods. Capturing life as it is lived. *Annual Review of Psychology.* 54(1): 679–616. https://www.annualreviews.org/content/journals/10.1146/annurev.psych.54.101601.145030

Bondas T and Hall EO (2007) Challenges in approaching meta-synthesis *Health Research.* 17(1): 113–121.

Booß C (2013) *Von der Stasi-Erstürmung zur Aktenöffnung. Konflikte und Kompromisse im Vorfeld der Deutschen Einheit.* [From storming the Stasi to the Opening of the Records. Conflicts and Compromises in prior to the German Unification]. Available at: https://www.bpb.de/themen/deutschlandarchiv/54118/von-der-stasi-erstuermung-zur-aktenoeffnung/ (accessed 13 April 2023).

Booth A, Sutton A, Clowes M and Martyn-St James M (2022) *Systematic Approaches to a Successful Literature Review*. 3rd Edition. Thousand Oaks, CA: Sage.

Borsboom D and Cramer AOJ (2013) Network analysis. An integrative approach to the structure of psychopathology. *Annual Review of Clinical Psychology.* 9: 91–121. https://doi.org/10.1146/annurev-clinpsy-050212-185608.

Borsboom D, Cramer AOJ, Schmittmann VD, Epskamp S and Waldorp LJ (2011) The small world of psychopathology. *PLoS One*. 6(11): Article e27407.

Borsboom D, Deserno MK, Rhemtulla M, Epskamp S, Fried EI, McNally RJ, Robinaugh DJ, Perugini M, Dalege J, Costantini G, Isvoranu AM, Wysocki AC, Van Borkulo CD, Van Bork R and Waldorp LJ (2021) Network analysis of multivariate data in psychological science. Primer. *Nature Reviews.* 1–58. https://doi.org/10.1038/s43586-021-00055-w.

Borsboom D, Fried EI, Epskamp S, Waldorp LJ, Van Borkulo C, Van der Maas HLJ and Cramer AOJ (2017) False alarm? A comprehensive reanalysis of "evidence that psychopathology symptom networks have limited replicability" by Forbes, Wright, Markon, and Krueger (2017). *Journal of Abnormal Psychology*. 126(7): 989–999.

Bose S (2017) Reflections on being a senior nurse and a reflective practice group conductor of nursing groups in the same traumatised and traumatising organisation. *Group-Analytic Contexts Special Issue: Reflective Practice in Organisations*. 75(1): 65–77.

Bosse H (1993a) Group analysis and anthropology I: using anthropology in group analysis and psychotherapy. II: using group analysis in social and cultural anthropology and related sciences. III: mutual influences. *Group Analysis*. 26(3): 227–228.

Bosse H (1993b) A group's bad self in Papua New Guinea. A true home in the modern world? *Group Analysis*. 26(3): 232–335.

Boud D, Keogh R and Walker D (1994) Promoting reflection in learning a model. In Boud D, Keogh R and Walker D (Eds.) *Reflection. Turning Experience into Learning*. New York: Routledge, pp. 18–40.

Bourdeau M (2022) *Auguste Comte*. Stanford Encyclopedia of Philosophy. Available at: https://plato.stanford.edu/entries/comte/ (accessed 6 January 2023).

Bourdieu P (1971) Systems of education and systems of thought. In Hopper E (Ed.) *Readings in the Theory of Educational Systems*. London: Hutchinson University Library, pp. 159–183.

Bouvier FB and Parcher R (2023) What should be done and what should be avoided when comparing two treatments? *Best Practice & Research Clinical Haematology*. 36(2): 101473. https://doi.org/10.1016/j.beha.2023.101473.

Bowen GA (2009) Document analysis as a qualitative research method. *Qualitative Research Journal*. 9(2): 27–40. https://doi.org/10.3316/QRJ0902027.

Bowlby J (1969) *Attachment and Loss. Attachment*. London: Hogarth Press.

Bowlby J (1973) *Attachment and Loss. Separation*. London: Hogarth Press.

Bowlby J (1980) *Attachment and Loss. Loss*. London: Hogarth Press.

Boyd J (2011) A non-QM explanation of Jacques' (2007) "Wheeler Gedanken experiment with delayed choice," without delayed choice. Session F Theory. Meeting of the APS. *Bulletin of the American Physical Society*. 56(17): 18–19.

Boyd J (2012) Rethinking a Wheeler delayed-choice Gedanken experiment. *Physics Essays*. 25(3): 390–396.

Boyd RD (1989) The developmental stages of the Anima and the Animus in small groups I. *Group Analysis*. 22(2): 135–147.

Boyer RI (2017) *Depth Insights Seeing The Word with Soul*. Available at: https://www.depthinsights.com/Depth-Insights-scholarly-ezine/on-romanticism-in-jungs-psychology-a-reflection-on-richard-tarnas-the-passion-of-the-western-mindby-ronald-l-boyer/

Boyle GJ, Mattews G and Saklofske DH (Eds.) (2008a) *The Sage Handbook of Personality Theory and Assessment. Personality Theories and Models. Volume 1*. Thousand Oaks, CA: Sage.

Boyle GJ, Mattews G and Saklofske DH (Eds.) (2008b) *The Sage Handbook of Personality Theory and Assessment. Personality Measurement and Testing. Volume 2*. Thousand Oaks, CA: Sage.

Bozalek V and Murris K (2022) Diffraction. In Murris K (Ed.) *A Glossary for Doing Postqualitative, New Materialist and Critical Posthumanist Research Across Disciplines*. New York: Routledge, pp. 54–57.

Bozalek V and Zembylas M (2017) Diffraction or reflection? Sketching the contours of two methodologies in educational research. *International Journal of Qualitative Studies in Education*. 30(2): 111–127. https://doi.org/10.1080/09518398.2016.1201166.

BPB (Bundeszentrale für Politische Bildung) (2003) *Dossier Weltfestspiele 1973*. [Dossier on the World Championships in 1973]. https://www.bpb.de/themen/deutsche-teilung/weltfestspiele-73/

BPB (Bundeszentrale für Politische Bildung) (2008) *Außerparlamentarische Opposition und Studentenbewegung*. [Exceptional parliamentary opposition and student movement]. https://www.bpb.de/themen/linksextremismus/geschichte-der-raf/49201/ausserparlamentarische-opposition-und-studentenbewegung/

BPB (Bundeszentrale für Politische Bildung) (2021) *Sport im DDR Fernsehen*. 1 June. [Sport on GR television]. https://www.bpb.de/themen/medien-journalismus/deutsche-fernsehgeschichte-in-ost-und-west/245678/sport-im-ddr-fernsehen/

BPS (2021) *BPS Guide to Human Research Ethics.* Leicester: The British Psychological Society. https://www.bps.org.uk/guideline/bps-code-human-research-ethics

Bracken HM (1978) Philosophy and racism. *Philosophia.* 8(2–3): 241–260.

Bradbury H, Mirvis P, Neilsen E and Pasmore W (2008) Action research at work: Creating the future following the path from Lewin In Reason P and Bradbury H (Eds.) *Handbook of Action Research: Participative Inquiry and Practice.* Thousand Oaks, CA: Sage, pp. 77–92.

Brady SR (2015) Utilizing and adapting the Delphi method for use in qualitative research. *International Journal of Qualitative Methods.* 14(5): 1–6.

Brandist C (n.d.) The Bakhtin circle. *The Internet Encyclopedia of Philosophy.* https://iep.utm.edu/bakhtin-circle/

Branley D, Seale O and Zacharias T (2018) Doing a literature review. In Seale C (Ed.) *Researching Society and Culture.* 4th Edition. Thousand Oaks, CA: Sage, pp. 63–78.

Brantlinger E, Jimenez R, Klingner J and Pugach M (2005) Qualitative studies in special education. *Exceptional Children.* 71(2): 195–207. https://doi.org/10.1177/001440290507100205.

Braun J (2007) "Very nice, the enemies are gone!". Coming to terms with GDR sports since 1989/90. *Historical Social Research.* 32(1): 172–185.

Braun V and Clarke V (2006) Using thematic analysis in psychology. *Qualitative Research in Psychology.* 3(2): 77–101.

Braun V and Clarke V (2021) One size fits all? What counts as quality practice in (reflexive) thematic analysis? *Qualitative Research in Psychology.* 18(3): 328–352. https://doi.org/10.1080/14780887.2020.1769238.

Braun V and Clarke V (2022a) *Thematic Analysis. A Practical Guide*. Thousand Oaks, CA: Sage.

Braun V and Clarke V (2022b) Toward good practice in thematic analysis: avoiding common problems and be(com)ing a *knowing* researcher. *International Journal of Transgender Health.* 24(1): 1–6. https://doi.org/10.1080/26895269.2022.2129597.

Breitman BD (2020) The Scarab. Jung Created a Coincidence within a Coincidence. *Psychology Today.* 16 November. Available at: https://psychologytoday.com/gb/blog/connecting-coincidence/202011/the-scarab-jung-created-coincidence-within-coincidence (accessed 7 July 2024).

Breitsprecher U (2020) *Der sozialistische Hochschullehrer. Die Berufungspolitik in der SBZ/DDR am Beispiel der Hochschullehrerschaft der Humboldt Universität in Berlin (1945–1990). [The socialist university lecturer. The professional politics in the SBZ/GDR. Example of the lecturers at Humboldt University in Berlin].* Dissertation, Universität Leipzig, Germany. https://www.fachportal-paedagogik.de/literatur/vollanzeige.html?FId=3363439

Bridger H (1990) The discovery of the therapeutic community. The northfield experiments. In Trist E, Murrary H and Trist B (Eds.) *The Social Engagement of Social Science. A Tavistock Anthology. Vol. 1. The Socio-Psychological Perspective.* Pennsylvania: Pennsylvania University Press, pp. 68–88.

Bridgman PW (1950) *Reflections of a Physicist.* New York: Philosophical Library Inc. [Republished 1980 by Arno Press; 2009 by Kessinger Publishing.]

Brink DA (2021) *Philosophy of Science And The Kyoto School. An Introduction to Nishida Kitaro, Tanabe Hajime and Tosaka Jun.* New York: Bloomsbury.

Britannica (2023) *10 Women scientists who should be famous (or more famous)*. The Editors of Encyclopedia Britannica. Science & Tech. 12 April 2023. Available at: https://www.britannica.com/list/10-women-scientists-who-should-be-famous-or-more-famous (accessed 29 November 2024).

Britannica (2024) *Kurt Koffka*. The Editors of Encyclopedia Britannica. 19 November 2024. Available at: https://www.britannica.com/biography/Kurt-Koffka (accessed 24 December 2024).

Brock A (2009) Producing the 'Socialist Personality'? Socialisation, education, and the emergence of new patterns of behaviour. In Fulbrook M (Ed.) *Power and Society in the GDR, 1961–1979: The Normalisation of Rule?* New York: Berghahn Books, pp. 220–252.

Brokensha D and Crowder M (Eds.) (1967) *Africa in the Wider World. The Interrelationship of Area and Comparative Studies.* Oxford: Pergamon Press.

Brokensha S, Kotzé E and Senekal B (2023) *AI in and for Africa: A Humanistic Perspective.* Boca Raton, FL: CRC Press.

Broodryk J (2005) *Ubuntu Management Philosophy: Exporting Ancient African Wisdom into the Global World.* Johannesburg: Knowles.

Brook AT, Garcia J and Fleming MA (2008) The effects of multiple identities on psychological well-being. *Personality and Social Psychology Bulletin.* 34(12): 1588–1600.

Brown CA and Detoy CJ (1988) A comparison of the personal constructs of management in new and experienced managers. In Fransella F and Thomas L (Eds.) *Experimenting with Personal Construct Psychology.* London: Routledge and Kegan Paul, pp. 426–433.

Brown D (1983) Dr S. H. Foulkes (1898–1976). *International Journal of Psychoanalysis.* 64(2): 109–109.

Brown D (1985) Bion and Foulkes. Basic assumptions and beyond. In Pines M (Ed.) (1992) *Bion and Group Psychotherapy.* London: Routledge, pp. 192–219.

Brown D (2001) A contribution to the understanding of the social unconscious. *Group Analysis.* 34(1): 29–38.

Brown LD, Tang X and Hollman RL (2014) The structure of social exchange in self-help support groups: development of a measure. *American Journal of Community Psychology.* 53(1–2): 83–95. https://doi.org/10.1007/s10464-013-9621-3.

Brown LM and Weidner RT (2024) Physics. Science. *Encyclopedia Britannica.* 9 December 2024. Available at: https://www.britannica.com/science/physics-science (accessed 17 December 2024).

Brown M, Downie A and Buckingham Shum S (2012) Mapping the matrix: Using compendium as a tool for recording the analytic group. *Group Analysis.* 45(1): 99–115.

Brown SR (1986) Q technique and methods. In Berry W and Lewis-Beck MS (Eds.) *Principles and Procedures. New Tools for Social Scientists: Advances and Application in Research Methods.* Thousand Oaks, CA: Sage, pp. 57–76.

Brown SR (2003) *Structural Phenomenology. An Empirically-Based Model of Consciousness*. Thesis, University of Southampton, UK. Available at: https://web-archive.southampton.ac.uk/cogprints.org/3061/1/Dissertation_Master.htm (accessed 7 April 2025).

Brown SR (2005) *Structural Phenomenology. An Empirically-Based Model of Consciousness. Monograph.* New York: Peter Lang.

Brumberg J and Gumz A (2012) Was sind Űbertragungsdeutungen und wie wirken sie? Eine systematische Űbersicht. [What are interpretations of transferences and how do they work? A systematic overview]. *Zeitschrift für Psychosomatische Medizin und Psychotherapie*. 58(3): 219–235.

Bryant A and Charmaz K (2007) Grounded theory research. Methods and Practices. In Bryant A and Charmaz K (Eds.) *The Sage Handbook of Grounded Theory.* Thousand Oaks, CA: Sage, pp. 1–28.

Buber M (1958) *I and Thou.* Trans. RG Smith. Scribner Classics. New York: Scribner Book Company.

Buber M (1993) *Between Man and Man.* New York: Routledge & Kegan Paul. [Published in 1947; Second Edition 2002, Routledge]. https://archive.org/details/dli.ministry.10198

Buchanan RD (2011) The controversial Hans Eysenck. *The Psychologist.* 24(4): 318–319.

Buckley P (1997) Psychoanalysis and its romantic rebellion. *Journal of the American Psychoanalytic Association.* 45(2): 577–587. https://doi.org/10.1177/00030651970450020601.

Budde G-F (1997) Paradefrauen. Akademikerinnen in Ost- und Westdeutschland. [Women on display. Female academics in East and West Germany]. In Budde G-F (Hrg.) *Frauen Arbeiten. Weibliche Erwerbstätigkeit in Ost- und Westdeutschland nach 1945. [Women work. Female employment in East and West Germany after 1945].* Göttingen: Vandenhoeck und Ruprecht, pp. 183–211. https://www.fachportal-paedagogik.de/literatur/vollanzeige.html?FId=2362385

Budde G-F (2002) Gelungener Elitenwechsel? Studentinnen in der DDR in den 50er und 60er Jahren. [Successful change of the elite? Female students in the GDR in the 1050s and 1960s]. *Journal für Wissenschaft und Bildung.* 11(2): 150–168. https://www.pedocs.de/frontdoor.php?source_opus=16524

Buescher T and McGugan S (2022) Standing out on the margins: Using dialogical narrative analysis to explore mental health student nurse identity construction and core modules. *Issues in Mental Health Nursing.* 43(8): 737–747. https://doi.org/10.1080/01612840.2022.2037174

Bujo B (1997) *The Ethical Dimension of Community. The African Model and the Dialogue between North and South.* Nairobi: Paulines Africa Publications.

Bujo B (2001) *Foundations of an African Ethic: Beyond the Universal Claims of Western Morality.* Nairobi: Paulines Africa Publications.

Bujo B (2009) Is there a specific ethic? Towards a discussion with western thought. In Murove MF (Ed.) *African Ethics. An Anthology of Comparative and Applied Ethics.* Scottsville: University of Kwazulu-Natal Press, pp. 113–128

Bundesarchiv (2023) *Was war die Stasi?* [What was the Stasi?]. Available at: https://www.bundesarchiv.de/themen-entdecken/online-entdecken/staatssicherheit/was-war-die-stasi/ (accessed 14 Juni 2023).

Burks M (2014) Practical philosophy. In Burks M and Mills J (Eds.) *Qualitative Methodology. A Practical Guide.* Thousand Oaks, CA: Sage, pp. 17–29.

Burks M and Mills J (Eds.) *Qualitative Methodology. A Practical Guide.* Thousand Oaks, CA: Sage.

Burlingame G, Strauss B, Joyce A, MacKenzie K, Ogrodniczuk J and Taylor S (2006) *CORE Battery: A Revision and Update.* Washington, DC: American Group Psychotherapy Association.

Burlingame GM and Strauß B (2021) Efficacy of small group treatments: Foundation for evidence-based practice. In Barkham M, Lutz W and Castonguay LG (Eds.) *Bergin and Garfield's Handbook of Psychotherapy and Behavior Change.* 7th Edition. Hoboken, NJ: John Wiley & Sons, pp. 583–624.

Burlingame GM, Gleave R, Erekson D, Nelson PL, Olsen J, Thayer S and Beecher M (2016) Differential effectiveness of group, individual, and conjoint treatments: An archival analysis of OQ-45 change trajectories. *Psychotherapy Research.* 26(5): 556–572. https://doi.org/10.1080/10503307.2015.1044583.

Burlingame GM, MacKenzie KR and Strauss B (2004) Small-group treatment: Evidence for effectiveness and mechanisms of change. In Lambert MJ (Ed.) *Bergin and Garfield's Handbook of Psychotherapy and Behavior Change.* 5th Edition. Hoboken, NJ: John Wiley & Sons, pp. 647–496.

Burlingame GM, McClendon DT and Yang C (2018) Cohesion in group therapy: A Metaanalysis. *Psychotherapy.* 55(4): 384–398. https://doi.org/10.1037/pst0000173.

Burlingame GM, Strauss BM and Clayton D (2024) The complexity of becoming an evidence-based group clinician: Introducing an evidence-based group treatment website. *Group Dynamics: Theory, Research, and Practice.* 28(3): 121–131. https://doi.org/10.1037/gdn0000228.

Burns RB (2000) *Introduction to Research Methods.* 4th Edition. London: Sage.

Burrow T (1913) Psychoanalysis and life. In Pertegato GE and Pertegato GO (Eds.) (2013) *From Psychoanalysis to Group Analysis: The Pioneering Work of Trigant Burrow.* London: Karnac, pp. 7–16. [Republished 2018 by Routledge].

Burrow T (1925) A relative concept of consciousness. An analysis of consciousness in its ethnic origin. Pertegato EG and Pertegato GO (Eds.) (2018) *From Psychoanalysis to Group Analysis. The Pioneering Work of Trigant Burrow.* New York: Routledge, pp. 71–86. [Originally published by Karnac 2013].

Burrow T (1926a) The laboratory method in psychoanalysis. Its inception and development. In Pertegato GE and Pertegato GO (Eds.) (2013) *From Psychoanalysis to Group Analysis: The Pioneering work of Trigant Burrow.* London: Karnac, pp. 145–156. [Republished 2018 by Routledge].

Burrow T (1926b) Our mass neuroses. In Pertegato GE and Pertegato GO (Eds.) (2013) *From Psychoanalysis to Group Analysis: The Pioneering work of Trigant Burrow.* London: Karnac, pp. 157–164. [Republished 2018 by Routledge].

Burrow T (1927) The Group method of analysis. In Pertegato GE and Pertegato GO (Eds.) (2013) *From Psychoanalysis to Group Analysis: The Pioneering work of Trigant Burrow.* London: Karnac, pp. 165–178. [Republished 2018 by Routledge].

Burrow T (1928a) The basis of group analysis, or the analysis of the reactions of normal and neurotic individuals. In Pertegato GE and Pertegato GO (Eds.) (2013) *From Psychoanalysis to Group Analysis: The Pioneering work of Trigant Burrow.* London: Karnac, pp. 179–188. [Republished 2018 by Routledge].

Burrow T (1928b) 'The autonomy of the "I" from the standpoint of group analysis. In Pertegato GE and Pertegato GO (Eds.) (2013) *From Psychoanalysis to Group Analysis: The Pioneering work of Trigant Burrow.* London: Karnac, pp. 189–206. [Republished 2018 by Routledge].

Burrow T (1958) *A Search for Man's Sanity. The Selected Letters of Trigant Burrow*. Edited by the Editorial Committee of the Lifwynn Foundation. New York: Oxford University Press.

Burt C and Stephenson W (1939) Alternative views of correlations between persons. *Psychometrika.* 4(4): 269–281.

Bustamante N (2023) What Is Gestalt Psychology? Theory, Principles & Examples. *Simply Psychology.* Available at: https://www.simplypsychology.org/what-is-gestalt-psychology.html (accessed 14 November 2023).

Butler J (1990) *Gender Trouble. Feminism and the Subversion of Identity.* New York: Routledge.
Butler T (1998) Towards a hermeneutic method for interpretative research in information systems. *Journal of Information Technology.* 13(4): 285–300.
Butler-Adam J (2015) The Weighty History and Meaning behind the Word 'Science'. *The Conversation.* 1 October. Available at: https://theconversation.com/the-weighty-history-and-meaning-behind-the-word-science-48280
Butto N (2021) Revealing the essence of electric permittivity constant. *Journal of High Energy Physics, Gravitation and Cosmology.* 7(1): 210–217. https://doi.org/10.4236/JHEPGC.2021.71011.
Butto N (2024a) A new theory exploring the internal structure of quarks. *Journal of High Energy Physics, Gravitation and Cosmology.* 10(4): 1713–1733. https://doi.org/10.4236/jhepgc.2024.104097.
Butto N (2024b) Unravelling the quantum Web. The vortex theory of mass and matter formation. *Journal of High Energy Physics, Gravitation and Cosmology.* 10(3): 1195–1225. https://doi.org/10.4236/jhepgc.2024.103072.
Bygstad B, Munkvold BE and Volkoff O (2016) Identifying generative mechanisms through affordances. A framework for critical realist data analysis. *Journal of Information Technology.* 31(1): 83–96. https://doi.org/10.1057/jit.2015.13.
Byrne D (2022) A worked example of Braun and Clarke's approach to reflexive thematic analysis. *Quality & Quantity.* 56(3): 1391–1412.
Byrne J (2016) Improving the peer review of narrative literature reviews. *Research Integrity and Peer Review.* 1(12): 1–4. https://doi.org/10.1186/ s41073-016-0019-2.
Byrne P (2007) The many worlds of Hugh everett. *Scientific American.* 297(6): 98–105.
Caddick N, Phoenix C and Smith B (2015) Collective stories and well-being: using a dialogical narrative approach to understand peer relationships among combat veterans experiencing post-traumatic stress disorder. *Journal of Health Psychology.* 20(3): 286–299. https://doi.org/10.1177/1359105314566612.
Cahan D (Ed.) (2003) *From Natural Philosophy to the Sciences. Writing the History of Nineteenth-Century Science.* Chicago, IL: Chicago University Press.
Cai S, Zhou J and Pan J (2021) Estimating the sample mean and standard deviation from order statistics and sample size in meta-analysis. *Statistical Methods in Medical Research.* 30(12): 2701–2719. https://doi.org/10.1177/09622802211047.
Cairns P and Cox AL (Eds.) (2008) *Research Methods for Human Computer Interaction.* Cambridge: Cambridge University Press.
Caldeira CM, Andrade RM, Silva LSP e and Polvarini and de Morais V (2022) Análise intertransferencial no manejo de ristotlerativo com funcionários de um hospital psiquiátrico [Intertransferential analysis on the management of an operative group with employees of a psychiatric hospital.] *Vínculo.* 19(1): 98–105. https://doi.org/issn.19982-1492v19n1a10.
Calder G (2014) Representing groups. In Calder G, Bessone M and Zuolo F (Eds.) *How Groups Matter. Challenges of Toleration in Pluralistic Societies.* New York: Routledge, pp. 17–33.
Callahan JL (2010) Constructing a manuscript: Distinguishing integrative literature reviews and conceptual and theory articles. *Human Resource Development Review.* 9(3): 300–304. https://doi.org/10.1177/1534484310371492.
Callahan JL (2014) Writing literature reviews: a reprise and update. *Human Resource Development Review.* 13(3): 271–275.
Callahan R (1985) *How Executives Overcome the Fear of Public Speaking and Other Phobias.* Wilmington, DE: Enterprise Publishing.
Callahan R (2001) *Tapping the Healer Within. Using Thought Field Therapy to Instantly Conquer your Fears, Anxieties, and Emotional Distress.* New York: Contemporary Books.
Cambridge International Education Team (2025) *Getting Started with Key Concepts.* Available at: https://cambridge-community.org.uk/professional-development/gswkey/index.html (accessed 5 February 2025).
Camilleri K (2007) Bohr, Heisenberg and divergent views of complementarity. *Studies in History and Philosophy of Modern Physics.* 38(3): 514–528. https://doi.org/10.1016/j.shpsb.2006.10.002.
Campbell J (2006) Chopping up the Rainbow. Quality assurance and the challenge to group-analytic training. *Group Analysis.* 39(3): 341–355.

Campbell M and Gregor F (2002) *Mapping Social Relations. A Primer in Doing Institutional Ethnography.* Toronto: University of Toronto Press.

Campbell MJ (2021) *Statistics at Square One*. 12th Edition. Chichester: Blackwell-Wiley. [Revised Edition of TD Swinscow, BMJ, 1997].

Campbell ML (2001) Textual accounts, ruling action: The intersection of knowledge and power in the routine conduct of community nursing work. *Studies in Cultures, Organizations and Societies.* 7(2): 231–250. https://doi.org/10.1080/10245280108523559.

Cañete M, Stormont F and Ezquerro A (2000) Group analytic therapy with the elderly. *British Journal of Psychotherapy.* 17(1): 94–105.

Cao X and Henderson EF (2020) The interweaving of diaries and lives: Diary-keeping behaviour in a diary-interview study of international students' employability management. *Qualitative Research.* 21(6): 829–845.

Caplan HL, Rohde PD, Shapiro DA and Watson JP (1975) Some correlates of repertory grid measures used to study a psychotherapeutic group. *The British Journal of Medical Psychology*. 48(3): 217–226. https://doi.org/10.1111/j.2044-8341.1975.tb02325.x.

Capra F (1991) *The Tao of Physics. An Exploration of the Parallels between Modern Physics And Eastern Mysticism.* 3rd Edition. London: HarperCollins.

Caputo JD (1996) *Deconstruction in a Nutshell. A Conversation with Jacques Derrida.* New York: Fordham University Press.

Cardno C (2018) Policy document analysis. A practical educational leadership tool and a qualitative research method. *Educational Administration: Theory and Practice.* 24(4): 623–640. https://eric.ed.gov/?id=EJ1305631.

Carey MA (1994) The group effect in focus groups. Planning, implementing, and interpreting focus group research. In Morse JM (Ed.) *Critical Issues in Qualitative Research Methods.* Thousand Oaks, CA: Sage, pp. 225–241.

Carminati GG and Carminati F (2019) The marauding paths of a group training. *Psychology.* 10(14): 1959–1983. https://doi.org/10.4236/psych.2019.1014126.

Carmines EG and Woods JA (2005) Validity assessment. In Kempf-Leonard K (Ed.) *Encyclopedia of Social Measurement*, New York: Elsevier, pp. 933–937.

Carnap R (1928/1967) *The Logical Structure of the World.* Chicago, IL: Open Court.

Carnap R (1958) *Introduction to Symbolic Logic and Its Applications.* New York: Dover Publications.

Carnap R (1963) Replies and systematic expositions. In Schilpp P (Ed.) *The Philosophy of Rudolf Carnap.* Chicago: Open Court, pp. 859–1013.

Carpiano RM and Daley DM (2006) A guide and glossary on postpositivist theory building for population health. *Journal of Epidemiological Community Health.* 60(7): 564–570. https://jech.bmj.com/content/60/7/564

Carreira J (2010) *Eight Confusing Philosophical Terms Explained.* Blog Series. Available at: https://web.archive.org/web/20170607131222/https://philosophyisnotluxury.com/2010/06/eight-confusing-philosophical-terms-explained/ (accessed 10 November 2024).

Carroll S (2022) How to Think About Relativity. *Quanta Magazine.* 14 November 2022. Available at: https://www.quantamagazine.org/how-to-think-about-relativitys-concept-of-space-time-20221114/ (accessed 8 August 2024).

Carter B (2009) Tick box for child? The ethical positioning of children as vulnerable, researchers as barbarians and reviewers as overly cautious. *International Journal of Nursing.* 46(6): 858–864.

Carter N (2014) The use of triangulation in qualitative research. *Oncology Nursing Forum.* 41(5): 545–547.

Carter RE (1989) *The Nothingness beyond God: An Introduction to the Philosophy of Nishida Kitaro.* New York: Paragon House. Available at: https://archive.org/details/nothingnessbeyon00robe

Caruana EJ, Roman M, Hernandez-Sanches J and Solli P (2015) Longitudinal Studies. *Journal of Thoracic Disease.* 7(11): E537–E540.

Carus P (Ed.) (1902) *Kant's Prolegomena to Any Future Metaphysics.* Available at: https://www.gutenberg.org/files/52821/52821-h/52821-h.htm (accessed 1 June 2024).

Cassirer E (2001) *Philosophie der Symbolischen Formen*, Bände 1–3. [Philosophy of Symbolic Forms. Volumes 1–3]. Hamburg: Meiner.

Castellano MB (2000) Updating aboriginal traditions of knowledge. In Dei GJ, Hall B and Rosenberg DG (Eds.) *Indigenous Knowledges in Global Contexts. Multiple Readings of Our World.* Toronto: Toronto University Press, pp. 21–36.

Castells M (1996) *The Rise of the Network Society. The Information Age, Economy, Society and Culture. Volume 1.* Oxford: Blackwell.

Catina A and Tschuschke V (1993) A summary of empirical data from the investigation of two psychoanalytic groups by means of repertory grid technique. *Group Analysis*. 26(4): 433–447. https://doi.org/10.1177/0533316493264005.

Catina A, Tschuschke V and Winter DA (1989) Self-reconstruing as a result of social interaction in analytic group therapy: Preliminary data with depressives. *Group Analysis*. 22(1): 9–72. https://doi.org/10.1177/0533316489221007.

Cedeño KE, Diaz SA and Aggarwal NK (2020) Using theories from group psychotherapy to understand group process in multicultural focus groups: A pilot study. *Group Analysis.* 53(2): 210–233. https://doi.org/10.1177/0533316419870125.

Celikates R and Flynn J (2023) *Critical Theory (Frankfurt School)*. Stanford Encyclopedia of Philosophy. Available at: https://plato.stanford.edu/entries/critical-theory (accessed 2 April 2024).

CERM (2025) Future Circular Collider. Available at: https://www.home.cern/science/accelerator/future-circular-collider (accessed 13 January 2025).

Chalmers DJ (1996) *The Conscious Mind. In Search of a Fundamental Theory*. New York: Oxford University Press.

Chalmers DJ (2022) *Reality+. Virtual Worlds and the Problems of Philosophy*. New York: W. W. Norton & Company.

Chan SY (2000) Gender relationship roles in the analectics and mencius. *Asian Philosophy.* 10(2): 115–132.

Chan SY (2017) Confucianism and care ethics. In Garry A, Khadar SJ and Stone A (Eds.) *The Routledge Companion to Feminist Philosophy.* New York: Routledge, pp. 556–567.

Chandler D (2006) *Semiotics for Beginners*. Available at: https://www.cs.princeton.edu/~chazelle/courses/BIB/semio2.htm (accessed 9 February 2025).

Chao Y-S, Wu C-J, Lai Y-C, Hsu H-T, Cheng Y-P, Wu H-C, Huang S-Y and Chen W-C (2022) Why mental illness diagnoses are wrong. A pilot study on the perspective of the public. *Frontiers in Psychiatry.* 13. https://doi.org/10.3389/fpsyt.2022.860487.

Charmaz K (2006) *Constructing Grounded Theory: A Practical Guide through Qualitative Analysis*. Thousand Oaks, CA: Sage.

Charmaz K (2008) The legacy of Anselm Strauss for constructivist grounded theory. In Denzin NK (Ed.) *Studies in Symbolic Interaction*. Bingley: Emerald Publishing, pp. 127–141.

Charmaz K (2014) *Constructing Grounded Theory.* 2nd Edition. Thousand Oaks, CA: Sage.

Charmaz K (2017) The power of constructivist grounded theory for critical inquiry. *Qualitative Inquiry* 23(1): 34–45.

Charmaz K (2020) “With constructivist grounded theory you can’t hide”: Social justice research and critical inquiry in the public sphere. *Qualitative Inquiry*. 26(2): 165–176.

Charmaz K and Belgrave LL (2015) *Grounded Theory*. The Blackwell Encyclopedia of Sociology. https://doi.org/10.1002/9781405165518.wbeosg070.pub2 (Previous version by Charmaz K 2007) https://doi.org/10.1002/9781405165518.wbeosg070.

Charmaz K and Henwood K (2008) Grounded theory. In Willig C and Stainton RW (Eds.) *The Sage Handbook of Qualitative Research in Psychology*. Thousand Oaks, CA: Sage, pp. 240–259.

Charmaz K and Thornberg R (2021) The pursuit of quality in grounded theory. *Qualitative Research in Psychology.* 18(3): 305–327.

Chasseguet-Smirgel J (1984) *The Ego Ideal.* New York: W. W. Norton & Company.

Chasseguet-Smirgel J and Grunberger B (1986) *Freud Or Reich? Psychoanalysis and Illusion.* Trans. C Pajaczkowska. London: Free Association Books.

Check J and Schutt RK (2012) Survey research. In Check J and Schutt RK (Eds.) *Research Methods in Education.* Thousand Oaks, CA: Sage Publications, Chapter 8.

Chen M (2023) The philosophy of the metaverse. *Ethics and Information Technology*. 25(3): 1–13. https://link.springer.com/article/10.1007/s10676-023-09714-w.
Chen ZL, Lawson RB, Gorden LR and McIntosh B (1996) Groupthink. Deciding with the leader and the devil. *The Psychology Record.* 46(4): 581–590. https://doi.org/10.1007/BF03395186.
Cheng TY (2023) On the quadrants of the thing-world relations: a critical revision of Hartmut Rosa's resonance theory in terms of thing-world. *Journal of Chinese. Sociology.* 10: 11. https://doi.org/10.1186/s40711-023-00191-8.
Chigevenga R (2022) Decolonising research methodologies in the Global South: Experiences of an African social scientist. *African Journal of Social Work.* 12(4): 199–206.
Chilisa B (2012) *Indigenous Research Methodologies*. Thousand Oaks, CA: Sage.
Chilisa B (2014) Indigenous research is a journey. *The International Journal of Narrative Therapy and Community Work.* 2(1): 41–44.
Chilisa B (2020) *Indigenous Research Methodologies.* 2nd Edition. Thousand Oaks, CA: Sage.
Chilisa B (2024) Philosophical underpinnings of mixed methods. Decolonizing evaluation practice through decolonizing paradigms. In Shan Y (Ed.) *Philosophical Foundations Of Mixed Methods Research. Dialogues between Researchers and Philosophers.* New York: Routledge, pp. 54–82.
Chilisa B and Tsheko GN (2014) Mixed methods in indigenous research: building relationships for sustainable intervention outcomes. *Journal of Mixed Methods Research.* 8(3): 222–233. https://doi.org/10.1177/1558689814527878.
Chilisa B, Major TE and Khudu-Petersen K (2017) Community engagement with a postcolonial, African-based relational paradigm. *Qualitative Research.* 17(3): 326–339. https://doi.org/10.1177/1468794117696176.
Chimakonam JO (2017) Conversationalism as an emerging method of thinking in and beyond African philosophy. *Acta Academica.* 49(2): 11–33. https://doi.org/10.18820/24150479/aa49i2.1.
Chiorazzi A (2015) The Spirituality of Africa. *The Harvard Gazette.* 6 October. Available at: https://news.hardvard.edu/gazette/story/2015/10/the-spirituality-of-Africa/ (accessed 24 December 2024).
Chisholm R (1964) The Myth of the Given. In Chisholm RM, Feigl H, Frankena WK, Passmore J and Thompson M (Eds.) *Philosophy. The Princeton Studies.* Englewood Cliffs, NJ: Prentice Hall, pp. 261–286. https://archive.org/details/philosophy0000unse/page/n3/mode/2up
Chisnall M (2020) Digital slavery, time for abolition? *Policy Studies*. 41(5): 488–506. https://doi.org/10.1080/01442872.2020.1724926.
Chita C (2025) Notes about resonance(s). *Group Analysis*. Online. https://doi.org/10.1177/05333164251353166.
Chong S and Plonsky L (2024) A typology of secondary research in applied linguistics. *Applied Linguistics Review*. 15(4): 1569–1594. https://doi.org/10.1515/applirev-2022-0189.
Chopra D (1989) *Quantum Healing. Exploring the Frontiers of Mind/Body Medicine.* New York: Bantam.
Choudhary P (2024) *Benefits and Limitations of LLM.* AIThority. Available at: https://aithority.com/machine-learing/benefits-and-limitations-of-llm/ (accessed 29 December 2024).
Chrastina J (2018) Meta-Synthesis of Qualitative Studies. Background, Methodology and Applications. *Education and Educational Research. US Department of Education*, pp. 113–121. Available at: https://files.eric.ed.gov (accessed 20 November 2024).
Chun Tie Y, Birks M and Francis K (2019) Grounded theory research: A design framework for novice researchers. *Sage Open Medicine.* 7(1): 1–8.
Ciere Y, Jaarsma D, Visser A, Sanderman R, Snippe E and Fleer J (2015) Studying learning in the health-care setting. The potential of quantitative diary methods. *Perspectives on Medical Education.* 4(4): 203–207. https://doi.org/10.1007/s40037-015-0199-3.
Cilasun J, Schlapobersky J, Papanastassiou M and Thomas A (2021) The large group in training Parts I and II. *Group Analysis*. 55(3): 407–440. https://doi.org/10.1177/05333164211037947 (Original work published 2022).
Clandinin DJ (Ed.) (2007) *Handbook of Narrative Inquiry. Mapping a Methodology*. Thousand Oaks, CA: Sage Publications.
Clandinin DJ and Connelly FM (2000) *Narrative Inquiry: Experience and Story in Qualitative Research.* San Francisco: Jossey-Bass.

Clare J and Zarbafi A (2009) *Social Dreaming in the 21st Century. The World we are Losing.* New York: Routledge.

Clark K and Holquist M (1984) *Mikhail Bakhtin.* Harvard: Harvard University Press.

Clarke JJ (1994) *Jung and Eastern Thought. A Dialogue with the Orient.* New York: Routledge.

Clarke V and Braun V (2017) Thematic analysis. Commentary. *Journal of Positive Psychology.* 12(3): 297–298. https://doi.org/10.1080/17439760.2016.1262613.

Clarke V and Braun V (2018) Using thematic analysis in counselling and psychotherapy research: A critical reflection. *Journal of Counselling and Psychotherapy Research.* 18 (2): 107–110. https://doi.org/10.1002/capr.12165.

Clarke V and Braun V (2019a) Feminist qualitative methods and methodologies in psychology: A review and reflection. *Psychology of Women and Equalities. Section Review.* 2(1): 13–28. https://www.researchgate.net/publication/341025758_Feminist_qualitative_methods_and_methodologies_in_psychology_A_review_and_reflection

Clarke V and Braun V (2019b) *Checklist to assess thematic analysis manuscripts.* Available at: https://www.thematicanalysis.net/editor-checklist/ (accessed 7 July 2024). (Guidelines published in Braun and Clarke 2020).

Clauser JF, Horne MA, Shimony A and Holt RA (1969) Proposed experiment to test local hidden-variable theories. *Physical Review Letters.* 23(15): 880–884. https://doi.org/10.1103/PhysRevLett.23.880.

Clegg B (2020) What is the human body made of? *BBC Science Focus Magazine.* 28 August 2020. Available at: https://www.sciencefocus.com/the-human-body/what-is-the-human-body-made-of/ (accessed 9 January 2025).

Cleland JA (2017) The qualitative orientation in medical education research. *Korean Journal of Medical Education.* 29(2): 61–71. https://doi.org/10.3946/kjme.2017.53.

Cohen IB and Whitman A (1999) *Isaac Newton's Principia. The Mathematical Principles of Natural Philosophy. A New Translation.* Berkeley: University of California Press.

Cohen J (1988) *Statistical Power Analysis for the Behavioral Sciences* 2nd Edition. Hillsdale, NJ: Lawrence Erlbaum Associates.

Cohen SM (2020) *Aristotle's Metaphysics.* Stanford Encyclopedia of Philosophy. https://plato.stanford.edu/enristotlestotle-metaphysics/ (accessed 10 January 2025).

Cole BC (2000) *The East German Sports System. Image and Reality.* PhD Thesis. University of Texas, US. https://ttu-ir.tdl.org/items/29bb35f2-a6b4-42eb-9437-84b9a9b24c1e

Colebrook C (2002) *Understanding Deleuze.* New York: Routledge.

Collins H (2010) *Creative Research. The Theory and Practice of Research for the Creative Industries.* Singapore: AVA Publications.

Collins PH (1990) *Black Feminist Thought. Knowledge, Consciousness, and Politics of Empowerment.* New York: Routledge.

Comte A (1988/1853) *Introduction to Positive Philosophy.* Ed. and Trans. F Ferre. Cambridge, IN: Hackett Publishing Company Inc.

Connolly K (2012) Ikea Says Sorry to East German Political Prisoners Forced to Make its Furniture. *The Guardian.* 16 November. Available at: https://www.theguardian.com/business/2012/nov/16/ikea-regrets-forced-labour-germany (accessed 8 March 2020).

Conway S, Audin K, Barkham, M, Mellor-Clarke J and Russell S (2003) Practice-based evidence for a brief time-intensive multi-modal therapy guided by group analytic principles and method. *Group Analysis.* 36(3): 413–435.

Coole D (2001) Thinking politically with Merleau-Ponty. *Radical Philosophy.* 108 (July/August): 17–28. https://www.radicalphilosophy.com/article/thinking-politically-with-merleau-ponty

Coombe P (2020) The Northfield experiments. A reappraisal 70 years on. *Group Analysis.* 53(2): 162–176.

Cooper K (2022) *Protons. The Essential Building Blocks of Atoms.* SpaceCom. 27 November. Available at: https://www.space.com/protons-facts-discovery-charge-mass (accessed 12 January 2025).

Cooper M (2011) Meeting the demand for evidence-based practice. *Therapy Today.* 22(4): 10–16.

Cooper PC (1998) The Disavowal of the Spirit. Integration of Wholeness in Buddhism and Psychoanalysis. In Molino A (Ed.) *The Couch and The Tree. Dialogues In Psychoanalysis And Buddhism.* London: Open Gate Press, pp. 231–246.

Cooper R (1999) Foulkes and Group Analysis. In Oakley C (Ed.) *What Is A Group? A New Look at Theory in Practice. Encyclopaedia of Psychoanalysis* 2. London: Rebus Press, pp. 39–70.

Cornell D and Muvangua N (Eds.) (2012) *uBuntu and The Law. African Ideals and Post-Apartheid Jurisprudence.* New York: Fordham University Press.

Cornell D and van Marle K (2005) Exploring ubuntu: tentative reflections. *African Human Rights Law Journal.* 5(2): 195–220. Available at: https://www.ahrlj.up.ac.za/cornell-d-van-marle-k

Cornell D and van Marle K (2015) Ubuntu feminism: tentative reflections. *Verbum et Ecclesia.* 36(2): Article 1444. https://doi.org/10.4102/ve.v36i2.1444.

Cortesão EL (1989) *Grupanálise. Teoria e Técnica.* [Group Analysis. Theory and Technique]. Lisboa: Fundaçao Calouste Gulbenkian. [2nd Edition SPG Sociedade Portuguesa de Grupanálise, 2008; Lisboa: Fundação Calouste Gulbenkian].

Cottone RR (1989) Defining the psychomedical and systemic paradigms in marital and family therapy. *Journal of Marital and Family Therapy*. 15(3): 225–235. https://doi.org/10.1111/j.1752-0606.1989.tb00804.x.

Cottone RR (1992) *Theories and Paradigms of Counseling and Psychotherapy*. Needham Heights, MA: Allyn & Bacon.

Cottone RR (2007) Paradigms of counselling and psychotherapy revisited. Is social constructivism a paradigm? *Journal of Mental Health Counseling*. 29(3): 189–203.

Cottone RR (2012) *Paradigms of Counseling and Psychotherapy*. Cottleville, MO: Cottone Publishing Company. https://www.smashwords.com/books/view/165398

Cottone RR (2017) *Theories of Counseling and Psychotherapy. Individual and Relational Approaches.* New York: Springer Publishing Company.

Cowen A (2024) Learn More About these 38 Scientists for Black History. *Blog Post. Science Buddies*. 23rd January. Available at: https://www.sciencebuddies.org/blog/black-history-month-scientists/ (accessed 29 December 2024).

Cox DR and Wermuth N (1996) *Multivariate Dependencies. Models, Analysis and Interpretation. Monographs on Statistics and Applied Probability. 67.* New York: Routledge.

Cox M (1989) *Coding the Therapeutic Process. Emblems of Encounter*. London: Jessica Kingsley.

Cramer AO, Van Borkulo CD, Giltay EJ, Van der Maas HL, Kendler KS, Scheffer M and Borsboom D (2016) Major depression as a complex dynamic system. *PLoS One*. 11(12): e0167490. https://doi.org/10.1371/journal.pone.0167490.

Cramer AO, Waldorp LJ, Van der Maas HL and Borsboom D (2010) Comorbidity: A network perspective. *Behavioral and Brain Sciences.* 33(2–3): 137–150. https://doi.org/10.1017/S0140525X09991567.

Creath R (2022) *Logical Empiricism*. Stanford Encyclopedia of Philosophy. Available at: https://plato.stanford.edu/entries/logical-empiricism/ (accessed 4 June 2023).

Crenshaw K (1989) *Demarginalizing the Intersection of Race and Sex: A Black Feminist Critique of Antidiscrimination Doctrine, Feminist Theory and Antiracist Politics. U. The University of Chicago Legal Forum.* 139–167. https://scholarship.law.columbia.edu/faculty_scholarship/3007/

Cresser JD (2011) *Quantum Physics Notes*. Sydney: Macquarie University Press.

Cresswell J (2003) *Research Design. Qualitative, Quantitative, and Mixed-Method Approaches.* 2nd Edition. Thousand Oaks, CA: Sage.

Cresswell J (2011) Being faithful: Bakhtin and a potential postmodern psychology of self. *Culture & Psychology*. 17(4): 473–490. https://doi.org/10.1177/1354067X11418540.

Creswell J (1994) *Research Design: Qualitative and Quantitative Approaches*. Thousand Oaks, CA: Sage.

Creswell J (2007) *Qualitative Inquiry and Research Design. Choosing among Five Traditions.* 2nd Edition. Thousand Oaks, CA: Sage.

Cribb M, Mika JP, Leberman S and Bennett A (2024) Tupua te Kawa: Indigenous methodologies for non-Indigenous (and Indigenous) organisations. *Qualitative Research.* 1–23. Online. https://doi.org/10.1177/1468794124129740.

Crits-Christoph P and Gibbons MB (2021) Psychotherapy process-outcome research. Advances in understanding causal connections. In Barkham M, Lutz, W and Castonguay LG (Eds.) *Bergin and Garfield's Handbook of Psychotherapy and Behavior Change.* Hoboken, NJ: John Wiley & Sons, pp. 263–296.

Cronin P, Ryan F and Coughlan M (2008) Undertaking a literature review: a step-by-step approach. *British Journal of Nursing.* 17(1): 38–43.

Crotty M (1998) *The Foundations of Social Research: Meaning and Perspective in the Research Process.* Thousand Oaks, CA: Sage. https://archive.org/details/foundationsofsoc0000crot

Crouch MC, Kim Z, Asquith-Heinz E, Decker Y, Andrew NT, Lewis JP and Rosich RM (2023) Indigenous Elder-centered methodology. Research that decolonizes and indigenizes. *Alter/Native.* 19(2): 447–456.

Cruwys T, Steffens NK, Haslam SA, Haslam C, Jetten J and Dingle GA (2016) Social identity mapping: A procedure for visual representation and assessment of subjective multiple group memberships. *The British Journal of Social Psychology.* 55(4): 613–642. https://doi.org/10.1111/bjso.12155.

Cui S, Li J, Mouchel L, Feng Y and Faltings B (2024) Nuance matters. Probing epistemic consistency in causal reasoning. In *Proceedings of the AAAI Conference on Artificial Intelligence*. 39(22): 23715–23723. https://arxiv.org/abs/2409.00103

Curry C (2017) 17 Famous Female Scientists Who Helped Change the World. *Global Citizen.* 10 February. Available at: https://www.globalcitizen.org/en/content/17-top-female-scientists-who-have-changed-the-world/ (accessed 29 December 2024).

Curtis JT, Silberschatz G, Sampson H and Weiss J (1994) The plan formulation method. *Psychotherapy Research.* 4(3–4): 197–207. https://doi.org/10.1080/10503309412331334032.

Cytrynbaum S and Noumair DA (Eds.) (2004) *Group Dynamics, Organizational Irrationality and Social Complexity: Group Relations Reader 3.* Jupiter, FL: A. K. Rice Institute for the Study of Social Systems.

D'Alfonso S (2020) AI in mental health. *Current Opinion in Psychology.* 36(2): 112–117. https://doi.org/10.1016/j.copsyc.2020.04.005.

Dagley JC, Gazda GM, Eppinger SJ and Stewart EA (1994) Group Psychotherapy Research with Children, Preadolescents, and Adolescents. In Fuhriman A and Burlingame GM (Eds.) *Handbook of Group Psychotherapy: An Empirical and Clinical Synthesis.* Hoboken, NJ: John Wiley, pp. 340–369.

Dahl H and Teller V (1994) The characteristics, identification, and application of FRAMES. *Psychotherapy Research.* 4(3–4): 253–276. https://doi.org/10.1080/10503309412331334082.

Dahlin O (2003) Group analysis has no theory! Foulkes failed us. Did He? *Group Analysis.* 36(3): 365–374.

Dalal F (1993) 'Race' and Racism. An attempt to organize difference. *Group Analysis* 26(3): 277–293.

Dalal F (1998) *Taking the Group Seriously: Towards a Post-Foulkesian Group Analytic Theory.* London and Philadelphia, PA: Jessica Kingsley.

Dalal F (2001) Insides and Outsides: A review of psychoanalytic renderings of difference, racism and prejudice. *Psychoanalytic Studies.* 3(1): 43–66.

Dalal F (2002) *Race, Colour and the Processes of Racialization. New Perspectives from Group Analysis, Psychoanalysis and Sociology*. Hove: Brunner.

Dalal F (2006) Racism. Processes of detachment, Dehumanization and hatred. *The Psychoanalytic Quarterly.* 75(1): 131–161.

Dalal F (2012) *Thought Paralysis. The Virtues of Discrimination.* London: Karnac.

Dalal F (2015) The statistical spin. Linguistic obfuscation. The art of overselling the CBT evidence base. *The Journal of Psychological Therapies in Primary Care.* 4(1): 1–25.

Dalal F (2016) Group analysis in the times of austerity. Neo-liberalism, managerialism and evidence-based research. *Group Analysis.* 50(1): 35–54.

Dalal F (2018a) CBT. *The Cognitive Behavioural Tsunami. Managerialism, Politics and the Corruptions of Science.* London: Routledge.

Dalal F (2018b) Back to the rough ground: From predictability to radical uncertainty. *Group Analysis.* 51(3): 315–333.

Dalal F (2023) It's not in the bottle: Research, ethics and psychotherapy. *Psychodynamic Practice*. 29(2): 101–116.

Dale A, Wathan J and Higgins V (2008) Secondary analysis of quantitative data sources. In Alasuutari P, Bickman L and Brannen J (Eds.) *The Sage Handbook of Social Research Methods.* Thousand Oaks, CA: Sage, pp. 530–535.

Dalissier M (2007) *Nishida Kitaro: The Philosopher, His Thought, and Its Stakes*. GIS ASIE French Academic Network on Asian Studies. Available at: https://www.gis-reseau-asie.org/en/article/nishida-kitaro-philosopher-his-thought-and-its-stakes (accessed 8 October 2024).

Dalissier M (2009) Nishida Kitaro and Chinese philosophy. In Lam W-K and Cheung C-Y (Eds.) *Facing the 21st Century. Frontiers of Japanese Philosophy. 4*. Nagoya: Chisokudo Publications, pp. 211–250.
Damasio AR (2005) *Descartes' Error. Emotion, Reason and the Human Brain*. Revised Edition. New York: Penguin Books.
Damschroder LJ (2020) Clarity out of chaos. Use of theory in implementation research. *Psychiatric Research*. 283: 112461. https://doi.org/10.1016/j.psychres.2019.06.036.
Daniels D (2011) *Decolonising The Researcher's Mind About Southern Research: Reflections From The Field*. Stellenbosch University. https://scholar.sun.ac.za/items/49f22429-13c3-4511-91ee-01bd607a032a, http://hdl.handle.net/10019.1/86800
Dauphinee E (2010) The ethics of autoethnography. *Review of International Studies*. 36(3): 799–818.
David SJ, Marshall AJ, Evanovich EK and Mumma H (2018) Intraindividual dynamic network analysis. Implications for clinical assessment. *Journal of Psychopathology and Behavioral Assessment*. 40(2): 235–248. https://doi.org/10.1007/s10862-017-9632-8.
Davidson B and Thomas A (2002) Buddhism and group analysis. *Group Analysis*. 35(1): 57–71. https://doi.org/10.1177/053331602400934025.
Davies R (1992) Gorbachev's Socialism in Historical Perspective. *The New Left Review*. Available at: https://newleftreview.org/issues/i179/articles/r-w-davies-gorbachev-s-socialism-in-historical-perspective.pdf (accessed 11 August 2022).
Davis BW (2022) Introduction. What Is Japanese Philosophy? In Davis BW (Eds.) *The Oxford Handbook of Japanese Philosophy*. New York: Oxford University Press, pp. 1–81.
Davis J, Mengersen K, Bennett S and Mazerolle L (2014) Systematic reviews and meta-analysis in social research through different lenses. *SpringerPlus*. 3: 511. https://springerplus.springeropen.com/articles/10.1186/2193-1801-3-511
Dawkins R (2021) Afterword. In Krauss LM (Ed.) *A Universe from Nothing. Why There is Something Rather than Nothing*. London: Simon & Schuster Ltd, pp. 187–191.
Dawson C (2019) *Introduction to Research Methods. A Practical Guide for Anyone Undertaking a Research Project*. 5th Edition. London: Robinson.
Day M and Thatcher J (2009) "I'm really embarrassed that you're going to read this …" Reflections on using diaries in qualitative research. *Qualitative Research in Psychology*. 6(4): 249–259.
Day SX (2014) A unifying theory for group counselling and psychotherapy. In DeLucia-Waack J, Kalodner CR and Riva MT (Eds.) *Handbook of Group Counselling & Psychotherapy*. 2nd Edition. Thousand Oaks, CA: Sage, pp. 24–33.
DDR Museum (2014) *Tamaras Asyl im Paradies. Die Rockgruppe Silly*. [Tamaras Asylum in Paradise. The Rock Group Silly]. 16 September 2014. Available at: https://www.ddr-museum.de/de/blog/archive/tamaras-asyl-im-paradies-die-rockgruppe-silly (accessed 2 April 2023).
de Beauvoir S (1949) *Le Deuxième Sexe. Les Fait Et Les Mythes. [The Second Sex. The classic manifesto of the liberated woman]*. Paris: Gallimard. [published in 1989 in English, trans. by HM Parshley. London: Vintage Books].
De Benedittis G (2020) From quantum physics to quantum hypnosis. A quantum mind perspective. *The International Journal of Clinical and Experimental Hypnosis*. 68(4): 433–450. https://doi.org/10.1080/00207144.2020.1799380.
De Benedittis G (2023) The (re)discovery of the unconscious: what we have learned from neuroscience. *International Journal of Cognition and Behavior*. 6(1): 1–7. https://clinmedjournals.org/articles/ijcb/international-journal-of-cognition-and-behaviour-ijcb-6-017.php?jid=ijcb
De Bono E (1973) *Lateral Thinking. Be More Creative and Productive*. New York: Harper Perennial.
De Haas W (2025) *Group Therapy and Group Dynamic Theory. A Professional Method For All Group Based Treatment*. New York: Routledge.
De Maré P (1972) *Perspectives in Group Psychotherapy. A Theoretical Background*. London: George Allen and Unwin.
De Maré P (1983) Michael Foulkes and the northfield experiment In Pines M (Ed.). *The Evolution of Group Analysis*. London: Routledge & Kegan Paul, pp. 218–231.
De Maré P (1985) Major Bion. In Pines M (Ed.) (1992) *Bion and Group Psychotherapy*. London: Routledge & Kegan Paul, pp. 108–113.

De Maré P (1989) The history of large group phenomena in relation to group-analytic psychotherapy. The story of the median group. *Group.* 13(3–4): 173–197.

De Maré P (1990) The development of the Median Group. *Group Analysis.* 23(2): 113–127.

De Maré P and Schőllberger R (2003) The larger group as a meeting of minds. In Schneider S and Weinberg H (Eds.) *The Large Group Re-Visited.* London: Jessica Kingsley Publishers.

De Maré P and Schőllberger R (2004) A case of mind. *Group Analysis.* 37(3): 339–352.

De Maré P, Piper R and Thompson S (1991) *Koinonia: From Hate, Through Dialogue, to Culture in the Large Group.* London: Karnac Books.

De Mendelssohn F (2000) The aesthetics of the political in group analytic process. The wider scope of group analysis. *Group Analysis.* 33(4): 438–458.

De Nooy W, Mrvar A and Batagelj V (2005) *Exploratory Social Network Analysis with Pajek.* New York: Cambridge University Press. [Revised and Expanded 3rd Edition, 2018]. http://mrvar.fdv.uni-lj.si/pajek/be3.htm

De Saussure F (1959) *Course in General Linguistics.* Trans. W Baskin. New York: Philosophical Library Inc.

De Schryver M, Vindevogel S, Rasmussen AE and Cramer AOJ (2015) Unpacking constructs. A network approach for studying war exposure, daily stressors and post-traumatic stress disorder. *Frontiers in Psychology.* 6(4): https://doi.org/10.3389/fpsyg.2015.01896.

De Vaus D (2008) Comparative and cross-national designs. In Alasuutari P, Bickman L and Brannen J (Eds.) *The Sage Handbook of Social Research Methods.* Thousand Oakes, CA: Sage, pp. 249–264.

De Vellis RF and Thorpe CT (2022) *Scale Development. Theory and Applications.* 5th Edition. Thousand Oaks, CA: Sage Publications.

De Witte M (2020) Psychological research has a racism problem Stanford scholar says. *Stanford Report.* 24 June. Available at: https://news.stanford.edu/stories/2020/06/psychological-research-racism-problem-stanford-scholar-says (accessed 29 December 2024).

De Zulueta F (2006) *From Pain to Violence. The Traumatic Roots of Destructiveness.* 2nd Edition. Chichester: John Wiley & Sons.

De Zuluetta F (1995) Bilingualism, culture and identity. *Group Analysis.* 28(2): 255–265.

Deaton A and Cartwright N (2018) Understanding and misunderstanding randomized controlled trials. *Social Science & Medicine.* 210(12): 2–21. https://doi.org/10.1016/j.socscimed.2017.12.005.

Debbane EG and de Carufel F (1993) The context of transference interpretations in analytical group psychotherapy. *American Journal of Psychotherapy.* 47(4): 540–553.

Debray TP, Damen JA, Snell KI, Ensor J, Hooft L, Reitsma JB, Riley RD and Moons KG (2017) A guide to systematic review and meta-analysis of prediction model performance. *British Medical Journal.* 356: i6460. https://www.bmj.com/content/356/bmj.i6460.

DeChavez MG, Gutierrez M, Ducaju M and Fraile JC (2000) Comparative study of the therapeutic factors of group therapy in schizophrenic inpatients and outpatients. *Group Analysis.* 33(2): 251–264. https://doi.org/10.1177/0533316400332006.

Deci EL and Ryan RM (2008) Hedonia, eudaimonia, and well-being. An introduction. *Journal of Happiness Studies.* 9(1): 1–11. https://doi.org/10.1007/s10902-006-9018-1.

Declaration of Helsinki by WMA (1964) *Declaration of Helsinki.* Available at: https://www.wma.net/what-we-do/medical-ethics/declaration-of-helsinki/ (accessed 8 August 2024).

Dei GJ (2000) Rethinking the role of indigenous knowledges in the academy. *International Journal of Inclusive Education.* 4(2): 111–132. https://files.eric.ed.gov/fulltext/ED479137.pdf

Del Medico B (2022) *From the Physical Universe to the Metaphysical Cosmos. The Quantum Entanglement and Synchronicity of Carl Jung. On the Way to the Era of Collaboration between Spirit and Matter.* Rome: Bruno Del Medico Publishers.

Deleuze G (1991) *Empiricism and Subjectivity.* Trans. C Boundas. New York: Columbia University Press.

Deleuze G (2002) *Negotiations: Interventions and Interviews 1971–2001.* Trans. E Rottenberg. Stanford: Stanford University Press.

Deleuze G and Guattari F (1984) *Anti-Oedipus. Capitalism and Schizophrenia.* Trans. M Seem, R Hurley and HR Lane. Minneapolis: University of Minneapolis.

Deleuze G and Guattari F (1987) *A Thousand Plateaus. Capitalism and Schizophrenia.* Trans. B Massumi. Minneapolis: University of Minneapolis.
Deleuze G and Guattari F (1991) *What Is Philosophy?* Trans. H Tomlinson and G Burchell III. New York: Columbia University Press.
Deleuze G and Guattari F (1994) *What Is Philosophy?* Trans. G Burchell and H Tomlinson. London: Verso.
Dennett DC (2012) Facing up to the hard problem of consciousness. *Philosophical Transactions of the Royal Society B.* 19(373): 1755–1762.
Dennis M and Laporte M (2003) *The Stasi. Myth and Reality. [The Stasi. Myth and Reality].* Trans. P Brown. Themes in Modern German History Series. London: Pearson Education Limited. [Published 2014 by Routledge].
Denzin NK (2003) *Performance Ethnography. Critical Pedagogy and the Politics of Culture.* Thousand Oaks, CA: Sage.
Denzin NK (2012) Triangulation 2.0. *Journal of Mixed Methods Research.* 6(2): 80–88. https://doi.org/10.1177/1558689812437186.
Denzin NK (2018) *Performance Autoethnography: Critical Pedagogy and the Politics of Culture.* 2nd Edition. New York: Routledge. https://doi.org/10.4324/9781315159270.
Denzin NK and Lincoln YS (1994) *Handbook of Qualitative Research.* Thousand Oaks, CA: Sage.
Denzin NK and Lincoln YS (1998) *The Landscape of Qualitative Research: Theories and Issues.* Thousand Oaks, CA: Sage.
Denzin NK and Lincoln YS (2000) *Handbook of Qualitative Research.* 2nd Edition. Thousand Oaks, CA: Sage.
Denzin NK and Lincoln YS (2005a) *Handbook of Qualitative Research.* 3rd Edition. Thousand Oaks, CA: Sage.
Denzin NK and Lincoln YS (2005b) Introduction: The discipline and practice of qualitative research. In Denzin NK and Lincoln YS (Eds.) *Handbook of Qualitative Research.* 3rd Edition. Thousand Oaks, CA: Sage, pp. 1–32.
Denzin NK and Lincoln YS (2011) Preface. In Denzin NK and Lincoln YS (Eds.) *The Sage Handbook of Qualitative Research.* 4th Edition. Thousand Oaks, CA: Sage, pp. ix–xvi.
Denzin NK, Lincoln YS and Smith LT (2008) *Handbook of Critical and Indigenous Methodologies.* Thousand Oaks, CA: Sage.
Derogatis LR (1975) *Brief Symptom Inventory.* Baltimore, MD: Clinical Psychometric Research.
Derogatis LR (1977) *The SCL-90 Manual I: Administration, Scoring and Procedures for the SCL-90.* Baltimore: Clinical Psychometric Research.
Derogatis LR (1993) *Brief Symptom Inventory: Administration, Scoring and Procedures Manual.* 4th Edition. Minneapolis: NCS Pearson Inc.
Derogatis LR (1994) *SCL-90-R: Administration, Scoring and Procedures Manual.* Minneapolis: NCS Pearson Inc.
Derogatis LR (2000) *The Brief Symptom Inventory–18 (BSI-18): Administration, Scoring and Procedures Manual.* Minneapolis: NCS Pearson Inc.
Derogatis LR (2017) Symptom checklist-90-revised, brief symptom inventory, and BSI-18. In Maruish ME (Ed.) *Handbook of Psychological Assessment in Primary Care Settings.* 2nd Edition. New York: Routledge, pp. 599–629.
Derogatis LR and Melisaratos N (1983) The brief symptom inventory: An introductory report. *Psychological Medicine.* 13(3): 595–605.
Derogatis LR and Savitz KL (1999) The SCL-90-R, brief symptom inventory, and matching clinical rating scales. In Maruish ME (Ed.) *The Use of Psychological Testing for Treatment Planning and Outcomes Assessment. Instruments for Adults.* 2nd Edition. New York: Lawrence Erlbaum Associates Publishers, pp. 679–724.
Derogatis LR and Spencer PM (1982) *The Brief Symptom Inventory (BSI). Administration and Procedures Manual 1.* Baltimore, MD: Clinical Psychometric Research.

Derr A (2024) *Using Network Density to Evaluate and Optimize Collaboration Intensity.* VisibleNetworkLabs. Available at: https://visiblenetworklabs.com/2024/11/13/using-network-density-to-evaluate-and-optimize-collaboration-intensity/ (accessed 20 March 2025).

Derrida J (1967a) *L'écriture et la Différence.* Paris: Editions du Seuil. [*Writing and Difference.* Chicago: The University of Chicago Press. published in English in 1980].

Derrida J (1967b) Violence and metaphysics. An essay on the thought of emmanuel levinas. In *Writing and Difference.* Trans. A Bass. Chicago, IL: The University of Chicago Press, chapter 4, pp. 79–153. [Republished in 1980].

Derrida J (1976) *Of Grammatology.* Trans. GC Spivak. Baltimore, MD: John Hopkins University.

Derrida J (1981) *Positions.* Trans. A Bass. Chicago, IL: Chicago University Press.

Derrida J (1990) Some statements and truisms about neologisms, newisms, postisms parasitisms, and small seisms. Trans. A Tomiche. In Carroll D (Ed.) *The States of 'Theory'. History, Art, and Critical Discourse.* New York: Colombia University Press, pp. 63–94.

Derrida J (1997) *Deconstruction in a Nutshell. A Conversation with Jacques Derrida.* Edited and with comments by JD Caputo. New York: Fordham University Press.

Derrida J (1998) *Of Grammatology.* Trans. GC Spivak. Baltimore, MD: John Hopkins University.

Descartes R (1637/1998) *Discourse on Method* and *Meditations on the First Philosophy.* 4th Edition. Trans. DA Cress. Cambridge, IL: Hackett Publishing Company.

Descartes R (1644/2009) *Principles of Philosophy.* Amsterdam: Elsevier.

Deshpande R (2022) What is Ahimsa? *Yoga Journal.* 15 February. Available at: https://www.yogajournal.com/lifestyle/what-is-ahimsa/ (accessed 24 January 2025).

Dettmer M, Röbel S and Sandberg B (2007) Der Tote von Zimmer 317. [The Dead in Room 317] *Der Spiegel,* 7 October, 41. https://www.spiegel.de/politik/der-tote-von-zimmer-317-a-40212bd8-0002-0001-0000-000053203432

Deutscher Bundestag (1994) *Beschlußempfehlung und Bericht des 1. Untersuchungsausschusses nach Artikel 44 des Grundgesetzes.* Drucksache 12/7600. [Recommendations and Report of the 1st Inquiry committee according to $44 of the Constitution, Print Matter 12/7600]. Autoren: Joachim Gres & Dr. Andreas von Bülow. Bonn: Druckservice Bonn. https://dip.bundestag.de/drucksache/beschlußempfehlung-und-bericht-des-1-untersuchungsausschusses-nach-artikel-44-des/122691

Deutsches Radio Archiv (DRA) (2021) Sport im Fernsehen. [Sport on Television]. Available at: https://www.dra.de/entdecken/fruehes-ddr-fernsehen/sport-im-fernsehfunk (accessed 4 March 2022).

DeVault ML (2006) Introduction: What is institutional ethnography? *Social Problems.* 53(3): 294–298. https://doi.org/10.1525/sp.2006.53.3.294; https://www.academia.edu/29049128/Introduction_What_is_Institutional_Ethnography

DeVault ML and McCoy L (2002) Institutional ethnography. Using interviews to investigate ruling relations. In Gubrium and Holstein (Eds.) *Handbook of Interview Research: Context and Method.* Thousand Oaks, CA: Sage, pp. 751–776.

Devereux G (1967) *From Anxiety to Method in the Behavioral Sciences.* Berlin: Walter de Gruyter Publishers.

Devers KJ (1999) How will we know "good" qualitative research when we see it? Beginning the dialogue in Health Services Research. *Health Services Research.* 34(5): 1153–1188.

Devi A and Fenn E (2012) Make sure you keep our house safe! Thematic analysis of a children's psychotherapy group. *Journal of Child Psychotherapy.* 38(3): 318–334. https://doi.org/10.1080/0075417X.2012.720104.

Dewey J (1910/1933) *How We Think.* Buffalo, NY: Prometheus Books. https://archive.org/details/dli.ernet.240488

Dewey J (1916/1944) *Democracy and Education.* New York: Collier Books, Macmillan. https://archive.org/details/democracyeducati1916dewe/page/n15/mode/2up

Dewey J (1938) *Experience and Education.* New York: Macmillan Company. https://archive.org/details/ExperienceAndEducation

Dewey J (1982) *Logic. The Theory of Inquiry.* New York: Irvington. https://archive.org/details/JohnDeweyLogicTheTheoryOfInquiry

Dey L (1999) *Grounding Grounded Theory. Guidelines for Qualitative Inquiry.* London: Academic Press.
Dharani B (2025) Fluidity of social identities: implications for applying intersectionality. *Equality, Diversity and Inclusion. An International Journal.* 44(5): 502–523. https://doi.org/10.1108/EDI-06-2022-0151.
Di Giuseppe M, Perry JC, Petraglia J, Janzen J and Lingiardi V (2014) Development of a Q-sort version of the Defense Mechanism Rating Scales (DMRS-Q) for clinical use. *Journal of Clinical Psychology.* 70(5): 452–462. https://doi.org/10.1002/jclp.22089.
Diamond G, Wlodek B, Arthey S and Parker S (2025) A systematic review of deliberate practice in psychotherapy: Definitions, operationalization, and preliminary outcomes. *Psychotherapy.* 62(2): 113–131. https://doi.org/10.1037/pst0000569.
Diamond J (1978) *Behavioural Kinesiology and the Autonomic Nervous System.* Valley Cottage, NY: Aschaeus Press.
Diamond J (1979) *Your Body Doesn't Lie.* Enfield: Eden Grove Publishers. https://archive.org/details/yourbodydoesntlidiam00diam
Diamond J (1985) *Life Energy.* St. Paul, MN: Paragon House. https://archive.org/details/lifeenergyusingm0000diam
Dick B (1981) The spin of the proton. *Group Analysis.* 14(2): 128–129.
Dictionary.com (2023) Theory. Available at: https://www.dictionary.com/browse/theory (accessed 17 April 2024).
Dienes Z (2008) *Understanding Psychology as a Science. An Introduction to scientific and statistical evidence.* New York: Palgrave MacMillan.
Dijksterhuis A and Nordgren LF (2006) A theory of unconscious thought. *Perspectives On Psychological Science.* 1(2): 95–109.
Dijksterhuis A, Bos MW, Nordgren LF and van Baaren RB (2006) On making the right choice: The deliberation without-attention effect. *Science.* 311(5763): 1005–1007. https://doi.org/10.1126/science.1121629.
Dillman DR, Symth JD and Christian LM (2014) *Internet, Phone, Mail, and Mixed-Mode Surveys. The Tailored Design Method.* 4th Edition. Hoboken, NJ: John Wiley & Sons.
DiMaggio P (1995) Comments on "What theory is not". *Administrative Science Quarterly.* 40(3): 391–397. https://doi.org/10.2307/2393790.
Dincel BK and Savur H (2019) Diary keeping in writing education. *Journal of Education and Training Studies.* 7(1): 48–59. https://eric.ed.gov/?id=EJ1199146.
Dladla N (2017) Towards an African critical philosophy of race. Ubuntu as a philo-praxis of liberation. *Filosofia Theoretica. Journal of African Philosophy, Culture and Religions.* 6(1): 39–68. https://doi.org/10.4314/ft.v6i1.3.
Doğmuş YU and Canpolat M (2024) Clients' experiences during three phases of a time-limited psychodrama group: A case study. *Group Analysis.* Online. https://doi.org/10.1177/05333164241258163.
Dolamo R (2013) Botho/ubuntu: The heart of African ethics. *Scriptura: Journal for Biblical, Theological and Contextual Hermeneutics.* 112(1): 1–10. https://doi.org/10.7833/112-0-78.
Dolgopolov MV and Zubarev AP (2011) Some aspects of the m-adic analysis and its applications to m-adic stochastic processes. *P-Adic Numbers, Ultrametric Analysis, and Applications.* 3(1): 39–51.
Dooley D and McCarthy J (2005) *Nursing Ethics: Irish Cases and Concerns.* Dublin: Gill and Macmillan.
Doran M (2001) *A Clinical Study of a 30 Week Group for Women Who Have Been Sexually Abused as Children.* MSc. London: Birkbeck College, University of London.
Doria N, Condran B, Boulos L, Maillet DG, Dowling L and Levy A (2018) Sharpening the focus. Differentiating between focus groups for patient engagement vs qualitative research. *BMC. Research Involvement and Engagement.* 4: 19. https://researchinvolvement.biomedcentral.com/articles/10.1186/s40900-018-0102-6.
Dorrien G (2012) In the spirit of Hegel. Post-Kantian subjectivity. The phenomenology of the spirit, and absolute idealism. *American Journal of Theology & Philosophy.* 33(3): 200–223.
Douglas A (2013) Growing a median group. *Group-Analytic Contexts.* Summer Issue: 29–36. https://groupanalyticsociety.co.uk/contexts/
Downe-Wamboldt B (1992) Content analysis. Method, applications, and issues. *Health Care for Women International.* 13(3): 313–321.

Dragovich B, Khrennikov AY, Kozyrev SV and Volovic IV (2009) On p-Adic mathematical physics. *P-Adic Numbers, Ultrametic Analysis and Applications*. 1(1): 1–17.

Droitcour J, Silberman G and Chelimsky E (2009) Cross-design synthesis. A new form of meta-analysis for combining results from randomized clinical trials and medical-practice databases. *International Journal of Technology Assessment in Health Care*. 9(3): 440–449.

Dudley DO and Stenbeck M (1988) Panels and cohorts: Design and model in the study of voting turnout. *Sociological Methodology*. 18(1): 1–35.

Duffy J (2016) Uncovered: The 'Forgotten' Stories of Scotland's Trailblazing Women Scientists. *The Herald Scotland*. 26th June. Available at: https://www.heraldscotland.com/news/14580545.uncovered-forgotten-stories-scotlands-trailblazing-women-scientists/ (accessed 20 December 2024).

Dunning H (2023) Double-slit Experiment that Proved the Wave Nature of Light Explored in Time. 3 April 2023. Available at: https://www.imperial.ac.uk/news/244037/double-slit-experiment-that-proved-wave-nature/) accessed 8 January 2025).

Dutta S and Kundu A (2021) Dialectics of homophily in the formation of friendship groups in Jawaharlal Nehru University, New Delhi, India. *Group Analysis*. 54(2): 244–264. https://doi.org/10.1177/0533316420959746.

Duval S and Tweedie R (2000) Trim and fill: a simple funnel-plot-based method of testing and adjusting for publication bias in meta-analysis. *Biometrics*. 56(2): 455–463. https://doi.org/10.1111/j.0006-341x.2000.00455.x.

Dyson H and Brown D (2016) The experience of mentalization-based treatment: an interpretative phenomenological study. *Issues in Mental Health Nursing*. 37(8): 586–595. https://doi.org/10.3109/01612840.2016.1155246.

Eagle MN (2013) The implications of conceptual critiques and empirical research on unconscious processes for psychoanalytic theory. *Psychoanalytic Review*. 100(6): 881–917. https://doi.org/10.1521/prev.2013.100.6.881.

Eccles JC (1994) *How the Self Controls Its Brain*. New York: Springer Verlag. https://archive.org/details/howselfcontrolsi0000eccl/page/n3/mode/2up

Eckardt J-N, Hahn W, Rőllig C Statik S, Platzbecke U, Müller-Tidow C, Serve H, Baldus CD, Schliemann C, Schäfer-Eckart K, Hanoun M, Kaufmann M, Burchert A, Thiede C, Schetelig J, Sedlmayr M, Bornhäuser M, Wolfien M and Middeke JM (2024) Mimicking clinical trials with synthetic acute myeloid leukemia patients using generative artificial intelligence. *NPJ Digital Medicine*. 7(1): 76. htpps://doi.org/10.1038/s41746-024-01076-x.

Eckert AM (2014) Geteilt, aber nicht unverbunden. Grenzgewässer als Deutsch-Deutsches Umweltproblem. [Separated but not unconnected. The border water shores as a German environmental problem]. *Zeitgeschichte*. 62(1): 69–99. https://www.ifz-muenchen.de/heftarchiv/2014_1_3_eckert.pdf

Eco U (1977) *A Theory of Semiotics*. London: Macmillan. https://raggeduniversity.co.uk/wp-content/uploads/2025/01/A-Theory-of-Semiotics-Umberto-Eco-1979.pdf

Edinger EF (1992) *Ego and Archetype. Individuation and the Religious Function of the Psyche*. Boston: Shambhala. https://www.obafemio.com/uploads/5/1/4/2/5142021/ego_and_archetype.pdf

Edwards LM (2003) Response to 'Buddhism and Group Analysis'. *Group Analysis*. 36(1): 157–160.

Egger M, Davey Smith G, Schneider M and Minder C (1997) Bias in meta-analysis detected by a simple, graphical test. *British Medical Journal*. 13 September. 315(629). https://doi.org/10.1136/bmj.315.7109.629.

Ehrlich S (2023) Unbounded worlds. A challenge for group relations? In Archer C, Kelly R, Strauss G and Triest J (Eds.) *The Ecosystem of Group Relations. Culture, Gender and Identity in Groups and Organizations. The Group Relations Conferences Series*. New York: Routledge, pp. 7–18.

Einhorn S (2021) From a woman's point of view. How internalised misogyny affects relationships between women. *Group Analysis*. 54(4): 481–498.

Einstein A (2005) Physics, philosophy, and scientific progress. *Physics Today*. 58(6): 46–48. https://doi.org/10.1063/1.1996474.

Einstein A (2013) *Relativity. Foreword by Derek Raine*. New York: Routledge.

Einstein A and Cohen ER (1956) The meaning of relativity. *Physics Today*. 9(10): 30–32. https://doi.org/10.1063/1.3059795.

Einstein A, Schilpp PA and Morrison P (1950) The proceedings of the American philosophical society; The meaning of relativity; Out of my later years and Albert Einstein: philosopher-scientist. *Physics Today.* 3(11): 30–32. https://doi.org/10.1063/1.3066685.

Einstein A and Schilpp PA (1950) Expectations of a definite form. *Physics Today*. 3(2): 6–11. https://doi.org/10.1063/1.3066809.

Eisold K (1995) *Psychoanalysis Today. Implications for Organizational Applications*. A Paper for the ISPSO International Conference. July 7–9, 1995, London. Published in *Free Associations.* 38(6): 174–191. Available at: https://www.psychoanalysis-and-therapy.com/human_nature/free-associations/eisold.html (accessed 18 June 2024).

Ekman P (1992) An argument for basic emotions. *Cognition and Emotion.* 6(3/4): 169–200.

Elias N (1939) *The Civilizing Process I: The History of Manners. II: State Formation.* Oxford.

Elias N (1978) *What Is Sociology?* New York: Columbia University Press. https://archive.org/details/whatissociology0000elia_v4s7

Elias N (1987) *Involvement and Detachment.* Oxford: Blackwell. https://archive.org/details/involvementdetac0000elia/page/n7/mode/2up

Elias N (1991) *The Symbol Theory.* London: Sage Publications.

Elias N (1994) *The Civilizing Process.* Oxford: Blackwell. https://archive.org/details/civilizingproces0000elia.

Ellaway RH, Kehoe A and Illing J (2020) Critical realism and realist inquiry in medical education. *Academic Medicine.* 95(7): 984–988. https://doi.org/10.1097/ACM.0000000000003232.

Elliott KC and McKaughan DJ (2014) Non-epistemic values and the multiple goals of science. *Philosophy of Science*. 81(1): 1–21. https://doi.org/10.1086/674345.

Elliott R (2010) Psychotherapy change process: Realizing the promise. *Psychotherapy Research.* 20(2): 123–135.

Elliott R (2012) Qualitative methods for studying psychotherapy change processes. In Thompson A and Harper D (Eds.) *Qualitative Research Methods in Mental Health and Psychotherapy: An Introduction for Students and Practitioners*. Chichester: Wiley-Blackwell, pp. 69–81.

Ellis C and Bochner A (2000) Analysing analytic autoethnography: An autopsy. *Journal of Contemporary Ethnography.* 35(4): 429–449. https://www.researchgate.net/publication/249714199_Analyzing_Analytic_AutoethnographyAn_Autopsy

Elo S and Kyngäs H (2008) The qualitative content analysis process. *Journal of Advanced Nursing.* 62(1): 107-115. https://doi.org/10.1111/j.1365-2648.2007.04569.x.

Emerson C (1997) *The First Hundred Years of Mikhail Bakhtin.* Princeton, NJ: Princeton University Press.

Emery F (1959) *Characteristics of Socio-Technical Systems. A Critical Review of Theories and Facts about the Effects of Technological Change on the Internal Structure of Work Organisations, With Special Reference to the Effects of Higher Mechanisation and Automation.* (Doc. 527). London: Human Resource Centre, Tavistock Institute of Human Relations.

Emery FE and Thorsrud E (1964) *Form and Content in Industrial Democracy. Some Experiences from Norway and Other European Countries*. Assen, Drenthe: Von Gorcum Publishers. [Republished 1969 with Trist EL, London: Tavistock Publications; Endler CP, Enzian A, Dietrich G, Schacht S and Sachs G (2022) Observers in analytic groups. A content analysis study from the participant perspective, *Group Analysis.* 55(3): 391–406.

Engler S and Gardiner MQ (2022) Theorizing and analysis. In Engler S and Stausberg M (Eds.) *The Routledge Handbook of Research Methods in the Study of Religion.* New York: Routledge, pp. 110–133.

Engler S and Stausberg M (Eds.) (2022) *The Routledge Handbook of Research Methods in the Study of Religion.* New York: Routledge.

Epskamp S (2019) Network Psychometrics. Current State and Future Direction. Available at: https://sachaepskamp.com/files/Taipei_Epskamp.pdf

Epskamp S (2020) Psychometric network models from time-series and panel data. *Psychometrika.* 85(1): 206–231. https://doi.org/10.1007/s11336-020-09697-3.

Epskamp S, Cramer AOJ, Waldorp LJ, Schmittnann VD and Borsboom D (2012) qgraph: Network visualizations of relationships in psychometric data. *Journal of Statistical Software*. 48(4): 1–18. https://www.jstatsoft.org/article/view/v048i04

Epskamp S, Maris G, Waldorp LJ and Borsboom D (2018) Network psychometrics. In Irwing P, Booth T and Hughes DJ (Eds.) *The Wiley Handbook of Psychometric Testing. A Multidisciplinary Reference on Survey, Scale and Test Development.* London: Wiley Blackwell, pp. 953–986.

Epstein M (1998) Beyond the oceanic feeling. Psychoanalytic study of Buddhist mediation. In Molino A (Ed.) *The Couch and The Tree. Dialogues In Psychoanalysis and Buddhism.* London: Open Gate Press, pp. 119–130.

Erikson TH (2001) *Small Places Large Issues. An Introduction to Social and Cultural Anthropology.* London: Pluto Press.

Erwin EJ, Brotherson MJ and Summers JA (2011) Understanding qualitative metasynthesis. Issues and opportunities in early childhood intervention research. *Journal of Early Intervention.* 33(3): 186–200. https://doi.org/10.1177/1053815111425493.

Escamilla M (2021) Neuroscience and Jung. In O'Brien N and O'Brien J (Eds.) *The Professional Practice of Jungian Coaching. Corporate Analytical Psychology.* New York: Routledge, pp. 44–56.

ESOMAR (European Society for Opinion and Market Research) (2018) *Guideline on Research and Data Analytics with Children, Young People, and Other Vulnerable Individuals.* Available at: https://esomar.org/code-and-guidelines/guideline-on-research-and-data-analytics-with-children-and-young-people-and-other-vulnerable-individuals (accessed 10 April 2025).

Ettin MF (2001) The deep structure of group life. Unconscious dimensions. *Group.* 25(4): 253–298.

Etymonline (2021) *Reality.* Updated 12 May 2021. Available at: https://www.etymonline.com/word/reality (accessed 5 January 2025).

Etymonline (2022a) *Research.* Available at: https://www.etymonline.com/word/research (accessed 7 March 2022).

Etymonline (2022b) *Science.* Available at: https://www.etymonline.com/word/science (accessed 7 March 2022).

Etymonline (2023) *Positivism.* Available at: https://www.etymonline.com/word/positivism (accessed 15 February 2023).

Etymonline (2024a) *Paradigm.* Available at: https://www.etymonline.com/word/paradigm (accessed 15 February 2024).

Etymonline (2024b) *Concept.* Updated 13 January 2024. Available at: https://www.etymonline.com/word/concept (accessed 15 April 2024).

Etymonline (2024c) *Framework.* Updated 13 January 2024. Available at: https://www.etymonline.com/word/framework (accessed 15 April 2024).

Etymonline (2024d) *Model.* Updated 13 January 2024. Available at: https://www.etymonline.com/word/model (accessed 15 April 2024).

Etymonline (2024e) *Theory.* Updated 13 January 2024. Available at: https://www.etymonline.com/word/theory (accessed 15 April 2024).

Etymonline (2024f) *Meta-.* Updated 13 January 2024. Available at: https://www.etymonline.com/word/meta- (accessed 15 April 2024).

Etymonline (2025) *Virtual.* Updated 04 January 2025. Available at: https://www.etymonline.com/word/virtual (accessed 5 January 2025).

Eubanks CF, Muran JC and Safran JD (2018) Alliance rupture repair. A meta-analysis. *Psychotherapy.* 55(4): 508–519. https://doi.org/10.1037/pst0000185.

Evans C (2001) Research as an Extended Group Phenomenon: Is "Hard Science" a Sexual Metaphor? *Group Analysis.* 34(2): 299–307.

Evans C, Connell J, Barkham M, Margison F, McGrath G, Mellor-Clark J and Audin K (2002) Towards a standardised brief outcome measure: Psychometric properties and utility of the CORE-OM. *British Journal of Psychiatry.* 180(1): 51–60.

Evans C, Margison F and Barkham M (1998) The contribution of reliable and clinically significant change methods to evidence-based mental health. *BMJ Mental Health.* 1(3): 2–5. https://mentalhealth.bmj.com/content/1/3/70

Evans CR and Dion KL (1991) Group cohesion and performance. A meta-analysis. *Small Group Research.* 22(2): 175–186.

Evans J (1988) Research findings and clinical practice with adolescents. *Group Analysis.* 21(2): 103–115.
Evans J (1998) *Active Group Analytic Group Therapy for Adolescence.* London: Jessica Kingsley Publishers.
Evans J and Benefield P (2001) Systematic reviews of educational research: Does the medical model fit? *British Educational Research Journal.* 27(5): 527–541.
Eysenck HJ (1967) *The Biological Basis of Personality*. Springfield, IL: Charles C Thomas Publishers Ltd.
Eysenck HJ (1981) General features of the model. In Eysenck HJ (Ed.) *A Model for Personality*. New York: Springer, pp. 1–37.
Eysenck HJ (1986/2017) *The Decline and Fall of the Freudian Empire.* Harmondsworth: Penguin Books.
Eysenck HJ and Eysenck MW (1985) *Personality and Individual Differences. A Natural Science Approach.* New York: Plenum.
Eze EC (Ed.) (1997) *Postcolonial African Philosophy. A Critical Reader.* Oxford: Blackwell.
Eze MO (2020) Ubuntu/Botho. Ideologie oder Verstehen? [Ideology or understanding?] *Deutsche Deutsche Zeitschrift für Philosophie.* 68(6): 928–942. https://www.degruyterbrill.com/document/doi/10.1515/dzph-2020-0063/html
Ezquerro A and Cañete M (2023) *Group Analysis throughout the Life Cycle. Foulkes Revisited from a Group Attachment and Developmental Perspective.* New York: Routledge.
Ezquerro A and Cañete M (2025) *The Power of Group Attachment: John Bowlby Revisited from a Group-Analytic Perspective.* New York: Routledge.
Ezriel H (1973) Psychoanalytic group therapy. In Wolberg LR and Schwartz EK (Eds.) *Group Therapy.* New York: Stratton International Medical Book, pp. 183–210.
Faflak J (2008) *Romantic Psychoanalysis. The Burden of the Mystery.* Albany: Suny Press.
Fals Borda O (2006) Participatory (action) research in social theory: Origins and challenges. In Reason P and Bradbury H (Eds.) *Handbook of Action Research: Participative Inquiry and Practice.* Thousand Oaks, CA: Sage, pp. 27–37.
Fannrich-Lautenschläger I (2014) *DDR Zwangsarbeiter. Ausbeutung nach Plan.* Deutschlandfunk. [Forced labor. Exploitation according to plan.] 15 June 2014. https://www.deutschlandfunk.de/ddr-zwangsarbeiter-ausbeutung-nach-plan-100.html
Fanon F (1963) *The Wretched of The Earth.* New York: Grove, Weidenfeld.
Faraday M (1859) *A Course of Lectures on the Various Forces of Matter, and their Relations to Each Other.* New York: Harper Brothers. (Republished in 2015 by Leopold Classic Library).
Farr J (1986) So vile and miserable an estate. The problem of slavery in Locke's political thought. *Political Theory*. 14(2): 263–289. https://doi.org/10.1177/0090591786014002005.
FAS Society (2012) *An Introduction to Hisamatsu Shin'Ichis's Religious Thought.* Translations edited by Tokiwa Gishin in collaboration with Tsukui Akemi. Kyoto. Available at: www.fas.x0.com (accessed 18 June 2023).
Faul F, Erdfelder E, Buchner A and Lang A-G (2009) Statistical power analyses using G*Power 3.1: Tests for correlation and regression analyses. *Behavior Research Methods*. 41(4): 1149–1160.
Faul F, Erdfelder E, Lang A-G and Buchner A (2007) G*Power 3: A flexible statistical power analysis program for the social, behavioral, and biomedical sciences. *Behavior Research Methods*. 39(2): 175–191.
Faulkenberry TJ (2022) *Psychological Statistics: The Basics.* New York: Routledge.
Faye J (2024) Copenhagen Interpretation of Quantum Mechanics. 31 May 2024. Available at: https://plato.stanford.edu/entries/qm-copenhagen/ (accessed 9 January 2025).
Faye J and Jaksland R (2011) Barad, Bohr, and quantum mechanics. *Synthese*. 199: 8231–8255. https://doi.org/10.1007/s11229-021-03160-1.
Fehr SS (2018) *Introduction to Group Psychotherapy A Practical Guide* 3rd Edition. London: Taylor & Francis Ltd.
Feilzer (2024) A pragmatist approach to mixed methods research. In Shan Y (Ed.) *Philosophical Foundations of Mixed Methods Research. Dialogues between Researchers and Philosophers.* New York: Routledge, pp. 13–29.

Ferguson G (2020) How the Five Skandhas Build Our Sense of Self. *Lion's Roar Magazine.* 11 March 2020. Available at: https://www.lionsroar.com/how-five-skandhas-build-sense-self/ (accessed 24 January 2025).

Fernandez E, Woldgabreal Y, Day A, Pham T, Gleich B and Aboujaoude E (2021) Live psychotherapy by video versus in-person: A meta-analysis of efficacy and its relationship to types and targets of treatment. *Clinical Psychology & Psychotherapy*. 28(6): 1535–1549.

Fernandez KV (2019) Critically reviewing literature: a tutorial for new researchers. *Australasian Marketing Journal*. 279(3): 187–196. https://doi.org/10.1016/j.ausmj.2019.05.001.

Ferrante MA (1993) Using anthropology in group analysis and psychotherapy. *Group Analysis.* 26(3): 229–325.

Ferreira AG (1980) Transference and transference neurosis in group analysis. *Group Analysis.* 13(2): 93–99.

Ferro S and França M (2020) The Portuguese school of groupanalysis. The integration of psychoanalytic concepts in groupanalysis. In Manso Netto S and França M (Eds.) *The Portuguese School of Group Analysis. Towards a Unified and Integrated Approach to Theory Research and Clinical Work.* New York: Routledge, pp. 53–72.

Festinger L, Schachter S and Back K (1974) *Social Pressures in Informal Groups: A Study of Human Factors in Housing.* Stanford, CA: Stanford University Press.

Feyerabend P (1975) *Against Method. Outline of an Anarchistic Theory of Knowledge.* London: Verso.

Feynman RP, Leighton RB and Sands M (1975) *The Feynman Lectures on Physics. Volumes 1–3.* Reading, MA: Addison-Wesley Publishing.

Fichte JG (1982) *The Science of Knowledge.* Ed. and Trans. P Heath and J Lachs. Cambridge: Cambridge University Press.

Field AP (2001) Meta-analysis of correlation coefficients: A Monte Carlo comparison of fixed and random-effects methods. *Psychological Methods*. 6(2): 161–180.

Field AP (2003a) Can meta-analysis be trusted? *The Psychologist*. 16(12): 642–645.

Field AP (2003b) The problems in using fixed-effects models of meta-analysis on real-world data. Understanding statistics. *Statistical Issues in Psychology, Education, and the Social Sciences.* 2(2): 105–124.

Field AP (2005a) *Discovering Statistics Using SPSS.* 2nd Edition. London: Sage.

Field AP (2005b) Is the meta-analysis of correlation coefficients accurate when population correlations vary? *Psychological Methods*. 10(4): 444–467.

Field AP (2005c) Meta-analysis. In Miles J and Gilbert P (Eds.) *A Handbook of Research Methods in Clinical and Health Psychology*. Oxford: Oxford University Press, pp. 295–308.

Field AP (2024) *Discovering Statistics Using IBM SPSS Statistics.* 6th Edition. New York: Sage.

Field AP and Gillett R (2010) How to do a meta-analysis. *The British Journal of Mathematical and Statistical Psychology*. 63(3): 665–694. https://doi.org/10.1348/000711010X502733.

Fielding JM (1975) A technique for measuring outcome in psychotherapy. *British Journal of Medical Psychology.* 48(3): 189–197. https://doi.org/10.1111/j.2044-8341.1975.tb02322.x.

Fierz M and Weisskopf VF (1960) (Eds.) *Theoretical Physics in the Twentieth Century. A Memorial Volume to Wolfgang Pauli.* New York: Interscience Publishers Inc.

Figal G (2007) Gadamer als Phänomenologe. [Gadamer as Phenomenologist.] *Phänomenologische Forschungen.* 1: 95–107. https://doi.org/10.28937/1000107937.

Figgess S (2018) A gestalt perspective on energy psychotherapy. *British Gestalt Journal*. 27(2): 30–36.

Filep CV, Turner S, Eidse N, Thompson-Fawcett M and Fitzsimons S (2018) Advancing rigour in solicited diary research. *Qualitative Research.* 18(4): 451–470. https://doi.org/10.1177/1468794117728411

Finlay J and Dela Cruz AM (2025) "This is my future?" Understanding the lives of emerging adult women living with chronic pain through a narrative inquiry. *Global Qualitative Nursing Research.* 12. Online https://doi.org/10.1177/23333936251335531.

Finlay L (2006) The embodied experience of multiple sclerosis: An existential-phenomenological analysis. In Finlay L and Ballinger C (Eds.) *Qualitative Research for Allied Health Professionals: Challenging Choices.* Chichester: John Wiley & Sons Ltd, pp. 185–199.

First MB, Gaebel, W, Mai M, Stein DJ, Kogan, CS, Saunders JB, Poznvak VB, and Gureie O, Lewis-Fernandez R, Marcker A, Brewin CR, Cloitre M, Claudino A, Pike KM, Baird, G, Skuse D, Krueger RB, Briken P, Burke JD, Lochman JE, Evans SC, Woods DW and Reed GM (2021) An organization- and category-level comparison of diagnostic requirements for mental disorders in ICD-11 and DSM-5. *World Psychiatry*. 20(1): 34–51.

Fisher RA (1921) On the "Probable Erro" of a coefficient of correlation deduced from a small sample. *Metron.* 1: 3–32.

Fisher RA (1935) *The Design of Experiments*. Edinburgh: Oliver & Boyd.

Fishman DB (2013) The pragmatic case study method for creating rigorous and systematic, practitioner-friendly research. *Pragmatic Case Studies in Psychotherapy.* 9(4). https://pcsp.nationalregister.org/index.php/pcsp/article/view/1833.

Fishman DB, Messer DJ, Edwards DJ and Dattilio FM (Eds.) (2016) *Case Studies Within Psychotherapy Trials*. New York: Oxford University Press.

Fiumara R (1976) Analytical psychology and therapeutic group analysis. *Journal of Analytic Psychology.* 21(1): 1–24.

Fiumara R (1983) Analytic psychology and group-analytic psychotherapy. Convergences. In Pines M (Ed.) *The Evolution of Group Analysis.* London: Routledge, pp. 109–127.

Fiumara R (1989) Jungian analysts and group analysis. *Group Analysis.* 22(2): 131–134.

Fiumara R and Zanasi M (1989) Depression of the group and depression in the group. *Group Analysis.* 21(1): 49–57.

Flax J (1990) Postmodernism and gender relations in feminist theory. In Nicholson LJ (Ed.) *Feminism/Postmodernism*. New York: Routledge, pp: 39–62.

Fletcher AJ (2017) Applying critical realism in qualitative research. Methodology meets method. *International Journal of Social Research Methods.* 20(2): 181–194.

Flikschuh K (2018) II - Philosophical racism. *Aristotelian Society. Supplementary Volume.* 92(1): 91–110. https://doi.org/10.1093/arisup/aky003.

Flikschuh K and Ypi L (Eds.) (2014) *Kant and Colonialism. Historical and Critical Perspectives.* Oxford University Press.

Flint MA, Eaton PW and Smithers LE (2023) (Navigating-circling-un/doing)~post-qualitative inquiry: a collective biography. *Qualitative Inquiry*. 29(6): 686–697. https://doi.org/10.1177/10778004221126699.

Flores Mosri D, Abrams A, Barry V, Biran I, Coetzer R, Moore P, Muñoz Zúñiga JF and Zellner M (2022) Clinical writing in neuropsychoanalysis. *Neuropsychoanalysis.* 24(2): 171–191.

Floridi L (2011) The informational nature of personal identity. *Minds and Machines.* 21(4): 549–566. https://link.springer.com/article/10.1007/s11023-011-9259-6.

Flowers P and Theopold K (2015) Tunneling. In Flowers P, Theopold K, Langley R and Austin SF (Eds.) *Chemistry.* Houston, TX: OpenStax College, pp. 722–727. https://openstax.org/books/chemistry-2e/pages/1-2-phases-and-classification-of-matter

Flyvbjerg B (2006) Five misunderstandings about case-study research. *Qualitative Inquiry*. 12(2): 219–245.

Fofana F, Bazeley P and Regnault A (2020) Applying a mixed methods design to test saturation in health outcome research. *PLoS One.* 19(6): e0234898. https://doi.org/10.1371/journal.pone.0234898.

Fonagy P (2004) Foreword. In Richardson P, Kächele H and Renlund C (Eds.) *Research on Psychoanalytic Psychotherapy with Adults.* London: Karnac, pp. xix–xxvii.

Fonagy P, Campbell C and Bateman A (2017) Mentalizing, attachment, and epistemic trust in group therapy. *International Journal of Group Psychotherapy.* 67(2): 176–201.

Fontana A and Frey J (1994) Interviewing. The art of science. In Denzin NK and Lincoln YS (Eds.) *The Handbook of Qualitative Research*. Thousand Oaks, CA: Sage, pp. 361–376.

Fontana A and Frey J (2005) The interview. From neutral stance to political involvement. In Denzin NK and Lincoln YS (Eds.) *The Handbook of Qualitative Research.* 3rd Edition. Thousand Oaks, CA: Sage, pp. 695–727.

Fontana A and Prokos AH (2016) *The Interview. From Formal to Postmodern.* New York: Routledge.

Forman J and Damschroder L (2008) Qualitative content analysis. In Jacoby L and Siminoff LA (Eds.) *Empirical Methods for Bioethics: A Primer.* New York: Elsevier, pp. 39–62.

Forness SR (2001) Special education and related services: What have we learned from meta-analysis? *Exceptionality*. 9(4): 185–197. https://eric.ed.gov/?id=EJ637179

Forsey M (2010) Ethnography and the myth of participant observation. In Hillyard S (Ed.) *New Frontiers in Ethnography. Studies in Qualitative Methodology. Vol. 11.* Bingley: Emerald, pp. 65–79.

Forshaw M (2010) *Easy Statistics in Psychology: A BPS Guide*. London: Wiley.

Forsyth DR (2019) *Group Dynamics.* 7th Edition. Boston, MA: Cengage.

Foucault M (1961) *Madness and Civilization. A History of Insanity in the Age of Reason.* Cambridge: Cambridge University Press. [Originally published in 1961, Paris: Editions Gallimard].

Foucault M (1966) *The Order of Things. An Archaelogy of the Human Sciences*. Trans. A Sheridan. London: Tavistock Publications 1970. Republished 1989, 2001, 2013 by Routledge; 1994 by Vintage Press. [Originally published in 1966, Paris: Editions Gallimard].

Foucault M (1969) *The Archaeology of Knowledge. And the Discourse of Language.* Trans. A Sheridan. London: Tavistock Publications 1972. Republished 1989, 2002, 2018 by Routledge.Foucault M (1977) *Language, Counter-Memory, Practice. Selected Essays and Interviews.* Ed. and Trans. D Bouchard. Ithaca, NY: Cornell University Press.

Foucault M (1978) *The History of Sexuality*. Vol. 1 An Introduction. New York: Pantheon.

Foucault M (1979) *Discipline and Punish. The Birth of the Prison.* London: Penguin Books, Reprinted 1991.

Foucault M (1980) *Power/Knowledge. Selected Interviews & Other Writings 1972–1977*. Ed. C Gordon. Trans. C Gordon, L Marshall, J Mepham and K Soper. Brighton: Harvester Press. [Originally published in 1972] [Published in 1972, 1975, 1976, 1977 by Pantheon Press, New York].

Foucault M (1983) The subject and power. In Dreyfus HL and Rabinov P (Eds.) *Beyond Structuralism.* Chicago, IL: University of Chicago Press, pp. 208–226.

Foucault M (1998) *The Will to Knowledge. The History of Sexuality.* London: Penguin.

Foucault M (1999) Michel Foucault and zen. A stay in zen temple. In Carrette JR (Ed.) *Religion and Culture.* Manchester: Manchester University Press, chapter 8, pp. 110–114.

Foucault M (2019) *Power: The Essential Works of Michael Foucault 1954–1984. Edited by P Rabinow.* London: Penguin.

Foulkes E (Ed.) (1990) *Selected Papers of S.H. Foulkes. Psychoanalysis and Group Analysis*. London: Karnac.

Foulkes SH (1936) Zum Stand der heutigen Biologie. Dargestellt in Kurt Goldstein. Der Aufbau des Organismus. [Regarding the view of contemporary biology. Represented in Kurt Goldstein. The structure of the organism.] *Imago. Zeitschrift für Psychoanalytische Psychologie. Ihre Grenzgebiete und Anwendungen.* 22(1): 21–60. [Republished in Foulkes E (Ed.) (2014) *Ausgewählte Schriften zu Psychoanalyse und Gruppenanalyse. Mit Übersetzungen von Elisabeth Vorspohl. Herausgegeben und mit einem Vorwort von Dieter Nitzgen.* Gießen: Psycho-Sozial Verlag, pp. 55–94.]

Foulkes SH (1946a) Group analysis in a military neurosis centre. *Lancet.* 247(6392): 303–306. https://doi.org/10.1016/s0140-6736(46)91386-4.

Foulkes SH (1946b/1990) On group analysis. In Foulkes E (Ed.) *Selected Papers of S.H. Foulkes. Psychoanalysis and Group Analysis.* London: Karnac, pp. 127–136.

Foulkes SH (1948) *Introduction to Group Analytic Psychotherapy*. [Reprinted in 1983]. London: Karnac.

Foulkes SH (1964) *Therapeutic Group Analysis*. London: George Allen and Unwin.

Foulkes SH (1969) Note on transference in groups. *Group Analysis.* 1(3): 135–146.

Foulkes SH (1971) The group as a matrix of the individual's mental life. In Foulkes E (Ed.) (1990) *Selected Papers of S.H. Foulkes. Psychoanalysis and Group Analysis*. London: Karnac, pp. 223–233.

Foulkes SH (1973) The group as matrix of the individual's mental life. In Wolberg LR and Schwartz EK (Eds.) *Group Therapy. An Overview*. New York: Intercontinental Medical Book Corporation, pp. 211–220.

Foulkes SH (1975a) *Group-Analytic Psychotherapy. Method & Principles*. London: Gordon and Breach.

Foulkes SH (1975b) Problems of the large group. In Foulkes E (Ed.) (1990) *Selected Papers of S.H. Foulkes. Psychoanalysis and Group Analysis.* London: Karnac, pp. 249–269.

Foulkes SH (1977) Notes on the concept of resonance. In Foulkes E (Ed.) (1999) *Selected Papers of S.H. Foulkes. Psychoanalysis and Group Analysis.* London: Karnac Books, pp. 296–306.
Foulkes SH (1983) *Introduction to Group-Analytic Psychotherapy.* London: Maresfield Reprints.
Foulkes SH (1984) *Therapeutic Group Analysis.* London: Karnac.
Foulkes SH (1990a) Biology in the light of the work of Kurt Goldstein. In Foulkes E (Ed.) *Selected Papers of S. H. Foulkes. Psychoanalysis and Group Analysis.* London: Karnac, pp. 39–56.
Foulkes SH (1990b) The leader in the group. In Foulkes E (Ed.) *Selected Papers of S. H. Foulkes. Psychoanalysis and Group Analysis.* London: Karnac, pp. 285–296.
Foulkes SH (2002) *Group Analytic Psychotherapy. Method and Principles.* Reprint. London: Karnac.
Foulkes SH (2003) Mind. (Preface by Malcolm Pines). *Group Analysis*. 36(3): 315–321.
Foulkes SH and Anthony EJ (1957) *Group Psychotherapy. The Psycho-Analytic Approach.* London: Karnac.
Foulkes SH and Anthony EJ (1965) *Group Psychotherapy. The Psychoanalytic Approach.* 2nd Edition. London: Penguin Books. [Reprinted in 1984 by Karnac. Republished in 2018 by Routledge]
Fourie L (2020) Technology and theology. Finding the real god. In Van Den Berg J (Ed.) *Engaging the Fourth Industrial Revolution. Perspectives from Theology, Philosophy and Education.* Bloemfontein: Sun Media, pp. 11–44.
Fox WP and Everton SF (2013) Mathematical modeling in social network analysis: Using TOPSIS to find node influences in a social network. *Journal of Mathematics and System Science.* 3(10): 531–541. https://www.davidpublisher.com/index.php/Home/Article/index?id=7362.html
Franco A, Malhotra N and Simonovits G (2014) Social science. Publication bias in the social sciences. Unlocking the file drawer. *Science.* 345(6203): 1502–1505. https://doi.org/10.1126/science.1255484.
Frank A (2023) How Einstein challenged quantum mechanics and lost. Available at: https://bigthink.com/13-8/quantum-mechanics-einstein/ (accessed 24 December 2024).
Frank AW (2005) What is dialogical research, and why should we do it? *Qualitative Health Research.* 15(7): 964–974. https://doi.org/10.1177/1049732305279078.
Frank AW (2006) Health stories as connectors and subjectifiers. *Health.* [An Interdisciplinary Journalfor the Social Study of Health, Illness and Medicine] 10(4): 421-440. https://doi.org/10.1177/1363459306067312.
Frank AW (2010) *Letting Stories Breathe. A Socio-Narratology*. Chicago, IL: University of Chicago Press.
Frank AW (2012) Practicing dialogical narrative analysis. In Holstein J and Gubrium J (Eds.) *Varieties of Narrative Analysis*. London: Sage, pp. 33–52.
Frank AW (2013) *The Wounded Storyteller. Body, Illness and Ethics*. 2nd Edition. Chicago: University of Chicago Press.
Franke U (2024) Two metaverse dystopias. *Res Publica.* 30: 825–843. https://doi.org/10.1007/s11158-024-09655-1.
Frankfort-Nachmias C and Nachmias D (1996) *Research Methods in The Social Sciences.* 5th Edition. London: Arnold.
Fransella F (1970) The self and the sterotype. In Bannister D (Ed.) (1977) *New* Perspectives in Personal Construct Theory. New York: Academic Press, pp. 39–66.
Fransella F and Bannister D (Eds.) (1977) *A Manual for Repertory Grid Technique.* London: Academic Press.
Fransella F and Joyston-Bechal MP (1971) an investigation of conceptual process and pattern change in a psychotherapy group over one year. *British Journal of Psychiatry.* 119(549): 199–206. https://doi.org/10.1192/bjp.119.549.199.
Fransella F and Adams B (1965) An illustration of the use of repertory grid technique in a clinical setting. *British Journal of Social and Clinical Psychology*. 5(1): 51–62.
Fransella F, Bannister D and Belly R (Eds.) (2003) *A Manual for Repertory Grid Technique.* 2nd Edition. New York: Wiley & Sons.
Fraser JS (2020) Shifting paradigms from the DSM to the process of change. In Hayes SC and Hoffman SG (Eds.) *Beyond the DSM. Toward a Process-Based Alternative for Diagnosis and Mental Health Treatment.* Oakland, CA: New Harbinger Publications, pp. 47–72.
Freeman LC (2004) *The Development of Social Network Analysis. A Study in the Sociology of Science.* Vancouver: Empirical Press.

Freire P (1967) *Educacao como practica da Liberdade.* Rio de Janeiro: Paz e Terra, Reprinted in 2011. [*Education The Practice of Freedom.* Trans. M Bergman Ramos. Published in 1976 by Writers and Readers Publishing Cooperative, London].
Freire P (1970) *Pedagogy of the Oppressed.* Trans. M Bergman Ramos. New York: Herder and Herder. [Republished 1996 by Penguin; With Introduction by Donaldo Macedo republished in 2000, 2005 by The Continuum International Publishing Group].
Freire P (1978) *Pedagogy in Process. The Letters of Guinea-Bissau.* New York: The Seabury Press. [Trans. Carman ST John Hunter, Republished in 2016 by Bloomsbury; With new introduction by Michael W Apple, republished in 2021].
Freud S (1895) *Project for a Scientific Psychology.* Ed. and Trans. J Strachey with A Freud, A Strachey and A Tyson. SE 1. London: Hogarth Press, pp. 281–391.
Freud S (1900) *The Interpretation of Dreams.* Ed. and Trans. J Strachey with A Freud, A Strachey and A Tyson. SE 4–5. London: Hogarth Press, pp. 34–606.
Freud S (1905a) Fragment of an analysis of a case of hysteria. In *A Case of Hysteria. Three Essays on Sexuality and Other Works.* Ed. and Trans. J Strachey with A Freud, A Strachey and A Tyson. SE 7. London: Hogarth, pp. 1–123.
Freud S (1905b) *Three Essays on Sexuality and Other Works.* Ed. and Trans. J. Strachey with A Freud, A Strachey and A Tyson. SE 7. London: Hogarth.
Freud S (1912) *Types of Onset of Neurosis.* Ed. and Trans. J. Strachey with A Freud, A Strachey and A Tyson. SE 12. London: Hogarth.
Freud S (1913) *Totem and Taboo.* Ed. and Trans. J. Strachey with A Freud, A Strachey and A Tyson. SE 13. London: Hogarth Press, pp. 7–162.
Freud S (1915a) *Instincts and their vicissitudes.* Ed. and Trans. J. Strachey with A Freud, A Strachey and A Tyson. SE 14. London: Hogarth, pp. 117–140.
Freud S (1915b) *Repression. SE 14.* Ed. and Trans. J. Strachey with A Freud, A Strachey and A Tyson. London: Hogarth, pp. 141–158.
Freud S (1915c) *The Unconscious.* Ed. and Trans. J. Strachey with A Freud, A Strachey and A Tyson. SE 14. London: Hogarth, pp. 159–190.
Freud S (1921) *Group Psychology and the Analysis of the Ego.* Ed. and Trans. J. Strachey with A Freud, A Strachey and A Tyson. SE 18. London: Hogarth, pp. 67–143.
Freud S (1927) *The Future of an Illusion.* In SE 21. London: Hogarth, pp. 1–56.
Freud S (1930) *Civilization and Its Discontent.* Ed. and Trans. J. Strachey with A Freud, A Strachey and A Tyson. SE 21. London: Hogarth, pp. 57–146.
Freud S (1933) *New Introductory Lectures on Psychoanalysis.* New York: W. W. Norton & Company.
Freud S (1940) *An Outline of Psychoanalysis.* Ed. and Trans. J. Strachey with A Freud, A Strachey and A Tyson. SE 23. London: Hogarth, pp. 2–63.
Freund A (2009) Oral history as process-generated data. *Historische Sozialforschung.* 34(1): 22–48. https://www.jstor.org/stable/20762332; https://nbn-resolving.org/urn:nbn:de:0168-ssoar-286344
Frey JH and Fontana A (1991) The group interview in social research. *Social Science Journal.* 28(2): 175–187. https://doi.org/10.1016/0362-3319(91)90003-M.
Fried EI (2020) Theories and models. What they are, what they are for, and what they are about. *Psychological Inquiry.* 31(4): 336–344.
Friedman B (1963) *The Feminine Mystique.* New York: W. W. Norton & Company.
Friedman R (2008) Dreamtelling as a request for containment: Three uses of dreams in group therapy. *International Journal of Group Psychotherapy.* 58(3): 327–343.
Friedman R (2015a) The soldier's matrix. A group analytic view of societies in war. *Group Analysis.* 48(3): 239–257.
Friedman R (2015b) Using the transpersonal in dreamtelling and conflict. *Group Analysis.* 48(1): 45–60.
Friedman R (2018) Beyond rejection, glory and the soldier's matrix. The heart of my group analysis. *Group Analysis.* 51(4): 389–405.
Friedman R (2019) *Dreamtelling, Reflections, and Large Groups. New Developments in Group Analysis.* New York: Routledge.
Friedman R and Doron Y (Eds.) (2017) *Group Analysis ilhe Land of Milk and Honey.* London: Karnac.

Froggett L (2020) Imagery and association in a group-based method: The visual matrix. In Reavey P (Ed.) *A Handbook of Visual Methods in Psychology Using and Interpreting Images in Qualitative Research.* 2nd Edition. London: Routledge, pp. 245–269.

Froggett L and Trustram M (2014) Object relations in the museum: A psychosocial perspective. *Museum Management and Curatorship*. 29(5): 1–16.

Froggett L and Wengraf T (2004) Interpreting interviews in the light of research team dynamics. A study of Nila's biographic interview. *Critical Psychology.* 10(1): 93–121. https://www.researchgate.net/publication/45637108_Interpreting_interviews_in_the_light_of_research_team_dynamics_A_study_of_Nila's_biographic_narrative.

Froggett L, Maley J and Roy A (2015) The visual matrix method. Imagery and affect in a group-based research setting. *Forum Qualitative Sozialforschung.* 16(3): 1–34. https://qualitative-research.net/index.php/fqs/article/download/2308/3849?inline=1

Froggett L, Muller L and Bennett J (2019) The work of the audience: Visual matrix methodology in museums. *Cultural Trends*. 28(2–3): 162–176.

Fromm E (1960) Psychoanalysis and zen buddhism. In Molino A (Ed.) (1998) *The CI and the Tree. Dialogues in Psychoanalysis and Buddhism.* London: Open Gate Press, pp. 65–71.

Fuentes C and Kahlo F (1995) *The Diary of Frida Kahlo. An Intimate Self-Portrait.* New York: Bloomsbury.

Fuhriman A and Barlow S (1994) Interaction analysis. Instrumentation and issues. In Fuhriman A and Burlingame GM (Eds.) *Handbook of Group Psychotherapy: An Empirical and Clinical Synthesis.* New York: John Wiley, pp. 191–222.

Fuhriman A and Burlingame GM (1994) Group psychotherapy. Research and practice. In Fuhriman A and Burlingame GM (Eds.) *Handbook of Group Psychotherapy: An Empirical and Clinical Synthesis.* New York: John Wiley, pp. 3–40.

Fulbrook M (2009) The concept of normalisation and the GDR in contemporary perspective. In Fulbrook M (Ed.) *Power and Society in the GDR, 1961–1979. The 'Normalisation' Rule.* New York: Berghahn Books, pp. chapter 1, pp. 1–30. https://ir101.co.uk/wp-content/uploads/2018/10/fulbrook-ch-1-power-and-society-in-the-gdr.pdf

Gabbard GO and Horowitz MJ (2009) Insight, transference interpretation, and therapeutic change in the dynamic psychotherapy of borderline personality disorder. *American Journal of Psychiatry.* 166(5): 517–521. https://www.researchgate.net/publication/24397941_Insight_Transference_Interpretation_and_Therapeutic_Change_in_the_Dynamic_Psychotherapy_of_Borderline_Personality_Disorder

Gabbard GO, Horwitz L, Allan JG, Frieswyk S, Newsom G, Colson GD and Coyne L (1994) Transference interpretation in the psychotherapy of borderline patients: A high-risk, high-gain phenomenon. *Harvard Review of Psychiatry*. 2(2): 59–69. https://doi.org/10.3109/10673229409017119

Gabriel R (2023) *A Suspicious Science. The Uses of Psychology.* New York: Oxford University Press.

Gad AF (2024) *Bayesian Decision Theory Explained.* 23 September. Available at: https://www.digitalocean.com/community/tutorials/bayesian-decision-theory (accessed 9 February 2025).

Gadamer HG (1966) The universality of the hermeneutical problem. In Linge DE (Ed.) (1977) *Philosophical Hermeneutics*. Berkeley, CA: University of California Press, pp. 3–17.

Gadamer HG (1976) *Philosophical Hermeneutics*. Berkeley: University of California Press. https://archive.org/details/philosophicalher0000gada

Gadamer HG (1979) Practical philosophy as a model of the human sciences. *Research in Phenomenology.* 9(1): 74–85.

Gadamer HG (1987) *Hegel Husserl Heidegger.* Tűbingen: JCB Mohr Verlag. https://archive.org/details/neuerephilosophi0000gada

Gadamer HG (2004) *Truth and Method.* 2nd Revised Edition. London: Continuum Publishing Group.

Galinsky MJ and Schopler JH (1989) Development patterns in open-ended groups. *Social Work with Groups.* 12(2): 99–114.

Gallagher LA (Ed.) (2007) *Thesaurus of Psychological Index Terms.* 11th Edition. Washington, DC: American Psychological Association.

Galli-Carminati GG, Martin F and Carminati F (2017) A very simple quantum model of mind and matter. *NeuroQuantology*. 15(2): 186–199. https://www.neuroquantology.com/open-access/A+Very+Simple+Quantum+Model+of++Mind+and+Matter_11486/

Gallistl A, Kirschner H, Paripovic G, Rauschenbach M, Storch M and Strauß B (2022a) Aufarbeitung der DDR Psychotherapie als transdisziplinäres Forschungsfeld. Teil I: chronologisch/historische Perspektiven [Reprocessing psychotherapy in the German Democratic Republic as a transdisciplinary field of research. Part I: chronological/historical perspectives]. *Psychotherapeut.* 67(5): 420–429. https://doi.org/10.1007/s00278-022-00599-6.

Gallistl A, Kirschner H, Paripovic G, Rauschenbach M, Storch M and Strauß B (2022b) Aufarbeitung der DDR Psychotherapie als transdisziplinäres Forschungsfeld. Teil II: Fachgebiet Vergangenheitsbewaltigung. Sozialwissenschaften; [Reprocessing the GDR. Psychotherapy as interdisciplinary field of research. Discipline Processing the past. Social Sciences. Part II]. *Psychotherapie.* 67(5): 430–438 https://link.springer.com/article/10.1007/s00278-022-00615-9

Gans HJ (1999) Participant observation in the era of "ethnography". *Journal of Contemporary Ethnography.* 28(5): 540–548. https://doi.org/10.1177/089124199129023532.

Garavaglia S and Sharma A (1998) A smart guide to dummy variables. Four applications and a macro. In *Proceedings of the Northeast SAS Users Group (NESUG) Conference*, 43, January 22-25, Nashville, TN, USA. https://www.academia.edu/101864932/A_smart_guide_to_dummy_variables_four_applications_and_a_macro

Gardiner M (1992) *The Dialogics of Critique. M.M. Bakhtin and the Theory of Ideology*. London: Routledge.

Garfinkel H (1967/1984) *Studies in Ethnomethodology*. Cambridge: Polity Press.

Garfinkel H (2002) *Ethnomethodology's Program. Working Out Durkheim's Aphorism.* Lanham, MD: Rowman & Littlefield.

Garland C (2010) *The Groups Book. Psychoanalytic Group Therapy. Principles and Practice. Including the Groups Manual: A Treatment Manual with Clinical Vignettes.* London: Karnac.

Garrison J (2019) The myth that dewey accepted "the myth of the given". *Transactions of the Charles S. Peirce Society.* 55(3): 304–325. https://muse.jhu.edu/pub/3/article/745416

Gauck J (1994) Das Erbe der Stasi Akten. [The Inheritance of the Stasi Records]. *German Studies Review.* 17: Fall 1994: 187–198. *Special Issue Totalitäre Herrschaft. Totalitäres Erbe* [Special Issue Totalitarian Governance Totalitarian Inheritance]. https://www.jstor.org/stable/40575005

Geels FW (2002) Technological transitions as evolutionary reconfiguration processes: a multi-level perspective and a case-study. *Research Policy*. 31(8–9): 1257–1274. https://www.sciencedirect.com/science/article/abs/pii/S0048733302000628

Geerts E and van der Tuin I (2021) Diffraction & reading diffractively. *Matterial Journal of New Materialist Research.* 1(2): 173–177. Available at: https://www.academia.edu/45178163/Diffraction_and_Reading_Diffractively_V2_2021_

Geipel I (2009) *Zensiert, verschwiegen, vergessen. Autorinnen in Ostdeutschland 1945–1989.* [Censored, silenced, forgotten. Female authors in East Germany 1945–1989]. Dűsseldorf: Patmos Verlag.

Geipel I (2019) *Umkämpfte Zone. Mein Bruder, der Osten und der Hass.* [Battled Zone. My brother, the East and the Hatred]. Stuttgart: Klett-Cotta.

Geipel I (2022) *Schöner Neuer Himmel. Aus dem Militärlabor des Ostens. [Beautiful New Sky. From the Military Laboratory of the East].* Stuttgart: Klett-Cotta.

Geller S (2020) Cultivating online therapeutic presence: Strengthening therapeutic relationships in teletherapy sessions. *Counselling Psychology Quarterly*. 34(3–4): 1–17.

Geller S (2023) Being present and together while apart: Therapeutic presence in telepsychotherapy. In Weinberg H, Rolnick A and Leighton A (Eds.) *Advances in Online Therapy: The Emergence of a New Paradigm.* New York: Routledge, pp. 21–34.

Gellner E (1990) *Nationen und Nationalismus. [Nations and Nationalism].* Berlin: Rotbuch.

Gelman A, Carlin JB, Stern HS, Dunson DB, Vehtari A and Rubin DB (2013) *Bayesian Data Analysis*. 3rd Edition. *Chapman & Hall/CRC Texts in Statistical Science Series.* New York: Routledge.

Geniusas S (2020) Towards a phenomenology of the unconscious. Husserl and fink on Versunkenheit. *Journal of the British Society for Phenomenology.* 53(1): 1–23. https://doi.org/10.1080/00071773.2020.1834334.

Geniusas S (2024) The unconscious in Husserl's phenomenology. *Human Studies.* 48: 91–115. https://link.springer.com/article/10.1007/s10746-024-09726-5.

Georgaca E and Avdi E (2011) Discourse analysis. In Harper D and Thompson AR (Eds.) *Qualitative Research Methods in Mental Health and Psychotherapy: A Guide for Students and Practitioners.* London: Wiley, pp. 147–161.
Gergen KJ (1973) Social psychology as history. *Journal of Personality & Social Psychology.* 26(2): 309–320. https://doi.org/10.1037/h0034436.
Gergen KJ (1978) Toward generative theory. *Journal of Personality & Social Psychol*ogy. 36(11): 1344–1360. https://doi.org/10.1037/0022-3514.36.11.1344.
Gergen KJ (1985) The social constructionist movement in modern psychology. *American Psychologist.* 40(3): 266–275. https://doi.org/10.1037/0003-066X.40.3.266.
Gergen KJ (1990) Toward a postmodern psychology. *The Humanistic Psychologist.* 18(1): 23–34. https://doi.org/10.1080/08873267.1990.9976874.
Gergen KJ (1991) *The Saturated Self. Dilemmas of Identity in Contemporary Life.* New York: Basic Books.
Gergen KJ (1994) Exploring the postmodern: Perils or potentials? *American Psychologist.* 49(5): 412–416. https://doi.org/10.1037/0003-066X.49.5.412.
Gergen KJ (2019) Qualitative psllogy and the new pluralism. In Schiff B (Ed.) *Situating Qualitative Methods in Psychological Science.* New York: Routledge, pp. 61–71.
Gergen KJ and Gergen M (1986) Narrative form and the construction of psychological science. In Sarbin TR (Ed.) *Narrative Psychology. The Storied Nature of Human Conduct.* New York: Praeger, pp. 22–44.
Gergen KJ, Josselson R and Freeman M (2015) The promises of qualitative inquiry. *American Psychologist.* 70(1): 1–9. https://doi.org/10.1037/a0038597.
Gerke F, Müller R, Bitzenbauer P, Ubben M and Weber K-A (2022) Requirements for future quantum workforce a delphi study. *Journal of Physics*. Conference Series 2297 012017. https://doi.org/10.1088/1742-6596/2297/1/012017.
Gerrad J, Rudolph S and Sriprakash A (2017) The politics of post-qualitative inquiry history and power. *Qualitative Inquiry.* 23(5): 384–394. https://doi.org/10.1177/1077800416672694.
Gfäller GR (1993) 'Figuration'. The contribution of Norbert Elias. *Group Analysis.* 26(3): 341–356.
Ghasemi A and Zahediasl S (2012) Normality tests for statistical analysis: A guide for non-statisticians. *International Journal of Endocrinology & Metabolism.* 10(2): 486–489. https://doi.org/10.5812/ijem.3505.
Giddens A (1976) *New Rules of Sociological Method.* London: Hutchinson and Company.
Giddens A (1984) *The Constitution of Society. Outline of a Theory of Structuration.* Cambridge: Polity Press.
Gidley B (2018) Doing historical and documentary research. In Seale C (Ed.) *Researching Society and Culture.* 4th Edition. London: Sage Publications, pp. 286–304.
Gieseke J (2014a) *The History of the Stasi. East Germany's Secret Police, 1945–1990.* New York: Berghahn Books.
Gieseke J (2014b) The stasi in the GDR. In Scott CE and Taylor FF (Eds.) *Totalitarianism on the Screen. The Art and Politics of the Lives of Others.* Lexington, KY: University of Kentucky Press, pp. 231–256.
Gigerenzer G (2000) *Adaptive Thinking. Rationality in the Real World.* Oxford: Oxford University Press.
Gillam L, Salo FT and Campbell P (2010) Infant observation and ethics. *AAIMHI Newsletter.* 23(2): 2–5. https://www.aaimh.org.au/resources/for-professionals/newsletter-archive/
Gillespie A and Cornish F (2010) Intersubjectivity. Towards a dialogical analysis. *Journal for the Theory of Social Behaviour*. 40(1): 19–46.
Gines KT (2011) Musings. Being a black woman philosopher. Reflections on founding the collegium of black women philosophers. *Hypatia.* 26(2): 429–437. https://www.jstor.org/stable/23016557
Ginner H, Werbart A, Levander S and Sahlberg B (2001) Tillförlitlighet i studier av subjektiva förklaringssystem: Ett kodningssystem för privata teorier om patogenes och kur [Reliability in studies of subjective explanatory systems: A coding system for private theories of pathogenesis and cure]. *Psykoterapi: Forskning och utveckling*. Research Report No. 19. Stockholm: Psychotherapy Institute, Section for Psychotherapy.
Giorgi A (1970) *Psychology as a Human Science. A Phenomenologically Based Approach.* New York: Harper & Row.
Giorgi A (1985) *Phenomenology and Psychological Research.* Pittsburgh, PA: Duquesne University Press. https://archive.org/details/phenomenologypsy00gior

Giorgi A (1991) *Phenomenology and Psychological Research.* 2nd Edition. Pittsburgh, PA: Duquesne University Press.

Giorgi A (2006) Facts, values and the psychology of the human person. *Indo-Pacific Journal of Phenomenology.* 6(1): 1–17. https://journals.co.za/doi/abs/10.10520/EJC46950

Giorgi A (2008) Difficulties encountered in the application of the phenomenological method in the social sciences. *Indo-Pacific Journal of Phenomenology.* 8(1): 1–9. https://www.tandfonline.com/doi/abs/10.1080/20797222.2008.11433956.

Giorgi A (2009) *The Descriptive Phenomenological Method in Psychology. A modified Husserlian Approach.* Pittsburgh, PA: Duquesne University Press.

Giorgi A (2010) Phenomenology and the practice of science. *Existential Analysis.* 21(1): 3–22. https://community.existentialanalysis.org.uk/product/existential-analysis-vol-21-1-january-2010-pdf

Giorgi A (2014) An affirmation of the phenomenological psychological descriptive method. A response to Rennie (2012). *Psychological Methods.* 19(4): 542–551. https://doi.org/10.1037/met0000015.

Giorgi A, Giorgi B and Morley J (2017) The descriptive phenomenological psychological method. In Willig C and Stainton Rogers W (Eds.) *The Sage Handbook of Qualitative Research in Psychology.* 2nd Edition. Thousand Oaks, CA: Sage, pp. 176–192. https://www.researchgate.net/publication/318451180_The_Descriptive_Phenomenological_Psychological_Method

Giovacchini PL (1979) *Treatment of Primitive Mental States.* New York: Jason Aronson.

Glaser BG (1998) *Doing Grounded Theory. Issues and Discussions.* Mill Valley, CA: Sociology Press.

Glaser BG (2001) *The Grounded Theory Perspective: Conceptualization Contrasted with Description.* Mill Valley, CA: Sociology Press.

Glaser BG (2008) *Doing Quantitative Grounded Theory.* Mill Valley, CA: Sociology Press.

Glaser BG (2013) *No Preconceptions: The Grounded Theory Dictum.* Mill Valley, CA: Sociology Press.

Glaser BG and Strauss AL (1965) *Awareness of Dying.* Chicago,IL: Aldine.

Glaser BG and Strauss AL (1967) *The Discovery of Grounded Theory: Strategies for Qualitative Research.* Mill Valley, CA: Sociology Press. [Republished 1999 Transaction Publisher, 2017 by Routledge].

Glaser BG and Strauss AL (1968) *Time for Dying.* Chicago, IL: Aldine.

Glenn ND (2005) *Cohort Analysis.* 2nd Edition. Thousand Oaks, CA: Sage.

Glesne C and Peshkin A (1992) *Becoming Qualitative Researchers.* Thousand Oaks, CA: Sage.

Glover N (2009) The Legacy of Wilfred Bion. In Glover N (2009) *Psychoanalytic Aesthetics: An Introduction to the British School.* London: Karnac, pp. 103–136. Available at: https://www.psychoanalysis-and-therapy.com/human_nature/glover/chap4.html (accessed 22 November 2024).

Godfrey-Smith P (2003) *Theory and Reality.* Chicago: The University of Chicago Press. Available at Understanding Science Website. The Philosophy of Science. University of California. https://undsci.berkeley.edu/the-philosophy-of-science/ (accessed 7 November 2024).

Godwin M, Ruhland L, Casson L, MacDonald S, Delva D, Birtwhistle R, Lam M and Seguin R (2003) Pragmatic controlled clinical trI in primary care: The struggle between external and internal validity. *BMC Medical Research Methodology.* 3(28). https://doi.org/10.1186/1471-2288-3-28.

Goffman E (1963) *Stigma. Notes on the Management of a Spoiled Identity.* Englewood Cliffs, NJ: Prentice-Hall. https://archive.org/details/stigmanotesonman0000goff/page/n5/mode/2up

Göktür E (2005) *What is "Paradigm"?* Oslo: University of Oslo, Department of Informatics. https://www.researchgate.net/publication/266068018_What_is_paradigm

Goldacre B (2012) *Bad Pharma. How Drug Companies Mislead Doctors and Harm Patients.* London: Fourth Estate.

Goldberg A (2012) *The Analysis of Failure. An Investigation of Failed Cases in Psychoanalysis and Psychotherapy.* New York: Routledge.

Goldkuhl G (2017) Pragmatism versus interpretivism in qualitative information systems research. *European Journal of Information Systems.* 21(2): 135–146.

Goldstein K (1925) Zur Theorie des Funktionden Nervensystems. [Regarding the Theory of the Functioning Nervous System]. *Archiv für Psychiatrie und Nervenkrankheiten.* 74(1): 370–405. https://link.springer.com/article/10.1007/BF01814194.

Goldstein K (1939/1995) *The Organism. A Holistic Approach to Biology Derived from Pathological Data in Man.* New York: Zone Books. https://archive.org/details/organismholistic00gold

Golm W (2022) *Satire im DDR Rundfunk. Ein Spiegel für die Welt Medien. Aus den Archiven.* Deutschlandfunk Kultur. [Satire on GDR radio. A Mirror to the World of the Media. From the Archives of the German Radio Culture]. Available at: https://www.deutschlandfunkkultur.de/satire-ddr-100.html (accessed 6 March 2023).

Gonggrijp P (1993) Black and white. Median and large groups. *Group Analysi*s. 26(3): 363–365. https://doi.org/10.1177/0533316493263016.

Goodheart GJ (1989) *You'll Be Better. The Story of Applied Kinesiology.* Geneva: AK Publishing.

Goodman G (2009) An attachment-based pathways model depicting the psychology of therapeutic relationships. In Culer E and Ackhart M (Eds.) *Psychology of Relationships.* Hauppauge, NY: Nova Science Publishers, pp. 471–491. https://www.researchgate.net/publication/329265532_An_attachment-based_pathways_model_depicting_the_psychology_of_therapeutic_relationships

Goraga Z (2023) *The Power Of AI For Research Transformation.* Silver Spring, MD: Zemelak Goraga Publishers.

Gosepath S (2020) Die Notwendigkeit globaler Philosophie. [The Necessity of Global Philosophy.] *Deutsche Zeitschrift für Philosophie.* 68(6): 943–956. https://doi.org/10.1515/dzph-2020-0064.

Goswami UC (2020) *What is neuroscience?* Available at: https://www.thebritishacademy.ac.uk/blog/what-is-neuroscience/ (accessed 4 March 2022).

Gough B (2003) Deconstructing reflexivity. In Finlay L and Gough B (Eds.) *Reflexivity: A Practical Guide for Researchers in Health and Social Sciences.* London: Wiley, pp. 21–35.

Gournelos T, Hammonds JR and Wilson MA (2019) *Doing Academic Research. A Practical Guide to Research Methods and Analysis.* New York: Routledge.

Graesser AC and Black JB (Eds.) (2019) *The Psychology of Questions.* New York: Routledge.

Gram -Hanssen I (2021) Individual and collective leadership for deliberate transformations: insights from Indigenous leadership. *Leadership.* 17(5): 519–541. https://doi.org/10.1177/174271502 1996486.

Grande T, Rudolf G, Oberbracht C, Jakobsen T and Keller W (2004) Investigating structural change in the process and outcome of psychoanalytic treatment. The Heidelberg-Berlin study. In Richardson P, Kächele H and Renlund C (Eds.) *Research on Psychoanalytic Psychotherapy with Adults.* London: Karnac, pp. 35–62.

Graneheim U and Lundman B (2004) Qualitative content analysis in nursing research. Concepts, procedures, and measures to achieve trustworthiness. *Nurse Education Today.* 24(2): 105–112. https://www.academia.edu/949954/Qualitative_content_analysis_in_nursing_research_concepts_procedures_and_measures_to_achieve_trustworthiness

Grant DC and Harari E (2005) Psychoanalysis, science and the seductive theory of Karl Popper. *Australian & New Zealand Journal of Psychiatry.* 39(6): 446–452.

Grant MJ and Booth A (2009) A typology of reviews: an analysis of 14 review types and associated methodologies. *Health Information and Libraries Journal.* 26(2): 91–108.

Grantt SP (2015) Functional subgrouping and the systems-centered approach to group therapy. In Kleinberg JL (Ed.) *The Wiley Blackwell Handbook of Group Psychotherapy.* Oxford: Wiley Blackwell, pp. 113–167.

Grawe K, Donati R and Bernauer F (1994) *Psychotherapie im Wandel. Von der Konfession zur Profession.* [Psychotherapy in Transition. From Confession to Profession]. Göttingen: Hogrefe.

Greaney A-M, Sheehy A, Heffernan C, Murphy J, Mhaolrúnaigh SN, Heffernan E and Brown G (2012) Research ethics application: A guide for the novice researcher. *British Journal of Nursing.* 21(1): 38–43. https://doi.org/10.12968/bjon.2012.21.1.38; https://www.researchgate.net/publication/221743358_Research_ethics_application_A_guide_for_the_novice_researcher

Grech V and Calleja N (2018) WASP (Write a Scientific Paper): parametric vs. non-parametric tests. *Early Human Development.* 123(1): 48–49. https://doi.org/10.1016/j.earlhumdev.2018.04.014. Available at: https://www.docdroid.net/oD4oKX7/parametric-vs-non-parametric-tests-pdf

Green C (2001) Operationalism again. What did Bridgman say? What did Bridgman need? *Theory and Psychology.* 11(1): 45–51.

Green J and Thorogood N (2005) *Qualitative Methods for Health Research.* London: Sage.

Green RH (1983) 'Things fall apart': the world economy in the 1980s. *Third World Quarterly.* 5(1): 72–94. https://www.jstor.org/stable/3991168

Greenberg LS (1986) Change process research. *Journal of Consulting and Clinical Psychology.* 54(1): 4–9.

Greene CJ, Morland LA, Macdonald A, Frueh BC, Grubbs KM and Rosen CS (2010) How does telemental health affect group therapy process? Secondary analysis of a noninferior trial. *Journal of Consulting and Clinical Psychology.* 78(5): 746–750.

Greene LR (2012) Studying the how and why of therapeutic change. The increasingly prominent role of mediators in group psychotherapy research. *International Journal of Group Psychotherapy.* 62(2): 325–331.

Greenwald AG (2012) There is nothing so theoretical as a good method. *Perspectives on Psychological Science.* 7(2): 99–108.

Greenwood DJ and Levin M (1998) *Introduction to Action Research. Social Research for Social Change.* Thousand Oaks, CA: Sage.

Greenwood DJ and Levin M (2001) Pragmatic action research and the struggle to transform universities into learning communities. In Reason P and Bradbury H (Eds.) *Handbook of Action Research.* London: Sage, pp. 103–113.

Greenwood DJ and Lewin M (2007) *Introduction to Action Research. Social Research for Social Change.* 2nd Edition. Thousand Oaks, CA: Sage.

Gregg C (2014) *Why Jung Threw The Yijing (Or I Ching) And Why Might You? Carl Greff and the Patheos.* Best of Patheos Channel. 27 December. Available at: https://www.patheos.com/blogs/carlgregg/2014/01/yijing-and-jung (accessed 23 July 2024).

Gregory AT and Denniss AR (2018) An Introduction to writing narrative and systematic reviews. tasks, tips and traps for aspiring authors. *Heart, Lung & Circulation.* 27(7): 893–898. https://doi.org/10.1016/j.hlc.2018.03.027.

Gregson J (2002) *Engendering the GDR. DEFA cinema 1956–1966.* PhD Thesis, University of Nottingham, UK. Available at: https://eprints.nottingham.ac.uk/14353/1/246478.pdf (accessed 11 August 2022).

Greig A and Taylor J (1999) *Doing Research with Children.* Thousand Oaks, CA: Sage.

Grencavage LM and Norcross JC (1990) Where are the commonalities among the therapeutic common factors? *Professional Psychology: Research and Practice.* 21(5): 372-378. https://doi.org/10.1037//0737028.21.5.372; https://www.academia.edu/52759009/Where_are_the_commonalities_among_the_therapeutic_common_factors

Gripsrud BH, Ramvi E, Froggett L, Hellstrand I and Manley J (2018) Psychosocial and symbolic dimensions of the breast explored through a visual matrix. *Nordic Journal of Feminist and Gender Research.* 26(3): 210–229. https://doi.org/10.1080/08038740.2018.1482958.

Grix J (2002) Introducing students to the generic terminology of social research. *Politics.* 22(3): 175–186. https://doi.org/10.1111/1467-9256.00173.

Grix J (2018) *The Foundations of Research.* 3rd Edition. Bloomsbury Study Skills Series. London: Bloomsbury Publishing PLC.

Groff R (2004) *Critical Realism, Post-Positivism and the Possibility of Knowledge.* London: Routledge.

Grossen M (2010) Interaction analysis and psychology: A dialogical perspective. *Integrative Psychological and Behavioral Science.* 44(1): 1–22. https://doi.org/10.1007/s12124-009-9108-9.

Grossen M and Salazar Orvig A (2011) Dialogism and dialogicality in the study of the self. *Culture & Psychology.* 17(4): 491–509.

Grossman J and FJ Mackenzie (2005) The Randomized Controlled Trial: gold standard, or merely standard? *Perspectives in Biology and Medicine.* 48(4): 516–534. https://dx.doi.org/10.1353/pbm.2005.0092.

Grosz E (1994) *Volatile Bodies. Toward A Corporeal Feminism.* Bloomington, IN: Indiana University Press. https://archive.org/details/volatilebodiesto0000gros_t4d0

Grosz E (1995) *Space, Time and Perversion. Essays on the Politics of Bodies.* New York: Routledge. https://archive.org/details/spacetimepervers0000gros_t8b0

Gruetzemacher R (2022) The Power of Natural Language Processing. AI and Machine Learning. *Harvard Business Review.* 19 April 2022. https://hbr.org/2022/04/the-power-of-natural-language-processing

Grűnbaum A (1984) *The Foundations of Psychoanalysis. A Philosophical Critique.* Berkely: University of California Press. https://archive.org/details/foundationsofpsy00grun

Grűnbaum A (1986) Précis of the foundations of psychoanalysis. A philosophical critique. *Behavioral and Brain Sciences.* 9(2): 217–228. https://doi.org/10.1017/S0140525X00022287

Grunther D (2024) *The Quantum Dream. VisionarInsciousness, AI, and the New Renaissance.* New York: Epigraph Books.

Guattari F (1992) *Chaosmose. [Chaosmosis. An Ethico-Aesthetic Paradigm.].* Paris: Galilée. [English Publication in 1995, Trans. P Bains and J Pefanis. Bloomington, IN: Indiana University Press.

Guba EG and Lincoln YS (1994) Competing paradigms in qualitative research. In Denzin NK and Lincoln YS (Eds.) *The Handbook of Qualitative Research.* Thousand Oaks, CA: Sage, pp. 105–117.

Guba EG and Lincoln YS (2005) Competing paradigms in qualitative research. In Denzin NK and Lincoln YS (Eds.) *The Handbook of Qualitative Research.* 3rd Edition. Thousand Oaks, CA: Sage, pp. 191–216.

Guest G, Namey E and McKenna K (2016) How many focus groups are enough? Building an evidence base for nonprobability sample sizes. *Field Methods.* 29(1): 3–22.

Gunnarsen G (2020) Setting up and running explicit Mentalization Groups 101: Simple Guidance and Clinical Considerations. *Group-Analytic Contexts. Summer Issue.* 88. Available at: https://groupanalyticsociety.co.uk/contexts/issue-88/articles/setting-up-and-running-explicit-mentalizing-groups-101-simple-guidance-and-clinical-considerations/ (accessed 28 March 2025).

Guo S, Yang Y and Fu L (2023) Interventions to reduce racial bias and discrimination in the United States. A scoping review. *Journal of the Society for Social Work and Research.* 14(1): 165–183. https://www.journals.uchicago.edu/doi/10.1086/723871.

Gupta VA, Scott S, Tonkinson M, Jonsson P, Goodburn L and Duffield S (2025) Quality in qualitative evidence: new best practice principles from NICE's real-world evidence framework. *Journal of Comparative Effectiveness Research.* 14(7): e250064. https://doi.org/10.57264/cer-2025-0064.

Gustavsen B (2003) Action research and the problem of the single case. *Concepts and Transformation.* 8(1): 93–99.

Gustavsen B, Hansson A and Qvale TU (2008) Action research and the challenge of scope. In Reason P and Bradbury H (Eds.) *Handbook of Action Research: Participative Inquiry and Practice.* Thousand Oaks, CA: Sage, pp. 63–76.

Gutland C (2018) Husserlian phenomenology as a kind of introspection. *Frontiers in Psychology.* 9: 896. https://www.frontiersin.org/journals/psychology/articles/10.3389/fpsyg.2018.00896/full

Guy-Evans O (2023) Gestalt Therapy. Definition, Types, Techniques and Efficacy. *Simply Psychology.* Available at: https://www.simplypsychology.org/what-is-gestalt-therapy.html (accessed 14 November 2023).

Gyekye K (1987) *An Essay on African Philosophical Thought: The Akan Conceptual Scheme.* New York: Cambridge University Press.

Habermas J (1975) *Legitimation Crisis.* Trans. T McCarthy. Boston, MA: Beacon Press.

Habermas J (1981) *The Theory of Communicative Action. Reason and the Realization of Society. Vol. 1.* Cambridge, MA: Polity Press.

Haddaway NR, Page MJ, Pritchard CC and McGuinness LA (2022) PRISMA2020. An R package and shiny app for producing PRISMA 2020-compliant flow diagrams, with interactivity for optimised digital transparency and open synthesis. *Campbell Systematic Reviews.* 18(2): e1230. https://doi.org/10.1002/cl2.1230.

Haenen H (2017) Inleiding. Dans, denken en zijn. Dynamiek van Afrokaanse filosofie. [Introduction. Dance, Thought, and Being: Dynamics of Afro-American Philosophy] In Ramose M (Ed.) (2017) *Ubuntu. Stroom van het bestaan als levensfilosofie*. [Stream of existence as a philosophy of life]. Utrecht: Uitgeverij Ten Have, pp. 10–27.

Hahn D, Weck F, Witthöft M and Kühne F (2021) Assessment of counseling self-efficacy: validation of the german counselor activity self-efficacy scale (CASES-R). *Frontiers in Psychology.* 12. https://doi.org/10.3389/fpsyg.2021.780088.

Hall JN (2024) The dialectic stance. Navigating difference. In Shan Y (Ed.) *Philosophical Foundations of Mixed Methods Research. Dialogues between Researchers and Philosophers.* New York: Routledge, pp. 83–99.

Hall RF (2013) Mixed methods in search of a paradigm. In Lê T and Lê Q (Eds.) *Conducting Research in a Changing and Challenging World.* Laboratory and Clinical Research Series. New York: Nova Science Publishers, chapter 7. Available at: https://www.researchgate.net/publication/259045135_Mixed_Methods_In_search_of_a_paradigm

Hall Z and Mullee M (2000) Undertaking psychotherapy research. *Group Analysis.* 33(3): 319–332.

Halton M (1999) Bion, Foulkes and the oedipal situation. In Oakley C (Ed.) *What is a Group?* London: Rebus Press, pp. 68–73.

Hamed S, Ezzat M and Hefny H (2020) A review of sentiment analysis techniques. *International Journal of Computer Applications.* 176(37): 20–24. https://www.ijcaonline.org/archives/volume176/number37/31444-2020920480/

Hamilton E and Cairns H (Eds.) (1961) *The Collected Dialogues of Plato. Including the Letters. With Introduction and Prefatory Notes.* Princeton: Princeton University Press. [Reprinted 1985; 1992 with A Cooper additional author].

Hammer L (2010) *Psychologie & Chinesische Medizin. Zukunfsweisende Erkenntnisse űber das energetische Zusammenspiel von Emotionen und Kőrperfunktionen. Vierte Auflage. [Psychology & Chinese Medicine, Future directive Insights into the energetic interplay between emotions and bodily functions.]* Mittelberg: Joy Verlag GmbH.

Hammersley M (1995) *Principles of Social and Educational Research. Block 1, Units 1–4. Introducing Social Research.* Milton Keynes: The Open University.

Hamston J (2006) Bakhtin's theory of dialogue. A construct for pedagogy, methodology and analysis. *The Australian Educational Researcher.* 33(1): 55–74. https://doi.org/10.1007/BF03246281.

Hanh TN (2001) *Essential Writings. Modern Spiritual Masters Series.* New York: Orbis Books. https://archive.org/details/thichnhathanhess0000nhat

Hanneman R and Riddle M (2005*) Introduction to Social Network Methods*. Riverside: University of California.

Hannes K and Lockwood C (2011) Pragmatism as the philosophical foundation for the joanna briggs meta-aggregative approach to qualitative evidence synthesis. *Journal of Advanced Nursing.* 67(7): 1632–1642. https://doi.org/10.1111/j.1365-2648.2011.05636.x.

Haraway D (1988) Situated knowledges. The science question in feminism as a site of discourse on the privilege of partial perspective. *Feminist Studies.* 14(3): 575–599. https://stores.modularmarket.com/fsonline/donna-haraway-situated-knowledges-p636.php

Haraway D (1992) The promises of monsters. A regenerative politics for inappropriate/d others. In Grossberg L, Nelson C and Treichler P (Eds.) *Cultural Studies,* New York: Routledge, chapter 18, pp. 295–337.

Haraway D (1997) *Modest_Witness@Second_Millennium. FemaleMan_Meets_OncoMouse. Feminism and Technoscience.* New York: Routledge.

Härdtle R and Schneider W (1999) Die Indentierte Dynamische Gruppenpsychotherapie als Paradigma der Psychotherapie in der DDR. Kontinuität oder Zänsur im Verhältnis zu psychoanalytischen Konzepten? [The Intended Dynamic Group psychotherapy as paradigm of psychotherapy in the GDR. Continuity or censorship in relation to psychoanalytic concepts?] *Forum der Psychoanalyse.* 15(1): 42–57. https://link.springer.com/article/10.1007/s004510050035.

Hardy GE and Barkham M (1994) The relationship between interpersonal attachment styles and work difficulties. *Human Relations*. 47(3): 263–281. https://doi.org/10.1177/001872679404700302.

Hardy GE and Llewelyn S (2015) Introduction to psychotherapy process research. In Gelo OC, Pritz A and Rieken B (Eds.) *Psychotherapy Research. Foundations, Process, and Outcome*. Vienna: Springer Verlag, pp. 183–193. https://download.e-bookshelf.de/download/0003/9326/79/L-G-0003932679-0013266322.pdf

Harper D (2012) Choosing a qualitative research method. In Harper D and Thompson AR (Eds.) *Qualitative Methods in Mental Health and Psychotherapy. A Guide for Students and Practitioners.* Chichester: John Wiley & Sons, pp. 83–98.

Harré R (1981) The positivist-empiricist approach and its alternative. In Reason P and Rowan J (Eds.) *Human Inquiry.* New York: John Wiley, pp. 3–17.

Harriden K (2022) Docoloyarning: You are not the messiah … you're a very naughty researcher (aka some reasons to, and tips for decolonizing writing). Australian National University. Fenner School. Available at: https://fennerschool.anu.edu.au/news-events/decoloyarning-some-reasons (accessed 9 December 2022).

Harriden K (2023) Decolonising your writing. Available at: https://i2insights.org/2023/05/02/decolonising-your-writing (accessed 6 November 2023).

Harris P (1994) *Designing and Reporting Experiments.* Milton Keynes: Open University Press.

Harris STG (2024) The fear of critical race methodologies. *The European Journal of Development Research.* Online. https://doi.org/10.1057/s41287-024-00667-4.

Harrison T (2000) *Bion, Rickman, Foulkes and the Northfield Experiments: Advancing on a Different Front.* London: Jessica Kingsley Publishers.

Harrison T (2018) Social fields, battle fields and Northfield: The legacy of the 'Northfield experiments'. *Group Analysis.* 51(4): 442–454.

Harrison T and Clark D (1992) The Northfield experiments. *British Journal of Psychiatry.* 160(5): 698–708.

Hartley P and Kennard D (2009) *Staff Support Groups in the Helping Professions. Principles, Practice and Pitfalls.* New York: Routledge.

Harvey L (2012) *Semiology.* Social Research Glossary, Quality Research International. Available at: https://www.qualityresearchinternational.com/socialresearch/ (accessed 7 January 2025).

Hass D (2001) Psychotherapy and research: An uneasy relationship. *Group Analysis.* 34(3): 387–393.

Hassin RR, Uleman JS and Bargh JA (2005) (Eds.) *The New Unconscious. Global intellectual Property and Developing Countries.* (Oxford Series in Social Cognition and Social Neuroscience). New York: Oxford University Press.

Hatch JM (1995) *Qualitative Research in Early Childhood Settings.* New York: Bloomsbury.

Hatfield G (2002) Psychology, philosophy, and cognitive science. Reflections on the history and philosophy of experimental psychology. *Mind & Language.* 17(3): 207–232. https://doi.org/10.1111/1468-0017.00196.

Hatfield G (2008) *René descartes.* Stanford Encyclopedia of Philosophy. Available at: https://plato.stanford.edu/entries/descartes/ (accessed 24 January 2020).

Hawking S (1989) *A Brief History of Time. From the Big Bang to Black Holes.* New York: Bantam Books. https://archive.org/details/briefhistoryofti0000hawk

Haye A and Torres-Sahli M (2025) Laughter as ideological symptom: dialogical analysis of older adults' discourse. *Frontiers in Psychology.* 16: 1606683. https://doi.org/10.3389/fpsyg.2025.1606683.

Headway (2025) *How to Use the Beck Anxiety Inventory and Interpret Scores.* 14 July 2025. Available at: https://headway.co/recourses/beck-anxiety-inventory

Heale R and Forbes D (2013) Understanding triangulation in research. *Evidence Based Nursing.* 16(4): 98. https://doi.org/10.1136/eb-2013-101494.

Heaton J (2011) *Reworking Qualitative Data.* New York: Sage. https://archive.org/details/reworkingqualita0000heat/page/n5/mode/2up

Heckmann M (2024) OpenRepGrid. An R package for the analysis of repertory grid data. *The Journal of Open Source Software.* 9(104): 6918. https://joss.theoj.org/papers/10.21105/joss.06918.

Hedges LV and Olkin I (1985) *Statistical Methods for Meta-Analysis.* San Diego, CA: Academic Press.

Hegel GWF (1948) *Early Theological Writings.* Trans. TM Knox. Chicago, IL: University of Chicago Press.

Hegel GWF (2018) *The Phenomenology of Spirit.* Trans. and Ed. T Pinkard. Cambridge: Cambridge University Press.

Heidegger M (1962) *Being and Time.* Trans. J Macquarie and E Robinson. New York: Harper and Row.

Heigl-Evers A (1971) *Psychoanalyse und Gruppe.* [Psychoanalysis and Group]. Göttingen: Vandenhoeck & Ruprecht.

Heigl-Evers A (1973) *Gruppendynamik.* [Group Dynamics]. Göttingen: Vandenhoeck & Ruprecht.

Heigl-Evers A (1978) *Konzepte der Analytischen Gruppenpsychotherapie.* [Concepts of Analytic Group Psychotherapy]. Göttingen: Vandenhoeck & Ruprecht.

Heigl-Evers A and Heigl F (1973) Gruppentherapie: Interaktionell–tiefenpsychologisch fundiert, analytisch orientiert–psychoanalytisch. *Ergebnisse und Berichte.* [Group Therapy. Interactional, in-depth, psychologically-based, analytically psychoanalytically oriented. Results and Reports.]. *Gruppenpsychotherapie und Gruppendynamik.* 7(2): 132–157. [*Group Psychotherapy and Group Dynamic.*]

Heigl-Evers A and Heigl F (1983) Das interaktionelle Prinzip in der Einzel- und Gruppenpsychotherapie. [The Interactional Principle in Individual andGroup Psychotherapy]. *Zeitschrift Für Psychosomatische Medizin Und Psychoanalyse.* [Journal of Psychosomatic Medicine] 29(1): 1–14. http://www.jstor.org/stable/23996469

Heigl-Evers A and Heigl F (1994) Das Göttinger Modell der Anwendung der Psychoanalyse in Gruppen unter besonderer Berücksichtigung der psychoanalytisch-interaktionellen Methode. [The Göttinger Model of the application of Psychoanalysis in Groups under specific consideration of the P sychoanalytic Interactional Method] *Gruppenpsychotherapie und Gruppendynamik.* 30(1): 1–29.

Heigl -Evers A and Ott J (2002) *Die psychoanalytisch-interaktionelle Methode. Vierte Auflage.* [The group analytic interactional Method. 4th Edition]. Göttingen: Vandenhoeck & Ruprecht.

Heigl -Evers A and Ott J (Hrgs.) (1994) *Die Psychoanalytisch-interaktionelle Methode. Theorie und Praxis. [Regarding the Psychoanalytic Interactional Method. Theory and Practice].* Göttingen: Vandenhoeck & Ruprecht.

Heigl-Evers A, Heigl F and Ott J (1994) *Lehrbuch Der Psychotherapie.* [Textbook of Psychotherapy]. Stuttgart: Fischer Verlag.

Heigl-Evers, A, Heigl FS and Ott J (1998) Zur Theorie und Praxis der psychoanalytisch-interaktionellen Gruppenpsychotherapie. (Regarding the Theory and Practice of the psychoanalytic-interactional group psychotherapy] In Heigl-Evers A and Ott J (Hrsg.) *Die psychoanalytisch-interaktionelle Methode. Dritte Auflage* [The group analytic interactional Method. 3rd Edition]. Vandenhoeck & Ruprecht. Göttingen, pp. 235–279.

Heim M (1993) *The Metaphysics of Virtual Reality.* New York: Oxford University. Press.

Heinemann C (2019) *Autorin Ines Geipel. "Friedensnobelpreis fur die Ostdeutschen". [Writer Ines Geipel. "Peace Nobel Prize for the East Germans"].* Deutschlandfunk Archiv. 29 December. Available at: https://www.deutschlandfunk.de/autorin-ines-geipel-friedensnobelpreis-fuer-die-ostdeutschen-100.html (accessed 11 August 2022).

Heinzel R, Breyer F and Klein T (2000) Outpatient psychoanalytic individual and group psychotherapy in a nationwide catamnestic study in Germany. *Group Analysis.* 33(3): 353–372.

Heinzel R, Breyer, F and Klein T (1998) Ambulante analytische Einzel- und Gruppenpsychotherapie in einer bundesweiten katamnestischen Evaluationsstudie. *Zeitschrift für Gruppenpsychotherapie und Gruppendynamik.* 34(2): 135–152.

Heisenberg W (1927) Über den anschaulichen Inhalt der quantentheoretischen Kinematik und Mechanik. [About the illustrative content of quantum theoretical kinematics and mechanics). *Zeitschrift für Physik.* 143(3–4): 172–198. https://ntrs.nasa.gov/citations/19840008978

Heisenberg W (1945) *Das Plancksche Wirkungsquantum.* Preussische Akademie der Wissenschaften. Vorträge und Schriften. [Planck's Effect Quantum. Prussian Academy of Science, Lecturers and Writings]. *Heft 21.* Berlin: Walter De Gruyter & Co. https://www.orellfuessli.ch/shop/home/artikeldetails/A1017797224

Heisenberg W (1949) *The Physical Principles of the Quantum Theory.* Trans. C Eckart and FC Hoyt. Chicago, IL: Dover Publications Inc.

Heisenberg W (1956) Die Entwicklung der Deutung der Quantentheorie. [The Development of the Interpretation of Quantum Theory]. *Physikalische Blätter.* 12(7): 289–304.

Heisenberg W (1960) Erinnerungen an die Zeit der Entwicklung der Quantenmechanik. [Memories about the time of the development of Quantum Mechanics]. In Fierz M and Weisskopf VF (Eds.) *Theoretical Physics in the Twentieth Century. A Memorial Volume to Wolfgang Pauli.* London: Interscience Publishers Inc., pp. 40–67.

Heisenberg W (1971) *Physics and beyond: Encounters and Conversations.* Trans. A Pomerans. London: Allen & Unwin.

Heisenberg W (1975) Bemerkungen über die Entstehung der Unbestimmtheitsrelation. [Remarks about the Emergence of Uncertainty Relations]. *Physikalische Blätter.* 31(5): 193–196.

Heisenberg W (1977) *Tradition in der Wissenschaft. Reden und Aufsätze.* [Tradition in Science. Speeches and Papers]. München: Piper.

Heisenberg W (2014) *Wandlungen in den Grundlagen der Naturwissenschaft.* Zehn Vorträge. 12. Auflage, Mit einem Beitrag von G Raschke und BL van der Waerden. [Changes in the basics of the physical science. Ten Lectures. 12th Edition. Including a contribution by Raschke and van der Waerden]. Stuttgart: Hirzel Verlag.

Hempel C and Oppenheim P (1948) Studies in the logic of explanation. *Philosophy of Science.* 15(2): 135–175.

Hendricks M (1994) Civility, barbarism and Aphra Behn's the widow ranter. In Hendricks M and Parker P (Eds.) *Women, "Race", and Writing in the Early Modern Period.* New York: Routledge, chapter 13, pp. 225–241.

Hennink MM, Kaiser BN and Weber MB (2019) What influences saturation? Estimate sample sizes in focus group research. *Qualitative Health Research.* 29(10): 1483–1496.

Henriksen AK, Ulberg R, Tallberg BP, Løvgren A and Johnsen-Dahl HS (2021) Conflicted anger as a central dynamic in depression in adolescents. A double case study. *International Journal of Environmental Research and Public Health.* 18(12): 6466. https://doi.org/10.3390/ijerph18126466.

Henry E and Pene H (2001) Kaupapa Māori: Locating indigenous ontology, epistemology and methodology in the academy. *Organization.* 8(2): 234–242.

Herbert N (1985) *Quantum Reality. Beyond the New Physics.* New York: Anchor.

Herder JG (1968) *Reflections on the Philosophy of the History of Mankind.* Chicago, IL: University of Chicago Press.

Herrmann B (2019) *West Autos in der DDR. [Western Car in the GDR].* Zeitlitz: Oktan.

Hersoug AG, Ulberg R and Høglend P (2014) When is transference work useful in psychodynamic psychotherapy? Main results of the first experimental study of transference work (FEST). *Contemporary Psychoanalysis.* 50(1): 156–174.

Hevey D (2018) Network analysis: A brief overview and tutorial. *Health Psychology and Behavioral Medicine.* 6(1): 301–328. https://doi.org/10.1080/21642850.2018.1521283.

Hevey D, Collins A and Brogan A (2013) Network analysis. *The Psychologist.* 26(6): 430–431.

Hickey-Moody A (2013) Affect as method. Feelings, aesthetic and affective pedagogy. In Coleman R and Ringrose J (Eds.) *Deleuze and Research Methodologies.* Edinburgh: Edinburgh University Press, pp. 79–95.

Hickling FW (2012) *Psychohistoriography. A Post-Colonial Psychoanalytic and Psychotherapeutic Model.* London: Jessica Kingsley Publishers.

Higgins JP, Thompson SG and Spiegelhalter D (2009) A re-evaluation of random-effects meta-analysis. *Journal of the Royal Statistical Society. Series A.* 172(1): 137–159. https://doi.org/10.1111/j.1467-985X.2008.00552.x.

Higgins JP, Thompson SG, Deeks JJ, Altman DG (2003) Measuring inconsistency in metaanalyses. *British Medical Journal.* 327(7414): 557–560. https://doi.org/10.1136/bmj.327.7414.557.

Higgins JPT, Thomas J, Chandler J, Cumpston M, Li T, Page MJ, Welch VA (Eds.) (2024) *Cochrane Handbook for Systematic Reviews of Interventions* version 6.5. Updated August 2024, Cochrane. https://www.cochrane.org/authors/handbooks-and-manuals/handbook

Highhouse S (2002) A history of the T-group and its early application in management development. *Group Dynamics Theory Research and Practice.* 6(4): 277–290.

Hildebrand D (2024) *John Dewey.* Stanford Encyclopedia of Philosophy. Available at: https://plato.stanford.edu/entries/dewey (accessed 2 December 2024).

Hill CE, Thompson BJ and Williams EN (1997) A guide to conducting consensual qualitative research. *Counseling Psychologist.* 25(4): 517–572. https://doi.org/10.1177/0011000097254001.

Hill D (2021) Dysregulation and its impact on states of consciousness. In Siegel DJ, Schore AN and Cozolino L (Eds.) *Interpersonal Neurobiology and Clinical Practice.* New York: W. W. Norton & Company, pp. 169–193.

Hill K, Wittkowski A, Hodgkinson E Bell R and Hare DJ (2016) Using the repertory grid technique to examine trainee clinical psychologists' construal of their personal and professional development. *Clinical Psychology & Psychotherapy.* 23(5): 425–437. https://doi.org/10.1002/cpp.1961.

Hill M (2005) Ethical considerations in researching children's experiences. In Greene S and Hogan D (Eds.) *Researching Children's Experiences. Methods and Methodological Issues.* London: Sage, pp. 61–86.

Hindle D and Klauber T (2006) Ethical issues in infant observation: Preliminary thoughts on establishing an observation. *Infant Observation.* 9(1): 7–19.

Hirschbiegel O (2017) *Der Gleiche Himmel.* 3-part series. [The Same Sky Series in 3 Parts]. ZDF. Available at: https://www.zdf.de/filme/der-gleiche-himmel (accessed 11 August 2022).

Hisamatsu S (1959) The characteristics of oriental nothingness. In Miyake G, Kishimoto H, Furuta S, Kosaka M, Shigizawa T and Kaneko T (Trans. and Eds.) (1961) *Philosophical Studies of Japan. Volumes 3.* Tokyo: Japan Society for the Promotion of Science, pp. 65–97.

Hisamatsu S (1965) Zen. its meaning for modern civilization. Trans. R DeMartino and G Tokiwa. *The Eastern Buddhist.* 1(1): 22–47. http://www.jstor.org/stable/44364446

Hisamatsu S (1971) Dialogues, east and west. Conversations between Paul Tillich and Hisamatsu Shin'Ichi. (Paul Tillich, Hisamatsu Shin'Ichi, Hannah Tillich, Richard DeMartino, Fujiyoshi Jikai). *The Eastern Buddhist.* 4(2): 89–107.

Hisamatsu S (1975) Ultimate crisis and resurrection. Sin and death. Trans. G Tokiwa. *The Eastern Buddhist.* 8(1): 12–29.

Hisamatsu S (1982) *Zen and the Fine Arts.* Trans. G Tokiwa. New York: Kodansha International. Available at: https://archive.org/details/zenfinearts0000hisa

Hisamatsu S (2002) *Critical Sermons of the Zen Tradition. Hisamatsu's Talks on Linji.* Ives C and Gishin T (Eds.) Manoha: University of Hawaii Press. https://archive.org/details/criticalsermonso0000hisa

Hisamatsu S (2005) *The Characteristics of Oriental Nothingness.* Trans. R De Martino in collaboration with Fujiyoshi Jikai and Abe Masao. Kyoto: F.A.S. Society. Available at: https://www.fas.x0.com (accessed 8 December 2024).

Hlatswayo NM, Adendorff H, Blackie M, Fataar A and Maluleka (Eds.) (2022) *Decolonizing Knowledge and Knowers. Struggles for University Transformation in South Africa.* New York: Routledge.

Ho L and Limpaecher A (2022) *Qualitative Content Analysis: Manifest Content Analysis vs Latent Content Analysis in Qualitative Research.* Delve Blog. December 15. Available at: https://delvetool.com/blog/manifest-content-analysis-latent-content-analysis (accessed February 2024).

Hoag MJ and Burlingame GM (1997) Evaluating the effectiveness of child and adolescent group treatment. A meta-analytic review. *Journal of Clinical Child Psychotherapy.* 26(3): 234–246.

Hoang LN (2013) Dynamics of Wave Function. Heisenberg, Schrődinger, Collapse. 4 March 2013. Available at: https://www.science4all.org/article/dynamics-of-the-wave-function/ (accessed 12 January 2025).

Hobson RP and Kapur R (2005) Working in the transference: Clinical and research perspectives. *Psychology and Psychotherapy: Theory, Research and Practice.* 78(3): 275–295.

Höck K (1969) 20 Jahre Psychotherapie in der DDR. [20 Years of Psychotherapy in the GDR]. *Medizinische Bildung.* 12: 161–162.

Höck K (1981a) Dynamische Gruppenpsychotherapie in Theorie, Forschung und Ausbildung. Referate des zweiten Gruppenpsychotherapiesymposiums mit internationaler Beteiligung vom 12. 10.-16. Oktober 1981 in Leipzig. Teil 1, *Heft 8/81. [Dynamic Group Psychotherapy in /theory, Research and Training. Lectures of the 2nd Group Psychotherapy Symposium with international Participation. Part 1].*

Höck K (1981b) Dynamische Gruppenpsychotherapie in Theorie, Forschung und Ausbildung. Referate des zweiten Gruppenpsychotherapeutischen Symposiums in Leipzig. Teil 2, *Heft 9/81. [Dynamic Group Psychotherapy in /theory, Research and Training. Lectures of the 2nd Group Psychotherapy Symposium with international Participation. Part 2].* Berichte űber die Psychotherapie und Neurosenforschung des Hauses der Gesundheit, Berlin. [Reports about the Psychotherapy and Neuroses Research of the Center of Health, Berlin].

Höck K (1981c) Untersuchungen zum Verlauf der intendierten dynamischen Gruppenpsychotherapie. Teil 1 Untersuchungsansatz, *Heft 7/81.* [Research regarding the duration of the Intentional Dynamic Psychotherapy. Part 1. Research Approach]

Höck K (1982) *Gruppenpsychotherapieforschung. Psychotherapie und Grenzgebiete, Bd 2.* Leipzig: Barth. [Group Psychotherapy Research. Psychotherapies and bordering areas].

Höck K, Szewczyk H and Wendt H (1973) (Hrsg.) *Neurosen. Ätiopathogenese, Diagnostik und Therapie.* [Neuroses, Etiopathogeneses, Diagnostic and Therapy]. Berlin: Deutscher Verlag der Wissenschaften.

Hoekstra R, Vugteveen J, Warrens MJ and Kruyen PM (2018) An empirical analysis of alleged misunderstandings of coefficient alpha. *International Journal of Research Methodology.* 22(4): 1–14.

Hofmann F (2015) *Pädagogische Kunstkommunikation zwischen Kunstaneignung und Kunstvermittlung. Fallspezifische empirische Untersuchungen zu zwei Schulklassen und einer Kita-Gruppe in Kunstausstellungen.* [Pedagogic Art Communication between Art, Acquisition and Art Teaching. Case Specific Empirical Study of two school classes and one Kindergarten Group in an Art Exhibition]. Műnchen: Kopaed.

Hofmann F (2016a) Social phenomenological analysis as a research method in art education. Developing an empirical model for understanding gallery talks. *International Journal of Education & the Arts.* 17(33). Available at: https://www.ijea.org/v17n33/ (accessed 5 February 2024). https://www.researchgate.net/publication/311653074_Social_Phenomenological_Analysis_as_a_Research_Method_in_Art_Education_Developing_an_Empirical_Model_for_Understanding_Gallery_Talks

Hofmann F (2016b) *Vermitteln und aneignen lassem im Spiel der Differenzen. Pädagogische Kunstkommunikation in Schule und Museum.* [Teaching and learning in the Play of Differences. Pedagogic Art Communication in School and Museum]. *Kulturelle Bildung Online.* https://doi.org/10.25529/92552.444. Available at: https://www.kubi-online.de/artikel/vermitteln-aneignen-lassen-spiel-differenzen-paedagogische-kunstkommunikation-schule-museum (accessed 5 February 2024).

Hofmann F (2016c) Developing the model of "pedagogical art communication" using social phenomenological analysis: An introduction to a research method and an example of its outcome. *Journal for Leaning through the Arts.* 12(1). Available at: https://escholarship.org/uc/item/6xw4f5c3 (accessed 5 February 2024).

Hofmann F and Preuβ K (Hrgs.) (2017) *Kunstvermittlung im Museum. Ein Erfahrungsraum. [Art Teaching in Museum. A Space of Experience].* Műnster und New York: Waxmann.

Hogarth I (2018) AI nationalisms. Available at: https://www.ianhogarth.com/blog/2018/6/13/ai-nationalism (accessed 24 December 2024).

Høglend P (1990) Dynamisk korttidsterapi (brief dynamic psychotherapy). In Alnes R, Ekern P and Jarval P (Eds.) *Poliklinikken Psykiatrisk Klinikk 25 a° r.* Oslo: University of Oslo, pp. 27–38.

Høglend P (2004) Analysis of transference in psychodynamic psychotherapy. A review of empirical research. *Canadian Journal of Psychoanalysis/Revue Canadienne de Psychanalyse.* 12(2): 280–300.

Høglend P (2014) Exploration of the patient-therapist relationship in psychotherapy. *American Journal of Psychiatry.* 171(10): 1056–1066.

Høglend P, Amlo S, Marble A, Bøgwald K-P, Sørbye Ø, Sjaastad MC and Heyerdahl O (2006) Analysis of the patient-therapist relationship in dynamic psychotherapy. An experimental study of transference interpretations. *American Journal of Psychiatry.* 163(10): 1739–1746.

Høglend P, Bøgwald KP, Amlo S, Heyerdahl O, Sørbye O, Marble A, Sjaastad MC and Bentsen H (2000) Assessment of change in dynamic psychotherapy. *Journal of Psychotherapy Practice and Research* 9(4): 190–199.

Høglend P, Bøgwald K-P, Amlo S, Marble A, Ulberg R, Sjaastad MC, Sørbye Ø, Heyerdahl O and Johansson P (2008) Transference interpretations in dynamic psychotherapy. Do they really yield sustained effects? *American Journal of Psychiatry.* 165(6): 763–771.

Høglend P, Dahl H-S, Hersoug AG, Lorentzen S and Perry JC (2011) Long-term effects of transference interpretation in dynamic psychotherapy of personality disorders. *European Psychiatry.* 26(2): 419–424.

Høglend P, Sørlie T, Heyerdahl O, Sørbye Ø and Amlo S (1993) Brief dynamic psychotherapy. *Journal of Psychotherapy Practice and Research.* 2(3): 230–241.

Hőhfeld K (2014) Aktuelle Gedanken zur Gruppenpsychotherapie in Deutschland. [Contemporary Thoughts on Group Psychotherapy in Germany]. *Gruppenpsychotherapie und Gruppendynamik.* 46(4): 274–285. https://doi.org/10.13109/grup.2010.46.4.274.

Hohls JK, König H-H, Quirke E, Hajek A (2021) Anxiety, depression and quality of life. a systematic review of evidence from longitudinal observational studies. *International Journal of Environmental Research and Public Health.* 18(22): 12022. https://doi.org/10.3390/ijerph182212022.

Hollway W and Jefferson T (2000) *Doing Qualitative Research DifferenI Free Association, Narrative and the Interview Technique.* London: Sage.

Hollway W and Jefferson T (2012) *Doing Qualitative Research Differently. A Psychosocial Approach.* 2nd Edition. Thousand Oaks, CA: Sage.

Holmes J (2019) On writing. Notes from an attachment-based psychotherapist. In Weegmann M (Ed.) *Psychodynamics of Writing.* New York: Routledge, pp. 6–16.

Holquist M (1990) *Dialogism: Bakhtin and His World.* London: Routledge. http://dx.doi.org/10.4324/9780203330340

Holstein J and Gubrium J (Eds.) (2012) *Varieties of Narrative Analysis*. London: Sage.

Holton G (1960) On the origins of the special theory of relativity. *American Journal of Physics.* 28: 627–636. https://doi.org/10.1119/1.1935922.

Holtz P (2020) Does postmodernism really entail a disregard for the truth? Similarities and differences in postmodern and critical realist conceptualizations of truth, progress, and empirical research methods. *Frontiers in Psychology.* 11(9): 545–556. https://doi.org/10.3389/fpsyg.2020.545959.

Honderich T (Ed.) (1995) Axiological Ethics. *The Oxford Companion To Philosophy.* Oxford and New York: Oxford University Press, p. 71.

Hong QN, Pluye P, Fabregues S, Bartlett G, Boardman, F, Corgo, M, Dagenais P, Gagnon M-P, Griffiths F, Nicolau B, O'Cathain A, Rousseau M-C and Vedel IV (2018) Mixed Methods Appraisal Tool (MMAT) Version 2018. User Guide. https://docs.edtechhub.org/lib/WJWIBS9S; http://mixedmethodsappraisaltoolpublic.pbworks.com/w/file/fetch/127916259/MMAT_2018_criteria-manual_2018-08-01_ENG.pdf

Hong X, Falter MM and Fecho B (2016) Embracing tension: using Bakhtinian theory as a means for data analysis. *Qualitative Research.* 17(1): 20–36. https://doi.org/10.1177/1468794116653800.

Hookway CJ (2008) *Pragmatism. Stanford Encyclopedia of Philosophy*. Archive Summer 2010 Edition. https://plato.stanford.edu/archIves/sum2010/entries/pragmatism/

Hopper E (1971) Notes on stratification education and mobility in industrial society. In Hopper E (Ed.) *Readings in the Theory of Educational Systems*. London: Hutchinson University Press, pp. 13–37.

Hopper E (1997) Traumatic experiences in the unconscious life of groups: A fourth basic assumption. *Group Analysis.* 30(4): 439–470.

Hopper E (2001) The social unconscious. Theoretical considerations. *Group Analysis.* 34(1): 9–27.

Hopper E (2003a) *The Social Unconscious. Selected Papers*. London: Jessica Kingsley Publishers.

Hopper E (2003b) *Traumatic Experience in the Unconscious Life of Groups.* London: Jessica Kingsley Publishers.

Hopper E (2003c) Aspects of aggression in large groups characterised by (ba) I:A/M. In Schneider S and Weinberg H (Eds.) *The Large Group Re-Visited. The Herd, Primal Horde, Crowds and Masses.* International Library of Group Analysis 25. London: Jessica Kingsley Publishers, pp. 58–72.

Hopper E (2007) Theoretical and conceptual notes concerning transference and countertransference processes in groups and by groups, and the social unconscious. Part III. *Group Analysis.* 40(2): 285–300.

Hopper E (2019) "Notes" on the theory of the fourth basic assumption in the unconscious life of—roups and group-like social syste–s - Incohesion: Aggregation/massification or (ba) I:A/M. *Group.* 43(1): 9–27.

Hopper E (2024a) Introduction. In Hopper E (Ed.) *The Tripartite Matrix ithehe Developing Theory and Expanding Practice of Group Analysis. The Social Unconscious in Persons, Groups and Societies: Volume 4.* London: Routledge, pp. 1–16.

Hopper E (Ed.) (2024b) *The Tripartite Matrix in the Developing Theory and Expanding Practice of Group Analysis. The Social Unconscious in Persons, Groups and Societies: Volume 4.* London: Routledge.

Hopper E and Weinberg H (Eds.) (2011) *The Social Unconscious in Persons, Groups and Societies Volume 1: Mainly Theory.* London: Karnac.

Hopper E and Weinberg H (Eds.) (2016) *The Social Unconscious in Persons, Groups and Societies. Volume 2. Mainly Foundation Matrices.* London: Karnac.

Hopper E and Weinberg H (Eds.) (2017) *The Social Unconscious in Persons, Groups and Societies Volume 3: The Foundation Matrix Extended and Re-configured.* New York: Routledge.

Horkheimer M (1999) Materialism and Metaphysics. In Horkheimer M (1999) *Critical Theory. Selected Essays. Max Horkheimer. Translated by MJ O'Connell.* New York: Continuum, pp. 10–46.

Horkheimer M (2004) *Eclipse of Reason.* London: Continuum.

Horowitz LM and Rosenberg SE (1994) The consensual response psychodynamic formulation. Method and research results. *Psychotherapy Research.* 4: 222–233.

Horowitz LM and Rosenberg SE (1994) The consensual response psychodynamic formulation. Method and research results. *Psychotherapy Research.* 4(3–4): 222–233. https://doi.org/10.1080/10503309412331334052.

Horowitz LM, Rosenberg SE, Baer BA, Ureño G and Villaseñor VS (1988) Inventory of interpersonal problems: Psychometric properties and clinical applications. *Journal of Consulting and Clinical Psychology.* 56(6): 885–892.

Horowitz LM, Rosenberg, SE, Baer BA, Ureño G and Villaseñor VS (1988) Inventory of interpersonal problems: psychometric properties and clinical applications. *Journal of Consulting and Clinical Psychology.* 56(6): 885–892. https://doi.org/10.1037/0022-006X.56.6.885.

Horvath AO and Greenberg LS (1989) Development and validation of the working alliance inventory. *Journal of Counselling Psychology.* 36(2): 223–233. https://doi.org/10.1037/0022-0167.36.2.223.

Houshmand Z, Livingston RB and Wallace BA (Eds.) (1999) *Consciousness at the Crossroads.* New York: Snow Lion Publications.

Howe KR (1988) Against the quantitative-qualitative incompatibility thesis or dogmas die hard. *Educational Researcher.* 17(8): 10–16. https://doi.org/10.3102/0013189X017008010.

Hsieh H-F and Shannon SE (2005) Three approaches to qualitative content analysis. *Qualitative Health Research.* 15(9): 1277–1288. https://doi.org/10.1177/1049732305276687.

Huang L-L (2016) Interpersonal harmony and conflict for Chinese people: A yin–yang perspective. *Frontiers in Psychology.* 7: 847. https://doi.org/10.3389/fpsyg.2016.00847.

Huber F and Laste S (2021) *Ein Tag im Augustoderntation1.* Available at: https://www.zdf.de/dokumentation/zdfzeit/zdfzeit-ein-tag-im-august-der-mauerbau-61-100.html (accessed 7 February 2023).

Hughes EA, Ellis S and Smith JR (2024) Connecting groups and behaviours: A network analysis of identity-infused behaviours. *British Journal of Social Psychology.* 631(1): 205–233. https://doi.org/10.1111/bjso.12674.

Hughes K and Tarrant A (2020) The ethics of qualitative secondary analysis. In Hughes K and Tarrant A (Eds.) *Qualitative Secondary Analysis.* London: Sage, pp. 37–58.

Hughes K, Hughes J and Tarrant A (2022) Working at a remove: Continuous, collective, and configurative approaches to qualitative secondary analysis. *Quality & Quantity.* 56(2): 375–394.

Hummelen B, Wilberg T and Karterud S (2007) Interviews of female patients with borderline personality disorder who dropped out of group psychotherapy. *International Journal of Group Psychotherapy.* 57(1): 67–91.

Humphreys M and Weinstein JM (2009) Field experiments and the political economy of development. *Annual Review of Political Science.* 12(1): 367–378.

Hunleth JM, Spray JS, Meehan C, Lang CW and Njelesani J (2022) What is the state of children's participation in qualitative research on health interventions? A scoping study. *BMC Pediatrics.* 22(1): 328. https://doi.org/10.1186/s12887-022-03391-2.

Husain N (2024) January 1928: The Dirac equation unifies quantum mechanics and special relativity. *APS News.* 19 November 2024. This Month In Physics History. Available at: https://www.aps.org/apsnews/2024/11/mathematical-intuition-dirac-quantum-mechanics (accessed 7 January 2025).

Husserl E (1936/2012) *Die Krise der Europäischen Wissenschaften und die Transzendentale Phänomenologie. Eine Einleitung in die Phänomenologische Philosophie.* Mit einer Einleitung und Registern, von der Hrg. Elizabeth Strőker. [The Crisis of the European Sciences and the Transcendental Phenomenology. An Introduction in the Phenomenological Philosophy. With an Introduction by the editor Elizabeth Strőker.] Hamburg: Meiner Verlag.

Husserl E (1950–2014) *Husserliana. Edmund Husserl. Gesammelte Werke. [Collective Works of Husserl].* Available at: https://www.springer.com/series/6062 (accessed 16 January 2021).

Husserl E (1980) *Phenomenology and the Foundations of the Sciences*. Trans. TE Klein and WE Pohl. Dordrecht: Kluwer.

Husserl E (1983) *Ideas Pertaining to a Pure Phenomenology and a Phenomenological Philosophy.* Trans. F Kersten. The Hague: Martinus Nijhoff.

Hutchinson S (2017) Group analytic identity. *Group Analysis.* 50(4): 419–435.

Hyers LL (2018) *Diary Methods. Understanding Qualitative Research.* New York: Oxford University Press.

IBM (2021) *What is a Chatbot?* Available at: https://www.ibm.com/think/topics/chatpots (accessed 4 December 2024).

IGA (2023–24) *Handbook for the Qualifying Course*. Available at: www.groupanalysis.org (accessed 6 February 2023).

IGA (2024–25) *Handbook for the Qualifying Course*. Available at: www.groupanalysis.org (accessed 20 August 2024).

Iida M, Shrout PE, Laurenceau J-P and Bolger N (2012) Using diary methods in psychological research. In Cooper H (Ed.) *APA Handbook of Research Methods in Psychology. Vol. 1. Foundations, Planning, Measures, and Psychometrics.* Washington, DC: The American Psychological Association, pp. 277–305.

Ikkos G (2000) Psychosomatics and psychodynamics: An introductory review. Group Analysis. 33(2): 235–250. https://doi.org/10.1177/05333160022077308.

IlNodo (2021) *Social Dreaming*. Available at: https://www.ilnodogroup.it/cosa-facciamo/ (accessed 2 April 2025).

Imbo (1998) *An Introduction to African Philosophy*. Lanham, MD: Rowman and Littlefield Publishers.

Inderhaug TS (2013) *Challenges in mentalization-based group therapy (MBTG): A video-based explorative case study.* (Graduate thesis). Trondheim: The Norwegian University of Science and Technology.

Inderhaug TS and Karterud S (2015) A qualitative study of a mentalization-based group for borderline patients. *Group Analysis*. 48(2): 150–163.

Ingham-Broomfield RB (2016) A nurses' guide to the hierarchy of research designs and evidence. *Australian Journal of Advanced Nursing.* 33(3): 38–43.

Ingold T (2008) Anthropology is not ethnography. Radcliffe-brown lecture in social anthropology. *Proceedings of the British Academy.* 154: 68–92. https://doi.org/10.5871/bacad/9780197264355.003.0003.

Iosefo F, Holman-Jones S and Harris A (2020) Introduction. In Iosefo, F, Jones, S and Harris A (Eds.). *Wayfinding and Critical Autoethnography*. New York: Routledge, pp. 1–11. Partially available at: https://www.academia.edu/77820876/Wayfinding_and_Critical_Autoethnography

Iqbal S and Pipon-Young L (2009) The Delphi method. A step-by-step guide. *The Psychologist.* 22(7): 598–600. https://www.bps.org.uk/psychologist/delphi-method

Iqbal S, Hackett S and Callanan M (2009) 'Normal' and 'inappropriate' childhood sexual behaviours: Findings from a Delphi study of professionals in the UK. *Journal of Sexual Aggression.* 15(3): 275–288. https://doi.org/10.1080/13552600902915984.

Irvine A (2024) First steps in qualitative secondary analysis: experiences of engaging with the primary research team. *International Journal of Social Research Methodology.* 27(6): 721–733.

Irvine JT (2018) Divided values, shadow languages: positioning and perspective in linguistic ideologies. *Signs and Society*. 6(1): 25–44. https://doi.org/10.1086/695142.

Irwin S (2013) Qualitative secondary analysis: Ethics, epistemology and context. *Progress in Development Studies.* 13(4): 295–306.

Isaacs W (1999) *Dialogue and the Art of Thinking Together. A Pioneering Approach to Communicating in Business and Life.* New York: Doubleday.

Island TK (1995) The role of the large group in creating a group analytic training community. In Peternel F (Ed.) *Median and Large Groups in Group Analytic Training*. Proceedings of E.G.A.T.I.N. Study Days. Ljubljana.

Island TK (2003) The large group and leadership challengers in a group analytic training community. In Schneider S and Weinberg H (Eds.) *The Large Group Re-Visited.* London: Jessica Kingsley Publishers, pp. 201–213.

Jackson AY and Mazzei LA (2012) *Thinking with Theory in Qualitative Research. Viewing Data across Multiple Perspectives.* New York: Routledge.

Jackson F (2024) Conceptual Analysis. In Frank MC and Majid A (Eds.) *Open Encyclopedia of Cognitive Science.* Cambridge, MA: MIT Press. https://doi.org/10.21428/e2759450.5ff2bcd7

Jackson L, Power K, Mitchell K, Duncan K, Graham L and Wilson K (2023) Understanding female survivors of interpersonal trauma and their experience of the 'survive & thrive' course. *Group Analysis.* 57(1): 23–49.

Jacobson NS and Truax P (1991) Clinical significance. A statistical approach to defining meaningful change in psychotherapy research. *Journal of Consulting and Clinical Psychology.* 59(1): 12–19.

Jacques V, Wu E, Grosshans F, Treussart F, Grangier P, Aspect A and Roch J-F (2007) Experimental realization of wheeler's delayed-choice gedanken experiment. *Science.* 315(2): 966–968.

James K (2007) Der Deutsche Liebling *Trabi Fährt Wieder Los.* 19 Mai. Deutsche Welle. Archiv. [The German Darling Trabi Runs Again]. Available at: https://web.archive.org/web/20080324052640/; http://www.dw-world.de/dw/article/0.2542584.00.html

Jamieson MK, Govaart GH and Pownall M (2023) Reflexivity in quantitative research: A rationale and beginner's guide. *Social and Personality Psychology Compass*. 17(4): e12735. https://doi.org/10.1111/spc3.12735.

Jammer M (1934) Quantenphysikalische Bemerkungen zur Biologie und Psychologie. *Erkenntnis.* 4(1): 215–252. https://link.springer.com/article/10.1007/BF01793491. Available at: https://www.jstor.org/stable/20011714

Janesick VJ (2000) The choreography of qualitative research design. In Denzin NK and Lincoln YS (Eds.) *Handbook of Qualitative Research.* 2nd Edition. Thousand Oaks, CA: Sage, pp. 379–433.

Janis IL (1971) Groupthink. *Psychology Today.* November. 5: 43–46/6: 74–76. Available at: https://pdfcoffee.com/janis-irving-l-groupthink-43-44-46-74-76-pdf-free.html.

Janowitz N (2018) Ancient ideologies of ineffability and their echoes. *Signs and Society.* 6(1): 45–63. https://doi.org/10.1086/695143.

Jansen WS, Otten S, Van Der Zee KI and Jans L (2014) Inclusion: Conceptualization and measurement. *European Journal of Social Psychology.* 44(4): 370–385.

Jarausch K, Hinrich S and David C (1997) "The presence of the past: Culture, opinion, and identity in Germany". In Jarausch K (Ed.) *After Unity: Reconfiguring German Identities.* Oxford: Berghahn Books, pp. 25–60.

Jarrett C (2014) *The 10 Most Controversial Psychology Studies Ever Published.* Research Digest, BPA. 19 September 2014. Available at: https://www.bps.org.uk/research-digest/10-most-controversial-psychology-studies-ever-published (accessed 3 December 2024).

JBI (Joanna Briggs Institute) (2023) *Critical Appraisal Tools.* Available at: https://jbi.global/critical-appraisal-tools (accessed 2 November 2024).

Johansson L (2016) Post-qualitative line of flight and the confabulative conversation: A methodological ethnography. *International Journal of Qualitative Studies in Education.* 29(4): 445–466. https://doi.org/10.1080/09518398.2015.1053157.

Johansson L and Werbart A (2009) Patients' views of therapeutic action in psychoanalytic group psychotherapy. *Group Analysis.* 42(2): 120–142.

Johnson EL, Mutti MF, Springham N and Xenophontes I (2016) Mentalization after mentalization based treatment. *Mental Health and Social Inclusion.* 20(1): 44–51.

Johnson JE, Burlingame GM, Olsen JA, Davies DR and Gleave RL (2005) Group climate, cohesion, alliance, and empathy in group psychotherapy. Multilevel structural equation models. *Journal of Counseling Psychology.* 53(3): 310–321.

Johnson JE, Pulsipher D, Ferrin SL, Burlingame GM, Davies DR and Gleave R (2006) Measuring group processes: A comparison of the GCQ and CCI. *Group Dynamics. Theory, Research, and Practice.* 10(2): 136–145.

Johnson RB (2017) Dialectical pluralism. A metaparadigm whose time has come. *Journal of Mixed Methods Research.* 11(2): 156–173.

Johnson RB (2024) Dialectical pluralism and integration in mixed methods research. In Shan Y (Ed.) *Philosophical Foundations of Mixed Methods Research. Dialogues between Researchers and Philosophers.* New York: Routledge, pp. 100–126.

Johnson RB, Onwuegbuzie AJ and Turner LA (2007) Toward a definition of mixed methods research. *Journal of Mixed Methods Research.* 1(2): 112–133.

Jones E (1987) *Die Theorie der Symbolik.* Frankfurt: Athenaeum.

Jones E (2000) *Therapeutic Action. A Guide to Psychoanalytic Therapy.* Northvale, NJ: Aronson.

Jones E (2004) War and the practice of psychotherapy. The UK experience 1939–1960. *Medical History.* 48(4): 493–510.

Jones EE and Windholz M (1990) The psychoanalytic case study. Toward a method for systemic inquiry. *Journal of the American Psychoanalytic Association.* 38: 985–1016. https://doi.org/10.1177/000306519003800405.

Jones M (1952) *Social Psychiatry: A Study of Therapeutic Communities.* London: Tavistock Publications.

Jones RK (2000) The unsolicited diary as a qualitative research tool for advanced research capacity in the field of health and illness. *Qualitative Health Research.* 10(4): 555–567.

Jones T (1976) East Germany under Honecker. *The World Today.* 32(9): 339–346. http://www.jstor.org/stable/40394943

Jones TL, Baxter MA and Khanduja V (2013) A quick guide to survey research. *The Annals of The Royal College of Surgeons of England.* 95(1): 5–7.

Jorm AF (2015) Using the Delphi expert consensus method in mental health research. *Australian & New Zealand Journal of Psychiatry.* 49(10): 887–897.

Joseph B (1983) On understanding and not understanding. Some technical issues. *International Journal of PsychoanalysI*64(3): 291–298.

Joseph B (1985) Transthence: The total situation. *International Journal of Psychoanalysis.* 66(12): 447–454.

Josselson R (2007) The ethical attitude in narrative research. In Clandinin DJ (Ed.) *Handbook of Narrative Inquiry. Mapping a Methodology.* Thousand Oaks, CA: Sage, pp. 537–566.

Joyce AS, MacNair-Semands R, Tasca GA and Ogrodniczuk JS (2011) Factor structure and validity of the therapeutic factors inventory–short form. *Group Dynamics: Theory, Research, and Practice.* 15(3): 201–219. https://doi.org/10.1037/a0024677.

Joyce RA (2004) Embodied subjectivity. Gender, femininity, masculinity, sexuality. In Meskell LM and Preucel RW (Eds.) *A Companion to Social Archaeology.* Oxford: Blackwell, pp. 82–95.

Joyce RA (2005) Archaeology of the body. *Annual Review of Anthropology.* 34: 139–158. http://www.jstor.org/stable/25064880

Judt M (2013) *Der Bereich Kommerzielle Koordinierung. Das DDR Wirtschaftsimperum des Alexander Schalck-Golodkowski. Mythos und Realität. [The Department Commercial Coordination. The GDR Economic Empire of Alexander Schalck-Golodkowski. Myth and Reality].*Berlin: Links Verlag.

Judt M (2015) *Ein kommunistischer Kapitalist. Zum Tode von Alexander Schalck-Golodkowski. [A communist capitalist. On the death of Alexander Schalck-Golodkowski].* 2 July. Deutschland Archiv. Berlin: Bundeszentrale für politische Bildung. https://www.bpb.de/themen/deutschlandarchiv/209006/ein-kommunistischer-kapitalist-zum-tode-von-alexander-schalck-golodkowski/

Julian LJ (2011) Measures of anxiety: state-trait anxiety inventory (STAI), Beck anxiety inventory (BAI), and Hospital anxiety and depression scale-anxiety (HADS-A). *Arthritis Care & Research.* 63(11): 467–472. https://doi.org/10.1002/acr.20561.

Jung CG (1912) *Psychology of the Unconscious. A Study of the Transformations and Symbolism.* New York: Moffat Yard and Company.

Jung CG (1917) *Die Psychologie der unbewussten Prozesse. Ein Überblick über die moderne Theorie und Methode der analytischen Psychologie.* [The Psychology of the unconscious Processes. An Overview of the modern Theory and Method of analytic Psychology.] Zürich: Rauscher.

Jung CG (1921/1971) *The Collected Works. Volume Six. Psychological Types. Edited and Translated by Gerhard Adler and R Hull*. Princeton: Princeton University Press.

Jung CG (1934/1969) *The Collected Works. Volume Eight. Structure and Dynamics of the Psyche. Edited and Translated by H Read and R Hull*. Princeton: Princeton University Press.

Jung CG (1938) *Psychology and Religion*. New Haven, CT: Yale University Press.

Jung CG (1950/1975) Foreword to the I-Ching. *The I Ching or Book of Changes. The Richard Wilhelm Translation. Rendered Into English by Gary F. Baynes.* Volume 11, Bollingen Series XIX. New York: Pantheon Books, pp. xxi–xxiv.

Jung CG (1960) Synchronicity. An Acausal Connecting Principle. In Jung CG (1960) *The Structure and the Dynamics of the Psyche*. Collected Works, Volume 8. Princeton: Princeton University Press, pp. 104–116. https://archive.org/details/synchronicityaca00cgju/page/n1/mode/2up

Jung CG (1961) *Memories, Dreams, Reflections*. Recorded and Ed. by A Jaffé. Trans. Richard and C Winston. London: Vintage Books.

Jung CG (1963) *Memories, Dreams, Reflections.* London: Random House.

Jung CG (1964) *Man and His Symbols.* Conceived and Edited by C Jung. London: Picador.

Jung CG (1968a) *Analytical Psychology Its Theory and Practice*. C.G. Jung. *The Tavistock Lectures.* Foreword by Bennet EA. London: Routledge & Kegan Paul.

Jung CG (1968b) *The Archetypes and the Collective Unconscious.* 2nd Edition. New York: Routledge.

Jung CG (1971) Studies in Word Association. *The Collected Works. Volume Two. Experimental Research. Edited and Translated by Gerhard Adler and R Hull*. Princeton: Princeton University Press.

Jung CG (1978) *Psychology and the East.* Trans. RFC Hull. Volumes, 10, 11, 13, and 18. Bollington Series XX. Princeton, NJ: Princeton University Press.

Jung CG (2011) Beiträge zur Symbolik des Selbst. Band 9. In *Jung* CG (2011) Gesammelte Werke. *Dritte Auflage*. [Contributions to the Symbolic of the Self]. Stuttgart: Patmos Verlag.

Jung CG and Riklin F (1904/1973) *The Associations of Normal Subjects*. Trans. L Stein and D Riviere. Princeton, NJ: Princeton University Press.

Jusdanis G (2001) *The Necessary Nation*. Princeton, NJ: Princeton University Press.

Kaba A, Wishart I, Fraser K, Goderre S and McLaighlin K (2016) Are we at risk of groupthink in our approach to teamwork interventions in health care? *Medical Education.* 50(4): 400–408.

Kächele H, Schachter J and Thomä H (2009) *From Psychoanalytic Narrative to Empirical Single Case Research. Implications for Psychoanalytic Practice.* New York: Routledge.

Kaës R (2011) *Um Singular Plural. A psicanálise à prova do grupo*. [A Singular Plural. Psychoanalysis to the Test of the Group]. São Paulo: Edições Loyola Jesuítas.

Kaës R (2017) *O aparelho psíquico grupal*. [The Group Psychic Apparatus]. São Paulo: Ideias & Letras.

Kaey J (2000) *India. A History.* Revised Edition. London: Harper Collins Publishers.

Kagel MR (2020) *Socialist Realignment. Correctional Education in East Germany's Youth Workhouses, 1949-1969.* PhD Thesis, Oberlin College, US. Available at: https://digitalcommons.oberlin.edu/honors/697/ (accessed 6 March 2023).

Kaiser J, Hanschmidt F and Kersting A (2021) The association between therapeutic alliance and outcome in internet-based psychological interventions: A meta-analysis. *Computers in Human Behavior.* 114, Article 106512. https://doi.org/10.1016/j.chb.2020.106512.

Kaklauskas FJ and Olson EA (2020) History and developments. In Kaklauskas FJ and Greene LR (Eds.) (2020) *Core Principles of Group Psychotherapy. An Integrated Theory, Research, and Practice Training Manual. American Group Psychotherapy Association Group Therapy Training and Practice Series.* New York: Routledge, pp. 3–24.

Kakoliris G (2017) Jacques derrida's deconstruction of western metaphysics. The early years. *Dia-noesis. A Journal of Philosophy.* 4: 43–62. Available at: https://dianoesis-journal.com/issue-4-2017/

Kaku M (2024) *Quantum Supremacy. How Quantum Computers Will Unlock the Mysteries of science and Address Humanity's Biggest Challenges.* Dublin: Penguin Books.

Kalleklev J and Karterud S (2018) A comparative study of mentalization-based versus psychodynamic group therapy session. *Group Analysis.* 51(1): 44–60.

Kamal SS (2019) Research paradigm and the philosophical foundations of a qualitative study. *International Journal of Social Sciences.* 4(3): 1386–1384. https://doi.org/10.20319/pijss.2019.43.13861394.

Kaminsky A (2016) *Frauen in der DDR.* [Women in the GDR]. Berlin: Links Verlag.

Kaminsky A (2019) *Berufstätigkeit von Frauen in der DDR. "Mit Gleichberechtigung hatte das weniger zu tun". [Employment of Women in the GDR. It had less to do with equality].* Deutschland Archiv. Deutschlandfunk. Available at: https://www.deutschlandfunk.de/berufstaetigkeit-von-frauen-in-der-ddr-mit-100.html (accessed 10 April 2023).

Kant I (1781/2003) *Critique of Pure Reason.* Trans. JMD Meiklejohn. Available at: https://gutenberg.org/files/4280/=4280h/4280-h.htm (accessed 4 March 2022)

Kant I (2016) *Kant's Prolegomena to Any Future Metaphysics.* Trans. and Ed. P Carus. EBook. Project Gutenberg. Available at: https://www.gutenberg.org/files/52821/52821-h/52821-h.htm (accessed 1 June 2024).

Karcher S (1999) Jung, the tao, and the classic of change. *Journal of Religion and Health.* 38(4): 287–304. https://www.jstor.org/stable/27511402

Karterud S (1989a) A comparative study of six different inpatient groups with respect to their basic assumption functioning. *International Journal of Group Psychotherapy.* 39(3): 355–376.

Karterud S (1989b) A study of Bion's basic assumption groups. *Human Relations.* 42(4): 315–335.

Karterud S (2000a) On the scientific foundation of group analysis. Commentary on an article by Ralph Stacey. *Group Analysis.* 33(4): 514–518.

Karterud S (2000b) The group emotionality rating. In Beck AP and Lewis CM (Eds.) *The Process of Group Psychotherapy. Systems for Analyzing Change.* Washington, DC: American Psychological Association, pp. 113–134.

Karterud S (2001) Group analysis in the age of evidence-based psychology/psychiatry. Commentary on 'research as an extended group phenomenon: Is "hard science" a sexual metaphor?' by Chris Evans'. *Group Analysis.* 34(2): 312–316.

Karterud S (2015) *Mentalization-Based Group Therapy. A theoretical, Clinical and Research Manual.* London: Oxford University Press.

Karterud S (2018) Case formulations in mentalization-based group therapy. *Research in Psychotherapy, Psychopathology, Process and Outcome.* 21(3): 132–136. https://doi.org/10.4081/ripppo.2018.318.

Karterud S (2024) *Group Analysis. A Modern Synthesis.* New York: Routledge.

Karterud S (2025) Some reflections on research and group analysis. *Group Analysis*. Online. https://doi.org/10.1177/05333164251357748.

Karterud S and Bateman AW (2012) Group therapy techniques. In Bateman AW and Fonagy P (Eds.) *Handbook of Mentalization in Mental Health Practice.* Washington, DC: American Psychiatric Association, pp. 81–105.

Karterud S and Foss T (1989) The group emotionality rating system. A modification of thelen's method of assessing emotionality in groups. *Small Group Research.* 20(2): 131–150.

Karterud S and Wilberg T (2007) From general day hospital treatment to specialized treatment programmes. *International Review of Psychiatry.* 19(1): 39–49.

Karterud S, Bjerke SN, Normann-Eide T and Ulland A (2025) Group treatment is favoured by Norwegian mental health leaders. *Group Analysis*. Online. https://doi.org/10.1177/05333164241300693.

Karterud S, Gunnarsen G, Kongerslev MT, Staun L and Schultz-Venrath U (2024) On the relationship between group analysis and mentalization-based group therapy. *Group Analysis.* 58(1): 115–129. https://doi.org/10.1177/05333164231218694.

Kastner M, Tricco AC, Soobiah C, Lillie E, Perrier L, Horsley T, Welch V, Cogo E, Antony J and Straus SE (2012) What is the most appropriate knowledge synthesis method to conduct a review? Protocol for a scoping review. *BMC Medical Research Methodology*. 12: 114. https://doi.org/10.1186/1471-2288-12-114.

Kasulis TP (1977) Zen Buddhism, Freud, and Jung. *The Eastern Buddhist.* 10(1): 68–91.

Kaur R and Li J (2023) How to conduct a randomized controlled trial. *Respiratory Care*. 69(1): 128–138. https://doi.org/10.4187/respcare.11351.

Kazdin AE (2007) Mediators and mechanisms of change in psychotherapy research. *Annual Review of Clinical Psychology.* 3(1): 1–27.

Kazis L, Anderson JJ and Meenan RF (1989) Effect sizes for interpreting changes in health status. *Medical Care*. 27(3): S179–S189. https://doi.org/10.1097/00005650-198903001-00015.

Keane W (2007) *Christian Moderns. Freedom and Fetish in the Mission Encounter.* Berkeley: University of California Press.

Keane W (2018) On semiotic ideology. *Signs and Society*. 6(1): 64–87. https://doi.org/10.1086/695387.

Kearney GP, Corman MK, Hart N, Johnston J and Gormley G (2019) Why institutional ethnography? Why now? Institutional ethnography in health professions education. *Medical Education.* 8(1): 17–24. https://pmejournal.org/articles/10.1007/S40037-019-0499-0

Kearney MH (1998) Ready-to-wear. Discovering grounded formal theory. *Research in Nursing Health.* 21(2): 179–186. https://doi.org/10.1002/(sici)1098-240x(199804)21:2<179::aid-nur8>3.0.co;2-g.

Kearney MH (2000) New directions in grounded formal theory. In Schreiber RS and Stern PM (Eds.) *Using Grounded Theory in Nursing*. New York: Springer, pp. 227–246.

Keeley T, Williamson P, Cllaery P, Joes LL, Mathers J, Jones J, Young B and Calvert M (2016) The use of qualitative methods to inform Delphi surveys in core outcome set development. *Trials.* 4(17): 230. https://doi.org/10.1186/s13063-016-1356-7.

Keen TR and Bell RC (1980) One thing leads to another: A new approach to elicitation in the repertory grid technique. *International Journal of Man–Machine Studies*. 13(1): 25–38. https://doi.org/10.1016/S0020-7373(80)80033-2.

Keet A (2014) Epistemic 'othering' and the decolonization of knowledge. *Africa Insight.* 44(1): 23–37.

Keevy I (2009) Ubuntu versus the core values of the South African Constitution. *Journal for Juridical Science.* 34(2): 19–58. https://doi.org/10.4314/jjs.v34i2.63129

Keiser RE (1980) Jung's Word Association Test: Response Norms And Patterns Of Disturbance. Master's Thesis. Loyola University Chicago. Available at: https://ecommons.luc.edu/luc_theses/3252 (accessed 4 January 2025).

Keller EF (1995) *Reflections on Gender and Science*. Yale: Yale University Press.

Kellermeyer L, Harnke B and Knight S (2018) Resource review. Covidence and rayyan. *Journal of the Medical Library Association.* 106(4): 580–583.

Kelly GA (1955) *The Psychology of Personal Constructs.* London: W. W. Norton & Company.

Kemmis S, McTaggart R and Nixon R (2014) *The Action Research Planner. Doing Critical Participator Action Research.* New York: Springer.

Kendall HO, Kendall FP and McCreary EK (1949) *Muscle Testing and Function.* Baltimore, MD: Williams & Wilkins.

Kennard D, Roberts J and Winter D (1993) *A Workbook of Group-Analytic Interventions.* London: Routledge.

Kennefick D (2005) Einstein versus the *Physical Review*. *Physics Today*. 58(9): 43–48. https://doi.org/10.1063/1.2117822.

Kent J (2021) Scapegoating and the 'angry black woman'. *Group Analysis.* 53(1): 1–18.

Kernberg OF (1975) *Borderline Conditions and Pathological Narcissism*. New York: Jason Aronson.

Kernberg OF (1989) The temptations of conventionality. *International Review of Psycho-Analysis.* 16(2): 191–205.

Kerr J (1993) *A most Dangerous Method. The Story of Jung, Freud & Sabina Spielrein.* London: Vintage Books.

Keyton J (2016) The future of small group research. *Small Group Research*. 47(2): 134–154.

Khoza RJ (2005) *Let Africa Lead. African Transformational Leadership for 21st Century Business*. Johannesburg: Vezubuntu Publishing Ltd.

Khoza RJ (2006) *Let Africa Lead: African Transformational Leadership for 21st Century Business*. 2nd Edition. Johannesburg: Vezubuntu Publishing Ltd.

Khrennikov A (2006) Quantum-like brain: "Interference of minds". *Biosystems.* 84(3): 225–241. https://doi.org/10.1016/j.biosystems.2005.11.005.

Khrennikov A (2007) Toward an adequate mathematical model of mental space: Conscious and unconscious dynamics on m-adic trees. 1–37. *Biosystems.* 90(3): 656–675. https://doi.org/10.1016/j.biosystems.2007.02.004.

Khrennikov A (2008) The quantum-like brain on the cognitive and subcognitive time scales. *Journal of Consciousness Studies.* 15(7): 39–77. https://www.researchgate.net/publication/262956136_The_Quantum-Like_Brain_on_the_Cognitive_and_Subcognitive_Time_Scales

Khrennikov A (2010) The quantum-like brain. In Khrennikov A (Ed.) (2010) *Ubiquitous Quantum Structure. From Psychology to Finance.* New York: Springer, pp. 65–78.

Khrennikov A (2023) Cooperative functioning of unconscious and consciousness from theory of open quantum systems. In Chakraborti A, Haven E, Patra S and Singh N (Eds.) *Quantum Decision Theory and Complexity Modelling in Economics and Public Policy. New Economic Windows.* New York: Springer, pp. 11–23.

Khurana D, Koli A, Khatter G and Singh S (2023) Natural language processing: State of the art, current trends and challenges. *Multimedia Tools and Applications.* 82(3): 3713–3744. https://pmc.ncbi.nlm.nih.gov/articles/PMC9281254/

Kim S (2024) What's the point of participant information sheets if no-one reads them? In Smyth BM, Martin MA and Downing M (Eds.) *The Routledge Handbook of Human Research Ethics and Integrity in Australia.* New York: Routledge, pp. 152–161.

Kimberlin CL and Winterstein AG (2008) Validity and reliability of measurement instruments used in research. *American Journal of Health-System Pharmacy.* 65(23): 2276–2284. https://doi.org/10.2146/ajhp070364.

King P (2013) Moderators/Moderating Factors. In Gellman MD and Turner R (Eds.) *Encyclopedia of Behavioral Medicine*. New York: Springer Nature, pp. 1256–1258.

King PR, Beehler GP, Donnelly K, Funderburk JS and Wray LO (2021) A practical guide to applying the Delphi technique in mental health treatment adaptation. The example of enhanced problem-solving training (E-PST). *Professional Psychology Research and Practice.* 52(4): 376–386.

Kinouani G (2019) Difference, whiteness and the group analytic matrix: an integrated formulation. *Group Analysis* 53(1): 60–74.

Kinouani G (2020) Silencing, power and racial trauma in groups. *Group Analysis.* 53(2): 145–161.

Kinouani G (2023) *White Minds. Everyday Performance, Violence and Resistance.* Bristol: Polity Press.

Kitcher PS (2024) Philosophy of Science. *Encyclopedia Britannica*. Available at: https://www.britannica.com/topic/philosophy-of-science (accessed 7 November 2024).

Klein M (1940/1988) *Love, Guilt, Reparation.* London: Virago Press.

Klein M (1946) Notes on some schizoid mechanisms. *International Journal of Psychoanalysis.* 27(1): 99–110.

Klein M (1946/1988) *Envy and Gratitude.* London: Virago Press.

Klein M (1952) The origins of transference. *International Journal of Psychoanalysis.* 33(4): 433–438.

Kleinheksel AJ, Rockich-Winston N, Tawfik H and Wyatt TR (2020) Demystifying content analysis. *American Journal of Pharmaceutical Education.* 84(1): Article 7113. https://doi.org/10.5688/ajpe7113.

Knauss LK (2007) Legal and ethical issues in providing group therapy to minors. In Christner RW, Stewart JL and Freeman A (Eds.) *Handbook of Cognitive Behavior Therapy with Children and Adolescents. Specific Settings and Presenting Problems.* New York: Routledge, pp. 65–85.

Knauss W (2000) Editorial introduction. Special edition: Empirical research. *Group Analysis.* 33(3): 317.

Knight ZG (2019) The researcher's transference in psychoanalytically informed qualitative research. *Qualitative Research in Psychology.* 16(4): 602–623. https://doi.org/10.1080/14780887.2019.1577520.

Knoke D and Yang S (2008) *Social Network Analysis.* 2nd Edition. Thousand Oaks, CA: Sage.

Kobe SL (2021) Ubuntu as a spirituality of liberation for black theology of liberation. *HTS Teologiese Studies/Theological Studies.* 77(3): 1–8. https://doi.org/10.4102/hts.v77i3.6176.

Kober M (2009) The copenhagen interpretation of quantum theory and the measurement problem. *History and Philosophy of Physics.* 5(1): 1–9. https://arxiv.org/abs/0905.0408

Kober M (2010) Über die Beziehung der begrifflichen Grundlagen der Quantentheorie und der Allgemeinen Relativitätstheorie. *[About the Relation of the terminological Foundations of Quantum Theory and General Relativity Theory].* Dissertation. Fachbereich Physik der Johann Wolfgang Goethe Universität in Frankfurt am Main. Frankfurt: Goethe Universität. https://arxiv.org/abs/1510.01196.

Koffka K (1935) *Principles of Gestalt Psychology.* Harcourt: Brace Jovanovich.

Kőhler W (1920) *Die physischen Gestalten in Ruhe und im stationären Zustand. Eine naturphilosophische Untersuchung. [The physical Forms in Tranquility and in a stationary Condition, A natural philosophical Study.].* Braunschweig: Friedrich Vieweg und Sohn.

Kőhler W (1940) *Dynamics in Psychology.* New York: Liveright.

Kőhler W (1947) *Gestalt Psychology. An Introduction to New Concepts in Modern Psychology.* New York: Liveright.

Kőhler W (1969) *The Task of Gestalt Psychology. Princeton Legacy Library.* Princeton, NJ: Princeton University Press.

Kohut H (1971) *The Analysis of the Self.* New York: International University Press.

Kohut H (1984) *How Does Psychoanalysis Cure?* Chicago, IL: University of Chicago Press.

Kőlbel M (2021) Varieties of conceptual analysis. *Analytic Philosophy.* 64(1): 20–38.

König K and Lindner WV (1993) *Psychoanalytische Gruppentherapie. Zweite Auflage.* Göttingen: Vandenhoeck & Ruprecht.

König K and Lindner WV (1994) *Psychoanalytic Group Therapy.* Northvale, NJ/London: Jason Aronson Inc. Publishers.

Koukis A (2016) *On Group Analysis and Beyond. Group Analysis as Meta-Theory, Clinical Social Practice, and Art.* London: Karnac.

Kovaly P (1977) Maurice Merleau-Ponty and the problem of self-accusations. *Studies in Soviet Thought.* 17(3): 225–241. https://www.jstor.org/stable/20098746

Krah H (2021) Karl Popper and modern cosmology. His thoughts and their impact. In Parusniková Z and Merritt D (Eds.) *Karl Popper's Science and Philosophy.* Cham: Springer, pp. 53–68.

Krämer K, Vetter A, Schultz-Venrath U, Vogeley K and Reut S (2021) Mentalization-based treatment in groups for adults with autism spectrum disorder. *Frontiers in Psychology.* 12: https://doi.org/10.3389/fpsyg.2021.708557.

Krauss LM (2012) *A Universe from Nothing. Why there is Something Rather than Nothing.* London: Simon & Schuster Ltd.

Kreeger L (1975) *The Large Group. Dynamics and Therapy.* London: Karnac.

Kreutzmann S (2012) Ikea entschuldigt sich bei der DDR über Zwangsarbeiten. [IKEA apologizes to the GDR for its forced labor]. *Wall Street Journal.* 16 November. Available at: https://www.wsj.com/articles/SB10001424127887324556304578122901995180378 (accessed 7 April 2022).

Krippendorff K (2004) Reliability in content analysis. *Human Communication Research.* 30(3): 411–433.

Krippendorff K (2019) *Content Analysis: An Introduction to Its Methodology.* 4th Edition. Thousand Oaks, CA: Sage Publications.

Krischer M, Smolka B Voigt B, Lehmkuhl G, Flechtner HH, Franke S, Hellmich M and Trautmann-Voigt S (2019) Effects of long-term psychodynamic psychotherapy on life quality in mentally disturbed children. *Psychotherapy Research.* 30(8): 1039–1047. https://doi.org/10.1080/10503307.2019.1695169.

Krogel J, Burlingame G, Chapman C, Renshaw T, Gleave R, Beecher M and MacNair-Semands R (2013) The group questionnaire. A clinical and empirically derived measure of group relationships. *Psychotherapy Research.* 23(3): 344–354.

Krois JM (2004) More than a linguistic turn in philosophy: the semiotic programs of peirce and cassirer. *Northern European Journal of Philosophy.* 5(2): 14–33.

Krueger RA (1994) *Focus Groups. A Practical Guide for Applied Research.* 2nd Edition. Thousand Oaks, CA: Sage.

Krueger RA (1998) *Moderating Focus Groups.* Thousand Oaks, CA: Sage.

Krueger RA and Casey MA (2000) *Focus Groups. A Practical Guide for Applied Research.* Thousand Oaks, CA: Sage.

Krueger RA and Casey MA (2008) *Focus Groups. A Practical Guide for Applied Research.* 4th Edition. Thousand Oaks, CA: Sage.

Krummenacher M (2019) *Der Preis der Freiheit. [Cost of Freedom] 3-part series.* Germany: Gabriela Sperl Produktion, Wiedermann & Berg Film Produktion, ZDF Enterprises, Wilma Film. Available at: https://www.zdf.de/play/filme/preis-der-freiheit-110/preis-der-freiheit-1-100; https://www.zdf.de/play/filme/

preis-der-freiheit-110/preis-der-freiheit-2-102; https://www.zdf.de/play/filme/preis-der-freiheit-110/preis-der-freiheit-3-102

Krzyzanowska N (2016) The discourse of counter-monuments: Semiotics of material commemoration in contemporary urban spaces. *Social Semiotics*. 26(5): 465–485.

Kuhn TS (1962) *The Structure of Scientific Revolutions.* Chicago, IL: University of Chicago Press.

Kühne F, Heinze PE, Ay-Bryson DS, Maaß U and Weck F (2021) Development of a scale for assessing basic psychotherapeutic skills. *Zeitschrift für Klinische Psychologie und Psychotherapie.* 50(3–4): 116–132. https://econtent.hogrefe.com/doi/10.1026/1616-3443/a000623

Kurtz A (2017) *How to Run Reflective Practice Groups. A Guide for Healthcare Professionals.* New York: Routledge.

Kurunmäki J and Marjanen J (2018) Isms, ideologies and setting the agenda for public debate. *Journal of Political Ideologies.* 23(3): 256–282.

Kyngäs H, Mikkonen K. and Kääriäinen M (Eds.) (2020) *The Application of Content Analysis in Nursing Science Research.* Basel: Springer.

Labbe JM and Smith C (2003) *Romanticism, Poetry, and the Culture of Gender*. Manchester: Manchester University Press.

Lacan J (1966) *Ecrits.* [Writings] Paris: Seul.

Lacan J (2000) *On Feminine Sexuality, the Limits of Love and Knowledge, 1972–1973. Encore. The Seminar of Jacques Lacan Book XX.* London: W. W. Norton & Company.

Lacan J (2007) *Ecrits.* Trans. B Fink. London: W. W. Norton & Company.

Lachal J, Revah-Levy A, Orri M and Moro MR (2017) Metasynthesis. An original method to synthesize qualitative literature in psychiatry. *Frontiers in Psychiatry*. 8(269). https://doi.org/10.3389/fpsyt.2017.00269.

Ladyman J (2002) *Understanding Philosophy of Science.* New York: Routledge.

Lagercrantz H (2014) The emergence of consciousness. Science and ethics. *Seminars in Fetal & Neonatal Medicine.* 19(5): 300–305.

Lagercrantz H and Changeux J-P (2009) The emergence of human consciousness. From fetal to neonatal life. *Pediatric Research.* 65(3): 255–260.

Laing RD (1990) *The Divided Self.* London: Penguin Books.

Lakatos I (1986) *The Methodology of Scientific Research Programmes. Philosophical Papers Volume 1.* Edited by Worrall J and Currie G. Cambridge: Cambridge University Press. (Originally published 1978).

Lam TY, Cheung MF, Munro YL, Lim KM and Sung JJ (2022) Randomized controlled trials of artificial intelligence in clinical practice. Systematic review. *Journal of Medical Internet Research.* 24(8): e37188. https://doi.org/10.2196/37188.

Landis JR and Koch GG (1977) The measurement of observer agreement for categorical data. *Biometrics*. 33(1): 159–174.

Lapp PJ (2013) *Grenzregime in der DDR. [Border Regimes in the GDR].* Aachen: Helios.

Lapp PJ (2014) *Offiziershochschule "Rosa Luxemburg". Kaderschmiede der DDR Grenztruppen. [Military Academy 'Rosa Luxemburg'. Elite training center of the border troops of the GDR].* Aachen: Helios Verlag.

Lapp PJ (2016) *Die Mauer. Eine Grenze durch Deutschland.* [The Wall. A border across Germany] 2. Auflage [Second Edition]. Thüringen: Landeszentrale für politische Bildung. https://www.bundesstiftung-aufarbeitung.de/de/publikationen/die-mauer-eine-grenze-durch-deutschland

Läpple C (2020) *Am Todesstreifen. DDR Grenzler erzählen. [At the Death strip. German border officers talk.]* Available at: https://www.Dokumentation-sonstige/am-todesstreifen-ddr-grenzler-erzählen-104.html (accessed 6 March 2023).

Larsson J, Williams P and Zetterqvist A (2019) The challenge of conducting ethical research in preschool. *Early Child Development and Care.* 191(4): 511–519. https://doi.org/10.1080/03004430.2019.1625897.

Lather P (1991) *Getting Smart. Feminist Research and Pedagogy with/in the Postmodern.* New York: Routledge.

Lawrence WG (1997) *Centering of the Sphinx for the Psychoanalytic Study of Organizations.* Lecture given at the ISPSO conference in Philadelphia, USA, 27 June 1997.
Lawrence WG (1998) *Social Dreaming @ Work.* London: Karnac.
Lawrence WG (2000) *Tongued with Fire. Groups in Experience.* London: Karnac.
Lawrence WG (2003) *Experiences in Social Dreaming.* London: Karnac.
Lawrence WG (2005) *Introduction to Social Dreaming. Transforming Thinking.* London: Karnac.
Lawrence WG (2007a) Infinite possibilities of social dreaming. In Lawrence WG (Ed.) *Infinite Possibilities of Social Dreaming.* London: Karnac, pp. 5–17.
Lawrence WG (2012) Social dreaming. Making the unconscious available in systems. *Presentation Written for a Policy Seminar at the Tavistock Clinic*. Unpublished.
Lawrence WG (Ed.) (2007b) *Infinite Possibilities of Social Dreaming.* London: Routledge.
Lawrence WG (Ed.) (2010) *The Creativity of Social Dreaming.* London: Routledge.
Lawrence WG and Biran H (2002) The complementarity of social dreaming and therapeutic dreaming. In Neri C, Pines M and Friedman R (Eds.) *Dreams in Group Psychotherapy.* London: Jessica Kingsley, pp. 46–67.
Lawson E (2020) Editor's briefing. *British Journal of General Practice.* 70(697): 371.
Lazaridou F and Fernando S (2022) Deconstructing institutional racism and the social construction of *whiteness*: A strategy for professional competence training in culture and migration mental health. *Transcultural Psychiatry*. 59(2): 175–187. https://doi.org/10.1177/13634615221087101.
Le Bon G (1896) *The Crowd. A Study of the Popular Mind.* London: Ernest Benn Ltd.
Le Mouel C (2021) Experiencing the Unus Mundus. *Psychological Perspectives.* 64(4): 437–442.
Leach C, Freshwater K, Aldridge J and Sunderland J (2001) Analysis of repertory grids in clinical practice. *British Journal of Clinical Psychology*. 40(3): 225–248. https://doi.org/10.1348/014466501163652.
Leach E (1961) *Rethinking Anthropology.* London: Athlone.
Lear T (1983) Spirit and psyche: Some afterthoughts of a group experience. *Group Analysis.* 16(1): 67–74.
Leask P (2019) The writer in the archives, empathy, trauma, ambivalence. In Weegmann M (Ed.) *Psychodynamics of Writing.* New York: Routledge, pp. 83–94.
Leavy SA (1973) Psychoanalytic interpretation. *The Psychoanalytic Study of the Child.* 28(1): 305–330.
Lee CS and Lee AY (2020) How artificial intelligence can transform randomized controlled trials. *Translational Vision Science & Technology.* 9(2): https://doi.org/10.1167/tvst.9.2.9.
Lee LH, Li JH and Yu LC (2022) Chinese EmoBank. Building valence-arousal resources for dimensional sentiment analysis. *ACM Transactions on Asian and Low-Resource Language Information Process.* 21(4): 1–18.
Lee RP, Hart RI, Watson RM and Rapley T (2014) Qualitative synthesis in practice: Some pragmatics of meta-ethnography. *Qualitative Research.* 15(3): 334–350.
Lee S and Kang H (2015) Statistical and methodological considerations for reporting RCTs in medical literature. *Korean Journal of Anesthesiology*. 68(2): 106–115. https://doi.org/10.4097/kjae.2015.68.2.106.
Leech NL, Dellinger AB, Brannagan KB and Tanaka H (2009) Evaluating mixed research studies: A mixed methods approach. *Journal of Mixed Methods Research.* 4(1): 17–31. https://doi.org/10.1177/1558689809345262 (Published 2010).
Legg C (2024) *Pragmatism.* Stanford Encyclopedia of Philosophy. Winter Edition. https://plato.stanford.edu/entries/pragmatism
Leggett AJ (2002) Testing the limits of quantum mechanics. Motivations, state of play, prospects. *Journal of Physics Condensed Matter.* 14(15): 415–451. https://iopscience.iop.org/article/10.1088/0953-8984/14/15/201
LeGrange L (2018) What is (post)qualitative research? *South African Journal of Higher Education.* 32(5): 1–14. https://doi.org/10.20853/32-5-3161.
Lehle HG (2025) "Was ist denn hier los?!" Abenteuerspielplatz Kindergruppenanalyse. Eine lohnende Zumutung. [What is happening here?! Adventure Space Playing Ground. Group Child Analysis. A beneficial imposition] *Gruppenanalyse.* 1(1): 113–131.

Leichsenring F and Rabung S (2011) Long-term psychodynamic psychotherapy in complex mental disorders: Update of a meta-analysis. *British Journal of Psychiatry*. 199(1): 15–22. https://doi.org/10.1192/bjp.bp.110.082776.

Leichsenring F, Abbass A, Hilsenroth MJ, Leweke F, Luyten P, Keefe JR, Midgley N, Rabung S, Salzer S and Steinert C (2017) Biases in research: risk factors for non-replicability in psychotherapy and pharmacotherapy research. *Psychological Medicine*. 47(6): 1000–1011.

Leichsenring F, Hiller W, Weissberg M and Leibing E (2006) Cognitive-behavioral therapy and psychodynamic psychotherapy: Techniques, efficacy, and indications. *American Journal of Psychotherapy*. 60(3): 233–259.

Leiman M (2002) Toward semiotic dialogism: The role of sign mediation in the dialogical self. *Theory & Psychology*. 12(2): 221–235. https://doi.org/10.1177/0959354302012002631.

Leiman M (2004) Dialogical sequence analysis. In Hermans HJ and Dimaggio G (Eds.) *The Dialogical Self in Psychotherapy*. London: Brunner & Routledge, pp. 255–269.

Leiman M (2011) Mikhail Bakhtin's contribution to psychotherapy research. *Culture & Psychology*. 17(4): 441–461. https://doi.org/10.1177/1354067X11418543.

Leiman M (2012) Dialogical sequence analysis in studying psychotherapeutic discourse. *International Journal of Dialogical Science*. 6(1): 123–147.

Leiss W, Kline S and Jhally S (1990) *Social Communication in Advertising. Persons, Products and Images of Well-Being*. 2nd Edition. London: Routledge.

Lem S (2014) *Summa Technologiae*. Trans. J Zylinska. Series Electronic Mediations. Minnesota: University of Minnesota Press.

LenkaBula P (2008) Beyond anthropocentricity. Botho/ubuntu and the quest for economic and ecological justice in Africa. *Religion & Theology*. 15(3–4): 375–394. https://brill.com/view/journals/rt/15/3-4/article-p375_10.xml

Leong D (2023) A new dialogue on Yijing - The book of changes in a world of changes, instability, disequilibrium and turbulence. *Asian Philosophy*. 33(3): 208–232.

Leong FT, Kalibatseva Z and Scott NA (2024) Dismantling racism in research methods and practices. *Review of General Psychology*. 28(4): 301–314. https://doi.org/10.1177/10892680241289574.

Lepper G and Riding N (2006) *Researching the Psychotherapy Process. A Practical Guide to Transcript-Based Methods*. New York: Palgrave Macmillan.

Leszcz M and Malat J (2015) The interpersonal model of group psychotherapy. In Kleinberg JL (Ed.) *The Wiley Blackwell Handbook of Group Psychotherapy*. Oxford: Wiley Blackwell, pp. 33–58.

Letourneau N and Allen M (1999) Post-positivistic critical multiplism. A beginning dialogue. *Journal of Advances in Nursing*. 30(3): 623–630. https://doi.org/10.1046/j.1365-2648.1999.01133.x.

Leung F-H and Savithiri R (2009) Spotlight on Focus Groups. *Canadian Family Physician*. 55(2): 218–219.

Lev G (2023) Conditions for Love. The psychoanalytic situation and the analyst's emotion. *International Forum of Psychoanalysis*. 32(2): 114–124.

Levac L, Baikie G and Hanson C (2018) *Learning Across Indigenous and Western Knowledge Systems and Intersectionality. Reconciling Social Science Research Approaches*. Guelph: University of Guelph.

Levin M and Greenwood D (2011) Revitalizing universities by reinventing the social sciences. In Denzin NK and Lincoln YS (Eds.) *The Sage Handbook of Qualitative Research*. 4th Edition. Thousand Oaks, CA: Sage, pp. 27–42.

Levine D (1979) Social theory as a vocation. Engaging with future challenges. *Perspectives*. 19(2): 1–8.

Lévi-Strauss C (1967) The structural study of myth. In *Structural Anthropology. Vol. 2*. Trans. C Jacobson and BG Schoepf. New York: Doubleday, pp. 206–231.

Levitt H (2016) Qualitative research and humanistic psychotherapy. In Cain DJ, Keenan K and Rubin S (Eds.) *Handbook of Research and Practice*. Washington, DC: American Psychological Association, pp. 81–113.

Levy KN and Scala JW (2012) Transference, transference interpretations, and transference-focused psychotherapies. *Psychotherapy*. 49(3): 391–403.

Lewin K (1935) *A Dynamic Theory of Personality*. New York: McGraw-Hill.

Lewin K (1936) *Principles of Topological Psychology*. New York: McGraw-Hill.

Lewin K (1946) Action research and minority problems. *Journal of Social Issues.* 2(4): 34–46.

Lewin K (1947) *Field Theory in Social Sciences.* New York: Harper & Brothers.

Lewin K (1948) *Resolving Social Conflicts.* New York: Harper and Row Publishers.

Lewin K (1951) *Field Theory in Social Science: Selected Theoretical Papers.* New York: Harper & Row.

Lewis P and Runde J (2001) Intersubjectivity in the socio-economic world. A critical realist perspective. In Fullbrook E (Ed.) *Intersubjectivity in Economics. Agents and Structures.* London: Routledge, pp. 198–215.

Li G (2012) Statistical testing techniques. In Dwyer L, Gill A and Seetaram N (Eds.) *Handbook of Research Methods in Tourism. Quantitative and Qualitative Approaches.* Cheltenham: Edward Elgar Publishing Ltd., pp. 13–30.

Li O (2024) Should we develop AGI? Artificial suffering and the moral development of humans. *AI and Ethics.* 5: 641–651. https://doi.org/10.1007/s43681-023-00411-4.

Librarianship Studies (2022) *Research.* Librarianship Studies & Information Technology. 23 October 2022. https://www.librarianshipstudies.com/2017/11/research.html

Likert R (1932) A technique for measurement of attitudes. *Archives of Psychology.* 140: 44–53. https://www.academia.edu/118125341/A_technique_for_the_measurement_of_attitudes

Lilienfeld S, Ritschel LA, Lynn SJ, Cauntin RL and Latzman RD (2013) Why many clinical psychologists are resistant to evidence-based practice. Root causes and constructive remedies. *Clinical Psychology Review.* 33(7): 883–900.

Lilienfeld SO, McKay D and Hollon SD (2018) Why randomised controlled trials of psychological treatments are still essential. *Lancet Psychiatry.* 5(7): 536–538.

Lilliengren P and Werbart A (2005) A model of therapeutic action grounded in the patients' view of curative and hindering factors in psychoanalytic psychotherapy. *Psychotherapy: Theory, Research, Practice, Training.* 42(3): 324–339. https://doi.org/10.1037/0033-3204.42.3.324.

Lin T, Heckman TG and Anderson T (2022) The efficacy of synchronous teletherapy versus in-person therapy: A meta-analysis of randomized clinical trials. *Clinical Psychology. Science and Practice.* 29(2): 167–178.

Lindberg D (2010) *The Beginnings of Western Science. The European Scientific Tradition in Philosophical, Religion, and Institutional Context, Prehistory to A.D. 1450.* Second Edition. Chicago, IL: University of Chicago.

Lindley DV (2001) Thomas Bayes. In Heyde CC, Seneta E, Crepel P, Fienberg SE and Gani J (Eds.) *Statisticians of the Centuries.* New York: Springer, pp. 68–71.

Lintott B (1983) Mind and matrix in the writing of S. H. Foulkes. *Group Analysis.* 16(3): 242–251.

Lischke S (2022) *Verlorene Kindheit. Weggesperrt in der DDR. [Lost Childhood. Locked Up in the GDR.]* 12 January 2022. Available at: https://www.zdf.de/video/dokus/zdf-info-100/verlorene-kindheit-weggesperrt-in-der-ddr-100 (accessed 26 March 2023).

Litowitz BE (2014) Peirce's semiotic and psychoanalysis. *Journal für Psychoanalyse.* 55: 48–55. https://www.seismoverlag.ch/en/daten/charles-sanders-peirce-und-die-psychoanalyse/journals/psychoanalyse/

Liu B (2015) *Sentiment Analysis. Miming Opinions, Sentiments, and Emotions.* New York: Cambridge University Press.

Lobo MA, Moeyaert M, Baraldi CA and Babik I (2018) Single-case design, analysis, and quality assessment for intervention research. *Journal of Neurologic and Physical Therapy.* 41(3): 187–197.

Loewenthal D (2007) *Case Studies in Relational Research. Qualitative Research Methods in Counselling and Psychotherapy.* New York: Palgrave MacMillan.

Lonargain DA, Hodge S and Line R (2017) Service user experiences of mentalization-based treatment for borderline personality disorder. *Mental Health Review Journal.* 22(1): 16–27. https://doi.org/10.1108/MHRJ-04-2016-0008.

Long S and Harney M (2013) The associative unconscious. In Long S (Ed.) *Socioanalytic Methods. Discovering the Hidden in Organisations and Social Systems.* London: Karnac, pp. 3–22.

Lopez A, Rothberg B, Reaser E, Schwenk S and Griffith R (2020) Therapeutic groups via video teleconferencing and the impact on group cohesion. *mHealth.* 6: 13–22. https://dx.doi.org/10.21037/mhealth.2019.11.04

Lorens A, Tzovara A, Bellier L, Bhaya-Grossman I, Bidet-Caulet A, Chang WK, Cross ZR, Dominguez-Faus R, Flinker A, Fonken Y, Gorenstein MA, Holdgraf C, Hoy CW, Ivanova MV, Jimenez RT, Jun S, Kam JW, Kidd C, Marcelle E, Marciano D, Martin S, Myers NE, Ojala K, Perry A, Pinjeiro-Chagas P, Ries SK, Saez I, Skelin I, Slama K, Staveland B, Bassett DS, Buffalo EA, Fairhall AL, Kopell NJ, Kray LJ, Lin JJ, Nobre AC, Riley D, Solbakk AK, Wallis JD, Wang XJ, Youval-Greenberg S, Kastner S, Knight RT and Dronkers NF (2021) Gender bias in academia. A lifetime problem that needs solution. *Neuron.* 109(13): 2047–2074. https://www.sciencedirect.com/science/article/pii/S0896627321004177.

Lorentzen S (2006) Contemporary challenges for research in group analysis. *Group Analysis.* 39(3): 321–340.

Lorentzen S (2012) Writing manuals for psychodynamic group treatments. *Group Analysis.* 45(1): 28–45.

Lorentzen S (2014) *Group Analytic Psychotherapy.* London: Routledge.

Lorentzen S (2020) Short-term focused group-analytic psychotherapy (SFGAP) An integrative approach to change based on research. *Group Analysis.* 50(3): 243–360.

Lorentzen S (2022) *Focused Group Analytic Psychotherapy. An Integration of Clinical Experience and Research.* New York: Routledge.

Lorentzen S, Fjeldstad A, Ruud T, Marble A, Klungsøyr O, Ulberg R and Høglend P (2015a) The effectiveness of short- and long-term psychodynamic group psychotherapy on self-concept. Three years follow-up of a randomized clinical trial. *International Journal of Group Psychotherapy.* 65(3): 362–385.

Lorentzen S, Ruud T, Fjeldstad A and Høglend P (2013) Comparison of short-term and long-term dynamic group psychotherapy. Randomized clinical trial. *British Journal of Psychiatry.* 203(4): 280–287.

Lorentzen S, Ruud T, Fjeldstad A and Høglend P (2015b) Personality disorder moderates outcome in short- and long-term group analytic psychotherapy. A randomized clinical trial. *British Journal of Clinical Psychology.* 54(2): 129–146.

Lorentzen S, Strauss B and Altmann U (2018) Process-outcome relationships in short- and long-term psychodynamic group psychotherapy: Results from a randomized clinical trial. *Group Dynamics: Theory, Research, and Practice.* 22(2): 93–107.

Lorenzer A (1970) *Kritik des Psychoanalytischen Symbolbegriffs.* [Critique of the Psychoanalytic Symbol Term]. Frankfurt: Suhrkamp.

Loux MJ (2006) *Metaphysics. A Contemporary Introduction.* 3rd Edition. New York: Routledge.

Loveridge R, Willman P and Deery S (2007) 60 years of human relations. *Human Relations.* 60(12): 1873–1888. https://doi.org/10.1177/0018726707084917.

Lu H-S (2018) The bodhisattva's path as gender-neutral practices: A case study of the buddhist Tzu Chi community in Taiwan. In Pang-White A (Ed.) *The Bloomsbury Handbook of Chinese Philosophy and Gender.* New York: Bloomsbury, pp. 357–376.

Luborsky EB and Baber JP (1994) Perspectives on seven transference-based measures applied to the interview with Ms Smithfield. *Psychotherapy Research.* 4(3–4): 152–154. https://www.tandfonline.com/doi/abs/10.1080/10503309412331333992

Luborsky EB, O'Reilly-Landry M and Arlow JA (2011) Psychoanalysis. In Corsini RJ and Wedding D (Eds.) *Current Psychotherapies.* 9th Edition. Belmont, CA: Brooks/Cole, pp.16–66.

Luborsky L and Barrett MS (2006) The history and empirical status of key psychoanalytic concepts. *Annual Review of Clinical Psychology.* 2: 1–19. https://doi.org/10.1146/annurev.clinpsy.2.022305.095328.

Luchins AS and Luchins EH (1999) Isomorphism in gestalt theory. Comparison of wertheimer's and Kőhler's concepts. *Gestalt Theory.* 21(3): 208–234.

Luck M and Aylett R (2000) Applying artificial intelligence to virtual reality: intelligence, virtual environments. *Applied Artificial Intelligence.* 14(1): 3–32. https://doi.org/10.1080/088395100117142.

Lüders A, Carpentras D and Quayle M (2024) Attitude networks as intergroup realities: Using network-modelling to research attitude-identity relationships in polarized political contexts. *British Journal of Social Psychology.* 63(1): 37–51. https://doi.org/10.1111/bjso.12665.

Lumsden A (2023) Group analysis and its application. In Graham P (Series Ed.) *Cambridge Guide to Psychodynamic Psychotherapy. Cambridge Guides to the Psychological Therapies.* Cambridge: Cambridge University Press, pp. 310–321.

Lundberg CC (2004) Is there really nothing so practical as a good theory? *Business Horizons.* 47(5): 7–14.

Lune H and Berg B (2017) *Qualitative Research Methods for the Social Sciences.* 9th Edition. New York: Pearson.

Lunt PK (1988) The perceived causal structure of examination failure. *British Journal of Social Psychology.* 27(2): 171–179. https://doi.org/10.1111/j.2044-8309.1988.tb00816.x.

Lunt PK (1991) The perceived causal structure of loneliness. *Journal of Personality and Social Psychology.* 61(1): 26–34. https://doi.org/10.1037//0022-3514.61.1.26.

Luo H, Li G, Feng Q, Yang Y and Zuo M (2019) Virtual reality in K-12 and higher education. A systematic review of the literature from 2000–2019. *Journal of Computer Assisted Learning.* 37(3): 887–901. https://www.researchgate.net/publication/350106651_Virtual_reality_in_K-12_and_higher_education_A_systematic_review_of_the_literature_from_2000_to_2019

Lutz A, Greischar L, Rawlings N, Ricard M and Davidson RJ (2004) Long-term meditators self-induce high-amplitude gamma synchrony during mental practice. *Proceedings of the National Academy of Sciences of the United States of America.* 101(46): 16369–16373. https://doi.org/10.1073/pnas.0407401101.

Lutz A, Slagter HA, Dunne JD and Davidson RJ (2008) Attention regulation and monitoring in meditation. *Trends in Cognitive Science.* 12(4): 163–169.

Lyndon P (1992) The black and white group. A group-analytic contribution to race relations? *Group Analysis.* 25(1): 117–120.

Lyndon P (1997) The median group. An appropriate setting for the negotiation of hatred. An elaboration of ideas from the work of PB de Maré. *Group Analysis.* 30(1): 131–137.

Ma SSY (2005) The I Ching and the psyche-body connection. *Journal of Analytical Psychology.* 50(2): 237–250.

Ma WJ (2019) Bayesian decision models. A primer. *Neuron.* 104(1): 164–175. https://doi.org/10.1016/j.neuron.2019.09.037.

Ma ZG (2016) Comparison between Hegel's being-nothing-becoming and I-Ching's Yin-Yang-I (Change). *Asian Research Journal of Arts & Social Sciences.* 16(6): 26–40.

MacDonald J and Mellor-Clark J (2015) Correcting psychotherapists' blindsidedness: Formal feedback as a means of overcoming the natural limitations of therapists. *Clinical Psychology & Psychotherapy.* 22(3): 249–257. https://doi.org/10.1002/cpp.1887.

Mace C (2006) Setting the world on wheels. Some clinical challenges of evidence-based practice. *Group Analysis.* 39(3): 304–320.

MacKenzie KR (1981) Measurement of group climate. *International Journal of Group Psychotherapy.* 31(3): 287–295. https://doi.org/10.1080/00207284.1981.11491708.

MacKenzie KR (1983) The clinical application of a group measure. In Dies RR and MacKenzie KR (Eds.) *Advances in Group Psychotherapy: Integrating Research and Practice.* New York: International Universities Press, pp. 159–170.

MacKenzie KR and Tschuschke V (1993) Relatedness, group work, and outcome in long-term inpatient psychotherapy groups. *Journal of Psychotherapy Practice Research.* 2(2): 147–156.

Mackenzie NM and Knipe S (2006) Research dilemmas. Paradigms, methods and methodology. *Issues in Educational Research.* 16(2): 193–205. https://www.academia.edu/1104997/Mackenzie_N_M_and_Knipe_S_2006_Research_dilemmas_Paradigms_methods_and_methodology_Issues_in_Educational_Research_16_2_

Mackereth K (2021) *A New AI Lexicon: AI Nationalism.* AINow. https://ainowinstitute.org/publication/a-new-ai-lexicon-ai-nationalism

MacKinnon DP (2011) Integrating mediators and moderators in research designs. *Research on Social Work Practice.* 21(6): 675–681.

MacNair -Semands R and Whittingham M (Eds.) (2023) *Group Psychotherapy Assessment and Practice: A Measurement-Based Care Approach.* New York: Routledge. https://doi.org/10.4324/9781003255482.

MacNair-Semands RR (2002) Predicting attendance and expectations for group therapy. *Group Dynamics. Theory, Research, and Practice.* 6(3): 219–228.

MacNair -Semands RR, Ogrodniczuk JS and Joyce AS (2010) Structure and initial validation of a short form of the therapeutic factors inventory. *International Journal of Group Psychotherapy.* 60(2): 245–281. https://doi.org/10.1521/ijgp.2010.60.2.245.

Macran S and Shapiro DA (1998) The role of personal therapy for therapists. A review. *British Journal of Medical Psychology.* 71(1): 13–25.

Macran S, Stiles WB and Smith JA (1999) How does personal therapy affect therapists' practice? *Journal of Counselling Psychology*. 46(4): 419–431.

Madill A (2008) Realism. In Given LM (Ed.) *The SAGE Encyclopedia of Qualitative Research Methods.* London: Sage, pp. 731–735.

Maeda Y, Caskurlu S, Kenney RH, Kazan K and Richardson JC (2022) Moving qualitative synthesis research forward I education: A methodological systematic review. *Educational Research Review.* 35: https://doi.org/10.1016/j.edurev.2021.100424.

Maeres R (2000) *Intimacy and Alienation. Memory, Trauma and Personal Being.* New York: Routledge.

Maeres R (2005) *The Metaphor of Play. Origin and Breakdown of Personal Being.* New York: Routledge.

Maeres R (2012) *A Dissociation Model of Borderline Personality Disorder.* New York: W.W. Norton & Company.

Maguire P (2006) Uneven ground: Feminisms and action research. In Reason P and Bradbury H (Eds.) *Handbook of Action Research: Participative Inquiry and Practice.* Thousand Oaks, CA: Sage, pp. 59–69.

Maharaj AS, Bhatt NV and Gentile JP (2021) Bringing it in the room: Addressing the impact of racism on the therapeutic alliance. *Innovations in Clinical Neuroscience*. 18(7–9): 39–43.

Mahmutovic J (2023) 18 Different Types of Survey Methods + Pros & Cons. Available at: https://www.surveylegend.com/types-of-surveys/types-of-survey-methods/ (accessed 6 December 2024).

Maier S (2019) *Der Preis der Freiheit. Die Dokumentation. [The Price of Freedom. The Documentary.]* April 2019. Available at: https://www.zdf.de/filme/preis-der-freiheit-110 (accessed 13 March 2023).

Main TT (1946) The hospital as a therapeutic community intervention. *Bulleting of the Meninger Clinic.* 10: 66–70.

Makkonen E (2006) Producing the past together. Group interview and Oral history. *Elore*. 13(1). http://cc.joensuu.fi/~loristi/1_06/mak1_06.pdf; https://www.academia.edu/108360797/Producing_the_Past_Together_Group_Interview_and_Oral_History

Malachowski C, Skorobohacz CH and Stasiulis E (2017) Institutional ethnography as a method of inquiry: A scoping review. *Qualitative Sociology Review*. 13(4): 121–184. https://czasopisma.uni.lodz.pl/qualit/article/view/11465

Malan DH, Balfour FGH, Hood VG and Shooter AMN (1976) Group psychotherapy. A long-term-follow up study. *Archive of General Psychiatry.* 33: 1303–1315. https://doi.org/10.1001/archpsyc.1976.01770110031002.

Malinowski B (1947) *Freedom and Civilization. Coral Gardens and their Magic. A Study of the Methods of Tilling the Soil and of Agricultural Rites in the Trobriand Islands. 2 Volumes.* London: George Allen & Unwin Ltd. https://www.berose.fr/IMG/pdf/malinowski_1947-freedom_and_civilization.pdf

Malinowski B (1948) *Magic Science and Religion and Other Essays. Selected and with an introduction by Robert Redfield.* Glencoe, IL: The Free Press. https://www.berose.fr/IMG/pdf/malinowski_1948-magic_science_and_religion.pdf

Malterud K (2019) *Qualitative Metasynthesis. A Research Method for Medicine and Health Sciences.* New York: Routledge.

Mandela N (2008) *Long Walk to Freedom. The Autobiography of Nelson Mandela*. London: Routledge.

Mangena F (2014) Ethno-philosophy is rational: a reply to two famous critics. *Thought and Practice.* 6(2): 23–38. https://www.ajol.info/index.php/tp/article/view/119731

Mangena F (2016) African ethics through ubuntu: A postmodern exposition. *Africology. Journal of Pan African Studies.* 9(2): 66–80. https://www.jpanafrican.org/archive_issues/vol9no2.htm

Manley J (2009) When words are not enough. In Clarke S and Hoggett P (Eds.) *Researching Beneath the Surface: Psycho-Social Research Methods in Practice.* London: Karnac, pp. 79–98.

Manley J (2010) The slavery in the mind: Inhibition and exhibition. In Lawrence WG (Ed.) *The Creativity of Social Dreaming*. London: Karnac, pp. 65–83.

Manley J (2014) Gordon Lawrence's social dreaming matrix. Background, origins, history, and development. *Organizational & Social Dynamics.* 14(2): 322–341.

Manley J and Roy A (2016) The visual matrix. A psychosocial method for discovering unspoken complexities in social care practice. *Psychoanalysis, Culture & Society.* 22(2): 132–153.
Manley J, Roy A and Froggett L (2015) Researching recovery from substance misuse using visual methods. In Hardwick L, Smith R and Worsley A (Eds.) *Innovation in Social Work Research.* London: Jessica Kingsley, pp. 191–211.
Marais EJ (1984) Philosophy African thought. *Africa Insight.* 14(4): 264–268. https://journals.co.za/doi/epdf/10.10520/AJA02562804_231
Maraldo JC (2005) *Nishida Kitaro.* Stanford Encyclopedia of Philosophy. Available at: https://plato.stanford.edu/entries/nishida-kitaro/ (accessed 9 September 2024).
Marbach E (2007) Towards integrating Husserlian phenomenology with cognitive neuroscience of consciousness. *Synthesis Philosophica.* 22(2): 385–400. https://hrcak.srce.hr/23582
Margolis E and Laurence S (2019) *Concepts.* Stanford Encyclopedia of Philosophy. Available at: https://plato.stanford.edu/entries/concepts (accessed 2 April 2024).
Maris CW (2020) Philosophical racism and ubuntu: in dialogue with Mogobe Ramose. *South African Journal of Philosophy.* 39(3): 308–326. https://www.tandfonline.com/doi/abs/10.1080/02580136.2020.1809124
Mark GT and Lyons AC (2010) Maori healers' views on wellbeing. The importance of mind, body, spirit, family and land. *Social Science & Medicine.* 70(11): 1756–1764.
Marková I (2003) *Dialogicality and Social Representations: The Dynamics of Mind.* Cambridge: Cambridge University Press.
Marks J (2017) *Is Science Racist?* Cambridge: Polity Press.
Marmarosh C (2024) Spirituality, security, compassion, and play. Innovative ways group psychotherapy addresses human suffering. *International Journal of Group Psychotherapy.* 74(2): 85–97.
Marrone M (1984) On integrating models: Response to Louis Zinkin. *Group Analysis.* 17(1): 22–32.
Marrone M (1998) *Attachment and Interaction. International Library of Group Analysis.* London: Jessica Kingsley Publishers.
Martin F, Carminati F and Galli Carminati G (2009) Synchronicity, quantum information and the psyche. *The Journal of Cosmology.* 3: 580–589. In Atmanspacher H and Primas H (Eds.) *Recasting Reality: Wolfgang Pauli's Philosophical Ideas and Contemporary Science.* New York: Springer-Verlag, pp. 227–243. ebook: https://download.e-bookshelf.de/download/0000/0131/33/L-G-0000013133-0002370649.pdf
Marx C (2002) Ubu and ubuntu. On the dialectics of apartheid and nation building. *Politikon.* 29(1): 49–69. https://www.tandfonline.com/doi/abs/10.1080/02589340220149434
Marx K (1867) *Das Kapital.* Hamburg: Otto Meissner.
Marx K (1997) *Writings of the Young Marx on Philosophy and Society.* Ed. and Trans. LD Easton and KH Guddat. Cambridge, IN: Hackett Publishing Company.
Masango M (2006) African spirituality that shapes the concept of ubuntu. *Verbum et Ecclesia.* 27(3): 930–943. https://doi.org/10.4102/ve.v27i3.195.
Masao A (1990) Introduction. In Nishida K (Ed.) *An Inquiry into the Good.* Trans. A Masao and C Ives. New Haven, CT: Yale University Press, pp. vii–xxvi.
Masao A and Ives CA (1981) Hisamatsu's philosophy of awakening. *The Eastern Buddhist.* 14(1): 26–42.
Masterman M (1965/1970) The Nature of a Paradigm. In Lakatos I and Musgrave A (Eds.) *Criticism and the Growth of Knowledge. Proceedings of the 1965 International Colloquium in the Philosophy of Science.* Cambridge: Cambridge University Press, pp. 51–58.
Materne M (2016) *Trabi, Wartburg und Ostrennwagen. Dokumentation. ZDF [Trabi, Wartburg and East Racing Cars. Documentation. ZDF].* 10 January 2016. https://www.imdb.com/title/tt29631747/
Mautner T (Ed.) (1997) Comte. *Penguin Dictionary of Philosophy.* London: Penguin Books, p. 102.
Max Planck Institute (2019) *What is Complexity in Particle Physics?* 8 July 2019. Available at https://www.aei.mpg.de/120719/what-is-complexity-in-particle-physics (accessed 24 December 2024).
Maxwell JA (2006) Literature reviews of, and for, educational research: A commentary on Boote and Beile's "Scholars before researchers". *Educational Researcher.* 35(9): 28–31. https://doi.org/10.3102/0013189X035009028.
Maxwell JC (1888/2010) *Matter and Motion.* New York: Cambridge University Press.
Maybin J (2001) Language, struggle and voice: The Bakhtin/Volosinov writings. In Wetherell M, Taylor S and Yates SJ (Eds.) *Discourse Theory and Practice. A Reader.* London: Sage, pp. 64–71.

Mayer K (2006a) After the fall of the wall. Living through the post-socialist transformation in East Germany. In Diewald M, Goedicke A and Mayer K (Eds.) *After the Fall of the Wall. Life Courses in the Transformation of East Germany.* Stanford: Stanford University Press, pp. 1–28.

Mayer K (2006b) Society of departure. The German democratic republic. In Diewald M, Goedicke A and Mayer K (Eds.) *After the Fall of the Wall. Life Courses in the Transformation of East Germany.* Stanford: Stanford University Press, pp. 29–43.

Mayne HG (1972) Discharges from the army on medical grounds. In Mellor WF (Ed.) *History of the Second World War. Casualties and Medical Statistics.* London: HMSO, pp. 438–453.

Mays N, Pope C and Popay J (2005) Systematically reviewing qualitative and quantitative evidence to inform management and policymaking in the health field. *Journal of Health Services Research & Policy.* 10(1): 6–20.

Mazzei LA (2013) Desire undone. Productions of privilege, power and voice. In Coleman R and Ringrose J (Eds.) *Deleuze and Research Methodologies.* Edinburgh: Edinburgh University Press, pp. 96–110.

Mbazzi FB (2023) Translating the ubuntu philosophy into practical disability inclusive interventions. The Obuntu bulamu experience from Uganda. In Mutanga O (Ed.) *Ubuntu Philosophy and Disabilities in Sub-Saharan Africa.* London: Routledge, pp. 139–149.

Mbembe J (2016) Decolonizing the university: New directions. *Arts & Humanities in Higher Education.* 15(1): 29–45.

Mbiti JS (1991) *Introduction to African Religion.* 2nd Edition. London: Heineman Educational Publishers.

Mbiti JS (1999) *African Religions and Philosophy.* 2nd Edition. Johannesburg: Heinemann. https://archive.org/details/africanreligions00john

McAdams AJ (1996) The Honecker trial. The East German past and the German future. *Review of Politics.* 58(1): 1–23.

McAdams DP (1988) *Power, Intimacy and the Life Story.* New York: Guilford Press.

McAdoo T (2024) *How to Cite ChatGPT.* APA Blog. Available at: https://apastyle.apa.org/blog-how-to-site-chatgpt (accessed 6 March 2025).

McCabe G (2008) Mind, body, emotions and spirit. Reaching to the ancestors for healing. *Counseling Psychology Quarterly.* 21(2): 143–152.

McCarthy J (2006) A proposal for the Dartmouth summer research project in artificial intelligence, 31 August 1955. *AI Magazine.* 4: 12–14. https://ojs.aaai.org/aimagazine/index.php/aimagazine/article/view/1904

McCraty R (2003) *The Energetic Heart. Bioelectromagnetic Communication within and between People.* Boulder Creek, CA: Institute of HeartMath. https://www.heartmath.org/research/research-library/energetics/energetic-heart-bioelectromagnetic-communication-within-and-between-people/

McDermid D (2024) Pragmatism. Internet Encyclopedia of Philosophy. Available at: https://iep.utm.edu/pragmati/ (accessed 10 November 2024).

McDermut W, Miller WI and Brown RA (2001) The efficacy of group psychotherapy for depression: A meta-analysis and review of empirical research. *Clinical Psychology Science and Practice.* 8(1): 98–116.

McDonnell N and Wildman N (2019) Virtual reality: Digital or fictional? *Disputatio.* 11(55): 371–397.

McFadden RD (2016) Margot Honecker, East German Hard Liner and Widow of Ruler, Dies at 89. *The New York Times.* 6 May. Available at: https://www.nytimes.com/2016/05/07/world/europe/margot-honecker-widow-of-east-german-ruler-dies-at-89.html (accessed 23 October 2022).

McGinn C (1999) *The Mysterious Flame. Conscious Minds in a Material World.* New York: Basic Books.

McGrath S, Zhao X, Steele R, Thombs BD and Benedetti A (2020) Estimating the sample mean and standard deviation from commonly reported quantiles in meta-analysis. *Statistical Methods in Medical Research.* 29(9): 2520–2537.

McGuigan J (2009) *Cool Capitalism.* London: Pluto Press.

McKay JP (1995) *The Official Concept of the Nation in the GDR. Theory Versus Pragmatism.* Thesis. London: London School of Economics and Political Science. https://etheses.lse.ac.uk/1376/1/U074613.pdf.

McLaughlin SPB, Barkowski S, Burlingame GM, Strauss B and Rosendahl J (2019) Group psychotherapy for borderline personality disorder: a meta-analysis of randomized-controlled trials. *Psychotherapy.* 56(2): 260–273. https://doi.org/10.1037/pst0000211.

McLeod J, Thurston M and McLeod J (2015) Case study methodology. In Vossler A and Moller N (Eds.) *The Counselling and Psychotherapy Research Handbook.* London: Sage, pp. 189–211.

McLeod S (2023a) Qualitative Vs Quantitative Research Methods & Data Analysis. *Simply Psychology.* Available at: https://www.simplypsychology.org/qualitative-quantitative.html (accessed 23 December 2023). (Updated May 16, 2025, https://www.simplypsychology.org/qualitative-quantitative.html)

McLeod S (2023b) P-Value and statistical significance: What it is & why it matters. *Simply Psychology.* Available at: https://www.simplypsychology.org/p-value.html (accessed 23 December 2023).

McLeod S (2024) Theories of Personality: Hans Eysenck, Gordon Allport & Raymond Cattell. *Simply Psychology.* Available at: https://simplypsychology.org/personality-theories.html (accessed 9 July 2024).

McMahon A (2023) A narrative review of group analytic literature on clinical supervision: Seeking coherence and correspondence. *Group Analysis.* 1–27. Online. https://doi.org/10.1177/05333164231153927.

McMillan SS, King M and Tully MP (2016) How to use the nominal group and Delphi techniques. *International Journal of Clinical Pharmacy.* 38(3): 652–655.

McStay A (2023) The metaverse: Surveillant physics, virtual realist governance, and the missing commons. *Philosophy and Technology*. 36(1): 1–26.

MDR (2019) Ostfrauen: Selbstbewusst. Unabhängig. Erfolgreich. [East German Women: Confident. Independent. Successful.] 10 December 2019. https://www.mdr.de/geschichte/zeitgeschichte-gegenwart/politik-gesellschaft/ostfrauen-karriere-beruf-familie-emanzipation-100.html

Mead GH (1934) *Mind, Self, and Society from the Standpoint of a Social Behaviorist.* Chicago: University of Chicago Press.

Meeussen L, Agneessens P, Delvaux E and Phalet K (2018) Ethnic diversity and value sharing: A longitudinal social network perspective on interactive group processes. *British Journal of Social Psychology.* 57(2): 428–447. https://doi.org/10.1111/bjso.12237.

Mehrpour A, Widmer ED and Staerklé C (2025) Social network analysis in social psychological research (1990–2020): A scoping review. *British Journal of Social Psychology.* 64: e12833. https://doi.org/10.1111/bjso.12833.

Meier HE (2018) Dopingbekämpfung als zentrale Aufgabe der Sportpolitik. [Fight against doping as central task of the politics of sports]. *Polis.* 22(1): 14–16. http://dvpb.de/wp-content/uploads/2018/11/POLIS_1-18_web.pdf

Meier HE and Mutz M (2016) Sport related national pride in East and West Germany 1992–2008. Persistent differences or trends toward convergence? *Sage Open.* 6(3): 1–10.

Meier HE and Mutz M (2018) Political regimes and sport related national pride. A cross-national analysis. *International Journal of Sport and Politics.* 10(3): 525–548.

Meier HE, Reinhard K, Konjer M and Leinwather M (2016) Deutschland, einig Fußballland? Ost-West Unterschiede in der Nachfrage nach Nationalmannschaften. [Germany, united football country? East-West differences in the demand of national teams]. *Leviathan.* 44(2): 247–279.

Mejeh M (2020) Cross-sectional network analysis. In Huber M and Froehlich DE (Eds.) *Analyzing Group Interactions. A Guidebook for Qualitative, Quantitative and Mixed Methods.* New York: Routledge, pp. 85–95. https://doi.org/10.4324/9780367321116-10

Menoutis V (2000) Median and large group-analytic groups in a naval academy. *Group Analysis.* 33(1): 49–61.

Merleau-Ponty (1962) *Phenomenology of Perception.* Trans. C Smith. London: Routledge.

Merleau-Ponty (1964a) *Sense and Non-Sense.* Trans. H Dreyfus. Evanston, IL: Northwestern University Press. https://archive.org/details/sensenonsense0000merl

Merleau-Ponty (1964b) *Signs.* Trans. R McCleary. Evanston, IL: Northwestern University Press. https://archive.org/details/20200305northwesternuniversitystudiesinphenomenologyexis/page/n5/mode/2up

Mersky RR (2008) Social dream-drawing: A methodology in the making. *Socio-Analysis.* 10: 35–50. https://search.informit.org/doi/10.3316/INFORMIT.296172059763109

Mersky RR (2012) Contemporary methodologies to surface and act on unconscious dynamics in organizations: An exploration of design, facilitation capacities, consultant paradigm and ultimate value. *Organisational and Social Dynamics.* 12(1): 19–43.

Mersky RR (2013) Social dream-drawing "drawing brings the inside out". In Long S (Ed.) *Socioanalytic Methods: Discovering the Hidden in Organisations and Social Systems*. New York: Routledge, pp. 53–78.
Mersky RR and Sievers B (2018) Social photo-matrix and social dream-drawing. In Stamenova K and Hinshelwood RD (Eds.) *Methods of Research into the Unconscious. Applying Psychoanalytic Ideas to Social Science.* London and New York: Routledge, pp. 145–168.
Mertens DM (2007) Transformative paradigm. Mixed methods and social justice. *Journal of Mixed Methods Research.* 1(3): 212–225.
Mertens DM (2008) *Transformative Research and Education.* London: Guilford Press.
Mertens DM (2012) Transformative mixed methods. Addressing inequities. *American Behavioral Scientist.* 56(6): 802–813.
Mertens DM (2017) Transformative research: Personal and societal. *International Journal for Transformative Research.* 4(1): 18–24.
Merton RK (1967) *On Theoretical Sociology.* New York: Free Press.
Metz T (2011) Ubuntu as a moral theory and human rights in South Africa. *African Human Rights Law Journal.* 11(2): 532–559.
Metz T (2019) *The African Ethic of Ubuntu. 1000-word Philosophy*. Available at: 1000wordphilosophy.com/2019/09/08/the-african-ethic-of-ubuntu/ (accessed 19 December 2024).
Metzinger T (2010) *The Ego Tunnel. The Science of the Mind and the Myth of the Self.* New York: Basic Books.
Metzinger T (2021) Artificial suffering. An argument for a global moratorium on synthetic phenomenology. *Journal of Artificial Intelligence & Consciousness.* 8(1): 43–66.
Michels MD (2011) Foreword. In Klein R, Bernhard HS and Schermer V (Eds.) *On Becoming A Therapist. The Personal and Professional Journey.* Oxford: Oxford University Press, p. viii.
Michels S, Hommersom A, Lucas P and Velikova M (2015) A new probabilistic constraint logic programming language based on generalized distribution semantics. *Artificial Intelligence.* 228: 1–44. https://www.sciencedirect.com/science/article/pii/S0004370215001009
Midgley N, Ansaldo F and Target M (2014) The meaningful assessment of therapy outcomes: Incorporating a qualitative study into a randomized controlled trial evaluating the treatment of adolescent depression. *Psychotherapy.* 51(1): 128–137. https://doi.org/10.1037/a0034179.
Midgley N, Mortimer R, Cirasola A, Batra P and Kennedy E (2021) The evidence-base for psychodynamic psychotherapy with children and adolescents: A narrative synthesis. *Frontiers in Psychology.* 12: 662671. https://doi.org/10.3389/fpsyg.2021.662671.
Migliorati PG (1989) The image and group relationships. *Group Analysis.* 22(2): 189–199.
Mignolo WD and Walsh CE (2017) *On Decoloniality. Concepts, Analytics, Praxis.* New York: Duke University Press.
Mikahere-Hall A (2017) Constructing research from an indigenous Kaupapa Māori perspective: An example of decolonizing research. *Psychotherapy and Politics International.* 1–14. https://doi.org/10.1002/ppi.1428.
Miles J and Banyard P (2007) *Understanding and Using Statistics in Psychology: A Practical Introduction.* New York: Sage.
Miles JR and Paquin JD (2014) Best practices in group counselling and psychotherapy research. In DeLucia-Waack JL, Kalodner CR and Riva MT (Eds.) *Handbook of Counselling and Psychotherapy.* 2nd Edition. Thousand Oaks, CA: Sage, pp. 178–192.
Miles MB and Huberman AM (1994) *Qualitative Data Analysis: An Expanded Sourcebook.* 2nd Edition. Thousand Oaks, CA: Sage.
Mill CW (2021) *Race, Philosophy, and Political Thought. Dialogue with Owen Williams, Sharon Achinstein, Charles W Mill, Jennifer I Morgan, Robert Bernasconi. 21 June 2021.* Transcript. A Folger Institute Fiftieth Anniversary Project. Supported by the Mellon Initiative in Collaborative Research. https://www.folger.edu/research/featured-research-projects-and-initiatives/critical-race-conversations/ (Critical Race Conversations). See also: https://www.youtube.com/playlist?list=PLR8P-dSNaJkXDYEqDI_AX-AKs7J2nPiqc

Miller P and Rose N (2001) The Tavistock programme. The government of subjectivity and social life. In Wetherell M, Taylor S and Yates SJ (Eds.) *Discourse Theory and Practice*. London: Sage, pp. 364–379.
Mills C (1997) *The Racial Contract.* Ithaca, NY: Cornell University Press.
Ming-Dao D (1990) *Scholar Warrior. An Introduction to the Tao in Everyday Life.* New York: HarperCollins. https://archive.org/details/scholarwarriorin0000deng
Mingers J and Willcocks L (2017) An integrative semiotic methodology for IS research. *Information and Organization.* 27(1): 17–78.
Minnick CL (2024) *Bion's Mother-Infant Model for Creating a Mental Apparatus.* Minnick's Klein Academy. Models for Understanding. The Baby Core of the Personality. Available at: https://minnickskleinacademy.com/module-2/bions-mother-infant-model-for-creating-a-mental-apparatus/ (accessed 29 November 2024).
Mirvis PH (1988) Organization development. Part I. An evolutionary perspective. In Woodman RW and Pasmore WA (Eds.) *Research in Organizational Change and Development, Vol. 2.* Greenwich, CT: JAI Press, pp. 1–58.
Mishra P, Pandey CM, Singh U, Gupta A, Sahu C and Keshri A (2019) Descriptive statistics and normality tests for statistical data. *Annals of Cardiac Anaesthesia.* 22(1): 67–72. https://doi.org/10.4103/aca.ACA_157_18.
Mishra S (2004) *Haunted Lines. Postcolonial Theory and the Genealogy of Racial Formations in Fiji.* New York: Routledge.
Mitchell J (1974) *Psychoanalysis and Feminism.* New York: Pantheon Books.
Mitchell S (2006) *Tao Te Ching.* Trans. S Mitchell. New York: HarperCollins Publishers. https://ia801704.us.archive.org/28/items/taoteching-Stephen-Mitchell-translation-v9deoq/taoteching-Stephen-Mitchell-translation-v9deoq_text.pdf
Mittwoch A (2001) Our place in the world of science: What Is at stake? *Group Analysis.* 34(4): 431–448.
Mkhize N (2008) Ubuntu and Harmony: An African approach to morality and ethics. In Nicolson R (Ed.) *Persons in Community. African Ethics in a Global Culture.* Scottsville, KY: University of KwaZulu-Natal Press.
Mncube Z (2017) Book review: Is science racist? *International Studies in the Philosophy of Science.* 31(3): 319–321. https://doi.org/10.1080/02698595.2018.1463695.
Mocombe PC (2017) Phenomenological structuralism: A structuralist theory of human action. *Sociology International Journal.* 1(1): 22–30.
Mohajan HK (2020) Quantitative research: A successful investigation in natural and social sciences. *Journal of Economic Development, Environment and People.* 9: 52–79. https://doi.org/10.26458/jedep.v9i4.679.
Mohamed S, Png M-T and Isaac W (2020) Decolonial AI: Decolonial theory as sociotechnical foresight in artificial intelligence. *Philosophy & Technology.* 33: 659–684. https://doi.org/10.1007/s13347-020-00405-8.
Mohr DC (2024) Standards for randomized controlled trials of efficacy of psychological treatments. *World Psychiatry.* 23(2): 286–287.
Mojović M (2007) The impact of the post-totalitarian social context on the group matrix. *Group Analysis.* 40(3): 394–403.
Mojović M (2019) Serbian reflective citizens and the art of psychosocial listening and dialogue at the caesura. *Journal of Psychosocial Studies.* 12(1–2): 81–95.
Mokoena K (2024) A holistic ubuntu artificial intelligence ethics approach in South Africa. *Verbum Et Ecclesia.* 45(1): 1–8. https://doi.org/10.4102/ve-v45i1.3100; https://verbumetecclesia.org.za/index.php/ve/article/view/3100/7364
Molenberghs P (2022) (Ed.) *The Neuroscience of Intergroup Relations. Global Perspectives on the Neural Underpinnings of Intergroup Behavior. Ingroup Bias and Prejudice.* New York: Routledge.
Möller HJ (2011) Effectiveness studies: Advantages and disadvantages. *Dialogues in Clinical Neuroscience.* 13(2): 199–207. https://doi.org/10.31887/DCNS.2011.13.2/hmoeller.
Mollon P (2008) *Psychoanalytic Energy Psychotherapy.* London: Karnac.

Molyneux J (1995) A modest proposal for portsmouth. In Miles M (Ed.) *Art and the City*. Portsmouth: University of Portsmouth, pp. 16–18.

Mondal S (2023) Theories of truth. *Journal of Research in Humanities and Social Science*. 11(5): 40–42.

Monge PR and Contractor NS (2003) *Theories of Communication Networks*. New York: Oxford University Press.

Montgomery A (2013) *Neurobiology Essentials for Clinicians. What Every Therapist Needs To Know*. New York: W. W. Norton & Company.

Moore R (2019) *Breaking the code of the archetypal self. An Introductory overview of the research discoveries leading to Neo-Jungian Structural Psychoanalysis*. Available at: https://jungchicago.org/blog/breaking-the-code-of-the-archetypal-self (accessed 24 December 2024).

Moreno JL (1933) What Is Structure? Cited in Rawlings CM, Smith JA, Moody J and McFarland DA (2023) *Network Analysis. Integrating Social Network Theory, Method, And Application with R*. New York: Cambridge University Press, p. 2.

Moreno JL (1934) *Who Shall Survive: A New Approach to the Problem of Human Interrelations*. Washington, DC: Nervous and Mental Disease Publishing Company.

Morgan DL (1996) Focus groups. *Annual Review of Sociology*. 22(1): 129–152. https://www.researchgate.net/publication/261773532_Focus_Groups

Morgan DL (2007) Paradigms lost and paradigms regained. Methodological implications of combining qualitative and quantitative methods. *Journal of Mixed Methods Research*. 1(1): 48–76.

Morgan SL and Lee J (2021) A rolling panel model of cohort, period, and aging effects for the analysis of the general social survey. *Sociological Methods & Research*. 53(1): 369–420. https://doi.org/10.1177/00491241211043135.

Morley G and Shashidhara S (2020) Debriefing as a response to moral distress. *Journal of Clinical Ethics*. 31(3): 283–289.

Morrell-Scott N (2018) Using diaries to collect data in phenomenological research. *Nurse Researcher*. 25(4): 26–29. https://doi.org/10.7748/nr.2018.e1527

Morris JB (1977) Appendix 1. The prediction and measurement of change in a psychotherapy group using the repertory grid. In F Fransella and Bannister D (Eds.) *A Manual for Repertory Grid Technique*. London: Academic Press. (cited in Winter, 1992).

Morris P (Ed.) (1994) *The Bakhtin Reader. Selected Writings of Bakhtin, Medvedev and Voloshino*. New York: Oxford University Press. http://www.europhd.net/sites/europhd/files/images/onda_2/07/27th_lab/scientific_materials/jesuino/bakhtin_reader.pdf

Morrison CA (2012) Solicited diaries and the everyday geographies of heterosexual love and home: Reflections on methodological process and practice. *Area*. 44(1): 68–75.

Morse JM, Stern PN, Cobin J, Bowers B, Charmaz K and Clarke AE (2009) *Developing Grounded Theory. The Second Generation*. Walnut Creek, CA: West Coast Press.

Morson GS and Emerson C (1990) *Mikhail Bakhtin: Creation of a Prosaics*. Stanford: Stanford University Press. https://archive.org/details/isbn_9780804718226

Moustakas C (1994) *Phenomenological Research Methods*. London: Sage. https://archive.org/details/phenomenological0000mous

Msaouel P, Lee J and Thall PF (2023) Interpreting randomized controlled trials. *Cancers*. 15(19): 4674. https://www.researchgate.net/publication/374122843_Interpreting_Randomized_Controlled_Trials

Muhammad M, Wallerstein N, Sussman AL, Avila M, Belone L and Duran B (2015) Reflections on researcher identity and power: the impact of positionality on community based participatory research (CBPR) processes and outcome. *Critical Sociology*. 41(7–8): 1045–1063.

Muhr T (2004) ATLAS.ti. The Knowledge Workbench, Version 5.0. [User Manual]. 2nd Edition. Berlin: Scientific Software Development GmbH. Manuals available at: https://atlasti.com/manuals-and-documents

Mulder R, Singh AB, Hamilton A, Das P, Outhred T, Morris G, Bassett D, Baune BT, Berk M, Boyce P, Lyndon B, Parker G and Malhi GS (2018) The limitations of using randomised controlled trials as a basis for developing treatment guidelines. *Evidence-Based Mental Health*. 21(1): 4–6. https://doi.org/10.1136/eb-2017-102701.

Muller JP (2013) *Beyond the Psychoanalytic Dyad. Developmental Semiotics in Freud, Peirce, and Lacan.* New York: Routledge. https://www.scribd.com/document/210409439/Beyond-the-Psychoanalytic-Dyad
Multon KD, Patton MJ and Kivlighan DM (1996) *Missouri Identifying Transference Scale (MITS).* Washington: APA. https://doi.org/10.1037/t04300-000.
Muncer SJ and Gillen K (1997) Network analysis and lay interpretation: Some issues of consensus and representation. *British Journal of Social Psychology.* 36(4): 537–551. https://www.researchgate.net/publication/229766804_Network_analysis_and_lay_interpretation_Some_issues_of_consensus_and_representation
Muncer SJ, Taylor S, Green D and McManus I (2001) Nurses' representations of the perceived causes of work-related stress: A network drawing approach. *Work and Stress.* 15(1): 40–52.
Munder T, Flűckiger C, Leichsenring F, Abbass AA, Hilsenroth MJ, Luyten P, Rabung S, Steinert C and Wampold WE (2019) Let's distinguish relative and absolute efficacy to move psychotherapy research forward. *Zeitschrift für Psychosomatische Medizin und Psychotherapie.* 65(2): 178–182. https://doi.org/10.13109/zptm.2019.65.2.178
Mungwini P (2022) *African Philosophy. Emancipation and Practice.* New York: Bloomsbury.
Mungwini P (2024) The global south framework and African philosophy: Epistemologies and struggles for emancipation. *African Identities.* 1–16. https://doi.org/10.1080/14725843.2024.2442630.
Münkel D (2015) Das Berichtswesen der Staatssicherheit 1953 bis 1989. [The nature of reporting of national security]. In Münkel D (Ed.) *Staatssicherheit. Ein Lesebuch zur DDR Geheimpolizei. [A Textbook about the Secret Service of the GDR].* Berlin: Bundesarchiv, pp. 94–103. https://www.bundesarchiv.de/publikationen/publikation/staatssicherheit/
Munn Z, Peters MDJ, Stern C, Tufanaru C, McArthur A and Aromataris L (2018) Systematic review or scoping review? Guidance for authors when choosing between a systematic or scoping review approach. *BMC Medical Research Methodology.* 18: 143. https://doi.org/10.1186/s12874-018-0611-x.
Munn Z, Porritt K, Lockwood C, Aromataris E and Pearson A (2014) Establishing confidence in the output of qualitative research synthesis: The ConQual approach. *BMC Medical Research Methodology.* 14: 108. https://doi.org/10.1186/1471-2288-14-108.
Munn Z, Stern C, Aromataris E, Lockwood C and Jordan Z (2018) What kind of systematic review should I conduct? A proposed typology and guidance for systematic reviewers in the medical and health sciences. *BMC Medical Research Methodo*logy. 18: 5. https://doi.org/10.1186/s12874-017-0468-4.
Munro H (1974) Section IV group- group analytic commentary. A historical account of the development of dynamic psychology. *Group Analysis.* 7(1): 179–184.
Murad MH, Asi N, Alsawas M and Alahdab F (2016) New evidence pyramid. *British Medical Journal.* 21(4): 125–127. https://www.researchgate.net/publication/283420404_The_New_Evidence_Pyramid
Murray DM, Varnell SP and Blitstein JL (2004) Design and analysis of group-randomized trials: A review of recent methodological developments. *American Journal of Public Health.* 94(3): 423–32.
Murray M (1995) *The Law of the Father? Patriarchy in the Transition from Feudalism to Capitalism.* London: Routledge. https://archive.org/details/lawoffatherpatri0000murr
Murray M and Sargeant S (2012) Narrative psychology. In Harper D and Thompson AR (Eds.) *Qualitative Methods in Mental Health and Psychotherapy. A Guide for Students and Practitioners.* Chichester: John Wiley & Sons, pp. 163–175.
Murris K and Bozalek V (2019) Diffracting diffractive readings of texts as methodology. Some propositions. *Educational Philosophy and Theory.* 51(14): 1504–1517.
Murris K and Zhao V (2022) Non/representational. In Murris K (Ed.) *A Glossary for Doing Postqualitative, New Materialist and Critical Posthumanist Research across Disciplines.* New York: Routledge, pp. 92–93.
Murtagh F (2014) Mathematical representations of Matte Blanco's Bi-logic based on metric space and ultrametric or hierarchical topology. Towards practical application. *Language and Psychoanalysis.* 3(2): 40–63. https://journals.ed.ac.uk/languageandpsychoanalysis/article/view/1581/2036
Mussolini B (1925) Speech delivered at La Scala on 28th October 1925. In *Mussolini as Revealed in his Political Speeches November 1914 – August 1923.* Benito Mussolini. Audiobook. LibriVox. Available

at: https://librivox.org/mussolini-as-revealed-in-his-political-speeches-by-benito-mussolini/ (accessed 11 March 2023).

Muthukrishna M and Heinrich J (2019) A problem in theory. *Nature Human Behaviour*. 3(3): 221–229. https://www.michael.muthukrishna.com/wp-content/uploads/2019/02/Muthukrishna-A-problem-in-theory.pdf

Myburgh S Tammaro AM (2013) Constructing a theoretical framework. In Myburgh S and Tammaro AM (Eds.) *Exploring Education for Digital Librarians. Meaning, Modes and Models. A Volume in Chandos Information Professional Series.* Chandos Publishing, pp. 133–172.

Nahm FS (2016) Nonparametric statistical tests for the continuous data. The basic concept and the practical use. *Korean Journal of Anesthesiology*. 69(1): 8–14. https://doi.org/10.4097/kjae.2016.69.1.8.

Napolitani D (1981) Struttura gruppale della psicoanalisi e analisi del gruppo. [Structure of the psychoanalytic group and analysis of the group]. In Angeli F (Ed.) *Le Frontiere Della Psicoanalisi. a cura di Carlo Ravasini*. [The boundary of the Psychoanalyst a cure by Carlo Ravasini]. Milano: Modena, pp. 89–136.

Narayan A, Purkayastha B and Khan K (2022) Intersectionality. In Engler S and Stausberg M (Eds.) *The Routledge Handbook of Research Methods in the Study of Religion.* New York: Routledge, pp. 72–87.

Natayanan V (2005) Hinduism. In Coogan MD (Ed.) *Eastern Religions. Hinduism, Buddhism, Taoism, Confucianism, Shinto.* London: Duncan Baird Publishers, pp. 10–109.

Nathan V and Poulsen S (2004) Group-analytic training groups for psychology students: A qualitative study. *Group Analysis.* 37(2): 163–177.

National Academy of Sciences (1993) *Assessment of the Possible Health Effects of Ground Wave Emergency Network.* New York: National Academies Press.

Nauenberg M (2016) Max Planck and the birth of the quantum hypothesis. *American Journal of Physics.* 84(9): 709–720. https://doi.org/10.1119/1.4955146.

Nayak S (2021) Black feminist intersectionality is vital to group analysis: Can group analysis allow outsider ideas in? *Group Analysis.* 54(3): 337–353.

Nayak S (2023) *Decolonising the Curriculum of Group Analysis (Phase 1). Report on Findings. December 2023.* London: Institute of Group Analysis. https://www.iga.co.uk

Nayak S and Forrest A (Eds.) (2024) *Intersectionality and Group Analysis. Explorations of Power, Privilege and Position in Group Therapy.* New York: Routledge.

Ndlovu-Gatsheni SJ (2018) *Epistemic Freedom in Africa. Deprovincialization and Decolonization.* New York: Routledge.

NDR (2021) *Musik in der DDR. Wie lenkbar is Musikkultur? [How controllable is the music culture?]* 4 June. Available at: https://www.ndr.de/geschichte/chronologie/Musik-in-der-DDR-Wie-lenkbar-ist-Musikkultur,weststars100.html (accessed 3 April 2023).

Neri C and Pines M (Eds.) (2002) *Dreams and Group Psychotherapy. Theory and Technique.* London: Jessical Kingsley Publishers.

Neumann E (1955) *The Great Mother.* Princeton, NJ: Princeton University Press. https://archive.org/details/greatmotheranaly0000neum_d6r3/page/n7/mode/2up

Neve M (2004) A commentary on the history of social psychiatry and psychotherapy in twentieth-century Germany, Holland and Great Britain. *Medical History.* 48(4): 407–412.

New World Encyclopedia (2022) *Logical Positivism.* 3 November 2022. Available at: https://www.newworldencyclopedia.org/p/index.title=Logical_positivism&oldid=1085378 (accessed 15 January 2024).

Nezlek JB (2012) *Diary Methods for Social and Personality Psychology.* Thousand Oaks, CA: Sage.

Ngubane-Mokiwa SA (2018) Ubuntu considered in light of exclusion of people with disability. *African Journal of Disability.* 7: 460–467. https://doi.org/10.4102/ajod.v7i0.460; https://ajod.org/index.php/ajod/article/view/460

Nguyen J, Rashid M and Forgie S (2023) Twelve tips for how institutional ethnography (IE) is conducted in health professions education research. *Medical Teacher*. 46(6): 763–768. https://doi.org/10.1080/0142159X.2023.2289852.

Nguyen T (2023) *Using Computer Simulations for Hypothesis-Testing and Prediction. Epistemological Strategies*. https://philpapers.org/rec/NGUEOC

NICE (2024a) *Glossary. Systematic Review*. Available at: https://www.nice.org.uk/Glossary?letter=S (accessed 6 December 2024).

NICE (2024b) *Glossary. Randomised Controlled Trial*. Available at: https://www.nice.org.uk/Glossary?letter=R (accessed 6 December 2024).

NICE (2024c) *Glossary. Meta-analysis*. Available at: https://www.nice.org.uk/Glossary?letter=M (accessed 6 December 2024).

NICE (2025a) *NICE Real-world Evidence Framework*. Updated January 2025. Available at: https://www.nice.org.uk/corporate/ecd9/chapter/overview#real-world-data-and-its-role-in-nice-guidance (accessed March 2025) (Originally published June 23, 2022).

NICE (2025b) *Conduct of Qualitative Research Studies. Appendix 4*. Available at: https://www.nice.org.uk/corporate/ecd9/chapter/appendix-4-conduct-of-qualitative-research-studies (accessed June 2025).

Nichol AD, Bailey M and Cooper DJ (2010) Challenging issues in randomised controlled trials. *Injury*. 41(S1): 20–S23. https://doi.org/10.1016/j.injury.2010.03.033.

Nickerson C (2024) What Is Face Validity? *Simply Psychology*. 1 November. Available at: https://www.simplypsychology.org/face-validity.html (accessed 5 December 2024).

Nietzsche F (1962) *Philosophy in the Tragic Age of the Greeks*. Republished in 1996 by Gateway. London. https://archives.org/detail-nietzsche-philosophy-tragic-age-greeks

Nietzsche F (2019) *Also Sprach Zarathustra*. Frankfurt/M: Pretorian Books. https://archive.org/details/alsosprachzarath0000frie

NIH (2024) *National Institute of Health. Research Methods Resources. Parallel Group- or Cluster-Randomized Trials*. Available at: https://researchmethodsresources.nih.gov/methods/grt (accessed 6 December 2024).

Nikolopoulou K (2022) *What Is Predictive Validity? Examples & Definitions*. 15 September. Available at: https://scribbr.co.uk/research-methods/predictive-validity-explained/ (accessed 5 December 2024).

Nikulin D (2002) Mikhail Bakhtin. A theory of dialogue. *Constellations*. 5(3): 381–402.

Nilsen P (2015) Making sense of implementation theories, models, and frameworks. *Implementation Science*. 10(1): 53. https://doi.org/10.1186/s13012-015-0242-0.

Nilsen P and Bernhardsson S (2019) Context matters in implementation science. a scoping review of determinant frameworks that describe contextual determinants for implementation outcomes. *BMC Health Services Research*. 19(1): 189–210. https://doi.org/10.1186/s12913-019-4015-3.

Ninan PA, Hirisave U and Girimaji SC (2019) Group interventions for children and adolescents with emotional problems: A review of the literature. *Indian Journal of Mental Health*. 6(1): 5–17.

Nisa -Waller A and Piercy G (2024) Autoethnography as a decolonising tool: bringing identity into the classroom. *Higher Education Research & Development*. 43(5): 1142–1155. https://doi.org/10.1080/07294360.2024.2307924.

Nishida K (1921/1990) *An Inquiry into the Good*. Trans. M Abe and C Ives. New Haven, CT: Yale University Press.

Nishida K (1923) *Art and Morality*. Trans. DA Dilworth and VH Viglielmo. Honolulu: University Press of Hawai'i, Published in 1973. Available at: https://archive.org/details/artmorality0000nish/page/n7/mode/2up

Nishida K (1927/1978–9) *Complete Works of Nishida Kitarô. 19 Volumes*. Tokyo: Iwanami.

Nishida K (1958/1966) *Intelligibility and the Philosophy of Nothingness: Three Philosophical Essays*. Tokyo: East-West Center Press. https://archive.org/details/intelligibilityp00nish/page/n11/mode/2up

Nishida K (1958/1973) *Intelligibility and the Philosophy of Nothingness*. Trans. R Schinzinger. Tokyo: Maruzen, 1958. Reprint. Westport, Conn: Greenwood Press, 1973.

Nishida K (1970) *Fundamental Problems of Philosophy. The World of Action and the Dialectical World*. Trans. DA Dilworth. Tokyo: Sophia University. Available at: https://archive.org/details/fundamentalprobl0000kita

Nishida K (1993) *Last Writings. Nothingness and the Religious Worldview*. Translated and with an Introduction by DA Dilworth. Honolulu: University of Hawai'i Press.

Nitsun M (1996) *The Anti -Group. Destructive Forces in the Group and their Creative Potential*. London: Routledge.

Nitsun M (2006) *The Group as an Object of Desire. Exploring Sexuality in Group Therapy.* East Sussex: Routledge.
Nitsun M (2015) *Beyond the Anti-Group. Survival and Transformation.* London: Routledge.
Nitzgen D (2006) Contemporary clinical challenges of group analysis. *Group Analysis.* 39(3): 295–303.
Nitzgen D (2010) The matrix reloaded: Ernst Cassirer - Kurt Goldstein - S.H. Foulkes. *Psychosozial.* 119: 25–37. https://psychosozial-verlag.de/programm/4000/4100/26191-detail
Noack A (2020) Treating psychotic anxiety in the group. *Group Analysis.* 3(3): 309–326.
Noah PD (2017) A systematic approach to qualitative metasynthesis. *Issues in Information Systems.* 18(2): 196–205.
Noble H and Heale R (2019) Triangulation in research, with examples. *Evidence Based Nursing.* 22(3): 67–68. https://ebn.bmj.com/content/22/3/67
Noblit GW (2018) Meta-ethnography: Adaptation and return. In Urrieta L and Noblit GW (Eds.) *Cultural Constructions of Identify: Meta-Ethnography and Theory*. Oxford: Oxford University Press, pp. 34–50.
Noblit GW and Hare DR (1988) *Meta-ethnography: Synthesizing Qualitative Studies*. Newbury Park, CA: Sage.
Norcross JC and Wampold BE (2019) Relationships and responsiveness in the psychological treatment of trauma. The tragedy of the APA clinical practice guidelines. *Psychotherapy.* 56(3): 391–399.
Norris M (1977) The use of repertory investigating change in trainees at a detention centre. *The British Journal of Criminology*. 17(3): 274–279. https://www.jstor.org/stable/23636187
Noyes J, Booth A, Flemming K, Garside R, Harden A, Lewin S, Pantoja T, Hannes K, Cargo M and Thomas J (2018) Cochrane qualitative and implementation methods group guidance series-paper 3: Methods for assessing methodological interventions, data extraction and synthesis, and confidence in synthesized qualitative findings. *Journal of Clinical Epidemiology.* 97: 49–58. https://www.jclinepi.com/article/S0895-4356(17)30719-9/abstract
Nussbaumer Streit B, Jesser, A, Humer E, Barke A, Doering BK, Haid B, Schimböck W, Reisinger A, Gasser M, Eichberger-Heckmann H, Stippl P, Gartlehner G, Pieh C, Probst T (2022) A web-survey assessed attitudes toward evidence-based practice among psychotherapists in Austria. *Scientific Reports.* 12(1): 9374–9381. https://doi.org/10.1038/s41598-022-13266-2.
Nyamathi A and Shuler P (1990) Focus group interview. A research technique for informed nursing practice. *Journal of Advanced Nursing.* 15(11): 1281–1288. https://doi.org/10.1111/j.1365-2648.1990.tb01743.x.
O'Beney R, Salm A-M and Lavender T (2019) An exploration of members' experiences of group therapy. An interpretative phenomenological analysis. *Group Analysis.* 52(1): 82–99.
O'Brien J and O'Brien N (2025) *Jung's Word Association Experiment. Manual for Training and Practice.* New York: Routledge.
O'Brien R (2001) An overview of the methodological approach of action research. In Richardson R (Ed.) *Theory and Practice of Action Research.* Joao Pessoa: Universidade Federal da Paraiba. Available at: http://www.web.ca/~robrien/papers/arfinal.html (accessed 5 October 2024).
O'Connor JJ and Robertson EF (2015) *Ernst Pascual Jordan.* University of St Andrews. July 2015. Available at: https://mathshistory.st-andrews.ac.uk/Biographies/Jordan_Pascual/ (accessed 9 January 2025).
O'Mahoney J and Vincent S (2014) Critical realism as an empirical project. A Beginner's Guide. In Edwards PK, O'Mahoney J and Vincent S (Eds.) *Studying Organizations Using Critical Realism. A Practical Guide.* Oxford: Oxford University Press, pp. 1–20.
OASH (Office of the Assistant Secretary for Health) (2024) *The International Compilation of Human Research Standards, 2024 Edition.* Washington: US Department of Health and Human Services (HHS), OASH, Office for Human Research Protection (OHRP) Available at: https://www.hhs.gov/ohrp/international/compilation-human-research-standards/index.html
Obholzer A and Roberts VZ (2005) *The Unconscious at Work. A Tavistock Approach to Making Sense of Organizational Life.* London: Routledge.
Obholzer A and Roberts VZ (2019) *The Unconscious at Work. A Tavistock Approach to Making Sense of Organizational Life.* 2nd Edition. London: Routledge.

Obiechina E (1992) Narrative Proverbs in the African Novel. *Research in African Literature.* 24(4): 123–140. https://www.jstor.org/stable/3820257

Ofer G (2017) Social Dreaming Matrix. GAD Blog. Available at: https://groupanalyticsociety.co.uk/social-dreaming-matrix/ (accessed 2 April 2025).

Ogden P (2021) The healing context. Philosophical spiritual principles of sensorimotor psychotherapy. In Siegel DJ, Schore AN and Cozolino L (Eds.) *Interpersonal Neurobiology and Clinical Practice.* New York: W.W. Norton & Company, pp. 195–239.

Ogden T (2005) On psychoanalytic writing. *International Journal of Psychoanalysis.* 86(1): 15–29.

Ogrodniczuk JS and Piper WE (2003) The effect of group climate on outcome in two forms of short-term group psychotherapy. *Group Dynamics. Theory, Research, and Practice.* 7(1): 64–76.

Ogrodniczuk JS, Piper WE, Joyce AS and McCallum M (1999) Transference interpretations in short-term dynamic psychotherapy. *Journal of Nervous and Mental Disease.* 187(9): 571–578.

Ohly S, Sonnentag S, Niessen C and Zapf D (2010) Diary studies in organizational research. *Journal of Personnel Psychology.* 9(2): 79–93. https://www.researchgate.net/publication/44218840_Diary_studies_in_organizational_research_An_introduction_and_some_practical_recommendations

Okada A (2025) *Knowledge Cartography for Young Thinkers. Sustainability Issues, Techniques and AI Tools.* Cham: Springer. Available at: https://link.Springer.com/book/10.1007/978-3-031-54677-8 (accessed 12 April 2025).

Okada A, Buckingham Shum S and Sherborne T (Eds.) (2008) *Knowledge Cartography: Software Tools and Mapping Techniques.* London: Springer.

Olabode J (2022) *Statistical Significance: P-Value and Confidence Interval.* Medium Blog. 25 September. Available at: https://gmust.medium.com/statistical-significance-p-value-and-confidence-interval-c297207fc2dc (accessed 2 July 2024).

Oldstone-Moore J (2005a) Taoism. In Coogan MD (Ed.) *Eastern Religions. Hinduism, Buddhism, Taoism, Confucianism, Shinto.* London: Duncan Baird Publishers, pp. 212–313.

Oldstone-Moore J (2005b) Confucianism. In Coogan MD (Ed.) *Eastern Religions. Hinduism, Buddhism, Taoism, Confucianism, Shinto.* London: Duncan Baird Publishers, pp. 314–415.

Oliveira A (2017) *The Digital Mind. How Science is Redefining Humanity.* Boston, MA: MIT Press.

Oliver C (2012) Critical realist grounded theory. A new approach for social work research. *British Journal of Social Work.* 42(2): 371–387.

Olsen RK (2025) The value of child participation in research, a qualitative child-centered approach to the early development of an empowerment inventory for children. *Child & Youth Services.* 46(2): 400–421. https://doi.org/10.1080/0145935X.2024.2336914.

Ono YA (1982) How I created the theory of relativity. *Physics Today.* 35(8): 45–47. https://doi.org/10.1063/1.2915203.

Onwuegbuzie AJ and Combs JP (2010) Data analysis in mixed methods research. A primer. In Tashakkori A and Teddlie C (Eds.) *Sage Handbook of Mixed Methods in Social & Behavioral Research.* 2nd Edition. Thousand Oaks, CA: Sage, pp. 397–430.

Onwuegbuzie AJ and Leech NL (2005) On becoming a pragmatic researcher: The importance of combining quantitative and qualitative research methodologies. *International Journal of Social Research Methodology: Theory and Practice.* 8: 375–387. https://doi.org/10.1080/13645570500402447.

Onwuegbuzie AJ, Dickinson WB, Leech NL and Zoran AG (2009) A qualitative framework for collecting and analyzing data in focus group research. *International Journal of Qualitative Methods.* https://doi.org/10.1177/160940690900800301.

Onwuegbuzie AJ, Dickinson WB, Leech NL and Zoran AG (2009a) A qualitative framework for collecting and analyzing data in focus group research. *International Journal of Qualitative Methods.* 8(3): 1–21. https://doi.org/10.1177/160940690900800301.

Onwuegbuzie AJ, Johnson RB and Collins KMT (2009b) A call for mixed analysis: A philosophical framework for combining qualitative and quantitative. *International Journal of Multiple Research Methods.* 3(2): 114–139. https://www.researchgate.net/publication/264274973_Call_for_mixed_analysis_A_philosophical_framework_for_combining_qualitative_and_quantitative_approaches

Open University (2024) *Modern Positivism*. (OpenLearn Create. Glossary). Available at: https://www.open.edu/openlearncreate/mod/glossary/showentry.php?eid=5935&displayformat=dictionary (accessed 29 December 2024).

Open University (2025) The science of nutrion and healthy eating. (OpenLearn), Available at: https://www.open.edu/openlearn/education-development/learning-how-learn/content-section-6.1 (accessed 5 January 2025).

OpenAI (2023) *ChatGPT* (Mar 14 version) [Large language model]. Available at: https://chat.openai.com/chat

OpenAI (2025) ChatGPT. Available at: https://openai.com/chatgpt/overview/ (accessed 8 January 2025).

Operario D and Fiske ST (1998) Racism equals power plus prejudice. A social psychological equation for racial oppression. In Eberhardt JL and Fiske ST (Eds.) *Confronting Racism. The Problem and the Response.* New York: Sage Publications Inc., pp. 33–53.

Orfanos S, Burn E, Priebe S and Spector A (2020) A systematic review and quality assessment of therapeutic group process questionnaires. *International Journal of Group Psychotherapy*. 70(3): 425–454. https://doi.org/10.1080/00207284.2020.1755292.

Orlov YF (1982) The wave logic of consciousness: A hypothesis. *International Journal of Theoretical Physics.* 21(1): 37–53.

Ormont LR (1992) *The Group Therapy Experience. From Theory to Practice.* New York: St. Martin's Press.

Ormont LR (2001) Meeting maturational needs in the group setting. *International Journal of Psychoanalysis.* 51(3): 343–359. https://doi.org/10.1521/ijgp.51.3.343.49890.

Osler L (2022) Reality+ Reality – A review of Reality+: Virtual worlds and the problems of philosophy. *Philosophical Psychology.* 37(5): 1281–1286.

Ostermann F, Cavalcanti CJ, Nascimento MM and Lima NW (2023) Speech analysis under a Bakhtinian approach: Contributions to research on physics education. *Physical Review Physics Education Research.* 19(1): https://doi.org/10.1103/PhysRevPhysEducRes.19.010141.

tern TP Jusslin S, Nødtvedt Knudsen K, Maapalo P and Bjørkøy I (2023) A performative paradigm for post-qualitative inquiry. *Qualitative Research.* 23(2): 272–289. https://doi.org/10.1177/14687941211027444.

Owen I and Morris N (1999) The Husserlian phenomenology of consciousness and cognitive science. We can see the path but nobody is on it. *Journal of Consciousness Studies.* 6(2–3): 269–273.

Own RK, Bradbury N, Xin Y, Cooper N and Sutton A (2019) MetaInsight. An interactive web-based tool for analyzing, interrogating, and visualizing network meta-analyses using R-shiny and netmeta. *Research Synthesis Methods.* 10(4): 569–581.

Ozaki M (2019) Kyoto school philosophy in relation to neo-confucian metaphysics. *Biocosmology Neo-Aristotelism*. 9(1–2): 137–152.

Paap D, Karel YHJM, Verhagen AP, Dijkstra PU, Geertzen JHB and Pool G (2022) The working alliance inventory's measurement properties: A systematic review. *Frontiers in Psychology.* 13: 945294. https://doi.org/10.3389/fpsyg.2022.945294.

Padmanathan P, Biddle L, Hall K, Scowcroft E, Nielsen E and Knipe D (2019) Language use and suicide: An online cross-sectional survey. *PLoS One*. 14(6): e0217473. https://doi.org/10.1371/journal.pone.0217473.

Page MJ, McKenzie JE, Bossuyt PM, Boutron I, Hoffmann TC, Mulrow CD, Shamseer L, Tetzlaff JM, Akt EA, Brennan SE, Chou R, Glanville J, Grimshaw JM, Hróbjartsson A, Lalu MM, Li T, Loder EW, Mayo-Wilson E, McDonald S, McGuinness LA, … Moher D (2021) The PRISMA 2020 statement: an updated guideline for reporting systematic reviews. *British Medical Journal.* 372(71). https://doi.org/10.1136/bmj.n71.

Page SE (2018) *The Model Thinker. What you Need to Know to Make Data Work for you.* New York: Basic Books.

Pais A (1979) Einstein and the quantum theory. *Reviews of Modern Physics*. 51(4): 863–914. https://doi.org/10.1103/RevModPhys.51.863.

Pais A (1988) The impact of Einstein's relativity theory. *American Scientist*. 76(2): 154–158. http://www.jstor.org/stable/27855069.

Palmer B (1992) Ambiguity and paradox in group relations conferences. In Pines M (Ed.) *Bion and Group Psychotherapy.* New York: Routledge, pp. 274–305.
Pang-White A (2006) Analogy and comparative philosophy. A hermeneutic retrieval of confucius and aquinas. *The SACP Forum: Asian and Comparative Philosophy.* 23(47): 127–147.
Pang-White A (2018a) Rereading the canon. In Pang-White A (Ed.) *The Bloomsbury Handbook of Chinese Philosophy and Gender.* New York: Bloomsbury, pp. 1–21.
Pang-White A (2018b) Neo-confucians and Zhu Xo on family and women: Challenges and potentials. In Pang-White A (Ed.) *The Bloomsbury Handbook of Chinese Philosophy and Gender.* New York: Bloomsbury, pp. 69–87.
Pang-White A (2018c) Non-self, agency, and women: Buddhism's modern transformation. In Pang-White A (Ed.) *The Bloomsbury Handbook of Chinese Philosophy and Gender.* New York: Bloomsbury, pp. 331–356.
Panorama (2009) *Margot Honecker: Der Sozialismus Kommt! [Margot Honecker: Socialism is Coming!]* Panorama. https://www.ndr.de/fernsehen/sendungen/panorama/archiv/2009/Margot-Honecker-Der-Sozialismus-kommt,panoramahonecker100.html (accessed 5 December 2010).
Park JS, O'Brien JC, Cai CJ, Morris MR, Liang P and Bernstein MS (2023) Generative Agents: Interactive Simulacra of Human Behavior. *UIST '23. Proceedings of the 36*th *Annual ACM Symposium on User Interface Software and Technology.* 7 April 2023. 1: 1–22. https://doi.org/10.1145/3586183.
Park P (1993) *Voices of Change: Participatory Research in the United States and Canada.* Westport, CT: Bergin & Garvey. https://archive.org/details/voicesofchangepa0000unse
Park PKJ (2013) *Africa, Asia, and the History of Philosophy. Racism and the Formation of the Philosophical Canon, 1780–1820.* New York: State University of New York Press.
Park S, Constantinides M, Aiello LM, Quercia D and Van Gent P (2020) WellBeat; A framework for tracking daily well-being using smartwatches. *IEEE Internet Computing.* 24(5): 10–17.
Park YS, Konge L and Artino AR (2020) The positivism paradigm of research. *Academic Medicine.* 95(5): 690–694.
Parker I (2005) *Qualitative Psychology. Introducing Radical Research.* Maidenhead: Open University Press.
Parker WS (2008) Franklin, holmes, and the epistemology of computer simulation. *International Studies in the Philosophy of Science.* 22(2): 165–183. https://doi.org/10.1080/02698590802496722.
Parkes G (2008) The definite internationalism of the Kyoto school changing attitudes in the contemporary academy. In Goto-Jones C (Ed.) *Re-Politicising the Kyoto School as Philosophy.* New York: Routledge, pp. 161–182.
Parlett M (1991) Reflections on field theory. *The British Gestalt Journal.* 1(2): 68–91.
Parr R (2002) *Te Matahauariki Methodology. The Creative Relationship Framework.* Hamilton, NZ: University of Waikato.
Parr S (2013) Integrating critical realist and feminist methodologies. Ethical and analytical dilemmas. *International Journal of Research Methodology.* 18(2): 193–207.
Parsons T (1949) *Essays in Sociological Theory: Pure and Applied.* Glencoe, IL: Free Press.
Pasby T (2013) Time and quantum theory: A history and a prospectus. Studies in history and philosophy of science Part B. *Studies in History and Philosophy of Modern Physics.* 52: 24–38. Available at: https://philpapers.org/rec/PASTAQ-2.
Pascal B (1958) *Pascal's Pensées.* Introduction by TS Eliot. New York: E. P. Dutton & Company. Available at: https://www.gutenberg.org/files/18269/18269-h/18269-h.htm (accessed 8 July 2024).
Pascual-Leone A, Greenberg LS and Pascual-Leone J (2009) Developments in task analysis. New methods to study change. *Psychotherapy Research.* 19(4–5): 527–542. https://doi.org/10.1080/10503300902897797.
Paterson T (2009) Dictator's wife defiant over forced adoptions. Margot Honecker, a Communist-era minister now living in exile in Chile, left a cruel legacy of separated families. *The Independent.* 10 November. Available at: https://www.independent.co.uk/news/world/europe/dictator-s-wife-defiant-over-forced-adoptions-1817710.html (accessed on 4 April 2023).

Patton MJ, Kivlighan DM and Multon KD (1997) The Missouri psychoanalytic counseling research project: Relation of changes in counseling process to client outcomes. *Journal of Counseling Psychology*. 44(2): 189–208.
Patton MQ (1999) Enhancing the quality and credibility of qualitative analysis. *Health Services Research*. 34(5): 1189–1208.
Patton MQ (2002) *Qualitative Research and Evaluation Methods*. 3rd Edition. Thousand Oaks, CA: Sage.
Peale SJ (2023) Celestial mechanics. Physics. *Encyclopedia Britannica*. 30 August 2023. Available at: https://www.britannica.com/science/celestial-mechanics-physics (accessed 7 January 2025).
Pearl J (2000) *Causality: Models, Reasoning, and Inference*. New York: Cambridge University Press.
Pearson MJ (2017) *The Group Readiness Questionnaire. A Practice-Based Evidence Measure?* Thesis. Faculty of Philosophy. Department of Counseling, Psychology and Special Education. Brigham Young University. Available at: https://scholarsarchive.byu.edu/etd/6485 (accessed 09 July 2024).
Peck MS (1987) *The Different Drum. Community Making and Peace*. New York: Simon & Schuster.
Pedrina F (2004) Group therapy with mothers and babies in postpartum crises: Preliminary evaluation of a pilot project. *Group Analysis*. 37(1): 137–151.
Peebles PJE and Ratra B (2003) The cosmological constant and dark energy. *Reviews of Modern Physics*. 75(2): 559–606.
Peirce CS (1868) Questions concerning certain faculties claimed for man. *Journal of Speculative Philosophy*. 2(2): 103–114. https://www.jstor.org/stable/25665643
Peirce CS (1931) *Collected Papers. Volumes I–VIII*. Edited by Hartshorne C and Weiss P. Cambridge, MA: Harvard University Press.
Peirce CS (1958) *Selected Writings. (Values in a Universe of Chance)*. New York: Dover Press. https://archive.org/details/selectedwritings0000peir_k0z4
Peirce CS (1968) Some consequences of four incapacities. *Journal of Speculative Philosophy*. 2(3): 140–157. https://www.jstor.org/stable/25665649?seq=1
Penna C (2023) *From Crowd Psychology to the Dynamics of Large Groups. Historical, Theoretical and Practical Considerations*. New York: Routledge.
Penrose R (1965) Gravitational collapse and space-time singularities. *Physical Review Letters*. 14(3): 57–59.
Penrose R (1989) *The Emperor's New Mind. Concerning Computers. Minds and the Laws of Physics*. Oxford: Oxford University Press.
Penrose R (2005) *The Road to Reality. A Complete Guide to the Laws of the Universe*. London: Vintage.
Penrose R (2014) On the gravitization of quantum mechanics 1: Quantum state reduction. *Foundations of Physics*. 44(5): 557–575.
Pepperell R (2024) *What Matter Feels. Consciousness, Energy and Physics. How Science Can Explain Minds*. London: Interdisciplinary Research Media, IRM.
Peres A (1997) *Quantum Theory. Concepts and Methods*. New York: Springer.
Pernecky T (2016) *Epistemology and Metaphysics for Qualitative Research*. London: Sage Publications Ltd.
Perren S and Richardson T (2018) Everybody needs a group: A qualitative study looking at therapists' views of the role of psychotherapy groups in working with older people with dementia and complex needs. *Group Analysis*. 51(1): 3–17.
Pertegato EG (2014) Foulkes' roots in Trigant Burrow's writings. *Group Analysis*. 47(3): 312–328.
Pertegato EG and Pertegato GO (2013) *From Psychoanalysis to Group analysis. The Pioneering Work of Trigant Burrow*. London: Karnac.
Pertegato EG and Pertegato GO (2018) *From Psychoanalysis to Group analysis. The Pioneering Work of Trigant Burrow*. New York: Routledge.
Peters JD and McCormick S (2008) Hermeneutics. *The International Encyclopedia of Communication*. Available at: https://doi.org/10.1002/9781405186407.wbiech016 (accessed on 12 November 2024).
Pfister G (2002) Sport for women. In Roland N and Hardman K (Eds.) *Sport and Physical Education in Germany*. New York: Routledge, pp. 136–145.

Pfohl M (2009) "Neptune Warnemünde". Das Hotel der Spione. *Der Stern.* 17 February. [Neptune Warnemunde. The Hotel of the Spies.] Available at: https://www.stern.de/gesellschaft/-neptun--warnemuende-das-hotel-der-spione-3423896.html (accessed 6 February 2023).

Philips B and Falkenström F (2021) What research evidence is valid in psychotherapy research? *Frontiers in Psychiatry.* 11: 625380. https://doi.org/10.3389/fpsyt.2020.625380.

Philips B, Werbart A and Schubert J (2005) Private theories and psychotherapeutic technique. *Psychoanalytic Psychotherapy.* 19(1): 48–70.

Phillips KA, Johnson FR and Maddala T (2002) Measuring what people value: A comparison of "attitude" and "preference" surveys. *Health Services Research.* 37(6): 1659–1679. https://doi.org/10.1111/1475-6773.01116.

Phipps J (2023) Finding words for it. The birth of group analytic training in Rwanda. In Noack A and Vincent D (Eds.) *Group Analytic Therapists at Work. Everyday Group Analysis.* New York: Routledge, Taylor & Frances, pp. 75–83.

Phyak P (2021) Epistemicide, deficit language ideology, and (de)coloniality in language education policy. *International Journal of the Sociology of Language.* 2021(267–268): 219–233. https://doi.org/10.1515/ijsl-2020-0104.

Pichon-Rivière E (2000) *Teoria do Vínculo.* [Theory of the Link]. São Paulo: Marins Fontes.

Pichon-Rivière E (2005) *O Processo Grupal.* 7th Edition. [The Group Process]. São Paulo: Martins Fontes.

Pichon-Rivière E, Bleger J, Liberman D and Rolla E (1960) Técnica de los grupos operativos. [Technique of operative groups], In *El proceso grupal. Del psicoanálisis a la psicología social (I)* [The group process: From psychoanalysis to social psychology (I)]. Buenos Aires: Nueva Visión, Reprinted 1971, pp. 107–120.

Pilgrim D (2014) Some implications of critical realism for mental health research. *Social Theory & Health.* 12(1): 1–21.

Pillow WS (2003) Confession, catharsis or cure? Rethinking the uses of reflexivity as methodological power in qualitative research. *The International Journal of Qualitative Research in Education.* 16(2): 175–196.

Pines M (1998) *Circular Reflections. Selected Papers on Group Analysis and Psychoanalysis.* London: Jessica Kingsley Publishers.

Pines M (2002) The coherency of group analysis. *Group Analysis.* 35(1): 13–26.

Pines M (2003) Preface. *Group Analysis.* 36(3): 315–321.

Pines M (2007) Group analysis and the affective disorders. *Group Analysis.* 40(3): 357–365.

Pines M (Ed.) (1983) *The Evolution of Group Analysis.* London: Routledge.

Pines M (Ed.) (1992) *Bion and Group Psychotherapy.* London: Tavistock, Republished by Routledge.

Pines M and Rafaelsen L (Eds.) (1982) *The Individual and the Group. Boundaries and Interrelations. Volume 1: Theory.* New York: Springer.

Pines M and Rafaelsen L (Eds.) (1984) *The Individual and the Group. Boundaries and Interrelations. Volume 2: Practice.* New York: Springer.

Pines M and Schermer V (Eds.) (1994) *Ring of Fire. Primitive Affects and Object Relations in Group Psychotherapy.* (Foreword by Otto Kernberg). London: Routledge.

Pinsonneault A and Kraemer KL (1993) Survey research methodology in management information systems. An assessment. *Journal of Management Information Systems.* 10(2): 75–105. https://doi.org/10.1080/07421222.1993.11518001.

Piper WE, Azim HF, Joyce AS and McCallum M (1991) Transference interpretations, therapeutic alliance, and outcome in short-term individual psychotherapy. *Archives of General Psychiatry.* 48(10): 946–953.

Piper WE, Debbane EG, Bienvenu J-P, de Carufel F and Garant J (1986) Relationships between the object focus of therapist interpretations and outcome in short-term individual psychotherapy. *British Journal of Medical Psychology.* 59(1): 1–11.

Piper WE, Ogrodniczuk JS, Joyce AS, McCallum M and Rosie JS (2002) Relationships among affect, work, and outcome in group therapy for patients with complicated grief. *American Journal of Psychotherapy.* 56(3): 347–361.

Pisani RA (1993) Neuroses and group culture in Southern Italy. The matrix of a 'real' large group. *Group Analysis.* 26(3): 239–250.

Pisani RA (2013) Large, small and median groups in group analysis. *Group Analysis*. 46(2): 132–143.

Pisani RA, Colangeli G, Giordani A and Popolla (2006) The median group: Training and supervision. *Group Analysis*. 39(4): 537–548.

Planck M (1900) *Zur Theorie des Gesetzes der Energieverteilung im normalen Spektrum. [On the Theory of the Law of Energy Distribution on the normal Spectrum].* Vertrag auf der Sitzung der Deutschen Physikalischen Gesellschaft 14 Dezember 1900. [Presented at a Meeting of the German Physical Society, 14th December]. *Newsletter of the Physical Society.* 17(2): 237–245.

Planck M (1958) *Physikalische Abhandlungen und Vorträge.* Braunschweig: Friedrich Wieweg & Sohn. [Physical Discussions and Lectures.]

Platt J, Holstein JA (2012) The history of the interview. In Gubrium JF, McKinney KD and Marvasti AB (Eds.) *The SAGE Handbook of Interview Research.* New York: Sage Publications, pp. 9–26.

Plus (2017) Physics in a minute: the double slit experiment. Plus, bringing mathematics to life project, University of Cambridge.5 February 2017. Available at: https://plus.maths.org/content/physics-minute-double-slit-experiment-0 (accessed 8 January 2025).

Plutchik R (1991) *The Emotions.* Lanham, MD: University Press of America.

Poincaré H (1902–8/2012) *The Foundation of Science. Science and Hypothesis. The Value of science. Science as Method.* New York: Science Press. Ebook, 2012. Available at: https://www.gutenberg.org/files/39713/39713-h/39713-h.htm (accessed 22 November 2014).

Poincaré H (2015) *The Foundation of Science. Science and Hypothesis. The Value of science. Science as Method.* New York: Arkose Press. https://www.hlevkin.com/hlevkin/90MathPhysBioBooks/Math/Poincare-ScienceAndMethod.pdf

Polkinghorne DE (1995) Narrative configuration in qualitative analysis. *International journal of qualitative studies in education.* 8(1): 5–23.

Polzin A (2015) Postkontrolle, Telefonüberwachung, Funkaufklarung. In Münkel D (Hrg.) *Staatssicherheit. Ein Lesebuch zur DDR Geheimpolizei. [*Control of Mail. Monitoring of Phones. Radio Reconnaissance. *In Munkel Editor. State Security. A Textbook on the Secret Service of the GDR]* Berlin: BPD, Der Stasi, pp. 104–112. https://www.bundesarchiv.de/publikationen/publikation/staatssicherheit/

Ponterotto J (2005) Qualitative research in counseling psychology. A primer on research paradigms and philosophy of science. *Journal of Counseling Psychology*. 52(2): 126–136.

Ponto J (2015) Understanding and evaluating survey research. *Journal of the Advanced Practitioner in Oncology.* 6(2): 168–171.

Poon JPH (2005) Quantitative methods: Not positively positivist. *Progress in Human Geography.* 29(6): 766–772.

Poppe G and Poppe N (2021) *Die Weggesperrten. Umerziehung in der DDR. Schicksale von Kindern und Jugendlichen. [The Locked-Up. Resocialization in the GDR. The Fate of Children and Teens.]* Berlin: Propyläen Verlag. https://www.amazon.de/Die-Weggesperrten-Umerziehung-Schicksale-Jugendlichen/dp/354910040X

Poppe G and Poppe N (2022) *Die Weggesperrten. Buchbesprechung in Berlin. [The Locked-up. Book Discussion in Berlin].* Available at: https://www.bundesstiftung-aufarbeitung.de/de/recherche/mediathek/die-weggesperrten-umerziehung-der-ddr-schicksale-von-kindern-und-jugendlichen (accessed 23 March 2023).

Popper K (1959) *The Logic of Scientific Discovery.* New York: Basic Books. [Original work published in 1935]. https://archive.org/details/logicofscientifi0000unse/page/50/mode/2up

Popper K (1962) *Conjectures and Refutations. The Growth of Scientific Knowledge.* New York: Basic Books.

Popper K (1972) *Objective Knowledge. An Evolutionary Approach.* Oxford: Clarendon Press.

Popper K (1983) *Realism and the Aim of Science.* Totowa,NJ: Rowman and Littlefield.

Popper K (1985) *Conjectures and Refutations. The Growth of Scientific Knowledge.* London: Routledge and Paul Kegan.

Porges SW (2001) The polyvagal theory. Phylogenetic substates of a social nervous system. *International Journal of Psychophysiology.* 42(2): 123–146.
Portelli A (2018) Living voices: the oral history interview as dialogue and experience. *The Oral History Review*. 45(2): 239–248.
Possati LM (2021) *The Algorithmic Unconscious. How Psychoanalysis Helps in Understanding AI.* New York: Routledge.
Potter E (1988) Modeling gender politics in science. *Hypatia.* 3(1): 19–33. https://www.jstor.org/stable/3810049
Potter E (2001) *Gender and Byle's Law of Gases.* Bloomington: Indiana University Press.
Potter E (2006) *Feminism and Philosophy of Science.* New York: Routledge.
Potter WJ and Levine-Donnerstein D (1999) Rethinking validity and reliability in content analysis. *Journal of Applied Community Research.* 27(3): 258–284.
Powell A (1982) Metaphor in group analysis. *Group Analysis.* 15(2): 127–134.
Powell A (1991) Matrix, mind, matter. From the internal to the eternal. *Group Analysis*. 24(3): 299–323.
Powell A (1993) The psychophysical matrix and group analysis. *Group Analysis.* 26(4): 449–468.
Power K (2017) On the primordial origins of group analysis and their relation to the creative nature of humanity. *Group Analysis*. 50(1): 91–103. https://doi.org/10.1177/0533316416685624.
Powers P (2007) The philosophical foundations of foucauldian discourse analysis. *Critical Approaches to Discourse Analysis across Disciplines*. 1(2): 18–34.
Pozzo R (2006) *Eco, Umberto (b. 1932).* Encyclopedia of Language & Linguistics. 2nd Edition, pp. 54–55. Available at: https://doi.org/10.1016/B0-08-044854-2/02548-7 (accessed 5 January 2025).
Pradhan RK (2018) Psychophysical interpretation and conscious observation in quantum field theory. *NeuroQuantology.* 16(9): 34–45. https://doi.org/10.14704/nq.2018.16.9.1258.
Praeg L (2009) An answer to the question: what is [ubuntu]? *South African Journal of Philosophy*. 27(4): 367–358. https://www.tandfonline.com/doi/abs/10.4314/sajpem.v27i4.31525
Praeg L and Magadla S (2014) (Eds.) *Curating the Archive.* Scottsville, KY: University of KwaZulu-Natal Press.
Prasad P (2005) *Crafting Qualitative Research: Working in the Postpositivist Traditions*. New York: Routledge.
Prashad V (2021) *Recovering East Germany's Social History.* Communist Party USA. Available at: Available at: https://www.cpusa.org/article/recovering-east-germanys-socialist-history/
Pretorius IM (2024) The value of direct child observation in a therapeutic parent-toddler group, for students of psychoanalysis. *Infant Observation*. 27(2): 102–116.
Preuβ K and Hofmann F (2019) Der Erfahrung Raum geben. Vorschläge zur Theoriebildung in der Kunstvermittlung und Museumspädagogik. [Giving space to Experience. Suggestions for Theory Development in teaching Art and Museum Pedagogy.]. *Kulturelle Bildung Online*. Available at: https://www.kubi-online/de/artikel/erfahrung-raum-geben-vorschlaege-zur-theoriebildung-kunstvermittlung-musumspaedagogik (accessed 3 September 2024).
Primas H (1998) Emergence in exact natural science. *Acta Polytechnica Scandinavica.* 91: 83–98. https://www.researchgate.net/publication/36443866_Emergence_in_exact_natural_science
Primas H (2003) Time-entanglement between mind and matter. *Mind and Matter*. 1: 81–119. https://www.researchgate.net/publication/233704344_Between_Mind_and_Matter
Primas H (2009) Complementarity of mind and matter. In Atmanspacher H and Primas H (Eds.) *Recasting Reality.* Berlin: Springer, pp. 171–209.
Principe LM (2011) *The Scientific Revolution. A Very Short Introduction.* Oxford: Oxford University Press.
Pross A (2016) *What is Life? How Chemistry Becomes Biology.* Oxford: Oxford University Press.
Pross A and Pascal R (2013) The origin of life: What we know, what we can know and what we will never know. *Open Biology*. 3(3): 120190. https://royalsocietypublishing.org/doi/epdf/10.1098/rsob.120190
Pule N (2024) Social dream drawing: a participatory action research methodology to study student leadership towards social justice. *Socio-Analysis.* 25: 17–37. https://search.informit.org/doi/10.3316/informit.T2024031600015290184877783

Pyle A and Danniels (2016) Using a picture book to gain assent in research with young children. *Early Child Development and Care.* 186(9): 1438–1452.

Quantum Physics Lady (2019) *Collapse of the wave function.* Encyclopedia of Quantum Physics and Consciousness. 10 March 2019. Available at: https://quantumphysicslady.org/glossary/collapse-of-the-wave-function/ (accessed 12 January 2025).

Quaye SJ (2007) Voice of the researcher. Extending the limits of what counts as research. *Journal of Research Practice.* 3(1): 1–14.

Quiroz JC, Geangu E and Yong MH (2018) Emotion recognition using smart watch sensor data. Mixed-design study. *JMIR Mental Health.* 5(3): e10153.

R Core Team (2017) R: A language and environment for statistical computing [Computer software manual]. Vienna, Austria. Available at: https://www.R-project.org/ (accessed 28 March 2025).

Rad D and Rad G (2023) Exploring the psychological implications of ChatGPT: A qualitative study. *Journal Plus Education.* 32(1): 43–55.

Rahman A (1993) *People's Self Development: Perspectives on Participatory Action Research. A Journey through Experience.* London: Zed Books.

Raile P (2024) The usefulness of ChatGPT for psychotherapists and patients. *Humanities and Social Sciences Communications.* 11: 47. Online. https://doi.org/10.1057/s41599-023-02567-0.

Ramarajan L (2014) Past, present and future research on multiple identities: Toward an intrapersonal network approach. *The Academy of Management Annals*. 8(1): 589–659.

Ramose MB (1999) *African philosophy through Ubuntu*. Harare: Mond Books.

Ramose MB (2001) An African perspective and justice and race. *Polylog: Forum for Intercultural Philosophy.* Available at: https://them.polylog.org/3/frm-en.htm [Please note that I could not locate this article in Polylog itself but only on the internet, when searching for it https://polylog.net/en/reading/show-all-issues].

Ramose MB (2002a) The philosophy of Ubuntu and ubuntu as a philosophy. In Coetzee PH and Roux APJ (Eds.) *Philosophy from Africa. A Text with Readings.* Cape Town: Oxford University Press, pp. 330–238.

Ramose MB (2002b) The Ethics of Ubuntu. In Coetzee PH and Roux APJ (Eds.) *Philosophy from Africa. A Text with Readings.* Cape Town: Oxford University Press, pp. 324–330.

Ramose MB (2003) I doubt, therefore African philosophy exists. *South African Journal of Philosophy.* 22(2): 113–127. https://doi.org/10.4314/sajpem.v22i2.31364.

Ramose MB (2009) Ecology through ubuntu. In Munyaradzi Felix Murove (Ed.) *African Ethics: An Anthology for Comparative and Applied Ethics.* Scottsville, South Africa: University of KwaZulu-Natal Press, pp. 69–77.

Ramose MB (2015) On the contested meaning of 'philosophy'. *South African Journal of Philosophy.* 34(4): 551–558.

Ramose MB (2016) Teacher and student with a critical pan-epistemic orientation: An ethical necessity for Africanising the educational curriculum in Africa. *South African Journal of Philosophy*. 35(4): 546–555.

Ramose MB (2017) *Ubuntu. Stroom van het bestaan als levensfilosofie*. [Ubuntu the Current of Existence as Philosophy of Life]. Utrecht: Ten Have.

Ramose MB and Mosupyoe B (2011) *The Development of Thought in Pan Africanism.* 2nd Edition. Dubuque, IA: Kendall Hunt Publishing Company.

Ramvi E, Gripsrud BH, Liveng A, Lading A, Froggett L, Manley J and Hollway W (2019) The visual matrix method in a study of death and dying: Methodological reflections. *Psychoanalysis, Culture & Society.* 24(1): 31–52. https://doi.org/10.1057/s41282-018-0095-y.

Rangell L (2004) *My Life in Theory.* New York: Other Press.

Rangell L (2017) An analysis of the course of psychoanalysis: The case for a unitary theory. *Psychoanalytic Psychology.* 23(2): 217–238.

Raphael-Leff J (2018) Configuring words. In Weegmann M (Ed.) *Psychodynamics of Writing.* New York: Routledge, pp. 105–120.

Rapley A (2020) Participant information – an ethics committee view. *Medical Writing.* 29(4): 30–31.

Rapley M (2012) Ethnomethodology/conversation analysis. In Harper D and Thompson AR (Eds.) *Qualitative Methods in Mental Health and Psychotherapy. A Guide for Students and Practitioners.* Chichester: John Wiley & Sons, pp. 177–192.

Rapoport A (1972) Explanatory power and explanatory appeal of theories. *Synthese.* 24: 321–324.

Rapoport RN (1960) *Community as Doctor.* London: Tavistock.

Ratnesar N and Mackenzie J (2007) The quantitative-qualitative distinction and the null hypothesis significance testing procedure. In Bridges D and Smith R (Eds.) *Philosophy, Methodology and Educational Research.* Oxford: Blackwell Publishing Ltd., pp. 107–115.

Rawlings CM, Smith JA, Moody J and McFarland DA (2023) *Network Analysis. Integrating Social Network Theory, Method, and Application with R.* New York: Cambridge University Press.

Reason P (2003) Pragmatist philosophy and action research: readings and conversation with Richard Rorty. *Action Research.* 1(1): 103–123.

Reason P (2005) Living as part of the whole. *Journal of Curriculum and Pedagogy.* 2(2): 35–41.

Reason P and Bradbury H (2008a) Introduction. In Reason P and Bradbury H (Eds.) *Handbook of Action Research. Participative Inquiry and Practice.* 2nd Edition. Thousand Oaks, CA: Sage, pp. 11–14.

Reason P and Bradbury H (2008b) Introduction to skills. In Reason P and Bradbury H (Eds.) *Handbook of Action Research. Participative Inquiry and Practice.* 2nd Edition. Thousand Oaks, CA: Sage, pp. 585–588.

Redman-MacLaren M and Mills J (2015) Transformational grounded theory. Theory, voice, and action. *International Journal of Qualitative Methods.* 14(3): 1–12.

Reed-Danahay DE (1997) *Auto/Ethnography: Rewriting the Self and the Social.* Oxford: Berg. https://www.researchgate.net/publication/249425519_AutoEthnography_Rewriting_the_Self_and_the_SocialAutoEthnography_Rewriting_the_Self_and_the_Social

Reeder J (1998) Hermeneutics and intersubjectivity. The interpreting dialogue. *International Forum of Psychoanalysis.* 7(2): 65–75.

Reeves A (2018) Dissemination of research. In Vossler A and Moller N (Eds.) *The Counselling and Psychotherapy Research Handbook.* London: Sage, pp. 227–289.

Reid C (2004) *The Wounds of Exclusion: Poverty, Women's Health, and Social Justice.* Edmonton: Qual Institute Press, International Institute for Qualitative Methodology.

Reid MD, Drummond P, Bowen W, Cavalcanti E, Lam PK, Bachor H, Anderssen UL and Leuchs G (2009) Colloquium: the Einstein-Podolsky-Rosen paradox: from concepts to applications. *Reviews of Modern Physics.* 81(4): 1727–1751. https://doi.org/10.1103/RevModPhys.81.1727.

Reischl J (2021) Triangulation von Dokumentarischer Methode und Tiefenhermeneutik. *Sozialer Sinn.* 22(2): 321–351. https://doi.org/10.1515/sosi-2021-0012.

Reischl J and Schmőlz A (2020) "Ich bin keine Pausenaufsicht, ich bin kein Retter … ich bin Lehrer." Eine dokumentarische Analyse zur Rolle von Lehrenden. ["I am not a break supervisor, I am no savior … I am a teacher". A documentary analysis of the role of educationalists.] *Medienimpulse.* 58(2): 1–40.

Reischl J and Schmőlz A (2020) "Ich bin keine Pausenaufsicht, ich bin kein Retter … ich bin Lehrer." Eine dokumentarische Analyse zue Rolle von Lehrenden. *Medienimpulse.* 58(2): 1–40.

Rennie DL (2006) The grounded theory method: Application of a variant of its procedure of constant comparative analysis to psychotherapy research In Fischer CT (Ed.) *Qualitative Research Methods for Psychologists.* Amsterdam: Academic Press, pp. 59–78.

Rennie DL, Phillips JR and Quartaro GR (1988) Grounded theory: A promising approach to conceptualization in psychology? *Canadian Psychology.* 29(2): 139–150.

Republished 1976, Emery FE and Thorsrud E. Leiden: Nijhoff.]

Rescheleit M and Krippendorf S (2002) *Der Weg ins Leben. DDR Strafvollzug im Jugendhaus Dessau.* [The way to Life. The GDR Penal system in the Youth House in Dessau.] Sachsen-Anhalt: Landesbeauftragte für die Unterlagen des Staatssicherheitsdienstes der ehemaligen DDR. [Saxony-Anhalt: State Representative for the Documents of the Security Services of the former GDR.]

Reser JP and Muncer S (2004) Sensemaking in the wake of September 11th: A network analysis of lay understandings. *British Journal of Psychology.* 95(3): 283–296.

Resneck JS (2024) Revisions to the declaration of Helsinki on its 60th anniversary. A modernized set of ethical principles to promote and ensue respect for participants in a rapidly innovative research ecosystem. *JAMA.* 333(1): 15–17. https://doi.org/10.1001/jama.2024.21902.

Rethlefsen ML and Page MJ (2021) PRISMA 2020 and PRISMA-S: Common questions on tracking records and the flow diagram. *Journal of the Medical Library Association.* 109(2): 174–200. https://doi.org/10.5195/jmla.2021.962.

Rethlefsen ML, Kirtley S, Waffenschmidt S, Ayala AP, Moher D, Page MJ, Koffel JB et al. (2021) PRISMA-S: An extension to the PRISMA statement for reporting literature searches in systematic reviews. *Systematic Reviews.* 10(1): 39. https://doi.org/10.1186/s13643-020-01542-z.

Reynolds CR (2010) Measurement and assessment. An editorial view. *Psychological Assessment.* 22(1): 1–4.

Reynolds J (2024) *Jacques Derrida (1930–2044).* Internet Encyclopedia of Philosophy. Available at: https://iep.utm.edu/jacques-derrida/ (accessed 15 December 2024).

Rezaii N, Walker E and Wolff P (2019) A machine learning approach to predicting psychosis using semantic density and latent content analysis. *Schizophrenia.* 5(9): 1–12. https://www.researchgate.net/publication/333753843_A_machine_learning_approach_to_predicting_psychosis_using_semantic_density_and_latent_content_analysis

Rice AK (1965) *Learning for Leadership. Interpersonal and Intergroup Relations.* New York: Routledge.

Rice AK (1969) Individual, group and inter-group processes. *Human Relations.* 22(6): 565–584. https://doi.org/10.1177/001872676902200606.

Richardson FC (2011) A hermeneutic perspective on dialogical psychology. *Culture & Psychology.* 17(4): 462–472. https://doi.org/10.1177/1354067X11418544.

Richardson R (2008) Reflections on reconciliation and ubuntu. In Nicolson R (Ed.) *Persons in Community: African Ethics in a Global Culture.* Scottsville, KY: University of KwaZulu-Natal Press, pp. 65–83.

Richter E (2000) Doping in der DDR. Nur die Medaillen zählten. [Doping in the GDR. Only the Medals Counted.] *Deutsches Ärzteblatt.* 97(30): 1598–1600.

Richter P, Werner J, Heerlein A, Kraus A and Sauer H (1998) On the validity of the beck depression inventory. A review. *Psychopathology.* 31(3): 160–168.

Ricoeur P (1981) *Hermeneutics and the Human Sciences: Essays on Language, Action, and Interpretation.* Ed. and Trans. JB Thompson. Cambridge: Cambridge University Press.

Ricoeur P (1991) The creativity of language. In Vales MJ (Ed.) *A Ricoeur Reader. Reflection and Imagination.* Toronto: University of Toronto Press, pp. 461–481.

Riedl D, Labek K, Gstrein I, Rothmund, MS, Sperner-Unterweger B and Kantner-Rumplmair W (2023) Large improvement of mental health during in outpatient short-term group psychotherapy treatment-a naturalistic pre-/post-observational study. *Neuropsychiatrie.* 37(2): 57–64. https://doi.org/10.1007/s40211-022-00449-6.

Riley D (2007) The paradox of positivism. *Social Science History.* 31(1): 115–126.

Ringrose J and Coleman R (2013) Looking and desiring machines. A feminist deleuzian mapping of bodies and affect. In Coleman R and Ringrose J (Eds.) *Deleuze and Research Methodologies.* Edinburgh: Edinburgh University Press, pp. 125–144.

Rioch MJ (1970) Group relations. Rationale and technique. *International Journal of Group Psychotherapy.* 20(3): 340–355.

Ritzer G (1975) Sociology. A multiple paradigm science. *The American Scientist.* 10(3): 156–167.

Ritzer G (1981) *Toward an Integrated Sociological Paradigm. The Search for an Exemplar and an Image of the Subject.* Boston, MA: Allyn & Bacon.

Riva G and Galimberti C (Eds.) (2001) *Towards Cyberpsychology. Mind, Cognition, and Society in the Internet Age*. Amsterdam: IOS Press.

Rivas C (2018) Writing a research report In Seale C (Ed.) (2018) *Researching Society and Culture.* 4th Edition. London: Sage Publications, pp. 534–565.

Robbins SB (1989) Validity of the superiority and goal instability scales as measures of defects in the self. *Journal of Personality Assessment.* 53(1): 122–132. https://doi.org/10.1207/s15327752jpa5301_13.

Robbins SB and Patton MJ (1985) Self-psychology and career development: Construction of the superiority and goal instability scales. *Journal of Counseling Psychology*. 32(2): 221–231. https://doi.org/10.1037/0022-0167.32.2.221.

Roberts SO, Barket-Shavit C, Dollins FA, Goldie PD and Mortenson E (2020) Racial inequality in psychological research. Trends of the past and recommendations for the future. *Perspectives on Psychological Science*. 15(6): 1295–1309.

Robinaugh DJ, Hoekstra RHA, Toner ER and Borsboom D (2020) The network approach to psychopathology: A review of the literature 2008–2018 and an agenda for future research. *Psychological Medicine*. 50(3): 353–366. https://doi.org/10.1017/S0033291719003404.

Robinson C and Seale C (2018) Research design. In Seale C (Ed.) *Researching Society and Culture*. 4th Edition. London: Sage Publications, pp. 101–121.

Roesler C (2018) *Research in Analytic Psychology. Empirical Research*. New York: Routledge, chapter 2.

Roesler C and Uffelen T (2018) Complexes and the unconscious. From the association experiment to recent fMRI studies. In Roesler C (Ed.) *Research in Analytic Psychology. Empirical Research*. New York: Routledge.

Rogers C (2013) Engaging with the median group. *Group Analysis*. 46(2): 183–195.

Rogers C (2017) Provocation in large groups: Reflective practice and organisational consultancy. In Thornton C (2017) (Ed.) *Group-Analytic Contexts*. Special Issue: Reflective Practice in Organisations. 75(1): 38–40. https://groupanalyticsociety.co.uk/contexts/

Rohr E (1993) In the church. Ethnopsychoanalytic research in Ecuador. *Group Analysis*. 26(3): 295–306.

Rohr E (2013) From conflict to recognition: Cultural transformation through group supervision in Guatemala. *Group Analysis*. 46(2): 272–285.

Rohr E (2016) Response to: 'Reshaping social identity: A qualitative report on experiences in an interracial median group' by Hilary Vice and Assie Gildenhuys. *Group Analysis*. 49(2): 183–187.

Rohr E (2019) Comments to Christoph's Seidler's 'East goes West. West goes East. Border border crossing and development'. *Group Analysis*. 52(2): 221–225. https://doi.org/10.1177/0533316419831150.

Rohr E and Cogoy R (2024) Women in group analysis. Group analytic training with Ilse Seglow: Experiences of the first training group of the Institute of Group Analysis, Heidelberg/Germany. *Group Analysis*. 57(1): 3–22. https://doi.org/10.1177/05333164231218146.

Roller MR and Lavrakas PJ (Eds.) (2015) *Applied Qualitative Research Design. A Total Quality Framework Approach*. London: Guilford Press.

Roos V (2008) The Mmogo-method TM. Discovering symbolic community interactions. *Journal of Psychology in Africa*. 18(4): 659–667.

Roos V (2016) Conducting the Mmogo-method. In Roos V (Ed.) *Understanding Relational and Group Experiences through the Mmogo-Method*. Cham: Springer, pp. 19–32.

Rorty R (1970) *The Linguistic Turn: Recent Essays in Philosophical Method*. Chicago: University of Chicago Press.

Rosa H (2013) *Social Acceleration: A New Theory of Modernity*. Columbia: Columbia University Press.

Rosa H (2016) *Resonanz. Eine Soziologie der Weltbeziehung. [Resonance, A Sociology of World Relations.]* Berlin: Surkamp.

Rosa H (2017) Gelingendes Leben in der Beschleunigungsgesellschaft. Resonante Weltbeziehungen als Schlűssel zur Űberwindung der Eskalationsdynamik der Moderne. [Successful Life in the Society of Acceleration. Resonant World Relations as the key to overcome the escalation dynamic of Modernity] In Kläden T and Schűßler M (Eds.) *Zu Schnell Fűr Gott? Theologische Kontroversen zu Beschleunigung und Resonanz. [Too fast for God? Theological Controversies about the Acceleration of Resonance.]* Freiburg: Herder, pp. 18–51.

Rosa H (2020) *The Uncontrollability of the World*. Oxford: Wiley.

Rosa H (2023) Resonance as a medio-passive, emancipatory and transformative power: a reply to my critics. *Journal of Chinese Sociology*. 10: 16. https://doi.org/10.1186/s40711-023-00195-4.

Rosa PJ (2023) Editorial for special issue psychophysiology and experimental psychology. *International Journal of Psychological Research*. 16(2): 1–3. https://doi.org/10.21500/20112084.6584.

Rose G (2001) *Visual Methodologies. An Introduction*. Thousand Oaks, CA: Sage.

Rosenberg MS (2005) The file-drawer problem revisited: A general weighted method for calculating fail-safe numbers in meta-analysis. *Evolution.* 59(2): 464–468.

Rosendahl J, Alldredge CT, Burlingame GM and Strauss B (2021) Recent developments in group psychotherapy research. *American Journal of Psychotherapy.* 74(2): 52–59. https://doi.org/10.1176/appi.psychotherapy.20200031.

Roseneil S (2019) Broader than psychoanalysis and deeper than sociology: the psychosocial promise of group analysis. *Psychoanalysis, Culture & Society.* 24(4): 493–501.

Rosenthal G (Ed.) (1998) *The Holocaust in Three Generations. Families of Victims and Perpetrators of the Nazi Regime.* London: Cassell. https://www.loc.gov/item/2021758529/; https://tile.loc.gov/storage-services/master/gdc/gdcebookspublic/20/21/75/85/29/2021758529/2021758529.pdf

Rosenthal R (1979) The file drawer problem and tolerance for null results. *Psychological Bulletin.* 86(3): 638–641. https://doi.org/10.1037/0033-2909.86.3.638.

Rost F (2020) Q-sort methodology: Bridging the divide between qualitative and quantitative. An introduction to an innovative method for psychotherapy research. *Counselling and Psychotherapy Research.* 21(1): 98–106. https://doi.org/10.1002/capr.12367.

Roth M (2023) The ethics of research with children on violence re-examined. In Roth M, Alfandari R and Crous G (Eds.) *Participatory Research on Child Maltreatment with Children and Adult Survivors.* Leeds: Emerald Publishing Ltd., pp. 65–81.

Rowan J (2006) The humanistic approach to action research. In Reason P and Bradbury H (Eds.) *Handbook of Action Research: Participative Inquiry and Practice.* Los Angeles, CA: Sage, pp. 114–123.

Rubinstein G (2005) From Logical Positivism to Scientific Realism. *Encyclopedia of Social Measurement,* pp. 409–416. Available at: https://www.sciencedirect.com/science/article/abs/pii/B0123693985005533 (accessed 19 July 2023).

Rush H (2023) The Logic of Human Intergroup Conflict. Knowns and Known Unknowns. https://doi.org/10.26481/umagsb.2023014.

Rustin M (1991) Psychoanalysis, racism and anti-racism. In *The Good Society and the Inner World.* London: Verso, pp. 57–84.

Rustin M (2019) *Researching the Unconscious. Principles of Psychoanalytic Method.* New York: Routledge.

Rutzou T and Steinmetz G (Eds.) (2018) *Critical Realism, History, and Philosophy in the Social Sciences.* New York: Emerald Publishing.

Rwelamila PD, Talukhaba AA and Ngowi AB (1999) Tracing the African project failure syndrome. The significance of 'ubuntu. *Engineering, Construction and Architectural Management.* 6(4): 335–346.

Ryan G (2018) Introduction to positivism, interpretivism and critical theory. *Nurse Researcher.* 25(4): 41–49.

Ryan M (2018) Explainer: how Romanticism rebelled against cold-hearted rationality. *The Conversation.* July 25. Available at: https://theconversation.com/explainer-how-romanticism-rebelled-against-cold-hearted-rationality-100242 (accessed 16 August 2023).

Ryle A and Lunghi ME (1969) The measurement of relevant change after psychotherapy: use of repertory grid testing. *British Journal of Psychiatry.* 115(528): 1297–1304. https://doi.org/10.1192/bjp.115.528.1297.

Ryu S (2020) The combination of critical discourse analysis and social network analysis. In Huber M and Froehlich D (Eds.) *Analyzing Group Interactions. A Guidebook for Qualitative, Quantitative and Mixed Methods.* New York: Routledge, pp. 96–106.

Sachse C, Knorr S and Baumgart B (2017) *Historische, rechtliche and psychologische Hintergründe des sexuallen Missbrauchs an Kindern und Jugendlichen in der DDR. [Historical, Legal, and Psychological Background of the Sexual Abuse of Children and Teenagers in the GDR].* Wiesbaden: Springer.

Sacks H (1995) *Lectures on Conversation. Volume I and II.* Ed. by Jefferson G. Introduction by Schegloff EA. Oxford: Blackwell Publishing.

Sade RM (2003) Publication of unethical research studies. The importance of informed consent. *Ethics in Cardiothoracic Surgery.* 75(2): 325–328.

Safran JD and Muran JC (1996) The resolution of ruptures in the therapeutic alliance. *Journal of Consulting and Clinical Psychology.* 64(3): 447–458.

Safran JD and Muran JC (2003) *Negotiating the Therapeutic Alliance: A Relational Treatment Guide.* New York: Guilford Press.

Safran JD and Muran JC (2006) Has the concept of the therapeutic alliance outlived its usefulness? *Psychotherapy, Theory, Research, Practice, Training.* 43(3): 286–291.

Safran JD, Muran JC and Shaker MA (2014) Research on therapeutic impasses and ruptures in the therapeutic alliance. *Contemporary Psychoanalysis.* 50(1–2): 211–232.

Safran JD, Muran JC, Samstag LW and Stevens C (2002a) Repairing alliance ruptures. *Psychotherapy.* 38(4): 406–412.

Safran JD, Muran JC, Samstag LW and Stevens C (2002b) Repairing alliance ruptures. In Norcross JC (Ed.) *Psychotherapy Relationships that Work.* New York: Oxford University Press, pp. 235–254.

Said SJ (2018) Knowing through being known: Reflections on indigenous epistemology and participatory consciousness. *Interventions International Journal of Postcolonial Studies.* 21(8): 1124–1138. https://www.researchgate.net/publication/329742160_Knowing_through_being_known_reflections_on_Indigenous_epistemology_and_participatory_consciousness

Sakthivel S (2021) *Sentiment Analysis. Sentiment Classification Adapting Multiple Domains.* Bangalore: Independently Published.

Salant P and Dillman DA (1994) *How to Conduct Your Own Survey.* New York: John Wiley and Sons.

Salgado J and Clegg JW (2011) Dialogism and the psyche: Bakhtin and contemporary psychology. *Culture & Psychology.* 17(4): 421–440. https://doi.org/10.1177/1354067X11418545.

Salmons J (2023) When you are the researcher and the participant with autoethnography. Sage Research Methods Community Blog. June 22, 2023. Available at: https://researchmethodscommunity.sagepub.com/blog/when-you-are-the-participant-collecting-autoethnographic-data (accessed 10 July 2023).

Salter-Townshend M, White A, Gollini I and Murphy TB (2012) Review of statistical network analysis: Models, algorithms, and software. *Statistical Analysis and Data Mining.* 5(4): 243–264.

Sandelowski M and Barroso J (2003) Creating metasummaries of qualitative findings. *Nursing Research.* 52(4): 226–233.

Sandelowski M and Barroso J (2007) *Handbook for Synthesizing Qualitative Research.* New York: Springer.

Sandelowski M, Docherty S and Emden C (1998) Qualitative metasythesis. Issues and Techniques. *Research in Nursing & Health.* 20(4): 365–371.

Sandner D (1995) Intendierte Dynamische Gruppenpsychotherapie und Gruppenanalyse – theoretische, behandlungstechnische und gesellschaftspolitische Aspekte. [Intentional Dynamic Group Psychotherapy and Group analysis – theoretical, treatment-technical and societal-political aspects.] In Benkenstein H, Kirchner R and Seidler C (Hrsg.) *Die Gruppe: eine verlorene Utopie? Gruppenpsychotherapie im Ost-West-Dialog. [The Group: A lost Utopia? Group psychotherapy in East-West Dialogue.]* Berlin: Pabst, Lengerich, pp. 71–80.

Sandner D (2018) Entwicklungslinien der Gruppenanalyse. *Gruppenpsychotherapie und Gruppendynamik. [Lines of development of Group analysis, Group psychotherapy and group dynamic.] Zeitschrift für Theorie und Praxis der Gruppenanalyse.* 54(1): 19–34.

Sanjuan T (2012) *Nishida Kitaro: the Philosopher, his thought, and its stakes.* GIS ASIE. European Alliance for Asian Studies. Available at: https://www.gis-reseau-asie.org/en/article/nishida-kitaro-philosopher-his-thought-and-its-stakes-0

Santos BDS (2014) *Epistemologies of the South: Justice Against Epistemicide.* New York: Routledge.

Sarkissian H (2018) Neo-confucianism, experimental philosophy and the trouble with intuitive methods. *British Journal for the History of Philosophy.* 26(5): 812–828.

Sattar R, Lawton R, Panagioti M and Johnson J (2021) Meta-ethnography in healthcare research: A guide to using a metaethnographic approach for literature synthesis. *BMC Health Services Research.* 21(50). https://doi.org/10.1186/s12913-020-06049-w.

Saturni S, Bellini F, Braido F, Paggiaro P, Sanduzzi A, Scichilone N, Santus PA, Morandi L and Papi A (2014) Randomized Controlled Trials and real life studies. Approaches and methodologies: a clinical point of view. *Pulmonary Pharmacology & Therapeutics.* 27(2): 129–138. https://doi.org/10.1016/j.pupt.2014.01.005.

Saunders B, Sim J, Kinestone T, Baker S, Waterfield J, Bartlam B, Burroughs H and Jinks C (2017) Saturation in qualitative research: Exploring its conceptualization and operationalize. *Quality & Quantity.* 52(4): 1893–1907.

Sayers J (1992) *Mothering Psychoanalysis Helen Deutsch, Karen Horney, Anna Freud, Melanie Klein.* London: Penguin Books.

Scally D (2016) Germany bids tearless farewell as Margot Honecker dies in exile. *The Irish Times*. 8 May. Available at: https://www.irishtimes.com/news/world/europe/germany-bids-tearless-farewell-as-margot-honecker-dies-in-exile-1.2640008 (accessed 11 March 2023).

Scanlon C (2015) On the perversity of an imagined psychological solution to very real social problems of unemployment (Work-lessness) and social exclusion (Worth-lessness): A group analytic critique. *Group Analysis.* 48(1): 31–44.

Scanlon C and Adlam J (2008) Refusal, social exclusion and the cycle of rejection: A cynical analysis? *Critical Social Policy.* 28(4): 529–549.

Scanlon C and Adlam J (2009) "Why do you treat me this way?": Reciprocal violence and the mythology of 'deliberate self-harm'. In Motz A (Ed.) *Managing Self-Harm: Psychological Perspectives*. London: Taylor and Francis, pp. 55–81.

Scanlon C and Adlam J (2011) 'Defacing the currency?': A group-analytic appreciation of homelessness, dangerousness, disorder and other inarticulate speech of the heart. *Group Analysis*. 44(2): 131–148.

Schaeffer NC (1991) Conversation with a purpose or conversation? Interaction in the standardized interview. In Biemer PP, Groves RM, Lyberg LE, Mathiowetz NA, Sudman S (Eds.) (2004) *Measurement Errors in Surveys. (Wiley Series in Probability and Statistics).* New York: Wiley, chapter 19, pp. 365–391. https://doi.org/10.10002/9781118150382.ch19.

Scharf JS (2013) *Psychoanalysis Online.* London: Karnac.

Scheidlinger S (1952) *Psychoanalysis and Group Behavior.* New York: Norton.

Schermer VL (1985) Beyond bion. The basic assumption states revisited. In Pines M (Ed.) (1992) *Bion and Group Psychotherapy.* London: Tavistock/Routledge, pp. 139–156.

Schermer VL (2011) Interpreting psychoanalytic interpretation. A fourfold perspective. *The Psychoanalytic Review.* 98(6): 817–842.

Schermer VL (2012) Group-as-a-whole and complexity theories: Areas of convergence. Part I: Background and literature review. *Group Analysis.* 45(3): 275–288. https://doi.org/10.1177/0533316412453701.

Schermer VL (2018) Four modalities of the experience of others in groups. *Group Analysis.* 51(2): 175–196.

Schermer VL and Pines M (Eds.) (1999) *Group Psychotherapy of the Psychoses. Concepts, Interventions and Contexts. International Library of Group Analysis* 2. London: Jessica Kingsley Publishers.

Schermer VL and Rice CA (2015) Towards an integrative intersubjective and relational group psychotherapy. In Kleinberg JL (Ed.) *The Wiley Blackwell Handbook of Group Psychotherapy.* Oxford: Wiley Blackwell, pp. 59–87.

Schick H (2013) From social alienation to mental health through koinonia via the median group. *Group Analysis.* 46(2): 171–177.

Schieffelin B, Woolard K and Kroskity P (1998) *Language Ideologies. Practice and Theory.* New York: Oxford University Press.

Schiermer B (2017) Acceleration and resonance. An interview with Hartmut Rosa. E-special four generations of critical theory in acta sociologica. *Acta Sociologica.* 47(4): 374–382.

Schindler W (1981) Some reflections on the informative element in the "working though" of analytical group therapy. *Group Analysis.* 14(3): 183–192.

Schlamm L (2014) Individuation. In Leeming DA (Eds.) *Encyclopedia of Psychology and Religion.* Boston, MA: Springer, pp. 866–870. https://doi.org/10/1007/987-1-4614-6086-2_329.

Schlapobersky JR (2016) *From the Couch to the Circle. Group-Analytic Psychotherapy in Practice.* London: Routledge.

Schlütter J (2016) Der Skandal wird Kleiner. Medikamententests in der DDR. 15 March. [Testing Medications in the GDR.] *Zeit Online.* Available at: https://www.zeit.de/wirtschaft/2013-05/medikamenten-tests-ddr (accessed 19 April 2023).

Schmittmann VD, Cramer AOJ, Waldorp LJ, Epskamp S, Kievit RA and Borsboom D (2013) Deconstructing the construct: A network perspective on psychological phenomena. *New Ideas in Psychology.* 31: 43–53. https://doi.org/10.1016/j.newideapsych.2011.02.007.

Schneider S (2003) The Mystical and the Spiritual in the Large Group. In Schneider S and Weinberg H (Eds.) *The Large Group Re-Visited.* London: Jessica Kingsley Publishers, pp. 163–185.

Schober P and Vetter TR (2020) Nonparametric statistical methods in medical research. *Anesthesia & Analgesia.* 131(6): 1862–1863. https://doi.org/10.1213/ANE.0000000000005101.

Schőllberger R (2009) Group analysis and the concept of mind. *Group Analysis.* 42(3): 290–294.

Schőllberger R (2013) Welcome. *Group Analysis.* 46(2): 116–119.

Schön DA (1983) *The Reflective Practitioner: How Professionals Think in Action.* London: Temple Smith.

Schore AN (2003) *Affect Dysregulation and Disorders of the Self.* New York: W.W. Norton & Company.

Schore AN (2009) Right-brain affect regulation. An essential mechanism of development, trauma, dissociation, and psychotherapy. In Fosha D, Siegel D and Solomon M (Eds.) *The Healing Power of Emotion. Affective Neuroscience, Development and Clinical Practice.* New York: W.W. Norton & Company, pp. 112–144.

Schore AN (2019) *The Development of the Unconscious Mind.* New York: W.W. Norton & Company.

Schrődinger (1926) An undulatory theory of the mechanics of atoms and molecules. *Physical Review.* 28(6): 1049–1070. Available in the Archives: https://journals.aps.org/pr/abstract/10.1103/PhysRev.28.1049

Schrődinger E (1944) *What is Life? The Physical Aspect of the Living Cell.* Cambridge: Cambridge University Press. https://archive.org/details/whatislifephysic0000schr

Schrődinger E (2020) *Collected Papers on Wave Mechanics. With an Introduction by Valia Allori.* Montreal, Quebec: Minkowski Institute Press.

Schröter O (2004) Erinnerungen an das Gefängnis in Dessau. Das Grab meiner Jugend. [Memories of Dessau Prison. The Grave of my Youth.] *Mitteldeutsche Zeitung.* 2 December. Available at: https://www.mz.de/lokal/dessau-rosslau/erinnerungen-an-dessauer-knast-das-grab-meiner-jugend-2950017 (accessed 7 April 2023).

Schudel M (2016) Margot Hocker, unrepentant widow of East Germany's leader, dies at 89. *Washington Post.* 7 May. Available at: https://www.washingtonpost.com/world/margot-honecker-unrepentant-widow-of-east-germanys-last-leader-dies-at-89/2016/05/07/1cc1cc08-13de-11e6-8967-7ac733c56f12_story.html (accessed 11 March 2023).

Schulhoff S (2025) LLM Limitations: When Models and Chatbots Make Mistakes. 6 March. Available at: https://learnprompting.org/docs/basics/pitfalls (accessed 13 March 2025).

Schulte CM (2018) Deleuze, concept formation, and the habit of shorthand inquiry. *Qualitative Inquiry.* 24(3): 194–202.

Schultz-Venrath U (2024) *Mentalizing the Body. Integrating Body and Mind in Psychotherapy.* New York: Routledge.

Schultz-Venrath U and Dőring P (2009) Hat die Ausbildung in Gruppenanalyse und analytischer Gruppenpsychotherapie eine Zukunft? [Does Training in Group Analysis and analytic Group Psychotherapy has a future?] *Gruppenpsychotherapie und Gruppendynamik. (Zeitschrift für Theorie und Praxis der Gruppenanalyse.)* 45(2): 139–163.

Schumann S (1997) *Vernichten oder Offenlegen? Zur Entstehung des Stasi-Unterlagen-Gesetzes. Eine Dokumentation der öffentlichen Debatte 1990/1991. [Destroy or Reveal? About the Emergence of the Stasi Documents Law. A Documentation of a public Debate.1990/1991.]* https://www.bundesarchiv.de/publikationen/publikation/vernichten-oder-offenlegen-zur-entstehung-des-stasi-unterlagen-gesetzes/

Schüssler G (2002) The current conception of the unconscious - empirical results of neurobiology, cognitive sciences, social psychology and emotion research. *Zeitschrift für Psychosomatische Medizin und Psychotherapie.* 48(2): 192–214. PMID: 11992328.

Schűtz A (1972) *The Phenomenology of the Social World.* London: Heinemann Publishers.

Schwartz S (2006) A theory of cultural value orientations: Explication and applications. *Comparative Sociology.* 5(2–3): 137–182.

Schwartze D, Barkowski S, Strauss B, Knaevelsrud C and Rosendahl J (2019) Efficacy of group psychotherapy for posttraumatic stress disorder: Systematic review and meta-analysis of randomized controlled trials. *Psychotherapy Research.* 29(4): 415–431.

Scientia (2019) Professor Wolf Singer. The Coordination of Neuronal Communication. 16 May 2019. Available at: https://www.scientia.global/professor-wolf-singer-the-coordination-of-neuronal-communication/ (accessed 5 November 2024).

Scotford Archer M and Vaughan M (1971) Domination and assertion in educational systems. In Hopper E (Ed.) *Readings in the Theory of Educational Systems*. London: Hutchinson University Press, pp. 56–70.

Scott D (2005) Critical realism and empirical research methods in education. *Journal of the Philosophy of Education.* 39(4): 633–646.

Scott J and Marshall G (2015) *neo-positivism*. Quick Reference, from: *Oxford Dictionary of Sociology.* 4th Edition. Oxford: Oxford University Press. Available at: https://www.oxfordreference.com/display/10.1093/acref/9780199533008.001.0001/acref-9780199533008-e-1541

Seale C (2018a) Grounded theory. In Seale C (Ed.) *Researching Society and Culture.* 4th Edition. Thousand Oaks, CA: Sage Publications, pp. 275–284.

Seale C (Ed.) (2018b) *Researching Society and Culture.* 4th Edition. Thousand Oaks, CA: Sage Publications.

Seale C, Gobo G, Gubrium JF and Silverman D (2004) Introduction: Inside qualitative research. In Seale C, Gobo G and Gubrium JF and Silverman D (Eds.) *Qualitative Research Practice.* London: Sage, pp. 1–11.

Searle J (1995) *The Construction of Social Reality*. New York: The Free Press.

Segawa TF (2017) Book review: From chemistry to consciousness. A legacy to Hans Primas *Journal of Consciousness Studies*. 24(3–4): 216–223.

Seidler C (2015) War corrupts empathy, guilt and shame. Considerations to Robi Friedman's are soldiers sick? *Group Analysis.* 48(3): 258–264.

Seidler C (2019) East goes West. West goes East. Border crossing and development. *Group Analysis.* 52(2): 172–189.

Sekuler R (1996) Motion perception. A modern view of Wertheimer's 1912 monograph. *Perception.* 25(10): 1243–1258.

Seth S (2009) Putting knowledge in its place: science, colonialism, and the postcolonial. *Postcolonial Studies*. 12(4): 373–388. https://doi.org/10.1080/13688790903350633.

Settles IH, Sellers RM and Alphonse D (2002) One role or two? The function of psychological separation in role conflict. *The Journal of Applied Psychology*. 87(3): 574–582.

Settles LH (2004) When multiple identities interfere: The role of identity centrality. *Personality and Social Psychology Bulletin.* 30(4): 487–500. https://doi.org/10.1177/0146167203261885.

Shajahan NS (2022) Crafting non-western ways for writing. 21 February. Available at: https://criticalinternationalization.net/2022/02/21/crafting-non-western-ways-for-writing (accessed 5 December 2023).

Shaked J (1995) Interplay between the Large Group and the Small Groups in Group Analytic Training. In Peternel F (Ed.) *Median and Large groups in Group Analytic Training. Proceedings of E.G.A.T.I.N.* Study days, Ljubljana. https://www.egatin.net/study-days/about-study-days

Shaked J (2003) The large group and political process. In Schneider S and Weinberg H (Eds.) *The Large Group Re-Visited. The Herd, Primal Horde, Crowds and Masses.* International Library of Group Analysis 25. London: Jessica Kingsley Publishers, pp. 150–161.

Shapiro DA and Barkham M (1993) *Relate. Information Needs Research. Report to the Department of Social Security.* London: HMSO.

Shapiro DA, Caplan HL, Rohde PD and Watson JP (1975) Personal questionnaire changes and their correlates in a psychotherapeutic group. *The British Journal of Medical Psychology*. 48(3): 207–215. https://doi.org/10.1111/j.2044-8341.1975.tb02324.x.

Sharma AC (2022) *A Textbook on Modern Quantum Mechanics*. Boca Raton, FL: CRC Press.

Shay J (2021) Terrified of group therapy: Investigating obstacles to entering or leading groups. *American Journal of Psychotherapy*. 74(2): 71–75.

Shear J (Ed.) (1999) *Explaining Consciousness. The Hard Problem.* Cambridge: MIT Press.

Shearing H (2020) *Seven female scientists you may not have heard of- but should know about.* BBC News. 6th February. Available at: https://www.bbc.com/news/uk-51399835 (accessed 29 December 2024).

Shechtman Z (2007) Group Counselling and Psychotherapy with Children and Adolescents. *Theory, Research and Practice.* New York: Routledge.

Shen H, Gao L and Cope TA (2006) The *I Ching's* psychology of heart, and Jungian analysis. *Psychological Perspectives.* 49(1): 61–78.

Sher M (2012) *In the Idiom of Tavistock Practice Approaches to Public Sector Psychotherapy.* Group Relations Organisational Development & Change and Board Evaluation. Thesis, University of East London in Collaboration with the Tavistock and Portman NHS Foundation Trust. https://repository.uel.ac.uk/item/85z7z

Shetterly ML (2017) *Hidden Figures: The History of Nasa's Black Female Scientists.* Glasgow: HarperCollins Publishers.

Shevrin H, Ghannam JH and Libet B (2002) A neural correlate of consciousness related to repression. *Conscious Cognition.* 11(2): 334–346. https://doi.org/10.1006/ccog.2002.0553.

Shingler J (2011) Rocking the Wall. East German Rock and Pop in the 1970s and 1980s. *The View East.* WordPress. Available at: https://thevieweast.wordpress.com/2011/07/15/rocking-the-wall-east-german-rock-and-pop-in-the-1970s-and-1980s/ (accessed 6 February 2020).

Shopes L (2011) Oral history. In Denzin NK and Lincoln YS (Eds.) *The Sage Handbook of Qualitative Research.* 4th Edition. Thousand Oaks, CA: Sage, pp. 451–465.

Shotter J and Gustavsen B (1999) *The Role of Dialogue Conferences in the Development of Learning Regions: Doing from within Our Lives Together What We Cannot Do Apart.* Stockholm: Swedish Centre for Advanced Studies in Leadership, Stockholm School of Economics. Cited in Olin A, Almqvist J and Hamza K (2021) To recognize oneself and others in teacher-researcher collaboration. *Educational Action Research.* 31(2): 248–264, p. 254. https://doi.org/10.1080/09650792.2021.1897949.

Shreffler J and Huecker MR (2025) Diagnostic testing accuracy: sensitivity, specificity, predictive values and likelihood ratios. In StatPearls. StatPearls Publishing, Treasure Island (FL). PMID: 32491423. [online book]

Shu FH (2024) Cosmology. Astronomy. *Encyclopedia Britannica.* 16 December 2024. Available at: https://www.britannica.com/science/cosmology-astronomy (accessed 7 January 2025).

Shukla V (2023) *Research in the Age of AI: Ultimate Guide to Using AI Tools.* San Francisco, CA: Vishal Shukla Publishers.

Shumeli G (2010) To explain or to predict? *Statistical Science.* 25(3): 289–310. https://papers.ssrn.com/sol3/papers.cfm?abstract_id=1351252.

Shun K-I (1997) *Menicus and Early Chinese Thought.* Stanford: Stanford University Press.

Shuttleworth M (2009) *Who invented the scientific method?* Explorable, Think outside the Box. Available at: https://explorable.com/who-invented-the-scientific-method (accessed 24 November 2024).

Si L (Ed.) (2017) *Yangming Theory of Mind. The Wisdom of the Integrative Knowing and Doing.* Beijing: Overseas Publication House.

Siddaway AP, Wood AM and Hedges LV (2019) How to do a systematic review: A best practice guide for conducting and reporting narrative reviews, meta-analyses, and meta-syntheses. *Annual Review of Psychology.* 7: 747–770. https://doi.org/10.1146/annurev-psych-010418-102803.

Siegel DJ (2010) *Mindsight. The New Science of Personal Transformation.* New York: Random House.

Siegel DJ, Sammons M and Dahl H (2002) FRAMES. The method in action and the assessment of its reliability. *Psychotherapy Research.* 12(1): 59–77. https://doi.org/10.1080/713869617.

Sievers B (2007) Pictures from below of the Surface of the University. The Photo-Matrix as a method for understanding organizations in depth. In Reynolds M and Vince R (Eds.) *Handbook of Experiential Learning and Management Education.* Oxford: Oxford University Press, pp. 241–257.

Sievers B (2008) Perhaps it is the role of pictures to get in contact with the uncanny. The social photo-matrix as a method to promote the understanding of the unconscious in organizations. *Organisational and Social Dynamics.* 8(2): 234–254.

Sievers B (2013) Thinking organisations through photographs. The social photo-matrix as a method for understanding organisations in depth. In Long S (Ed.) *Socioanalytic Methods. Discovering the Hidden in Organisations and Social Systems.* London: Karnac, pp. 129–151.

Sigler D (2020) Lacan's Romanticism. In Rabate J-M (Ed.) *Knots. Post-Lacanian Psychoanalysis, Literature and Film.* New York: Routledge, pp. 55–69.

Sigurðsson G and D'Ambrosio PJ (2023) Ritualized world relations: a Confucian critique of Rosa's limitations on resonance. *Journal of Chinese Sociology.* 10: 4. https://doi.org/10.1186/s40711-023-00184-7.
Sil A, Betkerur J and Das NK (2019) *P*-Value demystified. *Indian Dermatology.* 10(6): 745–750. https://doi.org/10.4103/idoj.IDOJ_368_19.
Silverberg LM (2020) Fragments of energy, not waves or particles, may be the building blocks of the universe. *The Conversation.* 9 December 2020. Available at: https://theconversation.com/fragments-of-energy-not-waves-or-particles-may-be-the-fundamental-building-blocks-of-the-universe/150730 (accessed 4 January 2025).
Silverman D (1998) Analysing conversation. In Seale E (Ed.) *Researching Society and Culture*. Thousand Oaks, CA: Sage, pp. 261–274.
Silverman D (2000) Analyzing talk and text. In Denzin NK and Lincoln YS (Eds.) (2000) *Handbook of Qualitative Research.* 2nd Edition. Thousand Oaks, CA: Sage, pp. 821–834.
Silverman K (1983) *The Subject of Semiotics.* Oxford: Oxford University Press.
Silverstein M (1998) The improvisional performance of culture in realtime discursive practice. In Swayer RK (Ed.) *Creativity in Performance.* Greenwich, CT: Ablex Publishing, pp. 265–311.
Silverstein M (2004) Cultural contexts and the language-culture nexus. *Current Anthropology.* 45(5): 621–652.
Silverstein M and Urban G (1996) *National Histories of Discourse.* Chicago: University of Chicago Press.
Sim J and Mengshoel M (2023) Metasynthesis. Issues of empirical and theoretical context. *Quality & Quantity*. 57(4): 3339–3361.
Simkus J (2023) Confounding variables in psychology. Definition & example. *Simply Psychology.* 31 July. Available at: https://www.simplypsychology.org/confounding-variable.html (accessed 8 May 2024).
Simmel G (1896) Superiority and subordination as subject-matter of sociology. *American Journal of Sociology.* 2(2): 167–189. https://www.jstor.org/stable/2761662
Simmel G (1923) The relative and the absolute in the problem of the sexes. In Oakes G (Ed.) (1984) *George Simmel on Women Sexuality and Love. Trans. and with Introduction.* New Haven, CT: Yale University Press, pp. 102–132.
Simmonds H and Gazley A (2018) Marketing systems: Critical realist interventions towards better theorizing. *Journal of Critical Realism.* 17(2). https://doi.org/10.1080/14767430.2018.1454684.
Simon MK and Francis JB (1998) *The Dissertation Cookbook: A Practical Guide to Start and Complete Your Dissertation.* 2nd Edition. Dubuque, IA: Kendall/Hunt.
Simons DJ (2014) The value of direct replication. *Perspectives on Psychological Science.* 9(1): 76–80.
Singer (2018) Neuronal oscillations: Unavoidable and useful? *European Journal of Neuroscience.* 48(7): 2389–2398. https://doi.org/10.1111/ejn.13796.
Singer W (2019) A naturalistic approach to the hard problem of consciousness. *Frontiers in Systems Neuroscience.* 13: 58. https://doi.org/10.3389/fnsys.2019.00058.
Singh K (2007) *Quantitative Social Research Methods.* New York: Sage Publications.
Single PB (2009) *Demystifying Dissertation Writing. A Streamlined Process from Choice of Topic to Final Text.* Sterling, Virgina: Stylus Publications LLC.
Sinha P, Calfee C and Delucchi K (2021) Practitioner's guide to latent class analysis. methodological considerations and common pitfalls. *Critical Care Medicine.* 49(1): 63–79.
Sjőberg B (1993) Prediction of valency and productivity. An empirical study of long-term group psychotherapy. *Scandinavian Journal of Psychotherapy.* 34(2): 161–173. https://doi.org/10.1111/j.1467-9450.1993.tb01111.x.
Skaife S and Martyn J (Eds.) (2022) *Art Psychotherapy Groups in The Hostile Environment of Neoliberalism: Collusion or Resistance?* New York: Routledge.
Skogstad W (2018) Psychoanalytic observation. The mind as research instrument. In Stamenova K and Hinshelwood RD (Eds.) *Methods of Research into the Unconscious. Applying Psychoanalytic Ideas to Social Science.* London and New York: Routledge, pp. 107–125.
Slavson SR (1950) Transference phenomena in group psychotherapy. *Psychoanalytic Review.* 37: 39–55.
Smaldino PE (2020) Tutorial. How to translate a verbal theory into a formal model. *Social Psychology.* 51(4): 207–218.

Small JF and Birnbaum M (1971) The structure group interview. *Training and Development Journal.* 25(9): 26–32.
Smith A (1776/2005) *An Inquiry Into The Nature and Causes of The Wealth of Nations.* An Electronic Classics Series Publication. Available at: https://www.gutenberg.org/ebooks/3300 (accessed 19 May 2024).
Smith A (2007) Children and young people's participation rights in education. *The International Journal of Children's Rights.* 15(1): 147–164.
Smith B (2016) Narrative analysis. In Lyons E and Coyle A (Eds.) *Analysing Qualitative Data in Psychology.* Thousand Oakes, CA: Sage, p. 202–221.
Smith D (1971) Power, ideology and the transmission of knowledge. An explorative essay. In Hopper E (Ed.) *Readings in the Theory of Educational Systems*. London: Hutchinson University Press, pp. 240–261.
Smith DE (1987) *The Everyday World as Problematic. A Feminist Sociology.* Toronto: University of Toronto Press.
Smith DE (1990) *The Conceptual Practices of Power. A Feminist Sociology of Knowledge*. Toronto: University of Toronto Press.
Smith DE (1996) The relations of ruling. A feminist inquiry. *Studies in Cultural Organization and Society.* 2: 171–190. https://doi.org/10.1080/10245289608523475.
Smith DE (1999) *Writing the Social. Critique, Theory, and Investigations*. Toronto: University of Toronto Press. https://www.degruyterbrill.com/document/doi/10.3138/9781442683747/html
Smith DE (2003) Making sense of what people do. A sociological perspective. *Journal of Occupational Science.* 10(1): 61–64. https://doi.org/10.1080/14427591.2003.9686512.
Smith DE (2005) *Institutional Ethnography. A Sociology for People.* Lanham, MD: Alta Mira Press.
Smith DE (2006) Introduction. In Smith DE (Ed.) *Institutional Ethnography as Practice*. Lanham, MD: Rowman and Littlefield, pp. 1–11.
Smith DE (2007) Making change from below. *Journal of the Society for Socialist Studies.* 3(2): 7–30. https://socialiststudies.com/index.php/sss/article/view/23779/17664
Smith H (1991) *The World's Religions. The Revised & Updated Edition of The Religions of Man.* New York: HarperCollins Publishers.
Smith JA (1996) Beyond the divide between cognition and discourse: Using interpretative phenomenological analysis in health psychology. *Psychology and Health.* 11(2): 261–271. https://doi.org/10.1080/08870449608400256.
Smith JA, Flowers P and Larkin M (2022) *Interpretative Phenomenological Analysis. Theory, Method and Research.* 2nd Edition. London: Sage.
Smith L (1999) *Decolonizing Methodologies. Research and Indigenous People.* London: Zed Books.
Smolensky P (1987) Connectionist AI, symbolic AI, and the brain. *Artificial Intelligence Review.* 1: 95–109. https://link.springer.com/article/10.1007/BF00130011
Snell R (2024) *Antonio Ferro. A Contemporary Introduction.* New York: Routledge.
Snijders TA (2001) The statistical evaluation of social network dynamics. *Sociological Methodology.* 31(1): 361–395. https://doi.org/10.1111/0081-1750.00099.
Snow KC, Hays DG, Caliwagan G, Ford DJ, Mariotti D, Mwendwa JM and Scott WE (2016) Guiding principles for indigenous research practices. *Action Research* 14(4): 357–375. https://doi.org/10.1177/1476750315622542.
Snyder H (2019) Literature review as a research methodology: An overview and guidelines. *Journal of Business Research.* 104: 333–339. https://doi.org/10.1016/j.jbusres.2019.07.039.
Snyder H (2023) Designing the literature review for a strong contribution. *Journal of Decision Systems.* 33(4): 551–558. https://doi.org/10.1080/12460125.2023.2197704.
Solms M and Turnbull O (2002) *The Brain and the Inner World.* London: Karnac Books.
Solms ML (2018) The neurobiological underpinnings of psychoanalytic theory and therapy. *Frontiers in Behavioral Neuroscience.* 12: 294. https://doi.org/10.3389/fnbeh.2018.00294.
Sommer BW and Quinlan MK (2024) *The Oral History Manual.* 2nd Edition. Plymouth: Rowman & Littlefield.

Sommers R and Miller FG (2013) Forging debriefing in deceptive research. Is it ever ethical? *Ethics & Behavior.* 23(2): 98–116.
Sonesson G (2013) The natural history of branching. Approaches to the phenomenology of sirstness, secondness, and thirdness. *Signs & Society.* 1(2): 297–325.
Song D (2020) Subjective Universe: Interweaving Matter and Mind through Cyclical Time. Peking: D Song. https://www.amazon.co.uk/Subjective-Universe-Interweaving-through-Cyclical/dp/1735317098
Song D (2021) Does observation create reality? *NeuroQuantology.* 19(1): 11–15. https://doi.org/10.14704/nq.2021.19.1.NQ21002; https://www.neuroquantology.com/open-access/Does+Observation+Create+Reality%253F_5890/
Sorrell S (2018) Explaining sociotechnical transitions. A critical realist perspective. *Research Policy.* 47(7): 1267–1282.
Spence S (2019) The birth of AI Nationalism. *New Statesman.* Available at: https://www.newstatesman.com/science-tech/2019/04/the-birth-of-ai-nationalism-2 (accessed 24 December 2024).
Spiegelhalter DJ, Best NG, Carlin BP and Van Der Linde A (2002) Bayesian measures of model complexity and fit. *Journal of the Royal Statistical Society. Series B.* 64(4): 583–639.
Spiegelhalter DJ, Myles JP, Jones DR and Abrams KR (2000) Bayesian methods in health technology assessment. A review. *Health Technology Assessment.* 4(38): 1–130.
Spinoza B (1677/2002) Ethics. In ML Morgan (Ed.) *Spinoza. Complete Works.* Trans. S Shirley. Cambridge, IN: Hackett Publishing.
Spinoza B (2001) *Ethics.* Trans. WH White and AK Stirling. Introduction by Don Garrrett. Ware: Wordsworth Edition.
Spiro M, Becker L and Beech T (2013) Small and large groups as containers for transformation in a group analytic training programme: Cape town, South Africa. *Group Analysis.* 46(3): 286–298.
Spivak GC (1993) *Outside in the Teaching Machine.* New York: Routledge.
Sporn M (2019) *Die großen Mythen der DDR. Wahrheit und Legenden. [The great myths of the GDR. Truth and Legends.]* ZDF 6 October. Available at: https://www.fernsehserien.de/filme/die-grossen-mythen-der-ddr (accessed 13 April 2023) https://www.youtube.com/watch?v=IXjUFRX-bxs
Spotnitz H (1967) *Psychotherapy of Preoedipal Disorders.* New York: Jason Aronson.
Spurling L (2015) *The Psychoanalytic Craft.* London: Palgrave.
Spurling L (2019) Clinical writing and the analyst's subjectivity. In Weegmann M (Ed.) *Psychodynamics of Writing.* New York: Routledge, pp. 61–73.
Srinath U, Kumar SK and Shakti Vidyalaya A (2011) Supervision and training of psychotherapists in an indian therapeutic community. *European Journal for Qualitative Research in Psychotherapy.* 5: 71–82. https://openjournals.ljmu.ac.uk/ejqrp/article/view/2885/1384
St Pierre EA (2011) Post qualitative research. The critique and the coming after. In Denzin NK and Lincoln YS (Eds.) *The Sage Handbook of Qualitative Research.* 4th Edition. Thousand Oaks, CA: Sage, pp. 611–626.
St Pierre EA (2014) A brief and personal history of qualitative research. *Journal of Curriculum Theorizing.* 30(2): 1–18.
St Pierre EA (2017) Post qualitative inquiry, the refusal of method, and the risk of the new. *Qualitative Inquiry.* 27(1): 3–9.
St Pierre EA (2017) Writing post qualitative inquiry. *Qualitative Inquiry.* 24(9): 603–608.
St Pierre EA (2021a) Why post qualitative inquiry? *Qualitative Inquiry.* 27(2): 163–166.
St Pierre EA (2021b) Post qualitative inquiry, the refusal of method, and the risk of the new. *Qualitative Inquiry*. 27(1): 3–9.
St Pierre EA (2023) Poststructuralism and post qualitative inquiry. What can and must be thought. *Qualitative Inquiry*. 29(1): 20–32.
Staats H (2018) One group analysis and many. Response to Farhad Dalal's 'one group analysis or many?' *Group Analysis.* 51(3): 334–342.
Staats H (2024) Mentalizing between groups. A response to 'On the relationship between group analysis and mentalization-based group therapy' by Karterud, Gunnarsen, Gordon, Kongerslev, Staun and Schultz-Venrath. *Group Analysis*. *58*(1): 130–137. https://doi.org/10.1177/05333164241241485.

Staats H, Bolm T and Dally A (2013) Variabilität mit Konzept: Gruppen leiten im Göttinger Modell. (Variability by Concept. Group analysis and group psychotherapy according to the Goettingen model of group psychotherapy). *Gruppenpsychotherapie und Gruppendynamik.* 49(1): 101–105.

Staats H, Bolm T and Dally A (Hrsg.) (2014) *Gruppenpsychotherapie und Gruppenanalyse. Ein Lehr- und Lernbuch für Klinik und Praxis.* Göttingen: Vandenhoeck & Ruprecht.

Stacey BC (2023) Whose Probabilities? About What? A Reply to Khrennikov. arXiv:2302.09475 [quant-ph].

Stacey R (2001) Complexity and the Group Matrix. *Group Analysis.* 34(2): 221–239. https://doi.org/10.1177/0533316401342003.

Stacey R (2003) *Complexity and Group Processes. A Radically Social Understanding of Individuals.* London and New York: Brunner-Routledge.

Stacey R (2006) Theories of change in therapeutic work. *Clinical Child Psychology and Psychiatry.* 11(2): 191–203. https://doi.org/10.1177/1359104506061446.

Stacey R (2010) *Complexity and Organizational Reality Uncertainty and the Need to Rethink Management after the Collapse of Investment Capitalism.* New York: Routledge.

Staczan P, Schmuecker R, Koehler M, Berglar J, Crameri A, Von Wyl A, Koemeda-Lutz M, Schulthess P and Tschuschke V (2015) Effects of sex and gender in ten types of psychotherapy. *Psychotherapy Research.* 27(1): 74–88. https://doi.org/10.1080/10503307.2015.1072285.

Stahnisch FW (2024) Assessing Kurt Goldstein's lasting influence in the neuropsycholgy of language versus his use of aphasic symptoms as diagnostic insights into injuries. *Frontiers in Psychology.* 15. https://doi.org/10.3389/fpsyg.2024.1356824.

Stamenova K (2018) Comparative analysis of overlapping psychoanalytic concepts using operationalization. In Stamenova K and Hinshelwood RD (Eds.) *Methods of Research into the Unconscious. Applying Psychoanalytic Ideas to Social Science.* London and New York: Routledge, pp. 183–196.

Stamenova K and Hinshelwood RD (2018) Introduction. In Stamenova K and Hinshelwood RD (Eds.) *Methods of Research into the Unconscious. Applying Psychoanalytic Ideas to Social Science.* London and New York: Routledge, pp. 1–16.

Stanford Encyclopedia of Philosophy (2009) *Feminist Perspectives on Science.* By Sharon Crasnow. Available at: https://plato.stanford.edu/entries/feminist-science/ (accessed 3 July 2024).Stanford Encyclopedia of Philosophy (2010) *Immanuel Kant.* By Michael Rolhf. Available at: https://plato.stanford.edu/entries/kant/ (accessed 8 June 2020).

Stanford Encyclopedia of Philosophy (2020) *Carnap.* By Hannes Leitgeb & Andre Carus. Available at: https://plato.stanford.edu/entries/carnap/ (accessed 11 February 2022).

Stanford Encyclopedia of Philosophy (2021) *Hans Reichenbach.* By Clark Glymour & Frederick Eberhard. Available at: https://plato.stanford.edu/entries/reichenbach/ (accessed 11 February 2022).

Stanford Encyclopedia of Philosophy (2022) *Johann Gottlieb Fichte.* By Dan Breazaele. Available at: https://plato.stanford.edu/entries/johann-fichte/ (accessed 1 January 2024).

Stark G (2022) *Light.* Encyclopedia Britannica. 27 December 2024. Available at: https://www.britannica/com/science/light (accessed 8 January 2025).

Stasi Mediathek (2023) *Rede von Minister Erich Mielke zum 8. Jahrestag des Ministeriums für Sicherheit. [Speech by Minister Erich Mielke at the 8th Annual Meeting at the Ministry of Security.]* Das Bundesarchiv. Stasi Mediathek. Signatur: BStU,MfS,ZAIE,Tb,NR.150. Available at: https://www.stasi-mediathek.de/medien/rede-von-minister-erich-mielke-zum-8-jahrestag-des-ministeriums-fuer-staatssicherheit/ (accessed 6 April 2023).

Stefon M (2012) *de.* Encyclopedia Britannica. 31 May 2012. Available at: https://www.britannica/com/topic/de (accessed 19 September 2024).

Stein V (2022) *Einstein's Theory of Special Relativity.* Space Com. Available at: https://www.space.com/36273-theory-special-relativity.html (accessed 24 December 2024).

Steinman RM, Pizlo Z and Pizlo FJ (2000) Phi is not beta, and why Wertheimer's discovery launched the Gestalt revolution. *Vision Research.* 40(17): 2257–2264.

Steinmetz G (2005a) Positivism and its others in the social sciences. In Steinmetz G (Ed.) *The Politics of Method in the Human Sciences. Positivism and its Epistemological Others.* Durham, NC: Duke University Press, pp. 1–56.

Steinmetz G (2005b) The epistemological unconscious of the U.S. sociology and the transition to post-Fordism. The case of sociology. In Adams J, Clemens ES and Orloff AS (Eds.) *Remaking Modernity. Politics, History, Sociology.* Durham, NC: Duke University Press, pp. 109–157.

Stepanyan K, Mather R and Dalrymple R (2014) Culture, role and group work. A social network analysis perspective on an online collaborative course. *British Journal of Educational Technology.* 45(4): 676–693.

Stephenson N (1992) *Snow Crash.* London: Penguin.

Stephenson W (1936) The foundations of psychometry: Four factor systems. *Psychometrika.* 1(3): 195–209. https://doi.org/10.1007/BF02288366.

Stephenson W (1953) *The study of behavior: Q-technique and its methodology.* Chicago: University of Chicago Press.

Stephenson W (1977) Factors as operant subjectivity. *Operant Subjectivity.* 1(1): 3–16. https://ojs.library.okstate.edu/osu/index.php/osub/article/view/9351/8398

Stern DN (2004) *The Present Moment in Psychotherapy and Everyday Life.* New York: W. W Norton & Company.

Stern PN (2007) On solid ground. Essential properties for growing grounded theory. In Bryant A and Charmaz K (Eds.) *The Sage Handbook of Grounded Theory.* Thousand Oakes, CA: Sage, pp. 114–126.

Sterne JAC, Savović J. Page MJ, Elbers RG, Blencowe NS, Boutron I, Cates JC, Cheng HY, Corbett, MS, Eldridge SM, Emberson JR, Hernán MA, Hopewell S, Hróbjartsson A, Junqueira DR, Jüni P, Kirkham JJ, Lasserson T, Li T, McAleenan A … Higgins JPT (2019) RoB 2: A revised tool for assessing risk of bias in randomised trials. *British Medical Journal.* 366: Article 4898. https://doi.org/10.1136/bmj.l4898.

Stevens J (2007) *Zen Bow, Zen Arrow. The Life and Teachings of Awa Kenzo, the Archery Master from Zen in the Art of Archery.* Boston, MA: Shambhala.

Stevenson S (2020) Psychodynamic intersectionality and the positionality of the group analyst. The tension between analytical neutrality and intersubjectivity. *Group Analysis.* 53(4): 498–514.

Stock Whitaker D (1981) Research issues in group psychotherapy. *Group Analysis.* 14(1): 38–41.

Stock Whitaker D (1982) A nuclear conflict and group focal conflict model for integrating individual and group level phenomena. In Pines M and Rafaelsen L (Eds.) (1982) *The Individual and the Group.* New York: Springer.

Stock Whitaker D and Lieberman M (1964) *Psychotherapy through the Group Process.* New York: Aldine.

Stocks H, Kyriakopoulos A and Ashton T (2020) Measuring meaningful markers of change. *Group Analysis.* 53(2): 177–193.

Stokes P (2005) *Philosophy 100 Essential Thinkers.* London: Enchanted Lion Books.

Stolorow RD, Brandschaft B and Atwood G (1987) *Psychoanalytic Treatment. An Intersubjective Approach.* Hillsdale, MI: The Analytic Press.

Stone Fish L and Busby D (2005) The Delphi method. In Sprenkle D and Piercy F (Eds.) *Research Methods in Family Therapy.* 2nd Edition. New York: Guilford Press, pp. 238–253.

Stone Fish L and Osborn J (1992) Therapists' views of family life: A Delphi study. *Family Relations.* 41(4): 409–416. https://doi.org/10.2307/585583; https://www.jstor.org/stable/585583.

Stone W (1995) Frustration, anger, and the significance of alter-ego transference in group psychotherapy. *International Journal of Group Psychotherapy.* 45(3): 287–302.

Story GW, Dalton F, Selway A, Caparrotta L, O'Reilly J, Colam A, Larney A, Ritchie S and Hillen T (2024) Effectiveness of group analytic and psychodynamic psychotherapy in routine secondary-care practice. *Group Analysis.* 57(4): 480–496. https://doi.org/10.1177/05333164241257239.

Strauss AL and Corbin J (1998) *Basics of Qualitative Research: Techniques and Procedures for Developing Grounded Theory.* Thousand Oakes, CA: Sage Publications.

Strauß B (2016) Prinzipien der psychodynamischen Gruppenpsychotherapie [Principles of Psychodynamic Group Psychotherapy]. *Psychotherapie, Psychosomatik, Medizinische Psychologie.* 66(12): 489–500. https://doi.org/10.1055/s-0042-120131.

Strauß B (2022) *Gruppenpsychotherapie: Grundlagen und integrative Konzepte. (Series Psychotherapie kompakt).* Stuttgart: Kohlhammer Verlag GmbH.

Strauß B and Burgmeier-Lohse M (1993) In-patient and ward psychosomatic psychotherapy: concepts, effectiveness and curative factors. *Psychotherapy and Psychosomatics*. 59(3–4): 144–155. https://doi.org/10.1159/000288658.

Strauß B and Schmidt S (2004) Differential treatment outcome of inpatient psychodynamic group work. In Richardson P, Kächele H and Renlund C (Eds.) *Research on Psychoanalytic Psychotherapy with Adults*. London: Karnac, pp. 15–34.

Strauß B, Burlingame GM and Bormann B (2008) Using the CORE-R battery in group psychotherapy. *Journal of Clinical Psychology*. 64(11): 1225–1237. https://doi.org/10.1002/jclp.20535.

Strauß B, Eckert J and Ott J (1993) Interpersonale Probleme in der stationären Gruppenpsychotherapie. [Interpersonal Problems in inpatient group psychotherapy.] *Gruppenpsychotherapie und Gruppendynamik*. 29(3): 223–226

Strauß B, Eckert J and Tschuschke V (Hrsg) (1996) *Methoden zur empirischen Forschung in der Gruppenpsychotherapie. [Methods of empirical Research in Group Psychotherapy]. Ein Handbuch*. Opladen: Westdeutscher Verlag.

Strauß B, Kirschner H, Paripovic G, Storch M and Gallistl A (2022) Aufarbeitung der DDR Psychotherapie als transdisziplinäres Forschungsfeld.Teil I: chronologisch/historische Perspektiven. [Processing the GDR. Psychotherapy as an interdisciplinary field of study. Part 1]. *Psychotherapeut*. 67(5): 420–429. https://link.springer.com/article/10.1007/s00278-022-00599-6; https://www.researchgate.net/publication/360426115_Aufarbeitung_der_DDR-Psychotherapie_als_transdisziplinares_Forschungs-feldReprocessing_psychotherapy_in_the_German_Democratic_Republic_as_a_transdisciplinary_research_field_Teil_I_chronologischhistoris

Streeck U (2024) *Die psychoanalytisch-interaktionelle Gruppenpsychotherapie. Intersubjektivität, Beziehungswissen und Zwischenleiblichkeit. [The psychoanalytic interactional Group Psychotherapy. Intersubjectivity, Relationship Knowledge and Intercoporeality.]* Gießen: Psychosozial Verlag. https://doi.org/10.30820/9783837962314

Strike K and Posner G (1983) Types of synthesis and their criteria. In Ward SA and Reed LJ (Eds.) *Knowledge, Structure and Use. Implications for Synthesis and Interpretation*. Philadelphia, PA: Temple University Press.

Strocchi F (2012) The physical principles of quantum mechanics. A critical review. *The European Physical Journal Plus*. 127(1): 1–12.

Strűngmann E (2023) Wolf singer. *Neuron*. 111(7): 927–932.

Stryker S and Serpe RT (1982) Commitment, identity salience, and role behavior: Theory and research example. In Ickes W and Knowles ES (Eds.) *Personality, Roles, and Social Behavior*. New York: Springer, pp. 199–218. https://www.researchgate.net/publication/279273409_Commitment_Identity_Salience_and_Role_Behavior_Theory_and_Research_Example

Stuchbury K (2021) Critical realism. An explanatory framework for small-scale qualitative studies or an ‘unhelpful’ edifice? *International Journal of Research and Method in Education*. 45(2): 113–128.

Stumptner K (Hrg.) (2022) *Gruppenanalytisch arbeiten mit Kindern und Jugendlichen. Impulse fűr eine kreative und vielfältige Praxis. [Working group-analytically with Children and Teenagers. Impulses for a creative and diverse Practice.]* Gőttingen: Vandenhoeck & Ruprecht.

Sue DW, Neville HA and Smith L (2024) Racism in counseling and psychotherapy: Illuminate and disarm. *The American Psychologist*. 79(4): 593–605. https://doi.org/10.1037/amp0001231.

Sultana M, Al-Jefri M and Lee J (2020) Using maschine learning and smartphone and smartwatch data to detect emotional states and transitions. Exploratory study. *JMIR mHealth and uHealth*. 8(9): e17818.

Sumsion T (1998) The Delphi technique. *British Journal of Occupational Therapy*. 61(4): 153–156.

Sundermier A (2015) The particle physics of you. *Symmetry Magazine*. 3 November. https://www.symmetrymagazine.org/article/the-particle-physics-of-you?language_content_entity=und

Suppe F (1977) *The Structure of Scientific Theories*. Urbana: University of Illinois Press.

Suppe F (2000) Understanding scientific theories. An assessment of developments, 1969–1998. *Philosophy of Science*. 67(3): S102–S115. https://www.jstor.org/stable/188661

Susen S (2007) *The Foundation of the Social. Between Critical Theory and Reflexive Sociology*. Oxford: Bardwell Press.

Susen S (2020) The resonance of resonance. Critical theory as a sociology of world relations? *International Journal of Politics, Culture and Society.* 33(3): 309–344. https://link.springer.com/article/10.1007/s10767-019-9313-6.

Sutherland JD (1985) Bion revisited. Group dynamics and group psychotherapy. In Pines M (Ed.) (1992) *Bion and Group Psychotherapy.* London: Tavistock/Routledge, pp. 47–86.

Sutton A, Clowes M, Preston L and Booth A (2019) Meeting the review family: Exploring review types and associated information retrieval requirements. *Health Information & Libraries Journal.* 36(3): 202–222

Sutton AI and Staw BM (1995) What theory is not. *Administrative Science Quarterly.* 40(3): 371–384.

Sutton C (2025) *Standard Model.* Encyclopedia Britannica. 31 January. Available at: https://www.britannica.com/science/standard-model (accessed 4 February 2025).

Synder CR and Fromkin HL (1980) *Uniqueness. The Huan Pursuit of Difference.* New York: Plenum Press.

Taherdoost H and Madanchian M (2023) Sentiment analysis. A review in competitive research. *Computers.* 12(2): 37–52.

Tajfel H and Turner JC (1986) The social identity theory of inter-group behavior. In Austin WG and Worchel S (Eds.) *Psychology of Inter-Group Relations.* Chicago, IL: Nelson-Hall Publishers, pp. 7–24.

Talbot D (2015) Teachers talk about their learning: A Bakhtinian analysis. *Knowledge Cultures.* 3(4): 171–187.

Tamdgidi M (2005) Orientalist and liberating discourses of east-west differences. Revisiting Edward Said and the Rubaiyat of Omar Khayyam. *The Discourse of Sociological Practice.* 7(1–2): 187–201.

Tan SY and Tatsumura Y (2014) Albert Schweitzer (1987-1965): A reverence for life. *Singapore Medical Journal.* 55(7): 351–352.

Tarasov L (2020) Semantic relativism and logical implication. *Erkenntnis.* 88(1): 1–21.

Tashakkori A and Teedlie C (1998) *Mixed-Methodology. Combining Qualitative and Quantitative Approaches.* Thousand Oaks, CA: Sage.

Taubner S, Klasen J and Munder T (2016) Why do psychotherapists participate in psychotherapy research and why not? Results of the attitudes to psychotherapy research questionnaire with a sample of experienced German psychotherapists. *Psychotherapy Research.* 26(3): 318–331.

Tavakol M and Dennick R (2011) Making sense of Cronbach's alpha. *International Journal of Medical Education.* 2(1): 53–55. https://www.ijme.net/archive/2/cronbachs-alpha/

Tavistock Institute (2020) *What's On. Experiences of Deepening Creative Practice.* Available at: https://www.tavinstitute.org/whats-on/experiences-of-deepening-creative-practice (accessed 27 November 2024).

Tavistock Institute (2024) *The Leicester Conference.* Available at: https://www.tavistockinstitute.org/professional:development/the-leicester-conference (accessed 17 November 2024).

Taylor C (2003) *Modern Social Imaginaries.* Durham, NC: Duke University Press.

Taylor C (2018) Resonance and the romantic era: a comment on Rosa's conception of the good life. In Rosa H and Henning C (Eds.) *The Good Life Beyond Growth.* 55–70. New York: Routledge, pp. 55–70.

Taylor C (2023) The ethical implications of resonance theory. *Journal of Chinese Sociology.* 10: 14. https://doi.org/10.1186/s40711-023-00186-5

Taylor SP (2008) Critical realism vs social constructivism & constructionism: Application to a social housing research study. *International Journal of Sciences Basic and Applied Research.* 37(2): 216–222.

Teddlie C and Tashakkori A (2011) Mixed methods research. In Denzin NK and Lincoln YS (Eds.) *The Sage Handbook of Qualitative Research.* 4th Edition. Thousand Oaks, CA: Sage, pp. 285–300.

Tenny S , Brannan JM and Brannan GD (2022) Qualitative Study. [Updated 2022 Sep 18]. In *StatPearls* [Internet]. Treasure Island (FL): StatPearls Publishing. Available from: https://www.ncbi.nlm.nih.gov/books/NBK470395/

Terlidou C, Moschonas D, Kakitsis P, Manthouli M, Moschona T and IK Tsegos (2004) Personality changes after completion of long-term group-analytic psychotherapy. *Group Analysis.* 37(3): 401–418.

Terwee C B, Bot SD, de Boer MR, van der Windt DA, Knol DL, Dekker J, Bouter LM and de Vet HC (2007) Quality criteria were proposed for measurement properties of health status questionnaires. *Journal of Clinical Epidemiology.* 60(1): 34–42. https://doi.org/10.1016/j.jclinepi.2006.03.012.

Thalassis N (2007) Soldiers in psychiatric therapy: The case of Northfield military hospital 1942–1946. *Social History of Medicine*. 20(2): 351–368.

Thambinathan V and Kinsella EA (2021) Decolonizing methodologies in qualitative research. Creating spaces for transformative praxis. *International Journal of Qualitative Methods*. 20(1): 1–9. https://doi.org/160940692110147.

The Editors (2022) *Diary*. Encyclopedia Britannica. 24 August. Available at: www.britannica.com/art/diary-literature (accessed 20 January 2024).

The Federal Archives (2021) *Stasi Unterlagen. [Stasi Records.]* https://www.bundesarchiv.de/stasi-unterlagen-archiv/ Also: Tasks and Structures. Available at: https://www.bundesarchiv.de/en/stasi-records-archive/tasks-and-structure/ (accessed 11 March 2023).

The Information Philosopher (2025) *Pascual Jordan (1902–1980)*. Chapter 1.5 – The Philosophers. The Information Philosopher. Solving philosophical problems with new information philosophy. Website. Available at: https://www.informationphilosopher.com/solutions/scientists/jordan/ (accessed 9 January 2025).

The Institute of Group Analysis (2024) *Foundation Course in Group Analysis 2024/25*. Available at: https://www.groupanalysis.org/courses/categories/foundation-course (accessed 17 November 2024).

Thompson B (2021) *An Interview with Mark Zuckerberg about the Metaverse*. October 28, 2021. Available at: https://stratechery.com/2021/an-interview-with-mark-zuckerberg-about-the-metaverse/ (accessed 9 January 2024).

Thompson C , Lewis DJ, Greenhalgh T, Smith NR, Fahy AE and Cummins S (2017) "I don't know how I'm still standing". A Bakhtinian analysis of social housing and health narratives in East London. *Social Science & Medicine*. 177: 27–34. https://doi.org/10.1016/j.socscimed.2017.01.054.

Thompson JD and Demerath NJ (1952) Some experiences with the group interview. *Social Forces*. 31(2): 148–152.

Thornburgh N (2009) In Berlin, A Peter Hacks Renaissance. *The New Yorker*. 9 November. Available at: https://www.newyorker.com/books/page-turner/in-berlin-a-peter-hacks-renaissance (accessed on 13 April 2023).

Thorne S (2017) Metasynthetic madness: What kind of monster have we created? *Qualitative Health Research*. 27(1): 2–12.

Thorne S (2022) Qualitative meta-synthesis. *Nurse Author & Editor*. 32(1): 15–18. https://doi.org/10.1111/nae2.12036.

Thornton C (2004) Borrowing my self. An exploration of exchange as a group-specific therapeutic factor. *Group Analysis*. 37(2): 305–320.

Thornton C (2010) *Group and Team Coaching*. New York: Routledge.

Thornton C (2017) Towards a group analytic praxis for working with teams in organizations. *Group Analysis*. 50(4): 519–536.

Thornton C (2018) Towards a group analytic praxis for working with teams in organizations II. *Group Analysis*. 51(1): 70–90.

Thornton, C (2025) *Group Coaching and Team Coaching*. 3rd Edition. London: Routledge.

Tiffin H (1995) Postcolonial literatures and counter discourse. In Ashcroft B, Griffiths G and Thiophen H (Eds.) *The Post-Colonial Studies Reader*. New York: Routledge, pp. 95–98.

Timulak L (2015) Introduction to research methodology. In Vossler A and Moller N (Eds.) *The Counselling and Psychotherapy Research Handbook*. Thousand Oaks, CA: Sage, pp. 74–87.

Tiryakian ED (1971) (Ed.) *Phenomenon of Sociology. A Reader in the Sociology of Sociology*. New York: Appleton Century Crofts.

Todd DM, Jacobus SI and Boland J (1992) Users of a computer database to support research-practice integration in a training clinic. *Professional Psychology. Research and Practice*. 23(1): 52–58.

Todd Z (2016) An indigenous feminist's take on the ontological turn: 'ontology' is just another word for colonialism. *Journal of Historical Sociology*. 29(1): 4–22.

Tong A, Flemming K, McInnes E, Oliver S and Craig J (2012) Enhancing transparency in reporting the synthesis of qualitative research: ENTREQ. BMC *Medical Research Methodology*. 12(181). https://doi.org/10.1186/1471-2288-12-181.

Tong A, Sainsbury P and Craig JC (2007) Consolidated criteria for reporting qualitative research (COREQ). A 32-item checklist for interviews and focus groups. *International Journal for Quality in Health Care.* 19(6): 349–357.

Tononi G and Koch C (2015) Consciousness here, there and everywhere? *Philosophical Transactions. The Royal Society.* 370(1688): 1–18. https://royalsocietypublishing.org/doi/10.1098/rstb.2014.0167

Toseland RW and Siporin M (1986) When to recommend group treatment: A review of the clinical and the research literature. *International Journal of Group Psychotherapy.* 36(2): 171–201.

Toulmin S (1990) *Cosmopolis. The Hidden Agenda of Modernity.* New York: Free Press.

Toye F, Seers K, Allcock N, Briggs M, Carr E and Barker K (2014) Meta-ethnography 25 years on. Challenges and insights for synthesising a large number of qualitative studies. *BMC Medical Research Methodology.* 14: 80. https://doi.org/10.1186/1471-2288-14-80.

Tranfield D, Denyer D and Smart P (2003) Towards a methodology for developing evidence-informed management knowledge by means of systematic review. *British Journal of Management.* 14(3): 207–222.

Trausan S (2010) The polyphonic model of hybrid and collaborative learning. In Wang F, Fong J and Kwan RC (Eds.) *Handbook of Research on Hybrid Leaning Models. Advanced Tools, Technologies, and Application.* Hershey, NY: Information Science Publishing, pp. 466–486.

Trausan S (2013) Collaborative and differential utterances, pivotal moments, and polyphony. In Suthers D, Lund K, Rose CP, Teplovs C and Law N (Eds.) *Productive Multivocality in the Analysis of Group Interactions.* New York: Springer, pp. 123–139.

Trausan- Matu S and Rebedea T (2010) A polyphonic model and system for inter-animation analysis in chat conversations with multiple participants. In Gelbukh A (Ed) *Computational Linguistics and Intelligent Text Processing. CICLing 2010.* Lecture Notes in Computer Science, Vol. 6008. New York: Springer. https://doi.org/10.1007/978-3-642-12116-6_29.

Trausan-Matu S, Dascalu M and Rebedea T (2014) PolyCaFe. Automatic support for the polyphonic analysis of CSCL chats. *International Journal of Computer Supported Collaborative Learning.* 9(2): 127–156.

Trausan-Matu S, Wegerif R and Major L (2021) Dialogism. In Cress U, Rose C, Wise F and Oshima J (Eds.) *International Handbook of Computer-Supported Collaborative Learning.* New York: Springer, pp. 65–84.

Travers KM (1996) The social organization of nutritional inequities. *Social Science and Medicine.* 43(4): 543–553.

Triantafyllidis A, Kondylakis H, Katehakis D, Kouroubali A, Alexiadis A, Seglouli S, Votis K and Tzovaras D (2024) Smartwatch interventions in healthcare. A systematic review of the literature. *International Journal of Medical Informatics.* 190. Online. https://doi.org/10.2026/j.ijmedinf.2024.105560.

Trinka Bog (2024) *Idea vs. Concept. How are they different?* Available at: https://www.trinka.ai/blog/idea-vs-concept-how-are-they-different/ (accessed 16 April 2024).

Trist E (1985) Working with bion in the 1940s. The group decade. In Pines M (Ed.) (1992) *Bion and Group Psychotherapy.* London: Tavistock/Routledge, pp. 1–46.

Trist E and Bamforth K (1951) Some social and psychological consequences of the longwall method of coal-getting. *Human Relations.* 4(1): 3–38.

Trist E and Murray H (1990) *Historical Overview. The Foundation and Development of the Tavistock Institute.* Philadelphia: University of Pennsylvania Press.

Trow M (1957) Comment on participant observation and interviewing. A comparison. *Human Organization.* 16(3): 33–35.

Tschuschke V (1993) *Wirkfaktoren stationärer Gruppenpsychotherapie. Prozess Ergebnis Relationen. [Effective Factors in inpatient Psychotherapy. Process. Results. Relations.]* Gőttingen: Vandenhoeck & Ruprecht.

Tschuschke V (1999) Gruppentherapie versus Einzeltherapie. Gleich wirksam? [Group Therapy vs Individual Therapy. Equally Effective?] *Gruppenpsychotherapie und Gruppendynamik.* 35(4): 257–274.

Tschuschke V (2005) Die Psychotherapie in Zeiten evidenzbasierter Medizin Fehlentwicklungen und Korrekturvorschläge. [Psychotherapy in Times of evidence-based Medicine. Mistaken development and suggestions for corrections.] *Psychotherapeuten Journal*. 2(2): 106–115.

Tschuschke V (2007) Psychodynamische Gruppenpsychotherapie. Evidenzbasierte Fakten. [Psychodynamic Groupsychotherapy. Evidence-based Factors.] *Gemeindenahe Psychiatrie*. 28(1): 21–32.

Tschuschke V (2016) *The Wrong Understanding of Evidence-Based Research in Psychotherapy. A Plea for Intensive Process-Outcome Research in Naturalistic Studies*. 17 February 2016. Speech in Vienna, conference of the Science and Research Committee of EAP, Research for Practitioners, 18–20 February, 2016. Available at: https://www.europsyche.org/About/Research/SARC-Conference-Vienna-2016 (accessed 13 November 2022).

Tschuschke V and Anbeh T (2000) Early treatment effects of long-term outpatient group therapies. First preliminary results. *Group Analysis*. 33(3): 397–411.

Tschuschke V and Dies RR (1994) Intensive analysis of therapeutic factors and outcome in long-term inpatient groups. *International Journal of Group Psychotherapy*. 44(2): 185–208.

Tschuschke V and Freyberger HJ (2015) Zur aktuellen Situation der Psychotherapiewissenschaft und ihrer Auswirkungen. Eine kritische Analyse der Lage. *Zeitschrift für Psychosomatische Medizin und Psychotherapie*. [On the present situation in psychotherapy and its implications. A critical analysis of the facts]. *Zeitschrift für Psychosomatische Medizin und Psychotherapie*. 61(2): 122–138. https://doi.org/10.13109/zptm.2015.61.2.122.

Tschuschke V and MacKenzie KR (1989) Empirical analysis of group development: A methodological report. *Small Group Behavior*. 20(4): 419–427. https://journals.sagepub.com/doi/10.1177/104649648902000403.

Tschuschke V, Anbeh T and Kiencke P (2007) Evaluation of long-term analytic outpatient group therapies. *Group Analysis*. 40(1): 140–159.

Tschuschke V , Bänninger-Huber E, Faller H, Fikentscher E, Fischer G, Frohburg, I, Hager W, Schiffler A, Lamprecht F, Leichsenring F, Leuzinger-Bohleber M, Rudolf G and Kächele H (1998) Psychotherapieforschung, Wie man es (nicht) machen sollte. Eine Experten/innen. Reanalyse von Vergleichsstudien bei Grawe et al. 1994. [Psychotherapy research. How it should (not) be done. An expert reanalysis of comparative studies by Grawe et al. 1994]. *Psychotherapie, Psychosomatik, Medizinische Psychologie*. 48(11): 430–444.

Tschuschke V , Catina A, Beckh T and Salvini D (1992) Wirkfaktoren in stationärer analytischer Gruppenpsychotherapie. [Effective Factors in inpatient analytic psychotherapy.] *Psychotherapie, Psychosomatik, Medizinische Psychologie*. 42(3/4): 91–101.

Tschuschke V, Crameri A, Koehler M, Berglar J, Muth K, Staczan P, Von Wyl A, Schulthess P and Koemeda-Lutz M (2014) The role of therapists' treatment adherence, professional experience, therapeutic alliance, and clients' severity of psychological problems: Prediction of treatment outcome in eight different psychotherapy approaches. Preliminary results of a naturalistic study. *Psychotherapy Research*. 25(4): 420–434.

Tschuschke V, Koemeda-Lutz M and Schlegel M (2014) *Rating Manual for the Objective Evaluation of Therapeutic Interventions of Psychotherapists Based on Various Theoretical Concepts. Schriftenreihe der Schweizer Charta für Psychotherapie Bd. 3.* Zurich: Schweizer Charta für Psychotherapie.

Tsur EE (2022) *Neuromorphic Engineering. The Scientist's Algorithms Designers' and Computer Architect's Perspectives on Brain-Inspired Computing.* Boca Raton, FL: CRC Press.

Tubert- Oklander J and Hernández-Tubert R (2004) *Operative Groups. The Latin-American approach to group analysis.* New York: Jessica Kingsley Publishers.

Tubert-Oklander J and Hernández-Tubert R (2014) The Social unconscious and the large group part II: A context that becomes text. *Group Analysis.* 47(3): 329–344.

Tubert-Oklander J and Hernández-Tubert R (Eds.) (2021) *Psychoanalysis, Group Analysis, and Beyond. Towards a New Paradigm of the Human Being.* New York: Taylor Francis Group.

Tuck E (2013) Commentary: decolonizing methodologies 15 years later. *Alter Native: An International Journal of Indigenous Peoples.* 9(4): 365–372.

Tuck E and Yang KW (2012) Decolonization is not a metaphor. *Decolonization: Indigeneity, Education & Society.* 1(1): 1–40.
Tucker JA (2020) Ancient learning. The Japanese revival of classical confucianism. In Davis BW (Ed.) *The Oxford Handbook of Japanese Philosophy.* New York: Oxford University Press, pp. 291–306.
Tucker S (2011) Psychotherapy groups for Traumatized Refugees and Asylum Seekers. *Group Analysis.* 44(1): 68–82.
Tuckman B (1965) Developmental sequence in small groups. *Psychological Bulletin* 65(6): 384–399.
Tuhiwai-Smith L (2021) *Decolonizing Methodologies. Research and Indigenous People.* 3rd Edition. London: Bloomsbury.
Tűrkcan B (2013) Semiotic approach to the analysis of children's drawings. *Educational Sciences: Theory & Practice.* 13(1): 600–607.
Turner C (2022) Augmented reality, Augmented epistemology, and the real-world Web. *Philosophy & Technology*. 35(1): 1–28.
Turner C (2023) The Metaverse: Virtual metaphysics, virtual governance, and virtual Abundance. *Philosophy & Technology*. 36(4): 1–8.
Turner HA (1992) *Germany from Partition to Reunification. A Revised Edition of the Two Germanies Since 1945.* Yale: Yale University Press.
Turoff M (2002) The Policy Delphi. https://www.researchgate.net/publication/265086472_The_Policy_Delphi. In Linstone H and Turoff M (Eds.) *The Delphi Method. Techniques and Application,* New Jersey: New Jersey Institute of Technology, pp. 80–96. Available at: http://is.njit.edu/pubs/delphibook (accessed 22 May 2009). https://www.researchgate.net/publication/272177922_The_Delphi_Method
Tutu D (2004) *God has a Dream. A Vision of Hope for Our Future.* London: Rider.
Twark J (2007) *Humor, Satire and Identity. East German Literature in the 1990s.* Berlin: DeGruyter.
Twark J (2011) *Negotiating the Politics of Satire: Satirical Novels in the GDR and beyond.* Conference 24 March 2011 in Oxford. Available at: https://public.mml.ox.ac.uk/gdrculture/abstracts7.html (accessed 1 April 2023).
Tweed A and Charmaz K (2012) Grounded theory methods for mental health practitioners. In Harper D and Thompson AD (Eds.) *Qualitative Research Methods in Mental Health and Psychotherapy: A Guide for Students and Practitioners*. Chichester: Wiley-Blackwell, pp.131–146.
Twigg E (2015) Quantitative methods. In Vossler A and Moller N (Eds.) *The Counselling and Psychotherapy Research Handbook.* Thousand Oakes, CA: Sage, pp. 131–182.
Twomey C and Dowling C (2025) Associations of group size with cohesion and clinical outcomes in group psychotherapy. A systematic review. *International Journal of Group Psychotherapy*. 75(2): 345–364. https://doi.org/10.1080/00207284.2025.2456020.
Tyndale A (1999) How far is transference interpretation essential to psychic change? In *Psychoanalytic Psychotherapy in the Independent Tradition*. New York: Routledge.
Tyndall J (2010) AACODS Checklist. Flinders University. https://dspace.flinders.edu.au/ dspace/
UCLA (2024) A Practical Introduction to Factor Analysis. Explorative Factor Analysis (UCLA Statistical Consulting Group) Advanced Research Computing. Statistical Methods and Data Analytics. Available at: https://stats.parc/ucla.edu/spss/seminars/introduction-to-factor-analysis/a-practical-introduction-to-factor-analysis/ (accessed 11 December 2024).
Uebel T and Limbeck-Lilienau C (Eds.) (2023) *The Routledge Handbook of Logical Empiricism.* New York: Routledge.
UKCP (2017) *Standards of Education and Training. The Minimum Core Criteria. Psychotherapy with Adults.* London: UK Council for Psychotherapy. https://www.psychotherapy.org.uk/ukcp-members/standards-guidance-and-policies/
Ulberg Amlo, Hummelen B, Hersoug AG, Midgley N, Høglend P and Johnsen Dahl HS (2021) The first experimental study of transference work in teenagers (FEST-IT). A multicentre, observer-and patient-blind, randomized controlled component study. *BioMedCentral Psychiatry*. 21: 106. https://doi.org/10.1186/s12888-021-03055-y.
Ulberg R, Amlo, S and Høglend P (2014) Manual for transference work scale. A micro-analytical tool for therapy process analyses. *BioMedCentral Psychiatry*. 14(1): 291–305.

UN (2002) 27th *Special Session of the General Assembly on Children, 10 May 2002, New York, United States. A World Fit for Children.* https://www.un.org/en/conference/children/newyork2002 (74th session in 2019, Rights of the Child Resolution; available at: https://digitallibrary.un.org/record/3848250 76th session in 2021 available at: https://digillibrary.un.org/record/3954144).
UNCRC (UN Convention on the Rights of the Child) (1989) *General Assembly Resolution 44/25. Convention on the Rights of the Child.* Available at: https://www.ohchr.org/en/instruments-mechanisms/instruments/convention-rights-child (accessed 7 April 2025).
United Nations (2013) *The United Nations Declaration on the Rights of Indigenous Peoples: A Manual for National Rights Institutions*. New York: United Nations.
Usandivaras R (1982) *Grupo, Pensamiento y Mito*. (Group, Thought and Myth). Buenos Aires: Eudeba.
Usandivaras R (1993) A new perspective in group analysis. *Group Analysis.* 26(3): 269–276.
Usandivaras RJ (1986) Foulkes' primordial level of clinical practice. *Group Analysis.* 19(2): 113–124.
Usandivaras RJ (1989a) Through 'communitas' to individuation. *Group Analysis.* 22(2): 161–170.
Usandivaras RJ (1989b) Therapeutic use of regression. *Group Analysis.* 22(2): 171–175.
Vahle-Hinz T, Baethge A and Van Dick R (2019) Beyond one work day? A daily diary study on causal and reverse effects between experienced workplace incivility and behaving rude towards others. *European Journal of Work and Organizational Psychology.* 28(2): 272–285.
Vaidyanathan U (2020) Theory, in practice. *Psychological Inquiry.* 31(4): 334–335.
Vaismoradi M, Turunen H and Bondas T (2013) Content analysis and thematic analysis: Implications for conducting a qualitative descriptive study. *Nursing & Health Sciences*. 15(3): 398–405. https://doi.org/10.1111/nhs.12048.
Valbak K (2003) 'Specialized psychotherapeutic group analysis: How do we make group analysis suitable for 'non-suitable' patients?' *Group Analysis*. 36(2): 73–86.
Valbak K (2022) Understandings, Misunderstandings and Illusions in the Research Matrix. *EGATIN Study Days in Rome 'Differences in the Didactic Matrix'*, 10–12 June 2022. Available at: https://egatin.net/studydays/2022
Valdez E (2023) *Electromagnet Fields in the Human Body*. Johnson Chiropractic Neurology & Nutrition. Blog. Available at: https://www.helpmychronicpain.com/blog/electromagnetic-fields-in-the-human-body/ (accessed 17 November 2024).
Van Binsbergen W (2001) Ubuntu and the globalisation of Southern African thought and society. *Quest. An African Journal of Philosophy.* 15(1–2): 53–89. Available on https://www.quest-journal.net/ at: https://www.quest-journal.net/2001.htm
Van den Heuvel BB, Dekker JJM, Daniëls M, Van HL, Peen J, Bosmans, J, Arntz A and Huibers MJH (2023) G-FORCE. The effectiveness of group psychotherapy for Cluster-C personality disorders. Protocol of a pragmatic RCT comparing psychodynamic and two forms of schema group therapy. *Bio Medical Central.* 24(1): 300–319.
Van der Braak A (2019) Hisamatsu Shin'ichi. Oriental Nothingness. In Kopf G (Eds) *The Dao Companion to Japanese Buddhist Philosophy. Vol. 8.* Dordrecht: Springer Nature, pp. 635–647. https://doi.org/10.1007/978-90-481-2924-9_28.
Van der Kolb B (2015) *The Body Keeps the Score. Mind, Brain and Body in the Transformation of Trauma.* New York: Penguin Books.
Van Deurzen E (1998) *Paradox and Passion in Psychotherapy. An Existential Approach to Therapy and Counselling.* London: Wiley.
Van Dijk TA (2015) Critical discourse analysis. In Tannen D, Hamilton HE and Schiffrin D (Eds.) *The Handbook of Discourse Analysis. Volume 1.* 2nd Edition. Chichester: Wiley Blackwell, pp. 466–485.
Van Egmond JRM (2022) *Resonance, Acceleration, And Phenomenology of the Feminine Body. A critical perspective on Hartmut Rosa's theory with Maurice Merleau-Ponty and Iris Marion Young.* Master Thesis, Tilburg University, School of Humanities and Digital Sciences. Netherlands. File 159608.R.M_van_Master_thesis_tilburguniversity.on-worldcat.org
Van Geert E and Wagemans J (2024) Prägnanz in visual perception. *Psychonomic Bulletin & Review.* 31(2): 541–567.

Van Hulst M, Metze T, Dewulf A, de Vries J, van Bommel S van Ostaijen M (2024) Discourse, framing and narrative: three ways of doing critical, interpretive policy analysis. *Critical Policy Studies*. 19(1): 74–96. https://doi.org/10.1080/19460171.2024.2326936.
Van Manen M (1990) *Researching Lived Experience: Human Science for An Action Sensitive Pedagogy*. Albany: State University of New York Press.
Van Manen M (2014) *Phenomenology of Practice. Mening-Giving Methods in Phenomenological Research and Writing.* New York: Routledge.
Van Manen M (2016) *Researching Lived Experience. Human Science for an Action Sensitive Pedagogy.* 2nd Edition. New York: Routledge.
Van Manen M (2017) But is it phenomenology? *Qualitative Health Research*. 27(6): 775–779.
Van Norden BW (2017a) Why the Western Philosophical Canon is Xenophobic and Racist. *Aeon.* Online Newsletter. 31 October 2017. Available at: https://aeon.co/essays/why-the-western-philosophical-canon-is-xenophobic-and-racist
Van Norden BW (2017b) *Taking Back Philosophy. A Multicultural Manifesto.* New York: Columbia University Press.
Van Rooij L and Baggio G (2020) Theory before the test. How to build high verisimilitude explanatory theories in psychological science. *Perspectives on Psychological Science.* 16(4): 682–697.
Van Wagoner SL (2015) From empathically immersed inquiry to discrete intervention: Are there limits to theoretical purity? In Kleinberg JL (Ed.) *The Wiley Blackwell Handbook of Group Psychotherapy.* Oxford: Wiley Blackwell, pp. 249–270.
Vandenberghe F (2023) Tuning into Harmut Rosa's systematic romanticism. *Journal of Chinese Sociology.* 10: 12. https://doi.org/10.1186/s40711-023-00189-2.
Vanheule S (2016) Capitalist discourse, subjectivity and Lacanian psychoanalysis. *Frontiers in Psychology*. 7: 1948. https://doi.org/10.3389/fpsyg.2016.01948.
Varadhan R and Weiss C (2011) Cross-design Synthesis for Extending the Applicability of Trial Evidence When Treatment Effect Is Heterogeneous. 1. Methodology. John Hopkins University. Dept. of Biostatistics Working Papers. Available at: https://biostats.bepress.com/jhubiostat/paper271 (accessed 4 January 2025).
Varkey B (2020) Principles of clinical ethics and their application to practice. *Medical Principles and Practice.* 4(30): 17–28.
Varzi AC (2011) On Doing ontology without metaphysics. *Philosophical Perspectives.* 25(1): 407–423. https://www.jstor.org/stabl/41329478
Veeser A (2024) Introduction. The question of the interview. *Journal of Postcolonial Writing.* 60(4): 431–438.
Vellem VS (2014) Spirituality of liberation. A conversation with African religiosity. *HTS Teologiese Studies/Theological Studies*. 70(1): 1–7. https://doi.org/10.4102/hts.v70i1.2752.
Veraart , W (2017) Het slavernijverleden van John Locke. Naar een minder wit curriculum? [The Slavery History in John Locke. Towards a less white curriculum?] In Van Beers B and Van Domselaar I (Eds.) *Homo Duplex. De dualiteit van de mens in recht, filosofie en sociologie*. [Homo Duplex. (double human). The duality of men in law, philosophy and sociology.] Den Haag: Boom, pp. 215–237.
Verde PE and Ohmann (2014) Combining randomized and non-randomized evidence in clinical research. A review of methods and applications. *Research Synthesis Methods.* 6(1): 45–62.
Verlinde E (2011) On the origin of gravity and the laws of Newton. *Journal of High Energy Physics.* 4, 029. https://doi.org/10.1007/JHEP04/(2011)1029.
Vetter TR and Schober P (2018) Regression: The Apple Does Not Fall Far From the Tree. *Anesthesia & analgesia*. 127(1): 277–283. https://doi.org/10.1213/ANE.0000000000003424.
Vezina B (2007) Universals and particulars. Aristotle's ontological theory and criticism of the Platonic forms. *Undergraduate Review*. 3(1): 101–103. https://www.scribd.com/document/566427475/Universals-and -Particulars.
Vice H and Gildenhuys A (2016) Reshaping social identity: A qualitative report on experiences in an intercultural median group. *Group Analysis*. 49(2): 101–123.
Viechtbauer W (2010) Conducting meta-analyses in R with the metafor package. *Journal of Statistical Software*. 36(3): 1–48.

Vitanova G (2013) Narratives as zones of dialogic constructions: A Bakhtinian approach to data in qualitative research. *Critical Inquiry in Language Studies*. 10(3): 242–261.

Vogt WP (2008) The dictatorship of the problem. Choosing research methods. *Methodological Innovations Online*. 3(1): 1–17. https://doi.org/10.4256/mio.2008.0006.

Vogt WP, Gardner DC and Haeffele LM (2012) *When to Use What Research Design*. New York: Guilford Press.

Volkan VD (1999) *Das Versagen der Diplomatie. [The Failure of Democracy.]* Gieβen: Psychosozial Verlag.

Volkan VD (2001) Transgenerational transmissions and chosen trauma: An aspect of large group identity. *Group Analysis*. 34(1): 79–97.

Volkan VD (2004) *Blind Trust. Large Groups and Their Leaders in Times of Crises and Terror.* Charlesville, VA: Pitchstone.

Volkan VD (2017) *Immigrants and Refugees. Trauma, Perennial Mourning, Prejudice and Border Psychology.* New York: Routledge.

Volkan VD (2021) Trauma, prejudice, large group identity and psychoanalysis. *The American Journal of Psychoanalysis*. 81(2): 137–154. https://doi.org/0.1057/s11231-021-09285-z.

Voloshinov VN (1976) *Freudianism: A Marxist Critique*. Trans. IR Titunik. New York, NY: Academic Press.

Voloshinov VN (1986) *Marxism and the Philosophy of Language*. Trans. L Matejka and IR Titunik. Cambridge, MA: Harvard University Press.

Von Bertalanffy (1950) An outline of general systems theory. *British Journal of Philosophy & Science*. 1: 134–165. https://doi.org/10.1093/bjps/I.2.134.

Von Glasersfeld (1981) An Introduction to radical constructivism. In Watzlawick P (Ed.) *The Invented Reality*. New York: Norton, pp. 17–40.

Von Glasersfeld E (1996) *Radical Constructivism. A Way of Knowing and Learning*. Washington, DC: The Falmer Press.

Von Sommaruga Howard T (2012) To stand sitting! Bi-cultural Dilemmas in a large group in Aotearoa, New Zealand. *Group Analysis*. 45(2): 219–243.

Von Sommaruga Howard T (2015) Dialogue in GASI? Thoughts after the Large Group in Lisbon. *Group-Analytic Contexts*. Summer Issue, pp. 33–35. Available on the Website of the Group Analytic Society, Group-Analytic Contexts Newsletter, International https://groupanalyticsociety.co.uk/

Von Sommaruga Howard T (2024) Lighting fires: On creating large group dialogue in organizations and society [CLGD]. *Group Analysis*. 57(1): 63–92.

Vorderer P and Halfmann A (2019) Why do we entertain ourselves with media narratives? A theory of resonance perspective on entertainment experience. *Annals of the International Communication Association*. 43(2): 79–96.

Vosmer S (2010) Group analysis and the virtual world: Communication in an expanding matrix. *Group Analysis*. 43(4): 505–522.

Vosmer S (2012) The usefulness of group analysis in the conceptualization and treatment of 'Personality Disorders' and 'Complex/Post-Traumatic Stress Disorder. *Group Analysis*. 45(4): 498–514.

Vosmer S (2015) Lessons learnt for group analysis from a group for adults with adult attention deficit hyperactivity disorder. *Progress and Communication in Sciences*. 2(1): 7–13.

Vosmer S (2016) What do dreams reveal about ourselves and 'the other'? *Group Analytic Contexts*. 73: 60–75. Available at the Group Analytic Society International. https://groupanalyticsociety.co.uk/contexts/

Vosmer S (2018) 'The Stone Mother Revisited'. A female group analytic reflection on working within male low-secure forensic inpatient settings in the United Kingdom. *Group Analysis*. 51(4): 500–514.

Vosmer S (2021) Why we should embrace positivism in group analysis. *International Journal of Psychotherapy. A Guide for Counsellors and Psychotherapists*. 25(3): 39–48.

Vosmer S (2022a) How (non)discriminatory are the institute of group analysis and group analysis? An institutional ethnography study. *Group Analysis*. 55(2): 233–252.

Vosmer S (2022b) Facets of love and love sickness. *Group Analysis*. 55(3): 272–290.

Vosmer S (2023a) Secondary Data. The Hidden Pearls of Wisdom. *Group Analytic Contexts* 102. Available at the Group Analytic Society International. https://groupanalyticsociety.co.uk/contexts/

Vosmer S (2023b) Scoping Reviews in Group Analysis. Group Analytic Contexts 101. Available at the Group Analytic Society International. https://groupanalyticsociety.co.uk/contexts/

Vosmer S (2023c) Expression of different kinds of love and their transformation in the interpretative encounter in the group. *Group Analysis.* 56(1): 28–51.

Vosmer S (2024a) How suitable is the analytic group for treating people Parkinson's? *Group Analysis.* Online. https://doi.org/10.1177/05333164241260368.

Vosmer S (2024b) Diary Studies As Empirical Method. Group Analytic Contexts 104. Available at the Group Analytic Society International. https://groupanalyticsociety.co.uk/contexts/

Vosmer S (2024c) Critical Realism. Group Analytic Contexts 103. Available at the Group Analytic Society International. https://groupanalyticsociety.co.uk/contexts/

Vosmer S (2024d) Lived experiences of diversity in group analytic training and as a qualified group analyst an autoethnographic study. *Group Analysis.* 57(2): 223–240.

Vosmer S Hackett S and Callanan M (2009) "Normal" and "inappropriate" childhood sexual behaviours. Findings from a Delphi study of professionals in the United Kingdom. *Journal of Sexual Aggression.* 15(3): 275–288.

Vossler A and Moller N (2014) Attitudes to and perceptions of research. In Vossler A and Moller N (Eds.) *The Counselling and Psychotherapy Research Handbook.* Thousand Oaks, CA: Sage, pp. 17–30.

Vromen S (1987) Georg Simmel and the cultural dilemma of women. *History of European Ideas.* 8(4–5): 563–579.

Vygotsky LS (1978) *Mind and Society. The Development of Higher Psychological Processes.* Cambridge, MA: Harvard University Press.

Wagemans J, Fider H, Kubovv M, Palmer, SE, Peterson MA, Singh M and Von der Heydt R (2021) A Century of gestalt psychology in visual perception I. Perceptual Grouping and Figure-Ground Organization. *Psychological Bulletin.* 138(6): 1172–1217.

Wahl DC (2020) *"Every -ism Creates a Schism". Avoiding the Habit of Othering*. Blog Medium 28 January 2020. Available at: https://medium.com/age-of-awareness-every-ism-creates-a-schism-avoiding-the-habit-of-othering-283594a5eb8c (accessed 1 January 2025).

Waite D (2022) Critical realist perspectives on the urban growth system. *Environment and Planning A: Economy and Space*. 54(6): 1219–1235. https://doi.org/10.1177/0308518X221102958.

Wajda Z, Kapinos-Gorczyca A, Lizinczyk S, Sitnik-Warchulska K and Izydorczyk B (2022) Online group psychodynamic psychotherapy. The effectiveness and role of attachment. The results of a short study. *Frontiers in Psychiatry.* 13: 1–16. https://doi.org/10.3389/fpsyt.2022.798991.

Waldenfels B (1992) *Einführung in die Phänomenologie. [Introduction to Phenomenology.]* Műnchen: Wilhelm Fink.

Waldherr A and Muck PM (2011) Towards an integrative approach to communication syles: the interpersonal circumplex and the five-factor theory of personality as frames of references. *Communications.* 36(1): 1–27. https://doi.org/10.1515/comm.2001.001.

Walker D (2019) What is indigeneity? Te Kaharoa. *Journal of Indigenous Specific Issues.* 12(1): 1–12.

Walker G (2024) *Operationalisation of Concepts in Psychoanalytic Research.* London: Routledge.

Walker G and Hinshelwood RD (2018) Is it a bird? Operationalization of unconscious processes. In Stamenova K and Hinshelwood RD (Eds.) *Methods of Research into the Unconscious. Applying Psychoanalytic Ideas to Social Science.* London and New York: Routledge, pp. 171–182.

Walker H, Trenoweth S, Martin C and Ramm M (2013) Using repertory grids to establish patients' views of psycho-education. *Journal of Psychology & Psychotherapy*. 3(1): 1–7. https://www.longdom.org/open-access/using-repertory-grid-to-establish-patients-views-of-psycho-education-2161-0487.1000108.pdf

Wall S (2006) An autoethnography on learning about autoethnography. *International Journal of Qualitative Methods.* 5(2): 1–12.

Wall S (2008) Easier said than Done. Writing an Autoethnography. *International Journal of Qualitative Methods.* 7(1): 38–53.

Wallace SS, Barak G, Truong G and Parker MW (2022) Hierarchy of evidence within the medical literature. *Hospital Pediatrics.* 12(6): 745–750.

Wallis SE (2010) Toward a science of metatheory. *Integral Review: A Transdisciplinary and Transcultural Journal for New Thought, Research, and Praxis.* 6(3): 73–120.

Wampold BE (2001) *The Great Psychotherapy Debate. Models, Methods, and Findings.* Mahwah, NJ: Lawrence Erlbaum Associates Publishers.

Wampold BW and Imel ZE (2015) *The Great Psychotherapy Debate. The Evidence for What Makes Psychotherapy Work.* 2nd edition. New York: Routledge.

Wan X, Wang W, LIU J and Tong T (2014) Estimating the sample mean and standard deviation from the sample size, median, range and/or interquartile range. *BMC Medical Research Methodology.* 14(1): 135. https://doi.org/10.1186/1471-2288-14-135.

Wang W, Stark T, Westaby JD, Parr AK and Newman DA (2023) Social network analysis in psychology: Recent breakthroughs in methods and theories. In Cooper H, Coutanche MN, McMullen LM, Panter AT, Rindskopf D and Sher KJ (Eds.) *APA Handbook of Research Methods in Psychology: Data Analysis and Research Publication.* Vol. 3. 2nd Edition. Washington, DC: American Psychological Association, pp. 501–537.

Wang Z (2024) Bridging Two Worlds. How to Unite Symbolic and Connectionist AI for the Future of LLM-Empowered Autonomous Agents? 19 August. Medium. Blog. Available at: https://medium.com/@wwzzyy9982/bridging-two-worlds-how-to-unite-symbolic-and-connectionist-ai-for-the-future-of-llm-empowered-5d6ec95ceccd (accessed 20 March 2025).

Wang Z, Huang D, Cui J, Zhang X, Ho S-B and Cambria E (2025) A review of Chinese Sentiment analysis: Subjects, methods, and trends. *Artificial Intelligence Review.* 58(75). https://doi.org/10.1007/s10462-024-10988-9.

Ware JE and Sherbourne CD (1992) The MOS 36-item short-form health survey (SF-36): conceptual framework and item selection. *Medical Care.* 30(6): 473–483.

Warr RL and Erich RA (2013) Should the interquartile range divided by the standard deviation be used to assess normality? *The American Statistician.* 67(4): 242–244. https://doi.org/10.1080/00031305.2013.847385.

Warren F and Norton K (2004) Henderson hospital democratic therapeutic community. Outcome studies and methodological issues. In Richardson P, Kächele H and Renlund C (Eds.) *Research on Psychoanalytic Psychotherapy with Adults.* London: Karnac, pp. 120–153.

Water T (2024) Ethical issues in participatory research with children and young people. In Coyne I and Cater B (Eds.) *Being Participatory. Researching with Children and Young People.* Cham: Springer, pp. 37–56. https://doi.org/10.1007/978-3-031-47787-4_3.

Watson JP (1970) A repertory grid method of studying groups. *British Journal of Psychiatry.* 117(538): 309–318.

Watson JP (1972) Possible measures of change during group psychotherapy. *British Journal of Medical Psychology.* 45(1): 71–77.

Watt R and Collins E (2019) *Statistics for Psychology. A Beginner's Guide.* 2nd Edition. New York: Sage.

Watts S (2015) Develop a Q methodological study. *Education for Primary Care.* 26(6): 435–437. https://doi.org/10.1080/14739879.2015.1101855.

Watts S and Stenner P (2005) Doing Q methodological research. Theory, method and interpretation. *Qualitative Research in Psychology.* 2(1): 67–91.

Watts S and Stenner P (2012) *Doing Q Methodological Research. Theory, Method and Interpretation.* Thousand Oaks, CA: Sage.

Wawrytko SA (2018) Buddhist Nondualism. Deconstructing gender and other Delusions of the discriminating mind through awareness. In Pang-White A (Ed.) *The Bloomsbury Handbook of Chinese Philosophy and Gender.* New York: Bloomsbury, pp. 307–330.

Weber J (2010) *Die Rückkehr der Rennpappe. [The Return of the Racing Cardboard/tarmac bubble.]* 7 May. Available at: https://www.dw.com/de/die-rűckkehr-der-rennpappe/a-5537892

Weber R and Strauß B (2015) Group psychotherapy in Germany. *International Journal of Group Psychotherapy.* 65(4): 513–525. https://doi.org/10.1521/ijgp.2015.65.4.513.

Webler T, Danielson S and Tuler S (2009) *Using Q Method to Reveal Social Perspectives in Environmental Research.* Greenfield, MA: Social and Environmental Research Institute. Available at: https://www.seri-us.org/content/primer-q-methodology-available-free-download (accessed 4 February 2025).

Weegmann M (2001) Working intersubjectively: What does it mean for theory and therapy? *Group Analysis.* 34(4): 515–530.

Weegmann M (2014) *The World within the Group. Developing Theory for Group Analysis*. London: Karnac.

Weegmann M (2016) *Permission to Narrate. Explorations in Group Analysis, Psychoanalysis, Culture.* London: Karnac.

Weick KE (1995) What theory is not, Theorizing is. *Administrative Science Quarterly.* 40(3): 385–390. https://www.jstor.org/stable/2393789

Weidling P, Von Villiez A, Loewenau A and Farron N (2016) The victims of unethical human experiments and Coerced research under national socialism. *Endeavour.* 40(1): 1–6.

Weinberg H (2006) *Group Analysis, Large Groups and the Internet Unconscious*. Thesis. Department of Psychology and Speech Therapy. Manchester: Manchester Metropolitan University, UK.

Weinberg H (2007) So what is this social unconscious anyway? *Group Analysis.* 40(3): 307–322.

Weinberg H (2014) *The Paradox of Internet Groups. Alone in the Presence of Virtual Others.* New York: Routledge.

Weinberg H (2020) Online group therapy. In search of a new theory? In Weinberg H and Rolnick A (Eds.) *Theory and Practice of Online Therapy: Internet-Delivered Interventions for Individuals, Families, Groups, and Organizations*. New York: Routledge, pp. 174–187.

Weinberg H (2021) Obstacles, challenges, and benefits of online group psychotherapy. *American Journal of Psychotherapy*. 74(2): 83–88.

Weinberg H (2023) Online training process groups for therapists: A proposed model. *International Journal of Group Psychotherapy*. 73(2): 141–165.

Weinberg H and Rolnik A (Eds.) (2019) *Theory and Practice of Online Therapy. Internet-delivered Interventions for Individuals, Groups, Families, and Organizations.* New York: Routledge.

Weinberg H and Schneider S (2003) Introduction. Background, structure and dynamics of the large group. In Schneider S and Weinberg H (Eds.) *The Large Group Re-Visited.* London: Jessica Kingsley Publishers.

Weinberg H, Rolnick A and Leighton A (Eds.) (2023a) *The Virtual Group Therapy Circle. Advances in Online Group Theory and Practice.* New York: Routledge.

Weinberg H, Rolnick A and Leighton A (Eds.) (2023b) *Advances in Online Therapy. Emergence of a New Paradigm.* New York: Routledge.

Weinberg RS and Gould D (2014) *Foundations of Sport and Exercise Psychology.* 7th edition. Champaign, IL.: Human Kinetics Publishers.

Weisser J (2024) *Beyond Methodology: What is Post Qualitative Inquiry?* Quirkos. Blog. November 25, 2024. Available at: https://www.quirkos.com/blog/post/beyond-methodology-what-is-post-qualitative-inquiry/ (accessed 7 May 2025).

Weisstein EW (n.d.) *Hilbert Space. MathWorld.* A Wolfram Web Resource. Available at: https://mathworld.wolfram.com/HilbertSpace.html (accessed 4 January 2025).

Weisstein EW (n.d.) *p-adic Number. MathWorld.* A Wolfram Web Resource. Available at: https://mathworld.wolfram.com/p-adicNumber.html (accessed 4 January 2025).

Welfel RE (2013) *Ethics in Counselling & Psychotherapy. Standards, Research, and Emerging Issues.* 5th Internal Edition. Cleveland: Brooks/Cole Central Learning.

Welldon E and Wilson P (2005) Introduction. *Group Analysis.* 38(3): 355–357.

Weller BE, Bowen NK and Faubert SI (2020) Latent class analysis. A guide to best practice. *Journal of Black Psychology.* 46(4): 287–311.

Weller S (2023) Fostering habits of care: Reframing qualitative data sharing policies and practices. *Qualitative Research.* 23(4): 1022–1041.

Wendt A (2015a) Non-local experience in time. In Wendt A (2015b) *Quantum Mind And Social Science. Unifying Physical and Social Ontology*. Cambridge: Cambridge University Press, pp. 189–205.

Wendt A (2015b) *Quantum Mind and Social Science. Unifying Physical and Social Ontology.* Cambridge: Cambridge University Press.

Wengraf T (2001) *Qualitative Research Interviewing. Biographic Narrative and Semi-Structured Methods.* New York: Sage.

Wengraf T (2011) Can psychoanalysis think about the psycho-social? *Journal of Psycho-Social Studies.* 5(1): 184–195.
Wengraf T (2018) Researching dated, situated, defended, and deciding/evolving subjectivities by biographic-narrative interview. Psychoanalysis, the psycho-societal unconscious, and biographic-narrative interview method and interpretation. In Stamenova K and Hinshelwood RD (Eds.) *Methods of Research into the Unconscious. Applying Psychoanalytic Ideas to Social Science.* London and New York: Routledge, pp. 211–238.
Wengraf T and Chamberlayne P (2013) Biography-using research, (BNIM), Sostris, institutional regimes and critical psychosocial realism. In Turk J and Mrozowicki A (Eds.) *Realist Biography and European Policy*. Leuven: Leuven University Press, pp. 63–92.
Werner N (2022) *Wie Schlack-Golodkowski von Politick und BND gedeckt wurde.* 1 March. Available at: https://www.mdr.de/geschichte/ddr/deutsche-einheit/wiedervereinigung/schalck-golodkowski-bnd-zerv-politik-100.html See also *ZERV Ermittler, Zeit der Abrechnung.* https://www.fernsehserien.de/zerv-zeit-der-abrechnung/folgen/zerv-die-ermittler-1532097; Documentary: https://www.crew-united.com/en/Geschichte-Mitteldeutschlands-Schalck-Golodkowski-und-die-Pleite-der-DDR__215132.html
Wertheimer M (1912) Experimentelle Studien über das Sehen von Bewegung.[Experimental studies on vision and movement.] *Zeitschrift für Psychologie.* 61(1): 161–265.
Wertheimer M (1922) Untersuchungen zur Lehre von der Gestalt I. [Study for the Teaching of Gestalt I.] *Psychologische Forschung.* 1(1): 47–58.
Wertheimer M (1923) Untersuchungen zur Lehre von der Gestalt II. [Study for the Teaching of Gestalt II.] *Psychologische Forschung.* 4(1): 301–350.
Wertheimer M (1944) Gestalt theory. *Social Research.* 11(1): 78–99.
Werts FJ, Charmaz K, McMullen LM, Josselson R, Anderson R and McSpadden E (2011) *Five Ways of Doing Qualitative Analysis. Phenomenological Psychology, Grounded Theory, Discourse Analysis, Narrative Research, and Intuitive Inquiry.* New York: The Guilford Press.
Wertsch JV (1991) *Voices of the Mind. A Sociocultural Approach to Mediated Action.* Cambridge, MA: Harvard University Press.
Weschler I, Massarik R and Tannenbaum R (1962) The self in process: A sensitivity training emphasis. In Weschler I and Schein E (Eds.) *Issues in Human Relations Training. (Selected Readings, No. 5).* Washington, DC: NTL, pp. 33–46.
Wetherell M, Taylor S and Yates SK (2001) *Discourse Theory and Practice. A Reader.* London: Sage.
Wheelan SA (Ed.) (2005) *The Handbook of Group Research and Practice.* Thousand Oaks, CA: Sage.
Wheeler B (1992) The Masculinity of King Arthur. From Gildas to the Nuclear Age. *Quondam et Futurus.* 2(4): 1–26.
White B (2025) *Methods Vignettes: Q Method (Q Methodology)*. Steps Centre. Available at: https://steps-centre.org/pathways-methods-vignettes/methods-vignettes-q-method/ (accessed 8 February 2025).
Whitinui P (2014) Indigenous autoethnography: Exploring, engaging, and experiencing 'self' as native method of inquiry. *Journal of Contemporary Ethnography.* 43(4): 456–487. https://doi.org/10.1177/0891241613508148.
Whittemore R and Knafl K (2005) The integrative review: Updated methodology. *Journal of Advanced Nursing.* 52(5): 546–553.
Whittingham M, Lefforge NL and Marmarosh C (2021) Group psychotherapy as a specialty: An inconvenient truth. *American Journal of Psychotherapy.* 74(2): 60–66. https://doi.org/10.1176/appi.psychotherapy.20200037.
WHO (2019) *Manual of the International Classification of Diseases, Injuries, and Causes of Death.* Geneva: World Health Organization.
WHO (2024) *Ethics and Governance of Artificial Intelligence for Health. Guidance on Large Multiple-Modal Models.* Geneva: World Health Organization.
Wibawa AP and Kurniawan F (2024) A survey text summarization: Techniques, evaluation and challenges. *Natural Language Processing Journal.* 7. https://doi.org/10.1016/j.nlp.2024.100070.
Wichert A (2023) *Mid, Brain, Quantum AI, and the Multiverse.* Boca Raton, FL: CRC Press.
Wickham RJ (2019) Secondary analysis research. *Journal of Advanced Practitioner in Oncology.* 10(4): 395–400.

Wikipedia (2024a) *Oedipus*. Available at: https://en.wikipedia.org/wiki/Oedipus (accessed 28th November 2024).

Wikipedia (2024b) *Concept*. Available at: https://en.wikipedia.org/wiki/Concept (accessed 27 March 2024).

Wikipedia (2024c) *Double Slit Experiment*. Available at: https://en.wikipedia.org/wiki/Double-slit_experiment (accessed 25 October 2024).

Wile DB, Bron, GD and Pollack, HB (1970) The group therapy questionnaire. An instrument for study of leadership in small groups. *Psychological Reports*. 27(1): 263–273.

Wilinski B (2017) Knowing and interpreting prekindergarten policy: A Bakhtinian analysis. *Education Policy Analysis Archives*. 25(27): 1–31. https://doi.org/10.14507/epaa.25.2211.

Wilinski B, Morley A and Landgraf J (2022) How policies and policy actors shape the pre-K Borderland: Implications for early childhood educators' work experiences. *Teachers College Record*. 123(10): 117–141. https://doi.org/10.1177/01614681211058962.

Wilke G (2003) Chaos and order in the large group. In Schneider S and Weinberg H (Eds.) *The Large Group Re-Visited*. London: Jessica Kingsley Publishers.

Wilke G (2016) The German social unconscious: Second generation perpetrator symptoms in organisations and groups. In Hopper E and Weinberg H (Eds.) *The Social Unconscious in Persons, Groups and Societies. Volume 2. Mainly Foundation Matrices*. London: Karnac, pp. 61–80.

Wilke G (2018) *The Art of Group Analysis in Organisations. The Use of Intuitive and Experiential Knowledge*. London: Routledge.

Will WC (2006) Was Einstein right? *Annalen der Physik*. 15(1): 19–33. https://doi.org/10.1002/andp.200651801-203.

Williams J (2004) Poststructuralism as deconstruction. Jacques Derrida's of Grammatology. In *Understanding Poststructuralism, Understanding Movements in Modern thought*. Chesham: Acumen Publishing, pp. 25–52.

Williams MH (2019) *Core Concepts of Bion*. PART ONE How the mind grows through processing thoughts. Writings and Artwork by Meg Harris Williams. https://www.artlit.info Available at: https://www.artlit.info/booksandpapers.html

Williams N (2021) Autoethnography: a decolonizing research methodological approach. In *SAGE Research Methods Cases*. Online. Sage Publications Ltd, pp. 1–14. https://doi.org/10.4135/9781529759563.

Wilson L and Ogston E (2017) To see ourselves as others see us: Thematic analysis of patient feedback following psychotherapy. *Group-Analytic Contexts*. 75(1): 116–125.

Wilson P and Wilson S (2000) Circles in the classroom. The cultural significance of structure. *Canadian Social Studies*. 34(2): 11–12.

Wilson RA (2016) *Quantum Psychology. How Brain Software Programs You and Your World*. Grand Junction, Colorado: Hilaritas Press.

Wilterdink NA (2002) The sociogenesis of postmodernism. *European Journal of Sociology/Archives Européennes de Sociologie*. 43(2): 190–216. https://www.jstor.org/stable/23999235 Published Online Cambridge Journals: https://www.cambridge.org/core/journals/european-journal-of-sociology-archives-europeennes-de-sociologie/article/abs/sociogenesis-of-postmodernism/3FC0AA6A88072E93986E7D0E3C7DE98D

Wilton D (2009) The 'Societalisation' of the state. Sport for the Masses and popular music in the GDR. In Fulbrook M (Ed.) *Power and Society in the GDR, 1961–1979: The Normalisation of Rule?* New York: Berghan, pp. 102–129.

Wing-Tsit C (1973) *A Source Book in Chinese Philosophy*. Trans. and Compiled by W-T Chan. 4th Edition. Princeton, NJ: Princeton University Press.

Winter DA (1992) Repertory grid technique as a group psychotherapy research instrument. *Group Analysis*. 25(4): 449–462

Wirth HJ (2007) Schismatic processes in the psychoanalytic movement and their impact on the formation of theories. *International Forum of Psychoanalysis*. 16(1): 4–11. https://doi.org/10.1080/08037060600888089.

Wittgenstein L (1921/1961) *Tractatus Logico Philosophicus*. London: Routledge & Kegan.

Wittgenstein L (1953) *Philosophical Investigations*. Oxford: Blackwell.

Witzenmann H and Wagemann J (Eds.) (2022) *Structure Phenomenology. Preconscious Formation in the Epistemic Disclosure of Reality.* New York: Bloomsbury.

WMA (World Medical Association) (1964) *Declaration of Helsinki.* Helsinki: WMA. Available at: https://www.wma.net/what-we-do/medical-ethics/declaration-of-helsinki/doh-jun1964/ (accessed 7 April 2025).

WMA (World Medical Association) (2024) WMA Declaration of Helsinki. Ethical Principles for Medical Research Involving Human Participants. Available at: https://www.wma.net/policies-post/wma-declaration-of-helsinki/ (accessed 7 April 2025).

Wölbern JP (2016) Haftarbeit in der DDR. Eine Zwischenbilanz. [Prison labor in the GDR.] *Zeithistorische Forschungen.* 13(1): 86–107. Available at: https://zeithistorische-forschungen.de/1-2016/5331

Wolf A and Schwartz EK (1962) *Psychoanalysis in Groups.* New York: Grame & Stratton.

Wolf F (2023) *Kampf im Klassenzimmer. Schulzeit in Ost und West Deutschland.* Terra X Geschichte. [Fight in the classroom. Time at School in East and West Germany. Terra X History.] Available at: https://schule.zdf.de/video/kampf-im-klassenzimmer--schulzeit-in-ost-und-west-100 (accessed 2 April 2023).

Wőlfer R and Hewstone M (2017) Beyond the dyadic perspective: 10 Reasons for using social network analysis in intergroup contact research. *British Journal of Social Psychology.* 56(3): 609–617. https://doi.org/10.1111/bjso.12195.

Wolle S (1999) *Die heile Welt der Diktatur. Alltag und Herrschaft in der DDR 1971–1989. [The intact World of the Dictatorship. Daily Life and Ruling in the GDR 1971-1989]* Bonn: BPB.

Wolle S (2004) *DDR. Eine kurze Geschichte. [GDR. A brief History]* Frankfurt/Main: Fischer Taschenbuch Verlag.

Wolle S (2013) *Der Groβe Plan. Alltag und Herrschaft in der DDR 1949–1961. [The great Plan. Daily Life and Ruling in the GDR from 1949 to 1961.]* Berlin: Links Verlag.

Wollstonecraft M (1792) *A Vindication of the Rights of Woman with Strictures on Political and Moral Subjects,* Boston: Peter Edges for Thomas and Andrews. [Republished in 2004 by Penguin Classics, London].

Wong SS and Jeffery TD (2015) Why theories do not turn into laws. *Science Scope.* 38(7): 34–41. https://www.researchgate.net/publication/273141746_Why_Theories_Do_Not_Turn_Into_laws

Wongpakaran T, Wongpakaran N, Intachote-Sakamoto R and Boripuntakul T (2013) The Group Cohesiveness Scale (GCS) for psychiatric inpatients. *Perspectives in Psychiatric Care.* 49(1): 58–64. https://doi.org/10.1111/j.1744-6163.2012.00342.x.

Wood C (2023) What is gravity? *Space Com.* 30 July. Available at: https://www.space.com/classical-gravity.html (accessed 5 August 2024).

Wood C and Sherman M (2022) Inside the Proton, the 'Most Complicated You Could Possible Imagine'. *Quanta Magazine.* 19 October 2022. Available at: https://www.quantamagazine.org/inside-the-proton-the-most-complicated-thing-imaginable-20221019/ (accessed 12 January 2025).

Wood N and Patel N (2017) On addressing 'Whiteness' during clinical psychology training. *South African Journal of Psychology.* 47(3): 280–291. https://doi.org/10.1177/0081246317722099.

Wood P (1997) Ethnography and ethnology. In Barfield T (Ed.) *The Dictionary of Anthropology.* Malden: Blackwell, pp. 157–160.

Woods J (1996) Group analysis with children, families, and young people. *Group Analysis.* 29(1): 5–7.

Woods J and Williams A (Eds.) (2014) *Forensic Group Psychotherapy. The Portman Approach.* London: Karnac.

Wooten NR, Fedina L and Hudson DL (2023) Introduction to the special section: Developing Antiracist research from research questions to dissemination. *Journal of the Society for Social Work and Research.* 14(1). https://doi.org/10.1086/724718.

Wróbel S (2019) Essay on indifference. Affect and thinking from Spinoza to Freud and Deleuze. *Philosophy Study.* 9(2): 65–73. https://www.davidpublisher.com/Public/uploads/Contribute/5cf8bf95d9701.pdf

Wynn D and Williams CK (2012) Principles for constructing critical realist case study research in information systems. *MIS Quarterly.* 36(3): 787–810.

Xavier de Aguiar TR (2005) The symmetries of the Hempelian model of explanation. *Scielo Social Sciences.* Article in English from *Kriterion Journal of Philosophy* 46(111): 138–152. http://socialsciences.scielo.org/scielo.php?script=sci_arttext&pid=S0100-512X2006000200010 (Túlio Roberto Xavier de Aguiar).

Xiang S (2023) *Chinese Cosmopolitanism. The History and Philosophy of an Idea.* Princeton, NJ: Princeton University Press.

Xiong H, Wang Z, Li X, Bian J, Xie Z, Mumtaz S, Al-Dulaimi A and Barnes E (2024) Converging Paradigms. The synergy of symbolic and connectionist AI in LLM-empowered autonomous agents. *Management International.* 28(2): 36–48. https://doi.org/10.48550/arXiv.2407.08516.

Xu R, Sun Y, Ren M, Guo S, Pan R, Lin H, Sun L and Han X (2024) AI for social science and social science of AI: A survey. *Information Processing & Management.* 61(3): 1–30. https://doi.org/10.1016/j.ipm.2024.103665.

Yager J, Kay J and Kelsay K (2021) Clinicians' cognitive and affective Biases and the practice of psychotherapy. *American Journal of Psychotherapy.* 74(3): 119–126. https://doi.org/10.1176/appi.psychotherapy.20200025.

Yalom ID (1975) *The Theory and Practice of Group Psychotherapy.* New York: Basic Books.

Yalom ID (1983) *Inpatient Group Therapy.* New York: Basic Books.

Yalom ID and Leszcz M (2005) *The Theory and Practice of Group Psychotherapy.* 5th Edition. New York: Basic Books.

Yalom ID and Leszcz M (2020) *The Theory and Practice of Group Psychotherapy.* 6th Edition. New York: Basic Books.

Yalom ID and Rand K (1966) Compatibility and Cohesiveness in therapy groups. *Archives of General Psychiatry.* 15(3): 267–275. https://doi.org/10.1001/archpsyc.1966.01730150043007; https://jamanetwork.com/journals/jamapsychiatry/article-abstract/489142

Yang J-M (2022) Qi and Bioelectromagnetic Energy. *YMAA.* Available at: https://ymaa.com/articles/2023/02/qi-and-bioelectromagnetic-energy (accessed 13 October 2024).

Yang Y (2022) Space, time and number as a holistic unity in the Yijing. *Cogent Psychology.* 9(1): 1–16. https://doi.org/10.1080/23311908.2022.2049130. Available on: https://www.researchgate.net/publication/366655984_SPACE_TIME_and_NUMBER_as_a_holistic_unity_in_the_Yijing

Yarkomi T (2020) Implicit realism impedes progress in psychology. Comment on Fried (2020). *Psychological Inquiry.* 31(4): 326–333.

Yarwood-Ross L and Jack K (2023) Building a classic grounded theory. Some reflections. *Grounded Theory Review.* 22(1): 49–65. https://groundedtheoryreview.org/index.php/gtr/article/view/107/77

Yasar K and Sheldon R (2024) *What is Virtual Reality? How It's Used and How It Evolved.* TechTarget Network. 14 August 2024. Available at: https://www.techtarget.com/whatis/definition/virtual-reality (accessed 1 October 2024).

Yazdani S and Hoseini AM (2019) Five decades of research and theorization on clinical reasoning: A critical review. *Advances in Medical Education and Practice.* 10: 703–716. https://doi.org/10.2147/AMEP.S213492. Available at: https://www.dovepress.com/five-decades-of-research-and-theorization-on-clinical-reasoning-a-crit-peer-reviewed-fulltext-article-AMEP

Yelle RA (2022) Semiotics. In Engler S and Stausberg M (Eds.) *The Routledge Handbook of Research Methods in the Study of Religion.* New York: Routledge, pp. 434–444.

Yeung HW (1997) Critical realism and realist research in human geography. A method or philosophy in search of a method? *Progress in Human Geography.* 21(1): 51–74. https://doi.org/10.1191/030913297668207944.

Yi V, Mac J, Na, VS, Venturanza RJ, Museus SD, Buenavista TL and Pendakur SL (2020) Toward an Anti-Imperialistic Critical Race Analysis of the Model Minority Myth. *Review of Educational Research.* 90(4): 542–579. https://doi.org/10.3102/0034654320933532. Available at: https://www.researchgate.net/publication/342288126_Toward_an_Anti-Imperialistic_Critical_Race_Analysis_of_the_Model_Minority_Myth

Yılmaz M, Türkarslan KK, Zanini L, Hasdemir D, Spitoni GF and Lingiardi V (2024) Transference interpretation and psychotherapy outcome. A systematic review of a no-consensus relationship. *Research in Psychotherapy. Psychopathology, Process and Outcome.* 27(1): 744–759. https://www.researchinpsychotherapy.org/rpsy/article/view/744/701

Yorks L (2005) Editorial nothing So practical as a good theory. *Human Resource Development Review.* 4(2): 111–113.

Zachariadis M, Scott S and Barrett M (2010) *Exploring critical realism as the theoretical foundation of mixed-method research: evidence from economics of IS innovations.* Jude Business School Working

Paper Series. Cambridge: Cambridge University Press. Available at: https://www.jbs.cam.ac.uk/wp-contet/uploads/2010/08/wp1003.pdf (accessed 30 December 2023).

Zachariadis M, Scott S and Barrett M (2013) Methodological implications of critical realism for mixed-methods research. *MIS Quarterly.* 37(3): 855–879.

Zahavi D and Overgaard S (2008) Phenomenological sociology. The subjectivity of everyday life. In Jacobsen MH (Ed.) *Encountering the Everyday. An Introduction to the Sociologies of the Unnoticed.* London: Palgrave, pp. 93–115.

Žalec B (2021) Rosa's theory of resonance. Its importance for (the science of) religion and hope. *Religions.* 12(10): 797. Available at: https://doi.org/10.3390/rel12100797 (accessed 11 March 2023). https://www.mdpi.com/2077-1444/12/10/797

Zapirain BT, Carminati F, Torres MA, de Mendivil EG, Fouassier C, Gex-Fabry M, Martin F, Labarere J, Demongeot J, Lorincz EN and Carminati GG (2014) Group unconscious common orientation: exploratory study at the basque foundation for the investigation of mental health group training for therapists. *NeuroQuantology.* 12(1): 139–150. https://doi.org/10.14704/nq.2014.12.1.709.

Zeigler H and Peak W (1971) The Political function of the educational system. In Hopper E (Ed.) *Readings in the Theory of Educational Systems.* London: Hutchinson University Press, pp. 212–239.

Zembylas M (2023) A decolonial approach to AI in higher education teaching and learning: Strategies for undoing the ethics of digital neocolonialism. *Learning, Media and Technology.* 48(1): 25–37. https://doi.org/10.1080/17439884.2021.2010094.

Zemmelman J (2021) *Making Mental Health Radically Accessible. A Conversation with Alison Darcy, Founder and President Of Woebot Health.* Available at: https://aifund.ai/insights/making-mental-health-radically-accessible-a-conversation-with-alison-darcy-founder-and-president-of-woebot-health/ (accessed 6 March 2025).

Zeng J (2023) The I Ching as a potential Jungian application: History and practice. *Journal of Analytical Psychology.* 68(5): 913–932. https://doi.org/10.1111/1468-5922.12958.

Zhai P (1998) *Philip Zhai, Get Real: A Philosophical Adventure in Virtual Reality.* Lanham, MD: Rowman & Littlefield.

Zhang Y and Wildemuth BM (2005) Qualitative analysis of content. *Human Brain Mapping.* 30(7): 2197–2206. Available at: https://pages.ischool.utexas.edu/yanz/Content_analysis.pdf

Zhang Y and Wildemuth BM (2009) Unstructured interviews. In Wildemuth BM (Ed.) *Applications of Social Research Methods to Questions in Information and Library Science.* Westport, CT: Libraries Unlimited, pp. 222–231. Available at: https://pages.ischool.utexas.edu/yanz/publication.html

Zhengkun G (n.d.) Dao De Jing and Western Science. *FutureLearn.* Available at: https://www.futurelearn.com/info/courses/taoism-and-western-culture/0/steps/84264 (accessed 23 January 2025).

Zhou Q, Chen Z-H, Cao Y-H and Peng S (2021) Clinical impact and quality of randomized controlled trials involving interventions evaluating artificial intelligence prediction tools. A systematic review. *Digital Medicine.* 4: 154. https://doi.org/10.1038/s41746-021-00524-2.

Zilcha-Mano S, Fisher H, Dolev-Amit T, Keefe JR and Barber JP (2023) A systematic review of the association between interpretations and immediate, intermediate, and distal outcomes. *Psychotherapy.* 60(3): 266–282.

Zilcha-Mano S, Keefe JR, Fisher H, Dolev-Amit T, Veler Poleg N and Barber JP (2024) Is the use of interpretations associated with treatment outcome? A systematic review and meta-analytic answer. *Clinical Psychology. Science and Practice.* 31(1): 1–13.

Zinkin L (1984) Three models are better than one. *Group Analysis.* 17(1): 17–21.

Zinkin L (1989) A Gnostic view of group analysis. *Group Analysis.* 22(2): 201–217.

Žižek S (1993) *Tarrying with the Negative. Kant, Hegel, and the Critique of Ideology.* Durham: Duke University Press.

Zuolo F (2014) Beyond groups? Types of sharing and normative treatment. In Calder G, Bessone M and Zuolo F (Eds.) *How Groups Matter. Challenges of Toleration in Pluralistic Societies.* New York: Routledge, pp. 199–218.

Zuzuki DT (1949/1998) The Zen Doctrine of no-mind. In Molino A (Ed.) (1998) *The Couch and the Tree. Dialogues in Psychoanalysis and Buddhism.* London: Open Gate Press, pp. 26–36.

Zuzuki DT (1993) *Zen and Japanese Culture.* Princeton, NJ: Princeton University Press.

APPENDIX 1

Group Analytic Psychotherapies, Conceptualizations & Developments

Development of Group Analytic Psychotherapies

Sigmund Freud first introduced Psychoanalysis toward the end of the 19th century. Subsequently, numerous individual and group psychotherapies were developed. Even though Freud himself was more interested in the individual than in groups, he developed methods (e.g. free association) that would be applied to groups. Additionally, social psychology, sociology, anthropology, physics, and philosophy, influenced talking therapies. Various theories developed out of studies that examined individual psychotherapies, groups, and group dynamics. All these developments laid the foundation for modern group psychotherapies.

They consist of different approaches, ranging from Positivist-oriented cognitive behavioral to group analytic psychotherapies, which have an interpretivist orientation. Group analytic psychotherapy itself developed from Psychoanalysis. It was founded by Trigant Burrow between 1924 and 1927 in the US. Exploring and addressing defense mechanisms forms a vital part of all psychoanalytic and group analytic approaches. According to Sandner (2018), three analytic methods arose from Burrow's approach: Wolf's psychoanalysis in the group (Wolf & Schwartz, 1962), Foulkes' (1948) Group Analysis, and Bion's (1961, 1962) analysis of the group-as-a-whole. Initially, concepts and techniques from Freudian Psychoanalysis were used in groups.

Having applied free association and dream interpretation to group psychotherapy, Slavson (1950) found that group dynamics could be utilized to understand individual group members (Van Wagoner, 2015). Kurt Lewin (1948) established the Center for Group Dynamics. He coined the term "group dynamics" after observing people's behavior in groups (what people did, talked about, which topics they avoided, who was active or silent, who had power over whom) (Day, 2014). Psychodynamic group approaches (e.g. Ezriel, Foulkes, Bion), which were influenced by Lewin's (1947) field theory, shifted the emphasis from understanding the emotions and behaviors of an individual group member to appreciating the operating forces in the whole group.

While Ezriel's (1973) object relations perspective focused on group tension, resistance, interpretation, and transference, Bion (1961) prioritized interpreting the group behavior, which interfered with the task of the group.

Interpretation, the foundation of Psychoanalysis (Leavy, 1973), is an important technique to understand defense mechanisms and other unconscious processes (Schermer, 2011). *Location* (therapists locate where problem occurs), *translation* (equivalent of making the Freudian repressed conscious), and *interpretation*, are at the heart of the group analytic model (Schlapobersky, 2016).

Bion (1965) also theorized knowing and reverie, often regarded as a dream-like state. Discussing emotional experiences, Bion (1962b) viewed the mother–infant feeding relationship as the primary site for reverie. It is the mother's capacity for reverie, her being the receptor and container of her baby's sensations, which enables thinking. Beta elements (sensations) are transformed through the process of reverie into alpha functions (thought) (Bion, 1962a,b). Bion linked the inability of thinking to Klein's notion of excessive projective identification.

Drawing on Melanie Klein's (1948) object relations theory, Bion also theorized the group. He had noticed that there was a sense of commonality amongst group members. At the same time, they also feared losing their individuality. To deal with this conflict, two types of groups develop in most groups, namely the "work group" and the "basic assumption group". Even though people behave rationally in the former, the group gets distracted by shared unconscious anxieties. Bion (1961) referred to these unconscious dynamics, which result from regressive mechanisms reminiscent of the earliest phase of life, as "basic assumptions". Identifying *dependency* (group is excessively dependent on the leader), *pairing* (group's focus is on one dyadic pair, or more pairs), and *fight/flight* (people retreat or argue aggressively), Bion found that these basic assumptions obstructed the task of the group. Their function served the protection from psychotic anxiety. The defense mechanisms of splitting, projection, and projective identification, dominate when a group operates at a basic assumptions level.

Opposing aspects of an experience can be separated in the mind (splitting). These are then projected into different people or groups, who identify with these aspects and act them out in projective identification. It is an unconscious process, whereby disowned feelings, actions, and motivations, are attributed to (projected into) others (Skogstad, 2018).

Although each individual has uniquely personal experiences of basic assumptions, each assumption is also common to the whole group. Bion (1961) introduced the idea that shared unconscious basic assumptions had the power to destroy a group's capacity for thinking. He suggested that groups gradually gained insight into these defensive processes, but that they would never be entirely free of these primitive modes of thinking and feeling.

Out of Bion's work developed the "Study Group", which is an essential element of the Tavistock Conferences (Palmer, 1992). It offers people the opportunity to learn about unconscious group processes a group setting.

According to Beveridge (2023), the Tavistock Clinic in London was established in 1920 to provide psychodynamic psychotherapy to the public. Freudian in orientation, from 1930 onwards, it incorporated ideas from Segal, Balint, Klein, Anna Freud, Bion, and others. The Tavistock Institute of Human Relations was formed during this period. It became responsible for teaching and research. This includes teaching psychotherapists to examine the how, what, and why of unconscious processes in groups, institutions, and organizations (Ehrlich, 2023).

Historically, Group Relations developed by broadening Lewin's (1947) field theory, integrating Von Bertalanffy's (1950) open systems theory, and by drawing on Bion's (1961, 1965) basic assumptions and conceptualizations of the group-as-a-whole. Group Relations regards understanding of, and working with, unconscious processes (e.g. social defenses against anxiety) as necessary for bringing about change (Sher, 2012).

Kenneth Rice (1965, 1969) used group experience as a method for understanding personal development and leadership roles. According to the Tavistock Institute (2020), the "forgotten giant" Rice had a good understanding of action research. He combined organizational design and consultancy practice into a unique blend of the theories of change and systems (including organizations). The A. K. Rice Institute for the Study of Social Systems in America was established by Margaret Rioch (1970) and Erich Miller in memory of Rice. Group Relations has expanded its reach in many countries.

Over the past decades, numerous group-analytically oriented therapies have been developed. The expanding field is diverse and vital to the treatment of the many problems that people experience.

According to Van der Heuvel et al. (2023), psychodynamic group therapy is an umbrella term for a variety of approaches, such as, Group Analysis (Foulkes, 1990), and interpersonal group therapy (Yalom, 1975; Yalom & Leszcz, 2005). The Institute of Group Analysis in London describes Group Analysis as a form of psychotherapy by the group, and of the group, including its conductor (group therapist). Achieving healthier integrations within individuals, and within their network of relationships, is an aim of therapy (Lumsden, 2023, p. 310). The "Study Day" provides group analysts with an opportunity for live exploration of identities (Hutchinson, 2017).

Rooted in the work of the American psychoanalyst Harry Stuck Sullivan, interpersonal group psychotherapy views the therapy group as a social microcosm that illuminates interpersonal patterns. Yalom (1975, 1983) radically departed from group-as-whole phenomena in favor of careful examination of interpersonal interactions (Van Wagoner, 2015). Like relational group psychotherapy, interpersonal psychotherapy values group cohesion (people's overall sense of belonging and participation in the group), but relational therapists focus more on the subjective experience of relatedness. Both approaches prioritize interactions in the here-and-now (Leszcz & Malat, 2015). That psychoanalytic data are mutually generated by both psychotherapists and patients, is a basic premise of the relational approach (Billow, 2003). Richard Billow (2017a) regards the need for acquiring emotional meaning as the primary organizer of group formation and processes. Relational therapists presume that much of their thinking is created jointly. Psychotherapists and patients unconsciously affect each other. Hence, they only may have a sense of what was happening retrospectively. By then, word and actions have already produced "enactments" (Billow, 2015, p. 170). Relational group psychotherapy has been influenced by relational psychology and intersubjectivity. It regards dynamics in supervision as a parallel process, mirroring what happens in the therapy group. However, the intersubjective-relational perspective is so eclectic that Schermer and Rice (2015) referred to it as "sensibility", rather than a specific school of thought.

Modern Group Analysis emphasizes communication and has shifted from monologue via dialogue to discourse, and to the relational dialogical approach to the Self (Schlapobersky, 2016).

The German model (e.g. Staats et al., 2014; Streeck, 2024) was developed by Heigl-Evers. It has a slightly different focus than group analytic therapy as practiced in Britain. The so-called "Gőttinger Model" (Heigl-Evers & Heigl, 1973, 1983, 1994; Heigl-Evers, 1971, 1973, 1978; Heigl-Evers & Ott, 1994, 2002; Heigl-Evers et al., 1994, 1998; Kőnig & Lindner, 1993, 1994; Strauß, 2022) is a type of psychodynamic therapy, whose clinical and empirical approach focuses on understanding (Staats et al., 2013). Different group theories within this integrative model were initially derived from psychoanalysis, social psychology, and empirical research.

Interestingly, in contrast to Foulkesain Group Analysis in the UK, more groups for children are offered (e.g. Lehle, 2025).

Although psychoanalysis and related therapies were discouraged in the former German Democratic Republic, Höck's (1969, 1981a,b,c; 1982; Hőck et al., 1973) Intentional Dynamic Group Psychotherapy (IDGP) was an influential model (Weber & Strauß, 2015). Despite its focus on symptom elimination, it seems to have some conceptual similarities with Foulkes' and Yalom's models (Härdtle & Schneider, 1999). Criticized for being too oriented toward socialist and collectivist ideologies (Gallistl et al., 2022a,b), after the German re-unification (Strauß et al., 2022), some queried whether the IDGT had also lost its home (see Grawe et al., 1994; Benkenstein et al., 1995; Sandner, 1995, 2018; Seidler, 2019).

Integrating field, communication, stress, and Bionian theories, Agazarian (1994, 1997) developed the method of functional subgrouping by applying her theory of living human systems to group psychotherapy. Systems Theory formulates operational definitions, which serve as hypotheses that are tested by the clinical method that implemented this definition. Since each intervention is designed to examine the validity of the theory (functional subgrouping), action research is built into systems-centered group therapy (Grantt, 2015).

If a group integrates its differences, Agazarian (1997) argued, it will not only survive but also develop. This contrasts with approaches that discourage subgrouping due to the risk of scapegoating.

Ormont's (2002) modern group analysis (Blanco Furgeri, 2001), which was originally based on Hyman Spotnitz (1976), relies on bridging. The therapist's reactions are regarded as a source of study. It is probably "the most technique-oriented" theory (Van Wagoner, 2015, p. 255).

More recently, mentalization, and short-term focused group analytic psychotherapy, have gained prominence (Karterud, 2015, 2018; Karterud et al., 2024; Krämer et al., 2021; Lorentzen, 2020; Schultz-Venrath, 2024). While the Norwegian group analyst Lorentzen (2022) developed focused-group analytic psychotherapy, the German Schultz-Venrath (2024) elaborated mentalization, integrating body and mind. Mentalization, which refers to the ability to grasp another person's subjectivity, is crucial to healthy relationships and intersubjectivity. The central idea of intersubjectivity is that the experiential and phenomenological worlds of individuals are jointly created through people's mutual exchanges with each other, and with their sociocultural worlds (Schermer & Rice, 2015, p. 60). Further variations of group analytic psychotherapy are found, for example, in South America and Portugal.

Studying why so many approaches were formed could be an interesting piece of research. Why Group Analysis has only recently recognized the need to decolonize its theories, practices, and structures, might be equally enlightening to find out.

Influence of the Gestalt School

Foulkes integrated concepts from the Gestalt School into Group Analysis. The Gestalt School is crucial to Gestalt psychology (Bustamante, 2023) and to Gestalt therapy (Guy-Evans, 2023). The Gestalt psychologists Kőhler (1920, 1940, 1947, 1969), Koffka (1935), and Wertheimer (1922, 1923, 1944) demonstrated that perception is based on the relationship between the figure perceived, and the background, in which it is embedded (Pepperell, 2024). Wertheimer (1912) discovered the "phi" phenomenon, showing that structured wholes are the primary units of mental life. Importantly, the whole tends to be grasped before the individual parts enter consciousness (Wagemans et al., 2021). This indicates that researchers need to adopt a holistic approach to understanding psychological phenomena.

The Gestalt School elaborated Field Theory and the Stability Principle, demonstrating that force fields compel systems toward stability. Luchins and Luchins (1999) noted the tendency for systems to achieve a thermodynamic equilibrium. Wertheimer's Law of "Prägnanz" (conciseness, exactness, pithiness) established a direct relationship between the organization of material objects, force fields, and their valence. Together, they determine our perceptual experience of objects (Pepperell, 2024). His Law explains why we are able to perceptually group ambiguous stimuli into precise figures, but further research is needed (Van Geert & Wagemans 2024; Arnheim 1971, 1985). Pithiness is essential to perceiving whole forms. Researchers could examine how different principles of perceptual organization interact in concrete situations, such as, psychotherapy groups or larger groups (institutions, society).

Viewing Gestalt therapy as a phenomenological approach, Parlett (1991) re-casted Field Theory, suggesting that five principles (organization, contemporaneity, singularity, changing process, possible relevance) are important for Gestalt therapy. Whether these are also relevant for psychodynamic group therapies would need to be researched first.

Bion & the Tavistock Group Relations' Methodology

In the 1950s–1960s, the Tavistock under Kenneth Rice, who had been a member of one of Bion's early study groups, shifted its focus from the roles that individuals assumed in work groups, to the dynamics of leadership and authority relations in groups. Rice (1965, 1969) suggested that individuals could not be understood, or changed, outside the context of the groups in which they lived. His colleague Emery (1959) aimed to develop a theory that could explain what the group was discovering, by examining the nature of technical systems, social systems, and the work relationship structures that brought these two systems together (Bradbury et al., 2008).

Lewin (1947, 1947, 1948), who had established the Center for Group Dynamics, was an active researcher, whose field theory shifted the emphasis from understanding the emotions and behaviors of an individual to focusing on the operating forces in the whole group (Lewin, 1935, 1936). Bion and Foulkes both integrated field theory into their group analytic approaches. Lewin (1951) postulated in his formulation of this theory that behavior was affected by the environment (context). His thinking was in line with Foulkesian Group Analysis, but posed a challenge to Freudian Psychoanalysis, which held that all behavior could be explained by deep-seated aspects of the personality.

Lewin's action research has demonstrated clearly that behavior varied across time and under the influence of different environmental forces. His theory and related findings became a central tenet of what would be called the socio-technical school, because it allowed for the possibility that by changing aspects of the workplace, behavioral changes could be produced.

Nowadays, the Tavistock's Group Relations Program regards the experiential study of groups and organizational processes as inseparable. It forms part of its research in the wider social sciences. There is, as Sher (2012) noted, a mutually beneficial cross-fertilization of research methods, data extraction methods, creation of knowledge, and dissemination.

Group Relations conferences focus on examining the nature of authority in organizations and leadership. However, the A. K. Rice Institute in America, the equivalent of the Tavistock Institute, moved toward personal growth and the study of interpersonal dynamics (Banet & Hayden, 1977).

"Learning from experience in groups" conferences have been held annually since 1957. In Britain, they are known as the "Leicester Conference". It is a 14-day experiential learning event that provides space to reflect and contemplate within a global cohort how to lead (Tavistock Institute, 2024). The current directors of the conference describe it as an international gathering, which offeres the opportunity to examine the depth of one's psyche within an intensity that is not overwhelming due to the luxury of time and space. Learning through experience means going deeper through exploration and experimentation.

According to Banet and Hayden (1977), the Tavistock method originated in the work of Bion, who conducted a series of small study groups at the Tavistock clinic in London. Influenced by Poincaré's (1951) science and method, as well as by Klein's conceptualization of the paranoid-schizoid and depressive positions (Glover, 2009), Bion combined their thinking when researching groups and developing his methodology.

The philosopher of science, Henri Poincaré (1902–1908/2012), who discovered the chaotic deterministic system, which became the foundation of Chaos Theory, argued that if a new result has any value, it must unite known elements. Suggesting that our mind was as frail as our senses, he held that the only facts worthy of our attention were those, which introduced order into the complexity of the world, and so made it accessible to us (Glover, 2009). For Bion (1962a,b), this exemplified a model of all creativity, where seemingly chaotic, disparate elements accumulate around a "selected fact". He referred to this fact as an "emotional experience".

The process whereby new (emotional) meaning arises is closely linked to his conceptualization of the "container-contained". In his theory of thinking, Bion (1962b, 1963, 1967, 1970) elaborated the "container-contained" relationship, stating that a thinking apparatus (container) was needed for thoughts to develop. Using Greek letters to denote the process by which babies learn to think, Bion proposed the following:

Beta elements, which are akin to raw sensory impressions that have no meaning or organization, are unmetabolized somatic and psychic experiences. They must be transformed into alpha elements (thoughts). For Bion (1962a), it was the mother who enabled this process. The infant's raw unthinkable states of mind, that are inseparable from bodily states, are communicated to her by crying. She tries to imagine what might be the matter and responds by incorporating her infant's state of mind into her own mental space. In so doing, she digests (contains) the infant's unmetabolized emotions. This process strips the beta elements of its unbearable quality and detoxifies the baby's experience. In other words, the mother has transformed an unthinkable experience (beta elements) into a meaningful experience (alpha elements), which can subsequently be used for thinking. Bion coined this transforming state of experience "reverie" (Minnick, 2024).

According to Williams (2009), just as Klein had regarded the mother–baby relationship as the basis for the adult's sexual relationships, Bion denoted "container and contained" by means of the accepted symbols for female and male. For him, the acquisition of true knowledge (thoughts) was something that happened through an internal male–female conjunction. It was similar to generating an embryo through sperm and ovum. Bion expressed this through mathematics, too. In his mathematical explication, points were the conjugate complex. The differing, two points, were simply being imposed over one another. For Bion (1962b, 1965, 1967), this was an organic, interpenetrating relationship, even if it could not be detected from the outside.

By articulating an account of thinking, Bion (1963) moved psychoanalytic theory more into the realm of Western epistemology (philosophy), according to Glover (2009). She suggested that Bion's conceptualization of "thoughts without a thinker" resembled Kant's notion of things-in-themselves. It was based on the conjecture that pure thoughts existed long before there was a mind to think them. However, a mind is nevertheless needed to think these thoughts.

Drawing attention to the epistemophilic impulse, K (knowledge), Bion (1992) made links between K, L (love), and H (hate), and between -K, -L, and -H. The latter is the antithesis to healthy relating.

Bion (1965) conceived of the inner space/world as arising from O (ultimate, unreachable, unknowable truth). Bion (1970) proposed that O could not be known but only known about, recognized, or felt. O's existence could not be scientifically discovered, even though it was an essential postulate of science that truth existed. He also referred to the Tao, the principle of the universe that is known by a sense of direction (Williams, 2019).

Glover (2009) suggested that Bion's language echoed his metaphysical beliefs. Bion stressed the emotional experience of words and regarded their intellectual understanding as secondary. To put it differently, ideas were transformed into an emotional experience instead of being merely cognitively assimilated.

Becoming oneself, or aligning with O, is what Bion meant by learning from experience, according to Williams (2019). Having, and digesting, thoughts that bring us in touch with reality, both internally and externally, happens through the operation of alpha-functions in the context of internal object relations. Reverie (dreaming whilst awake) is a state of mind in which alpha-function (symbol formation) can take place. With the concept of alpha function, Bion introduced a new understanding of how the unconscious comes into being.

Observation had an important place in Bion's theory of thinking. There could be no alignment with O, no contact with reality, without true and accurate observation. What is observed in psychoanalysis was the hidden psychic turbulence, which indicated the presence of a potential thought/idea. However, this kind of observation is difficult, requiring learning how, and where, to look, so that the place of conflict can be understood. For Bion, the detection of psychic turbulence was possible by learning from experience.

Early Tavistock pioneers believed that "learning from experience methods" should be applicable to various kinds of processes, which are investigated in the social sciences. Initially, Group Relations was based on Bion (1961), who asserted that the psychoanalytic approach, whether through the individual or the group, was dealing with different facets of the same phenomena. Bion coined the term "binocular vision" to combine the individualistic psychoanalytic with his group approach. Such vision enabled a more comprehensive understanding. In Freudian Psychoanalysis, examination of events centered on the oedipal situation. It is akin to the unconscious defense of pairing in the group. When situations were examined in the analytic therapy group, elucidations are related to the Sphinx, that is, knowledge and scientific method (Lawrence, 1997), because the Sphinx spoke in riddles.

Freud based his conceptualization of the Oedipus Complex (boys fall in love with their mothers and want to "kill" their fathers), on Sophocles' tragedy *Oedipus Rex.*

Oedipus was a Greek mythical king, who fulfilled the prophecy that he would kill his father and marry his mother. Unknowingly, he killed his father (king Laius) and married his mother. The city was at the mercy of the Sphinx, a monster, whose riddle Oedipus answered correctly.

Thereby he defeated the monster, won the throne, and married the queen, Jocasta, his mother (Wikipedia, 2024).

Bion's novel approach of viewing a group as a collective entity was evolving gradually into a method (Banet & Hayden, 1977). Kenneth Rice (1965, 1969), and others, developed Bion's thinking further. According to Sher (2012), Bion's psychoanalytic approach to understanding groups was applicable mainly to those groups, which had the task of self-examination. Even though he sometimes drew analogies between other types of groups (the army, church, aristocracy), the group Bion deeply thought about was nevertheless the psychotherapy group. This type of group could recover through a process of self-examination to discovery (Sher, 2012). To achieve this, group members had to gain insight into defenses, such as the basic assumptions (dependency, fight/flight, pairing).

According to Banet and Hayden (1977), when functioning at the level of basic assumptions, the group behaves, as if certain assumptions were true, and as if, certain behaviors were vital to the group's survival. While the word "basic" points to primitive survival motivations of the group, the term "assumption" underscores Bion's postulate that they are based on the collective projections of group members, rather than on reality (p. 15).

In a psychotherapy group, basic assumptions interfere with the exploration of feelings and problems of the individual members within the group (Brown, 1985). In the Fight and Flight basic assumption mode, splitting and projection are prominent (Schermer, 1985). The group perceives its survival as depending on either active aggression, scapegoating, physical attack, or on withdrawal, passivity, avoidance, or ruminations. The ineffectiveness of this solution can sometimes lead to a different activity, namely pairing (Sutherland, 1985). At other times, anyone who has a valency for the aggressive forces of the group assumes leadership. However, such leadership is short-lived due to the persistent arguing and competitive dynamics. In Flight mode, when an intruding threat is fled from (Brown, 1985), leadership may be bestowed on an individual, who minimizes the importance of the task, and facilitates a movement away from the here-and-now in the group (Banet & Hayden, 1977).

In contrast, when the group operates in Dependency mode, it attempts to attain security by gratifying the group's longing through magic (Sutherland, 1985). Alternatively, it seeks protection from the group facilitator, or another member, who takes on this role. The group behaves, as if it was stupid and incompetent, or even mad (psychotic). It hopes to be rescued from feeling impotent by a powerful, God-like leader (Schermer, 1985), who will instruct and direct the group toward task completion. Bion (1961) clarified that group members, who have a "valency" for certain emotions, or ideas, felt compelled to behave accordingly. Hence, they may take on the leader role in the group. However, when they fail to meet these impossible demands, members may express their disappointment and hostility in numerous ways. As Banet and Hayden (1997) suggest, the dependency mode often serves as a lure for a charismatic leader, who exerts authority through personal characteristics. It is noteworthy that groups can also oscillate between different basic assumptions. Pairing, where a bond between two people in the group is fostered, can result in comfortable feelings for a certain period of time. The pair may express warmth and affection toward each other, resulting in an intimate atmosphere and closeness. The whole group watches the pair (or pairs), who often provide mutual intellectual support to each to the extent that other members become inactive. The pair does not have to be of the same sex (Sutherland, 1985), even though survival is perceived as contingent on reproduction in this basic assumption mode. A "Messiah" will miraculously be born to save the group and help it complete its task (Banet & Hayden, 1977).

Balint Groups

In Britain, Balint groups use an analytic approach to explore the emotional aspects of the doctor-patient relationship, fostering self-awareness and empathy among healthcare professionals (Balint, 1964). These groups may consist of 6-12 people, last 1-2 hours, and take place weekly or less frequently. They offer healthcare professionals the opportunity to learn about unconscious dynamics in their relationships with patients, and how unconscious factors may affect their feelings and functioning (Balint, 1979). The primary focus is on emotional and interpersonal aspects of the relationships. These groups aim to move beyond diagnosis to enabling doctors to understand their patients better. Whilst one person describes a clinical case, the others gain an impression of the doctor-patient relationship. The facilitator refrains from making direct interpretations. Instead, s/he creates a good working atmosphere, in which silence is tolerated. Once fully trained in the Balint method, professionals can become a member of the Balint Society (https://balintsociety.org.uk/accreditation).

T-Groups

During his association with colleagues at the National Training Laboratories (NTL), Lewin (1935, 1936, 1947) started to study training groups (T-groups) until his untimely death in 1947. These were small, experiential groups designed to explore and develop interpersonal relationships, self-awareness, and group dynamics. The NTL adopted methods of open and honest participative inquiry amongst members of the T-Group (Bradbury et al., 2008).

Initially, the T-group was a form of "laboratory" education, where approx. 8–15 people would join together in a leaderless group. Self-study in T-groups was based on the idea that it would broaden their awareness of "taken for granted assumptions", which, in turn, would allow them to make choices about their behavior. The labs were considered as therapy for "normal" people (Weschler et al., 1962). Variations in labs and more psycho-analytically oriented programs offered by the Tavistock Institute, and a variety of encounter groups, developed from the 1950s to 1960s. These included stranger and familiar labs, involving supervisors and subordinates in leaderless groups.

Describing the history of the T-Group, Highhouse (2002) explained that the purpose of T-groups was to study how individuals behave in groups, how groups function, as well as how norms, roles, and power dynamics, arise. Their lack of structure aimed at allowing group members to explore their interactions and behavior freely, so that it could lead to organic learning experiences. However, participants frequently struggled to reflect and understand the impact of their own behavior in these unstructured groups without any agenda. Lewin (1948) realized that people required help to re-examine cherished assumptions about themselves and in relation to others. Hence, a facilitator (trainer) was used to guide the group process without domineering it. Facilitators encouraged self-discovery, helped participants reflect on their behavior and their effects on others, and fostered open communication. Participants explored issues such as trust, conflict, leadership, and cooperation. Increased self-awareness was a primary goal of these groups (see Bradbury et al., 2008; Reason & Bradbury, 2008b).

Methods used to achieve this included a focus on the here-and-now, observing, analyzing, and direct feedback from others (how a person's behavior was perceived and affected the group), which fostered learning from the immediate behavior, emotions, and dynamics in the group.

Areas of Application of Group Analytic Conceptualizations

Group analytic conceptualizations been applied to *small groups* (Behr & Hearst, 2005; Foulkes, 2002; Foulkes & Anthony, 1964; Schermer & Pines, 1999), as well as to *median and large groups* (De Maré et al., 1991; Gonggrijp, 1993; Kreeger, 1975; Lawrence, 2000; Lyndon, 1992; Penna, 2023; Tubert-Oklander & Hernández-Tubert, 2021; Volkan, 2004). Group Analysis has been theorized in relation to desire and sexuality (Nitsun, 2006), including the use of online pornography

(Vosmer, 2010). Additionally, group analysts have applied group analytic thinking to the *wider political arena* (Friedman, 2015a, 2018; Mojović, 2019; Volkan, 1999), and also offered *critiques of societal problems* (Scanlon, 2015; Scanlon & Adlam, 2008, 2009, 2011). The group analytic literature has shed light on the *traumatic origins of violence* (De Zulueta, 2006; Hopper, 1997, 2003a, b; Volkan, 2001, 2004, 2021; Volkan & Greer, 2002). It enabled a good *understanding of race, ethnicity and coloniality* (Aiyegbusi, 2021a,b; Blackwell, 2003, 2015, 2018, 2020, 2021; Dalal, 1993, 2001, 2002, 2006; Kent, 2020, Kinouani, 2019, 2020, 2023; Nayak, 2021; Stevenson, 2020). Furthermore, it allowed some understanding of both *destructive* (Nitsun, 1996), and of *healing un/conscious group processes* (Barwick & Weegmann, 2018; Nitsun, 2015). Recent explorations of power, privilege, and position in group therapy fostered an appreciation of the importance of intersectionality (Nayak & Forrest, 2024). Group analytic psychotherapy has been used to address many *mental health* (Fiumara & Zanasi, 1989; Noack, 2020; Pines, 2007; Vosmer, 2012), *relational and neurological* difficulties (Anderson, 2011), and *neurodiversity* (Avila & Macedo, 2012; Vosmer, 2015). Its applicability is broad. Modified group analytic psychotherapy could be suitable for working with people who have *Parkinson's* (Vosmer, 2024). Group analysts work with the *forensic and prison population* (Adlam et al., 2012; Adshead, 2002, 2012; Vosmer, 2018; Welldon & Wilson, 2005; Woods & Williams, 2010), with *refugees and asylum seekers* (Tucker, 2011; Volkan, 2017), with *staff groups* (Kurtz, 2017), *organizations* (Stacey, 2001, 2003, 2006, 2010; Thornton, 2010), and *governments* (Volkan, 2004). They have run *groups for children, adults, and the elderly* (Bacha, 2018; Ezquerro & Cañete, 2023; Cañete et al., 2000).

Furthermore, *online groups and online group analytic psychotherapy* have been developed (Weinberg, 2014; Weinberg et al., 2019, 2023a,b)

Important Concepts

Matrix

The Group-analytic matrix is a core concept of group analysis. Foulkes (1964, 1975a) emphasized the foundation matrix. Due to this invisible cultural network, when strangers meet in groups, they are able to relate to each other and communicate with each other, because we all share basic characteristics, such as language, culture and our biological make-up.

The matrix has a relational and semantic field, thus, pertaining to both systems and structure. Possibly reaching for a concept that transcended Freudian Psychoanalysis, as Powell (1991) put it, Foulkes formulated the matrix. His focus shifted away from psychic determinism toward communication and meaning. It is through the foundation matrix (Foulkes, 1971), the biological and cultural properties of our species (Foulkes, 1975, p. 131), that all human beings are connected. Even though Foulkes prioritized social factors, it is unclear whether he theorized the matrix within a materialist ontology (Powell, 1991).

Rejecting the Cartesian division of matter and mind, it seems that quantum mechanics captured his imagination. Just as particle and wave are inseparable, so too are the relational and semantic fields of the matrix. Powell (1991) wrote "… that advances in physics make plain that human beings exist in, and are part of, a matrix of awesome energy" (p. 314).

Transference & Countertransference

Freud (1905) was the first to identify transference. Referring to transference as facsimiles of impulses and phantasies that arise during psychoanalysis (p. 116), Freud noted the peculiar nature of transferences. The physician is replaced by another person from the analysand's early life. Past experiences are revived and applied to the physician at the present moment (p. 116).

Melanie Klein (1952) insisted that the patient is bound to have to deal with reexperienced conflicts and anxieties. These are directed at the psychoanalyst in the same way as s/he experienced them in the past. Withdrawing from the psychoanalyst, as the patient turned away from her/his primal objects (parents), for example. Or, trying to split the relationship to the psychoanalyst, keeping the psychotherapist either as a good, or, as a bad figure. Hence, analyzing both negative and positive transferences, as well as the inextricable connection between them, is an indispensable aspect of treatment (p. 436). In unraveling details of the transference, it is essential to think about the "total situation" that is being transferred from the past to the present. This includes emotions, defenses, and object relations (relationships with others), and countertransference (pp. 437–438). Unsurprisingly, counter/transference are important concept in Group Analysis (Hopper, 2007). Karterud (2024) describe how their conceptualizations have been broadened, refined, or devised, over the past decades (see Belinkoff et al., 1964; Black & Wright, 2024; Ferreira, 1980; Karterud, 2024; Stolorow et al., 1987; Stone, 1995;).

Originally, the term "countertransference" was used by psychoanalysts to designate their unconscious reactions to wards their analysands' transferences (Reeder, 1998). Frequently, *unresolved* past relational difficulties are transferred.

Historically, the pioneering work of Bion (1962, 1963), particularly, his effort to conceptualize the group dynamically, and the systematic application of psychoanalytic concepts to the treatment of individuals in the context of a group by Foulkes (1948), had given transference interpretation a new impetus. In the 1990s, group psychotherapists (e.g. Ormont, 1992) elaborated transference and countertransference.

Debbane and de Carufel (1993) viewed transference as a total situation, based on Joseph's (1985) and Klein's (1952) work, who had clinically and theoretically elaborated these two simultaneously occurring phenomena. Debbane and de Carufel's (1993) reasoning is in line with leading Kleinian thinkers (e.g. Wilfrid Bion, Herbert Rosenfeld and Hanna Segal), who adopted Melanie Klein's (1946/1988) conceptualization of the "paranoid-schizoid" (P-S) and the "depressive" phase. While the P-S is characterized by splitting, envy, hate, and other primitive defense mechanisms, the more mature depressive phase involves guilt, sadness, and mourning. In contrast to Freud's sequential developmental stages, Klein thought that people oscillate between the P-S and the depressive phase throughout life. Bion (1962, 1963) applied her thinking to groups. Bion's (1961) theoretical framework of the "workgroup" (p. 157), and "basic assumption mentality (p. 173), outline fundamental ways of avoiding real thought and true feeling. These determine group members' ability to relate to, and engage with, each other, and with the purpose for which the group was formed (Loveridge et al., 2007).

Interestingly, Betty Joseph (1983, 1985) recommended short and simple interpretations. She demonstrated that patients in the P-S phase resisted certain transference interpretations. Namely, interpretations aimed at making patients aware that they were splitting and projecting. Furthermore, in projective identification with their patients, psychoanalysts acted out the patients' phantasies. This happened when they failed to understand that their patients were psychologically in the P-S position. Envy, hate, and other primitive feelings, need to be really understood, so that they are not acted upon as a result of countertransferences (Joseph, 1985).

Resonance

Primarialy, Foulkes (1977) introduced this term to do justice to the fact that each individual member picks out of the common pool of communication something that is relevant to her/him.

The person responds, according to her/his individual disposition, for example, being prone to regression. Fixating on something, or developmental arrest, may have occurred. These then form the basis for the main disturbances and conflicts that are apparent in a group. If most group members had experienced a similar developmental arrest, a specific conflict dominates the group.

So, unconscious, highly specific reactions occur in response to a "stimulus". Basically, this is resonance. Foulkes believed that such a response may correspond to pre-/oedipal levels. What happens is that at any of the different phases of libidinal development, (oral, anal, oedipal), for example, the destructive behavior of the unruly Id in the oral stage, are evoked. Equivalent defensive and protective reactions occur in the group. At times, narcissistic character formations happened during childhood (ego and superego are affected). Any defense mechanism (e.g., repression, denial, somatization, acting out, projection, introjection, projective identification) may be deployed (Birchmore, 2015). Foulkes insisted that the individual resonates in the 'key, to which he is attuned', and according to how his specific personality structure is organized. This means that specific resonances are evoked, which are relevant to an individual person.

Valence is a related concept. A person has a valency for something. This becomes apparent, when an individual experiences resonance in the group.

Mirroring

Psychological resonance phenomena are often explained in terms of mirror neurons. Due to mirror neurons, people have the ability to recognize that an action performed by someone else, resembles their own. We can differentiate between this action and similar/dissimilar actions, because something is mirrored. We can identify ourselves in another person (see Cosmin, 2025 for more detail).

Miorroring is related to, but also distinct from, resonance. In the group, mirror reactions are characteristically triggered when a number of people meet and interact, Foulkes (1964) noticed. The person sees her/himself (or an aspect of her/himself) reflected in the interactions of other group members. When the person sees others re-/acting in the way s/he does, s/he gains insight into her behavior and feelings. This is a fundamental process of ego development (see Birchmore, 2015b; Cosmin, 2025 for further detail).

Communication

For Foulkes (1964), communication was of primary clinical, and theoretical, importance for the group-analytic situation. Group analysts are often believed to be primarily *communication-seeking*.

Foulkes developed four levels of communication: Current, Transference, Projective, and Primordial. These levels represent different layers of interaction, and unconscious processes, within a group setting (see Power, 2017 for further detail).

Condenser phenomenon

This refers to a sudden discharge of primitive material, when something suddenly erupts into consciousess. Foulkes and Anthony (1957) suggested that it was almost, as if all the different unconscious operated as a condenser. It first stores the strong emotional charges generated by the group secretly and then discharges them in the form of typical shared group events.

Chain phenomena tend to precede such events. Chain phenomena occur when the group pools its associations, and the resistance in the group is weakened. The discharge of unconscious material happen.

The Social Unconscious

The social unconscious is a cornerstone of Group Analysis. Foulkes used it in reference to our internalized and external social world, i.e., all the things that we are unaware of.

It has been conceptualized similar to, but also in contrast to the individual unconscious, although the individual unconscious is located inside the social unconscious. However, the social unconscious has also been defined as a property of society itself by Hopper (2001). The group analyst Weinberg offered an intersubjective definition. It situates the social unconscious in a transitional space. Weinberg suggestes that the social unconscious is the co-constructed shared unconscious of members of a particular social system (community, society, nation, culture) (Weinberg, 2008, p. 150). Social trauma is common across the world, and it forms a part of the social unconscious of societies, and other social systems, including organizations (Hopper, 2012). Often, group analysts consider the collective defenses against shared anxieties, which have been caused by social trauma, and address these in the group.

Neuroscientific Research Findings

Due to advances in neuroimaging, we know more about the neurobiological bases of instinctual drives, our basic emotions, and mental life (Berlin, 2011). Research results (Berlin & Montgomery, 2017; Roesler, 2018; Roesler & Uffelen, 2018) support the view support that mental activity is rooted in phylogenetically old emotional systems, which influence psychic development in early childhood, as suggested by Freud (1895, 1915c). Emotions can be triggered by unconscious processes. People can feel angry, or hostile, without being aware that they do, and act on emotions that are outside their awareness (see De Benedittis, 2020, 2023). Research (e.g., Hassin et al., 2005) also indicates that affective, motivational information can be processed subliminally. However, the unconscious cannot organize anything into meaningful and coherent representations of reality.

No specific brain structures, or circuits, seem to be dedicated to processing unconscious thought, but the right hemisphere and the limbic system, seem to be involved in the processing of emotions. Subliminal perception occurs when stimuli are processed by our sensory systems without them reaching the threshold of consciousness. This process seems to be based on the same mechanism as conscious vision (De Benedittis, 2023). Moreover, the neural mechanisms underlying repression remain unknown. But people, who require a longer time for neural activation to develop conscious experiences of stimuli, and have fewer verbal associations to subliminal stimuli (Shevrin et al., 2002), may be prone to developing repression as a defense against unacceptable unconscious desires. De Benedittis (2023) suggest that highly intelligent people may develop intellectualization as a defense mechanism.

APPENDIX 2

Where Can Group Analytic Psychotherapy Be Situated?

Group analytic psychotherapy has been described as a "broad church". According to Hutchinson (2017), Group Analysis accommodates the differences between group analysts' professional backgrounds, their psychoanalytic persuasion, and how they balance individual conceptualization with that of the group: "I" vs "We"; internal, instinct or fantasy vs the external, social context/environment.

There is no agreement regarding the status of Group Analysis. Whereas Hass (2001) mainly commented on the differing debates in Group Analysis, Evans (2001) discussed hard science as a sexual metaphor, and Mittwoch (2001) viewed Group Analysis as a "science (Wissenschaft), which relates to wisdom" (p. 446). While Michels (2011) claimed that psychotherapy is practice and not gnosis, Schermer and Rice (2015, p. 84) wrote that Group Analysis is "an art rather than a science".

Such differing views reflect an inherent dilemma within the field of group analytic psychotherapies. Although training courses have been established worldwide, and group analytic psychotherapy is practiced in more countries (e.g. Rwanda, India, New Zealand, Russia, Italy, Norway, Denmark, Finland, the US, South America, Serbia, Spain, Portugal, Greece, Germany), Hőhfeld (2014) described institutional resistance toward unity, and the adoption of the term "group analysis", in Germany.

Disagreements about appropriate research methodologies seem like inevitable consequences. While researchers, who regard group analytic psychotherapy as an art, advocate the use of qualitative methods, those who view it as a science adopt quantitative methods. To the latter, the scientific status of group analytic psychotherapy is more likely to matter than to the former.

However, the many theoretical and empirical foci of the broad field of group analytic psychotherapies make it difficult to situate it within philosophy, humanities, social science, or the arts. Contemporary group analytic psychotherapy encompasses, for example, ideas or theories from psychoanalysis (e.g. Freud, 1921; Klein, 1940; Kohut 1971), neurology (e.g. Foulkes, 1936; Goldstein, 1939), neuroscience (e. g, Bacha, 2017), sociology (e.g. Elias, 1978, 1991), Gestalt Theory (e.g. Koffka, 1935), Systems Theory (see Agazarian, 1997), Field Theory (e.g. Lewin, 1947), Attachment Theory (e.g. Bowlby, 1969, 1973, 1980; see Marrone, 1998), the Frankfurt

School, Rhetoric Theory (see Weegmann, 2016), mentalization (Karterud, 2015), and intersectionality (Crenshaw, 1989; see Nayak & Forrest, 2024).

Considering the scientific orientation of many of these theories, modern group analytic psychotherapy could be situated within the social sciences.

Historically, the German, integrative Göttinger Model (Heigl-Evers & Heigl, 1973, 1983), has been very research-oriented due to links to the Department of Clinical Psychotherapy at Göttingen University. It is associated with prominent academics and research figures (e.g. Karl König, Reinhard Kreische, Falk Leichsenring, Gerlinde Herdieckerhoff-Sanders, Joachim Biskup, Herman Staats).

Furthermore, psychodynamic groups in inpatient settings have been researched by the German Working Group on Inpatient Group Psychotherapy, which was founded by Strauß and Eckert (for details see Strauß & Schmidt, 2004).

Studies have shown that inpatients with interpersonal difficulties do benefit from psychodynamic treatment. Strauß and Schmidt (2004) suggested that the mutual interaction in group psychotherapy may enable patients to better reflect on interpersonal aspects of their selves and of others.

The Group Relations approach, influenced by Bion (1961), which uses an experiential learning methodology, is also research oriented. This would also support the view that group analytically informed approaches ought to be situated within the social sciences.

One of Bion's (1961, 1962a) major contributions was the application of the psychoanalytic approach to both the individual and the group. It provided practitioners with a rudimentary binocular vision, and was used subsequently to study groups and organizations by Rice. Advocating to "learning from experience", methods should be applied to the examination of all kinds of group processes. Rice has been instrumental in advancing this method. It has been applied worldwide.

The Tavistock Institute of Human Relations is committed to the integration of the social sciences and Psychoanalysis, favoring transdisciplinary co-operation to produce knowledge. However, its contribution to research has been disappointing. Cytrynbaum's (1993) wrote that "Group Relations is widely considered to have the potential to make a bigger contribution to research than it does" (p. 40).

Sher (2012) stated that an interpretive stance might be more relevant to clinical practice than to research, because it may compromise the scientific (objective) observer role. She suggested that Group Relations was guided by a "spiritual philosophy" of "wholeness", that forms part of consultancy, experiential learning, and research. It is aimed at understanding and working with the tension between people's freedom and accountability (pp. 125–126).

An affiliation between psychoanalytic therapy and the arts (poetry) is also apparent in Bion's (1962a,b) use of the poetic concept of "reverie", which describes the psychotherapist's unbiased state of receptiveness. Holmes (2019) wrote that the therapist, like the poet, allows thoughts and feelings to arise spontaneously. Reverie is like daydreaming. Memories, images, and roads not taken, appear in states of reverie. Free association in the group could be compared to dreaming aloud. Writing good clinical case studies (Ogden, 2005) also involves the conjunction of an interpretation. And it is a work of art (p. 15). Group analytic psychotherapists must use language in an artful way to convey the real/true analytic experience (Spurling, 2019). All these features highlight the similarity between group analytically oriented approaches and the arts.

On the other hand, due to their empirical traces, the opposite argument could be made, further strengthening the view that group analytic psychotherapies are more appropriately situated within the social sciences than the arts.

Burrow's group analytic procedures involved consensual observations and empirical experimentations (Pertegato & Pertegato, 2013, p. 157). The German, Jewish, psychiatrist, Foulkes (1948) regarded group analytic therapy as the most valuable tool for scientific investigation (Foulkes & Anthony, 1957). Gfäller (1993) highlighted the contribution of the sociologist Norbert Elias to group analytic psychotherapy and to the social sciences. Both Karterud (2000) and Vosmer (2021) noted that Foulkes' metaphors of neurology (networks, nodal points) support a footing in the natural (Positivist) sciences.

The past president of the Group Analytic Society International, Knauss (2000), also referred to Group Analysis as a "science", stating that its "survival" would depend considerably on empirical research (p. 317). However, the method of Group Analysis is a peculiar science, because it lacks (or has little) predictive power, and only produces causal claims retrospectively (Dalal, 2018b). Should Group Analysis, therefore, be placed in the humanities? Considering the overlap between philosophical ideas and group analytic psychotherapies, this would make sense.

Schermer (2018) noted that the discipline of philosophy was already engrained in group analytic psychotherapy. Indeed, we encounter many differing philosophical ideas in psychodynamic group therapy and research. Without elaborating his claim, Barwick (2018) stated that Foulkes drew on the philosophy of Edmund Husserl (1859–1938), whose phenomenology tried to be true to the phenomena, as they are experienced.

Etymologically, phenomenology stems from the Greek words "φαινόμενον" (that which appears) and "λόγος" (study). Transcendental (Husserl), Hermeneutic Phenomenology (Heidegger), and the Phenomenology of Perception (Merleau-Ponty), are distinct types of phenomenology. The ontological and epistemological positions of phenomenology suggest a reality, which is formulated by the human mind, necessitating an interaction between the world and the human being. Phenomenology also rejects Positivism.

Like phenomenology, spiritually informed dynamic group psychotherapy could be situated within the humanities, considering the incompatibility of spirituality and traditional views of science.

In his discussion of spirituality and interpersonal group psychotherapy, Abernethy (2015) pointed out that spirituality was a cultural experience. Although spirituality and religion are commonly contrasted, a sacred core and search process are central to both. Subjective feelings, thoughts, and behaviors, which arise from a search for "the Sacred", are crucial aspects of spirituality and religion. Due to their focus on "the Sacred", that is, a sense of ultimate reality related to some "divine being" (see Abernethy, 2015), they are incompatible with conceptualizations of modern science. This would be another argument for situating analytically oriented group psychotherapies in the humanities.

According to Popper (1959), non-scientific theories or systems, such as religion, are never wrong, because it is impossible to falsify God's existence. Hence, Popper argued that religion was not a science, because it can only make predictions that can never be falsified. But Popper also suggested that "historically speaking all … scientific theories originate from myth" (p. 50). His idea that a myth may contain important anticipations of scientific theories could offer interesting avenues for developing a framework that straddles the divide between hermeneutics and science. The term "hermeneutics" is related to Hermes, the God of Communication, who ferried messages between the gods and humans. It descends from the Latin "hermeneutica". Hermeneutics is the philosophy of textual interpretation and human understanding, and the art of reading text (Peters & McCormick, 2008).

Considering that many quantitative studies have been carried out by group analytic psychotherapists over the past two decades, which could be a sign that they have become more scientifically minded, one could argue that this scientific focus has shifted group analytic psychotherapies away from the humanities toward the social sciences. If we accept that it has empirical foundations, it could be argued that group analytic psychotherapy belongs to the social sciences. Why does this matter? Science is linked to power and prestige.

APPENDIX 3

Questionnaires, Software & Resources

Group Questionnaires, Inventories & Tests for Psychotherapy Research

Recent Review of Measures

Orfanos et al. (2020) reviewed therapeutic group process questionnaires. They assessed 13 questionnaires and scored them according to Terwee et al.'s (2007) criteria. Based on the total scores, the Group Cohesiveness Scale (Wongpakaran et al., 2013), Therapeutic Factor Inventory-Short (MacNair-Semands et al., 2010), Therapeutic Factor Inventory-19 (Joyce et al., 2011), Group Questionnaire (Krogel et al., 2013), and the Group Sessions Rating Scale scored highest in terms of *scale development quality*. All measures except for the Social Exchange Scale (Brown et al., 2014) demonstrated good internal consistency (p. 434). However, it was the only scale that was given a positive rating for content validity, which is regarded by Terwee et al. (2007) as the most important psychometric property.

Orfanos et al. (2020) note that the ability for the identified measures to assess change over time and longitudinal validity is limited or unclear. So, when considering the applicability of the reviewed measures for assessing therapeutic change, this must be borne in mind. All measures scored a "no rating" for the "floor and ceiling effects" criterion, making interpretation of the content validity further difficult (p. 438). In terms of therapeutic processes, the Group Cohesiveness Scale (Wongpakaran et al., 2013) appears to be a suitable measure of helpful group processes and the Group Questionnaire (GQ) (Krogel et al., 2013) to be the most suitable questionnaire available for researchers seeking to measure group processes beyond those experienced as curative.

Popular measures are not necessarily psychometrically robust, the authors commented. The Group Climate Questionnaire-Short (GCQ-S) (MacKenzie, 1983) is commonly used. It is validated (Burlingame et al., 2004; Johnson et al., 2006; Strauss et al., 2008). Like the TFI, it is recommended in the AGPA's CORE-R battery of group process measures (Burlingame et al., 2006; Strauss et al., 2008). Nevertheless, the reviewers highlight that the Group Climate Questionnaire (MacKenzie, 1981) and the Group Climate Questionnaire-Short (MacKenzie, 1983) have relatively low scale development quality scores compared to other available tools.

The discrepancy between the GCQ-S' low psychometric properties and high popularity might be due to the GCQ-S being an extremely user-friendly tool. It consists of only 12 items. It can be flexibly used by a group member, group leader, or observer (DeChavez et al., 2000)

Measures

The Group Climate Questionnaire (GCQ) measures how group members regard their experience in their psychotherapy group. Developed by MacKenzie (1983), the GCQ provides information on the group atmosphere. It identifies tension and anger in the group, as well as indicating avoidance of assuming personality responsibility of working in the group.

The GQ can be used to identify group members' perception of the group relationship and cohesiveness. The GQ is a 40-item self-report measure based on Johnson et al.'s (2005) 3-Factor Model (positive bonding and working; negative relationship). It has been used to gain insight into positive bonds/work and negative relationships between members in the group and with the group conductor(s).

Krogel et al. (2013) developed a shorter 30-item version.

The 16-item Perceived Group Inclusion Scale (PGIS) can be used in inclusion research and is found in Jansen et al. (2014). It consists of group membership, group affection, room for authenticity, and value in authenticity, subscales.

The Group Readiness Questionnaire identifies those clients who are ready to commence group therapy. And it can guide the group facilitator to better prepare clients for group therapy. It was developed by Pearson (2017).

While these are important measures, rating scales that have been developed in psychology or by psychodynamic researchers can also be useful. Such scales have been widely used in individual and group psychotherapy.

Rating Scales to Measure Transference & Transference Interpretations

The Missouri Identifying Transference Scale (MITS) (Multon et al., 1996) identifies different forms of transference, using a 5-point Likert scale.

Bøgwald et al. (1999) developed the Specific Therapeutic Technique Scale. It is designed to measure specific use of transference with a focus on interpretations. The 15-item STT is a useful tool for measuring and monitoring these psychodynamic interventions.

Ulberg et al. (2014) developed a manual for the Transference Work Scale (TWS). This scale focuses on the transference work (analysis of the patient-therapist relationship). The TWS was developed to identify and categorize relational interventions (transference work).

The 26-item scale has subscales, which rate timing, content and valence of the transference interventions, and the response from the patient.

Semi-Structured Interview

The Private Theories Interview (Ginner et al., 2001; Werbart & Levander, 2005, 2006), PTI, is a semi-structured interview, which aims to gather concrete examples and illustrative episodes regarding problem formulation, private theories of pathogenies and cure, and descriptions of change (Philips et al., 2005).

Inventories

Widely used scales for measuring depression and anxiety are the Beck Depression Inventory-II (BDI-II) (Beck et al., 1978, 1996) and the Beck Anxiety Inventory (BAI) (Beck et al., 1988).

Richter et al. (1998) discussed the validity of the initial BDI in *Psychopathology*, volume 31, pp. 160–168.

The symptom checklist 90-R (SCL90-R) (Derogatis, 1977, 1994, 2017; Derogatis & Savitz, 1999) is a 90-item self-report symptom inventory to measure psychological symptoms and psychological distress in individuals from the community, and with medical or psychiatric conditions. The SCL-90-R assesses psychological distress in terms of nine primary symptom dimensions and three summary scores termed global scores. The principal symptom dimensions are labeled Somatization (SOM), Obsessive-Compulsive (OBS), Interpersonal Sensitivity (INT), Depression (DEP), Anxiety (ANX), Hostility (HOS), Phobic Anxiety (PHOB), Paranoid Ideation (PAR), and Psychoticism (PSY). The global measures are referred to as the Global Severity Index (GSI), the Positive Symptom Distress Index (PSDI), and the Positive Symptom Total (PST).

The Brief Symptom Inventory (BSI; Derogatis, 1975, 1993; Derogatis & Melisaratos, 1983; Derogatis & Spencer, 1982) was developed from the SCL-90-R. It is a 53-item self-report symptom inventory. Clients rate the extent to which a given symptom has been distressing them on a 4-point Likert scale (0=not at all to 4=extremely). The BSI assesses primary psychiatric symptomatology. A higher score represents greater severity of symptoms. The mean provides an overall measure of symptomatology.

The BSI has been found reliable and valid. Patton et al. (1997) offer details about its validity and reliability.

The Brief Symptom Inventory-18 (BSI-18: Derogatis, 2000) is an abbreviated version of the nine dimension, 53-item BSI (Derogatis, 1993), which is a shortened form of the 90-item Symptom Checklist-90-Revised (SCL-90-R: Derogatis, 1994).

An advantage of the SCL-90-R, BSI, and BSI-18 is that the scales are available in more than two dozen languages and have been extensively utilized worldwide.

The 127-item Inventory of Interpersonal Problems (IIP) (Horowitz et al., 1988) is a self-report scale, which measures interpersonal problems. While the first 78 items begin with "It is hard for me to", the remaining 49 items describe "things you do too much". Clients rate their level of distress for each item on 4-point Likert scale, ranging from 0 (not at all) to 4 (extremely). This scale is reported to be sensitive to measuring changes resulting from brief psychotherapy.

The 10-item Goal Instability Scale (GIS) (Robbins, 1989; Robbins & Patton, 1985) is a self-report measure to assess the clients' lack of goal directedness.

The 10-item Superiority Scale (SS) (Robbins, 1989; Robbins & Patton, 1985) assesses how clients view themselves in relation to others. They indicate on a 6-point Likert scale their agreement with items.

The Working Alliance Inventory (WAI) (Horvath & Greenberg, 1989) is used to assess client–therapist bond and other aspects of the working alliance on a 7-point Likert scale.

The Short Form-36 (SF-36; Ware & Sherbourne, 1992) was designed for use in clinical practice and research, health policy evaluations, and general population surveys. The SF-36 includes one multi-item scale that assesses eight health concepts: (1) limitations in physical activities because of health problems; (2) limitations in social activities because of physical or emotional problems; (3) limitations in usual role activities because of physical health problems; (4) bodily pain; (5) general mental health (psychological distress and well-being); (6) limitations in usual role activities because of emotional problems; (7) vitality (energy and fatigue); and (8) general health perceptions.

It is used for self-administration by persons 14 years of age and older, and for administration by a trained interviewer in person or by telephone.

Aims of Therapy Inventory (ATI; Shapiro & Barkham, 1993). The ATI comprises 8 items rated on a 0–4 scale where a higher score represents the extent to which they want to achieve a particular aim. The mean item total indicates the extent to which patients aim to benefit from the therapy overall. Sample items include: "I want to understand myself better", "I want to find possible ways of coping with my problems", and "I want to feel supported by my group".

Inventory of Interpersonal Problems-Attachment Styles (Hardy & Barkham, 1994; IIP-AS). The IIP-AS comprises two scales measuring avoidance (7 items) and anxious-ambivalence (14 items).

The Clinical Outcome Routine Evaluation (CORE) is a widely used scale. The initial CORE-OM was developed by Evans et al. (2002). Details are found in their article, published in the *British Journal of Psychiatry*, volume 180, pp. 51–60.

Inventory of Interpersonal Problems-32 (IIP-32; Barkham et al., 1996; Barkham & Mellor-Clark, 2000, 2003) comprises 32 items rated on a 0–4 scale with a higher score representing greater severity of interpersonal difficulties. The mean item total provides an overall measure of interpersonal functioning. A higher score represents greater severity of interpersonal difficulties. The mean item total provides an overall measure of interpersonal functioning. The CASES-R assesses how counselors/psychotherapists perceive their ability to perform specific counseling or therapy-related tasks (e.g., helping clients set realistic goals): Hahn et al. (2021). Assessment of Counseling Self-Efficacy: Validation of the German Counselor Activity Self-Efficacy Scale (CASES-R). Available at: https://www.uni-potsdam.de/en/clinicalpsychology-psychotherapy/forschungsschwerpunkte/psychologische-messinstrumente

The Preferred Reporting Items for Systematic Reviews and Meta-Analyses & Other Checklists to Appraise a Paper

The PRISMA 2020 is a 27-item list, detailing the elements a high-quality paper should have, which are classified into essential and additional criteria. The latter provide supplementary information that may enhance the completeness and usability of systematic review reports (for more information, visit: http://www.prisma-statement.org/).

The new PRISMA-S (Rethlefsen et al., 2021) is a 16-item checklist for reporting items, each of which is detailed with exemplar reporting and rationale. It is an extension to the PRISMA statement 2020, which can be used by interdisciplinary authors, peer reviewers, and editors to verify that each component of a search is completely reported and, therefore, reproducible. Results are normally depicted in a flow chat.

Templates of the PRISMA Flow Diagram can be found at https://www.prisma-statement.org/prisma-2020-flow-diagram and further information is available in Haddaway et al. (2022).

Several other JBI (2023) checklists are useful, and their website offers information.

Checklist of Quasi-Experimental Studies,
Checklist for Analytical Cross-Sectional Studies,
Checklist for Qualitative Research,

Checklist for Text and Opinion.

The Mixed Methods Appraisal Tool (MMAT; Hong et al., 2018) can be used to appraise mixed-method studies

The AACODS Checklist (Tyndall, 2010) is useful when searching gray literature.

Checklists for Meta-Synthesis

The Joanna Briggs' Qualitative Appraisal and the Review Instrument (JB-QARI) (https://jbi-global/critical-appraisal-tools), as well as the Clinical Appraisal Skills Program (CAPS) (2024), are frequently used checklists for the evaluation of qualitative studies. They are available at https://casp-uk.net/casp-tools-checklists/qualitative-studies-studies-checklist/.

Furthermore, the ENTREQ Statement is useful. This framework consists of 21 items, grouped into 5 domains (introduction, methodology and methods, literature search and selection, appraisal, and synthesis of findings). It can be used to report the stages of the meta-synthesis (see Tong et al., 2012).

Moreover, the COREQ (Consolidated Criteria for Reporting Qualitative Research) is a 32-item checklist for assessing interviews and focus group studies (Tong et al., 2007).

Software

Covidence streamlines the production of systematic review. All searches and records can be imported into Covidence, which can be used for screening abstracts and to complete data extraction. It removes duplicates and automatically populates them into your PRISMA flowchart. When using referencing management software (e.g. EndNote, RefWorks), they can also be populated into Covidence (see Kellermeyer et al., 2018). The software Covidence is available at www.covidence.org.uk.

AI Tools for Meta-Analysis

OpenMeta[Analyst], developed by Brown University (http://www.cebm.brown.edu/open-meta/), JASP, a free statistical software (https://jasp-stats.org/) and MetaInsight, a free software package designed specifically for conducting network meta-analyses (see Owen et al., 2019).

Software for Qualitative Data Analysis

The software program NVivo is a "Qualitative Data Analysis Software" (CAQDAS). It can be useful for organizing and managing the data, memos, and literature (https://lumivero.com/products/nvovo). NVivo 15 has a Lumivero AI assistant, which enables automatic text summarization and provides coding suggestions. Automated coding can also be used for thematic and sentiment analysis. A variety of material from the internet can be imported, organized, and centralized with NVivo Collaboration Cloud, which additionally allows the members of a research team to code simultaneously and all contributions appear in real time. Data can be quickly converted into diagrams and charts. NVivo directly integrates data from Citavi as well, which is a knowledge and reference management software. Apps like SurveyMonkey can also be used. Automated NVivo transcription can increase the accuracy of transcription from audio and video formats (see Lumivero website). However, researchers must learn to use the NVivo software and pay for it. An alternative is ATLAS.ti (https://atlasti.com/), which was originally designed for Grounded Theory analysis. Nowadays, it has similar capability as NVivo, but excels at memoing and other tools for theory building (see info guides at George Mason University, infoguides.gmu.edu). A comparison between ATLAS.ti, NVivo, and DELVE could be useful (https://delvetool.com/blog/atlasti-vs-nvivo-vs-delve). Guides from John Hopkins University compare QDAS (https://guides.library.jhu.edu/QDAS).

Further Reading for Grounded Theory

If you would like to gain a deeper understanding, the original book by Glaser and Strauss (1967), as well as publications by Strauss and Corbin (1998), Charmaz (2006, 2008, 2014, 2017, 2020), Charmaz and Kenwood (2008), and Charmaz and Thornberg (2021) could be useful. Furthermore, Chun Tie et al. (2019) have written a brief article for novice nurse researchers that is easy to understand. Yarwood-Ross and Jack (2023) explain the classic version, where researchers seek to identify latent patterns of behavior in the data by utilizing open and selective coding, constant comparison, theoretical sampling, constant memoing, and theoretical coding. They provide a good overview of the extant literature. Morse et al. (2009) discuss versions of Grounded Theory and important aspects.

Network Analysis Publications/Resources

Rawlings et al.'s (2023) book for in-depth information on the application of Network Analysis with R. Current network research in clinical psychology stems from Denny Borsboom and colleagues. They provide tutorials, reviews, and information on the application of NA. Borsboom has applied NA to mental health and psychopathology symptoms (e.g. Borsboom, 2017; Borsboom & Cramer, 2013; Cramer et al., 2010; Cramer et al., 2016). Sacha Epskamp has written extensively on psychometric network models, including tutorials (see http://sachaepskamp.com). Publications, research information, including R software and packages, are also found on the Psychosystems website (https://psychosystems.org).

For review of statistical NA see, for example, Salter-Townshend et al. (2012). Hevey (2018) presented an example of how to conduct NA on empirical data in R, which is an open-source statistical programming language that facilitates statistical analysis and data visualization. The R manual (R Core Team, 2017), relevant information, and CRAN are available on the R Foundation website (https://www.r-project.org). Hevey (2018) noted that many NA methods can be implemented in the generic software MATLAB and Stata. Other software packages are UCINET and Gephi (https://www.gephi.org). The Stanford Network Analysis Platform (SNAP) provides an NA library. Most research on psychological networks has used R packages, Igraph, or qgraph. Data can be imported directly into R, using common formats and program (Excel, SPSS, SAS and Stata). Other software or tools: Cytoscape (www.cytoscape.org), SocNetV (www.socnetv.org), sDNA (www.sdna.cardiff.ac.uk), i2 Group documentation (www.docs.i2group.com), NodeXL, Graphviz, PARTNER CPRM, UCINET, Netlytic, Pajek, Pollinode, Kumu, and draw.io (https//app.diagrams.net).

Further Reading on Questionnaire Development

DeVellis and Thorpe (2022) *Scale Development. Theory and Applications. Fifth Edition.* The authors suggest how to develop scales, discuss validity and reliability, and emphasize logical understanding of concepts.

Kühne et al. (2021) Development of a Scale for Assessing Basic Psychotherapeutic Skills. *Zeitschrift für Klinische Psychologie und Psychotherapie* 50(3–4): 116–132.

They developed an instrument (Clinical Communication Skills Scale, CCSS), and described how they investigated its content validity and applicability. Scale is available at: https://www.uni-potsdam.de/en/clinical-psychology-psychotherapy/forschungsschwerpunkte/psychologische-messinstrumente

Boateng et al. (2018) Best Practices for Developing and Validating Scales for Health, Social, and Behavioral Research: A Primer. *Frontiers in Public Health. 11 June.* 6(149): 19 pages.

Adams and Cox (2008) have written a chapter on Questionnaires, in-depth interviews and focus groups, published in Cairns and Cox (Eds.) *Research Methods for Human Computer Interaction.* Cambridge: Cambridge University Press, pp. 17–34.

Andy Field (2024) *Discovering Statistics Using IBM SPSS Statistics. 6th Edition.* Sage.

In addition to explaining how to use the Statistical Package for Social Sciences (SPSS), you also learn about statistics. Online resources are also available.

Authors in Graesser and Black's (2019) book approach questioning from many perspectives, covering the influence of adjunct questions, problematize comprehension and theories, and discuss methods and application.

Learning More about Focus Groups

"How do focus groups work?" is a Ted-Ed video by Hector Lanz, which offers a brief introduction, available on YouTube. https://youtu.be/3TwgVQIZPsw?si=ruFqvqz1tBG1BMWb

Richard Krueger's "Moderating focus groups" shows a group discussion. All of Richard Krueger's books explain focus groups well. https://youtu.be/xjHZsEcSqwo?si=Sp-UeconzvjydDWU

Useful Information on the Q-Sort

Watts and Stenner (2005, 2012) provide a very good guide on how to use the Q-Methodology. The International Society for the Scientific Study of Subjectivity actively promotes research within that tradition: https://qmeth od.org/. Free software packages are also available, which can be found on Peter Schmolck's website (http://schmolck.org/qmethod/) along with other helpful references on Q-methodology. Also useful is Block's (1961ab, 2008) approach to Q-Methodology, the Defence Mechanism Rating Scale Q-sort (DMRS-Q; Di Giuseppe et al., 2014), the Psychotherapy Process Q-set (PQS; Ablon et al., 2011; Ablon & Jones, 2000), Armelius and Armelius (1980, 1992), Sjőberg (1993).

Software

Free Software is available for Q-studies, such as PQMethod, KenQ, and other analysis tools can be found on the website Q method (https://qmethod.org/resources/software/). Software can assist researchers in conducting studies, including data entry, analysis, and visualization.

For focus groups, QDA Miner, a mixed-method and qualitative data analysis software can be used, Provalis Research (https://provalisresearch.com/products/qualitative-data-analysis-software/). Python, with libraries such as Pandas, NumPy, and Matplotlib, offer tools for handling and visualizing matrix data (https://www.python.org).

Although AI tools for MRG analysis are limited, they could be used as general data analysis and visualization tools, for example, R Programming Language from CRAN, which is freely available (https://cran.r-project.org). Moreover, OpenRepGrid is an R package designed to analyze and visualize repertory grid data, also available from CRAN (Heckmann, 2024). Many other tools exist.

Useful Resources for Secondary Data

The UK Data Service (https://ukdataservice.ac.uk)

Timescapes Archive (https://timescapes-archive.leeds.ac.uk)

Federal German Archives (https://www.bundesarchiv.de). The online Stasi media center holds 1,300 documents, 160 photo series, 42 audios, 53 videos, and 288 publications. All information is available in both German and English (Bundesarchiv, 2025).

Word Association Experiment (WAE) & Word Association Test (WAT)

Jungian trained group analytic practitioner–researchers may find Jung's method useful. Word association tests have a long history in research and there seem to be a renewed interest in Jung's WAT/WAE. If researchers wanted to study complexes and the underlying archetypes, it could be a suitable empirical method for group analytic practitioner–researchers with a Jungian orientation, or for Jungian analysts with an interest in groups. The WAE/WAT can be used on its own or in combination with other tests.

Jung's (1968b) collective unconscious forms part of the social unconscious. It is characterized by archetypes. For Jung (1934), complexes were the living units of the unconscious psyche. He empirically demonstrated the existence of complexes (Escamilla, 2021) by using the Word Association Test (WAT). Jung (1963, 1971) regarded complexes as patterns of libidinally charged clusters of thoughts, feelings, memories, and behavior. They operate independently of conscious awareness. Known also as the Word Association Experiment (WAE), Jung (1971) originally developed it to gain insight into the unconscious, including complexes and archetypes. The WAE has been further developed and validated (e.g. Roesler, 2018; Roesler & Uffelen, 2018). Jung and Riklin (1904/1973) developed the term "feeling toned complex" (p. 116). He used galvanic skin response and other measures as well. Hence, he noticed physiological disturbances in heart rate, breathing, and skin. He viewed "complexed reactions" as signs of repression. "… Jung and Riklin provided an experimental demonstration of the efficacy of dynamic subconscious ideas … [they] were studying not only emotions but unconscious emotions …" (Kerr, 1993, p. 59).

Whereas psychotherapists often amplify, deepen, intensify, and enrich archetypal material with clients, researchers could explore such material with their participant through interview. Or they may study videotaped therapy sessions. Archetypes could be conceptualized as universal organizing principles. They could be defined as underlying motion patterns, manifesting as typical behavior patterns, and automatic unconscious reactions. The Self is regarded as the main archetype of our psyche. Jung (2011) held that the archetype is merely a possibility of representation of a given a priori. Only the forms of representations are inherited. The underlying meaning of words, and the postulate that they enable insights into our ancestral, cultural, and historical other, ultimately rests on the idea that archetypes are a source of unconscious knowledge (O'Brien & O'Brien, 2025). As Edinger (1992) noted, the unconscious creates the ego but never knew that it did. Only when the ego is sufficiently developed can it assume responsibility for all that happens in the psyche. Then the ego is no longer identical with the psyche.

O'Brien and O'Brien (2025) used the terms "WAE" and "WAT", referring to the latter when applied in research. The Word Association Test is easier to administer than to interpret. Training is required for the administration and interpretation of findings. Normally, the test is carried out over a minimum of three separate meetings, according to O'Brien and O'Brien (2025, p. 12). It involves discussion of the personal history, the administration of the 100-word list (50 nouns, 25 verbs, and 25 adjectives/adverbs) or a shortened 50-word list, the reviewing results, sharing findings with the participant, and offering him/her the opportunity to comment on the insights gained about the complexes (e.g. Mother, Father, or Siblings complex). Considering Counter-/ transference also forms part of the WAE interpretation process.

Words are read out aloud and participants have to offer an association. This is timed. A delayed reaction time and failure of association indicate that the stimulus word is somehow connected to a complex (Keiser, 1980). The longer the reaction time, the more pronounced is the underlying disturbance. Other aspects, such as perseveration, repetition or misunderstanding of the stimulus word, mimicry, exclamations and interjections, stuttering, slips of the tongue, no apparent connection between the stimulus word, multi-word or reactions in foreign languages, were also interpreted (pp. 15–16). Jung's WAT could be utilized when studying assessment or preparation sessions for group analytic therapy. When clients leave the group, they could be re-tested. A comparison of findings from the assessment, possibly from the individual preparation sessions, and from the completion of therapy would indicate whether complexes have changed.

Researchers could also integrate AI (see O'Brien & O'Brien, 2025) and give participants watches that monitor physiological processes, such as heart rate. Bodily responses would offer further insight. They were recorded by Jung.

Complexes, words, and other information are mapped by using pen and paper, and/or by drawing images. As part of the interpretation process, the researcher regards all the words as relevant images. They are interpreted like other images from dreams or artifacts. Emotional, bodily, and other effects that the image has on the researcher are taken into consideration. The researcher reflects on these within the context of the participant's own reflections and the wider environment. In this way, layers of the unconscious background of the complexes and the archetypal forces central to each complex can be revealed (pp. 49–50). The WAE/WAT can be used on its own or in combination with other tests.

Measurement of Multiple Group Memberships

A variety of measures have been designed to index multiple group memberships. These include open-ended measures of identity quantity (Brook et al., 2008), as well as scale measures of relations among pairs of identities (e.g. conflict; Benet-Martínez & Haritatos, 2005; Settles, 2002) and the overall structuring (e.g. hierarchy and relative identification; Stryker & Serpe, 1982) of group memberships (see Ramarajan, 2014 for a review). They measure the multiplicity of an individual's social group network more generally. They are relatively easy to administer and score.

More recent measurement tools aim to offer more comprehensive information on a person's social group networks. Social Identity Mapping (SIM; Bentley et al., 2020; Cruwys et al., 2016) explores the number of group memberships an individual has, the importance of each social group, the similarity among these groups, and their compatibility.

Individuals are asked to write down the name of each group they belong to on different-sized poster notes (the bigger the note, the more important the group). On one page, they write down spatially cluster similar groups near one and other, and dissimilar groups far apart. Compatible groups are to be joined by straight lines, and incompatible groups by jagged lines. Procedures such as SIM adopt a bottom-up, idiographic approach, where their own social identities are described and people draw their own conclusions regarding their interrelations (see Hughes et al., 2024).

APPENDIX 4

A Group Analyst's Journey to Master the Basics of Statistics

Let us consider the fictitious example of the group analytic psychotherapist Jackie. She wants to carry out a study but has no idea how to go about searching for articles. So, a friend tells her about *common* ***Platforms and Databases*** *that can be used for searches:*

PsycNET has been designed specifically to access content of the American Psychological Association (APA). It includes the database PsycINFO. It is the largest resource worldwide, devoted to peer-reviewed literature in the behavioral and social sciences. In addition to abstracts, full texts of articles and book chapters are available on PsycARTICLES.

PsycNET can also be accessed indirectly via EBSCO, Ovid Technologies, and ProQuest.

Most databases use Boolean logic. So, Boolean modifiers, such as AND, OR, and NOT can be used. Familiarity with the *Thesaurus of Psychological Index Terms* (Gallagher, 2007), which provides a standardized wording, is essential. It is the key to the vocabulary used to index entries. It was updated in 2024 (https://blog.apapubs.org/tag/apa-thesaurus/).

Other platforms and databases include Psychiatry Online, ScienceDirect, ProQuest, the Web of Science, Scopus, Google Scholar, and ERIC, Embase, Cinahl, the NHS Economic Evaluation Database, and the National Technical Information Service. RCTs can also be found on the Cochrane register (www.cochranelibrary.com), and on the Cochrane website (www.cochrane.org), which offers useful research information.

To access gray/grey literature (unpublished literature), Google, OpenGrey (https://opengrey.eu/), BASE (https://www.base-search.net/), and the free deep web database MedNar, which is a helpful complement to use together with the standard medical databases PubMed and MedlinePlus, are available at https://mednar.com/.

Jackie locates relevant papers. Then she encounters further difficulties. She wants to conduct a quantitative study. Until she stumbles over the words "power", "probability", "error", and "rejection". Power and rejection are important to group analysts and researchers. Of course, I do not know what others associate with power and rejection. However, there is a 0.999999 probability that every middle-aged group analyst has encountered power struggles, or rejection, at one point in her/his life. Probability is expressed by a number between 0 and 1. If the event is almost certain to occur, then it is near 1.

But what is this power, and what are errors about, in statistics? Jackie sighs. She decides to suppress her fear of rejection for a moment and attends to ***Power, Type I and Type II Error & Effect Size***, because these are important for her study. She reads Banerjee et al. (2009), who suggested that power (ability to detect an effect if there is one present) is an important consideration to reduce the chances of a Type II error (wrongly accepting the null hypothesis, a false positive). Think about power as sensitivity. So, the more power, the more likely it is that you will detect an effect, if there is one (e.g. Banerjee et al., 2009).

Jackie then considers the alpha level (cut-off value for deeming something significant), which is important. The standard is .05. Lower alpha values will decrease the amount of power. In turn, this increases the chance of a Type II error. But, if she uses higher alpha levels, then the chance of a Type I error (incorrect rejection of a true null hypothesis, a false negative) is higher as well.

Jackie also reads about Cohen's *d* (Cohen, 1988), which is a means to calculate the magnitude of an observed effect, the effect size (see Field, 2005c). The effect size statistic assesses the size of impact of an intervention, where an effect size of 1.0 is equivalent to a difference of 1 standard deviation (SD). Such statistics allow direct comparisons with other outcome studies.

Effect sizes can refer to differences either between two groups, or within one group across time (i.e. pre-post change). As a general convention, a between-group effect size of 0.2 indicates small change, 0.5 indicates moderate change, and 0.8 or above, indicates considerable change (Cohen, 1988; Kazis et al., 1989).

Jackie wants to use only a few participants. The more people (data), the greater the power. But she gets hung up on effect size, because how large a difference is, also impacts power. If there is a large enough effect size, there is a greater difference between the groups. Hence, power will be greater. But a small effect size will require more power to be able to detect an effect.

However, the statistical test itself can impact on power, Jackie discovers. Some tests have more sensitivity. The simpler the test, the more power it has to detect an effect. She knows that power analysis is done prior to data collection, so that she can determine the minimum sample size (participants), she needs to detect an effect. This can be done by using specific software, known as G*power (Faul et al., 2007, 2009). Jackie can use their free statistical software that allows her to determine statistical power by using G* power for correlation and regression analyses. She can specify the type of test she wants to run, the desired power and alpha level to determine the sample size needed. This software can be found at https://www.psychologie.hhu.de/arbeitsgruppen/allgemeine-psychologie-und-arbeitspsychologie/gpower.

So far, so good. Jackie plays around with power and starts to feel the effect of Cohen. Until she has no more energy to fight against the return of the repressed. The old White rivals re-appear: Cronbach, Spearman, and Eysenck.

Cronbach's Alpha, Pearson's Correlation Coefficient & Factor Analysis

Jackie must read more. So, she finds out that Charles Spearman introduced Factor Analysis, which became the ultimate method of individual personality psychology, and still is. Eysenck promoted experimental methods, trying to anchor personality, IQ, and race, in summaries of Factor Analysis (Buchanan, 2011). Eysenck (1981, 1985) developed the Eysenck Personality Questionnaire (EPQ), consisting of 90 items. By using the statistical technique "Factor Analysis", he revealed different traits and dimensions of personality (extraversion, neuroticism and psychoticism) (Boyle et al., 2008).

In contrast to the idiographic view that each person has some unique traits (Weinberg & Gould, 2014), the nomothetic approach toward personality emphasizes comparability among individuals and has developed inventories to assess personality (McLeod, 2024).

Jackie does not particularly like statistics. However, Factor Analysis is a statistical technique, which reduces a set of variables into a smaller number of factors by extracting all their communalities (see UCLA, 2024). Developed by Lee Cronbach in 1951 to provide an internal consistency of a test or scale, Cronbach's alpha is the most frequently used measure to examine the reliability of a measurement instrument (Hoekstra et al., 2018), expressed as a number between 0 and 1. This number indicates the internal consistency of a questionnaire (extent to which all the items in a questionnaire/test/scale measure the same concept). The closer to 1, the better. Good internal consistency is an essential condition that ensures the homogeneity/unidimensionality of items.

Jackie sighs, while concerning herself with Cronbach's alpha. It is grounded in the tau equivalent model, which assumes that each test item measures the same latent trait of the same scale. If multiple factors underlie the items for a scale, as revealed by Factor Analysis, alpha underestimates the reliability of the test. Thankfully, most computer packages for statistics can compute Cronbach's alpha. Calculating alpha is common practice in psychological and medical research (Tavakol & Dennick, 2011), so Jackie feels relieved. But how about Pearson?

Pearson's correlation coefficient, *r*, is used to measure linear relationships in parametric testing. It requires data to be normally distributed, to be interval at least, and to have similar variance. Jackie ponders whether a correlation is like a relation she has with her group.

No, it isn't, she concludes. A correlation coefficient is a single value that summarizes the relationship between two variables. Correlation coefficients lie between -1 and 1. A coefficient close to zero means that there is little/no relationship between the two variables of interest. Coefficients close to 1 indicate a strong relationship (Twigg, 2015).

But if she had a cohesive therapy group (coded numerically as 1) and a non-cohesive control group (coded numerically as 0), and she calculated a Pearson correlation between this variable and their sense of belonging, the resulting correlation would have the same *p*-value as a *t*-test on the same data (see Field & Gillett, 2010). There are direct relationships between *r* and statistics that quantify group differences (e.g. *t* and *F*), associations between categorical variables (x2), and the *p*-value of any test statistic. Jackie jots down that the conversions between r and these various measures, are discussed in Field (2005a,c).

For a long moment, Jackie is lured into the world of questionnaire design and ***Forms of Validity & Reliability.*** She likes validity, because she likes certainty. When designing questionnaires, different forms of validity are important. Validity is the extent to which the measurements of an instrument are robust (Simon & Francis, 1998), i.e., that it measures what it intends to measure.

Jackie quite likes all these different forms of validity. Face Validity refers to the extent to which researchers subjectively believe that a measuring instrument, such as a questionnaire, measures what it purports to measure. So, it is a superficial assessment and not a technically rigorous form of validity (Nickerson, 2024). Sampling validity means whether a given population, which is the total number of cases of e.g., depressed people in the world, is adequately sampled (represented) in your study. Content validity refers to whether the items of a questionnaire adequately measure the content they are intended to measure. Whether they represent the entire domain or property that the questionnaire is designed to measure (Frankfort-Nachmias & Nachmias, 1996). Jackie also likes prediction. Nikolopoulou (2022) said that predictive validity examines whether the test can predict a future outcome, i.e., the test must be correlated with a variable that can only be assessed in the future (e.g. a mental health issue). That is what Jackie would like to establish. When future respondents of a test have mental health issues, there is a high correlation between the scores and mental health. This means that the test can predict future mental health.

After giving it some thought Jackie stumbles over concurrent validity, which refers to the correlation between e.g., survey results and results from other sources, Nikolopoulou (2022) says. Jackie gets distracted by the author's name. Greek holidays, Greek wine and music.

Nothing to do with predictive and concurrent validity. These are both subtypes of criterion validity, pertaining to the validation of a test. Tests are dry, not like a good dry wine. Jackie struggles to concentrate. For establishing concurrent validity, scores of a test and the criterion variables are obtained at the same time, Nikolopoulou (2022) says. Predictive validity is measured by comparing the test scores against the scores of an already valid test.

Jackie decides to read up on statistics, before turning to Pearson's r correlation coefficient again. It can be used to calculate the strength between two variables. She can use Statistical Package for Social Science (SPSS), Excel, or other software (see Nikolopoulou, 2022). How many forms of validity are there?!? Jackie lets out a deep sigh.

Construct validity refers to whether the survey items accurately measure the hypothetical constructs they are supposed to measure. Or the extent to which a measure accurately represents the theoretical construct, which it intends to measure. Item consistency determines whether the items are consistent across constructs (Carmines & Woods, 2005). This was getting tedious.

Factorial validity is the degree to which the structure of a test matches its underlying theoretical structure. Jackie feels like throwing both her book and computer out of the window. But then she comes across the word "interpretation".

Reynolds (2010, p. 3) highlighted that reliability relates to test scores and validity to the accuracy of test score *interpretations.* Each interpretation attributed to a test score must be validated. No longer fascinated by questionnaires, Jackie decides to give them a miss. She will design a different type of quantitative study instead. Power tick, errors tick, and so on. Not too difficult, Jackie mumbles.

Until doubts creep in. What if … Jackie is in full catastrophizing mode when thinking about missing data. There is no possibility of "let's ask the audience", or "call a friend". But she has ChatGPT to tell her about missing data.

How can she ***reference*** it? *Citing generated text* is different. Unlike other non-retrievable human data/quotations, in the American Psychological Association, APA, 7th Edition Style articles, ChatGPT generated texts are not cited as "personal communication". Instead, full text of responses can be appended. Shorter replies, for example, "When prompted with …. The ChatGPT generated text … (OpenAI, 2023)" can be referenced and cited as OpenAI (2023). *ChatGPT* (Mar 14 version) [Large language model]. https://chat.openai.com/chat. So, the author is OpenAI, the year refers to the version you used, and the URL is https://chat.openai.com/chat. Referencing tick.

ChatGPT has told Jackie about ***"funnel plot" and "fill analysis***". Missing data and bias are problematic for any quantitative study. Procedures to address these problems have been devised. Bias can be detected via visual examination of a funnel plot. Jackie also gets a link to a paper by Egger et al. (1997). They pointed out that the value of meta-analyses could be limited when they are based on only a few small trials. A simple analysis of funnel plots (plots of the trial's effect estimates against sample size) is a useful test to detect bias in meta-analyses.

Looking for asymmetry that might suggest a specific omission of nonsignificant results is a useful way to assess bias, Jackie learns. When there is no bias, the plot resembles a symmetrical inverted funnel. When bias is present, the funnel plot is skewed and asymmetrical. This does not sound too complicated. So, she turns to fill analysis, which can be carried out to add missing data. This provides an adjusted effect estimate (Duval & Tweedie, 2000).

Oh dear, Jackie can feel anxiety in her chest. This is not that easy. Egger et al.'s (1997) regression test can be run to statistically analyze the relationship between study effect size and standard error (Egger et al., 1997). Aha. Jackie starts to have doubts about whether she will be able to grasp this: Rosenthal's (1979) ***Fail-Safe N*** can be used to estimate the number of unpublished studies with effect sizes of zero or low sizes. Such an inclusion could result in the mean effect size being nonsignificant. Effect sizes can be considered robust, if the required number of unpublished studies is greater than, or equal to $5n + 10$, where n is the number of studies in a meta-analysis (Rosenberg, 2005). Jackie is unsure whether she understands this.

Cochrane is straightforward. A risk of bias assessment for the primary outcome measure can be carried out by using the Cochrane Risk of Bias Tool (see Sterne et al., 2019).

As more doubts creep in, fear of rejection is surfacing. Jackie ***hypothesizes*** that it was wrong to reject Emma. Otherwise, why would she agonize over it? Peter highlights that she is having a confidence crisis. That's his "hypothesis" (referred to as alternative hypothesis, or H_1), which is a statement that can be tested to ascertain whether it is true.

(Hypothesis testing involves stating $H_{1,}$ figuring out the null hypothesis (H_0), stating it, choosing the right test, which must be performed, and rejecting the $H_{0,}$ or not.)

"Wouldn't it be great to know whether Peter's hypothesis is true?" Emma asks, suggesting that they could use ***statistical tests*** (*t*-tests, ANOVA, *Z*-test, regression tests, Mann-Whitney, Kruskal-Wallis, Wilcoxon, Chi-Square). Because they are scientific. "Too many tests!" Peter points out, looking at Jackie. "Regression, now that is relevant", he says. Jackie grabs a cigarette. "Oral stage", Peter comments, "you've reverted to the oral stage, no wonder that you don't understand probability tests".

Probability tests assess how likely it is that the observed data (e.g. confidence crisis) could occur under a given hypothesis. Does this mean that these tests will enable us to answer Peter's hypothesis that Jackie is having a confidence crisis? Alas, they don't. This is a very crucial point that many get wrong (see Vickers, 2010).

They do not, because probability tests focus on the null hypothesis and not on the alternative hypothesis (H_1). Probability tests provide a framework for making decisions under uncertainty. They help to assess evidence against the null hypothesis. However, they can't establish an absolute truth, because they are based on probabilities, assumptions, and data variability. So, remember that hypothesis testing is based on probabilities only.

Jackie is not impressed by Peter. Her new ***hypothesis*** is that "all group analysts are more neurotic than ordinary people". No sane person would sit in a psychotherapy group for months and months.

The null hypothesis is that "there is no difference between group analysts and ordinary people regarding neuroticism". Assume Jackie has assessed people's neuroticism and collected relevant data. When interpreting her results, Jackie works out whether to accept or reject the null hypothesis. The null hypothesis is the opposite of Jackie's statement. Her accepting the H_0 would mean that there is no significant difference between her sample of group analysts and ordinary people (in terms of neuroticism).

Rejecting the H_0 would mean that there is a significant difference between group analysts and ordinary people when it comes to sanity, which is expressed by the *p*-value (probability value; it's a cut-off point). In technical language, the *p*-value is the probability of finding the observed results (both groups are neurotic) when the null hypothesis is true. If the p-value is 0.05 or below, the null hypothesis is rejected (i.e. only group analysts are neurotic).

The p-value is a fundamental concept in science. But remember that the null hypothesis can't be proven. It is rejected or not rejected. Failing to reject does not translate into the null hypothesis being true.

Let's think about this scenario to better understand ***hypothesis testing***.

Peter is the head of the psychotherapy department. He states that the patients under their care suffer from "above average depression". A random sample of thirty patients had a mean depression score of 112.5.

(Michael Campbell's (2021) book is the latest revision of the 1997 BMJ book on statistics, used for some of my statistical explanations, as well as Vickers, (2010), ChatGPT for verification, and the BMJ resources: https://www.bmj.com/about-bmj/resources-readers).

Emma wonders whether there was enough evidence to support Peter's claim. She knows that the mean population depression score is 100, with a SD of 15. So, she states 1) the null hypothesis. H_0: $\mu = 100$ (because the population mean, expressed as μ, is 100); and 2) the alternative hypothesis (that patients have above average depression scores): H_1: $\mu > 100$. Emma is looking for scores that are "above average", i.e., greater than a certain point, which suggest that she must use a one-tailed t-test. Emma uses a graph to visually show this, which can be found on the internet. Then Emma states an alpha level of 5% (0.05), because she does not know the exact levels. She finds the rejection region area given by the alpha level from the z-table. An area of .05 is equal to a z-score of 1.645. Emma finds the relevant test statistic, using the appropriate formula:

$$Z = \frac{\bar{x} - \mu_0}{\sigma / \sqrt{n}}$$

In other words, the z-score reflects the SD of the sample minus the known population mean, divided by the SD from the square root of the sample size.

For Emma's dataset: $z = (112.5 - 100) / (15/\sqrt{30}) = 4.56$.

If this value is greater than the z-score from the rejection area ($4.56 > 1.645$), Emma can reject the H_0 (If it was smaller, she would have to accept the null hypothesis).

Emma and Jackie consult various statistic books. In statistics, ***lower and uppercase letters are used to distinguish between concepts***. Therefore, x denotes an observation in a dataset, n is the sample size/number of observations in the population, $\bar{x}$ (x-bar) is the SD of a sample, and μ the population mean. The known/hypothesized value of the population mean is represented by μ_0. While the population mean is the average of all values in a population, the sample mean is the average of a sample from that population, and σ is the SD of the population. Capital letters, such as X, denote the population random variable, N is the total number of observations in a population and n is the total number of observations in a sample. S is usually used for the SD of the population and s (or sigma) is the SD of a sample, and x is used to represent raw scores (individual data value). A series of data values are often presented as $x_1 + x_2, + x_i$.

Let's consider this ***research question, Emma asks: "Are group analysts frightened of ghosts?"*** Jackie has always been wary of ghosts. Hence, she believes that "ghosts frighten all group analysts". For her, this is a true hypothesis and a good research question.

Peter rejects this statement. He offers an alternative hypothesis, namely that she is experiencing visual hallucinations, because she was experimenting with psychedelic drugs. Jackie disagrees. She had been taking drugs for years without hallucinating. Obviously, she does not want to tell him. He would only question her ego strength and will power. But, she is absolutely certain that ghosts do exist. She also believes that "CBT therapists are more afraid of ghosts than group analysts". This is her new hypothesis. So, Jackie thinks of designing a ***randomized controlled trial (RCT)*** due to its high status in the traditional evidence hierarchy (only trumped by meta-analysis and systematic reviews, no political inuendo intended).

After re-defining "frightened" as "to make anxious", she chooses the Beck Anxiety Inventory (BAI) as an outcome measure (see Appendix 3).

Scores range from 0 (no anxiety) to 63 (severe), and scores above 36 indicate severe anxiety. The BAI is proven to be a good instrument for measuring anxiety, and items are scored on a scale between 0 and 3. A total score between 0 and 63 can be achieved. Scores indicate Normal Level of Anxiety (0–9), Mild Anxiety (10–18), Moderate Anxiety (19–29), Severe Anxiety (30–63) (Julian, 2011). (36–63 cut-off for severe reported by Headway, 2025).

Jackie recruits participants (group analysts) and chooses a method of randomization: using a list with random numbers. So, she randomizes her sample (first group consists of group analysts; the second of CBT therapists). Then everybody completes the BAI. Jackie sums up the scores and all scored 0. So, nobody suffers from anxiety.

In Jackie's designed study, both groups will discuss uncanny occurrences involving ghosts, watch scary ghost movies, and discuss these with the group facilitators.

Jackie expects all her participants to be frightened. However, the second group (CBT therapists) will be more frightened.

Wryly, Peter enquires how many participants she has recruited. She looks at him smugly. "I will be sure that the null hypothesis can be rejected and that my study has sufficient power, because I did a power calculation." More group therapy for Peter so that he can address his power issues and fear of rejection. Power and rejection are as crucial for research, as they are for psychotherapy. "There will be no difference between the two groups", that's the null hypothesis". The main purpose of her study is hypothesis testing. Determining the sample size (number of participants) depends on power. Nothing to do with group analysts having more power than clients. Statistical power is the probability of correctly rejecting the null hypothesis, when Jackie's hypothesis is true.

Expressed as $1 - \beta$, Jackie decides to choose 0.80. This means that there is an 80% chance of detecting a true effect in her study. Ensuring adequate (at least 80%) power is crucial, because the sample size plays a central role in ensuring that a study is not underpowered. This directly affects the study's ability to detect true effects and to draw robust conclusions. Effect size measures the magnitude of the difference.

Jackie thinks about power calculation. "To use a formula, or not, that's the question", she mumbles. "You hate math, use software", Emma says. If there truly is an effect of a given size, then all her rejection can be saved for the null hypothesis, instead of rejecting Emma.

"There is strength in numbers", Jackie comments, when being asked how many group analysts and CBT therapists she wants to recruit. "There's something to be said about greed", Emma retorts. "Nothing to do with greed. Plain statistics. The more participants I'll have in my study, the more the standard error will be reduced. It makes it easier to detect true effects and increases my power." Obviously, Jackie is no longer suffering from a lack of confidence. "I'll go for a frequential power analysis, because it's the most widely used method to calculate the sample size", she says in a matter-of-fact tone, as if she knew what she was talking about.

Jackie may choose one of the commonly used tests (the two-sample t-test for continuous data, the two-proportion Z-test formula for binary data, Cox proportional hazards models for survival, or intraclass correlation coefficient for cluster RCTs).

Jackie wants to ***estimate*** how many group analysts are frightened of ghosts compared to CBT therapists (purpose of her study is estimation). So, she is actually more interested in ***estimation*** than hypothesis testing. Hence, her sample size depends on how precise she would like her estimate to be. Precision refers to the width of the "***confidence interval***" (CI). CI is a statistical term and has nothing to do with Jackie's fluctuating confidence levels. CIs are essential in RCTs for evaluating the precision, magnitude, and significance of the difference between the two groups (group analysts, CBT therapists). The smaller the width, the better. If the CI would be wide in Jackie's study, it would indicate greater imprecision about the estimated effect size.

When the ghost story/films effect is ***estimated*** as 3 with a CI of (−1 to 7), the actual effect could range from a slight negative impact (–1) to a significant positive impact (7). Then her data would not provide a very precise estimate of the true value of the parameters that are being measured (whether group analysts or CBT therapists are more frightened of ghosts). Because there would be a high variability in her data. To put it simply, if there is a significant variability (large SD) in the outcome measures (some therapists are very scared, others hardly, or a bit), the confidence interval widens.

Luckily, Jackie's data are ***normally distributed***. In her study, two-thirds of her observations fall within one SD of the mean. Trusting Vicker's (2010) and not her psychotherapy group, this means that 66.67% lie within a 0.97 SD of the mean. Jackie finds the corresponding z-score. The z-score corresponding to a cumulative probability of 0.83335 is approx. $z = 0.97$. Furthermore, 90% of Jackie's observations are greater than the mean minus 1.28 SD. (I double-checked this with ChatGPT, which was suffering a confidence crisis, giving me different calculations, some of which were false. When I pointed this out, ChatGPT apologized, saying it was wrong. It proves my point, trust humans.)

The mean BAI score of the group analysts is 30, SD = 8. So, 66.67% of group analysts' scores fall between $30 \pm (0.97 \cdot 8) = [22.24, 37, 76]$. The mean BAI score for CBT therapists is 36, SD = 8. This indicates that 66.67% of their scores fall between $36 \pm (0.97 \cdot 8) = [28.24, 24, 76]$.

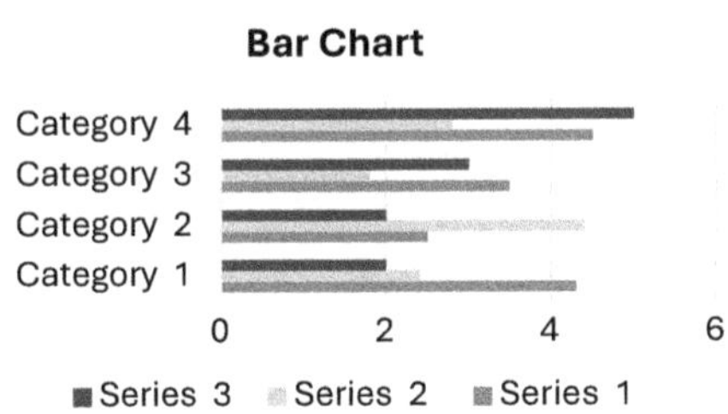

FIGURE 4A1 Bar Chart

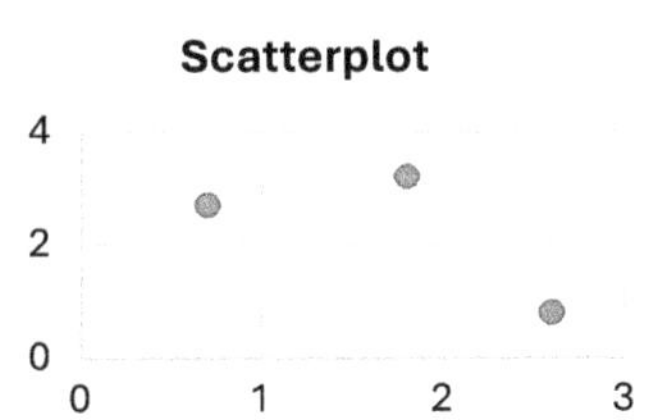

FIGURE 4A2 Scatterplot

Jackie draws this conclusion: While most group analysts' scores fall below the severe fear threshold of 38, a larger proportion of CBT therapists exceed this threshold or are near to exceeding it ($\pm$ 0.97 SD and $\mu - 1.28\ \sigma$). If Jackie used a t-test to compare the scores between the two groups, the higher mean score and tighter clustering of CBT therapists' scores near/above the threshold are likely to indicate a significant result, so Jackie concludes that CBT therapists are more afraid of ghosts. (Ignore that Jackie used a wrong cut-off score).

Jackie often worries about graphs, which show the data of a study in various formats. Most graphs have an x-axis and y-axis. When you draw a line, you state the value of y in terms of x. So, both x- and y-axis represent something (see Vickers, 2010). The x-axis is the bottom line, and the y-axis is the horizontal line on the left side).

A scatterplot (many dots are scattered around) and a bar chart are typical graphs, shown in Figures 4A2 and 4A1, respectively:

Jackie works with clients who have an eating disorders service, where it is common to measure weight and height. To calculate the "mean" (average) measurements of 20 clients, she adds up all the values for weight and height separately, then dividing each (weight and height that is) by 20 (number of clients). When planning service provisions for people with eating problems, calculating the mean is better than using the median (midpoint of weight numbers: half of your sample have values higher, and half have lower values).

However, when she has a very skinny client (39 kg) and three clients are toward the fuller size (together 230k), her data has "outliers". Then the median reflects the data better than the mean.

As such, the mean is the most commonly used measure of central tendency in group psychotherapy research (e.g. see Mishra et al., 2019 for discussion of descriptive statistics). It is particularly useful for continuous data (symptom scores, session attendance), often used in therapy outcome studies. The mean can account for every value in the dataset, providing the average level of a variable (symptom reduction). It is useful when the data are not heavily skewed. If they are, then the mean is less representative and may exaggerate the overall symptom severity. Unlike the mean, the median is not influenced by extreme values, making it a better measure for skewed data. The median provides the central value that reflects the middle of the dataset. If some group members report extremely high and others very low anxiety, the median provides the best measure of central tendency (Mishra et al., 2019).

In psychotherapy research, the mode can be useful when analyzing categorical or discrete data. While the mean and median are used for measures like symptom severity or therapy outcome, the mode provides valuable insight into specific contexts. To identify the most frequently utilized therapeutic approach, or to analyze variables, such as, diagnosis, age group, or preferred therapy type, the mode could reveal useful information. Furthermore, session attendance can be expressed by the mode, it provides a quick snapshot of typical attendance levels. Many variables in psychotherapy are nominal (e.g. therapy type) or ordinal (satisfaction ratings). Hence, the mode can offer useful understanding of the data. When summarizing the most frequent occurrences of something, analyzing the mode is essential. However, if multiple modes exist, it can be challenging to interpret the results (particularly in datasets with evenly distributed cases).

The above are called "***descriptive statistics***". In group psychotherapy research, the mean, median, and mode serve complementary purposes. It depends on the data type and distribution. Choosing the right measure ensures the accurate and meaningful representation of results (Mishra et al., 2019).

If Jackie conducted an RCT with 300 participants (250 improved but 50 got worse), there would be outliers. The mean would not really tell her what was happening. The median would provide better insight. In research papers, "measures of spread" (mean and median) are often reported. SDs are reported for the mean, and interquartile ranges for medians.

Jackie has learnt about normality in her psychotherapy group and stumbles over the "Bell Curve". It has this name, because it looks like a bell. The Bell Curve shows the "normal distribution" (Gaussian distribution) of data (see Grech & Calleja, 2018 for discussion).

It is a symmetrical probability distribution in statistics, representing a graph where the data cluster around the mean. The highest frequency is in the center, and it decreases toward the tails, so the bulk of data are clustered around the center. The normal distribution is a continuous probability, which is symmetrical. Left and right sides are mirror images. The further away from the mean a value is, the less likely it is to occur. For a normal distribution, the mean, median, and mode are the same value (peak of the curve) (e.g. see Ghasemi & Zahediasl, 2012).

The total area under the curve is 1, so the curve represents 100% of all possible data. The left side is 50% or .5, so the probability of a random variable appearing in the left half of the curve is .5, but this is not the case for every data.

Jackie looks at *Z*-tables. In essence, a *z*-score is a measure that converts a raw score into SDs to determine the probability (Jackie calculates the *z*-score by subtracting the mean from her X value and divides it by the SD).

In a normal distribution, the mean is the center of the normal standard distribution (abbreviated SD, σ, or s). A probability of 50% equals zero SDs. (The SD is the square root of variance.)

Jackie sighs. Not only is philosophy heavily influenced by the Greeks, but also many statistical symbols are expressed in Greek letters. Jackie favors the Romans, so she uses "SD". This is as arbitrary as the SD of 1, it would seem. The normal distribution is determined by two parameters, by the mean and the variance. The normal distribution has a mean of 0 and a SD of 1. It is used as a baseline for all distributions. The choice of SD of 1 for the standard normal distribution simplifies calculations.

In a normal distribution, 5% of the data fall into the left, and 5% into the right tails of the curve, and 90% will be in between. For example, when BAI test scores of clients are normally distributed, 2.5% score very high and 2.5% very low, then 95% of scores will be in the middle. The SD allows Jackie to compare different distributions of different types of data.

Many continuous data (IQ scores, salaries, outcome scores of group questionnaires) will display the Bell Curve. Jackie is keen to use powerful tests, because her confidence has hit rock bottom, while working through statistical assumptions and rules. In projective identification with the power of parametric tests, she carries out an analysis. After all, her data are normally distributed and continuous, which is a prerequisite for using parametric tests. (e.g. see Baghban et al., 2013 how to test for normal distribution).

They are considered more powerful but assume a normal distribution. Commonly *t-tests, ANOVA,* and ***regression*** tests are used. Non-parametric tests, such as, Wilcoxon U, Wilcoxon, or Mann-Whitney tests, and Kruskal-Wallis (techniques to analyze variants) are used for ranked data that are not normally distributed (e.g. see Nahm, 2016; Schrober & Vetter, 2020).

Jackie wonders whether she should do regression analysis. Did Peter not tell her that she was regressed? He did. But regression analysis has nothing to do with regressing to the oral, anal, or oedipal stage. Instead, it is used to assess the relationship between two variables (simple linear regression), or between multiple independent variables (different types of psychotherapy) to

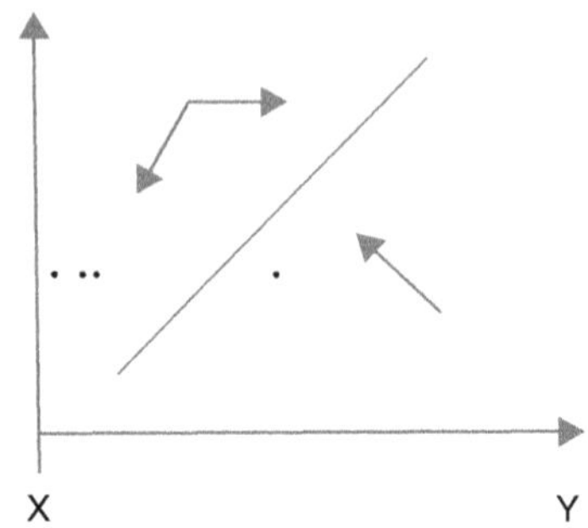

FIGURE 4A3 "Phallic" Regression Line Graph

predict the outcome (anxiety) of a single dependent variable (ghost stories) (Vetter & Schrober, 2018).

Jackie is more interested in *z*-scores. Having done the regression analysis, a statistical not a group analytic regression analysis, she looks at the pictorial representation. The linear regression line (line without arrows) is much too phallic for her taste (Figure 4A3).

Raw scores can be converted into *z*-scores (e.g. see Andrade, 2021), as mentioned above. This allows her to determine the proportion of values that fall within a specified number of SDs from the mean. In other words, the *z*-score tells her how far above or below the mean the individual score is, which is expressed in SDs. There is the 68-95-99.7 empirical rule, which describes the percentages of the data that fall within specific SDs. A small SD indicates that the data are tightly clustered around the mean, so it is shaped like a bell. A large SD indicates that the data are spread out, so the curve will be flatter and wider, or taller and thinner. This rule allows Jackie to get an idea about the likelihood of randomly obtaining a score that falls within a normal distribution.

Wikipedia tells her all about SDs (https://en.wikipedia.org/wiki/Standard_deviation).

What it means is this: 68% of data fall within the first SD from the mean. There is a 68% probability that a score will be between –1 and +1 SDs from the mean. So, when 95% of values fall within 2 SDs from the mean, there is a 95% probability that a score will be between –2 and +2 SDs from the mean. Similarly, when 99.7% of data fall within 3 SDs from the mean, there is a 99.7% probability that a score will be between –3 and +3 SDs from the mean. SPSS checks if the dataset is normally distributed and Jackie can do all other calculations with SPSS. As impressive as SPSS is, ultimately it is software. It does whatever she tells it to do. She is the brain behind it.

Kolmogorov Smirnov and Shapiro-Wilk tests can be used for smaller data sets. They quantify the difference between the distribution.

Regression coefficients (using t-test) enable a comparison of normally distributed data and provide a *p*-value.

When Jackie checks her data, and they are not normally distributed, this is bad news. She does not want this. She scans a few papers. Considering that 95% of observations fall within two SDs of the mean, SDs and means are useful to know. If a paper does not report them, but provides summary data providing the median, the range or percentiles, Jackie can estimate the mean and SDs, using formulas (see Wan et al. 2014; Bland, 2015; McGrath et al., 2020; Cai et al., 2021; BMJ, https://www.bmj.com/about-bmj/resources-readers/publications/statistics-square-one/2-mean-and-standard-deviation).

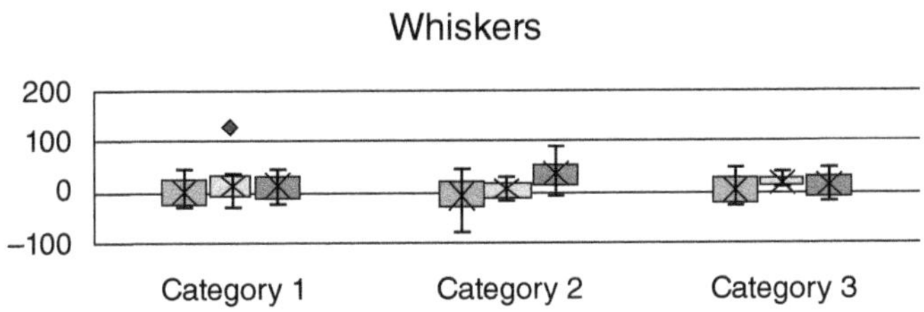

FIGURE 4A4 Whiskers Chart

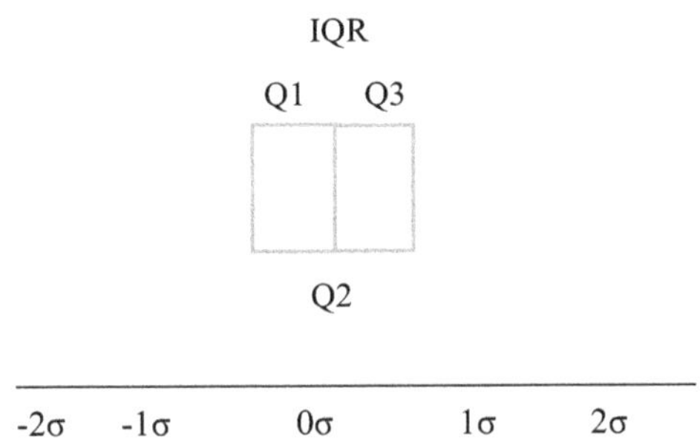

FIGURE 4A5 IQR

If she has the range (minimum and maximum values), as well as the median, Jackie can use this approximation: Mean (if normal distribution, symmetric):

Mean ≈ Min + Max value divided by 2 (with two values).

SD ≈ Max – Min value divided by 4 (with two values). This assumes a normal distribution roughly.

If Jackie finds percentiles reported in the paper, (e.g. 25th, 50th, 75th percentiles), she can estimate the interquartile range (IQR). It is a measure of spread, of where the bulk of the values lie and useful for reporting test scores. The IQR is the central half of any dataset, shown below on a box and whiskers chart (Figure 4A4) and drawing (Figure 4A5):

So, Jackie uses this formula, calculating the difference between the 75th and 25th percentiles, measuring the spread of the middle 50 percent:

IQR = 75th – 25th percentile

For a normal distribution: SD ≈ IQR divided by roughly 1.35.

Why roughly 1.35? Debray et al. (2017, p. 10) suggested it was approx. 1.35. It is the approximate ratio of the Interquartile range to the standard distribution for a normal distribution. But Warr and Erich (2013) disagree.

Jackie accepts 1.35. The IQR is the difference between the 76th and the 25th percentile in a dataset. Expressed as $IQR = Q_3 - Q_1$.

In the standard distribution, Q_3 corresponds to a *z*-score of +0. 674 and Q_1 to a *z*-score of –0.674.

(Jacke used the z-score calculator https://www.calculator.net/z-score-calculator.html)

The distance between these two *z*-scores is + 0.674 – (–0.674) = 1.348. Hence, for the normal distribution, the IQR is approximately 1.35 times the SD.

Rearranging this relationship gives SD ≈ IQR divided by 1.35.

This works when the data is normally distributed. Otherwise, this approximation would not be accurate, and Jackie would have to simply report the IQR as a measure of spread. Or transform it into a log, square root, or do a reciprocal transformation.

She decides to have a relationship with a statistician instead, who does the calculations for her. But she can't live on statistics alone and he turns out to be rather boring. Jackie focuses on her career. Working in an eating disorders unit, she ponders how to utilize her newly acquired statistical skills.

If Jackie's clients are too thin, she can answer questions like "what weight is exceeded by 69% of clients" and "what proportion falls below the critical body mass index" by using the mean and SDs. Her clients' mean weight is 45 kg and the SD is 5 kg. Jackie calculates the weight exceeded by 69% of clients and the proportion of clients below the critical mass index (40 kg). She finds the z-score for 31% cumulative probability (z-score corresponding to $P(Z \leq z) = 0.31$ is $z = 0.50$). (She rounds up from 0.496 to 0.50.)

Then she converts the z-score to a weight, using this formula: $W = \mu + z(\sigma)$.

The z-score formula ($z = (x - \mu) / \sigma$) is used to standardize a raw score (x) into a z-score. From a z-score Jackie returns to a raw score, rearranging the formula:

She starts with the z-score formula: $z = (x - \mu) / \sigma$.

Then she multiplies both sides by σ: $z\sigma = x - \mu$

Finally, she adds μ to both sides: $x = \mu + z\sigma$

(https://courses.lumenlearning.com/introstats1/chapter/the-standard-normal-distribution)

She substitutes the values: $W = 45$ kg + (−0.50 kg) (5 kg). This makes $W = 45$ kg – 2.5 kg = 42.5 kg.

So, 69% of clients' weight ***exceeds*** 42.5 kg.

Jackie presents these figures in the multi-disciplinary team meeting. She makes the clever argument that the majority of clients have benefited from her analytic group, that is why 69% of them have gained weight. So, statistics are useful for all kinds of things.

Jackie has learnt another lesson about the so important ρ-value. While it can tell her if there is an effect, it won't tell her how large this effect is, so must use Cohen's *d*.

P-values are used to test hypotheses, nothing else. Convention says that values equal to 0.05 (5 out of 100) or below ($\rho = 0.01$, 1 in 100; $\rho = 0.001$, 1 in 1000) are "statistically significant". The smaller the value, the better, because it is less likely that the results occurred by random chance that that the null hypothesis can be rejected (e.g. Sil et al., 2019; McLeod, 2023b).

If Jackie gets a value of $\rho = 0.051111$, it is not statistically significant. If this doesn't make a lot of sense, well, it's because the *ρ-value* has been defined somewhat arbitrarily.

So, when she comes across a psychotherapy trial which reports a value of $\rho \geq 0.05$ for shouting at your group members as intervention, it's a bad idea to shout at them in the hope that they'll improve. When it says $P \leq 0.05$, trust the group, or whatever intervention was used. But remember that a more significant result does not mean a more important result, or a larger effect. It just means that a result was detected, which is statistically significant.

She reads a paper in which the authors report 6 ρ-values. If many ρ-values are reported, it means that the researchers have tested many hypotheses, Vickers (2010) pointed out.

It's easy to forget that tests rely on assumptions. They can be broadly divided into parametric and non-parametric tests. Both groups have their advantages and limitations. However, when using advanced study designs, as is often the case in psychotherapy research, parametric tests are more useful, because they allow researchers to carry out more sophisticated analyses and to produce more robust results. Regression analysis, for example. Several variables can be analyzed when doing a regression analysis (Li, 2012).

When intending to evidence that a causal relationship exists between a *dependent variable* (e.g. depression) and one or more *independent variables* (e.g. stress, sleeplessness, anxiety), regression analysis can be useful. It allows Jackie to ***explain and quantify variations*** in the dependent variable (mild, moderate, severe depression) by finding out which of the independent variables may have caused severe depression. Many other statistical techniques can be applied. Reading introductory books on statistics or some of the articles mentioned here can give you an idea how to carry out a regression analysis.

Books on Statistics

Faulkenberry T (2022) *Psychological Statistics: The Basics*. New York: Routledge.

Field A (2024) *Discovering Statistics Using IBM SPSS Statistics*. New York: Sage.

Forshaw M (2010) *Easy Statistics in Psychology: A BPS Guide*. London: Wiley.

Miles J and Banyard P (2007) *Understanding and Using Statistics in Psychology: A Practical Introduction*. New York: Sage.

Watt R and Collins E (2019) *Statistics for Psychology. A Beginner's Guide Second Edition*. New York: Sage.

APPENDIX 5

Supplement to Chapter 2 Part 2: Development of Modern Physics & Quantum Mechanics

According to Brown and Weidner (2024), classical physicists regarded the universe as a mechanical system governed by deterministic laws of motion and interactions. One could say that they were realists. For them, reality was a phenomenon that could be described with total accuracy and certainty through empirical observation and experimentation. Classical physics (Greek "φύσις", natural world) is based on Newton's mechanical model of the world. The Newtonian world consisted of material particles that moved in an absolute space and absolute time. In mathematical equations, these were treated as mass points. For Newton, matter consisted of small, solid, and indestructible objects (Capra, 1991). In contrast, modern physics has modified classical laws, such as Newton's laws of motion, and Maxwell's electromagnetism, which describe the motion of macroscopic bodies, and unified electricity, and magnetism. Capra (1991) highlighted that the period from 1900 to 1930 changed the entire discipline dramatically. The work of Albert Einstein and other Nobel Prize Laureates marked the beginning of modern physics, which studies particles under a variety of conditions (Herbert, 1985).

Einstein's famous Special Theory of Relativity ($E = mc^2$) states that energy equals mass times the speed of light squared. It explains the impossibility that matter travels faster than light (Holton, 1960; Stein, 2022). Subsequently, Einstein published his General Relativity Theory, a mathematical model of the universe, in which the total volume of space is finite, yet has no boundary or edge (Shu, 2024). Relativity Theory and atomic physics shattered the Newtonian world and with it, ideas about the strictly causal nature of physical phenomena (p. 71).

General Relativity Theory is Einstein's (1915) understanding of how gravity affects the fabric of space and time. It still seems to be the best theory of gravity that physicists have. Gravity is the universe's fundamental force that keeps us grounded. When Einstein said that objects move in curved spacetime, we perceive this as the effects of gravity (Wood, 2023). Einstein expanded the Theory of Special Relativity, demonstrating the inextricable link between space and time. Spacetime, a four-dimensional continuum, is a mathematical model that fuses the three dimensions of space and the one dimension of time (Einstein, 1982). So, there is no universal flow of time, as in the Newtonian model, which has important implications, as Capra (1991) explained. Different observers will order events differently in time, if they move with different velocities relative to the observed events. Then two events, which are seen to occur simultaneously by one observer, might occur in different temporal sequences by another observer (p. 72).

Cresser (2011) stated that the fundamental building blocks on which modern physics rests are Quantum Theory and Einstein's theory. Each of these has resulted in new insights (Brown & Weidner, 2024). Unfortunately, Einstein's Theory of General Relativity and Quantum Theory are incompatible. While the former describes gravity as a continuous spacetime curvature, the latter describes forces in terms of discrete quanta. Einstein's theory is deterministic and Quantum Theory probabilistic.

One encompassing "Theory of Everything" has not yet been fully formulated. Quantum Field Theory is one possibility, and String Theory is the most favorable candidate for a quantum theory of gravity (Becker, 2022).

Kaku (2024) notes that quantum physics studies subatomic particles (fermions, bosons, leptons, such as positrons and neutrinos; baryons, such as neutrons and protons). They are believed to be formed from indivisible elements, known as "quarks". All matter is made of elementary particles (quarks, leptons, fermions, bosons). Essentially, particles are just lumps of energy. Subatomic particles interact with each other, and with themselves, in quantum fields, consisting of "quanta". Quantum mechanics derives its name from them (Herbert, 1985). It is attributed to the German physicist Max Planck (Brown & Weidner, 2024).

In quantum mechanics, mass is described in terms of wave equations and point particles. Energy is concentrated as a mathematical point. Both Quantum Theory and Quantum Field Theory are based on quantum mechanics. Quantum Field Theory, the quantum theory of subatomic particles at high energies, is the relativistic version of Schrődinger's equation (Kaku, 2024). Schrődinger (1944, 2020) formulated the mathematical equation of the probability that a particle would behave as a wave and coined the term "entanglement", the paradox of interlinked quantum states. A wavefunction is a mathematical description of the quantum state of an isolated quantum system (Byrne, 2007, p. 99). So, it explicates the wave characteristics of a particle.

Hoang (2016) described how the Fourier analysis (mathematical technique that allows the identification, quantification, and removal of the time-based cycles in data) was carried out by use of the Fourier transform. It provided a mapping of every wave number with an amplitude. It was possible then to deduce a mapping of every momentum.

Furthermore, the reduction of the state vector (wavefunction collapse) is one of the two processes by which quantum systems evolve over time. It takes a system from being a superposition of states (e.g. spin up and spin down states) to a definite state (Cresser, 2011). Various experiments in quantum optics, the branch of physics that studies how individual quanta of light (photons) interact with atoms and molecules, have demonstrated this. Combining quantum mechanics with optics, it uses lasers that measure the wavelength and frequency of light. It concerns itself with spectroscopy, the study of the absorption and emission of light and other radiation by matter (ATA, 2020). This involves the splitting of light into its constituent wavelengths through spectrometers, which act like a sophisticated form of *diffraction*, the spreading out of waves as they pass through an aperture or pass an obstruction. In other words, spectrometry is the practical measurement of matter at atomic and molecular levels (ATA, 2020).

Experiments, where a photon was shot from a laser gun, found that the photon left a little dark dot on the photographic plates. Physicists call this event "measured", that is, the photon has had an interaction with something in the physical universe (Wichert, 2023). This interaction allows the detection of the photon. Upon measurement, the probabilities calculated by the wavefunction equation instantaneously become 100%, meaning that the dark spot occurs where it does. And 0% that it occurs somewhere else. In quantum terminology, one says that the wavefunction has "collapsed". Before measurement, a quantum system is in Superposition, multiple outcomes are possible. During measurement, the photon settles into one definite state, the system seems to collapse (Quantum Physics Lady, 2019). Unfortunately, Schrődinger's equation can neither calculate when the collapse will occur, nor where the photon will leave its mark. The position the photon has selected appears random. This omission in the equation is called the "measurement problem".

Thus, various interpretations and further theories have been proposed (Everett rejects collapse, postulating possible outcomes in parallel universes; Pilot Wave Theory/Bohmian Mechanics postulates a hidden variable that guides the particle, eliminating the need for wavefunction collapse; the Ghirardi-Rimini-Weber (GRW) Theory postulates a spontaneous collapse, is a real physical process caused by gravity). These theories differ from Bohr's and Heisenberg's interpretation that the wavefunction collapses upon measurement, and that quantum states are only defined when observed.

Even though the problems have not been totally solved, the Quantum Theory of Decoherence offers a mathematical description of the interaction between the photon with the physical universe (Wichert, 2023). It explains why superpositions disappear in large systems, suggesting that collapse might be an emergent, instead of a fundamental, effect. Moreover, Roger Penrose's Gravity Theory postulates that gravity itself triggers collapse (see Penrose, 1965, 2005, 2014).

Einstein severely disliked the idea of a reality, in which objects lacked definitive states, and could be in two places at the same time. To him, this was too much indeterminacy. In vain would Einstein, Podolsky, and Rosen (known as EPR) attempt to challenge the consequences of Superposition and measurement. Although they presented a serious objection to quantum weirdness, instead of proving that it was wrong, they opened the door to the Bell Theorem. John Stewart Bell (1964) re-examined the EPR and debunked the local hidden variables theory. He calculated relationships that would allow experiments to distinguish between classical and quantum reality. Bell proved mathematically that certain quantum phenomena cannot have a local cause. His Theorem asserts that reality must be non-local. Quantum objects must be linked by non-local effects, which are faster than the speed of light (Bell, 2004). Whereas Einstein, Podolsky, and Rosen advocated a philosophy of science called *local realism*, Bell's Theorem proved that they were wrong. The unintended outcome of the EPR publication was that physicists would recognize that widely separated systems can act as a single quantum entity, nowadays known as entanglement (Frank, 2023), the "spooky action at a distance" as Einstein called it. Innovative Bell-type inequalities (Bell, 1964; Clauser et al., 1969) and delicate experiments (Aspect et al., 1982) have supported Bell's theory. They strongly suggest that certain quantum phenomena have a non-local property, a non-local cause. Bell's Theorem is an integral component of quantum theory and relevant to many areas of life. It accounts for the weirdness of quantum mechanics. Its mystery is illustrated in the double slit experiment (Becker, 2018).

Particles are fired toward a barrier that has two narrow slits and a screen behind it to detect where the particles land. When fired individually, the particles create an interference pattern on the screen, suggesting that each particle passes through both slits simultaneously, interfering with itself, as would be expected for waves passing through the slits. Originally performed by Thomas Young in 1801, and repeated in several variations since then, the double-split experiment has provided evidence that light and matter can behave like particles and waves (Wikipedia, 2024c). When a parallel beam of light passes through a single slit, experiments have shown that the emerging beam is no longer parallel but starts to diverge, known as *diffraction* (Stark, 2024).

An experiment, which involved directing light at an opaque screen with two thin parallel slits in it, offered intriguing insight. Behind the screen was a detector for the light that passed through, as Dunning (2023) explained. To travel through the slits as a wave, light splits into two waves that go through each slit. When these waves cross over again on the other side, they interfere with each other. Where peaks of the wave meet, they enhance each other. However, where a peak and a trough meet, they cancel each other out. This creates a striped pattern on the detector of regions of more light and less light. Light also consists of bundled photons, which can be recorded as they hit the detector one at a time (as in the photon experiment described above). Photons gradually built up a striped interference pattern. Even when researchers fired just one photon at a time, the interference pattern still emerged, as if the photon split into two and traveled through both slits. So, the wave essentially splits into two new waves, each spreading out from one of the slits. In the classic version of the experiment, light emerging from the physical slits changed its direction. The "interference pattern" was written in the angular profile of the light (Dunning, 2023).

Electrons seem to somehow split, passing through both slits at once. Interfering with itself, they also can recombine, when hitting a second screen (behind the first), as a single localized particle. When a detector was put near the slits to see which slit an electron would pass through, the particle pattern of two strips appeared (Plus, 2017). The interference pattern disappeared. Possibly, through the act of measuring did the electrons start to travel in an orderly way. The conclusions drawn from those experiments were that particles, such as electrons, can take on characteristics of both, a particle or a wave (wave-particle duality). Some scholars believe that the very act of measuring a quantum system has a profound effect on it. The propensity to behave as if a system can be two places at once, or even in different states at the same time, is known as "the Superposition of states".

Quantum *complementarity* is a cornerstone of the Copenhagen Interpretation. Influenced by Kantian philosophy and Pragmatism (our knowledge of reality is structured by how we observe it, we do not have access to reality independently of measurement), as well as by classical logic (A is either A, or not -A), Bohr used the term "complementarity" in 1927. He introduced a new kind of logical relationship (wave and particle are not contradictions but context-dependent truths).

The word "complementarity" is rather unfortunate, because it is counterintuitive. In quantum mechanics, it describes how the characteristics of a particle appear to be mutually exclusive but are nonetheless needed. So, complementarity means that something is necessary for a full description of an object, or of reality. The two entities Bohr considered (particle and wave) are only mutually exclusive in classical physics. To fit the paradoxical quality of particles into a model of reality, quantum mechanics utilizes the "wavefunction" (Becker, 2018).

Examples of complementary observables include wave vs particle, position vs momentum, or energy vs time. Light and matter exhibit both wave and particle behavior, *but not simultaneously*. But both wave and particle are necessary to describe them fully. Or, the precise measurements of energy require indefinite time, and vice versa. These three pairs correspond to incompatible quantum measurements, meaning that no experiment can measure them at the same time. What is important is the way we set up an experiment, what we observe, and that nature does not reveal all properties at once. This captures the concept of "complementarity". Bohr intended to express that quantum mechanics requires a shift in thinking about reality.

> To *rule out a too native interpretation of quantum complementarity,*

as Jacques et al. (2007, p. 967) put it, John Wheeler produced the "delayed choice Gedanken" (thoughts) experiment. Building on the double-split experiment, it introduces a twist: the choice of measurement is made after the photon (particle) has already passed through the splits. This should rule out that the photon was influenced by the measurer.

Jacques et al. (2007) found that, if we choose not to measure which slit the photon passes through, it behaves like a wave and creates an interference pattern. If we choose to measure which slit it went through, it behaves like a particle, and the interference pattern disappears. The surprising result was that although the particle has already passed the slits, it retroactively adjusts its behavior, depending on our future measurement choice. One important implication for quantum reality is that reality is shaped by our choices, even if these are made afterwards. This has a bit of an esoteric touch, because it seems, as if nature waits to decide what happened, until we look, also casting doubt on the linearity of time. As Jacques et al. (2007) put it:

> [Considering that] *no signal traveling at a velocity less than that of light can connect these two events, there is a strange inversion of the normal order of time.*
>
> *(p. 968)*

In other words, the past has been influenced by the experiment, meaning that the experimenters have an

> *unavoidable effect on the already past history of the photon.*
>
> *(p. 968)*

Offering an alternative explanation that did not lead to all those counter intuitive notions, Boyd (2011) commented that the solidity of those conclusions would depend on whether quantum mechanics provides the "only" available explanation of the experiment. For him, the duality of the particle wave is incorrect (Boyd, 2012).

Relativistic quantum interpretations of the double-split experiment, and duality of particle and wave, suggest that there is no reality apart from observation. Such view does not reflect how researchers typically think of an experiment (Cresser, 2011).

From a realist perspective, the observer looks at a phenomenon, or physical systems, from the outside, taking measurements and making objective observations. This conceptualization of reality has been thrashed by quantum mechanics. Some scholars have argued that quantum measurements disturb the system they measure. An intriguing assumption of the spacetime process model is that there is no objective reality out there to measure, contrary to what realists commonly postulate (Cresser, 2011).

Interestingly, the notion of duality, or unification, is already found in classical physics (in the unification of electricity and magnetism, which are disparate phenomena). However, in contrast to classical physics, seemingly contradictory appearances of one and the same particle can be justified by Heisenberg's (1927, 1971) Uncertainty Principle ($\Delta x \Delta p \geq \frac{1}{2}$ h). As Feynman (1975) so rightly noted, the Uncertainty Principle protects quantum mechanics. Nothing has to be totally certain. Human beings do not like uncertainty and unpredictability, so it seems that they resort to unconscious defense mechanisms to defend against this unsettling reality. They dislike the kind of randomness, which is found in experiments performed with electrons. Nonetheless, it is hard to ignore findings that point to randomness being an intrinsic part of the physical system itself. They are an inherent aspect of the universe (Cresser, 2011). When testing what is known as the "Bell Inequality", experiments have yielded results, again and again, that disprove classical realism (see Cresser, 2011). Nature behaves in line with quantum explanations, and non-locality has been proven. So, one is faced with "having to accept that certain aspects of the physical world are not explainable by classic physics". Theories can only predict the probabilities of the outcome of any measurement (p. 37).

As discussed, Schrődinger's mathematical equation describes how the wavefunction of a quantum system evolves over time. It has two aspects: one in which time explicitly appears (describes how the wave function of a particle will evolve), and the other, where time dependence has been "removed" (used to describe the allowed energies of a particle). While the equation has enormous significance regarding the quantization (mapping a large set of input values to a smaller set of output values) of energy, it falls short in describing the intrinsic spin of elementary particles (Cresser, 2011).

In 1928, Paul Dirac formulated the Dirac Equation, describing the behavior of electrons in a way that was consistent with quantum mechanics and Special Relativity Theory, laying the foundation for quantum electrodynamics (Husain, 2024). He theorized that space was filled with negative energy states, called the "Dirac Sea". So, the vacuum would be a seething turmoil of creation and annihilation. Dirac devised a relativistic wave equation with four components, divided into two energy states, positive and negative. For every particle, there exists a corresponding antiparticle, exactly matching it, but with opposite charge. For the electron, there should be a corresponding "positron". These pairs explain that an electron can spin in two ways, clockwise and anticlockwise (Berry, 1998). In Dirac's equation, the spin emerged as an inevitable property of an electron, reconciling seemingly contradictory characteristics of atoms, i.e., they can behave as localized particles and as waves that are spread out. It laid the foundation for the *Standard Model of Particle Physics* and was one of the greatest breakthroughs in physics (Amaral, 2024). Remarkably, Dirac predicted antimatter and his concept of the Sea of negative energy states was a way to explain why antimatter exists.

One consequence of modern physics was that the reductionists had to admit that the whole physical world is fundamentally a quantum system, even if the effects may be washed away in the macroscopic world (Carminati et al., 2017). Therefore, the barrier to regarding physics and psyche as a fundamental ontic unity were partly removed with the development of quantum theories.

The *Standard Model* is a specific application of Quantum Field Theory. The Standard Model explains three of the four fundamental forces that govern the universe, namely, the electromagnetic force, strong nuclear force, and the weak nuclear force (Sutton, 2025). It explains all fundamental types of particles:

a fermions, building blocks of matter that obey the Pauli Exclusion Principle, that is, two fermions can occupy the same quantum state (American Physical Society, 2025)
b six types of quarks
c six types of leptons that do not experience the strong force
d bosons (Gauge bosons, Higgs boson), which mediate the fundamental forces of nature and do not obey the Pauli Exclusion Principle (Sutton, 2025).

However, the Standard Model does neither explain gravity, nor dark matter and dark energy. Therefore, it is "not entirely the Theory of Everything" (Kaku, 2024, p. 273). Although Physicists hypothesize a "graviton" (quantum particle that mediates gravity), it has not been observed. Therefore, the search for a quantum theory of gravity is ongoing. String Theory and Loop Quantum Gravity are continuously elaborated.

The Large Hadron Collider is the most powerful particle accelerator, playing a crucial role in testing and expanding the Standard Model by colliding protons at extremely high energies to probe fundamental forces and particles. New colliders are envisaged, aiming to move beyond the Standard Model toward a *Theory of Everything*. In Geneva, the Future Circular Collider feasible study is developing designs for higher performance particle colliders and expected to conclude in 2025. The building of a new tunnel and a second machine are envisaged, which aim to be operational by the 2070s (CERN, 2025).

Recently, the Many-Worlds Interpretation (MMI) of quantum mechanics has received much attention. Originally proposed by Hugh Everett III in the 1950s (Barrett & Byrne, 2012), the collapse of a quantum system into one of its components of the Superposition is questioned (Segawa, 2017). Instead, a quantum measurement creates a new Superposition, which also includes the measurement apparatus and the experimenter. Every measurement splits the world into different components, creating many more worlds. Philosophers, who accept this interpretation, often regard this theory as a way to reduce the mental to the physical (Segawa, 2017).

Whereas Everett's thesis of the wavefunction was rejected by Bohr, and an abridged thesis about the relative state of the wave function was accepted, Everett's work was promoted in the 1970s and in 1985. David Deutsch proposed a quantum computer that exploited Everettian parallelism (Byrne, 2007). Everett's methods in devising the MMI presaged the concept of quantum decoherence. As Byrne (2007) noted, it explains why the probabilistic weirdness of quantum mechanics resolves itself into the concrete world of our experience (p. 98).

According to Faye (2024), the Copenhagen Interpretation was the first general attempt to understand the world of atoms. It reflects Bohr's insistence on using classical concepts to describe experimental results, while endowing quantum formalism with an empirical interpretation.

Classical concepts in quantum mechanics are *not* the same as in classical mechanics (Kober, 2010). However, Bohr's Correspondence Principle postulates that quantum mechanics must match classical physics in the limit of large numbers, which ensures that it does not contradict classical mechanics. Quantum mechanical symbolism also links it to experimental observations.

Ever since Quantum Theory was first introduced about a century ago, its exact character has resulted in many debates. While it is still ambiguous, the Copenhagen Interpretation can be regarded as the standard way of understanding Quantum Theory (Kober, 2009). Nowadays the Copenhagen Interpretation is mostly regarded as synonymous with indeterminism, Bohr's Correspondence Principle, Born's intrinsically probabilistic statistical interpretation, with the wavefunction determining likelihoods of measurement outcomes, as well as Bohr's complementarity interpretation of certain atomic phenomena (Faye, 2024).

Song (2021) noted a tendency whereby the measurements of the Copenhagen Interpretation are minimized so that it can be relegated to philosophy. However, measurement forms a central part in its scientific description of the universe. Quantum Theory implies that experience is subjective. To specify subjective reality, Song (2020) conceptualized time as cyclical (where past leads to future, and future to past), differentiating between matter and mind. In the classical (physical) macroscopic view, matter is moving forward. In the systemic quantum microscopic view, mind is moving backward.

Building Blocks of the Universe

The fundamental building blocks of nature are continuous liquid substances that are distributed throughout space, known as fields (e.g. electromagnetic fields). Hence, Quantum Field Theory holds that the vacuum of the universe is not an empty void. The universe is permeated by "dark energy" (Peebles & Ratra, 2003, p. 559), filling all its space, according to cosmology, astronomy, and celestial mechanics. Celestial bodies are objects in space such as the sun, moon, planets, and the stars (Stanton, 2023).

Both dark energy and dark matter are hypothetical forms of energy and matter. Dark energy is thought to make up 68%, dark matter 27%, Hydrogen and Helium 5%, and Higher Elements 1% of the universe (Kaku, 2024, p. 273). The substance of dark matter lies outside the Standard Model.

Quantum Chromodynamics is a fundamental theory that describes the interactions between quarks and gluons. Advanced computational methods, often performed on super (quantum) computers, are required for detailed predictions (Butto, 2024a). Experiments in high energy physics (using the Large Hadron particle Collider) have confirmed the predictions of this theory. Quarks can be viewed as the essential building blocks of matter in the universe.

Butto (2021) explicated how the vacuum behaves like a frictionless superfluid with extremely high thermal conductivity, which extends everywhere without any defined size, shape, center, or direction. Consequently, energy manifests in tangible, measurable ways. Butto (2024a) explained that the superfluid plays a crucial role in the formation of elementary particles, such as quarks. The ultimate reality of the universe before the Big Bang was a superfluid vacuum with high density. Everything else emerged from this state (Butto, 2021, p. 1221). Immediately afterward, this density caused intense fluctuations in the quantum fields. Regions of high energy concentration led to the formation of vortices. The properties of these vortices (charge, spin, mass) are determined by the dynamics of the quantum field (Butto, 2024a). Viewing quarks as vortices in a superfluid vacuum might offer new insight into their behavior and interactions (Butto, 2024b).

Quantum Computers

Even though classical Turing machines, which are the foundation of all modern computers, have been revolutionary, a quantum computer can solve problems that are beyond the reach of digital computers. And it is faster, since it can compute many states simultaneously (Wichert, 2023). Future generations of researchers will need to know quantum technologies (Greinert et al., 2022). They are advancing at a breathtaking speed and have numerous consequences. Globally, governments, private companies, and Startups have invested one trillion dollars in the development of quantum computers. The physicist Michio Kaku (2024) argued that quantum computers might codify the universe and simulate any phenomenon of the physical world, from subatomic particles, DNA, and black holes to the Big Bang.

Hilbert Space, P-Adic & M-Adic Numbers

These numbers are relevant to understanding studies that examine the unconscious.

A Hilbert space is a vector space H with an inner product (f, g). Hilbert spaces must be complete insofar that the norm, defined by a specific formula, turns H into a complete metric space.

If the metric defined by the norm is not complete, then H is known as an inner product space instead (Weisstein, n.d.). A p-adic number is an extension of the field of rational numbers (numbers written as fraction), such that congruences modulo powers of a fixed prime p are related to proximity in the so-called "p-adic metric" (Weisstein, n. d.). An m-adic number can be thought of as a number expressed in terms of powers of m, where m is a fixed positive integer greater than 1. Specifically, an m-adic integer is a number that can be represented as an infinite series of digits, each multiplied by a power of m. M-adic numbers are used in m-adic analysis. This is akin to p-adic analysis (see Dolgopolov et al. (2011) for discussion of these).

INDEX

Note: *Italic* page numbers refer to figures.

For Product Safety Concerns and Information please contact our EU
representative GPSR@taylorandfrancis.com
Taylor & Francis Verlag GmbH, Kaufingerstraße 24, 80331 München, Germany

www.ingramcontent.com/pod-product-compliance
Ingram Content Group UK Ltd.
Pitfield, Milton Keynes, MK11 3LW, UK
UKHW050230200926
475702UK00020B/2958
9781041003830